KU-267-668

GREAT POWER DIPLOMACY
1814–1914

GREAT POWER DIPLOMACY

1814-1914

❑

Norman Rich

Professor of History, Emeritus
Brown University

McGRAW-HILL, INC.

New York St. Louis San Francisco Auckland Bogotá Caracas
Lisbon London Madrid Mexico Milan Montreal New Delhi
Paris San Juan Singapore Sydney Tokyo Toronto

GREAT POWER DIPLOMACY
1814-1914

Copyright © 1992 by McGraw-Hill, Inc. All rights reserved.
Printed in the United States of America. Except as permitted under the
United States Copyright Act of 1976, no part of this publication may be
reproduced or distributed in any form or by any means, or stored in a data
base or retrieval system, without the prior written permission of the
publisher.

1 2 3 4 5 6 7 8 9 0 DOC DOC 9 0 9 8 7 6 5 4 3 2 1

ISBN 0-07-052254-5

This book was set in Garamond Book by Arcata Graphics/Kingsport.
The editors were David Follmer and Elaine Rosenberg;
the production supervisor was Kathryn Porzio.
The cover was designed by Joan Greenfield.
R. R. Donnelley & Sons Company was printer and binder.

Library of Congress Cataloging-in-Publication Data

Rich, Norman.
    Great power diplomacy, 1814-1914 / Norman Rich.
      p.   cm.
    Includes bibliographical references and index.
    ISBN 0-07-052254-5
    1. Europe—Politics and government—1815-1871.   2. Europe—
Politics and government—1871-1918.   3. World politics—19th
century.   4. World politics—1900-1918.   I. Title.
D363.R45   1992
327'.094'09034—dc20   91-38951

◻

About the Author

Norman Rich is Professor of History, Emeritus, at Brown University. After receiving his Ph.D. in history from the University of California, Berkeley, in 1949, he served for five years on the Board of Editors of the captured German Foreign Office documents, a project sponsored by the U.S. Department of State, the British Foreign Office, and the French Foreign Ministry. He has taught history at Bryn Mawr College, Michigan State University, and Brown University, where he helped direct the program in International Relations. He has been awarded research fellowships at the Center of International Studies, Princeton, and St. Anthony's College, Oxford, and in addition has been awarded Guggenheim and Fulbright fellowships for research in Germany.

His publications include *Friedrich von Holstein: Politics and Diplomacy in the Era of Bismarck and Wilhelm II,* 2 vols. (1965); *The Age of Nationalism and Reform* (1970, 2nd edition 1977); *Hitler's War Aims,* vol. I, *Ideology, the Nazi State, and the Course of Expansion;* vol. II, *The Establishment of the New Order* (1973–74); and *Why the Crimean War? A Cautionary Tale* (1985, paperback edition, 1990). He is a co-editor of *Documents on German Foreign Policy,* in many volumes, (1949 ff.) and, with M. H. Fisher, of *The Holstein Papers. Memoirs, Diaries, Correspondence,* 4 vols. (1954–61). He has contributed numerous articles and book reviews to American, Canadian, and European journals.

To My Students

Contents in Brief

Contents

Introduction

This survey of the foreign relations of the great powers is essentially a straightforward diplomatic history: an attempt to describe how statesmen over the past century and a half have conducted foreign policy, how they dealt with crisis situations, and how they succeeded or failed to resolve them. It concentrates on the foreign relations of the *great* powers because during the period under discussion their policies not only determined the fate and fortunes of their own peoples but affected, often critically, the destinies of peoples throughout much of the rest of the world.

A study of great power diplomacy is necessarily Europe-centered because throughout the nineteenth and much of the twentieth centuries Europe was the power center of the world and the world's great powers were the great powers of Europe: Britain, France, Russia, Austria (from 1867, Austria-Hungary), and Prussia (from 1871, Germany); Italy arrived on the scene in the 1860s with the pretensions but lacking the wherewithal to become a power of the first rank.

The European great powers had achieved their status through economic, administrative, and cultural developments that enabled them to harness their human and economic resources more effectively than other countries. So preponderant was their strength that by the end of the nineteenth century they had extended their authority and influence, directly or indirectly, over the greater part of the world. Only two major states outside Europe evaded European domination, the United States and Japan, and both did so through the use or adoption of European methods. In the United States, where wave upon wave of European immigrants had ruthlessly thrust aside the native inhabitants, Europeanization was largely a matter of transplantation. Far more revolutionary was the case of Japan, where a group of remarkable statesmen recognized that the only way to escape European dominion was to Europeanize. So successful were they in readjusting their country's institutions along European lines that Japan not only retained its independence but by the early twentieth century had become one of the world's great powers in its own right.

The status of a great power is based on its strength, whose most obvious manifestations are the size and quality of its armies and navies, the productive capacity of its economy, and its ability to mobilize its military and economic resources for war. Besides a country's military and economic establishments, however, its strength depends on the morale, ideological commitment, and educational level of its population, and on such impersonal factors as climate and geography. To these could be added a multitude of other qualities, but even the most comprehensive standards of measurement can be fatefully misleading; the American experience in Vietnam is a notable case in point.

Standards of measurement are particularly elusive when considering another integral and often decisive component of a state's power, namely, its leadership. For the actual effectiveness of power, like that of any other instrument, depends on how wisely and well it is used and thus on the quality of the leaders who exercise it. That political leaders are never completely free agents is obvious. They are obliged to work within the structures of their societies and political systems, even if their aim is to destroy them, and they have to deal with a multitude of existing and unforeseen problems as well as the moves and countermoves of rivals and opponents. But the importance of *how* a particular leader operates within given structural boundaries should be equally obvious. This is particularly true in the realm of foreign policy, where a country's security and vital interests are most frequently at risk and where faulty leadership may dangerously weaken even the strongest powers or plunge them into outright catastrophe.

This survey begins with a discussion of great power diplomacy at the close of the Napoleonic wars—world wars in the sense that they involved all the great powers of that era including that incipient great power, the United States. The statesmen who made peace in 1814-1815 laid the basis for an international order that endured for an entire century. Major changes took place within that order, a few through negotiation, many more through revolution and war, but the peacemakers of 1814 and their successors managed to prevent these conflicts from developing into a general war and successfully resolved a multitude of serious crises through diplomacy. This book is largely a record of those crises, and while it inevitably deals with the revolutions and wars of the period, it is concerned far more with examining the strategies employed for the preservation of peace.

In the century after 1814, peace was constantly threatened and frequently disrupted by the dramatic social and economic developments that played so great a role in the forging of European global predominance. But the problems that gave rise to many of the most serious international crises of this period are for the most part frighteningly familiar and seem to confirm Talleyrand's cynical observation about the human experience: the more things change, the more it's the same old story. Then as now peace was threatened by religious and ethnic fanaticism and by the revolutionary ferment of nationalism. Then as now there was pathological concern about national security, arms buildups justified by the need to defend that security, and the formation of alliances with foreign powers to counter or undercut the alliances of one's opponents. There was the question of whether to intervene in foreign revolutions that were perceived as threats to the interests and security of one's own state, and in this connection the most significant episode may well have been a nonevent: the decision of the British and French governments not to intervene in the American civil war. There was the Eastern Question, which in this period was largely a struggle over the heritage of a decaying Ottoman empire, whose territories in the early nineteenth century included the greater part of the Balkans, North Africa, and the Near and Middle East, regions that remain centers of international conflict and crisis. There was the Russian colossus that impinged on the very existence of its neighbors along its vast frontiers, looming as a threat to its rivals among the great powers—all, with the exception of the United States, far smaller in size and far more limited in human and natural resources.

In addition to the changes wrought by the nineteenth-century economic and social revolutions, there were political developments that would have a profound impact on the future: the growth of the United States into the world's greatest economic power; the unification of the German states and their metamorphosis into the world's greatest military power; the Europeanization of Japan and that state's entry into the arena of global politics.

There was imperialism: the continental expansion of the United States and Russia; the American claim to supremacy in the Western Hemisphere and the extension of American interests to the Caribbean and the Pacific; the European takeover and partition of Africa, which gave that continent much of its present-day political configuration; the struggle between Boers and British over southern Africa and the establishment of white supremacy; the European and American incursion into East Asia; the French takeover of Indochina (Vietnam and Cambodia); the immense Russian territorial gains at the expense of China and the great power struggle over the remainder of the once mighty Chinese empire. Most important of all, there was European cultural imperialism, the export of the ideologies of European-style nationalism and Marxism, European administrative, military, economic, and social structures—in fact that entire panoply of cultural phenomena now generally known as Modernism, which the rest of the world has adopted or felt constrained to adopt even as it shook off European political dominion.

It is one of the ironies of history that Germany's embarkation on a course of global politics in the last decade of the nineteenth century and its construction of a great battle fleet to support that policy should have turned the attention of its great power rivals back to Europe. For the British saw in the German fleet a threat to the security of their home islands, to which all Britain's own imperial concerns were subordinate; to counter that threat the British not only built up their own fleet but formed alliances with their archrivals in the imperial field, France and Russia. The formation of these alliances, and the German belief that they had been formed for the encirclement and destruction of their newly formed empire, set the stage for World War I, a conflict that could more accurately be called a European civil war and one that hastened the end of Europe's global primacy.

These and all other subjects discussed in this book constitute the background of problems that still confront the modern world. The study of this background and how statesmen dealt with crisis situations in the past will not necessarily contribute to a solution of contemporary problems—these must be dealt with on their own terms and in their contemporary context—but some knowledge of how those problems developed and the experiences of the past should contribute to our ability to cope with them. Indeed, the lack of such background knowledge has long stood out as a glaring weakness in our handling of contemporary crises. Quite apart from any practical value such knowledge may have, however, the history of international affairs is fascinating in its own right, and I can only hope that I have managed to communicate some of that fascination to the reader.

This book ends with the failure of diplomacy and the coming of World War I, which accelerated the transformation of the world's power structure and laid the basis of new global political configurations. A second volume will deal with those changes and take the story through World War II, the Cold War, and to what may prove to be the disintegration of the last of the great European colonial empires.

The political and national upheavals that have taken place in the world in the nineteenth and twentieth centuries have been accompanied by large-scale alterations of the names of persons and places. Both usage and spelling have thus become sensitive and controversial issues.

In dealing with place names, I have used the English name when this is the common practice: Vienna, not Wien. Otherwise I have used the name most commonly employed at the time of the events under discussion: Aix-la-Chapelle, not Aachen; Canton, not Guangzhou. I have generally anglicized given names: William and Francis, not Wilhelm and Franz. For surnames, I have used the spelling employed by the bearers of those names. For transliterations of both place and proper names, I have used the most simple and literal form: Pashich, not Pašić; Taiping, not T'ai-p'ing.

In quotations, I have used the spelling and punctuation found in the documents from which they were taken, except of course for translations. All additions of my own are in square brackets. All dates have been standardized to accord with the calendar in use in Europe and the United States in our era.

My thanks to Donald Lamm, president of W. W. Norton and Co., and to the University Press of New England for permission to use material from my books *The Age of Nationalism and Reform* (2nd edition, New York, 1977) and *Why the Crimean War?* (Hanover, N.H., 1985). My thanks also to colleagues who provided valuable criticism and correction for one or more chapters of this work: John Thomas and James Patterson (the United States); Lea Williams (East Asia); Newell Stultz (South Africa); Robert Padden (Latin America); Anthony Molho (Italy); and Volker Berghahn, who read the chapters dealing with Germany and thus a large part of the book. Particular thanks are due to my former colleague and good friend Ralph Menning, who read the entire manuscript and offered many stylistic as well as substantive suggestions. Harriett Prentiss was an invaluable and supportive editor. My wife, Joan Hitchcock Rich, volunteered to take on the onerous but critical task of preparing the index. For this, as for so much else, this terse acknowledgment is a sadly inadequate token of appreciation.

Norman Rich

GREAT POWER DIPLOMACY
1814-1914

ONE

◻

Peacemaking, 1814-1815

By the end of the first decade of the nineteenth century, Napoleon appeared to have achieved what no previous conqueror had been able to accomplish: supremacy over continental Europe. He had defeated the armies of all major continental powers, shattered all international coalitions that had been formed against him, and consolidated his military triumphs through diplomacy. In June 1807, following victories over Prussia and Russia, he imposed conditions on Prussia designed to render that state militarily impotent and permanently subservient to France. With Russia, however, he concluded an alliance that detached the most formidable continental military power from the ranks of his opponents and at the same time enlisted Russian cooperation in his continental economic embargo against Britain, the only major power still in the field against him. And in 1809, following the latest of many military victories over Austria, he concluded an alliance with Austria sealed by his marriage to Archduchess Marie Louise, the daughter of the Habsburg emperor Francis I. Through this marriage the parvenu Napoleon gained the prestige he craved of being united to one of the most ancient of Europe's ruling houses, but the terms of the Austrian alliance were designed to reduce the proud Habsburg empire, too, to a position of permanent subservience. Napoleon's European supremacy was challenged only by the British, who had defeated the French and their allies at sea and who continued what by now seemed a futile struggle against him by sending an army to the Iberian Peninsula to support guerrilla uprisings against French occupation forces in Spain.

There remained, however, the potential challenge of Russia, which despite repeated defeats was still a formidable military power. Moreover, the tsar was not proving to be a docile junior partner in the alliance with France, as Napoleon had expected, but was pursuing policies that loomed as a serious threat to French interests. He had gone to war with Turkey with the obvious intention of realizing the ancient Russian ambition of capturing Constantinople and establishing Russian supremacy in the Near East; he had seized Finland (albeit with Napoleon's blessing) and was now poised to extend Russian influence in Scandinavia; he was raising objections to Napoleonic policy in Poland, which the Russians themselves had long sought to dominate; and he was condoning his subjects' flagrant violations of Russian treaty obligations with respect to the economic embargo of Britain. Determined to eliminate what he by now regarded as the only serious threat to his dominion over

1

the continent, Napoleon invaded Russia in the spring of 1812 with an army of over half a million men, the largest military force ever assembled. Further, to supplement his invasion army and safeguard his flanks, he had dragooned Austria and Prussia into treaties promising France military support in the Russian campaign.

In Russia Napoleon finally met defeat, beaten by the Russian space, the Russian winter, and the dogged tenacity of the Russian people in defending their homeland. Only remnants of Napoleon's Grand Army succeeded in making their way back to western Europe.

Military defeat was followed by diplomatic defeat. In December 1812, during Napoleon's disastrous retreat from Moscow, the commander of the Prussian contingent of Napoleon's invasion forces had taken the initiative in deserting the French and concluding a neutrality agreement with Russia. Not until February of the following year, however, did the Prussian government overcome its fears of a Napoleonic resurgence by severing its diplomatic ties with France and concluding a formal alliance with Russia. Shortly afterward the British, who had been at war with Napoleon all along, concluded subsidy agreements with Prussia and Russia, bringing Britain into alliance with these two continental powers.

Metternich, the Austrian foreign minister, thought it necessary to play a more cautious game. Napoleon was still a formidable foe. After his return from Russia he had raised another powerful army, and if Austria once again took the field against him a victorious Napoleon would be certain to wreak vengeance on the Habsburg realm. But even if Napoleon were defeated, would his defeat necessarily be to Austria's advantage? Austria was now linked to France by political as well as marital ties and might therefore expect to continue to enjoy a secure if not honorable place in Napoleonic Europe. In the event of an allied victory, on the other hand, it seemed all too likely that French hegemony over Europe would be replaced by the hegemony of Russia, which would leave Austria, whether or not allied with Russia, in a position of even more abject subservience. As Metternich saw it, the interests of Austria, and of Europe too, could best be served if Austria used what influence it possessed on behalf of a negotiated peace that would preserve France, even a Napoleonic France, as a counterweight to Russia. Only through the reestablishment of the European equilibrium could Austria and all other weaker continental states maintain some semblance of independence and authority within the European states system.

Metternich's diplomatic campaign on behalf of a negotiated peace was complex and devious, but his basic strategy was simple enough. By holding out the prospect of Austria's entry into the war on the side of the allies, he hoped to persuade them to formulate peace terms that would serve as a basis for negotiation; and by threatening to join the allies, he hoped to persuade Napoleon to agree to negotiate. His major obstacle in dealing with the allies was the tsar, whose determination to crush Napoleon confirmed Metternich's fears that an allied victory would mean that Russia would replace France as the arbiter of Europe. In the spring of 1813, however, the tsar was sufficiently chastened by a succession of military defeats to enable Metternich to extract remarkably lenient terms from both him and his Prussian ally, terms which he persuaded them to make even more lenient by promising to bring Austria into the war if Napoleon rejected them.

It was Napoleon who proved the greater and in the end insuperable obstacle to Metternich's mediation efforts: the conqueror of Europe refused to compromise or abandon his imperial pretensions. In response to the terms offered by Metternich, which would still have left France a considerable extension of its prewar boundaries, he would agree to no more than an armistice and a conference, whereby his purpose was not to negotiate but to gain time to rest and reinforce his army. On August 10, as the time limit of the armistice ran out, Metternich resorted to an ultimatum to which Napoleon did not deign to reply. The Austrian minister was thus left with no alternative but to declare war on France in accordance with his promises to Prussia and Russia.

Metternich did not abandon his efforts to arrange a negotiated peace, and in this endeavor he received substantial support from Castlereagh, the British foreign secretary, who also saw the desirability of preserving France, if necessary a Napoleonic France, as a counterweight to Russia. Although not so generous as Metternich—he objected above all to leaving France in possession of the left bank of the Rhine and the channel coast opposite England—he too was prepared to allow France a considerable extension of its prewar boundaries, in this case the frontiers established in 1792.

The terms proposed by Castlereagh, which were endorsed by all the allied governments, were presented to Napoleon on February 17: if he accepted the frontiers of 1792 he might keep his throne if not repudiated by the French people, and as an additional incentive Castlereagh offered to return various colonial territories Britain had seized from France in the course of the recent wars. Once again Napoleon procrastinated. Twice Metternich persuaded his allies to extend the time limit for a French reply, but on March 18, when no satisfactory response from Napoleon had yet been received, the allies broke off negotiations, this time for good. Napoleon made a last desperate effort to divert an allied advance into France by attacking them in their rear in Lorraine, but the odds against him were now too great. On March 31, 1814, the allied armies entered Paris; on April 11 Napoleon was persuaded to abdicate. The allies granted him the island of Elba as a sovereign principality with an annual income of two million francs; he was to retain his title as emperor.

❑ *The Role of Wartime Alliance Treaties in Postwar Peacemaking*

Napoleonic France was defeated by a coalition of major and minor European states drawn together through their common opposition to France and formally united through a succession of wartime alliance treaties. The importance of these wartime treaties was far greater than their immediate purpose of putting together and maintaining an anti-French coalition. Like the treaties negotiated among the allies in World Wars I and II, they were intended to ensure the loyalty of the members of this coalition to one another, to sustain the willingness of its members to fight the war through to a successful conclusion, and to prevent its members from making a separate peace with France at the expense of one another. They therefore contained political, territorial, and economic provisions that all members deemed essential to safeguard and promote their individual interests and to ensure the future stability of Europe as a whole. These wartime treaties thus already determined in broad outline the terms of future peace settlements and laid the foundations of the postwar European states system.

The most important and far-reaching of these agreements, and the first con-cluded among all four of the major allied powers (Austria, Britain, Prussia, and Russia), was a treaty signed in the French town of Chaumont on March 19, 1814, which reaffirmed commitments made in previous agreements, including a pledge not to make a separate peace with France until all their objectives had been achieved. These objectives were defined in secret articles dealing with matters of concern to them all. They provided for the establishment of a confederation of sovereign German states; for the independence of the existing Swiss Confederation; and for the independence of an enlarged Holland, Spain, and the states of central and southern Italy, where the governments deposed in the recent wars were to be restored. The treaty provided further that the four-power alliance was to remain in force for twenty years after the conclusion of peace with the specific purpose of maintaining a united front against France. With some pride Castlereagh wrote to the British prime minister, Lord Liverpool, that this treaty was to be regarded "not only as a systematic pledge of preserving concert among the leading powers, but a refuge under which all the minor States, especially those on the Rhine, may look forward to find their security upon the return of peace relieved of the necessity of seeking a compromise with France."

Not covered in the Treaty of Chaumont were the provisions of earlier agree-ments dealing with matters of regional concern. In separate treaties concluded by Russia with Austria and Prussia, these states had been promised a restoration of their prewar territorial status, though not necessarily their exact prewar configuration, and all three powers had agreed to guarantee their respective postwar territories. In Scandinavia, Russia had promised to compensate Sweden for the loss of Finland (seized by Russia four years earlier) by supporting Swedish claims to Norway (at this time under the rule of Denmark, an ally of Napoleon).

In terms of outright gain endorsed in the wartime treaties, the greatest benefi-ciary was Britain, which had been able to pick up overseas territory in every part of the world in the course of the recent wars thanks to its naval supremacy. Well before the defeat of Napoleon, Britain had secured the agreement of its major allies that the question of Britain's maritime rights was not even to be discussed during any forthcoming peace negotiations. This meant that Britain alone could decide the future status of the colonial possessions of all the other European states taken over and occupied by Britain in wartime, and that Britain alone could formulate and interpret maritime regulations. Further, to restrict future maritime competition from France, Britain demanded the exclusion of France from any naval establishment on the Scheldt River, especially the great port of Antwerp.

❑ *The Peacemakers*

Despite the success of allied diplomats in settling many of the most important Euro-pean political and territorial questions in their wartime treaties, they still had to deal with difficulties that habitually arise after a war that is won by a coalition of powers: once the common foe has been defeated, the divergent interests of the victorious powers again come to the surface. This clash of interests was to make for dangerous differences among Napoleon's conquerors, but in contrast to the sit-uation after World Wars I and II, when the difficulties of coalition peacemaking were to be far more tragically evident, the statesmen of 1814 had interests in common that enabled them to overcome their immediate differences and continue their diplomatic cooperation into the postwar era. They were all agreed on the desirability, indeed the necessity, of preserving and defending the existing political, social, and economic system. Therefore, although they might engage in bitter controversy in seeking to defend or promote the interests of their respective states, they were all receptive to arguments about the need to avoid conflict that would threaten the existing order and to cooperate for the mutual defense of their common interests.

Foremost among the peacemakers of 1814 were the representatives of the four major allied powers: Alexander I, tsar of Russia, the only chief of state to take a leading part in the negotiations; Robert Stewart, Viscount Castlereagh and Second Marquis of Londonderry, the British foreign secretary; Prince Clement von Metternich-Winneburg, foreign minister of Austria; and Prince Carl August von Hardenberg, chancellor and foreign minister of Prussia, ably assisted by the renowned scholar and educator Wilhelm von Humboldt. Prominent from the first, and soon to take his place officially among the Big Four, was Charles Maurice de Talleyrand-Périgord, prince of Benevento, the representative of defeated France.

Alexander I, tsar of all the Russias and supreme autocrat, personally directed his country's foreign policy, and he alone made all major policy decisions. As is the case with all rulers, however, no matter how great their apparent power, the tsar depended on his bureaucracy for the execution of his orders and was subject to the influence of his advisers and associates. Alexander was particularly susceptible in this respect, and his own ministers as well as foreign statesmen were often disconcerted by his sudden shifts in policy inspired by people who enjoyed his favor. Yet no matter how great the vagaries of his personal inclinations, he consistently yielded to the arguments of those who urged him to cooperate in preserving the postwar treaty system and the peace of Europe, and to the end of his reign he remained a loyal member of the European concert.

Far more obviously consistent was Castlereagh, the British foreign secretary, who was allowed virtually a free hand in the conduct of British foreign policy by a monarch and ministerial colleagues who did not choose to interfere in foreign affairs so long as British interests were properly safeguarded. Born in 1769, the same year as Napoleon and the Duke of Wellington, the victor over Napoleon at Waterloo and thus in a sense Castlereagh's military counterpart, Castlereagh also shared with Wellington a common Irish heritage. Both were members of the Irish aristocracy, attended the same schools, and sat at the same time in the Irish parliament. Unlike Wellington, however, Castlereagh was never popular. In Ireland he was denounced by Irish patriots as the assassin of his country for his rigorous suppression of a French-supported Irish rebellion against British rule in 1799, when he was chief secretary for Irish affairs, and for securing the passage of the Act of Union of 1801 uniting the British and Irish parliaments. In England he was vilified by liberal idealists for supporting the policies of his conservative colleagues.

Dignified and austerely aloof, Castlereagh gave the impression of being imperturbable and indifferent to unpopularity and criticism. In reality he appears to have been a solitary and lonely man who hid his shyness beneath a mantle of patrician arrogance. In public gatherings, where most of his colleagues were distinguished by their flamboyant uniforms and proliferation of medals, Castlereagh stood out for his somber, almost puritanical appearance. A plodding and ponderous speaker, he was unable to stimulate the enthusiasm or imagination of his audience, yet his sheer mastery of the subjects he chose to address made him effective in debate. He was at his best at the negotiating table, where the penetrating quality of his intellect, his cool rationality, and his appreciation of the problems of Europe as a whole earned him the respect and confidence of his colleagues.

Closest to Castlereagh in his willingness and ability to see foreign affairs in a pan-European perspective was Metternich, the foreign minister of Austria, who remained in office longer than any of the other peacemakers of 1814 and who gave his name to the entire postwar era. As a student in Strasbourg, Mainz, and Brussels, he had seen the effects of the French Revolution at firsthand when French revolutionary armies had overrun these cities. Henceforth the idea of revolution was inseparably associated in his mind with violence, the subversion of law and order, and the destruction of established forces of society and government.

Metternich too was an impressive figure, but unlike his British counterpart his appearance of imperturbable self-confidence and immunity to criticism appears to have been genuine. In public and private discourse he could express himself easily and fluently in a variety of languages, and in dealing with people he had the rare gift of being able to sense intuitively their most pressing interests and concerns. Essential to his staying power and success was a prodigious physical and intellectual vigor, which allowed him to cope with crises as well as the daily routine of foreign affairs over a period of forty years. Praised by his admirers for his coherent political philosophy, he was denounced for this same consistency by his critics, who regarded him as a doctrinaire reactionary. Metternich himself took some pride in his adherence to fundamental principles, and he believed the most important of these to be the preservation of law, order, and international peace, which he considered the first requirements of a civilized society.

Hardenberg, the senior Prussian representative, agreed with Castlereagh and Metternich about the desirability of subordinating the interests of individual states to those of Europe as a whole, but as the representative of the weakest of the great powers he was also convinced that Prussia could not be satisfied with a mere restoration of its prewar territories; in order to remain a great power, Prussia required a consolidation and extension of its territorial base. His views in this regard coincided with those of his sovereign, King Frederick William III, who was willing to give Russia dominion over the greater part of Poland, including Prussian Poland, provided that Prussia be allowed to annex Saxony, whose king had made the mistake of remaining loyal too long to his alliance with Napoleon.

Invaluable to Hardenberg was the support of the second Prussian representative, Wilhelm von Humboldt, the most distinguished intellectual figure among the peacemakers of 1814. Poet, philosopher, classics scholar, educational reformer, and one of the greatest philologists of his age, he was also an experienced diplomat and expert on German political affairs. Although concerned primarily with shoring up Prussia's position through postwar treaties, he was at the same time eager to organize the entire body of German states into an effective defensive confederation. His memoranda on this subject remain monuments of German constitutional history, but his proposals for the constitution of a future confederation of German states went far beyond precedent and included provisions for an extensive bill of rights, freedom of religion, and full civil rights for Jews who fulfilled their civic obligations.

The German Confederation eventually established was based to a large extent on the ideas of Humboldt.

Among the peacemakers of 1814, the man who most obviously deserved the label of opportunist was Talleyrand, the French representative. A bishop of the Roman Catholic church before the French Revolution, he lived a thoroughly secular life. In the course of his long and checkered career he served five regimes—the Bourbon monarchy, a succession of revolutionary governments, Napoleon, the restored Bourbon monarchy, and the Orléans monarchy, which succeeded the Bourbons after the revolution of 1830.

Talleyrand's admirers maintain that despite these vagaries in his political loyalties he adhered to a consistent guiding principle throughout his career, namely, to serve the interests of France. His critics, on the other hand, observe that Talleyrand's conception of the interests of France corresponded remarkably closely with his own. Indeed, there is abundant evidence that he shamelessly exploited his official positions for the sake of personal gain. He solicited and accepted bribes on a lavish scale, he used his sources of political information for purposes of speculation and investment, and he succeeded in amassing an immense personal fortune. His one-time colleague Mirabeau said of him that he would sell his soul for money and in doing so would have made a good bargain, for he would have exchanged dung for gold.

Yet even the most hostile estimate of Talleyrand's character and the record of his pecuniary peculations cannot obscure the fact that he possessed political and diplomatic talents of the highest order. Self-assured, a brilliant and witty conversationalist, a man of unusual charm when he chose to exercise it, he combined an acute native intelligence with an uncanny sense of political timing and a flair amounting to genius for turning unfavorable political situations to his advantage. Whatever his guiding principles may have been (and critics question whether he had any), there can be no doubt of the value of his services to France, and the greatest of those services were performed in the course of the peacemaking process of 1814–1815.

❑ *Peace with France, 1814*

In their task of restoring peace and stable political and economic conditions throughout Europe, the peacemakers of 1814 were obliged to deal first with the problem of France. As we have seen, allied armies entered Paris on March 31, 1814, Napoleon abdicated twelve days later, and allied occupation forces were in control of much of the country. A settlement with France was therefore an obvious priority among allied concerns.

Peace with France posed three major questions:

1. *Territorial:* Should France be partitioned or stripped of much of its territory in order to break the power of France permanently, or should France be allowed to retain its prewar territorial status and take its place once again among the great powers of Europe?

2. *Economic:* Should France be obliged to pay reparations for the damage its armies had caused throughout Europe and for the exactions levied by French armies of occupation?
3. *Political:* Should Napoleon's infant son be allowed to succeed him, should the Bourbon dynasty be restored, or should an entirely new dynasty be established in France under allied auspices?

The process of peacemaking with France immediately exposed the conflicts of interest among the allies and the divergent political conceptions of the allied leaders. Broadly speaking, they were divided between advocates of a harsh peace and advocates of a peace of moderation and reconciliation.

The demand for a harsh peace was voiced most forcefully by Holland, Prussia, and other German states that had been the victims of repeated French invasions over the past century and a half, had been among the principal victims of the recent wars and French economic exploitation, and remained most immediately exposed to the danger of future French aggression. To ensure their security, these states demanded that France be so weakened as to be rendered incapable of waging future wars of aggression against its neighbors. To this end several proponents of a harsh peace demanded the outright partition of France, but all were agreed that France should be stripped of its most important strategic frontier territories and subjected to a long-term military occupation to guarantee France's good behavior. The advocates of a harsh peace demanded further that France be required to pay an indemnity to compensate the allies for their own economic sacrifices, for the destruction wrought by the French armies, and for the immense sums the French had exacted from the states they had conquered or occupied during the recent wars.

In favor of a peace of reconciliation were the representatives of Austria, Britain, and Russia. These states were not immediate neighbors of France and were therefore not so directly exposed to the danger of French aggression. Further, all three, but especially Britain and Russia, had already assured themselves of substantial territorial gains and influence in the postwar world, whereas their geographical position prevented them from making territorial gains at the expense of France in Europe. But these were not the primary or even very important considerations of the advocates of a conciliatory peace. Although far from agreement about specific plans for the future of France, the advocates of moderation recognized that a country such as France, with its powerful political and cultural traditions, could be neither permanently divided nor permanently weakened by the loss of a few frontier territories or the imposition of reparations. Harsh and humiliating peace terms would only foster a spirit of hatred and revenge, which would lead inevitably to a renewal of war as soon as France had recovered its strength, which a country with the resources of France was certain to do very quickly. The greatest guarantee of future security against France, the moderates insisted, was the creation of a conciliatory spirit in France itself and the reincorporation of France into the community of European states. The moderates did not neglect the need for more solid guarantees for security against France, but instead of weakening France they proposed strengthening the neighbors of France, whose sovereignty and independence were to be guaranteed by all the powers of Europe.

In considering the question of the future government of France, the moderates were generally agreed that they should seek to establish whatever government seemed most likely to cooperate in the preservation of peace. The manifest desirability of installing a cooperative government in France was an additional reason for lenient peace terms. For that government to attain the prestige it would require to establish its authority and gain the support of the French people, that government would have to be able to demonstrate its ability to secure an honorable peace for France and safeguard French interests.

In desiring the reconciliation and restoration of France, the advocates of a moderate peace had an even more profound and far-reaching purpose in mind. In surveying the past and looking to the future, they realized that France was not the only threat to European peace and security, that other states had waged wars of aggression and were likely to do so in the future, and that the cooperation of France would be essential in coping with such future threats. The great threat all percipient statesmen of western Europe had in mind when thinking of the future was Russia, that steadily expanding territorial colossus which had established itself as the successor to France as Europe's greatest military power and which could only grow more powerful as the years went by. In any case there was the undeniable fact that France existed, that it remained potentially the most powerful state in western Europe, and that France would have to be given its place in the reestablishment of the European balance of power.

❑ *The Role of Talleyrand*

The leaders of Austria, Britain, and Russia favored a peace of moderation as well as the installation of a cooperative government in France. Thus Talleyrand, who was to represent France at the forthcoming peace negotiations, had the great good fortune that the arguments he put forward on behalf of these same causes had already been accepted in principle by the governments of the most powerful allied states. His success in these negotiations was therefore not quite such a personal triumph or diplomatic *tour de force* as he and his admirers claimed. But there is no denying that in the complex political situation in which he was obliged to operate, he displayed remarkable skill and resourcefulness.

When it became obvious that Napoleon's collapse was imminent, Talleyrand took care not to remain in the entourage of the emperor. Unlike almost all other top-ranking French officials, he remained in Paris, where he was in position to deal with allied leaders when their armies entered the city. One of these leaders was Tsar Alexander I, whose confidence Talleyrand was fortunate to have won during the period of the Franco-Russian alliance by warning him not to place his trust in Napoleon but to work for the restoration of the European equilibrium. Talleyrand was thus assured access to the most powerful of the allied leaders, but he did not rest satisfied with this advantage. Upon hearing rumors that the Elysée Palace, where the tsar intended to reside, had been mined, he invited Alexander to live in his own palace on the rue St. Florentin. Thus Talleyrand maneuvered himself into an even more favorable position to convey his own ideas about the future of France to the impressionable Russian ruler.

On April 1, only one day after the tsar's arrival in Paris, Talleyrand took advantage of Alexander's residence in the rue St. Florentin to raise the question of the future government of France with him. The allies could never impose a king on

France, Talleyrand said. To select a ruler acceptable to the French people and therefore able to establish a durable government, it was necessary to act in accordance with the principle of legitimacy. This meant the restoration of the Bourbons, the only legitimate kings of France. When the tsar asked how he could know for certain that this was indeed the wish of the French people, Talleyrand replied that it was the wish of the only institution that could still speak for the French people, the French Senate, and that he would take it upon himself to secure a Senate resolution requesting the return of the Bourbons.

On that same day, April 1, Talleyrand, in his capacity of vice grand-elector, convened the Senate under his chairmanship. Undeterred that only 64 of 140 senators had responded to his summons, he arranged the passage of a Senate resolution on April 2 proclaiming the deposition of Napoleon and inviting the head of the Bourbon dynasty, Louis XVIII (the brother of the executed King Louis XVI), to return to France.

Upon hearing of the resolution of the Senate, Napoleon sent emissaries to Paris offering to abdicate in favor of his infant son. According to Talleyrand, the tsar was inclined to accept this offer, but Talleyrand denounced it as a transparent ruse. Napoleon the father would direct the government of his son, and within a year he would once again resume personal control of affairs and go to war to recover his lost empire. The only hope for stability in France and the peace of Europe was the restoration of the Bourbons. Convinced by Talleyrand's arguments, the tsar rejected Napoleon's offer and demanded that he abdicate unconditionally, which he did on April 11.

Meanwhile the Senate under Talleyrand's direction passed a constitutional charter expressing the desire of the people of France, "truly and without restraint," for the recall of the Bourbons. The allied governments respected this resolution, and in the first days of May 1814 King Louis XVIII made his ceremonial entry into the French capital.

Talleyrand had acted with skill and dispatch, but it is probable that the allies would have settled on a restoration of the Bourbons even without his intervention, for there were serious objections to all other candidates, whereas the Bourbons fulfilled all allied political and ideological requirements. Their restoration ensured the establishment of a conservative monarchy in France, their rule could be justified on the basis of the principle of legitimacy (the allies had not needed Talleyrand to recognize the desirability of this qualification), and a Bourbon government installed by the allies might be expected to cooperate with them in maintaining future peace treaties with France.

❏ *The First Treaty of Paris*

While awaiting the return of the Bourbons, Talleyrand persuaded the French Senate to authorize a provisional government, which he would preside over, to assume immediate executive responsibilities. As the representative of this provisional government he negotiated a preliminary treaty of peace with the allies; it was signed on April 23, 1814.

By the terms of this treaty, France undertook to evacuate its troops from all fortresses still held by the French beyond the French boundaries of 1792. The allies for their part agreed to withdraw their troops beyond these same boundaries. This meant that the allies agreed to evacuate French territory before a final peace treaty with France had been signed or even negotiated, a tremendous concession by the allies and a correspondingly great diplomatic triumph for Talleyrand. In pleading for leniency for France, Talleyrand's most telling argument had played into the self-interest of the allies: by giving the Bourbon government prestige, the allies would demonstrate to the people of France the advantages the Bourbon regime could secure for their country.

Talleyrand remained the principal French negotiator for the final treaty of peace between France and the allies, signed May 30, 1814, which on the allied side represented a complete triumph for the advocates of a peace of reconciliation. France was allowed to retain the territories it had conquered up to 1792, including Avignon, Venaissin, and parts of Savoy, the Palatinate, and Belgium. Thus defeated France, far from being forced to give up territory, saw its prewar boundaries extended substantially at the expense of the southern Netherlands (Belgium) and the states of Italy and Germany. The allies also restored to France all its overseas colonies captured in the course of the recent wars with the notable exception of the valuable island bases of Tobago and Santa Lucia in the West Indies, and Mauritius, Rodriguez, and the Seychelles in the Indian Ocean, all of which were retained by Britain.

Although the allies were bitterly divided on the question, in the end they refrained from imposing any kind of monetary indemnity on France. Further, they relinquished demands for compensation for the immense sums the French had exacted from the countries they had conquered or occupied in the course of the recent wars or for the destruction caused by their armies. The allies did not even require that the French return the works of art they had systematically looted from museums and private collections throughout Europe. No restriction of any kind was placed on the future size of the French armed forces.

Talleyrand was astounded by the leniency of these terms and justifiably elated by the success of his negotiations. In his memoirs he wrote that thanks to this treaty "France's territory was again secure, foreign soldiers had left French soil." With the return of French garrisons from fortresses they had manned abroad and of French prisoners of war, France would once again possess a superb veteran army. And as icing on the cake, France had succeeded in preserving "the admirable works of art carried off by our armies from nearly all the museums of Europe."

The May 30 treaty with France was only the first step in the process of peacemaking, for the allies still had to deal with the reorganization of the rest of Europe conquered or occupied by the French in the course of the recent wars. Accordingly, the final article of the May 30 treaty provided that "all the powers engaged on either side in the present war, shall, within the space of two months, send plenipotentiaries to Vienna, for the purpose of regulating, in general congress, the arrangements which are to complete the provisions of the present treaty."

Some of these "arrangements" were already spelled out in separate secret articles attached to the treaty of May 30. The territory given up by France (meaning French conquests in the rest of Europe) was to be disposed of in such a manner as to create a system that would permit the operation of a "real and permanent Balance of Power in Europe . . . upon the principles determined by the Allied Powers among themselves."

To assist in the establishment of such a balance, the allies undertook to strengthen the neighbors of France to make them more capable of defending them-selves against France or any other potential aggressor. To this end the separate articles of the May 30 treaty provided for the strengthening of Holland through the annexation of the southern Netherlands (Belgium), Luxemburg, and a strip of ter-ritory along the left bank of the Rhine; the strengthening of Piedmont-Sardinia, the Italian state bordering directly on France, through the annexation of the Republic of Genoa (although Sardinia was also obliged to cede part of the province of Savoy to France); and the strengthening of Switzerland through an international guarantee of the sovereignty and independence of the members of the Swiss Confederation.

Also attached to the treaty of May 30 was a separate Franco-British agreement to unite their efforts to persuade all the powers of Christendom to decree the ab-olition of the slave trade, a "Traffic repugnant to the principles of natural justice and of the enlightened age in which we live." This agreement was subsequently embodied in a declaration issued in the name of all eight signatories of the Paris treaty.

The Treaty of Paris of May 30 was thus not only a settlement with France, but together with its separate articles already contained numerous provisions for the settlement of other European problems. As specified in the final article of the Treaty of Paris, the details of these provisions were to be worked out at a forthcoming congress in Vienna, where arrangements for a general European settlement were to be completed.

❑ The United States and the Napoleonic Wars: Louisiana, Florida, and the Anglo-American War of 1812

Before turning to the Congress of Vienna, it is essential to take into account the repercussions of the Napoleonic wars in North America, where events of momen-tous long-term significance were taking place that were intrinsically connected with the conflicts in Europe.

In 1682 the French had laid claim to the entire watershed of the Mississippi River, a territory they called Louisiana in honor of King Louis XIV. A century later they ceded this territory to Spain, but in October 1800, in the complicated aftermath of a war between revolutionary France and Spain, Napoleon, who had become de facto dictator of France in the previous year, arranged for the restoration of Louisiana to France. At this time Napoleon was thinking about reestablishing a great French empire in the Western Hemisphere. This ambition had to be reined in sharply when a renewal of the war with Britain in Europe seemed imminent. Fearing that in the event of war Britain would simply seize French territory in America, Napoleon de-cided to cut his potential losses and on April 30, 1803, he sold Louisiana to the United States. "This accession of territory affirms forever the power of the United States," he said, "and I have just given England a maritime rival that sooner or later will lay low her pride."

Although by this time "Louisiana" was no longer considered to include the entire Mississippi watershed (the actual boundaries of the territory remained vague), its purchase nevertheless represented an immense increase in the size of the United States, for besides the present state of Louisiana it included Arkansas, Missouri, Iowa, Nebraska, North and South Dakota, as well as the greater part of Kansas, Colorado,

Wyoming, Montana, and Minnesota. Not without reason the French statesman and historian Adolphe Thiers would write in later years that the United States "owed the birth of its greatness to the long struggles between France and England."

Not content with these acquisitions, the Americans claimed that the Louisiana Purchase also included Texas and West Florida. American ambitions with respect to Texas had to remain in abeyance for another four decades, but in 1810 the United States took advantage of an insurrection against Spanish rule in West Florida and the French occupation of Spain itself to annex the area. Eight years later (to round out the Florida story) the Americans used the pretext of raids on American territory by East Florida Indians to demand that Spain maintain order in East Florida or cede it to the United States. The Spanish government, beset by domestic problems and revolution throughout much of its overseas empire, saw no alternative but to submit. By a treaty of 1819 Spain formally ceded both East and West Florida to the United States, a treaty ratified in 1821 when the United States took formal possession.

Meanwhile, the Americans had cast their eyes on even bigger game, for in 1812, while Britain was still involved in war with France, they launched a war of their own against Britain for the conquest of Canada. The Americans had ample pretext for hostility to Britain. In their great contest with Napoleon, the British had attempted to curtail the shipment of goods on American vessels to the French and their allies, or to countries from which such goods could be transshipped to the French. They had done so by blockading the American coast and seizing American ships which the British claimed were violating laws (formulated by the British themselves) regulating neutral trade with belligerents.

The Americans, who were making immense profits through their shipping and trade with belligerents, naturally resented British interference with this lucrative commerce. Even more did they resent the British impressment of seamen from American ships, many of whom were not Americans at all but deserters from British naval and merchant vessels, where life and discipline were far harsher than on American merchantmen. The British, who needed ten thousand new recruits annually to maintain their fleet at full strength, could ill afford the mass desertions occasioned by the lure of better pay and better living conditions on American vessels. But in boarding American ships to flush out deserters they seized a good many genuine Americans, so that American indignation over British impressment tactics was thoroughly justified. American hostility to Britain was fueled still further by reports that the British in Canada were encouraging the native Indians to attack American settlements.

Reports of this kind, and American grievances against Britain in general, were eagerly exploited by the many Americans who were seeking an excuse to invade and annex Canada. In an atmosphere of patriotic fervor stimulated by resentment and greed, and confidently believing that the conquest of Canada would be simply a matter of marching into that country, the Congress of the United States declared war on Britain on June 18, 1812.

Both the American army and navy were ill-prepared for war, American military leadership proved inept, American soldiers were poorly disciplined, and in some parts of the United States, notably New England, there was little support for a war against Britain which injured commerce and confronted Americans with the moral predicament of fighting on the side of Napoleon. New Englanders and other opponents of the war blocked the recruitment of troops for the American army, sold military supplies and provisions to the British, and generally hampered the American cause. The Canadians, on the other hand—many of them the descendants of British loyalists who had been expelled from the United States during and after the American war of independence—fought valiantly to defend their lands and homes. Instead of an American invasion of Canada, the British invaded the United States, and in the summer of 1814 they succeeded in burning much of Washington. The Americans did better at sea, but the British blockade of American ports remained effective and by retaining their overall superiority at sea the British were able to land troops at will almost anywhere on the American coast.

The American government soon regretted its decision to go to war and attempted to make peace, but all efforts to do so foundered during the next two years over Britain's refusal to give up the practice of impressment. "The Government could not consent to suspend the exercise of a right upon which the naval strength of the empire mainly depends," Castlereagh told the American representative in London.

With the defeat of Napoleon in Europe and faced with the prospect that British forces in North America would soon be heavily reinforced, the American government decided to drop its condition that the British abandon their practice of impressment, and in the summer of 1814 American delegates journeyed to the Flemish city of Ghent to undertake peace negotiations with the British. Castlereagh, preoccupied with the forthcoming negotiations in Vienna, was in no hurry to deal with the Americans, and when British delegates finally arrived in Ghent they posed such extreme territorial and commercial conditions that the negotiations seemed doomed from the start. The British, however, soon relaxed their conditions. In Vienna, Castlereagh found himself obliged to cope with a serious crisis arising from Russian and Prussian demands to annex Poland and Saxony which threatened to disrupt the anti-Napoleonic coalition, and from America came news of serious British reverses. The British government turned for advice to the Duke of Wellington, now at the height of his prestige following his victories over the French. Offered the command of the British forces in Canada, Wellington expressed his willingness to accept if ordered to do so, but he recommended instead that in view of the military situation in America Britain would do better to drop its territorial demands and make peace with the United States on the basis of the prewar status quo. This advice was accepted by a British government wearied by years of warfare against France and confronted with serious financial and other economic difficulties. On December 24, 1814, after much haggling over such issues as fishing rights, American and British delegates signed a treaty of peace which ended what American historians have called the War of 1812, and Canada remained a possession of Britain.

With the signing of the Treaty of Ghent, the American delegate John Quincy Adams expressed the hope that a peace treaty between Britain and the United States would never again be necessary. This hope seemed on the way to fulfillment with the signature in April 1817 of an Anglo-American treaty (the Rush-Bagot agreement) providing for mutual disarmament on Lake Champlain and the Great Lakes, but disagreements over boundaries, trade, and fishing rights continued to plague Canadian–American relations, as did American differences with Britain, which reached crisis proportions during the American Civil War (see Chapter 9). American quarrels with Britain and Canada continued to simmer until an overall settlement was reached in the Anglo-American Treaty of Washington of May 8, 1871 (see pp. 348, 380), which cleared the way for the relatively amicable relations that have continued to the present day. It was only after the signature of the Washington treaty that the principle of mutual disarmament, first embodied in the treaty of April 1817, was extended to the entire Canadian–American frontier.

❏ *The Congress of Vienna*

At all international congresses to which a large number of states, major and minor, have been invited, the representatives of the great powers, if they genuinely desire to resolve outstanding international problems, generally attempt to reach agreement on major issues among themselves. They are motivated not only by the selfish desire to safeguard and advance their own interests, but by the realistic recognition that if all the minor states represented at the congress were allowed a voice, the negotiating process would be far slower and more complicated and the success of the negotiations themselves perhaps jeopardized.

The conduct of the representatives of the great powers at the Congress of Vienna was to be no exception to this general behavioral pattern. As we have seen, well before the delegates assembled in September 1814 the representatives of the four major allied powers had concluded treaties among themselves over numerous important problems, and they left no doubt of their intention to make all major decisions at the congress. In a treaty of September 22, they agreed that the four major powers *alone* should determine the distribution of territories to be disposed of, their sole concession being that two other states, France and Spain, should be permitted to register objections to all decisions made by the Big Four.

Upon his arrival in Vienna Talleyrand was informed of the allied agreement of September 22 and immediately denounced it as both illegal and improper. Declaring that France intended to operate on the principle that *all* states represented at the congress should participate in the formulation and ratification of decisions, Talleyrand made France the leader and spokesman of all the minor states at the congress with the obvious intention of using their support to enhance France's bargaining power. His stratagem has been much admired as an example of his diplomatic skill, but it is doubtful whether he would have gained much by it if the Big Four had continued to maintain a united front. But they did not.

Despite their resolutions to cooperate and idealistic pronouncements about their desire for international peace and stability, the allied powers were soon entangled in familiar and far from idealistic quarrels over the division of the spoils. The most significant of these involved the Russian desire to control the greater part of the territories of the former state of Poland and Prussia's desire to annex the entire Kingdom of Saxony. These territorial aspirations clashed with the interests of Britain and especially Austria. Both objected to so great an extension of Russian influence into central Europe, and Austria in particular opposed so great an increase in the size and strength of Prussia, its major rival for influence among the German states.

To block the territorial aspirations of Prussia and Russia, which had joined forces to back up each other's claims, Metternich and Castlereagh found themselves obliged to seek the support of France. To a delighted Talleyrand, they proposed that in return for French support against Prussia and Russia, Austria and Britain would see to it that nothing was done at the congress to injure the vital interests

MAP 1   EUROPE IN 1815

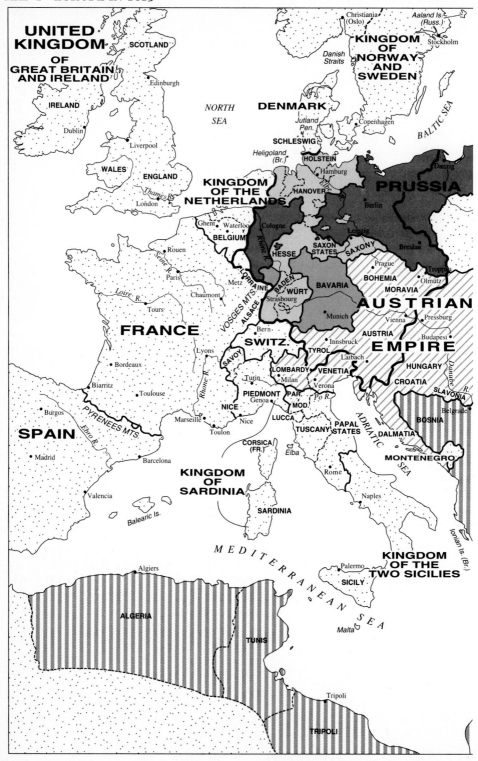

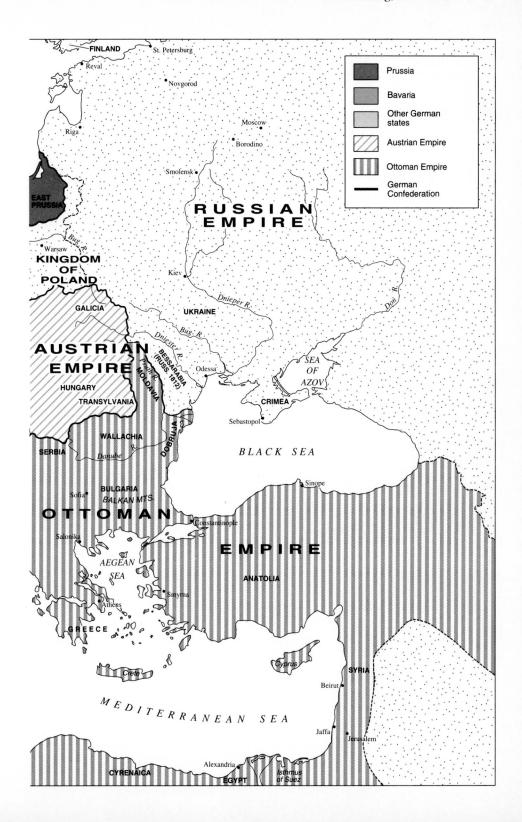

of France. Early in October 1814, on the motion of Austria and Britain, France was admitted to the secret conferences of the Big Four, and on January 3, 1815, Austria and Britain concluded a military alliance with France which was to come into effect if Prussia and Russia refused to abandon their claims to Poland and Saxony or to negotiate a compromise acceptable to Austria and Britain. Although this alliance was supposed to be secret, the Prussians and Russians learned of it almost immediately, as they were certainly intended to do. Faced with this formidable union and the threat of war if they persisted in their demands, they finally agreed to a compromise settlement.

Talleyrand was now invited to all the meetings of the Committee of Four, which thus became the Committee of Five. Nothing further was said about France's championship of the rights of the smaller states of Europe.

Although one of the most famous of international conferences, the Congress of Vienna was never really a congress at all. The congress was never officially opened, the plenipotentiaries of the states represented at the congress never met as a body for negotiation or debate, the principal negotiations were carried on and the major decisions made by the four (later five) great powers. To deal with special problems such as the future organization of the German states or international waterways, ten special committees were set up composed of the representatives of all the states concerned with these problems. Beyond that, the representatives of the lesser states had nothing to do but enjoy the lavish hospitality provided by the emperor of Austria for the delegates and their entourages, a hospitality his impoverished empire could ill afford—but which was to pay off handsomely in political dividends.

The entire congress did not even meet together for the signature of the Vienna treaty because the Final Act of the Congress of Vienna, as the document was called officially, was so long that not enough copies were available on June 9, 1815, the date officially assigned to its signature; it was estimated that twenty-six secretaries were required to produce even a single copy per day. Thus on June 9 the document was actually signed by the plenipotentiaries of the five great powers along with Portugal and Sweden. The other states were invited to adhere separately, which they all did eventually with the exception of the Holy See.

❑ *The Treaty of Vienna*

The Treaty of Vienna, or Final Act of the Congress of Vienna, represented that completion of the arrangements for a general European settlement which had been envisaged in the last article of the first Treaty of Paris. A large number of the articles in the treaty simply gave international sanction to territorial readjustments already made by the victorious powers in the course of the recent wars and confirmed the terms of the first Treaty of Paris and its supplementary articles. Besides confirming faits accomplis and previous agreements, however, the Vienna treaty contained provisions for the settlement of a great many other outstanding problems affecting the states of Europe, both in Europe itself and overseas.

In dealing with the task of restructuring the states and governments of Europe, the statesmen of Vienna spoke much about the principle of legitimacy, which, if scrupulously observed, would have meant the reestablishment of all states in existence before 1789 and the restoration of their ruling dynasties. In fact the principle of legitimacy, which Talleyrand had championed to such effect in securing favorable peace terms for France and the restoration of the Bourbons, was to be largely ignored elsewhere because it was simply impossible to apply. In almost every other part of Europe and European possessions overseas, legitimacy gave way to the more practical principles of security against France, the establishment of an operational balance of power, and self-interest.

For purposes of security against France, the Vienna treaty confirmed previous agreements providing for the enlargement (and presumably the strengthening) of two states on the frontiers of France, Holland and Piedmont-Sardinia. Further, it reaffirmed international guarantees of the sovereignty and independence of these and all other states contiguous to France: Spain, Switzerland (the Helvetic Confederation), and the states of Italy and Germany as reconstituted by the congress.

The most conspicuous feature of the arrangements for Italy was the role assigned to Austria as chief defender of the Italian states against France. The province of Lombardy, including Milan and Mantua, under Habsburg dominion before the Napoleonic wars, was restored to Austria, but in addition Austria was now awarded the province of Venetia, including a lengthy strip of territory along the Dalmatian coast. In being given direct control over the contiguous territories of Lombardy and Venetia, Austria not only acquired the most prosperous provinces of Italy but was placed in a strategic position to defend as well as dominate the entire peninsula.

Immediately in the path of any future French invasion of Italy was the Kingdom of Piedmont-Sardinia, now strengthened through the annexation of the Republic of Genoa but still not nearly strong enough to resist French aggression without the support of another major power, a role clearly assigned to Austria. The recently restored or newly established rulers of the other Italian states were even more heavily dependent on Austrian support to maintain their authority and defend their territories, a dependence the Austrian government reinforced in traditional Habsburg fashion through family ties.

Napoleon's empress, Marie Louise, the daughter of the emperor of Austria, did not accompany her husband into exile but accepted instead the rulership of the Italian states of Parma, Placentia (Piacenza), and Guastalla. Another Habsburg, the Archduke Ferdinand, a grandson of the Austrian empress Maria Theresa and brother of the present emperor of Austria, was reinstated as Grand Duke of Tuscany. Yet another Habsburg and another grandson of Maria Theresa, Grand Duke Francis IV, was reinstated as ruler of Modena, Reggio Emilia, and Mirandola. In the Kingdom of the Two Sicilies (Naples and Sicily), the allies had allowed Napoleon's former general and brother-in-law, Joachim Murat (who had been installed as King of Naples by Napoleon), to retain his throne as a reward for his desertion of Napoleon in the last stage of the recent wars. But Murat had made the error of rejoining Napoleon during the Hundred Days (see p. 23), and in 1815 he was ousted in favor of Ferdinand IV of Bourbon, the "legitimate" ruler. Although the head of one of the largest Italian states and geographically farthest removed from Austria, Ferdinand too was something of an Austrian satrap. He was married to yet another daughter of Maria Theresa,

Austria had helped him regain his throne, and because of the unpopularity of his government he depended on Austrian support for keeping it. Even the pope, Pius VII, newly restored as ruler of the papal states, looked to Austria for support of his regime, for as secular ruler he was quite as unpopular as any of his nonecclesiastical colleagues.

In no part of Europe was the principle of legitimacy more conspicuously ignored than in the states of Germany. Here as in Italy much of the reorganization was carried out with a view to security against France. Before 1789 there had been roughly three hundred sovereign states in the venerable Holy Roman Empire of the German Nation, the only political institution that could be said to represent "Germany" at that time. Most of those states and the Holy Roman Empire itself had been abolished by Napoleon in the interest of more efficient administration and to facilitate French exploitation and control. The statesmen of Vienna made no move to restore the former states or their legitimate rulers, but instead engaged in some far-reaching territorial reorganization of their own which reduced the number of sovereign states in Germany to thirty-nine.

The most significant territorial reorganization in Germany involved Prussia, which was expected to assume the task of holding the line against France along the Rhine. For this purpose Prussia was allotted extensive territory on the left and right banks of the Rhine. This was a territorial distribution of fateful significance, for this Rhineland area was to become the heartland of Germany's industrial revolution and was to provide Prussia with the economic resources that enabled it to supplant France as the most formidable military power in Europe. Prussia was strengthened further along its southern frontiers by being assigned two-fifths of the territory of the Kingdom of Saxony.

It was primarily to provide still further security against France, but also to bolster the strength and stability of their territorial reorganization of Germany in general, that the Vienna statesmen arranged for the organization of the thirty-nine states of Germany in a federal union, the so-called German Confederation, whose purpose was defined by the Vienna treaty as the "maintenance of the external and internal safety of Germany and of the independence and inviolability of the confederated states." All member states were obliged "to defend not only the whole of Germany but each individual state of the union" and to promise "not to make war on each other."

The German Confederation was composed of the territories of the sovereign princes and the free towns of Germany. Among these sovereign princes were the kings of Denmark, Great Britain, and the Netherlands, in their capacity as rulers of Holstein, Hannover, and Luxemburg, respectively. Also included were those territories of the King of Prussia and the Emperor of Austria that had been part of the old Holy Roman Empire. Significantly not included were the Polish provinces of Prussia and those Habsburg territories that lay outside the boundaries of the old empire, notably Lombardy, Venetia, Polish Galicia, and Hungary. Altogether, the confederation embraced almost all the German-speaking peoples of Europe with the exception of the German-speaking Swiss and Alsatians and the German inhabitants of East Prussia, which lay beyond Prussia's Polish provinces and had not been part of the Holy Roman Empire. It excluded almost all non-German peoples, the most notable exception being the Czechs and Moravians of the ancient Kingdom of Bohemia, which had been part of the Holy Roman Empire and was still regarded by most Europeans, certainly by most Germans, as part of "Germany."

The central administrative body of the German Confederation was a federal parliament to which the government of each member state sent representatives. This parliament met in the free city of Frankfurt under the presidency of Austria, whose emperor was still regarded as the traditional leader of Germany. Through this presidency the Austrians may have hoped to exercise control over the confederation and thus to dominate Germany as they expected to dominate Italy. Such a hope was never fulfilled because each member state jealously protected its sovereign rights and refused to allow Austria or any other member state to control the federal parliament and transform it into an instrument for domination. As it proved, this situation may actually have been an advantage to the Austrians, for through the confederation they were able to defeat or diffuse all attempts on the part of other German states, notably Prussia, to dominate the confederation in their own right and to exclude Austrian influence. Thus the confederation enabled Austria to retain a powerful even if not a dominant position in German affairs.

Among the provisions of the constitution of the German Confederation was a guarantee of civil and political rights and the equal treatment of all Christian sects. It is noteworthy that the constitution also charged the parliament of the confederation to make special efforts to secure and guarantee the civil rights of Jews on the condition that they submit to obligations imposed on other citizens.

Although the German Confederation has the appearance of a national organization, it was not set up in deference to the principle of nationality. It was simply an expedient way of reorganizing that potpourri of states in west central Europe that had been part of the Holy Roman Empire and whose principal language happened to be German.

Even though not conceived as a national institution, the German Confederation, when analyzed in retrospect, may well have been the best solution to the "German Question" that has ever been devised. It consisted almost exclusively of territories where a majority of the inhabitants spoke German, or some form of German dialect, and regarded themselves as German. Although not a perfect defender of the interests of its member states or of German interests in general, it nevertheless fulfilled its territorial defensive purposes effectively, backed up as it was by the guarantees of all the great powers of Europe. From the point of view of Europe as a whole, however, its greatest merit was that it proved impossible to organize for purposes of aggression in its own right. And because the confederation could never be regarded as a threat by Germany's neighbors, they had no valid reason to disregard their guarantees to that institution or attack it on the grounds of defending their own interests and security. The very weakness of the confederation, its lack of a centralized and efficient governing body, was thus an additional source of defensive strength.

It is unfortunate but understandable that German nationalists did not see the confederation in this light, and that in the course of the nineteenth century, as nationalist sentiment grew more intense and strident, they should regard the confederation with growing hatred and contempt because of its inability to mobilize

German power. What they craved was a national organization capable of representing German interests on the world stage in the manner of the governments of Britain, France, and Russia.

The thorny questions of Poland and Saxony, which had led to the most serious breach among the victorious allies, were resolved by compromise. The province of Galicia, acquired by Austria in the first partition of Poland in 1772, was once again awarded to Austria. Prussia relinquished to Russia all the territory it had acquired in the third partition of Poland (1795), but it regained the territories acquired in the first and second partitions (1772 and 1793), including Polish Prussia, Danzig, and the Grand Duchy of Posen (Poznan), which together gave Prussia a solid block of territory linking its western provinces to East Prussia. Cracow, the ancient city of the Polish kings, together with a small block of adjacent territory, was set up as a free republic under the joint protection of Austria, Prussia, and Russia. All the rest of Poland, which had constituted the greater part of Napoleon's Grand Duchy of Warsaw, was set up as a new Kingdom of Poland with the tsar of Russia as its king.

In the settlement over Saxony, Prussia was awarded the northern half, which included the territory around Wittenberg and northern Thuringia with the city of Erfurt and contained about two-fifths of Saxony's population. What was left of Saxony remained an independent kingdom under its legitimate sovereign, the unfortunate Frederick Augustus, who had remained loyal too long to his alliance with Napoleon.

As mentioned earlier, the state that gained most from the international treaties concluded during and after the Napoleonic wars was Britain. Thanks to its naval supremacy, Britain had been able to pick up territory in every part of the world while retaining everything that it desired. Among those territories the British retained were strategic bases throughout the world that would help them preserve their naval supremacy and safeguard their trading stations and trade routes. These bases included the island of Heligoland in the North Sea, which dominated the entrance to two major German rivers, the Elbe and the Weser, and Germany's two major seaports, Hamburg and Bremen; the island of Malta in the Mediterranean, which dominated the channel between Sicily and North Africa; the Cape Colony at the southern tip of Africa, which dominated trade routes around the Cape of Good Hope, the only sea lanes between Europe, India, and East Asia before the construction of the Suez Canal; the island of Ceylon, which dominated trade routes around the southern tip of India; the islands of Mauritius, the Seychelles, and Rodriguez in the Indian Ocean; and the islands of Santa Lucia, Tobago, and Trinidad at the southern entrance to the Caribbean Sea. Besides their importance as strategic bases, most of these territories represented valuable economic assets, an advantage that the representatives of the legendary nation of shopkeepers had certainly not ignored in their calculations.

Finally, the Vienna treaty dealt with such general European problems as emigration, indemnities to rulers or other persons deprived of property or rights through the provisions of the treaty, and rights of transport across the territories of sovereign states. It provided for freedom of navigation and commerce on all European rivers, it stipulated the obligations and services to be supplied by the states through which these rivers flowed or which bordered on them, and it set up a uniform system for the collection of dues and the regulations of tariffs. As most of these problems were too complex to be settled quickly, the treaty provided for the establishment of commissions of experts which should adopt the principles set forth in the Vienna agreement as the bases for their proceedings.

❏ *Napoleon's Hundred Days*

The final deliberations at Vienna and the signature of the treaty that brought the congress to an end took place against the background of the last and one of the most dramatic episodes of Napoleon's flamboyant career. Well informed about the rifts among the great powers at Vienna—in particular the bitter controversy over Poland and Saxony—and encouraged by reports about the unpopularity of the Bourbon government in France, Napoleon resolved to exploit these favorable circumstances to regain his throne and empire. In late February 1815 he escaped from Elba, and on March 1 he arrived in France. His enthusiastic reception in France seemed to confirm all reports about the unpopularity of the Bourbons, and his progress from the south of France to Paris took the form of a triumphal procession. Throughout France his veteran soldiers and patriotic youths flocked to his banner; within weeks he had once again assembled a formidable army. On March 20 he arrived in Paris, from which the Bourbon monarch had fled without making even a token defense of his regime, and took over the leadership of the French government. Thus began the famous Hundred Days, the final chapter of the Napoleonic saga.

Napoleon hastened to lead his forces into the field, realizing that his best chance for success lay in destroying the armies of his enemies piecemeal before they had an opportunity to reunite against him. On June 14 he marched into Belgium, where he scored a number of minor victories. Four days later, on June 18, 1815, he attacked the main body of the British army under the Duke of Wellington at Waterloo. For the greater part of the day Wellington succeeded in holding his own against the furious onslaughts of the French. Then toward evening the tide of battle shifted decisively in favor of the allies with the arrival of a Prussian army under the redoubtable General Blücher. The French were completely defeated, Napoleon was obliged to flee from the field, and after vain attempts to escape to America he surrendered to the British.

On June 22, 1815, Napoleon abdicated a second time, unconditionally and for good. Taking no chance of another Napoleonic restoration, the allies sent him to the tiny Atlantic island of St. Helena, roughly one thousand miles off the coast of southern Africa. Here he was to remain for the rest of his life. He died on May 5, 1821, presumably of cancer, although stories persist that he was poisoned.

Napoleon's Hundred Days did not halt the deliberations of the statesmen in Vienna, where the final treaty of the congress was signed on June 9, 1815, nine days before Waterloo. Napoleon's bold bid to regain his throne, however, and the French people's display of support for him, were to result in a new peace settlement with France and a second Treaty of Paris that was to contain far harsher peace terms than the first.

❑ *The Second Treaty of Paris*

Napoleon's violation of the first treaty of Paris and his enthusiastic reception by the French people, despite the leniency of that treaty, gave fresh impetus to the arguments of allied leaders who had advocated a harsh peace during the initial negotiations with France. They contended that the French people themselves had now provided irrefutable proof of their militarism and insatiable ambition, and that the French threat to the peace of Europe could be eliminated permanently only by the destruction of France.

As in 1814, the representatives of Prussia advocated a harsh peace, and again Talleyrand argued the case for leniency. The Bourbon monarch was now more than ever the rallying point for everyone in France who desired peace and order, he declared. "All will depend on the moderation of the allies. If France is treated with consideration, and the people believe that it is to the king we owe it, all will be well."

Once again Talleyrand was fortunate that the most powerful allied leaders still agreed with him about the desirability of moderation. A memorandum setting forth the views of the tsar in favor of leniency, but drawn up after full consultation with his own ministers and the representatives of Britain (in this case Castlereagh and the Duke of Wellington), was submitted to the representatives of Austria and Prussia on July 28, 1815. The primary objectives of this final stage of the war, this memorandum stated, had been to defeat Napoleon, to restore Louis XVIII to the throne, and to restore the European equilibrium established by the Vienna settlement. Hence the overriding objective of the current negotiations should be to ensure the stabilization of the Bourbon regime as quickly as possible, an aim that could be accomplished only if the French people perceived this regime to be the one that best served the interests of the nation. To impose drastic territorial sacrifices on France not only would undermine the Bourbons at home but would upset the equilibrium so delicately achieved at Vienna. Hence only modest demands should be made. France should be required merely to make a financial contribution to aid France's neighbors to strengthen their fortifications, and allied troops should be allowed to occupy certain French fortifications until this financial indemnity had been paid.

Humboldt, the Prussian representative, responded to the tsar's "pernicious" memorandum with anger and indignation. The very foundation of the Russian argument—that the war had been waged against Napoleon and not against the French people—was false. The French nation had enthusiastically associated itself with Napoleon's cause and had thereby forfeited every right to a generous peace. Whether the terms of peace with France were lenient or harsh, the French people would remain hostile to the allies and particularly to Prussia. Humboldt pointed to the long and consistent history of French aggrandizement at the expense of Germany, a rapacious policy made all the easier because, unlike the French, the Germans were essentially a peace-loving nation. Somewhat inconsistently, Humboldt also objected to the proposal that allied forces be allowed to occupy France on the grounds that this would permit the passage of Russian troops over German territory for years to come. He evidently regarded this potential Russian threat to German security as too high a price to pay for additional security against France.

Castlereagh swept aside the Prussian arguments in a trenchant analysis of the entire problem of a harsh versus a soft peace. The business of the allies was not to collect trophies but to restore the world to peaceful habits, and he did not think the French people would be rendered more docile if their country were placed in a straitjacket. Besides, considering the astonishing growth of some states in recent times, especially Russia, it was in the interest of the other states of Europe to make France a useful rather than a dangerous member of the European community. A harsh policy would arouse the entire French nation, foster a permanent thirst for revenge, and compel the allies to remain permanently in France to keep the country pacified. "It is curious to observe the insatiable spirit [among the neighbors of France] for getting something without a thought of how it is to be preserved," he said. "They seem to have no dread of a kick from the lion when his toils are removed, and are foolish enough to suppose that the Great Powers of Europe are to be in readiness to protect them in the enjoyment of their petty spoils."

With the government of Austria joining the governments of Britain and Russia in favoring a peace of reconciliation and moderation, Prussia and other advocates of a punitive peace were powerless to secure acceptance of their more extreme demands. Even so, the second treaty of peace with France, signed in Paris on November 20, 1815, was a good deal harsher than the first. The French frontiers were moved back to those of 1790 rather than 1792 (which still left France larger than it had been before the revolution), and France was forced to give up additional frontier territory and fortresses. France was now to pay an indemnity of 700 million francs and to bear the costs of an allied army of occupation for three to five years, depending on the country's progress in the reestablishment of order and tranquillity.

An additional article of the November 20 treaty once again expressed the desire of the signatory powers to give effect to measures deliberated at the Congress of Vienna relative to the complete and universal abolition of the slave trade, and to explore without loss of time the most effective methods "for the entire and definitive abolition of a Commerce so odious, and so strongly condemned by the laws of Religion and Nature."

❑ *The Holy and Quadruple Alliance*

While the terms of a second treaty of peace with France were being deliberated, the tsar took the initiative in proposing a new alliance among the four allied powers that was to be based on religious principles. The treaty embodying these tsarist proposals was called the Holy Alliance and was signed on September 18, 1815, by the rulers of Austria, Prussia, and Russia. By the terms of this treaty, the signatory powers resolved to take as their sole guide, both in the administration of their respective states and in their political relations with other governments, the precepts of the Christian religion: justice, Christian charity, and peace. These principles should guide princes at every step as the only means of consolidating human institutions and remedying their imperfections. Conforming to the words of the Holy Scriptures which commanded all men to consider each other as brothers, the three contracting monarchs would remain united by bonds of true and indissoluble fraternity and would lend each other assistance on all occasions and in all places. Regarding themselves as fathers of families in their relations with their subjects, they would lead them in the same spirit of fraternity to protect religion, peace, and justice. The contracting monarchs agreed that they would resort to force only in service to one another. All other powers that chose to adhere to these principles would be received into their Holy Alliance with equal ardor and affection.

The rulers of almost all the Christian states of Europe responded to this invitation by acceding to the Holy Alliance. Among the rulers who did not join was the pope, presumably because he felt he needed no treaty to ensure that he acted according to Christian principles. The prince regent of Britain also refused to join, despite urgent personal appeals from his fellow monarchs, on the grounds that accession would be contrary to the forms of the British constitution. He nevertheless declared that he was in full agreement with the principles his fellow sovereigns had laid down and would endeavor to regulate his own conduct in accordance with them and cooperate with his allies in all measures likely to contribute to the peace and happiness of mankind. The prince's ministers may have given him a more specific reason for not joining, for the treaty provided that its members would assist one another on all occasions and in all places, a commitment that might prove embarrassing as well as dangerous if the terms of the treaty were ever to be invoked.

Castlereagh, to be sure, saw no danger in the Holy Alliance, which he dismissed as meaningless, "this piece of sublime mysticism and nonsense," a point of view shared by Metternich. Many contemporary critics, on the other hand, professed to see in it a sinister conspiracy for the preservation of tyrannical governments and the suppression of popular liberties, a hypocritical disguise for defending the interests of the rulers who espoused it. Only a few years after the signature of the Holy Alliance, this hypercritical view became commonly accepted, especially by the British, who used the term "Holy Alliance powers" to refer, disparagingly, to the conservative governments of Austria, Prussia, and Russia.

On the same day as the signature of the second Treaty of Paris, November 20, 1815, a treaty of far greater practical significance than the Holy Alliance was signed by the representatives of Austria, Britain, Prussia, and Russia. This was the so-called Quadruple Alliance, essentially a renewal of the wartime coalition of the four major allied powers, whereby they promised to enforce their peace treaties with France and, if necessary, to use all their forces to prevent Napoleon or any member of his family from coming to power in France. In this same treaty, the four allied powers also agreed "to renew their meetings at fixed periods . . . for the purpose of consulting upon their common interests, and for the consideration of the measures which at each of these periods shall be considered the most salutary for the repose and prosperity of Nations, and for the maintenance of the Peace of Europe."

With this agreement, formal provision was made for the postwar meetings of the representatives of the allied powers for the purpose of taking joint action to deal with international crises and reducing the danger of conflict among themselves. This was the essential feature of what came to be called the Concert of Europe, which, with the process of peacemaking completed, now faced the far more complex task of peacekeeping.

❑ *General Observations on Peacemaking, 1814–1815*

Through their peace treaties ending the French revolutionary and Napoleonic wars, the statesmen of 1814 had not solved the major problems with which they had been confronted—political problems are never permanently solved—but they had provided intelligent and practical means for dealing with them.

They had made peace with France and established a government in France that seemed most likely to cooperate in the preservation of peace and the existing European political and economic system. For purposes of security against France they had strengthened the neighbors of France through territorial enlargement and international guarantees; they had reestablished a balance of power in Europe; and they had renewed their wartime anti-French coalition. Far more significantly, they had endeavored to lay the basis for the reconciliation of France and the restoration of France as a cooperative partner in the community of European states, the most effective as well as salutary means to ensure security against France in the long run.

In the reconstruction of Europe, they had restored the sovereignty and independence of well-established states such as Spain and Portugal and placed them under their legitimate monarchs, meaning rulers who could command recognition at home and abroad. Elsewhere they had found it necessary to engage in a good deal of territorial rearrangement to honor wartime commitments, strengthen the balance of power, or satisfy the demands of their own governments and those of their allies for the spoils of victory. For the most part these territorial rearrangements were not based on the desires of the populations involved or on their nationality, a neglect that was to lead to serious difficulties with the rise of national self-consciousness in the course of the nineteenth century.

It was to deal with just such unforeseen problems, however, that the statesmen of 1814 agreed by treaty to meet in conference in the event of future international or revolutionary crises in order to allow themselves the opportunity to settle such crises through consultation and negotiation and prevent their eruption into a general European war.

TWO

Peacekeeping, 1815–1823: The Concert of Europe

❏ *The Preservation of Peace and the Forces of Change*

In considering the problem of the preservation of peace, analysts tend to forget or overlook the fact that peace is closely linked with the preservation of the status quo—the maintenance of the existing political and international order. The policies of statesmen genuinely concerned with the preservation of peace therefore tend to be fundamentally conservative, in the correct sense of that much abused term. Idealists who profess to desire peace but at the same time call for revolution against the existing political and social order fail to perceive the inconsistency of their aims, for revolution (genuine revolution as opposed to a mere change in political leadership) is domestic warfare and frequently attracts foreign intervention, resulting in international war.

The rigid preservation of the political or any other status quo is manifestly impossible, however, for neither time nor anything else stands still. Forces of change are present in every society, and never before had those forces been more powerful than in nineteenth-century Europe. New technology, new methods of agricultural and industrial production, of construction, transportation, and communication, new methods for raising capital to finance economic enterprise—these and a multitude of other innovations were transforming European society and were soon to begin transforming the societies of much of the rest of the world, more radically and at a faster pace than ever before in the course of recorded history.

The forces of economic and social change exerted immense pressure for political change and fostered the development of political ideologies and programs to meet the needs and aspirations of a changing society. Preeminent among these were the doctrines of liberalism and socialism.

Liberalism is a philosophy of freedom, a belief that human beings can be trusted to govern themselves with a minimum of interference from outside authority, whether church, state, or labor union. Left to their own devices, human beings will act in accordance with their own best interests, and the sum of these individual efforts will enhance the welfare of all. Liberal theories reflected this individualism, for there were almost as many varieties of liberalism as there were liberals, and one of the great weaknesses of liberalism as a political movement is the perennial lack of unity or agreement among its adherents.

In emphasizing freedom of the individual, liberals stressed the need for laws and written constitutions to guarantee the rights, liberties, and property of all members of society and to protect them from arbitrary government interference and the rapacity of others. At the same time many liberals, whether for religious, humanitarian, or practical reasons, were also among the foremost advocates of social as well as political reform—the abolition of serfdom and slavery, improved working conditions in mines and factories—all of which required government interference in the affairs of the individual. So closely did liberals become associated with programs of government-instituted reform that over time liberalism has been perceived—especially by its critics—as merging into socialism, which in theory at least is the very antithesis of liberalism.

Liberalism has been called the political ideology of the middle class because most liberals were members of that class and the principal beneficiaries of the free enterprise system. Political leaders who professed to speak for laborers exploited by that system rejected free enterprise as anarchic and unjust. To ensure an equitable distribution of wealth to all members of society, spokesmen for labor turned to some form of socialism and the concept of a planned, government-regulated economy and society which might include the communal ownership of all property (communism).

The various forms of liberalism and socialism, as well as most other political doctrines that flourished in nineteenth-century Europe, appealed by and large to distinct social classes and were of primary importance in the domestic affairs of a particular country. The ideology of nationalism was not similarly restricted but was to stir the emotions of people of every class and almost every variety of political opinion in every part of the world. Because of its importance in the modern world and because it has been the subject of much confusion and misunderstanding, the ideology of nationalism requires discussion in some detail. This is especially necessary before addressing the problems of peacekeeping in the years after the Napoleonic wars, for nationalism was to prove one of the most serious and persistent threats to peace.

❑ *Nationalism*

Nationalism is a belief that every nationality is entitled to its own national state governed by members of that nationality. Indeed, its more extreme proponents contend that nationality is the only legitimate basis for a sovereign state. As it emerged from the Napoleonic wars, nationalism was a movement for national freedom in much the same way as liberalism was a movement for the freedom of the individual. At that time its appeal was still limited to a relatively small number of intellectuals and idealists, but as the century wore on, nationalism, with its emphasis on exclusive national values and interests, was to become an explosive force in European and ultimately in global society. Nationalism was to provide the principal ideological rationale for the political unification of Italy and Germany, for the revolutions against Turkish, Austrian, and Russian rule in eastern Europe and the Near East, and it may be argued that it was not communism but nationalism—the desire to assert national values and throw off the rule and influence of despised foreigners—that provided the ideological mainspring for many of the major revolutions of the twentieth century.

Contrary to popular belief and the assumption of many modern statesmen and political theorists, the nation is not a fundamental or unique component of human society. People are not born with feelings of national self-consciousness. The desire to be part of a community, and a sense of loyalty to that community, appear to be natural human characteristics; but the object of that loyalty has varied widely from age to age and country to country; it has taken the form of tribes and clans, city states, kingdoms, and empires. The nation is simply one of many forms of social organization, and the modern belief that nationhood is the essential basis for a state is a comparatively recent development.

A nation is composed of individuals with feelings of solidarity based on language, customs, and traditions, feelings that may develop as the result of the accident of birth into a particular society but that have also been systematically propagated in the modern nation state through systems of compulsory education, military training, and other methods of thought control. In similar fashion, people within a given society who come from a separate ethnic, cultural, religious, or geographical background and who consider themselves to be oppressed, rejected, or simply different, have been systematically encouraged by members of their own society to develop their own sense of national identity. It is no accident that the development of modern national self-consciousness has been accompanied by a great increase in the study of history and folklore as national groups seek to discover their common origin, their culture, and the triumphs and tragedies of their national heritage, a resurrection of the past that frequently owes far more to the fervor of nationalist imagination than to scholarship.

Because no scientific or other objective standards exist (or conceivably could exist) for determining national identity, nationality can be defined only as a state of mind. People are members of a particular nationality because they believe they are members of that nationality. Thus nationalism is a matter of faith, and it is in fact nothing less than a secular religion, complete with its own symbols, rituals, hymns, and doctrines. What is remarkable is its seemingly universal appeal and the fact that it has engaged the loyalty of modern man far more completely than most transcendental religions are still able to do. Indeed, many transcendental religions that have retained their appeal appear to have done so largely because they are closely linked with nationalism.

It is the emotional and essentially irrational appeal of nationalism that has made it such a revolutionary force within traditional nonnational societies and such a threat to international peace. Because nationalism inspires an absolute and frequently fanatic loyalty, and because nationalist programs require the fulfillment of nationalist political ideals and aspirations, however these may be defined, nationalist leaders and their constituents have not been amenable to negotiated or compromise solutions to nationality problems. This has meant that if nationalist aims were to be realized, they could be realized only through revolution and war.

A particularly sinister aspect of nationalism has been its association with theories of race, the belief that entire groups of people—whites or blacks, Teutons or Slavs, Europeans or Asians—are inherently superior to other groups in terms of intellectual capacity, creativity, or any other standard of comparison, and thus inherently entitled to dominate inferior peoples and take over their lands and property.

In the late nineteenth century, theories of national and racial superiority were buttressed by the ideology of Social Darwinism, a crude oversimplification of the theories of the naturalist Charles Darwin that all living organisms evolve, that they are engaged in a constant struggle for existence, and that in this struggle the organisms with the best developed qualities for obtaining food, for reproduction, and for self-defense are "naturally selected" to survive. From these theories came the notion of "survival of the fittest," which Darwin's popularizers used to explain every kind of social phenomenon, including differences between social classes, and which nationalists seized on to justify their subjugation of foreign peoples who, because they were vulnerable to conquest, were presumed to be less fit to survive.

❏ *Peacekeeping After 1815*

In turning now to the principal topic of this chapter—peacekeeping between 1815 and 1823—the point must be reiterated that the appeal of nationalism was still limited to a comparatively small number of politically conscious individuals, although Napoleon himself and several of his more perceptive adversaries had already recognized its potential force. But for the conservative statesmen of this period, nationalism was as yet seen as only one of many threats to peace and the existing world order. With the experience of the French Revolution behind them, they had a pathological fear of *all* popular ideologies and political movements and systematically sought their suppression in their own countries or spheres of influence. These men were not myopic reactionaries obsessed with the rigid preservation of the status quo. They understood the inevitability of change. They themselves, after all, had implemented major changes in the political and international order that had existed before 1789, and many of them, including Metternich, advocated further change to overcome shortcomings and weaknesses in their own systems of government. Their conservatism lay in their insistence that all change should be instituted by responsible leaders accustomed to the exercise of power and authority—in other words by men like themselves, who could be trusted to carry out necessary changes in an orderly manner within the existing political and social framework.

Because any changes in the laws and institutions of a country inevitably impinge on the rights and powers of vested interests, all governments, even the most autocratic, have trouble implementing new programs within their own societies; the parliamentary system of Britain was to prove the most resilient in this respect. Further, governments have been afraid that any changes they might undertake would unleash popular forces they would be unable to control, fears perennially reinforced by popular agitation and outright revolution. Even in their domestic affairs, therefore, governments have always had difficulty reconciling their desire to preserve the existing order with their recognition of the need for and the inevitability of change.

In the anarchic world of foreign affairs, that difficulty has been infinitely greater.

In their peace settlements of 1814–1815, the governments of the great powers had not attempted anything so ambitious as the establishment of an all-embracing international organization for the defense of these settlements or permanent international institutions through which peaceful changes in the international system might be effected. Instead, they depended on the Quadruple Alliance, on the successful operation of the balance of power, and on the security system they had built up around France. For arranging changes in the international order by peaceful means, they had only the general agreement embodied in their Quadruple Alliance to meet periodically to consult upon common interests "and for the consideration of measures which . . . shall be considered most salutary for the repose and prosperity of Nations, and for the maintenance of the Peace of Europe."

The cooperation among the allies for the restoration and preservation of peace after the Napoleonic wars has been called the Concert of Europe, and the allies' practice of meeting in congress to deal with problems of mutual concern has been given the somewhat misleading title of the Congress "system." Although the allies did succeed in preventing a general European war for many years, their concert was often more notable for its discords than its harmonies, and their periodic meetings in congress were no system at all, for they were not held regularly and there was no general agreement as to how they should be conducted or what their authority should be.

❑ *The Problem of France*

In the years immediately following the Napoleonic wars, the most serious threat to international peace still appeared to be France. Despite the lenient peace terms the allies had granted France in their postwar treaties, the French people remained embittered by defeat, they resented the government imposed on them by the allies, but most of all they resented the allied army of occupation that had been stationed in France after Napoleon's Hundred Days.

French resentment, which French patriots expressed eloquently and often, served to keep alive allied suspicions of France and fears that the French people were only waiting for an opportune moment to overthrow the treaties of 1815 and once again plunge Europe into war. The allies' fear of France was fueled by rumors that the tsar was seeking an alliance with France in order to acquire the Polish territories denied him by his allies in 1814–1815. This rumor seemed all the more credible because Talleyrand, who had resigned in September 1815, had been succeeded as French foreign minister by the Duke of Richelieu, who had entered the service of the Russian government while a refugee from France during the revolutionary era and had become the tsar's trusted adviser and friend.

To meet the potential danger of a Franco-Russian alliance, Metternich in April 1817 proposed the formation of a separate alliance between Britain and Austria. Castlereagh turned aside Metternich's proposal, confident that the tsar could be persuaded to continue to cooperate with his wartime partners. The best way to deal with the tsar, he said, would be to flatter his vanity, remind him how great his contribution had been to the reestablishment of peace in Europe and how incalculable the consequences would be if the existing alliance system were weakened and other powers were thereby encouraged to alter the territorial settlements arranged in 1815. Instead of forming a separate alliance, Castlereagh said, Austria and Britain should work together to keep the tsar "grouped" with powers dedicated to the preservation of peace and the political and territorial status quo.

Castlereagh's advice was followed and the policy he proposed was successful. The tsar, if he had ever seriously considered a separate alliance with France, made no move in that direction. Yet the problem of how to deal with France remained. In the summer of 1818 Wellington reported that the allied army of occupation in France was so intensely resented that he feared it might be defeating the very purpose for which it had been sent there, namely, to discourage French efforts to overturn the 1815 treaties.

The Duke of Richelieu had long appealed to the allies to remove their occupation forces, arguing that the restored monarchy could never gain the confidence or support of the French people so long as it seemed to rest on foreign bayonets. The second Treaty of Paris had provided that the allied army of occupation might be withdrawn within three years depending on the success of the French government in restoring order and tranquillity. By the autumn of 1818 three years would have elapsed, and Richelieu now addressed an especially urgent plea to the allies to act in accordance with the provision to withdraw their army of occupation and thereby remove this most obvious target of French resentment.

❑ *The Conference of Aix-la-Chapelle: International Collective Guarantees and the "Grouping" of France*

In response to Richelieu's plea and because of their concern about the dangers brewing in France, the allied governments for the first time took advantage of the provision in their Quadruple Alliance to meet in conference to consider measures to preserve European peace. On September 30, 1818, representatives of the allied governments met in Aix-la-Chapelle (in German, Aachen) with the primary purpose of dealing with the problem of France. At Aix the allies agreed unanimously that the withdrawal of the allied army of occupation was necessary and desirable, and on October 9 they concluded a treaty with France promising to withdraw all their troops by November 30 at the latest. In this same treaty they also fixed the final sum of French reparations payments at 265 million francs.

The allies had no illusions that their latest concessions would calm militant agitation in France, and they remained fearful that the more moderate French leaders might succumb to popular pressure for a more aggressive policy. As a warning to French militants and to strengthen the hand of moderate elements, the tsar proposed that the Quadruple Alliance be renewed to demonstrate that the anti-French wartime coalition was still intact and still determined to oppose any French threat to the 1815 treaties and the peace of Europe.

In addition to a renewal of the Quadruple Alliance, the tsar proposed the formation of a second alliance, to include all the signatories to the Vienna treaties; the purpose would be to guarantee the sovereignty, territorial integrity, and the very existence of the governments of all the members of this new coalition. Freed from all danger of foreign aggression and domestic revolution, member governments could afford to offer their peoples a constitution extending their personal liberties. To back up the guarantees his proposed alliance would provide, the tsar envisaged the formation of an international army with the Russian army as its nucleus.

Superficially the tsar's plan seemed an admirable amalgam of practicality and idealism, but Castlereagh was quick to point out its shortcomings. He thought the blessings of perpetual peace might be too dearly bought at the price of subjecting Europe to an international police force dominated by the armies of Russia, and that the alliance proposed by the tsar would give Russia an almost irresistible claim to march through the territories of member states to the most distant parts of Europe to fulfill its guarantee. He suspected that the tsar was disguising even to himself "under the language of evangelical abnegation" the ambition of playing the dominant role in the Confederation of Europe. Castlereagh also objected to the admission of all the small states to the councils of the great powers, for such a move would open the way to endless intrigue and confusion.

In a memorandum submitted to the plenipotentiaries of the other powers attending the conference at Aix, Castlereagh addressed the problem of granting one state or group of states the right to interfere in the internal affairs of another in order to guarantee peace and order. He conceded that if the domestic conditions in one state endangered its neighbors, these neighbors had a right to intervene in its internal affairs, but he was inexorably opposed to providing guarantees of support for all existing governments. Nothing would be more immoral or prejudicial to the character of governments generally than the idea that their force was collectively to be prostituted to the support of established power without any consideration of the extent to which it was abused. "The problem of an universal Alliance for peace and happiness of the world has always been one of speculation and of hope," Castlereagh said, "but it has never yet been reduced to practice, and if an opinion may be hazarded from its difficulty, it never can."

The reservations expressed by Castlereagh were shared by the representatives of Austria and Prussia, although they hesitated to state their suspicions and fears of Russia so clearly. Finding that he lacked support for his pan-European peace plan, the tsar was obliged to settle for his more modest proposal for a renewal of the Quadruple Alliance. Although this alliance was supposed to be secret, the allies communicated its terms to the French government, stressing that its purpose was to guard against revolutionary outbreaks in France that might once again threaten the peace of Europe. The warning to warmongers could not have been more clear.

The allies did not restrict themselves to a mere renewal of their Quadruple Alliance but proposed to take the potentially more effective step toward greater mutual security by bringing France into their great power alliance. Such a move would strengthen the hand of responsible members of the French government against militant agitators, it would make the French feel less threatened and isolated, and it would enhance France's own sense of security. In addition, by admitting France to their councils the allies would be in a position to exercise a certain amount of supervision and control over French policies.

To implement this political course, the allies addressed a note to the king of France on November 4, 1818, inviting him to join them in the task of preserving peace and upholding the treaties on which that peace was based. This invitation was accepted, and by a second treaty signed at Aix on November 15, 1818, France was formally admitted as an equal partner in the Quadruple Alliance, which henceforth became the Quintuple Alliance. "The object of this Union," the treaty stated, "is as simple as it is great and salutary . . . it has no other object than the maintenance of Peace, and the guarantee of those transactions on which the Peace was founded and consolidated." By this treaty France was brought into the Confederation of Europe and joined in the guarantee of the 1815 treaty settlements.

The treaty of November 15 was a diplomatic triumph for the allies, but it was also enormously advantageous to France. The alliance constrained France, to be sure, but at the same time it guaranteed France's own security. France would now be associated in all major international decisions, the allies would be obliged to take into account the interests of France, and France would be in a position to defend and promote those interests. Altogether, the treaties arranged at Aix were notable achievements in the process of peacekeeping.

The congress was less successful in dealing with a number of other important questions, in particular the abolition of the slave trade, the rebellions of the Spanish and Portuguese American colonies, and the suppression of the Barbary pirates. The powers had already agreed in previous treaties to take measures to ensure the abolition of the slave trade, but they refused to accept the principle of mutual right of search, the only way the slave trade might have been effectively suppressed, because this would have given the dominant sea power—Britain—an excuse to interfere with the shipping of every other state. The powers were unable to agree, in principle or otherwise, on what should be done about the American rebellions. Nor were they able to agree on measures to deal with the Barbary pirates because of British fears that international action would give Russia an excuse to play an active role in the Mediterranean. Suppression of the Barbary pirates was a major motive, or pretext, for the French expedition to Algeria in 1830, the first step in France's eventual takeover of the country (see p. 77).

❑ *The Congresses of Troppau and Laibach: Revolution and Foreign Intervention*

The achievements of subsequent congresses of the European great powers were considerably less impressive than those of Aix. They dealt primarily with the problem of revolutions in Europe and the Ottoman empire and the threat these revolutions posed to international peace and security. In the deliberations of the delegates over this question, the discords among the powers tended increasingly to drown out the harmonies of the concert. Although the powers had rejected the tsar's proposal for a treaty sanctioning intervention to suppress every revolution against an established government, it soon became evident that they did not object to the principle of intervention as such but were concerned primarily about how intervention would affect their own interests.

The primacy of interest over principle was clearly revealed when the statesmen of the concert were confronted with the first revolution to take place in western Europe following the Napoleonic wars—an uprising in Spain in January 1820 against the Bourbon king Ferdinand VII. At the time he was restored to his throne in 1814, King Ferdinand had sworn to uphold a constitution drawn up by the Spanish parliament in 1812 during the struggle with Napoleon which provided for a parliament elected by limited manhood suffrage and which severely restricted the authority of the king. Ferdinand had not kept his word but had governed the country autocratically, and his corrupt and incompetent rule had aroused widespread discontent. In the Spanish army this discontent was fanned into flame when Ferdinand attempted to mobilize an expeditionary force to undertake the reconquest of Spain's American colonies, which had broken away from Spanish rule when the Napoleonic wars cut

Spain off from its overseas empire. Disgusted with the king's incompetence and angered by the prospect of being shipped off to America, a group of army officers rebelled. Their mutiny set off uprisings in other parts of Spain, and on March 8, 1818, the king yielded to the demands of the revolutionaries to restore the constitution of 1812.

The tsar immediately called for allied intervention to suppress the uprising in Spain, which he regarded as a clear-cut case of revolution against a legitimate monarch. In a state paper of May 5, 1820, Castlereagh eloquently expressed the British government's opposition to intervention. Much as one might deplore revolution, he said, there was no area in Europe of equal magnitude where a revolution was less likely to menace the peace of Europe and the security of other states than Spain. Moreover, the Spanish were less likely than any other people of Europe to tolerate foreign intervention in their domestic affairs, as the French experience during the Napoleonic wars had demonstrated. Any intervention in Spain was therefore likely to be difficult and might even fail. Even if successful, however, it would hopelessly compromise the position of the king, and the problem would remain of how the country was to be governed after the allied armies were withdrawn. In any case, the Grand Alliance "was never intended as an Union for the Government of the World, or for the Superintendence of the Internal Affairs of other States." To make into a system the principle of interfering by force in the internal affairs of another state to uphold governmental authority, or to impose it as an obligation, was a scheme which Castlereagh denounced as "utterly impracticable and objectionable."

There were other reasons for Britain's opposition to allied intervention in Spain, which Castlereagh did not spell out so clearly. Britain's own interests would be seriously compromised if the tsar were given international sanction to march his armies across Europe, or if France were given an excuse to intervene in Spain and thus restore French influence in the Iberian Peninsula with the blessing of the Concert of Europe. The British also saw reason to fear that if the allies suppressed the revolution in Spain, they might go further and attempt to aid the rulers of Spain and Portugal to suppress the revolutions in their Latin American colonies. These revolutions had been condoned and even encouraged by Britain, where popular sympathy for liberation movements (when not directed against Britain) had been reinforced by traditional prejudice against Spain and, more materially, by a desire to take advantage of these revolutions to break the Spanish and Portuguese trading monopolies with their American colonies.

Metternich, otherwise such a staunch defender of legitimate government and bitter foe of revolution, supported Castlereagh for the simple reason that allied intervention in Spain was potentially an even greater threat to Austrian than to British interests. Austria had even more reason to fear the prospect of Russian armies marching across Europe; and to allow France to intervene in Spain and thus have the opportunity to reassert its dominion over the Iberian Peninsula would jeopardize the entire 1815 treaty system. These dangers might be neutralized to some extent if Austria and Prussia participated in an allied intervention in Spain, but neither state had troops to spare for that purpose or sufficient interests at stake to justify the costs of such an undertaking. It was therefore in the interest of Austria as well as Britain to prevent any kind of intervention in Spain, a policy that Metternich and Castlereagh pursued successfully for the next two years.

There was a notable shift in lineup on the question of intervention when a revolution broke out in Naples in July 1820. Inspired by the Spanish example, a group of Neapolitan army officers rose against their Bourbon ruler, King Ferdinand I, and compelled him to grant the country a constitution. Now it was Metternich who urged intervention, for this was a revolution in the Austrian sphere of interest; if allowed to succeed, it would undermine Austrian authority elsewhere in Italy and encourage revolutions generally. The great difficulty here was that French and Russian participation in an intervention in Naples would be even more dangerous for Austria than their intervention in Spain. Metternich therefore insisted that Austrian troops alone should be empowered to suppress this revolution on the grounds that Italy was an exclusively Austrian concern.

Castlereagh, who had opposed intervention in Spain, supported Metternich over Naples because he believed it was in Britain's interest to keep Austria as strong as possible as a counterweight to both France and Russia. Castlereagh, however, was overruled by his own government, which remained more consistent than its foreign secretary in opposing intervention of any kind in Naples. Thus Metternich found himself isolated on the question and obliged to submit the problem to a congress of the great powers which convened on October 20, 1820, in Troppau (in Czech, Opava), the capital of what was at that time the Austrian duchy and crown land of Silesia.

Before the representatives of the powers assembled at Troppau, the lineup over intervention shifted yet again. The French, who had hoped to use the congress to undermine the Austrian position in Italy, were dismayed to find that the tsar along with the king of Prussia had become so alarmed by the threat of revolution that they were inclined to side with Austria on the Naples question. Accordingly France joined Britain in refusing to send official delegates to Troppau and sent only unofficial observers instead. Metternich was thus left a free hand to exercise his considerable skill in personal diplomacy in dealing with Alexander I and to confirm the tsar's fears of an international revolutionary conspiracy. According to Metternich's account of a conversation he had with the tsar on the afternoon of October 24, the Russian monarch was completely convinced by Metternich's arguments and assured him that henceforth he would allow himself to be guided by the Austrian minister. "Tell me what you desire and what you wish me to do and I will do it." Whether the tsar ever made a statement of that kind is doubtful, but there is no question that Troppau initiated a new period of Austro-Russian cooperation.

In a preliminary protocol signed at Troppau on November 15, 1820, the governments of Austria, Prussia, and Russia reaffirmed the principle of intervention by the great powers if revolution in one state posed a threat to others, and at the close of the conference they agreed on the need for intervention in Naples. A decision on how that intervention was to be carried out was postponed, however, in order to consult beforehand with the king of Naples, who was invited to attend a second congress on the Naples question, which convened on January 11, 1821, in Laibach (in Slovenian, Ljubljana), the capital of the Austrian duchy of Carniola.

The Congress of Laibach was essentially a continuation of the meeting at Troppau. Once again the British and French governments refused to send official delegates, so that once again the governments of Austria, Prussia, and Russia were left a free hand to make all the decisions. By this time the tsar was even more willing to support Metternich's policies, for he had received news of the mutiny of one of his regiments in St. Petersburg and of a revolution against Turkish rule that had broken out in the Balkan province of Wallachia (part of the future state of Romania). He was now convinced of the existence of an international revolutionary committee

"which gives the signal for revolutions in countries which have been carefully prepared by intrigues and agitations." Metternich therefore had little trouble convincing
the tsar that the congress should authorize Austrian intervention in Naples.

Austrian troops were duly dispatched to Italy, and by March 1821 they had
succeeded in suppressing the revolution in Naples. Eventually these troops were to
serve a dual purpose, for upon their return through northern Italy they aided the
government of Piedmont-Sardinia in suppressing a revolution that had meanwhile
broken out in that state.

While the three northern powers were conferring at Laibach, Castlereagh once
again set forth the views of the British government opposing the principle of intervention and any attempt to make intervention part of a system of international law.
The British government, he said, was prepared to uphold the right of any state to
interfere where its security and interests were seriously endangered by the transactions of another state, but it refused to accept the principle that this right could
be applied generally and indiscriminately to all revolutionary movements. With respect to Naples, the British government strongly disapproved of the manner in
which the revolution there had been effected but did not feel justified in advising
British intervention. Castlereagh, however, scrupulously refrained from any criticism
of Austria and even expressed qualified approval of the Austrian action. While opposing intervention on principle, he said, the British government "fully admitted,
however, that other European States, and especially Austria and the Italian Powers,
might feel themselves differently circumstanced; . . . Britain would not interfere
with the course which such States might think fit to adopt, with a view to their
own security, provided only that they were ready to give every reasonable assurance
that their views were not directed to purposes of aggrandizement subversive to the
Territorial System of Europe, as established by the late Treaties." In other words,
Britain reserved the right of intervention when its own interests or those of its
friends appeared to be threatened, but at the same time reserved the right to oppose
intervention when it was contrary to Britain's interests, as in the case of Spain's
American colonies.

While the Austrians were suppressing uprisings in Italy, further rebellion broke
out in the Balkan provinces of the Ottoman empire. This additional evidence of the
spread of the forces of revolution buttressed Metternich's influence over the tsar
and enabled him to persuade the Russian ruler of the necessity of continuing to
allow Austria a free hand to preserve order in Italy. In gaining the tsar's consent to
Austrian intervention in Austrian spheres of interest, however, Metternich paid the
price of giving up the possibility of opposing intervention elsewhere and henceforth
found himself obliged to support the principle of intervention no matter what the
circumstances. At the conclusion of the Congress of Laibach this principle, which
had already been accepted at Troppau, was embodied in a more elaborate declaration that was signed by the plenipotentiaries of Austria, Prussia, and Russia on May
12, 1821.

❑ *Castlereagh Succeeded by Canning*

The British government's refusal to participate officially in the congresses of Troppau and Laibach, and Castlereagh's repudiation of the general principle of interven-

tion, have been interpreted by many historians as a British withdrawal from the Concert of Europe and the beginning of the end of the Congress system. It is true that Britain now refrained from participating actively in dealing with questions that did not directly affect British interests. But the moment British interests were affected, as they were to be in the crises already brewing in the Near East, British representatives immediately assumed their usual prominent position in the deliberations of the great powers.

There were to be notable changes in the conduct of British foreign policy after Laibach, but those changes were primarily the result of a change in British leadership. After Laibach, Metternich had counted on the continued support of Castlereagh to keep the tsar "grouped" and to counter French efforts to break out of the constraints of the 1815 treaty system. But on August 12, 1822, Castlereagh committed suicide in a fit of depression brought on by years of overwork and virulent abuse by opponents of his policies. Metternich mourned his death as "one of the worst catastrophes that could have befallen me." There was no one among the statesmen of Europe whose political convictions corresponded so closely with his own, no one who possessed a comparable grasp of affairs combined with a personal knowledge of the European statesmen entrusted with their conduct. "Many matters which would have been easy to settle with him," Metternich lamented, "will require fresh study and additional effort with his successor, whoever he may be."

Metternich's fears proved justified. Castlereagh's successor as foreign secretary was George Canning, a highly able and energetic diplomat, but a man far more inclined than Castlereagh to view international politics from the point of view of British interests rather than in terms of their overall European implications and one who disagreed profoundly with Metternich's most cherished ideas. Metternich acknowledged Canning's intelligence but believed him to be totally lacking in principle, a statesman whose chief ambition was to make a great name for himself and win the approval of his countrymen. Canning for his part described Metternich as "the greatest rogue and liar in Europe, perhaps in the civilized world." This mutual antipathy, which was to endure throughout their relationship, did not promote harmony within the Concert of Europe, and Canning's pursuit of a British rather than European policy contributed to the impression that Britain had withdrawn from the concert. But this impression was quite mistaken, for, as mentioned previously, the moment British interests were at stake British diplomats were once again in the thick of European negotiations.

❑ *The Congress of Verona: Intervention in Spain, 1823*

Having endorsed the general principle of intervention, and now deprived of the support of Castlereagh, Metternich found himself powerless to continue his resistance to the tsar's pressure for allied intervention in Spain. In response to that pressure, representatives of the five great powers assembled in October 1822 in yet another congress, this one in the northern Italian city of Verona, to renew discussions about how to deal with the revolutions in Spain and the Spanish colonies. While at Verona, the delegates were also called upon to consider what measures they should take in response to the revolution that had meanwhile broken out against Ottoman rule in Greece. As in all previous negotiations on the subject, the question of the principle of intervention was overshadowed by the question of who was to intervene.

The British government continued to oppose intervention of any kind in Spain. The instructions of the British representative at Verona had been drawn up by Castlereagh before his suicide and now served as guidelines for the Duke of Wellington, who took Castlereagh's place at the congress. With respect to Spain, Castlereagh had advocated "a rigid abstention from any interference in the internal affairs of that country." As for the Spanish colonies, if Spain did not succeed in establishing its authority over them within a reasonable time, the powers would sooner or later be obliged to recognize their independence. The trade that had grown up between Britain and the Spanish colonies made it only a question of time before British interests would require official recognition of the Latin American republics.

The Bourbon government of France, eager to enhance its prestige, offered the services of French troops to restore the authority of the Bourbon monarchy in Spain, although there was serious disagreement among French leaders about the wisdom of intervention—Napoleon's debacle in Spain was still a vivid memory. As was to be expected, the governments of the other great powers also opposed French intervention, at least unilateral French intervention, fearing that France might use this opportunity to restore its own control over the Iberian Peninsula and perhaps over the Spanish and Portuguese colonies in America as well. To neutralize the dangers of French intervention, the tsar once again proposed collective intervention in Spain, but the prospect of allowing Russian armies to march across the length of Europe was no more attractive to the powers in 1822 than it had been earlier, and the French declared that under no circumstances would they allow any foreign troops to cross French territory. The British government continued to oppose intervention of any kind, while Austria and Prussia, although supporting intervention in principle as they were obliged to do by treaty, still insisted that they could not spare the necessary troops or afford the costs of such action.

Metternich's solution to the problem of Spain was a proposal that the powers should address simultaneous notes to the Spanish government announcing their agreement to intervene in principle, a diplomatic gesture he hoped would overawe the revolutionaries, induce them to restore the authority of the king, and thus avert the need for allied intervention altogether. The British government, however, refused to be associated with this diplomatic action and formally withdrew from the congress, and the French government, which had no desire to be thwarted of an opportunity to intervene in Spain, refused to send a French note simultaneously with the other powers. With the rifts within the concert thus clearly exposed, the Spanish revolutionaries naturally paid no attention to the separate notes sent by the three other continental powers. The tsar still urged collective action, but France's adamant refusal to allow the passage of foreign troops across French territory remained an insuperable barrier to such a course.

Canning, the new British foreign secretary, was delighted to see the cracks in the concert. "The issue of Verona," he wrote on January 3, 1823, "has split the one and indivisible Alliance into three parts as distinct as the constitutions of England, France, and Muscovy . . . and so things are getting back to a wholesome state again. Every nation for itself and God for us all."

Canning soon found that this wholesome state of affairs was not so healthy as he assumed. Metternich, deprived of British support and unable to dampen Russian or French eagerness to intervene in Spain, evidently decided that French intervention represented the lesser danger for Austria. To overcome the opposition of the tsar, he pointed out that France's refusal to permit the passage of foreign troops across French territory left French unilateral intervention as the only possible course if intervention in Spain were to be effected at all. Furthermore, Russian troops might soon be needed to deal with the revolution in Greece, where Russian interests were far more directly affected than in Spain. With these arguments he persuaded the tsar to allow France to act alone in Spain, and through the tsar he also secured the consent of the king of Prussia.

Once the continental powers had agreed on a course of action in Spain, Canning could do no more than attempt to minimize the potential dangers of the situation for Britain. In April 1823 he issued a declaration that Britain would not oppose the entry of French troops into Spain if the French government observed three conditions:

1. French forces would be withdrawn from Spain as soon as their political objectives had been achieved.
2. France should abstain from any interference in the internal affairs of Portugal, which Britain was pledged to defend.
3. France should make no attempt to assist Spain to recover its colonial empire in Latin America.

The French government agreed to these conditions and faithfully observed them, so that none of the fears of the other powers about the dangers of French intervention were realized. The intervention itself took place without further international incident. The French troops that marched into Spain in April 1823 encountered none of the popular opposition that had caused them such difficulties during the Napoleonic wars. By the end of August the last rebel forces had been crushed and the authority of King Ferdinand fully restored. The French armies, having carried out their mission to suppress revolution and restore "legitimate" government in Spain, retired across the Pyrenees.

A revolution in Portugal in August 1820 should have alarmed the powers quite as much as the revolution in Spain, which it resembled in many ways. Alarmed though they may have been, they found themselves unable even to consider intervention in Portugal for the simple reason that Britain claimed Portugal as a sphere of influence, and, while safeguarding its own interests in that country, resolutely excluded all other powers from any voice in Portuguese affairs.

❑ *The Monroe Doctrine*

As the last rebel armies were being defeated by the French in Spain, Canning once again saw reason to fear that the continental powers, having intervened successfully to suppress revolution in Spain, might attempt to suppress the revolutions against Spanish and Portuguese rule in Latin America.

On August 16, 1823, Canning had a conference with Richard Rush, the American minister to London, which he followed up with three "personal and confidential'' notes. In these he proposed that Britain and the United States come to some agreement to oppose any action the continental powers might take in Latin America and to oppose the transfer of any Spanish colonial territory to another power. The U.S. president, James Monroe, was inclined to go along with Canning's proposal, but both Rush and Secretary of State John Quincy Adams were suspicious of British motives. They feared that cooperating with Britain on this issue might develop into the equivalent of an entangling alliance, or that the British might exploit such an agreement to extend their own influence in the Western Hemisphere. Adams thought that Canning much exaggerated the danger of European intervention in Latin America, that the agreement he desired was only ''ostensibly'' directed against the Holy Alliance, and that his real purpose was to obtain a self-denying pledge from the United States that would prevent the extension of American influence in the Western Hemisphere. Adams therefore advocated a unilateral American declaration against European intervention in the New World, which he deemed more dignified and honorable than ''to come in as a cockboat in the wake of the British man-of-war.''

Adams succeeded in winning the president and his colleagues over to his point of view. His own desire for such a declaration, however, was motivated far more by concern over the possible extension of Russian influence in the Western Hemisphere than about European intervention in Latin America. Russia had substantial territorial claims in the Pacific Northwest, and the Russian government had intimated that it might soon move to take possession of these areas. In the first draft of a declaration that Adams prepared for the president he did not even mention Latin America. It was Monroe himself who introduced this topic in the declaration, which after much further discussion with Adams and other advisers was delivered by the president as a message to Congress on December 2, 1823, and has become known in history as the Monroe Doctrine. This document stated that the government of the United States refused to condone further colonization in the Western Hemisphere by any European power and would regard any European intervention in this hemisphere ''as the manifestation of an unfriendly disposition toward the United States.''

Canning resented disregard of Britain's overtures by the United States, but he could only welcome this exposition of an American policy toward Latin America that corresponded so closely with his own. It is doubtful whether the United States at this time would have been powerful enough to withstand determined action by a European coalition, but Britain's own interest in preventing European intervention in Latin America was to assure the United States the support of the British navy, even without a formal agreement, and it was the British navy that for many decades was the most redoubtable defender of the Monroe Doctrine.

In view of the subsequent course of U.S. expansion, it is important to note that the Monroe Doctrine, while denying the states of Europe, including Britain, the right to acquire additional colonies in the Western Hemisphere, did not preclude the United States from further expansion in that hemisphere or deny that country the right to intervene in the internal affairs of the states of Latin America. Moreover, by denying the states of Europe this right, the United States severely limited their ability to put into effect one of the more admirable resolutions agreed upon in Vienna and subsequent European congresses, namely, the suppression of the slave trade.

Thanks largely to British opposition to European intervention in the revolutions against Spanish and Portuguese rule in Latin America, these revolutions did not produce crises that might have developed into major international conflicts. The most serious threats to international peace among the great powers continued to be revolutions in Europe itself and above all the perennial crises in the Near East, which were all part of what came to be called the Eastern Question.

❑

THREE

The Eastern Question

❑ *The Decline of the Ottoman Empire and the Response of the Great Powers*

In the past two centuries the so-called Eastern Question has been one of the most dangerous sources of conflict in international affairs. The Crimean War, the most serious of European mid-nineteenth-century conflicts, was essentially a struggle over the Eastern Question; an incident in the Eastern Question struck the spark that set off World War I; and crises over the Eastern Question since that time have exploded into a steady succession of lesser but nonetheless dangerous wars.

There is no uniform definition of the geographical area of the Eastern Question, but most scholars would agree that it embraces the Balkan region of southeastern Europe, the Middle East, as bounded by the Caucasus Mountains in the northeast and the Red Sea in the south, and the eastern part of North Africa. Politically this entire area was part of the Ottoman empire at the beginning of the nineteenth century.

A glance at the map reveals the strategic importance of this region. The heart of the Ottoman empire (Anatolia, present-day Turkey) lies across the major land and sea routes between Europe, Asia, and Africa. The capital of that empire, Constantinople, lies across the most important of those sea routes, the Straits of the Bosporus and the Dardanelles, which flow between the Black Sea and the Mediterranean, forming the only warm-water outlet for the maritime commerce of European Russia and the entire Black Sea hinterland. The disintegration of the Ottoman empire, the rise of successor states, and the conflicts among great and small powers for control of this area are the central themes in the history of the Eastern Question in modern times.

At its greatest extent in the late seventeenth century, the Ottoman empire held suzerainty over the greater part of the Balkan peninsula and Hungary, over the north shore of the Black Sea to the Caucasus Mountains, over all of Asia Minor to the Caspian Sea in the east and the Persian Gulf in the south, and over the coastal states of North Africa to Algeria. In addition to this territorial dominion, the ruler of the Ottoman empire, the Turkish sultan, in his capacity as spiritual leader of the world's

MAP 2   THE TURKISH STRAITS

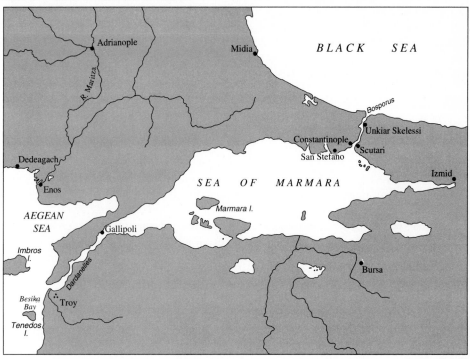

Muslims, held nominal sway over the entire Islamic world, from the Atlantic coast of Africa to India, the East Indies, and the islands of the Pacific.

By the end of the seventeenth century, the Ottoman empire had begun to decline in comparison with the European powers. The defeat of the Ottoman armies during the second siege of Vienna in 1683 marked the end of the empire's successful wars of conquest in eastern Europe and the beginning of a European counteroffensive. Within the empire ambitious local potentates managed to shake off all but the nominal authority of the sultan and establish themselves as quasi-independent rulers. In the course of the nineteenth century the empire was to be weakened still further by the growing self-consciousness of religious and national minorities, which engaged in a long succession of rebellions and frequently received foreign aid to free themselves from Ottoman dominion. Burdened with an antiquated and corrupt administration, faced with rebellion throughout its heterogeneous provinces, surrounded by large and small states eager to take over its territories, the Ottoman empire was in a perpetual state of crisis and was scornfully referred to as the Sick Man of Europe.

By the beginning of the nineteenth century, Austria and Russia had already seized large chunks of Ottoman territory. After turning back the Turks in their second siege of Vienna in 1683, the Austrians had advanced the boundary of their empire far to the south through the reconquest of Hungary, Transylvania, and large parts of Croatia and Slavonia. The Russians had done even better in acquiring the Crimean peninsula, the territory around the Sea of Azov, including control of the passage between the Sea of Azov and the Black Sea, and the entire north coast of the Black Sea. They had established a protectorate over a large part of the Caucasus, which they were later to annex, and with the acquisition of Bessarabia in 1812 they advanced their holdings along the west coast of the Black Sea as far as the Danube. These territorial gains gave Russia control of the mouths of the rivers which served as the principal channels of commerce and communication for the hinterlands of central and eastern Europe—the Danube, Dniester, Bug, and Dnieper, which flowed into the Black Sea, and the Don, which flowed into the Sea of Azov.

In addition the Russians had compelled the Turks to grant them important economic privileges, including freedom of navigation on the Black Sea, which had been closed to all but Turkish vessels since the end of the sixteenth century, and the right to send merchant ships through the Turkish Straits (the Bosporus and the Dardanelles) into the Mediterranean.

Russia's large-scale expansion at the expense of the Ottoman empire was checked by the end of the Napoleonic wars, not because of a revival of Turkish strength, but because other European powers had begun to fear the Russian threat to their own interests in the Near East and were prepared to shore up the tottering Ottoman empire to halt the Russian advance.

In contrast to Austria and Russia, which had steadily extended their dominions at the expense of the Ottoman empire, Britain and especially France had extended their influence in the Near East by establishing close political, military, and commercial ties with the Turks.

Since the fifteenth century, France had maintained close diplomatic relations with the Ottoman empire, which had served as a valuable ally in France's long struggles with the Habsburgs. Diplomatic ties were reinforced by commerce, and in the course of the eighteenth century French trade with Turkey increased so rapidly that France acquired a major economic stake in the Near East, especially in Asiatic Turkey.

The long tradition of Franco-Turkish friendship was disrupted when Napoleon led his expedition into the Ottoman province of Egypt in the summer of 1798 to strike at Britain's commercial lifelines and ensure the predominance of France in the Near East. His orders were to drive the British from as many of their Oriental possessions as he could reach, to cut a canal through the Isthmus of Suez, and "to ensure the French Republic the free and exclusive possession of the Red Sea."

French efforts to extend and consolidate their influence in the Near East were abruptly halted and French influence was substantially reduced when a British fleet under Nelson succeeded in destroying France's Mediterranean fleet in 1798. With the establishment of their naval supremacy in the eastern Mediterranean, the British proceeded to establish their commercial supremacy as well. In 1799 and 1809 Britain concluded two commercial treaties with Turkey which dramatically increased trade between the two countries, and for the duration of the Napoleonic wars the British navy effectively cut off Ottoman trade with France.

By the end of the Napoleonic wars, the British government had become convinced that British commercial as well as strategic interests required the prevention of further seizures of Turkish territory by rival powers, and that Britain must therefore seek to preserve the territorial integrity of the Ottoman empire. This British policy was supported by the Austrians, who had heretofore been busily engaged in the spoliation of the Ottoman realm and who as recently as 1781 had concluded a treaty with Russia providing for its partition. But by 1815 the Austrians were fully occupied with preserving their influence in Germany and Italy, and they had even greater reason than Britain to be apprehensive about further Russian expansion. Metternich in particular was obsessed by the fear that Russia would follow in the footsteps of France in seeking to dominate Europe, and he foresaw having to go to war to prevent Russia from becoming even more powerful through the extension of its dominion over strategic areas now controlled by Turkey. Like the British, he believed that this danger could be prevented most easily by preserving the sovereignty and territorial integrity of the Ottoman empire. The Ottoman empire, he said, was "a natural frontier which never claims our attention or dissipates our energies. We look upon Turkey as the last bastion standing in the way of another power." What *did* claim Metternich's attention was the weakness of the Ottoman empire. If it were allowed to collapse, he predicted it would break up into several parts, some of which would attempt to set themselves up as independent states. The result would be political anarchy followed by major wars among the European powers over the Turkish inheritance.

Russian policy toward the Ottoman empire veered between two alternatives. Among the great powers, Russia was in the most favorable geographical position to exercise influence over that empire and take advantage of its weakness. This weakness was a constant temptation to Russian expansionists, who had long sought to acquire Constantinople. The development of that city into a naval and commercial base would enable Russia to push its own sea power into the Mediterranean, prevent the entry of foreign warships into the Black Sea, and control the flow of commerce into the Black Sea and its hinterland. These territorial and economic temptations were stimulated further by a powerful messianic fervor among the Russians to protect their fellow Orthodox Christians in the Ottoman empire, and as racial and national consciousness developed in the course of the nineteenth century, this concern for fellow Christians was extended or transferred to fellow Slavs languishing under the rule of the Muslim Turks.

At the same time, the Russians also recognized the advantages of preserving the Ottoman empire, which formed an enormous buffer zone along Russia's southwestern flank, an empire too weak to threaten Russian security in any way but which through its very existence shielded Russia from more powerful neighbors. A further Russian advance at the expense of the Ottoman empire might well result in its collapse and partition among the European great powers, with the result that Russia would have dangerous rivals on its frontiers instead of the hapless Turks. There was also the consideration that by preserving the Ottoman empire, Russia, because of its favorable geographical position, might someday be able to take over all of it should a future international crisis temporarily immobilize Russia's rivals.

With the European great powers in general agreement about the desirability of preserving what was left of the Ottoman empire, and after the conclusion of the agreements of Troppau and Laibach to defend existing governments and their territories, the powers were confronted in the early 1820s with a major crisis in the Eastern Question resulting from a rebellion against Ottoman rule in Greece.

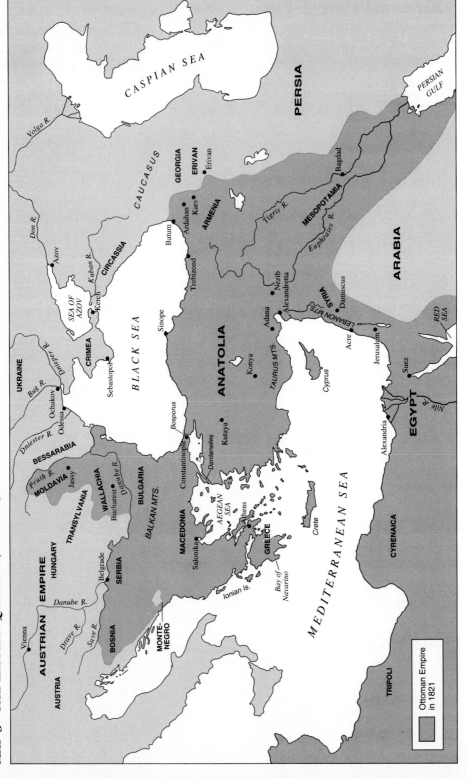

MAP 3 THE EASTERN QUESTION, 1821–1854

❑ *The Greek Revolution and the Dangers of Foreign Intervention*

The Greek revolution was one of a succession of revolutions against Ottoman rule in Europe that took place in the nineteenth century. These revolutions were all complicated by a multitude of local problems, and every generalization made about them is riddled with exceptions, but by and large it is possible to say that they shared the common qualities of being revolutions of native ethnic (largely Slavic) peoples against the foreign rule of the Turks and their satraps; of Christians (largely Greek Orthodox) against Muslims; and of native peasants and merchants against foreign landlords and a corrupt and exploitative administration. All were complicated by bitter factional rivalries among the revolutionaries themselves, by the appeals of factional leaders for the support of foreign powers, and by the direct or indirect intervention of these powers to protect their interests.

The Greek uprising aroused widespread sympathy among educated Europeans, who, in the early nineteenth century, still studied the language as well as the history and culture of ancient Greece and who saw in the struggle of contemporary Greeks against the Turks a parallel to the heroic wars of the ancient Greeks against the Persians. The Greeks also enjoyed widespread support from European Christians, especially from the Orthodox Christians of Russia and southeastern Europe, who regarded the Greek revolution as a latter-day crusade against the Muslim Turks.

Sentimental sympathy for the Greeks never overwhelmed the calculations of the leaders of the European great powers, who were far more concerned with the political implications of the Greek uprising. Far more clearly than the earlier revolutions in Spain and Italy, the Greek revolution showed why the statesmen of the great powers considered the suppression of revolution essential to preserve the general peace of Europe and maintain the balance of power. For Greece was a strategic area where the political and economic interests of all the great powers (apart from Prussia) might be critically affected.

In any revolution—and the revolution in Greece was no exception—leaders of revolutionary factions seek the support of foreign powers to strengthen their own position in the revolutionary movement and contribute to the success of the revolution itself. And any such effort on the part of revolutionary leaders tempts the statesmen of foreign powers to provide such support in the expectation that a revolutionary government which owes its success to a foreign state will in the future look to that state for protection and guidance. Precisely this temptation represented a threat to the peace of Europe in the Greek crisis, for if any single power gained undue influence in this critical strategic area, the European balance of power would be disrupted and rival powers might feel constrained to go to war to protect their own interests.

As the diplomats of that time saw it, the simplest way to eliminate such temptation and the hazards it might engender was to adhere to the principle to which all the continental powers had already agreed, namely, to support legitimate rulers in the suppression of revolution. In the case of Greece, this meant supporting the Turkish sultan and making certain Greece remained part of the Ottoman empire.

The temptations which European statesmen had feared the Greek revolution would produce made their appearance almost immediately. The Greeks addressed a passionate appeal for support to the tsar, who came under intense pressure from influential advisers to intervene in some fashion on behalf of the Greeks. In the summer of 1821 the tsar appeared on the verge of succumbing to this pressure. As so often happens in the atmosphere of violence and hatred engendered by revolution, both Greeks and Turks committed frightful atrocities. Greeks ruthlessly slaughtered the Turkish minority in many parts of the country, and the Turks retaliated by massacring Greeks in Constantinople and hanging the Greek patriarch. Incensed by reports of Turkish atrocities, the Russian government issued an ultimatum to Turkey on July 27, 1821, demanding protection for the Christian population and Christian churches in the Ottoman empire. The Turks rejected this ultimatum, Russia severed diplomatic relations with Turkey, and war seemed imminent.

❑ *The Efforts of Metternich and Castlereagh to Prevent Foreign Intervention*

Metternich was profoundly alarmed by the Greek crisis, for by rising up against their legitimate sovereign the Greeks had opened the floodgates to the forces of revolution and to further Russian expansion into southeastern Europe. In Metternich's view, there was every reason to fear that the impressionable tsar would fall completely under the influence of his Grecophile advisers and would use this opportunity to establish Russian control over the Greek peninsula under the guise of conducting a crusade on behalf of the Greek Christians against the heathen Turks. So great a threat to the European balance of power would be certain to unleash a general war that Austria could not afford to wage, and—far worse—a war in which Austria would have nothing to gain and a great deal to lose. The primary objective of Metternich's diplomacy during the Greek crisis, therefore, was to prevent Russia or any other power from intervening on behalf of the Greek revolutionaries and to aid the Turks in their suppression.

Metternich's fears were shared by Castlereagh (the Greek crisis had erupted a year before his suicide), who, now that British interests were at stake, assumed a much less hostile attitude toward the principle of foreign intervention for the suppression of revolution. The Greek revolution was not merely a question of a change of a particular form of government such as the revolution in Naples, he said. "The question of Turkey is of a totally different character and one which in England we regard not as a theoretical but practical consideration." Castlereagh's statement of the British government's position on the question of revolution could hardly have been more candid: revolutions where British interests were not involved were a theoretical consideration; but they became a practical consideration the moment British interests were affected, as was the case in Greece. The British now rejoined the Concert of Europe as though they had never been away.

Throughout the summer and autumn of 1821, Metternich and Castlereagh worked together to prevent Russian intervention on behalf of the Greek revolutionaries. This meant above all convincing the tsar of the dangers of such a course. Metternich's arguments all rested on the fundamental proposition that Russia's own interests were best served by seeking to preserve the existing political and social order, and for this purpose it was essential that the tsar cooperate in the suppression of revolution and not seek to avenge Turkish atrocities in the Ottoman empire, no matter how strongly he might feel about them.

Castlereagh's arguments ran along similar lines. He expressed confidence that in the present crisis the Russian ruler would afford yet another proof of his determination to maintain the inviolability of the European system as consolidated by the peace treaties of 1814–1815. The Greek rebellion represented no isolated phenomenon but was part of that "organized spirit of insurrection which is systematically propagating itself throughout Europe." Castlereagh did not deny the atrocities of the Turks, which were such as to make humanity shudder, but like Metternich he insisted that humanitarian considerations were subordinate to maintaining the "consecrated structure" of Europe, which would be jarred to the core by any radical insurrection.

To the relief of Metternich and Castlereagh, the tsar proved receptive to their arguments and eventually expressed complete agreement with them. His primary interest, he said, lay in preserving the peace and stability of Europe. War with Turkey would be a war on behalf of rebels against their legitimate ruler, it would fatally weaken the fragile conservative order established in Europe and allow the forces of disorder and revolution with their center in France to sweep once more over the continent. In response to the appeal of one of his pro-Greek advisers at the height of the crisis with Turkey in August 1821 he declared: "If we reply to the Turks with war, the Paris directory committee [by which he meant the revolutionary party in France] will triumph and no government will be left standing. . . . At all costs, means must be found of avoiding war with Turkey."

The tsar kept his word and did not intervene, despite a good deal of Turkish provocation. "I could have allowed myself to be swept along by the enthusiasm for the Greeks," he told the Prussian envoy to St. Petersburg in May 1822, "but I have never forgotten the impure origin of the rebellion or the danger of my intervention for my allies. Egotism is no longer the basis of policy. The principles of our truly Holy Alliance are pure."

❑ *The Accession of Tsar Nicholas I, the Intervention of Mehemet Ali, and the Policy of Canning*

Tsar Alexander I adhered to this course to the end of his reign, but in December 1825 he was succeeded on the throne of Russia by his brother, Nicholas I. With the accession of Nicholas there was a shift in Russian foreign policy. The new tsar did not subscribe to the principles of the Holy Alliance with the same enthusiasm as his brother; instead, he attempted to conduct a foreign policy more in line with Russian national interests as he understood them.

Nicholas has been described as an unimaginative bureaucrat, a simple and straightforward military man who believed the state should be organized and administered like a well-drilled army. It is difficult to understand how he could have acquired this reputation, for in many ways he was as complex and unpredictable as his brother. He was possessed by sudden hatreds and enthusiasms; he suffered from severe bouts of depression; his ideas could veer with disconcerting suddenness from one extreme to another; and like his brother he could be easily influenced by his advisers. Among his weaknesses as a diplomat was his predilection for dealing directly with other monarchs or their representatives and his confidence that he could solve the most complicated international problems through such personal diplomacy. This habit was to lead to serious misunderstandings with foreign governments and to some of his own most disastrous political miscalculations.

Nicholas's accession coincided with a decisive change in the situation in Greece. Unable to subdue the Greek rebellion, the sultan of Turkey appealed for aid to his nominal vassal, Mehemet Ali, the pasha of Egypt, who had built up a formidable army and navy by imposing immense tax burdens on his own people, borrowing heavily in European money markets, and employing European experts. Mehemet Ali responded to the sultan's appeal, and in February 1825 an Egyptian army under his son Ibrahim Pasha (who had been promised the island of Crete as a reward for his assistance) landed in Greece. By the end of the year Ibrahim, who was to prove a highly capable military leader, had subdued almost the entire peninsula. With the principal Greek revolutionary armies defeated and demoralized and the Turks once again in control of a large part of the country, the complete collapse of all Greek resistance seemed imminent.

Nicholas I quickly made it clear that, unlike his brother, he would not be constrained by the principles of monarchical solidarity; he intended to intervene to save the Greeks. Moreover, he saw reason to believe that his policy would be supported or at least condoned by Britain, where Canning had succeeded Castlereagh as foreign secretary. In the years since he took office, Canning had acquired an international reputation as a champion of liberty and foe of oppression. He had supported the cause of constitutional government in Portugal, and he had taken the lead in recognizing the revolutionary governments of Latin America. It was therefore natural to expect that he would be sympathetic to the cause of the Greeks, especially since as early as 1823 he had recognized the Greek revolutionaries as belligerents, which meant Britain no longer regarded them as rebels but as equals in their war with the Turks.

Canning, however, was as tenacious a guardian of British interests as Castlereagh and quite as aware of the dangers to those interests in the Greek situation. In recognizing the Greeks as belligerents, Canning had announced that he had taken this step to bring "within the bounds of a civilized war a contest which had been marked at the outset on both sides by disgusting barbarity." Canning had never explained how his recognition of the Greeks as belligerents might curb this barbarity, and his real motive in doing so appears to have been to put an end to Greek attacks on British shipping. He had done nothing further to aid the Greeks, and despite increasing pressure from British public opinion, incited by reports of Turkish atrocities, Canning had remained resolutely neutral. Early in 1825 he turned down a request from the Greek revolutionaries to be placed under British protection, and later in the year the British government issued a proclamation forbidding British subjects to take part in the war. When it appeared that the new tsar of Russia intended to intervene in the Greek revolution, Canning reacted exactly as Castlereagh might have done. If Russia declared war on behalf of the Greeks, he said, "she would gobble up Greece at one mouthful and Turkey at the next."

Canning, however, was unable to deal with Nicholas as Castlereagh had dealt with Alexander, for Nicholas showed no inclination to yield to diplomatic pressure or persuasion. Canning was therefore obliged to use different diplomatic tactics. To prevent unilateral Russian intervention against Turkey, he offered to collaborate with the tsar in dealing with the Greek problem, a stratagem that would enable him to exercise some control over Russian policy and thereby continue to keep Russia "grouped"—he even used the same term for this procedure as Castlereagh. Early in 1826 he sent the prestigious Duke of Wellington to St. Petersburg to assure the Russians that Britain was prepared to join them in using force to realize their joint objectives. At the same time the British ambassador to Constantinople (Canning's cousin Stratford Canning) was instructed to persuade the sultan to yield to future Anglo-Russian demands with respect to Greece and thus remove every possible excuse for Russia to intervene there or go to war with Turkey.

By April 1826 Wellington had succeeded in his mission. On the fourth of that month, Britain and Russia signed an agreement (the St. Petersburg Protocol) providing that Britain should offer to mediate between the Turks and Greeks with the object of making Greece an autonomous state where the Greeks should enjoy "complete freedom of conscience" and "complete commercial freedom" and be governed by authorities of their choice. To make these terms more palatable to the Turks, the agreement provided that the new Greek state was to remain technically a part of the Ottoman empire and pay an annual tribute to the sultan. The Turkish government was also conceded "a certain influence" in the nomination of the leaders of the Greek government. The agreement said nothing about the boundaries of the new state. In case British mediation failed, Britain and Russia reserved the right to act separately or together to force Turkish acceptance of these terms.

The great weakness of the Anglo-Russian agreement, as Canning well realized, was that it did not preclude a Russian attack against other parts of the Ottoman empire even if British mediation on behalf of the Greeks should be successful. To hold Russia in check, Canning now attempted to reactivate the European concert which he had heretofore so much despised. The terms of the Anglo-Russian agreement were revealed in confidence to the governments of Austria, France, and Prussia, which were asked to join in a guarantee of an eventual Greek-Turkish settlement.

Metternich, profoundly suspicious of Canning's motives, would have nothing to do with the Anglo-Russian agreement. He remained adamantly opposed to any program that would encourage rebellion, weaken Turkey, or contribute to any extension of Russian influence in the Balkans, and he persuaded the Prussian government to go along with Austria. The French, however, eager to protect their own interests in the Near East and always happy to promote rifts within the concert—which they still regarded as being primarily a coalition for the containment of France—joined the Anglo-Russian partnership in a formal treaty signed in London on July 6, 1827.

Canning had ample reason for apprehension about the future course of Russian policy. The day after the St. Petersburg Protocol was signed, the tsar sent a de facto ultimatum to the Ottoman government containing demands that had nothing to do with Greece, and the Turks, believing that Britain was now in partnership with Russia, yielded unconditionally. By the Convention of Akkerman of October 7, 1826, the Turks conceded Russia a virtual protectorate over Serbia and the Danubian Principalities of Moldavia and Wallachia (the future Romania) by granting Russia the authority to guarantee the rights and privileges of the inhabitants of these Balkan provinces of the Ottoman empire. They agreed further to recognize Russia's right to retain former Ottoman territories on the east coast of the Black Sea and the Caucasus region, acquired prior to the Russo-Turkish war of 1806–1812. Finally, they granted Russian merchantmen complete freedom of navigation on all domestic waterways of the Ottoman empire, including the all-important Turkish Straits.

Russia's success in extracting these concessions from the Turks was a blow to

Canning, whose policy of collaboration with Russia now appeared to have been a serious miscalculation, especially as the Turks still refused to yield to Anglo-Russian demands over Greece. Enrolling France in the Anglo-Russian partnership through the Treaty of London seemed to strengthen Britain's hand in dealing with both Russia and Turkey, but even with the addition of French pressure the Turks persisted in their refusal to make the desired concessions with respect to Greece.

To convince the Turks of their determination and unity of purpose, Britain, France, and Russia sent fleets to the eastern Mediterranean in the summer of 1827, and early in September they established a naval blockade around Greece to halt the shipment of supplies and reinforcements to the Turkish-Egyptian armies. By this time Canning was no longer in charge of British policy. He died suddenly in August 1827, barely five months after having succeeded the aged Earl of Liverpool as British prime minister. An interim government under Viscount Goderich was formed in September, giving way in January 1828 to a new government under the Duke of Wellington.

Meanwhile British policy in Greece continued along the course set by Canning. As the allied fleets proceeded to build up a naval blockade around Greece, a large Egyptian fleet with transports of men and supplies arrived at the Greek harbor of Navarino on September 8, 1827. Four days later a British squadron arrived off Navarino, where it was joined by French and Russian naval forces. On October 20 the allied navies entered the harbor of Navarino to compel the Egyptian fleet to return to Egypt. The Egyptians refused, fighting broke out, and within hours the allies had annihilated the combined Turkish-Egyptian fleets.

The allied victory at Navarino was anything but a triumph for British policy, which had been designed to prevent a conflict with Turkey and anything else that might serve as a pretext for a further extension of Russian influence in the Near East. Metternich viewed Navarino as a major catastrophe that might result in Russia's total domination of the Balkans, the collapse of the Ottoman empire, and a general European war.

The Turks, instead of being intimidated by Navarino and finally yielding to allied demands on Greece, were goaded to indignant fury by this allied act of war while their governments were still nominally at peace, and they were now more determined than ever to resist. In November they repudiated the Convention of Akkerman with Russia, and in December the allied ambassadors left Constantinople.

❏ The Russo-Turkish War of 1828 and the Treaty of Adrianople

The Russians can only have welcomed the Turkish repudiation of Akkerman, which gave them an excuse to take military action against the Ottoman empire while still aligned with Britain and France. On April 26, 1828, as soon as the snow had melted in the passes of the Balkan mountains, Russia declared war on Turkey.

Contrary to their expectations, the Russians did not score a quick military victory that would have enabled them to dictate terms to the Turks before other powers could intervene with offers of mediation. The tsar, who took personal command of his armies, was an inept military leader, the Russian supply system was abominable, and the Russian armies were soon to be decimated by disease. The war dragged on for over a year, but by the summer of 1829 the Turkish military position on both the eastern and western fronts of the Black Sea had deteriorated so seriously that the Turkish government was obliged to sue for peace. On September 14, 1829, Russian and Turkish plenipotentiaries signed the Treaty of Adrianople, which formally brought the war to an end.

The Russians did not exploit their victory over the Turks as fully as they might have because they feared other European powers might yet intervene on the side of the Turks. Even so, the Treaty of Adrianople was anything but moderate or lenient.

To avoid a direct challenge to the interests of other powers, the Russians restored to Turkey most of their conquests of Turkish territory in Europe, but the treaty reaffirmed the provisions of the Convention of Akkerman which gave Russia a de facto protectorate over Serbia and the Danubian Principalities. It also advanced the frontier of Russia to the southernmost channel of the Danube delta, thus giving Russia control of the entrance to the most important artery of transportation and communication of central and southeastern Europe. Russian troops were to occupy the Danubian Principalities pending Turkish payment of an indemnity of ten million Dutch ducats, the Turks were to raze all their own fortresses in the Principalities, and, in a provision foreshadowing the horrendous population transfers of the twentieth century, the Turks were required to remove the entire Muslim population from the Principalities. By the terms of this treaty, too, the Turks were compelled to recognize the autonomy of Greece, which the Russians undoubtedly hoped would now also become part of their sphere of influence in the Balkans.

Russian gains were even greater on the eastern side of the Black Sea. They acquired control of the entire Black Sea coast from the Kuban River (south of the Sea of Azov) to a point just north of Batum; they gained a better strategic frontier in the provinces of Kars and Ardahan; and they secured Turkish recognition of Russian claims to Erivan. Altogether this treaty represented an immense extension of Russian territory in the Caucasus region along the northeastern frontiers of the Ottoman empire.

Fear of foreign intervention was not the only reason the Russians did not exploit their victory over the Turks even more fully. Shortly before the end of the war, the tsar had set up a special committee to consider the future course of Russian policy toward the Ottoman empire. That committee had recommended the speedy conclusion of peace and a policy of restraint. By continuing the war or attempting to make still further gains, Russia ran the risk of the intervention of one or more of the European great powers on behalf of the Turks, or their participation in a wholesale partition of the Ottoman empire, which would mean that the weak and ineffective Turkish government would be replaced by powerful and dangerous rivals. The interests of Russia would be best served, the tsar's advisers believed, by preserving the Ottoman empire, whose existence represented no threat to Russian security but was on the contrary a valuable safeguard of Russia's southern frontier. Meanwhile the decline of Turkey should be allowed to continue unhindered and unassisted, leaving Russia in a position to absorb the entire Ottoman empire at some time when its rivals were occupied elsewhere or some other propitious opportunity should present itself.

The tsar accepted this advice, and for the next two decades Russia refrained from further advances at the expense of the Ottoman empire and cooperated to prevent the encroachments of other states.

❑ *The Recognition of Greek Independence*

In the course of the Russo-Turkish war, Metternich had attempted to resurrect the European concert through a general congress on Near Eastern affairs. He hoped that such a congress would dissolve the Anglo-French partnership with Russia and compel Russia to make peace with Turkey on terms satisfactory to the other powers, Austria in particular. Metternich's refusal to compromise in any way on the question of Greek independence, however, made it impossible for him to secure the support of the British and French governments for a congress. Both were confronted with serious domestic difficulties (which in France led to the revolution of 1830, in Britain to the franchise reform bill of 1832) and neither could afford to ignore the powerful pro-Greek sentiment in their respective countries. In an effort to cater to this sentiment and, more importantly, to prevent Russia from claiming sole credit for helping the Greeks and thereby gaining a predominant influence in their country, Britain and France concluded another treaty with Russia. The so-called New London Protocol, signed February 3, 1830, provided for the establishment of a completely autonomous Greek state that would no longer be even nominally under Turkish suzerainty. This treaty also defined the future boundaries of the new state (which inevitably were far narrower than the Greeks desired), it stipulated that the future Greek government should be a hereditary monarchy, and it provided that the independence of Greece be safeguarded by a joint guarantee of the signatory powers.

Freedom from Turkish rule and national independence did not usher in a new era of peace and harmony in Greek domestic affairs. On the contrary, factional strife continued and the first years of independence were marked by frequent riots, bloodshed, and general instability. In February 1832 the three allied governments at last managed to agree on a candidate for the throne of Greece, Prince Otto of Bavaria. To make the rule of this foreign prince more palatable to the Greeks, the allies promised to negotiate an extension of the Greek boundaries and to arrange a substantial loan to the new government. On February 6, 1833, Prince Otto landed in Greece accompanied by thirty-five hundred Bavarian soldiers, who were thought necessary to protect the new regime and maintain order.

The leaders of the allied governments expressed considerable satisfaction about their handling of the Greek affair and "on having come to a perfect agreement, in the midst of the most serious and delicate circumstances." Palmerston, British foreign secretary since November 1830, was particularly euphoric about his own contribution to the settlement, especially his success in securing better boundaries for Greece, which he believed would enable that country to defend itself more effectively and thus be more truly independent. In August 1832 he reported enthusiastically to the House of Commons that "the interests of civilization, the interests of commerce, and the interests of political independence are all in the interests of England, and all have been signally promoted by the emancipation of Greece."

The allies' actual achievements were a good deal less impressive than their own estimation of them. Their settlement over Greece was not regarded as satisfactory or final by either the Greeks or the Turks; they had not succeeded in establishing a stable government in Greece; and they had contributed substantially to increasing the instability within the Ottoman empire. Already in November 1831 another serious crisis erupted in the Near East when Mehemet Ali, the pasha of Egypt, encouraged by the successes of Russia and Greece, attacked his nominal overlord, the sultan of Turkey, to make some territorial gains of his own (see Chapter 5).

Yet, given the complexity of the problems in the Near East and the passions aroused in the course of the Greek revolution, it is impossible to see how the allies could have worked out a more satisfactory settlement. Unable to unite in suppressing the Greek revolution as Metternich had advocated, the powers found themselves compelled to condone and even support it, and in the end to recognize Greek autonomy. The establishment of an independent Greek state marked the first major change in the map of Europe since 1815, but that change had taken place without unleashing a major European war, as Metternich had feared it would. It had nevertheless severely shaken the international system, it had exposed the weakness of the Ottoman empire and therewith encouraged other states and revolutionary movements to take advantage of this weakness, and it had once again aroused general apprehension about the ambitions of Russia and the Russian threat to the security and interests of all the states of Europe.

FOUR

❑

The Revolutions of 1830 and the Revolutions in Portugal and Spain

❑ *The July Revolution in France*

In the councils of the great powers, the final negotiations over Greece were completely overshadowed by the outbreak of revolution in France in July 1830, an uprising that set off a chain reaction of revolution in almost every part of Europe. These insurrections, which involved all the powers in serious domestic as well as international difficulties, largely explain why the great powers allowed settlements to be made in the Near East that they might otherwise have opposed vigorously, and why they delayed so long in dealing with the new crisis in the Near East arising from the Egyptian attack on the Ottoman empire in November 1831.

The 1830 revolution in France, unlike the great revolution of 1789, was scarcely more than a coup d'état. The unpopular Bourbons were ousted with relative ease and were succeeded by a collateral branch of the royal family, the House of Orléans. The difference between Orléans and Bourbon (and at that time the difference seemed very great indeed) was that the former had come to power through revolution and that the new king, Louis Philippe, the head of the House of Orléans, claimed to rule by the grace of the sovereignty of the people instead of by the grace of God or the principle of legitimacy.

Louis Philippe, however, proved to be a cautious, unimaginative, and essentially conservative ruler, whose pronouncements about the sovereignty of the people did not mean that he intended "the people," or even their popularly elected representatives, should actually govern the country.

At the news of the July Revolution in France, the tsar immediately appealed to his fellow monarchs for joint action to overthrow the revolutionary regime. He found no support from the governments of the other great powers, however, whose leaders took a surprisingly calm view of events in France. Upon receiving assurances from Louis Philippe that he had no intention of embarking on an adventurous foreign policy and would scrupulously observe the 1815 treaties, they decided to overlook this violation of the principles of Troppau and Laibach. Very shortly after the establishment of the Orléans government in France, Austria, Britain, and Prussia accorded it diplomatic recognition. Four months later Russia did so as well, although with very bad grace on the part of the tsar, who continued to regard Louis Philippe as a usurper.

The great powers, with an unwilling Nicholas in tow, condoned the 1830 revolution in France because they did not perceive the new French government as a threat to their own interests and because intervention would have been a costly and potentially dangerous undertaking. An allied invasion of France would certainly have aroused the wrath of the French people and might have unleashed a far more dangerous revolution. All proposals to intervene were in any case shortly laid to rest when the other European powers were confronted with revolutions in their own spheres of interest as well as with serious domestic crises.

T he 1830 uprisings in the smaller states of Germany and Italy were to have a good deal of significance for the political development of those countries, but they had no serious international repercussions and were soon brought under control with the aid of Austria and Prussia.

❑ *The Belgian Revolution*

Of all the revolutions of 1830, the one that was to prove the most serious threat to the general peace of Europe was an uprising in the Belgian provinces of the Netherlands, whose aim was the breakup of their union with Holland. This union had been arranged in the peace settlements of 1814–1815 with the object of creating a more formidable bulwark in the Low Countries against France and a state more capable of defending its independence against all comers.

From the beginning the Belgians had felt restive in the new union. Although more than half the population of the Belgian provinces was Flemish, these people, who spoke a language closely akin to Dutch, by and large felt little affinity to the Dutch of Holland, and there was even less feeling of kinship on the part of the other half of the Belgian population, the French-speaking Walloons. Predominantly Roman Catholic in religion, the Flemish and Walloons both resented the assumption of moral superiority on the part of the Protestant Dutch, and they believed that in every other way they had been relegated to a subservient position in the new partnership. The king of the Netherlands was Dutch and a Calvinist, the seat of the government was in Holland, the administration, the economy, and the majority of public institutions were dominated by the Dutch. Although the Belgians accounted for well over half of the population, the Dutch were allotted an equal number of seats in the lower chamber of the Netherlands parliament.

Inspired by the example of the July Revolution in France, the Belgians rose up against the Dutch in August 1830, and in October they proclaimed the independence of the new state of Belgium. The king of the Netherlands, William I, immediately appealed to the great powers to honor the guarantees embodied in their 1814–1815 treaties and come to the aid of the Netherlands to suppress the Belgian revolution. Tsar Nicholas I once again took the lead in calling upon his fellow monarchs to join in the suppression of revolution, but the other great powers were as reluctant as ever to welcome the passage of Russian troops over their territories or to allow the tsar to bring his power to bear in western Europe.

Foreign intervention was impossible in any case because Britain and France, the countries whose interests were most immediately affected in the Netherlands, flatly refused to allow intervention of any kind. In the case of Belgium, however, they were not so much concerned about Russia as about each other. Talleyrand, once again on the diplomatic stage as ambassador of the new Orléans government to London, informed the British that France could not tolerate the intervention of another great power in a country so close to its own borders. The British for their part feared that France would take advantage of this crisis to annex Belgium and therewith gain a springboard for further expansion in western Europe—or for an invasion of England.

In France, despite pressure from many quarters to intervene on behalf of the Belgians and in particular the French-speaking Walloons, Louis Philippe pursued a policy of restraint. He realized that his new government could not afford a conflict or even a serious altercation with Britain or any other power, which a French move in the Netherlands would be certain to provoke. He therefore proposed that the powers settle the Belgian question as they had so recently settled the question of Greece by agreeing to the establishment of an independent Belgian state under a monarchical form of government. This solution would have the advantage for France of breaking up the Netherlands union created as a barrier against France, and it would improve the chances of France's absorption of Belgium at some more propitious opportunity. Louis Philippe's proposal was not favorably received by the leaders of the other great powers, who saw as clearly as he did its advantages for France, but they did agree to deal with the Belgian question through an international congress which convened in London on November 4, 1830.

The first move of the London congress was to arrange an armistice between the Belgians and the Dutch. This would allow the great powers to work out a solution to the Belgian question most satisfactory to themselves while avoiding the danger that one side or the other would suddenly gain a decisive military advantage. The British prime minister, the Duke of Wellington, whose government fell soon after the congress convened, favored maintaining the Netherlands union as a bulwark against France. This was also the position of Palmerston, the foreign secretary in the cabinet of Wellington's successor, Lord Grey. But Palmerston soon came to realize that imposing union on the Belgian rebels might drive them into the arms of France and thus create the very situation the British most feared. To avoid this possibility, Palmerston came forward as an advocate of Belgian independence, a policy stoutly seconded by France, which had favored this solution all along. The governments of Austria, Prussia, and Russia would have preferred the suppression of revolution in Belgium, but, occupied as they were with revolutions in their own spheres of interest, they found themselves obliged to agree to the solution favored by the powers most immediately concerned with the Belgian problem.

By an agreement of December 20, 1830, the powers recognized the de facto separation of the Belgian provinces from the Kingdom of the Netherlands. The intricate question of the boundaries between the two countries was settled in January of the following year, and in June 1831 the powers announced the selection of Prince Leopold of the tiny German state of Saxe-Coburg as the first king of the Belgians.

The Belgian crisis was not yet over. King William of the Netherlands rejected the settlement arranged by the powers, and in August 1831 he broke off the armistice with the Belgians and launched an attack on the unprepared Belgian forces. The powers now reluctantly authorized French intervention on behalf of the Belgians, but not before imposing strict limitations on the scope and duration of that intervention. By the end of the year the last Dutch forces had been driven from Belgium, the French withdrew in accordance with their agreements, and with that this final danger of a confrontation between the great powers over the Belgian question came to an end.

On November 15, 1831, the great powers and Belgium signed the Treaty of London, which provided for the establishment of an independent and neutral Belgium, defined the frontiers of the new state, and placed it under the joint guarantee of the signatory powers. Not until August 1839 did the government of Holland finally recognize Belgian independence.

The subsequent history of Belgium showed that the fears of the peacemakers of 1814–1815 had not been without justification. The Belgian provinces, standing alone, were a constant temptation to the territorial ambitions of more powerful neighbors. They proved to be a seductive lure to Napoleon III in the 1860s, and it was Germany's violation of Belgian neutrality in 1914 that propelled Britain into World War I.

The resolution of the Belgian crisis and avoidance of a general European war over this strategic region once again demonstrated the efficacy of the Congress system: the settlement of international problems at the conference table through negotiation and compromise. It is also noteworthy that the British, who had professed to shun the European concert in earlier crises, not only participated but played a leading role in cooperating with the other great powers to impose their decisions on the Dutch, and, far more important, to impose mutual restraint upon each other.

❑ *The Revolution in Poland*

A major reason why Tsar Nicholas I was unable to press more vigorously for international intervention to preserve the settlements of 1815 in the Low Countries was the outbreak of revolution within his own dominions: an uprising against Russian overlordship in Poland that began in November 1830.

At the Congress of Vienna, the greater part of the former state of Poland (or those territories inhabited by a majority of Polish-speaking peoples) had been reestablished as a kingdom under the protection of Russia with the tsar of Russia as king. Although granted a constitution more liberal than any conceded the peoples of Russia, Polish nationalists resented Russian overlordship. Their 1830 revolution aimed at complete independence from Russia and the restoration of the Polish state as it had existed before the partitions of the late eighteenth century. The Polish revolution thus threatened the interests not only of Russia, but of Austria and Prussia, Russia's partners in the spoliation of Poland. The Polish revolution nevertheless evoked widespread popular sympathy throughout the states of Germany, as it did in most other parts of Europe. Liberals and Roman Catholics joined in expressions of support for the predominantly Roman Catholic Poles against autocratic Orthodox Russia.

Despite the international reverberations of the Polish revolution, the uprising did not lead to serious international complications. The governments of Austria and Prussia did not allow their policies to be affected by popular sympathy for the Poles, they kept a watchful eye on their own Polish populations, and they stood by as the tsarist government ruthlessly crushed the rebellion. By September 1831 the principal Polish revolutionary armies had been defeated, and the Russian general Paskievich informed the tsar that "Warsaw is at Your Majesty's feet." The constitution granted the Poles in 1815 was now revoked and replaced in February 1832 by the so-called Organic Statute, which made the Kingdom of Poland an "indivisible part of the Russian Empire."

A tragic addendum to this unhappy chapter in Polish history took place fifteen years later when the only independent Polish state left in existence by the statesmen of 1815, the minute Republic of Cracow, was extinguished. This action took place in the wake of a Polish uprising against Austrian rule in Galicia, the principal Austrian spoil from the eighteenth-century partitions of Poland. One of the first acts of the Galician insurgents had been to proclaim the establishment of a provisional government in Cracow, long a center of Polish nationalist agitation and propaganda.

In Galicia itself the local peasants, most of them Ruthenians, did not join in the rebellion against Austria but instead used this occasion to rise against their Polish landlords. Their savage destruction of life and property profoundly shocked the Austrian authorities, who were nevertheless accused by Polish nationalists of having encouraged these attacks on the Polish gentry. This charge, although readily believed by the many European liberals who sympathized with Polish nationalist aspirations, had no effect on Tsar Nicholas, who called upon the Austrians to eliminate the Cracow hotbed of revolution and annex it to Galicia. With a considerable show of reluctance, which may well have been genuine, Metternich agreed to violate the provisions of the Vienna treaty regarding Cracow (and thus also the public law of Europe), and by a Convention of November 6, 1846, signed by representatives of the governments of Austria, Prussia, and Russia, the free city of Cracow was united to the Austrian monarchy.

❑ *The Revolutions in Portugal and Spain; the Policies of Palmerston*

Independent of the revolutions of 1830 in terms of strict chronology—although certainly part of the general revolutionary ferment of this era—were domestic upheavals in the states of the Iberian Peninsula, Portugal and Spain. Here the principal interventionist power was Britain; the chief architect of Britain's Iberian policy was Henry John Temple, Viscount Palmerston.

Palmerston, whom we met in connection with the problems of Greece and Belgium, was one of the most influential British statesmen in the quarter century after 1830. When he became foreign secretary in November 1830, he had already had many years of experience in government. Elected to the House of Commons in 1807, he was appointed lord of the admiralty shortly afterward and then secretary for war, a post he held under five prime ministers until 1829. His tenure at the foreign office was to be almost as long. Apart from one brief interlude, he served as foreign secretary from 1830 to 1841 and again from 1846 to 1851. In December 1852 he became home secretary in the cabinet of Lord Aberdeen, whom he succeeded as prime minister in 1855 in the darkest days of the Crimean War, a position he was to hold, again with brief interludes, until his death in office on October 18, 1865, in his eighty-first year.

A man of prodigious energy, Palmerston wrote all important policy directives himself and rarely sought or accepted the advice of colleagues or professional experts on his own staff. Although a member of the post-Napoleonic generation of statesmen, Palmerston was not one of those who saw international crises in a pan-European perspective or who believed in cooperation among the great powers in trying to resolve them through negotiation or compromise. Dogmatically certain of the correctness of his own views, he felt similar certainty about the moral primacy of England and sincerely believed that in furthering the interests of England he was at the same time serving the interests of humanity. Like George Canning, the foreign secretary and prime minister who had died in 1827, he believed in bold and unquestioning championship of British interests on every conceivable issue in every part of the world. Palmerston's consistent and often dramatic advocacy of a forceful and active British foreign policy made him one of the most popular statesmen of his day in his own country. These same qualities made him one of the most formidable and dangerous figures in world affairs.

❑ *Britain and Portugal*

Britain had a long history of involvement in the affairs of the Iberian Peninsula, and in the course of the Napoleonic wars it had gained an unusual degree of influence in both Portugal and Spain as a result of its leading role in driving out the French. In Spain, British influence had given way to that of France after troops of the Bourbon monarchy intervened to restore the authority of King Ferdinand VII in 1823 (see p. 41), but the British had retained their dominant position in Portugal.

In the late 1820s and early 1830s the influence of both Britain and France in Iberia was challenged by conservative pretenders to the thrones of Portugal and Spain who enjoyed the support of conservative elements within those countries and who looked for support to Europe's conservative powers. In Portugal the conservative challenge came from Dom Miguel, who became regent of the country in 1826 upon the accession to the crown of his seven-year-old niece as Queen Maria II.

In January 1827 George Canning, who so self-righteously condemned the intervention of rival powers in the domestic affairs of foreign governments, sent an expeditionary force of four thousand men to Lisbon to prevent any attempt on the part of Dom Miguel to overthrow what Canning termed the "legal-constitutional" (and pro-British) government of Portugal. These troops were withdrawn in April of the following year upon Dom Miguel's promise to respect the constitution, but he promptly violated this promise, abolished the constitution, and had himself proclaimed king.

Queen Maria fled to the court of her father, Dom Pedro, who had renounced the throne of Portugal to become emperor of the former Portuguese colony of Brazil when that country declared its independence in 1822. In April 1831, Dom Pedro, confronted with serious Brazilian domestic discontent, thought it prudent to abdicate in favor of his infant son, and together with Maria he went to England where he sought British aid to regain the throne of Portugal for his daughter.

Dom Pedro's efforts were warmly supported by Palmerston, who saw in his campaign to oust Dom Miguel a means to restore constitutional government (and British influence) in Portugal. Dom Pedro was allowed to recruit a sizable army in Britain, and in July 1833 Sir Charles Napier, a British admiral masquerading under the name of Carlos Ponza, defeated the fleet of Dom Miguel off Cape St. Vincent. This naval victory enabled Dom Pedro's army to land and capture Lisbon. In September 1833 Maria II was restored to her throne. It was to be another eight months, however, before Dom Miguel himself was finally defeated.

❏ *Britain and Spain*

The British effort to regain influence in Portugal had meanwhile merged with a parallel effort to take advantage of a civil war in Spain for a similar purpose. The troubles in Spain had begun almost immediately after the death in September 1833 of King Ferdinand VII, that same monarch whose authority had been restored by the French in 1823. Ferdinand had been married three times without producing an heir, and it was generally assumed that he would be succeeded by his brother, Don Carlos, whose political views were if anything even more reactionary than those of Ferdinand himself. But in 1829 Ferdinand married Maria Cristina, the daughter of the Bourbon king Ferdinand II of Naples (and a granddaughter of Empress Maria Theresa of Austria), who bore him two daughters: Isabella in 1830 and Luisa Fernanda in 1832.

In June 1833, to secure the succession for her daughter, Queen Maria Cristina persuaded Ferdinand to set aside the Salic law, which prohibited succession through the female line, thereby thwarting the hopes of Don Carlos. Upon the death of Ferdinand three months later, Maria Cristina became regent for her infant daughter, whose succession was immediately recognized by the governments of Britain and France. Just as immediately, her succession was challenged by Don Carlos, who joined forces with Dom Miguel in Portugal where he hoped to raise an army to assert his own claim to the Spanish crown.

Palmerston opposed the pretensions of Don Carlos in Spain as he opposed the regime of Dom Miguel in Portugal, and in both countries he championed the cause of what he chose to regard as liberal-constitutional governments. Such a policy, quite apart from its high moral purpose, would have the additional advantage of establishing governments in Portugal and Spain that could henceforth be expected to look to Britain for guidance and support. In pursuing this course he believed he could count on the cooperation of the new government of Louis Philippe in France, which Palmerston also chose to classify as a liberal-constitutional regime and one which had also recognized the succession of Isabella. Further, because the new French government was the product of revolution, it was regarded with hostile suspicion by Europe's conservative powers. To avoid complete diplomatic isolation, it would therefore have no alternative but to enter into what Palmerston called an *entente cordiale* with Britain.

"The great object of our policy," Palmerston informed his ambassador to Madrid in February 1834, "ought now to be to form a Western confederacy of free states as a counterpoise to the Eastern League of arbitrary governments. England, France, Spain and Portugal, united as they now must be, will form a political and moral power in Europe which will hold Metternich and Nicholas in check . . . and all the smaller planets of Europe will have a natural tendency to gravitate towards our system."

The French, who since 1823 had regarded Spain as *their* sphere of influence in Iberia and compensation for Britain's paramount influence in Portugal, had no desire to be relegated to the position of junior partner in Madrid, as Palmerston clearly intended they should be. But Talleyrand, ambassador of the Orléans monarchy to London, recognized as well as Palmerston that France in its diplomatic isolation had no alternative to alignment with Britain. He therefore persuaded his reluctant monarch to agree to Palmerston's proposal of an alliance that would include Portugal and Spain, but at the same time he took care to ensure that French policy in Iberia should not be subordinated to that of Britain and that France should preserve its freedom of action.

According to the terms of the Quadruple Alliance of April 22, 1834, all four states agreed to join forces to expel Dom Miguel from Portugal. Spain promised to provide troops for this purpose that were to leave Portugal as soon as their mission was accomplished; Britain was to provide naval support; and France was to join in military operations if this should be necessary. Talleyrand thus left France the option to intervene or not, as its interests seemed to require.

Palmerston was delighted with his success in putting together the Quadruple Alliance, which he described as a "capital hit, and all my own doing." It would settle the problem of Portugal and possibly that of Spain as well, but "what is of more permanent and extensive importance, it establishes a quadruple alliance among the constitutional states of the west, which will serve as a powerful counterpoise to the Holy Alliance of the east." Palmerston wrote in the same vein to his brother, adding, "I should like to see Metternich's face when he reads it."

Soon after the signature of the Quadruple Alliance, the problem of Portugal, or more accurately the problem of Dom Miguel, was indeed settled. The British-supported expeditionary force that had landed in Portugal in July of the previous year restored Queen Maria to her throne in September. In the spring of 1834 the army of Dom Miguel was decisively defeated, and both he and Don Carlos agreed to leave Portugal permanently.

The defeat of Dom Miguel did not usher in an era of peace and political stability—or of political liberalism—in Portugal, where the political situation remained unsettled and the government became increasingly authoritarian, but it did ensure the restoration of British influence. This was to be reinforced in 1836 through the marriage of Queen Maria II to Duke Ferdinand of Saxe-Coburg, whose family the French were soon to call the "Coburg tribe" because of its association with so many of the royal houses of Europe: Ferdinand's uncle Leopold had become king of the Belgians in 1831; his cousin Victoria would become queen of England in 1837; and she in turn married another Coburg cousin, Albert, in the following year.

The problem of Spain was not settled so easily. After the defeat of his ally Dom Miguel, the Spanish pretender Don Carlos went into exile briefly (in England), but in July 1834 he returned to Spain. Here he found refuge and support in the northern provinces, traditionally hostile to the central government, and he proceeded to rally conservative forces throughout the country to his cause. His return marked the beginning of the so-called Carlist War, which was to continue for another five years and was waged with fearful brutality on both sides.

The regent Maria Cristina appealed for support from Britain and France under the terms of the Quadruple Alliance, but intervention in Spain involved far more complicated international problems than similar action in Portugal. Palmerston, much though he might desire the defeat of the Carlists, feared that French intervention would ensure the restoration of French primacy in Madrid. He therefore rejected a French request for a guarantee of British aid in case French action in Spain should provoke an attack on France by Europe's conservative powers. Without such a guarantee, the cautious Louis Philippe decided against French intervention and in the end did no more than allow four thousand members of the French Foreign Legion to volunteer for service in Spain.

Palmerston saw no need to exercise similar caution. The British government gave the Maria Cristina regime an interest-free loan of three million pounds and arranged for the Rothschild bank to lend another three million in return for concessions in Spain's mercury mines. Britain also supplied direct military aid. Shortly after the signature of the Quadruple Alliance, the British government had suspended the Foreign Enlistment Act and cast a benevolent eye on the recruitment of a British Legion of ten thousand men. Formed too late for service in Portugal, the British Legion was sent to Spain under the command of a British officer, Sir George de Lacy Evans, but it was so poorly trained and equipped and was soon to be so decimated by disease that its impact on the fighting was negligible. It was the British navy that was the most important instrument of British intervention in Spain, as it had been in Portugal, by making it impossible for Europe's conservative powers to come to the aid of the conservative pretender.

Even without substantial British or French military support, the government of Maria Cristina gradually gained the upper hand in the Spanish civil war thanks to the competence of its own generals and to growing dissension and disaffection in the Carlist camp. Following a succession of Carlist military defeats in 1838 and 1839, the Carlists finally gave up the struggle and with the signature of the Convention of Vergara of August 31, 1839, the Carlist War came to an end. Don Carlos again went into exile, this time to France.

In Spain as in Portugal, the defeat of the conservative pretender did not put an end to domestic turmoil or ensure the triumph of liberal institutions, nor did it put an end to Anglo-French rivalry for influence in that country, which was to develop into an ugly crisis in the following decade.

❑ *The Affair of the Spanish Marriages*

For the sake of continuity, albeit at the expense of chronology, that crisis might best be described here. It arose over the question of the marriages of Queen Isabella and her sister, Luisa Fernanda, her immediate successor to the Spanish crown. The French feared that the marriage of either sister to a member of the Coburg tribe would consolidate British influence at the Madrid court, while the British harbored identical fears about a Spanish marriage to a member of the royal family of France.

In September 1841, however, the conciliatory Lord Aberdeen succeeded Palmerston at the British foreign office. In the interests of better relations with France, he concluded a gentlemen's agreement with his French counterpart, François Guizot, restricting the candidacy for the Spanish marriages to members of the Spanish or Neapolitan branches of the Bourbon family, thus specifically excluding the candidacy of a Coburg or a French prince. When shortly afterward the pro-French party in the Spanish parliament, the *moderados,* successfully displaced the pro-British faction, the *progresistas,* Aberdeen made no move to intervene and even seemed to concede France still further influence in Madrid by agreeing to the marriage of Luisa Fernanda to a son of King Louis Philippe, though with the proviso that this marriage should not take place until after Isabella had been married and produced an heir. The entire marriage question was "not an adequate cause of national quarrel," Aberdeen said.

The conciliatory policy of Aberdeen was abruptly reversed with the return of Palmerston to the foreign office in July 1846. In Palmerston's view "the independence of Spain would be endangered, if not destroyed, by the marriage of a French Prince into the Royal Family of Spain," and to counter this danger he revived the prospect of a Coburg candidacy for the hand of Isabella. In great alarm Guizot convinced Louis Philippe that Palmerston's repudiation of Aberdeen's promises had nullified all previous French commitments, and he proceeded to engineer the simultaneous engagement of Isabella to a Spanish Bourbon and of Luisa Fernanda to a son of Louis Philippe. Both marriages took place on October 10, 1846.

Guizot evidently regarded the Spanish marriages as a masterful diplomatic stroke on his part, but they proved to be as unfortunate for Guizot as for the women involved. Isabella detested her husband and blamed the French for her unhappy fate so that French influence in Madrid was actually endangered by the marriage coup. Far worse, Guizot had made an implacable enemy of Palmerston, who from this time forward rejected all overtures to revive Anglo-French cooperation and did everything in his power to frustrate French policy at every turn. Failures in foreign policy contributed to a steady decline in the prestige and popularity of the Orléans monarchy, accounting in part for its helplessness when confronted with the revolutionary crisis of 1848. Louis Philippe's first move to appease the revolutionaries was the dismissal of Guizot, but only hours later he and his entire government were to be swept away (see p. 80).

The British managed to retain firmer control over Portugal. They kept a squadron in Portuguese waters to watch over their interests, and ten years after the Coburg marriage they again intervened directly in Portuguese affairs in response to an appeal for aid from Queen Maria, who was confronted with rebellion provoked by the increasingly authoritarian policies of her government. Metternich observed this action on the part of Britain, which had so frequently decried Austrian interventionist policies, with wry amusement, and even Palmerston admitted that the "moral" distinction between British intervention and that of other powers had ceased to exist.

The Miguelist and Carlist wars and the political problems arising in their aftermath loom large in the history of Portugal and Spain, and as we have seen they were closely monitored by the governments of Britain and France. But throughout this period of civil strife in Iberia, and even as the great powers were working out the final details of the Belgian settlement, the attention of all the European governments was concentrated on a renewed crisis in the Near East, this one set off by the ambitions of Mehemet Ali, the pasha of Egypt.

FIVE

The Eastern Question, Continued

❑ *The Egyptian Crisis, 1831–1841*

In 1825 Mehemet Ali had responded to the appeal of his nominal overlord, the sultan of Turkey, for help in suppressing the Greek revolution, and in return he had been promised that his son Ibrahim would be awarded lordship over the island of Crete. The Egyptian campaign in Greece had been thwarted by the intervention of the European great powers and the destruction of the Turkish-Egyptian fleets at Navarino.

Having been burned once in a contest with the great powers, Mehemet Ali ignored the sultan's even more frantic appeal for aid in Turkey's war with Russia in 1828. Instead he took advantage of Turkey's difficulties to extend his dominion south into the Sudan and east into Arabia. In 1831 he sought to exploit Turkey's weakness still further by demanding that the sultan give him Syria in return for services rendered by the Egyptians in Greece. When the sultan refused, he launched an attack against the Ottoman empire in November 1831 to seize Syria by force.

By the end of July 1832 the Egyptian armies had overrun Syria and Mehemet Ali renewed his demand that the sultan formally cede Syria to Egypt. After five months of futile negotiation Mehemet Ali resumed his attack on the Ottoman empire, and in December 1832 his son Ibrahim decisively defeated the Turkish army at Konya. So complete was the Egyptian victory that it seemed probable Constantinople itself might fall to the Egyptian invaders.

During this period of crisis in the Near East, the Concert of Europe was immobilized by indecision and conflicts of interest among its members. After Konya, Metternich attempted to rally the concert to support the sultan against his rebellious vassal, but his enthusiasm for this policy was dampened when he found that the only power prepared to intervene was Russia. The British ambassador in Constantinople had urged his government to send a fleet to the Turkish capital when the Egyptians first invaded the Ottoman empire, confident that such a move would deter the Egyptians from advancing further and thus eliminate any Russian excuse for intervention. But the British government was preoccupied with a major parliamentary crisis over the extension of the franchise that was to end with the passage of the great reform bill of 1832. In any case the British had no ships to send to the Near East, for the greater part of the British fleet was being held in the Atlantic to keep watch over events in the Netherlands and the civil war in Portugal.

The French government of Louis Philippe not only refused to come to the aid of the sultan but had decided that French interests in the Near East could be promoted more effectively by supporting Mehemet Ali. The Egyptian ruler, who had filled his government's coffers through the ruthless exploitation of his people and the lucrative export of high-grade Egyptian cotton, had looked to France for officers, engineers, and other technical experts to build up a modern army and navy and for the purchase of arms and munitions. So dependent had Mehemet Ali become on French advisers and armaments that the French evidently believed he could be used as an instrument of French policy and that any extension of his dominion would mean a corresponding extension of their own influence.

The only European power willing and able to aid the sultan against Egypt was Russia, which offered to send warships to the Bosporus whenever the sultan should ask for them. Receiving no offers of aid from the Western powers, the sultan now found himself in the hapless position of having to accept the support of the perennial predator of the Ottoman empire, and in February 1833 he asked the Russians to send the promised aid. The Russians responded at once, and by the end of the month Russian warships and troop transports had arrived at Constantinople.

To the dismay of the sultan, the Russians did not immediately set about driving the Egyptians from the Ottoman territory they had conquered. Instead, the tsar compelled the sultan to make peace with Egypt on the basis of concessions Mehemet Ali had sought in vain a year earlier. By the Convention of Kutahya of May 5, 1833, Mehemet Ali was given administrative jurisdiction over Syria during his lifetime and de facto control of the strategic province of Adana, the gateway from the Fertile Crescent into Anatolia.

At this point Nicholas might have been expected to demand major concessions from the sultan in return for having come to the rescue of the Ottoman empire. The tsar, however, adhered to the policy recommended by his advisory commission when making peace with Turkey in 1829: to preserve the existing empire and steadily build up the influence of Russia while seeking to exclude that of rival powers. Instead of making fresh demands, therefore, the Russians now offered Turkey a defensive alliance. As summed up by Count Nesselrode, the Russian foreign minister, the purpose of that alliance would be to justify the presence and use of Russian forces in the Ottoman empire as circumstances arose so that they would always be able to arrive first in any theater of operations. Russia would thus be in control of any given situation, "either admitting the preservation of the Ottoman Empire as possible or finally admitting its dissolution as inevitable."

The fruit of Russian policy was the Treaty of Unkiar-Skelessi, signed in Constantinople on July 8, 1833. This treaty, a defensive alliance for mutual protection, emphasized Russia's desire to ensure the "permanence, maintenance, and entire independence" of the Ottoman empire and Russia's willingness to come to its defense with as many military and naval forces as both governments might deem necessary. A separate secret article provided that Russia would spare Turkey "the expense and inconvenience" of having to come to the aid of Russia in a defensive war. All that Russia required of Turkey in the event of such a war was that Turkey close the

Straits of the Dardanelles and not allow foreign warships to enter under any pretext whatever. The treaty was to run for eight years and could be renewed.

The Treaty of Unkiar-Skelessi achieved exactly what Nesselrode wanted. It established Russia as the chief guarantor and protector of the Ottoman empire; it allowed Russia to intervene in any crisis in that empire; and as an extra bonus it provided for the closure of the straits to the warships of the only powers capable of rapid intervention in the Near East or of challenging Russia's naval domination of the Black Sea.

Shortly after Unkiar-Skelessi, to demonstrate their goodwill toward Turkey still further, the Russians agreed to withdraw their armies from the Danubian Principalities (Moldavia and Wallachia) and to cancel Turkish reparations to Russia as provided by the Treaty of Adrianople.

Having established Russia as the chief guarantor of what was left of the Ottoman empire, the tsar tried to mend Russia's relations with the government of Austria, which had endeavored consistently to preserve that empire and had been alarmed and alienated by Russia's previous Near Eastern policies. In a treaty signed at München-grätz (in Czech, Mnichovo Hradiste) on September 18, 1833, to which Prussia later adhered, the tsar and the emperor of Austria proclaimed their joint desire to maintain the territorial integrity of the Ottoman empire. In a secret article appended to that treaty, they agreed further that if the Ottoman empire collapsed despite their best efforts, they would cooperate to arrange a new political system in the Near East and preserve the balance of power.

Encouraged by Russia's apparent desire to return to a policy of collaboration with Austria and Prussia, Metternich attempted to reconstruct his favorite instrument for the peaceful resolution of international problems, the Concert of Europe. In July 1834 he proposed the formation of a new European great power alliance to deal with future crises in the Near East. His purpose clearly was to include Britain and France in guarantees of the Ottoman empire, thus dissolving the treaties of Unkiar-Skelessi and Münchengrätz in a more general agreement.

Nothing came of Metternich's initiative. The Russians did not want to give up the favorable position acquired through Unkiar-Skelessi; the British—Palmerston in particular—distrusted the motives of both Metternich and the tsar; and the French did not want to be bound by treaties that would have restricted their freedom to support Mehemet Ali.

Metternich's proposal for a general European alliance was revived in August 1838 by none other than Palmerston, who had scornfully rejected it four years earlier. By this time Palmerston too had come to perceive the desirability of a general European agreement to preserve the Ottoman empire, dissolve the influence of Russia, and restrain France and Mehemet Ali. Palmerston's proposal failed as Metternich's had, and for the same reasons. Both Russia and France refused to be "grouped."

Meanwhile Palmerston had also taken more direct steps to bolster the Ottoman empire and increase British influence there. He sent advisers to help reorganize the Ottoman army and navy, he arranged a far-reaching Anglo-Turkish commercial agreement, and in general he sought to demonstrate the British government's concern for the welfare of the Ottoman empire and its desire to aid in shoring up that empire's defenses.

❑ *The Renewal of the Turkish–Egyptian War, the Intervention of the Powers, and the International Crisis of 1840*

Palmerston's gestures of British goodwill may have contributed to the development of precisely the kind of situation his policy had been designed to prevent. Encouraged by gestures of British support and evidently believing that Unkiar-Skelessi guaranteed him the support of Russia as well, Sultan Mahmud II decided the time had come to regain the Ottoman territories lost to Egypt during the past decade. Disregarding all advice and warnings from the governments of Europe, he ordered a Turkish attack against Egyptian occupation forces in Syria in April 1839.

Once again the Ottoman army proved no match for the armies of Egypt, skillfully commanded by Mehemet's son Ibrahim Pasha. On June 24 the Turks were humiliatingly defeated at Nezib in northern Syria. Military disaster was shortly followed by naval disaster. The Turkish fleet, which had been ordered to sail to Alexandria to support a Turkish military invasion of Egypt, surrendered to the Egyptians without firing a shot, an act motivated either by treachery or by fear on the part of the Turkish admiral that his government intended to hand the fleet over to the Russians.

Sultan Mahmud II died before the news of these calamities reached him. He was succeeded by Abdul Medjid, a boy of sixteen. With the Turkish government and its armed forces in a state of demoralization, the Ottoman empire once again seemed on the verge of collapse. Mehemet Ali, however, was unable to take advantage of this situation. Contrary to his own expectations and those of his French supporters, the other European powers, chastened by this latest threat to their interests in the Near East, finally put aside their differences and agreed to take collective action to preserve the Ottoman empire.

Metternich led this reconstruction of the Concert of Europe. On receiving news of the Battle of Nezib, he proposed that the great powers cooperate to end the war between Turkey and Egypt in a manner corresponding to their own interests. Palmerston, fearful of the intentions of both Russia and France in the Near East, now put aside his suspicion and dislike of Metternich and agreed to join in collective action. More surprisingly, the Russians and French agreed as well, the Russians because their interests were also threatened by Egypt and might be threatened even more by the armed intervention of rival great powers in the Near East, and the French because by taking part in collective action they would be in a better position to sow discord among the other European powers and secure more favorable terms for Egypt.

On July 27, 1839, a Collective Note of the five great powers was presented to the sultan informing him that they had agreed to act together on the Eastern Question and inviting the Ottoman government "to suspend any final determination [of a settlement with Egypt] without their concurrence, awaiting the result of the interest which those Powers feel for the Porte [the Ottoman government]." On August 22 the Ottoman government accepted the Collective Note and in effect asked the European powers to make peace with Egypt on its behalf.

With the governments of four of the European great powers (Austria, Britain, and Russia, with Prussia in tow) favoring the preservation of the Ottoman empire and opposing the ambitions of Mehemet Ali, there seemed little possibility that the powers could craft a Turkish-Egyptian peace treaty that would be acceptable to

Mehemet Ali and his French supporters. To avoid differences among themselves, which the French must have counted on and hoped to exploit, and in anticipation of a serious crisis with France, they moved to close ranks by reaching agreements designed to eliminate mutual suspicion and conflicts of interest. In September the Russians informed the British government of their willingness to allow the Treaty of Unkiar-Skelessi to lapse when it expired in 1841 and to replace it with a more general treaty involving all the great powers. This new treaty would include a provision for the closure of the Turkish Straits to all warships in peacetime, a provision that would henceforth be part of the public law of Europe. The British could only welcome these Russian offers, which were so much in line with their own policy objectives. By the end of the year the British as well as the Austrian government concluded agreements with Russia on the basis of these Russian proposals. The three powers agreed further that Mehemet Ali should henceforth be confined to Egypt and be compelled to give up most of his gains in Asia Minor.

As expected, the French were infuriated when informed of these conditions. In March 1840 the ministry of the aged Marshal Soult in France was replaced by a more belligerent government under Adolphe Thiers, who rejected all appeals to join the other European powers to coerce Mehemet Ali. The powers therefore proceeded to act without France. On July 15, 1840, the governments of Austria, Britain, Prussia, Russia, and Turkey signed a Convention for the Pacification of the Levant, which embodied their recent agreements concerning the Ottoman empire, the Straits, and the terms to be imposed on Mehemet Ali. He and his descendants were to be recognized as hereditary rulers of Egypt, though the country remained under the suzerainty of the sultan, and he was to be left in control of southern Syria and Acre during his lifetime. He was to withdraw his forces immediately from Arabia and its holy cities, Crete, the district of Adana, and all other parts of the Ottoman empire, and he was to return the Turkish fleet with its crews and equipment. If he did not accept these terms within ten days, he was to forfeit both southern Syria and Acre and be confined exclusively to Egypt.

Thiers vigorously opposed Egypt's capitulation to these terms and encouraged Mehemet Ali to consolidate his position in Syria and defy the powers to eject him. He realized that France could do little to support Mehemet Ali in the Near East with the fleets of the other great powers in control of the Mediterranean, but he let it be known that France could launch an attack across the Rhine and strike at the German members of the coalition ranged against him, a threat that provoked a nasty war scare in Europe.

Thiers's policy and the resulting war scare alarmed his monarch, Louis Philippe, who was acutely aware of his country's diplomatic isolation. In October 1840 the king addressed a note to the powers assuring them of France's love of peace and disinterestedness in the Orient, and later that month Thiers was obliged to resign. "The retirement of Thiers and his colleagues from office," Palmerston wrote on October 27, "is a sure pledge to Europe that France is not going to make war in defense of Mohemmed Ali."

Mehemet Ali had meanwhile followed Thiers's advice to reject the terms of the powers and to resist, but he and his French supporters had overestimated the strength of his position. The maintenance of his army and navy and the recent wars of conquest had overstrained Egypt's resources, the Egyptian armies were unpaid and insubordinate, and Mehemet Ali's efforts to exact tribute from the conquered provinces had led to increasing unrest and outright rebellion. In September 1840 a British squadron bombarded the coasts of Syria and Lebanon, and shortly afterward Austrian and British forces landed in Syria to support local insurgents and a Turkish army that was advancing into Syria. By November the Egyptians were in full retreat, and on November 27 Mehemet Ali submitted to the terms formulated by the European powers in the preceding summer; he was to be recognized as hereditary ruler of Egypt, but he was to give up all other claims and conquests in the Ottoman empire and to restore the Turkish fleet. The powers then proceeded to impose these same terms on a reluctant sultan, who had deposed Mehemet Ali two months earlier and was now compelled to reinstate him and to forgo the greater gains he had hoped to make at the expense of Egypt.

❑ The Straits Convention of 1841

More delicate was the problem of assuaging the pride of the French and persuading them to accept the settlements arranged by their rivals. On July 10, 1841, the four European great powers invited France to concur in the agreements they had reached "to afford to Europe a pledge of the union of the Five Powers." The French government accepted this olive branch, and three days later France joined the other European powers and Turkey in signing the Straits Convention, a new general treaty to regulate affairs in the Near East.

In the Straits Convention of July 13, 1841, the monarchs of the five great powers expressed the conviction that their union and agreement offered Europe the most certain pledge for the preservation of the general peace. They declared they were also united in the desire to give the sultan manifest proof of their respect for the inviolability of his empire. For this purpose they had therefore agreed to comply with an invitation of the sultan "in order to record in common by a formal Act, their unanimous determination to conform to the ancient rule of the Ottoman Empire, according to which the passage of the Straits of the Dardanelles and of the Bosphorus is always to be closed to Foreign Ships of War so long as the Porte is at peace." The sultan for his part expressed his resolve to uphold this "ancient rule of his Empire" and reserved the right to invite other powers to adhere to the agreement.

The peaceful coercion of France and the Straits Convention of 1841 were among the more notable achievements of the Concert of Europe in the nineteenth century. The French effort to advance their interests in the Near East through Mehemet Ali had been thwarted, and the international crisis resulting from this threat to the interests of rival powers had been peacefully resolved. The agreement of the powers to preserve the Ottoman empire temporarily ended the danger of a general European war over the spoils of that empire and left it as a great buffer zone along the southern frontiers of both the Austrian and Russian empires. The exclusive Russian guarantee of the Ottoman empire, which gave Russia a predominant position and special privileges, had been dissolved and superseded by a general great power guarantee. Through the Straits Convention all European states were assured of equal commercial opportunities in the Ottoman empire with freedom of access to that empire's roads and waterways. The closure of the Straits to the naval vessels of foreign powers in peacetime safeguarded Russia from the deployment of Western sea power in the Black Sea, while the Western powers were protected from potential Russian naval competition in the Mediterranean. Altogether it was a treaty that seemed to fulfill the intentions of the statesmen who drafted it to protect the interests of all the powers involved and eliminate the major sources of conflict and suspicion in the Near East.

❑ *The Tsar's Proposals for a New Near East Contingency Agreement, 1843–1844*

Although the Straits Convention expressed the agreement of the five powers to preserve and guarantee the Ottoman empire, it did not put an end to the doubts of many European statesmen about the viability of that empire or their fears about international complications in the event of its collapse. They therefore continued as before to consider alternative policies in the Near East and to confer on how they might best cope with future crises.

Preeminent among the doubters about the capacity of the Ottoman empire to survive was Nicholas I, who in 1843 and 1844 discussed the problems of the Near East with leaders of the Austrian and British governments. The tsar emphasized his continued sincere desire for the preservation of the Ottoman empire, but at the same time he raised the question of whether it would not be salutary to conclude agreements providing for its peaceful partition in the event that its dissolution could not be prevented. Metternich, who continued to believe that the preservation of the Ottoman empire was essential to Austrian security and who opposed any extension of Russian territory and influence in the Near East—which would certainly result from a partition of that empire—politely turned aside the tsar's overtures. At the same time, to avoid jeopardizing Austria's present good relations with Russia, Metternich assured the tsar of the Austrian government's continued desire for close cooperation with the European powers and left the tsar with the impression that he could count on Austria's agreement to any scheme he might work out with respect to the Ottoman empire. This was the first of several serious misconceptions the tsar was to form in the course of his efforts to forestall future Eastern crises.

In the spring of 1844, in the course of a visit to England, the tsar raised the question of the future of the Ottoman empire with the British prime minister, Sir Robert Peel, and his foreign secretary, Lord Aberdeen. According to a memorandum drawn up by the tsar's foreign minister, Count Nesselrode, the British and Russian governments agreed that it was in their common interest to maintain the sovereignty and territorial integrity of the Ottoman empire. The tsar, however, feared the danger of international complications that might result from a catastrophe in Turkey, and he believed this danger might be lessened or avoided altogether if Britain and Russia came to an understanding about how to deal with the situation. Such an understanding would be all the more beneficial since it would have the full approval of Austria, for between Austria and Russia "there exists already an entire conformity of principles in regard to the affairs of Turkey in a common interest of conservatism and peace."

The British agreed in principle about the advantage of an Anglo-Russian understanding to anticipate future crises in the Ottoman empire. "The result," Nesselrode's memorandum continued, "was the eventual engagement, that if anything unforeseen occurred in Turkey, Russia and England should previously concert together as to the course which they should pursue in common." The object of their understanding would be to seek to maintain the Ottoman empire in its present state as long as possible; if, however, the collapse of that empire seemed imminent, they would agree in advance to see that any changes that might occur should not injure the security and interests of their own states or the maintenance of the balance of power in Europe. If England acted in concert with Russia and Austria, whose policies were already "united by the principles of perfect identity," then France would find itself obliged to conform with the course agreed to by St. Petersburg, London, and Vienna. Conflict between the great powers would thus be avoided, and it could be hoped that the peace of Europe could be maintained even in the midst of the most serious crises.

Nesselrode's summary of the tsar's discussions with the British leaders was subsequently submitted to Peel and Aberdeen, who accepted it as accurate. The tsar, who was profoundly ignorant of British government procedures, believed that the British statesmen's acceptance of this memorandum meant that they had concurred with his views and thus made a gentleman's agreement with him, which he regarded as the equivalent of a treaty. This was another grave misconception.

Quite apart from the tsar's misconception about the nature of his agreement with Britain, his program for the Near East in general was an unfortunate example of political naïveté. He seemed totally unaware of the fears and suspicions Russia's earlier aggressive policies in the Near East had aroused or how great was the burden of the legacy of Adrianople and Unkiar-Skelessi. He also failed to perceive that Austria and Britain, and France too, might be opposed to *any* further extension of Russian influence in the Near East no matter how great the compensation for themselves. Even if the leaders of the other European powers believed in the sincerity of his intentions, which they had no reason to do (and which he had no reason to believe that they should), they could not ignore the possibility that Russia, if allowed to acquire an even stronger strategic position in the Near East through a partition of the Ottoman empire, might subsequently be tempted to run roughshod over its rivals and would then be even more capable of doing so.

Nevertheless, the professed objectives of the tsar's policy to sustain the Ottoman empire as long as feasible and to ensure the peaceful resolution of future crises corresponded with the fundamental interests of the other European powers. There was no reason why they could not have cooperated with Russia to realize these objectives, since in doing so they would not have needed to accept Russia's leadership or agree to any contingency plans the tsar might concoct for the partition of the Ottoman empire.

As it happened, apart from revolutions in the Danubian Principalities in 1848, the situation in the Near East remained relatively calm for the rest of the decade, so there was no occasion for the great powers to confer about the future of the Ottoman empire or intervene in its affairs. Meanwhile the tsar remained blithely confident that he could count on Britain and especially Austria in dealing with future crises in the Near East. He was to be sorely disillusioned.

❑ *The Problem of Algeria*

Algeria does not fit conveniently into the history of the Eastern Question either geographically or chronologically. But the French conquest of this outpost of the Ottoman empire needs to be mentioned because of its intrinsic importance and future international repercussions.

In July 1830, in the last days of the reign of the Bourbon king Charles X, the French had established a foothold in the coastal cities of Algeria. During the reign of Louis Philippe they endeavored, without conspicuous success, to extend their control over the rest of the country. Late in the year 1840, however, to compensate for their setback over Egypt, the French sent a large expeditionary force to Algeria and initiated a systematic program of conquest.

French expansion in North Africa alarmed the British, who regarded Algeria as part of the Ottoman empire and who saw in the French action another threat to the integrity of that realm. Worse still, in 1844 the French opened hostilities against Morocco, where Algerian resistance forces had sought refuge and where they had received the support of the sultan of Morocco. The great threat to British interests involved here was that if the French should now conquer Morocco, France would be established at the southern entrance of the Straits of Gibraltar. It would therewith be in a position to challenge British control over this strategic gateway to the Mediterranean which the British had dominated since their takeover of the Rock of Gibraltar in 1713.

British fears with respect to Morocco proved groundless. The French, diplomatically isolated and fully occupied in dealing with Algeria, were in no position to challenge Britain at Gibraltar. In response to British pressure, they formally renounced any intention to take over Morocco, and after defeating the Algerian resistance army and its Moroccan supporters they withdrew from the country. A treaty between France and Morocco of March 18, 1845, fixed the boundary between Algeria and Morocco on the Mediterranean coast. Not until early in the twentieth century did the French at last gain control of Morocco, this time in alliance with Britain, a move that touched off one of the gravest diplomatic crises in the years before 1914. Even then, the British made certain that the French should not control the coast opposite Gibraltar.

SIX

The Revolutions of 1848

Among the many threats to peace and to the international order established in 1815, the statesmen of Europe regarded domestic revolution as one of the most dangerous, not only because it imperiled the existing order in a particular country but because of its possible international repercussions. That they had ample reason for their fears was demonstrated by the revolutions that took place after 1815, above all the revolution in Greece and the chain reaction of revolution that followed the July uprising in France in 1830.

A revolutionary epidemic comparable to that of 1830 broke out in 1848, but on an even larger scale. The significance of these revolutions eventually proved to be far greater for the domestic development of the countries concerned than for their impact on the European international order, but they nevertheless produced a number of serious international crises and laid the groundwork for even greater crises in the decades that followed.

In the background of the revolutions of 1848 were three years of economic depression. Crop failures, especially that of the potato, which had become the primary source of food in many parts of Europe, resulted in sharp increases in the price of food and brought outright famine to some areas, such as Ireland, where 1846 was the year of the Great Hunger.

Agricultural depression was accompanied by financial crises and business failures, which in turn caused a sharp rise in unemployment. Hunger and unemployment exacerbated the already miserable condition of the poor throughout Europe and contributed to an atmosphere of anger and discontent, especially in those cities that had been growing with unprecedented rapidity in the course of the nineteenth century. This growth was due in large part to the influx of rural populations attracted by new trades and industries, opportunities which gave way to mass unemployment during this period of economic depression. As a result of these developments a large segment of the urban population in the capitals and major cities of Europe was poised to demonstrate in the streets when the spark of revolution was struck in 1848. This reservoir of popular support contributed to the initial success of all of the 1848 revolutions, and in many areas the revolutions themselves were to be metamorphosed and radicalized by popular involvement.

The 1848 revolutions can be divided into two general categories: the liberal-social and the national. The former were revolutions against native governments that were considered oppressive. In the liberal phase, the most common objective was a constitution that would guarantee fundamental political liberties and civil rights and provide for the establishment of a government responsive to the people's needs and wishes. As these revolutions gained the support of the urban masses, their objectives became increasingly social and included programs for the redistribution of land, the abolition of private property, and other measures designed to guarantee all people the basic necessities of life and a more equitable share of their countries' resources. These social objectives, however, frequently conflicted with the interests of liberal revolutionaries, many of them middle-class property owners, and led to divisions among the revolutionaries, which contributed substantially to their ultimate failure.

The national revolutions, as the name implies, were essentially uprisings of nationalities living under foreign rule against their foreign governments. Although these national revolutions shared many of the objectives of their liberal-social counterparts, their political and social goals were always subservient to the overriding purpose of overthrowing foreign rule and winning national autonomy and independence.

The actual conditions of revolution differed widely from country to country, but there were two curious features common to almost all of them: they do not appear to have been the product of carefully laid plots, as most conservative statesmen and their police agents were convinced they were; and they were successfully conducted against established governments that had army and police forces capable of suppressing them. That these revolutions were not suppressed appears to have been due above all to a loss of nerve on the part of leaders of the existing regimes, whether as a result of physical fear of the revolutionary mobs, uncertainty as to whether their army and police forces would obey their orders, or the more worthy sentiment of reluctance to shed the blood of their subjects.

The story of the 1848 revolutions, each one complicated enough in itself, is further confounded by the fact that they all overlapped chronologically and that developments in one area were affected, often decisively, by events taking place elsewhere. In this chapter each revolution is discussed separately in the hope that such treatment will make for greater clarity, but the interacting nature of the various revolutionary movements must constantly be borne in mind.

❏ *The Revolution in France*

The 1848 revolution in France was directed against the government of King Louis Philippe, who had come to the throne as a result of the revolution of 1830. Opponents of his regime had long agitated for thoroughgoing reforms of the government, the elimination of its manifest corruption, and an extension of the franchise.

In Paris on February 22, 1848, opposition leaders staged a political rally disguised as a banquet to evade a government ban on public political meetings. Police efforts to break up the rally erupted in violence and attracted a large urban mob, which joined in the fighting against the police. The National Guard was called in, but instead of obeying orders to bring the situation under control, the soldiers, most of them ordinary citizens of Paris, fraternized with the people.

The king still had thirty thousand troops of the regular army at his disposal in Paris as well as a large and reliable police force. His failure to use them to restore law and order was the first of the curious exhibitions of loss of nerve on the part of established governments in the course of the 1848 uprisings. On February 23 Louis Philippe dismissed his unpopular prime minister, Guizot, but when that gesture failed to quell the rioting he lost heart altogether. On February 24, a mere two days after the disturbances in Paris began, he abdicated and fled in disguise to England.

On that same evening of February 24, in an atmosphere of considerable confusion, opposition leaders, surrounded by a crowd of urban demonstrators, proclaimed that France was now a republic and set up a provisional government. The guiding spirit of the new government was the poet Alphonse de Lamartine, who took the office of foreign minister, a critical post because the revolutionary regime was immediately confronted with the danger of foreign intervention. Well aware of this danger, Lamartine reassured the governments of Europe of the peaceful intentions of the new French regime, but his messages of reassurance were contradicted by the proclamations of more enthusiastic revolutionaries calling for the overthrow of the 1815 treaty system and promising support for revolutionary movements everywhere. Lamartine himself found it necessary to cater to this sentiment, and in a manifesto of March 10 he declared that "the treaties of 1815 no longer exist in the eyes of the French Republic."

The alarm in the cabinets of Europe aroused by this declaration was hardly lessened by Lamartine's statement in that same manifesto that France nevertheless regarded the 1815 treaties "as a basis and starting point in its relations with other powers." Upon learning of the revolution in France, the tsar called upon Austria and Prussia to join him in its suppression, but these powers were soon to be engulfed in revolutions of their own. Moreover, as these revolutions threatened to spread to Russia, the tsar too became so preoccupied with events in central Europe that he could no longer consider intervention in France. By the end of March 1848 the only great power still in a position to intervene in France was Britain, but the British government saw no reason to do so because it did not regard the revolutionary regime as a threat to British interests.

The new republican government had greater difficulty dealing with unrest at home. Elections in April 1848 to a new constituent assembly had resulted in victory for moderate republicans, most of them representatives of the propertied middle classes. These moderates were not receptive to the programs of spokesmen for the rural and urban masses calling for a radical redistribution of land and property to relieve the miseries of the poor. When the new government moved to cut existing welfare programs, the frustration of the masses boiled over in the final week of June 1848 and led to some of the bloodiest street fighting of the century.

The republican government now demonstrated a determination to defend itself and to restore law and order, which the government of Louis Philippe had so conspicuously lacked. A state of martial law was declared and the task of restoring order entrusted to General Louis Cavaignac, a sound republican and a veteran of the brutal French wars for the conquest of Algeria. Cavaignac proceeded to put down the insurrection with savage ferocity. After organized resistance had been broken, his troops engaged in a large-scale massacre of the rebels, and of the twelve thousand persons arrested for taking part in the riots almost half were sentenced to long prison terms or deported to labor camps in Algeria. Throughout the country rigid controls were imposed on all political organizations, public meetings, and the press.

In the months of relative calm that followed the suppression of the radical revolution in France, the constituent assembly finished drafting a constitution for France. This constitution, while providing for a popularly elected single-chamber legislature, gave supreme executive power to the office of the president, presumably to enable him to deal more effectively with future revolutionary disturbances. The president was to be chosen through direct election by universal manhood suffrage. Elections to the presidency in December 1848 brought overwhelming victory to Louis Napoleon Bonaparte, a nephew of the first Napoleon, a victory that appears to have been due in large part to the magic of his name. The new president swore to uphold the constitution and the republican form of government, but on December 2, 1851, the anniversary of his uncle's great victory at Austerlitz and his coronation as emperor, Louis Napoleon carried out a coup d'état and made himself virtual dictator of France. Exactly a year later he cast aside all trappings of republicanism and himself assumed the imperial title as Emperor Napoleon III.

The revolution to overthrow the monarchy in France thus ended in a military dictatorship and restoration of the empire. Far more fateful, the election of another Napoleon as chief of state and his assumption of the imperial title aroused popular expectations of a new era of glory and empire for France, expectations which the new Napoleon proved unwilling or unable to resist. The 1848 revolution in France itself, however, had at no time posed a serious threat to international peace and stability.

❑ *The Revolutions in the Habsburg Empire*

Far more serious threats to peace, and to the entire European states system, were the revolutions that broke out in the Habsburg empire. With the exception of the revolution in Vienna, these were predominantly national revolutions whose primary objective was national independence and freedom from Habsburg rule.

The spark for the 1848 revolutions in the Habsburg empire was struck by the Hungarian nationalist leader Louis Kossuth. Inspired by the February revolution in France, he made an impassioned speech to the Hungarian parliament on March 3 calling for an end to repressive government and the establishment of representative institutions for all parts of the empire. For the Hungarians, however, he demanded far more: recognition of the special position of the Kingdom of Hungary within the empire and complete national autonomy under a separate ministry responsible only to the Hungarian people.

Nationality problems in the Habsburg empire were always complicated, and in the case of Hungary it should be pointed out that the Hungarian nationalists who purported to speak for the entire Hungarian people were in fact Magyars, who constituted a majority of the population of the ancient kingdom of Hungary. That kingdom, however, included large numbers of Croats, Slavonians, Romanians, and other national minorities, most of whom deeply resented Magyar domination.

The agitation of the Magyars for political reform stirred Austrian liberals into action. On the morning of March 13 several thousand university students marched on the Austrian parliament in Vienna demanding reforms and the dismissal of Metternich, whose name had become synonymous with the old regime. The student demonstrations were soon reinforced by urban crowds eager to voice their own grievances.

Metternich had long recognized the desirability, indeed the necessity, for instituting far-reaching reforms in the Habsburg empire, but he believed these should be granted by the government, not extracted under pressure from student or urban mobs. At a meeting of the imperial council on the afternoon of March 13, Metternich urged prompt and vigorous suppression of the demonstrations. He was supported by Prince Alfred von Windischgrätz, the military commander in Bohemia and an experienced general, who was prepared to use the substantial military force available in Vienna to restore order. But the council, many of whose members had long resented Metternich's influence in the government, decided instead to yield to the demonstrators' demand for Metternich's dismissal. That same evening the old statesman fled in disguise from the Austrian capital. He too went to England.

As was the case in France, the Austrian government's decision to yield did not put an end to disorder—or to popular demands. The imperial government itself was not overthrown at this time, but its position was obviously precarious, and further uprisings in May and October forced the court to flee from Vienna, in the first instance to Innsbruck, in the second to Olmütz (in Czech, Olomouc) in Moravia.

With the failure of the imperial government to provide effective leadership during these revolutionary months, imperial military commanders took over many of the government's decision-making functions and proceeded to save the Habsburg monarchy in spite of itself. In June Windischgrätz suppressed the revolution that had meanwhile broken out in Bohemia; in July the Habsburg general Joseph Radetzky defeated revolutionaries in northern Italy and the army of Piedmont-Sardinia, which had come to their support; and at the end of October Windischgrätz put down the latest uprising in Vienna, thereby enabling the court to return to the capital.

Windischgrätz did more. On his recommendation the emperor entrusted the leadership of the Habsburg government to Prince Felix zu Schwarzenberg, a vigorous, determined, and highly intelligent young nobleman, who had no scruples about using force or any other means that seemed necessary for the suppression of revolution and the restoration of order throughout the empire. One of Schwarzenberg's first moves was to secure the abdication of the feeble-minded Emperor Ferdinand in favor of his eighteen-year-old nephew Francis, who upon becoming emperor in December 1848 assumed the name of Francis Joseph. He thus linked the names of the popular emperor of the Napoleonic wars, Francis I, with that of Joseph II, the enlightened despot and author of wide-ranging reforms designed to bring more humane and just rule to the Habsburg lands. Joseph II, however, had also advocated a strong centralized government, which he had deemed essential for the implementation of his reforms.

The creation of such a strong centralized government was the most immediate objective of Schwarzenberg, not so much for the purpose of implementing reforms as to reestablish the authority of Vienna over the entire Habsburg realm. Early in March 1849 Schwarzenberg dissolved the Austrian parliament, which had just drawn up a constitution reorganizing the empire as a federal union and giving considerable local autonomy to its various regions. In its stead he promulgated his own constitution, which provided for a strong centralized government and the creation of a single administrative system for the entire empire, including Hungary.

Schwarzenberg and the Austrian generals between them performed something of a miracle. By the end of August 1849 the entire Habsburg realm, which had been on the verge of dissolution only a few months earlier, was back under control of the Vienna government; all revolutions within the empire had been suppressed (although for the suppression of the revolution in Hungary, the Austrians had been obliged to seek the aid of Russia). As in France, the revolutions in the Habsburg empire ended with a stronger centralized government more determined than its predecessor to preserve law and order and suppress popular unrest.

Bohemia

Although the population of Bohemia was predominantly Czech, the revolution in that area was in the beginning far more a liberal than a national (i.e., anti-German) movement. The Bohemian aristocracy and bourgeoisie included large numbers of Germans, many of them liberals who were as eager for reforms and greater local autonomy as were the Czechs. It was only after it became evident in the course of the revolution that the Czechs wanted not only reforms but complete autonomy from the German-dominated government of Vienna that the Germans abandoned the cause of revolution in Bohemia and the revolution took on a predominantly national character.

The leading spokesmen for the Czech nationalists were the historian Francis Palacký and a young journalist named Carl Havliček. Encouraged by the success of Hungarian nationalists, whose demands for national autonomy had been conceded in their entirety by the Vienna government in mid-March, Palacký and Havliček drew up a petition of their own on March 22 calling for an autonomous Czech state which was to include Bohemia, Moravia, and Austrian Silesia.

It soon became apparent that the Czech nationalist movement as conceived by Palacký had serious weaknesses. There was little unity of feeling and purpose among the various people Palacký proposed to unite. Moravians and the peoples of Silesia (for the most part Poles and Ruthenians), not to mention the Germans, had no desire to be included in a Czech-dominated state. Most Germans, in fact, entirely failed to comprehend the nature of Czech nationalism. For centuries Bohemia had been part of the Holy Roman Empire and as such it had been included in the German Confederation by the peacemakers of 1815. The Germans had come to take it for granted that Bohemia was in fact just another of the many diverse lands which together constituted their conception of "Germany."

At about the same time that Palacký had drafted his petition on behalf of Czech autonomy, German nationalists had formed a self-constituted committee to conduct elections throughout the German Confederation to a German national parliament, which they conceived as the prelude to the formation of a German national state. At the end of March 1848 these German nationalists held the first meeting of a so-called preliminary parliament (Vorparlament) to make arrangements for these pan-German elections, and Palacký was invited to attend as a representative of Bohemia. Palacký's reply of April 11 to this invitation was a noble statement on behalf of his Czech nationality, but it also contained a penetrating analysis of the value of the Habsburg empire for all the nationalities of central Europe, an appreciation which contrasts markedly with the narrow-minded conceptions of other nationalist leaders of his own time and since.

Palacký informed the Germans that he regarded himself as a Czech, not a German, but he then went on to deplore the fact that their nationalist activity on behalf of a German national state would inevitably undermine the Habsburg empire, "whose preservation, integrity and consolidation is, and must be, a great and important matter not only for my own nation, but also for the whole of Europe, indeed for humanity and civilization itself." Only through the Habsburg empire could the peoples of eastern Europe be protected against Russian expansion and domination, "an infinite and inexpressible evil, a misfortune without measure or bound." Because none of the nationalities of the Danube basin was strong enough to stand by itself, their union in one state was essential. "Assuredly, if the Austrian state had not already existed, the interests of Europe and indeed of humanity would have required that we create it, and that as soon as possible."

The attempt of Czech nationalists to block the holding of elections to a German national parliament in Bohemia was not motivated primarily by fear of undermining the Habsburg empire, however. What they dreaded was the prospect of the inclusion of Bohemia in a German national state, and it was over this issue that Czech and German reformers parted company.

To counter the influence of the Germans in the Habsburg realm, Palacký and other Czech leaders attempted to create a union of all the Slavic peoples of the empire. In June 1848 they organized a Congress of Slavs, held in Prague, which was attended by representatives of all the empire's Slavic ethnic groups. At this congress the ideas of Palacký prevailed. The delegates agreed on a program calling for the reorganization of the Habsburg empire along federal lines, but they made it clear that they wanted this reorganization to take place within the existing empire and that they did not desire its fragmentation into separate national states.

This program was not nearly radical enough for the younger members of the Czech nationalist movement, chiefly Prague university students, who on June 12, the day the Slavic Congress dissolved, rose in rebellion against the Habsburg government in Prague with the declared purpose of establishing an independent Czech republic. As in the case of the uprisings in Paris and Vienna, the Prague revolutionaries received widespread support from disaffected urban workers, and with their aid they set up a revolutionary government in the city.

The uprising in Bohemia proved to be the weakest and briefest of the revolutions in the Habsburg empire. Unlike Louis Philippe in Paris or the imperial government in Vienna, Windischgrätz, the military governor of Bohemia, did not hesitate to use the troops at his disposal. Once the uprising had begun, he deliberately allowed it to develop to expose the revolutionary elements—so that he could suppress them more completely. On June 16 he began an artillery bombardment of Prague; soon his troops were storming the city. All popular assemblies were dissolved and martial law was imposed until order was completely restored.

Hungary

In Hungary, the Hungarian (predominantly Magyar) parliament had responded enthusiastically to Kossuth's speech of March 3, 1848, calling for Hungarian autonomy, and by March 15 the parliament had drawn up a program for a new Hungarian government.

According to this program, Hungary was to be governed by a ministry responsible to a Hungarian parliament elected by the Hungarian people on a basis of limited manhood suffrage. The Hungarian government was to control its own budget and foreign policy, and Hungarian units were to be withdrawn from the imperial army to form a separate Hungarian army. The Hungarians would continue to recognize the Habsburg emperor as king of Hungary (he was to be represented in Hungary by a viceroy), but for all practical purposes Hungary was to be completely independent.

While seeking independence for themselves, however, the Magyar Hungarians demanded the incorporation into their new state of Croatia-Slavonia, Transylvania, and the military frontier districts set up for defense against the Turks. In all of these territories, Magyars formed only a minority of the population. Their disregard for the sentiments of nationalities other than their own was unfortunately typical of most of the world's nationalist movements.

The Habsburg government, which by this time was faced with a revolution in Vienna itself, yielded to all the demands of the Magyar nationalists. By the end of August 1848, however, with the successful suppression of revolutions elsewhere in the empire, the Habsburg government renounced its earlier concessions and initiated measures to suppress the revolution in Hungary as well. For this purpose it exploited the disaffection of the non-Magyar peoples of Hungary, notably the Croatians. In September a Croatian general, Baron Joseph Jellachich, who had been made governor (ban) of Croatia, launched an invasion of the Hungarian heartland at the head of an army of fifty thousand men consisting largely of Croatians. The Hungarians not only repulsed this invasion, but, aided by new uprisings in Vienna and other parts of the Habsburg realm, they were able to take the offensive. On April 14, 1849, in response to the promulgation of Schwarzenberg's constitution providing for the centralization of the entire Habsburg realm, including Hungary, the Hungarian parliament severed its final ties with Vienna. The Habsburg dynasty was deposed and Hungary declared a republic.

Throughout the upheavals of 1848–1849, Tsar Nicholas I, that passionate foe of revolution, had expressed his readiness to come to the aid of his fellow monarchs. In May 1849, as the Hungarian armies recaptured Budapest and seemed prepared to advance on Vienna, Emperor Francis Joseph set aside his pride and formally appealed to the tsar for assistance. Nicholas responded immediately and generously. He had been especially alarmed that two Polish generals who had participated in the 1830 revolution against Russia had joined the Hungarians and feared that Hungary would become a springboard for revolution throughout eastern Europe. "The symptoms of a general plot against everything sacred, and especially against Russia, are clearly visible in the Hungarian rebellion," he wrote on May 7, 1849, to General Paskievich, who had suppressed the 1830 revolution in Poland. "At the head of the rebellion, and acting as the principal instruments of it, are our eternal foes, the Poles." Early in June the tsar sent a 110,000-man army under Paskievich into Hungary, which he steadily reinforced to over 350,000. Against so formidable a force, the Hungarian revolution was doomed. The main Hungarian army surrendered on August 13 (to the Russians, not the Austrians) and the Habsburg government placed Hungary under martial law.

Once the Hungarian revolution had been suppressed, the tsar withdrew his armies from Habsburg territory without asking for payment of any kind. Following this selfless action on behalf of the Habsburg empire and the monarchical principle, the tsar was confident that he in turn could count on Austria's friendship and support in future crises affecting his own realm. He was to find that gratitude is a singularly volatile component in the calculations of statesmen. When Russia looked to Austria for support at the time of the Crimean War, the Austrian government believed its own interests would best be served by remaining neutral, and in the end Austria even addressed an ultimatum to Russia, which finally compelled the tsarist government to sue for peace (see p. 118).

Although to a far lesser extent than Russia, Britain too was concerned about the revolution in Hungary. Palmerston, the British foreign secretary, opposed the Hungarian independence movement because it threatened the Habsburg empire, whose preservation he considered essential to the interests of Britain and Europe as a whole. "Austria is a most important element in the balance of European power," he told the House of Commons on July 21, 1849. "Austria stands in the centre of Europe, a barrier against encroachment on the one side, and against invasion on the other. The political independence and liberties of Europe are bound up in my opinion with the maintenance and integrity of Austria as a great European Power, and therefore anything which tends by direct or even remote contingency to weaken and to cripple Austria, but still more to reduce her from the position of a first rate power to that of a secondary State, must be a great calamity to Europe, and one which every Englishman ought to deprecate and try to prevent."

While opposing the revolution in Hungary, Palmerston at the same time was sympathetic to the revolutions against the Habsburg empire in Italy, an inconsistency that many contemporary observers ascribed to the fact that Britain could not expect to benefit from the revolution in Hungary, whereas there were all kinds of political and economic advantages to be gained by the removal of Austrian control in Italy. Palmerston's concern for the preservation of the Habsburg empire appears to have been genuine, however, and he himself explained his inconsistency with respect to the revolutions in Hungary and Italy as stemming from that concern. In his view, Austria's Italian provinces were an undesirable diversion of Austrian resources, and he believed their loss would actually strengthen the Habsburg empire's ability to defend its position in eastern Europe. The loss of Hungary, on the other hand, would destroy its position in eastern Europe and remove Austria from the ranks of the great powers. When in December 1848 an emissary of Kossuth arrived in London to appeal for British aid, Palmerston refused to see him and instructed that he be informed that "Her Majesty's Government . . . has no diplomatic relations with Hungary except as a component of the Austrian Empire." Two months later Palmerston relented so far as to grant another Hungarian emissary a secret audience, but he did so only to reiterate that the maintenance of the Habsburg empire was a vital concern for Britain, and "that if it did not exist already it would have to be invented. . . . Austria was a European necessity and the natural ally of England in the East." He therefore advised the Hungarians to reconcile themselves with Austria "because in the framework of the European states system it would be impossible to replace Austria by small states."

Palmerston's views thus corresponded closely with those of Palacký, and for the same reason: the Habsburg empire constituted a great power which for centuries had stood guard for Europe against the Turks and which now served as a bulwark against the Russians; only through the maintenance of that empire could the peoples of east central Europe be safeguarded from Russian dominion and the European balance of power be preserved.

Palmerston's attitude toward Austria changed abruptly after the suppression of the Hungarian revolution, primarily because he feared precisely what the tsar believed he had achieved through his intervention in Hungary: that Austria, out of gratitude to Russia, would now join forces with Russia in the international arena, and that its usefulness in the balance of power system would thus be destroyed. Following the defeat of the Hungarian revolutionary armies, British public opinion was shocked by reports of Austria's repressive policies in Hungary, and Palmerston, always responsive to public opinion, was quick to express the outrage of the British government. But it was only when Austria and Russia acted together in demanding the extradition of Hungarian revolutionaries who had fled to the Ottoman empire that Palmerston took a firm stand against Austria. In this policy he was staunchly supported and indeed anticipated by the British ambassador in Constantinople, Stratford Canning, who on his own initiative had summoned a British naval squadron to Turkish waters to counter Austro-Russian pressure on the Ottoman government. This British naval demonstration was shortly joined by the French, who were as eager as the British to counter Russian influence and defend their own interests in the Near East.

The Austrian and Russian governments had meanwhile settled the Hungarian refugee question through direct negotiations with Turkey. Some three thousand Hungarians were granted amnesty and allowed to return, while Kossuth and other prominent revolutionary leaders were allowed to remain in Turkey. Palmerston, who had secured the approval of the British cabinet for Stratford Canning's summons of the fleet, was jubilant about the Austro-Russian compromise with Turkey, which he regarded as a triumph of British policy. "We have forced the haughty autocrat to go back from his arrogant pretensions," he wrote Canning. "We have obliged Austria to forgo another opportunity of quaffing her bowl of blood, and we have saved Turkey from being humbled down to absolute prostration."

Italy

Of all the upheavals in the Habsburg empire in 1848, the revolutions in Italy attracted the greatest international attention and represented the greatest threat to the peace of Europe.

In terms of chronology, the first of the 1848 revolutions had actually taken place in Italy: a revolution in Sicily on January 12 against the rule of Naples (Sicily and Naples were joined together politically as the Kingdom of the Two Sicilies). This Sicilian effort to break away from the government of Naples was essentially a separatist movement, but it nevertheless gave impetus to the agitation of liberals throughout the peninsula who were demanding constitutions in their various states which would guarantee fundamental political rights and liberties. In response, the king of Naples granted his state a constitution on February 10, 1848, an example followed on February 17 by the grand duke of Tuscany, and in March by the king of Sardinia and by Pope Pius IX in the Papal States.

News of the March revolution in Vienna and the ouster of Metternich set off revolutions in Lombardy and Venetia, the Austrian provinces of Italy, and against the Habsburg rulers of Parma and Modena. In contrast to the agitation elsewhere in Italy, which was concerned primarily with domestic reform, the revolutions in Lombardy and Venetia, directed as they were against foreign rule, were predominantly nationalist in character. On March 18 an Italian revolutionary government was established in Milan, the capital of Lombardy, and four days later revolutionaries in Venice proclaimed the restoration of the independent Republic of Venetia. These nationalist revolutions against Austria aroused an enthusiasm throughout Italy far greater than any previous domestic revolutions had done, and the governments of all Italian states now came under intense pressure from public opinion to support the anti-Austrian uprisings.

In the Kingdom of Sardinia (an amalgam of the island of Sardinia, the northern Italian state of Piedmont, and the former Republic of Genoa, joined to the kingdom in 1815) King Charles Albert was torn between his fear of revolution on the one hand and his greed and ambition on the other. For with the Habsburg empire seemingly on the verge of disintegration, he now had a splendid opportunity to place himself at the head of the Italian nationalist movement, come to the aid of Lombardy and Venetia, and extend Sardinian dominion over all of northern Italy and beyond. Greed and ambition triumphed. On March 22 Sardinia declared war on Austria. The Austrian forces under the command of the eighty-one-year-old General Radetzky retired to a ring of fortresses along the northern borders of Lombardy and Venetia (the so-called Quadrilateral), and for the time being the revolutionary governments were in control of the situation.

Charles Albert was not the only statesman attracted by the opportunities which the revolutions in northern Italy seemed to present. The leaders of the revolutionary government of France, who proclaimed support for revolutionary movements everywhere, were especially eager to provide such support in Italy and were under great popular pressure to do so. In France the idealistic desire to aid the cause of revolution in Italy was powerfully reinforced by two more practical motives: the desire to exploit these revolutions to reestablish French influence in Italy at the expense of Austria; and to prevent their exploitation by Sardinia, which, if allowed to annex Austria's Italian provinces, would become a disconcertingly powerful state directly on the French frontier. Precisely because he feared that France would attempt to frustrate Sardinian ambitions in Italy, Charles Albert sought to prevent French intervention. To stop the appeals of Italian revolutionaries for French aid, he declared that Italy had no need for French support: Italians alone would liberate Italy—*L'italia farà da sé.*

It is doubtful that Charles Albert's steadfast rejection of French support would have been sufficient to deter French intervention, but the British too had no desire to see Austrian influence in Italy replaced by that of France. Throughout the crisis Palmerston did his best to mediate a settlement of the Italian question so as to deprive the French of any excuse for intervention. Keeping the French out of Italy, however, did not mean that Palmerston favored keeping Austria in, for, as mentioned, he believed that giving up the Italian provinces would allow the Habsburg empire to concentrate on defending its vital interests in central and eastern Europe. He accordingly tried to persuade the Austrians to relinquish the provinces voluntarily, a policy that would serve two purposes: it would eliminate the danger of French intervention; and it could be expected to enhance British influence and benefit British interests in Italy.

While these diplomatic negotiations were in progress, Sardinian military commanders failed to take advantage of the initial demoralization of the Austrians to drive them from the fortresses of the Quadrilateral and expel them from Italy altogether. The Sardinian government, on the other hand, exploited the political situation in Italy with great success. At least in part because of the activity of Sardinian political agents, the revolutionary government of Lombardy voted in favor of union with Sardinia on May 29, 1848, an example quickly followed by the revolutionary regimes of Parma, Modena, and Venetia.

This large-scale increase in the size and strength of Sardinia was most unwelcome to the French, who now joined the British in attempting to persuade the Austrians to give up their Italian provinces voluntarily on the understanding that they should not enter into a union with Sardinia.

All negotiations with the Austrians failed. The Austrians procrastinated because they still hoped to recoup their position in Italy, but they might nevertheless have yielded had not the Italians insisted that any Austrian offer of independence to Lombardy and Venetia include the whole of Italy. By this the Italians meant all Habsburg territory south of the Alps, much of which had been part of the Habsburg domain for centuries and was inhabited by large numbers of Germans, Slavs, and other non-Italian nationalities. There was in any case little time for Anglo-French pressure to take effect, for on July 24, 1848, the entire situation in Italy abruptly changed when the aged General Radetzky, whose army in Italy had been heavily reinforced, overwhelmingly defeated the Sardinian-Italian armies at Custoza (just south of Lake Garda). Radetzky's handling of his troops at Custoza confirmed his reputation as a brilliant strategist, although the completeness of his victory appears to have been due quite as much to the incompetence of the Italian military commanders. Before the battle he is supposed to have told his gunners: "Spare the enemy generals—they are too useful to our side."

Charles Albert, though still fearful of French intervention, was now obliged to seek French mediation, a move which just a few weeks earlier might well have led to French intervention. But as will be recalled, the situation in France had also changed. At the end of June 1848 France suffered further revolutionary convulsions, which were brought under control by General Cavaignac, who now governed the country under martial law.

The situation in Italy placed Cavaignac in a dilemma. He was aware of British opposition to French intervention and was himself reluctant to commit his troops to adventures in Italy while they might still be needed to suppress revolution at home; but he also knew it would be difficult to resist popular clamor in France for intervention. He escaped this dilemma by proposing joint Anglo-French mediation in Italy, to which London responded positively.

The Austrians, however, were now in a position of strength. Although they agreed to accept Anglo-French mediation, they turned aside all proposals the Anglo-French negotiators put forward. Meanwhile the Austrians conducted direct negotiations with the Sardinians, and on August 9 they concluded an armistice on the basis of conditions they had formulated. Because the Austrians still feared Anglo-French intervention, these conditions were remarkably moderate. Austria demanded only the restoration of the prewar status quo; Sardinia was not required to cede any territory or pay an indemnity.

The Italian question was reopened by Charles Albert. Encouraged by the success of the Hungarian revolutionary armies and once again under intense pressure from Italian patriots, he denounced the armistice on March 12, 1849, and again declared war on Austria. Again his armies were overwhelmingly defeated by Radetzky, this time at Novara on March 23. After this second disastrous military humiliation, Charles Albert abdicated in favor of his son, Victor Emanuel II, who asked Radetzky for another armistice.

Again Radetzky showed restraint. Still acutely conscious of the danger of French intervention, he turned aside the demands of Austrian leaders who favored a harsh peace and again asked for no more than the restoration of the prewar status quo. This time, however, Sardinia was required to pay a sizable indemnity and Austrian troops were to occupy the frontier fortress of Alessandria until the indemnity was paid. These armistice terms were embodied in a final peace treaty between Austria and Sardinia signed in Milan on August 6, 1849.

After their second victory over Sardinia, the Austrians moved against the revolutionary governments that had been set up in the other states of Italy. They reestablished their authority over much of Lombardy, including the city of Milan, and by April 1849 brought the entire province under control; by July the revolutionary regime in Tuscany was ousted and the government of Grand Duke Leopold reinstated; and by August Venetian resistance was broken, the Venetian Republic abolished, and Habsburg authority restored.

In Rome, where a revolution against the papal government had compelled the pope to flee in November 1848, Austrian efforts to restore the secular authority of the papacy were forestalled by France, though only in the city of Rome itself and its surrounding territory (the so-called Patrimony of St. Peter); elsewhere in the Papal States papal authority was restored by the Austrians. The French intervention was a gesture on the part of the new government of Louis Napoleon to curry favor with Roman Catholic interests in France, but it was also a move to substitute French for Austrian influence in Italy and was in fact the prelude to substantial French intervention in the peninsula in the next decade.

The French forces sent to suppress the revolutionary government in Rome met with unexpectedly strong resistance. Toward the end of April 1849 the republican garrison was reinforced by volunteers from the north, including twelve hundred troops under the redoubtable guerrilla fighter Giuseppe Garibaldi, who conducted a stubborn defense of the city. Early in July, after heavy reinforcement, French troops finally captured Rome, but so intense was popular discontent that it was not until almost a year later that sufficient order was restored for the pope to return to his capital. Even then a French garrison remained in Rome to protect the person of the pope—and to ensure the continuation of French influence.

The results of the revolutions in Italy of 1848-1849 appear pathetically meager in proportion to the scope of the revolutionary activity during those years. There was no change whatever in the political map of the peninsula. Austria reestablished its rule over Lombardy and Venetia. "Legitimate" rulers were restored in Tuscany, Parma, Modena, and the Papal States, and Austrian garrisons were now stationed in all those states (apart from the Patrimony of St. Peter) to prop up their newly restored regimes. Ferdinand II reestablished his authority in Naples and Sicily. The only big change was that in the Patrimony of St. Peter, papal rule was now supported by the French rather than the Austrians.

There were nevertheless significant changes stemming from the revolutionary experiences of 1848-1849, although their full significance was not obvious at the time. They had stimulated Italian political as well as national consciousness, and they had greatly enhanced the prestige of the state of Sardinia. Despite its two disastrous defeats at the hands of the Austrians, Sardinia had gained much credit among Italian patriots for having dared take the field against Austria at all. Sardinia was the only Italian state ruled by a native Italian dynasty (the House of Savoy), and the Sardinian government was the only regime in Italy (apart from Naples) that did not require the support of foreign bayonets. Moreover, Sardinia was the only Italian government that had not abrogated the constitution granted by its rulers during the revolutionary era. That constitution, modeled on the French constitution of 1830, was hardly a liberal document. It gave the vote to only two and a quarter percent of the population, the parliament elected on the basis of this narrow franchise was conceded few powers, and government ministers proved in practice to be responsible to the king, not to parliament. The essential thing, however, was that the constitution provided for a parliament at all, for this parliament was to serve as a forum for Italian nationalists and reformers. Thus Sardinia was the only state in Italy that still had some attraction to both nationalists and liberals, and the only state that could be seriously considered to lead a pan-Italian nationalist movement or a future Italian national union.

❑ The Revolutions in Germany: Prussia

News of the February revolution in France, which had ignited revolutions throughout much of the Habsburg empire, set off similar revolutions in the states and free cities of the German Confederation. Mass demonstrations in major German cities were accompanied by peasant revolts in rural areas, creating an atmosphere of panic among the German ruling classes. In all the German states, existing governments attempted to stave off outright revolution by yielding to popular demands for constitutional representative government and guarantees of political and civil liberties. In many of these states the governments did indeed avoid violent revolution by making sweeping concessions and by appointing liberals to top positions in their administrations to carry out the promised changes. Even before the revolution in Vienna, liberal governments had been installed in many of the smaller states of Germany.

Prussia delayed longer than most in making concessions, but news of the revolution in Vienna stirred up mass agitation in Berlin to such an alarming degree that the king of Prussia, too, was convinced of the necessity of yielding to popular demands. On March 18 he promised to grant a constitution and far-reaching reforms. Revolutionary activity in Prussia continued throughout the spring and summer of 1848 and a succession of reform ministries were installed in Berlin in response to popular agitation. But in November the king, encouraged by the success of the Austrian government in suppressing revolution in Vienna, finally used his troops to restore order in Berlin and appointed a prime minister dedicated to the restoration of royal authority. Thus in Prussia, as in all other major states of Europe where revolution had broken out in 1848, the revolution was suppressed and government authority firmly reestablished.

As in Sardinia, however, the revolution in Prussia resulted in the promulgation of a constitution that was to have great importance in the future. King Frederick William IV, believing that a monarch's word was sacred, rejected the advice of his conservative advisers and resolved to live up to the promise he had made in the previous March to grant his people a constitution. That constitution, first promulgated in December 1848, was to be revised several times in a conservative sense, but it retained two features of crucial significance: it provided for a popularly elected parliament; and it gave that parliament the power to approve new laws and taxes and thus control over two fundamental legislative functions. The government never expected the parliament to make use of this power, however, for to ensure the election of conservative candidates who could be relied on to endorse government policies, it inserted provisions in the new constitution establishing a three-class system of voting that gave decisive representation to citizens who paid the highest taxes.

The Prussian government was soon to discover that it had made a grievous error in setting up this electoral system, for the majority of the highest taxpayers proved to be members of the increasingly wealthy middle class, who, inspired by the example of parliamentary government in England, wanted a share of political power commensurate with their growing economic strength. Within a decade the parliamentary representatives of this class would use the powers given them by the Prussian constitution to challenge the authority of the king and engage in a constitutional struggle for supreme authority in Prussia that would have profound significance for the future course of Prussian-German history (see p. 188).

❑ *Prussian Foreign Policy in the Revolutionary Era*

The revolution in Prussia produced no international crises that seriously threatened the existing international order or the peace of Europe, but it was not for want of trying on the part of the self-professed liberals who had been brought into the Prussian government to appease the revolutionaries.

Directly after the formation of a liberal government in March 1848, the new foreign minister, Heinrich von Arnim-Suckow, previously Prussian minister to Paris, concocted a scheme that not merely threatened the peace of Europe but was deliberately designed to provoke a general European war. In the manner of idealists elsewhere in Europe who breathed the heady atmosphere of power in 1848, Arnim and other liberals in unaccustomed positions of influence proposed to use that influence to spread the benefits of political and national liberty (as they conceived it) to the rest of the world. In the first stages of the 1848 revolutions, they enthusiastically supported the claims of Italians, Hungarians, Poles, and other nationalities to political and national freedom, if necessary even at the expense of the interest of their own states.

Central to Arnim's scheme was the unselfish objective of reestablishing an independent Polish state consisting of the Polish territories seized by Austria, Prussia, and Russia in the three partitions of the late eighteenth century. On behalf of this cause, Arnim was prepared to surrender Prussia's share voluntarily, but he saw no hope of securing freedom for Russian Poland except through another Polish revolution, which he envisaged as the beginning of a European liberal crusade against Russia. To rekindle the flame of revolution in Poland, Arnim proposed to encourage the organization of a Polish revolutionary army in Prussian Poland, which would come to the aid of revolutionaries in Russian Poland. This activity was expected to provoke a Russian attack on Prussia, but before such an attack took place Arnim intended to secure assurances of support from Britain and France in the event of Russian aggression. The provocation of a Russian attack would thus bring two of Europe's major powers into the war on the side of Prussia. The most important factor in Arnim's calculation, however, was his expectation that the entire German people would rally to the banner of Prussia in this crusade against the common foe of European political and national liberty, and that in the enthusiasm generated by the conflict a united Germany would be forged under Prussian leadership.

On March 21, 1848, immediately after taking office, Arnim proceeded to put this bizarre scheme into operation. He successfully provoked the desired revolt in Prussian Poland, and at the end of March he sounded out the British and French governments about his project. "Baron d'Arnim and his colleagues appear to overlook every consideration but that of favouring the Poles . . . in their enterprise for the rescue of Poland from the dominion of Russia," the British emissary in Berlin reported to his government. "They are ready to incur the risk of a war with Russia for this object. They hope eventually to obtain the countenance and support of England. They reckon with confidence upon having that of France."

From the revolutionary government of France Arnim expected far more than eventual countenance and support. He wanted "first, a solemn declaration of alliance and political solidarity concerning the restoration of Poland" and "the despatch, when asked for, of a French squadron to the Baltic." If France, Britain, and the German states united in this enterprise, "legitimate in its aims, and feasible seeing the formidable strength of such a combination, then fear of war with Russia among the countries of western and central Europe would disappear."

Arnim's scheme was as unrealistic as it was irresponsible. The French revolutionary government was still fully occupied with domestic problems and its chief foreign policy concern was the prevention of foreign intervention in France. It certainly had no intention of provoking such intervention by taking part in a Polish or German national war against Russia, and it never responded officially to Arnim's request for a declaration of alliance, though unofficially France promised military support in the event of a Russian attack on Prussia, a response that still allowed Arnim to hope for an alliance.

The British took a much firmer line against Arnim's enterprise, which they correctly regarded as "fraught with peril" to the general peace of Europe, and they sent a stern warning to the Prussian government "to abstain from any proceeding which could justly be considered by Russia as aggressive." The king of Prussia welcomed this British warning, for he too opposed Arnim's Polish policy as "too likely to become the subject of a serious quarrel between this country and Russia."

Meanwhile the situation in Poland was not developing at all as Arnim had planned. Polish peasants and artisans, inspired by Polish nationalist rhetoric, turned against Germans and Jews, many of them the local landlords and moneylenders, and a newly formed Polish National Committee informed the king of Prussia "that it is their aim to reestablish the Kingdom of Poland. They will transform Posnania [Prussian Poland] into a recruiting centre, a training ground, an arsenal, a supply base." Confronted with these developments, German enthusiasm for the Polish national cause soon faded. Even the most idealistic liberals were increasingly concerned with defending German interests and their sense of German nationalism was soon to override their sympathy for Polish liberation or, indeed, for liberalism in general. In Prussian Poland, Polish property owners were as concerned as the Germans about the popular unrest unleashed by the Polish nationalist movement, and they were particularly fearful of a war with Russia, the avowed objective of the Polish revolutionaries.

By early April the Prussian government had resolved to put an end to the dangers posed by the Polish revolutionary movement. Because of the rifts within the movement itself as well as the growing antirevolutionary sentiment on the part of the Polish as well as German gentry, Prussian troops had little difficulty in suppressing it. By the middle of May 1848 all organized resistance had been overcome and the authority of the Prussian government firmly reestablished.

By this time Arnim himself had abandoned the Polish cause, and soon after the suppression of the revolution in Prussian Poland he boasted shamelessly about how the Prussian government had labored unaided to combat "the perfidious Polish onslaught on the peace of Europe." On June 17, 1848, the Prussian government eliminated the Arnim menace to the peace of Europe by dismissing him from his position as foreign minister.

❑ *The Revolution in Schleswig-Holstein*

More dangerous to the peace of Europe than Arnim's irresponsible war plot and the abortive rising in Prussian Poland was the 1848 revolution in the northern duchies of Schleswig, Holstein, and Lauenburg against their dynastic overlord, the king of Denmark.

The 1848 revolution in Schleswig-Holstein belongs in the category of the national revolutions of that year, in this case a clash between Danish and German nationalism. The geographic position of the duchies and their strategic importance to the great powers made the crisis a matter of general European concern. The duchies form a land bridge between Germany and the Danish peninsula, which dominates the sea lanes between the North and Baltic seas. These Danish Straits are often compared to the Turkish Straits for their strategic and commercial importance, affecting as they do the interests of all the states of northern Europe and three of Europe's great powers, Britain, Prussia, and Russia. The duchies themselves, located at the base of the Danish peninsula, had long been considered as the site for a canal which would shorten the sea route between the North and Baltic seas, as great a strategic and economic asset as the Danish Straits themselves.

The crisis in Schleswig-Holstein began in January 1848 when their dynastic overlord, King Frederick VII of Denmark, announced a new constitution that included provisions designed to make the duchies an integral part of the Kingdom of Denmark. The incorporation of the duchies would have been a breach of international law, for according to ancient traditions and recent treaties, the duchies were independent of Denmark, their only link being that the king of Denmark was also duke of Schleswig and Holstein. According to these same traditions and treaties, the duchies were also supposed to remain indissolubly linked to each other, a situation complicated still further by the statesmen of Vienna in 1815, who had made Holstein, with its predominantly German population, a member of the German Confederation, whereas Schleswig, whose population included a substantial Danish minority, had been left out of the German union.

When informed of the new constitution of Frederick VII, the German representatives in the assemblies of Schleswig and Holstein refused to accept it and demanded instead a new and separate constitution for the duchies and the admission of Schleswig into the German Confederation. These demands were rejected by the Danish government, whereupon the Germans in the duchies rose in revolt on March 28, 1848, proclaimed their independence from Denmark, set up a provisional government, and appealed to the states of the German Confederation for support. The government of Prussia, its foreign policy under the direction of Heinrich von Arnim, responded to this appeal, as did the governments of several other German states, despite dire warnings from Britain and Russia.

Prusso-German forces quickly drove the Danish troops from the duchies and began an invasion of Denmark itself. The Danes countered by blockading the German coasts and attacking German shipping, which the Germans were unable to prevent because of their total lack of sea power, a vulnerability that made German nationalists fatefully conscious of the need for a German navy. The decisive engagements were fought on land, however, and as the Prusso-German forces pushed forward into Denmark it seemed likely that they would soon be in control of the entire peninsula.

The Danes were saved by the diplomatic intervention of the European powers. From the beginning of the crisis, Prussia was under intense pressure from Britain, Russia, and Sweden to submit the entire Schleswig-Holstein question to international arbitration. Especially indignant was the tsar of Russia, who could not understand how his brother-in-law, the king of Prussia, could lend his support to a revolutionary movement. Confronted with the diplomatic pressure of so formidable a coalition, King Frederick William IV, who had never been enthusiastic about the Schleswig-Holstein adventure and was anxious above all to preserve good relations with Russia, yielded to the pressure of his fellow monarchs and agreed to international arbitration.

In the subsequent negotiations over the duchies, the Danes rejected all proposals for their partition or any other changes that would have compromised Danish chances for gaining complete control over them. This Danish recalcitrance was eventually rewarded, for the other powers involved in the negotiations were also opposed to any change in the status of the duchies and dismissed all German claims based on the language and nationality of their inhabitants—"that dreamy and dangerous nonsense called German nationality," as the British statesman Benjamin Disraeli referred to it in the House of Commons.

Prussia was obliged to yield all along the line, and to the fury of German nationalists signed an armistice at Malmö on August 28, 1848, that met virtually all the conditions of the Danes. It provided for the withdrawal of all German forces from the duchies, the annulment of all acts of their provisional governments, and their administration by a joint Danish–German commission under the chairmanship of a man known to be pro-Danish.

The armistice of Malmö, advantageous to the Danes in almost every respect, was nevertheless denounced by the Danes in February 1849. Confident that they had the diplomatic support of Russia and Sweden and that the German states, in view of their recent diplomatic setbacks, would no longer dare to intervene, they believed they were now in a position to establish complete and exclusive control over the duchies. Their confidence proved ill-founded. The German states did intervene and were restrained from renewing their invasion of Denmark only by the diplomatic pressure of other powers. There followed three years of intermittent warfare, armistice, and negotiation, but on May 8, 1852, it seemed that the Schleswig-Holstein question was finally settled with the signature of a treaty in London (the so-called London Protocol) by the representatives of the governments of Austria, Britain, France, Prussia, Russia, Sweden, and Denmark. The tortuous circumlocutions in the wording of that treaty reflected a desire to save face by all concerned parties, but essentially it provided for the restoration of the pre-1848 status quo, with the powers "taking into consideration that the maintenance of the Integrity of the Danish Monarchy, as connected with the general interests of the Balance of Power in Europe, is of high importance to the preservation of Peace."

It was not the fault of the negotiators of 1852 that their solution to the Schleswig-Holstein question proved to be only temporary. In 1863 the Danes once again moved to incorporate the duchies and provoked a renewal of the Schleswig-Holstein crisis, which this time was to be resolved in a very different manner (see pp. 194–197).

❑ The Frankfurt Parliament

The most famous and from the point of view of Germany's future political development the most significant of the 1848 revolutions in Germany was not strictly speaking a revolution at all, but a peaceful political movement. Its aim was the creation of a constitutional government for all the peoples of Germany and the unification of Germany through a popularly elected all-German parliament. Despite its peaceful nature, however, the movement was unquestionably revolutionary, for it aspired to nothing less than the liquidation of the German Confederation and of all existing German states and governments. In this contradiction between its peaceful parliamentary nature and its fundamentally revolutionary program lay the fatal weakness of the German national parliamentary movement, for the movement quite simply lacked the power to impose an all-German government on the states of the German Confederation and enforce its legislation. This basic weakness doomed the German national parliament to eventual failure.

The original impetus for the movement to establish an all-German parliamentary government came from a self-constituted committee of German liberals that met in Heidelberg early in March 1848 to discuss how such a government might be created. This group decided to convene a larger and more representative assembly which was to serve as a preliminary parliament (Vorparlament) and arrange for elections to be held in all the states of the German Confederation, thereby ensuring the formation of a genuinely representative German national parliament. The Heidelberg committee chose from among its members a Committee of Seven, which was to draw up an agenda for the proposed preliminary parliament. To ensure that that parliament was as representative as possible, the committee invited all present and past members of existing German legislative assemblies as well as a number of distinguished individual Germans to participate.

For both the Committee of Seven and the Vorparlament there immediately arose a question that was to remain critical to the German national movement: What constituted a *German* state? There was no problem about the German quality of most member states of the German Confederation. But what was to be done about

Bohemia and Moravia, which were part of the confederation but whose population was predominantly Czech? What about East and West Prussia, Posnania, and Schleswig, which were not part of the confederation but which nevertheless included a large proportion of Germans? What about the German-speaking Swiss, and the Germanic Dutch and Flemings, who were also outside the confederation? And most important of all, what was to be done about Austria, the leading power within the confederation but also part of a largely non-Germanic empire?

The Vorparlament avoided dealing with most of these critical questions, and for the moment followed the example of the Committee of Seven by deciding to invite representatives from all the states of the existing German Confederation, and thus also from Bohemia and Moravia. After a good deal of debate, the Vorparlament also decided to invite representatives from both East and West Prussia and from Schleswig, despite their large Polish and Danish populations. Posnania was the subject of some of the most heated discussion, but for the time being the ideals of liberal nationalism still prevailed on this issue. Despite the impassioned pleas of a few German nationalists not to abandon the German population of Posnania, the Vorparlament passed a resolution declaring the dismemberment of Poland to have been a "shameful wrong" and its restoration "a sacred duty of the German nation." Because political conditions differed so greatly in the various states or provinces that were to be invited to elect representatives to the German national parliament, the Vorparlament left the actual election procedures to the individual German governments and insisted only that all elections be held on the basis of universal manhood suffrage. Before 1848 such elections would not have been permitted, but the governments of all these states were intimidated by revolution and many of them now included liberals who strongly supported the idea of a German national parliament. It therefore proved possible to hold elections in all the states of Germany, and on May 18, 1848, the first all-German parliament began its deliberations in the church of St. Paul (Paulskirche) in the free city of Frankfurt. Its principal task was to draft a constitution and establish a government for a united and democratic Germany.

The Frankfurt Parliament has special significance in German history: it was not only the first all-German popularly elected government, but it was also the sole one ever to be created entirely through German initiative. The Frankfurt Parliament was thus a landmark in the history of German parliamentary government and remained the prototype of the kind of government many German liberals continued to desire for their country. The colors of the national symbol of the Frankfurt Parliament— black, red, and gold, which had been the colors of the radical student leagues earlier in the century—were to become the colors of the first flag of the Weimar Republic, they were adopted as the colors of both East and West Germany after World War II, and they remain the colors of a united Germany.

The parliamentarians of Frankfurt have been severely criticized for giving way to excessively nationalist sentiments in the course of their debates and for allowing their concern for German national interests to override their liberal principles. Nationalists of all countries, however, have a distressing tendency to ignore the rights and interests of other nationalities while making demands on behalf of their own. In the case of the Germans at Frankfurt, it is difficult to imagine how they could have avoided an excessive emphasis on nationalism, since nationalism was the predominant ideological force that brought and held them together.

The German parliamentarians have also been criticized for being excessively theoretical in their conceptions of government, and for wasting precious time by indulging in debate over questions of detail and procedure. It is true that the debates in the Paulskirche were long and frequently petty, but the problems of drafting a constitution for a politically divided country still torn by religious differences and a multitude of conflicting interests were complex in the extreme. Moreover, although some of the parliamentarians were excessively theoretical and verbose, most of them were pragmatic politicians with a good deal of practical experience in governing their various states. The Frankfurt Parliament as a whole proved to be a remarkably realistic and effective body, and within less than a year it had completed its task of drawing up a constitution for Germany.

The fundamental weakness of the Frankfurt Parliament, as noted earlier, was its lack of power, and most of the delegates were acutely aware of it. The parliament did not have a police force, it had no bureaucracy to put its legislation into effect, and most important of all, it had no army to enforce its decisions at home or abroad. The remedy to this fundamental weakness was itself a dilemma whose solutions were distasteful to the more liberal of the Frankfurt parliamentarians: the leadership of a united Germany would have to be offered to one of the two states capable of providing the necessary power, either Austria or Prussia.

The partisans of Austria became known as the Greater Germany (Grossdeutsch) party. Austria, however, was part of a large, multinational empire, and for the Grossdeutsch party a problem arose: If Austria were to be the leader of a German national union, what was to be done about the non-German peoples of the Habsburg realm? Many partisans of Austria were willing to compromise their national principles and proceed to the formation of a supernational union, but members of the Greater Germany party remained bitterly divided on this issue. Opposed to them were the advocates of a Little Germany (Kleindeutsch) party, who favored an exclusively or at least predominantly German union. Many members of the Little Germany party were willing to accept Austrian leadership if Austria separated itself from the Habsburg empire, but as Austria was unlikely to agree to this condition, the Kleindeutsch party looked to Prussia for leadership and was prepared to accept a German union that might not include Austria. When the Austrian government made clear in March 1849 that its membership in a new German union would depend on the inclusion of the entire Habsburg empire, a majority of delegates to the Frankfurt Parliament swung over to the Kleindeutsch party, and on March 28, 1849, they voted to offer the imperial crown of a united Germany to the king of Prussia.

King Frederick William IV quickly declared that he had no intention of making Prussia the instrument of a popularly elected parliamentary regime. Although he was gracious enough in rejecting the imperial crown, in communications with his fellow monarchs he expressed the utmost scorn for this "crown from the gutter." The Frankfurt delegates were unfortunate that the man who happened to be king of Prussia in 1849 was a ruler who still harbored romantic medieval notions about the divine origins of kingship and who had little understanding of or sympathy for the concept of popular sovereignty or the institutions of parliamentary government.

Even a less romantic and more practical or ambitious ruler, however, might well have hesitated to accept the crown offered by the Frankfurt delegates. Their parliament was after all a revolutionary body, and the creation of a united Germany would have been a revolutionary act—a breach of the treaties of 1814–1815 and the principles embodied in the treaties of Troppau and Laibach, as well as a major threat to the European balance of power. By assuming the leadership of such a union, the king of Prussia would have faced the hostility of all the powers of Europe, the almost certain prospect of war with Austria, and the high probability of war with France and Russia as well, for neither power could be expected to tolerate the creation of a powerful German union on its frontier. Frederick William IV may not have been fully aware of the magnitude of these dangers, but he was sufficiently aware of the revolutionary nature of the movement he was being called upon to lead to reject it on ideological as well as practical grounds.

The Prussian rejection of German leadership killed the Frankfurt Parliament, and therewith the movement to achieve German unity on the basis of popular sovereignty through a popularly elected assembly. When the offer of the imperial crown was made to Prussia, the Austrian government recalled its delegates from Frankfurt, and when Prussia rejected the offer, the Prussian delegates and those of several other German states were withdrawn as well. The remaining delegates now moved to Stuttgart, where a rump parliament continued to meet, but by this time it had become little more than a debating society and soon its members simply dispersed.

How correct the king of Prussia had been to reject the crown of a united Germany was demonstrated shortly afterward. In May 1849 the Prussian government put forward a scheme for the union of the states of northern Germany with the obvious objective of extending Prussian influence in Germany while Austria was still embroiled in Hungary. Austria, however, now under the resolute leadership of Schwarzenberg, refused to allow the implementation of any part of the Prussian proposal or to make any kind of compromise that would have admitted an increase of Prussian influence in Germany. Throughout the ensuing crisis Austria was staunchly supported by Russia, which wanted no change in the balance of power within Germany. Faced with the prospect of a war with Austria and possibly with Russia as well, the Prussian government gave in. In a convention with Austria signed at Olmütz in Moravia on November 29, 1850, Prussia agreed to abandon the Prussian union program and to reestablish the old German Confederation under the presidency of Austria, a diplomatic setback that patriotic Prussians henceforth denounced as the "humiliation of Olmütz." Thus in Germany, as in almost all other parts of Europe, the pre-1848 status quo had been restored.

❑ *The 1848 Revolutions and the Foreign Relations of the Great Powers*

It was due in large measure to what might be called a rump Concert of Europe, in which Britain and Russia played the principal roles, that none of the 1848 revolutions set off a general European war, and that the widespread domestic upheavals did not destroy the international order established in 1815 or upset the European balance of power. Both Britain and Russia exercised great restraint in not taking advantage of their neighbors' predicaments to advance their own interests, and their diplomats spent months at conference tables to prevent other states from doing so. Britain and Russia held the ring around the areas of revolution to allow the states affected to deal with their own affairs, always on guard to prevent them from threatening the interests of others or the general peace of Europe.

The greatest positive achievement of this rump concert was its handling of the crisis over Schleswig-Holstein, where the war was kept localized through diplomacy and where peace and the status quo were eventually restored through negotiation. The only place where the international status quo was not restored was Rome, where France took the place of Austria as the principal guardian of the temporal interests of the Holy See.

In the realm of international affairs, the most significant result of the 1848 revolutions was the change of leadership in many of the great powers. The last of the elder statesmen whose views on foreign policy had been conditioned by the experiences of the French Revolution and Napoleonic wars were swept away and succeeded by younger men who were less conscious of the desirability of preserving the existing international order and were prepared to embark on more adventurous courses in foreign policy. Metternich, whose name had become synonymous with the old order and who had been the most consistent champion of concert diplomacy, was replaced by Schwarzenberg, a brilliant and energetic statesman, but a diplomat without Metternich's sense of perspective in international affairs. With ruthless determination he advanced the interests of Austria without regard for the interests of other powers or the sensibilities of their leaders. He therewith ignored one of the fundamental principles of Metternich's diplomacy: the need to respect the interests of other powers so that they remained convinced that those interests were best defended by cooperation within the existing international system and through the preservation of that system. Given a false sense of Austrian strength following Austria's miraculous recovery from the 1848 upheavals, Metternich's successors failed to bear in mind that Austria, more than any other power, depended on the preservation of peace and the support of the European concert to maintain its status and influence.

In France, King Louis Philippe had learned about the perils of isolation during the Near Eastern crisis of 1840, and his chief minister, Guizot, had resolved to cooperate with the concert. The regime of Louis Philippe, however, was overthrown in 1848 and succeeded by the government of Napoleon III, whose foreign policy was actually dedicated to disrupting the concert and destroying the 1814–1815 treaty system.

In Prussia, Frederick William IV remained in nominal control of the government for another decade, but in 1858 he was displaced for reasons of insanity. He was succeeded by his brother William, whose ministers were determined not to suffer another diplomatic defeat at the hands of Austria or any other power and who were to embark on far-reaching reforms of the Prussian army that would enable Prussia to undertake major changes in the international order.

In Britain, the leadership of Aberdeen was to alternate with that of the more forceful Palmerston, who was happy enough to cooperate with the European concert when such cooperation served the interests of Britain, but who was prepared to ignore and eventually destroy it when he thought British interests could be defended or promoted more effectively through other means. After 1848, in fact, only the government of Nicholas I, who had abandoned an aggressive foreign policy after Russia's victory over the Turks in 1829, remained a staunch defender of the concert and the post-Napoleonic international order.

SEVEN

❑

The Crimean War

❑ *The Background of the Conflict*

Shortly after the midpoint of the nineteenth century, concert diplomacy broke down over one of the perennial crises in the Near East, and a major international conflict took place that has become known in history as the Crimean War. In international affairs at least, this war proved to be a far more significant turning point in European history than the revolutions of 1848.

The Crimean War was a conflict between Russia and the Ottoman empire, which was supported by Britain and France and ultimately also by the northern Italian state of Piedmont-Sardinia. Contemporary explanations of the war were for the most part variations of the well-worn slogans associated with all modern wartime propaganda, confidently set forth at the time and almost certainly sincerely believed by most of the leaders of the belligerent powers and the majority of politically aware people in their respective countries. This was a war of civilization against barbarism, of freedom against tyranny, of self-defense against ruthless aggression, of Islam or Christianity (whether Orthodox, Protestant, or Roman) against the forces of darkness. Many of these simplistic slogans, though not always so crudely expressed, may still be found in some national histories and even in works of scholars purporting to seek more profound explanations for the war. Such studies tend to find Europe divided between the liberal and enlightened nations of the West, Britain and France, and the autocratic "Holy Alliance" powers, Austria, Prussia, and Russia. The war thus becomes one between liberalism and autocracy, a war on behalf of the nationalities of Europe and national freedom and self-determination against foreign rule and oppression.

All historical judgments, of course, are based on a historian's personal values and prejudices, but ideological explanations for the war must be dismissed for the most part as nonsense. So-called liberal states, Britain and France, were major colonial powers, busily suppressing freedom and national self-determination in many parts of the world and fighting on behalf of the preservation of the Ottoman empire, a Muslim state whose government was hardly a model of liberal enlightenment. The government of Britain itself was as yet a tight aristocratic oligarchy, that of France

101

MAP 4 THE CRIMEAN WAR

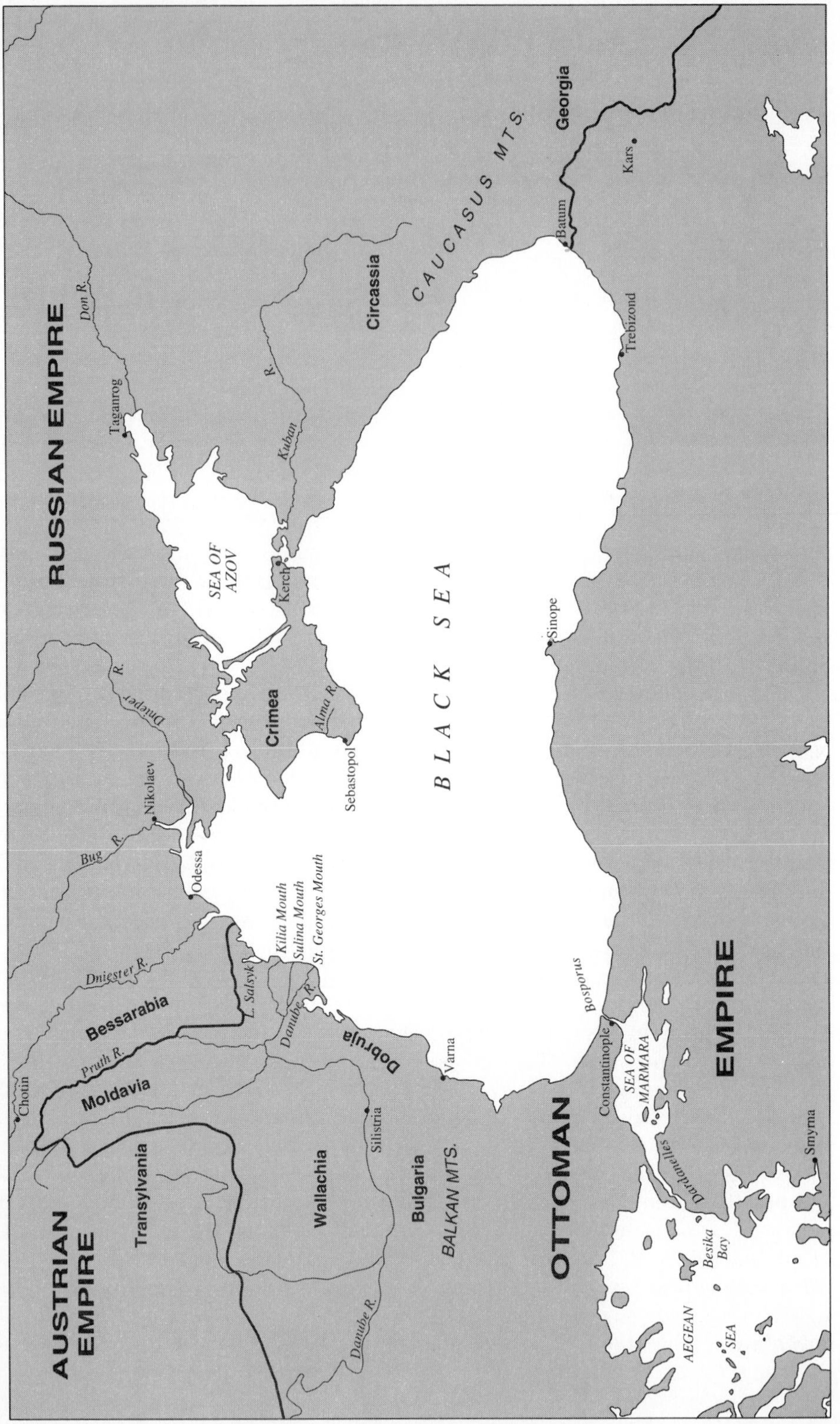

under Napoleon III a military dictatorship. A far better case can be and has been made that this was a war on behalf of great power economic and strategic interests in the Near East, and so it was, but all these considerations may be subsumed under the heading of fear of Russia, which was seen as the primary threat to the interests of the European powers in this area at that time.

Fear of Russia is no new phenomenon in history. Since the days of Peter the Great, foreign statesmen have looked with increasing apprehension at the mammoth power arising in the east, and at the gradual but steady extension of Russia's frontiers in every direction. Finland, the east coast of the Baltic, and a large part of Poland had come under Russian control in the late eighteenth and early nineteenth centuries. For two hundred years there had been a war between Russia and Turkey almost every twenty years, as Russia extended its influence at the expense of the Ottoman empire into the Middle East, the Balkans, and toward the Mediterranean. In Asia, too, Russia had steadily expanded eastward to the Pacific, Alaska, and the North American coast, and southward to the boundaries of Persia, Afghanistan, and China, where it was to loom as a threat to these countries comparable to the threat it posed to the Ottoman empire and the states of Europe.

It was primarily to halt Russian expansion and eliminate the Russian threat to the security and interests of the states of Europe and the Ottoman empire that the Crimean War was fought. The tragedy of that war was that it was both unnecessary and useless. It was unnecessary because it accomplished nothing that could not have been, and in fact actually had been, accomplished through peaceful negotiation. It was useless because it did not halt Russian expansion or even diminish, much less eliminate, Russia's capacity to pose a threat to other states. Even more tragic were the political repercussions of that war. The hatreds it engendered dealt a catastrophic blow to the precarious international stability established after the Napoleonic wars and to the Concert of Europe, which, for all its weaknesses, provided an arrangement for the peaceful settlement of international disputes at the conference table. The Crimean War destroyed the confidence among the statesmen of Europe that their own as well as their mutual interests were best served through respect for international treaties designed to preserve international order and therewith also international peace. The destruction of the European concert opened the gates for wars and revolutions that during the next two decades permanently altered the European states system and the international balance of power.

The process whereby the chief powers of Europe became involved in the Crimean War was complicated and many issues remain unclear and controversial. One theory about its origins, however, can definitely be eliminated: the war was not an accident, the result of bungling incompetence or misunderstandings on the part of the statesmen involved, although all of them can be charged with serious miscalculations. Yet rarely in history has a war been preceded by so lengthy a period of diplomatic crisis which provided time for passions to cool and statesmen to settle their differences at the conference table; and rarely in history were so many sincere and vigorous efforts made by responsible leaders of the great powers to arrange a compromise settlement throughout the period of prewar crisis and the entire course of the war itself.

Efforts to preserve or restore peace through negotiation failed because there were statesmen in Europe who did not want them to succeed, who were dedicated to the breakup of the existing international order or were not content merely to halt Russian expansion but wanted to eliminate the Russian threat permanently. Neither of these aims could be achieved through peaceful negotiation, for both required revolutionary changes in the European power structure that could be made only through war. The latter objective especially—the permanent elimination of the Russian threat—would have required the annihilation of the Russian armed forces and the dismemberment of the Russian empire or equally radical measures that would have necessitated not just war but war on an immense scale.

Among those who blocked efforts to arrange a peaceful resolution of the Near Eastern crises of the 1850s and who believed in the desirability or necessity of war with Russia, the most obvious were the Turks, who over the past two centuries had suffered a succession of military defeats and territorial losses at the hands of Russia. But the Turks would hardly have ventured war with Russia to recoup their losses had they not received strong support from the great powers.

Foremost among the leaders of the European powers providing such support was Napoleon III, nephew of the first Napoleon, who had been elected president of the Second French Republic in December 1848 and had subsequently made himself dictator and emperor. The Napoleonic name had been an important and perhaps decisive political asset in Louis Napoleon's rise to power. But the name Napoleon was also a fateful political legacy, for it aroused popular expectations of a new era of glory and empire. Few remaining records can be considered reliable guides to the political thinking of Napoleon III, but the entire course of his foreign policy suggests that he believed his regime was obliged to fulfill popular expectations and restore France to a position of predominance in Europe.

In seeking to realize this objective, Napoleon III was to employ three major strategies in his foreign policy:

1. He was resolved to cultivate good relations with Britain, the country he thought had been the major obstacle to his uncle's success, in the belief that the removal of that obstacle would facilitate the success of his own policies.
2. He endeavored to harness to his cause the ideological principle of nationalism, whose potential power his uncle had recognized but failed to exploit, by making himself the champion of nationalities seeking freedom from foreign rule and reorganizing Europe along the lines of nationality under the political and moral leadership of France.
3. Closely linked with his nationalities program, he sought to disrupt the international order that had been established after the Napoleonic wars to prevent future French aggression and that still constituted the major obstacle to re-establishing French predominance in Europe.

Because Russia was the foremost champion of this international order, a primary objective of Napoleon's foreign policy was to weaken Russia's ability to defend it. It was Napoleon's good fortune that he came to power at a time when fear of Russia overshadowed fear of France among the states of Europe, and he soon discovered that France would not lack for support in pursuing an anti-Russian policy.

Curiously enough it was Britain, farthest from Russia and least directly menaced, that was to become the most rabid opponent of Russia in the course of the Crimean crisis, the staunchest supporter of the Turks and Napoleon's anti-Russian policy, and the most vigorous advocate of imposing conditions on Russia that made a peaceful resolution of the crisis impossible. British suspicion of Russia had been vigorously stoked by journalists and other spokesmen for British vested interests in the Near East, but the British had legitimate reasons for concern. They feared the Russian threat to the European balance of power, the possibility of Russian control over the Ottoman empire, and the consequent threat to their overland routes to India, their trade in the Near East, and their sea power in the Mediterranean. These British fears were compounded by the belief that Russia had gained control of the Concert of Europe and that Austria, Prussia, and other conservative powers had fallen under Russian influence and would support or at least not hinder Russian efforts to extend that influence still further.

Since the Napoleonic wars, British statesmen had generally acted on the assumption that British interests in the Near East could be defended most cheaply and effectively through the preservation of the Ottoman empire. British support had been limited for the most part to diplomatic intervention and naval demonstrations; it was not designed to roll back Russian influence or recoup previous Turkish losses to Russia. There was no sign in the early 1850s that British leaders saw any need for more active support, much less war, on behalf of the Ottoman empire, and during the initial phase of the Franco-Russian crisis they attempted to cooperate with other powers eager to arrange a peaceful settlement. In the course of that crisis, however, the more pacific British leaders, notably Lord Aberdeen, the prime minister, allowed the direction of British foreign policy to slip away to more bellicose spirits, men who needed no prompting from Napoleon III to arouse their suspicions of Russia and who were eventually to advocate far more radical measures against Russia than anything conceived by the French ruler. Among the anti-Russian forces in the British government, two men played critical roles in influencing the course of British policy before and during the Crimean War: Viscount Palmerston and Stratford Canning (since 1852 Viscount Stratford de Redcliffe).

At the time of the Crimean crisis, Palmerston, who had held the post of secretary for war and foreign secretary in so many earlier governments (see p. 62), was home secretary in the cabinet of Lord Aberdeen. But even as home secretary, this doughty champion of British interests was the foremost advocate of a vigorous foreign policy dedicated to the permanent elimination of the Russian menace.

Stratford Canning, a cousin of George Canning, the foreign secretary and prime minister who had died in 1827, had served as a member of the British House of Commons for twelve years, but it was primarily through his diplomatic career that he earned his reputation as a statesman, especially through his service in Constantinople, where he had represented his country intermittently since 1810 and where over the years he had gained enormous prestige and influence. Stratford's attitude toward the crisis that led to the Crimean War was more parochial than Palmerston's, for he had spent so much time in the Near East that he had come to regard the region as something of a personal preserve. Although he agreed with Palmerston in perceiving the tsar's policies in the Near East as a threat to Britain, he appears to have resented them far more as an intrusion into his own domain, a personal insult that made the crisis in the Near East a power struggle between himself and the Russian autocrat. In 1832, Stratford had been appointed ambassador to St. Petersburg, a more prestigious post than Constantinople, but the tsar had refused to accept him because of Stratford's well-known hostility to Russia, a rejection which can only have fed the flames of his Russophobia. In 1853, his ambitions of becoming foreign secretary or ambassador to Paris recently frustrated, he agreed to return to Constantinople, evidently determined to demonstrate his diplomatic prowess to the world and frustrate the designs of Russia, whatever these might be.

Unlike Napoleon III, Palmerston and Stratford did not desire the breakup of the existing international order. On the contrary, they were primarily concerned with its preservation; it was their fear of the Russian threat to that order that motivated them to frustrate suspected Russian designs in the Near East. As the crisis with Russia developed, they became convinced that Russia could be stopped only through war, and the only objective that could justify waging war was the permanent elimination of the Russian menace.

Another force working against a peaceful resolution of the Crimean crisis was public opinion in Britain, where hostility to Russia had long been nourished by reports of Russian threats to British interests in the Near East and by the popular conception of tsarist Russia as a land of tyranny and oppression. In the mid-nineteenth century that hostility had been inflamed anew, this time against Austria as well as Russia, when these countries demanded the extradition of Hungarian and Polish refugees who had fled to the Ottoman empire after the brutal Austro-Russian suppression of the 1848 revolution in Hungary. Encouraged by Stratford, the Ottoman government had refused to yield to these demands, and the British government (in which Palmerston at that time served as foreign secretary) had sent a naval squadron to the Near East to back up Turkish resistance.

How justified were Turkish and Western fears of Russia? As the Turkish experience over the past two centuries had shown—and as had the experience of almost every other neighbor of Russia—they were very justified indeed. Russia, by its very existence, because of its sheer size and power, constituted a permanent threat to the security of the states of Europe and the Ottoman empire. But how immediate was that threat in the 1850s? Was the tsar actually planning another incursion into the Ottoman empire at this time? Was he unwilling to compromise and prepared to risk war to realize his ambitions?

As we have seen, when he first ascended the throne in December 1825, Nicholas I had certainly seemed prepared to pursue a radical policy in the Near East to promote the exclusive interests of Russia as he understood them. He intervened frequently in the affairs of the Ottoman empire, and in 1828 he went to war with Turkey because of Turkey's repudiation of previous treaty agreements. In the course of that war, however, a number of the tsar's ministers had warned of the dangers to Russia of this aggressive policy: any further Russian advance risked the danger of foreign intervention and war with one or more of the European great powers, or the participation of those powers in the partition of the Ottoman empire with the result that instead of the hapless Turks, Russia would have powerful and dangerous rivals along its southern frontiers.

The tsar had accepted this advice, made peace with Turkey, and over the next two decades had observed a policy of restraint in dealing with the Ottoman empire. This was still Russian policy when Napoleon deliberately provoked a crisis with Russia in the Near East in the spring of 1850.

❑ *The Development of the Crisis*

The incident that set off the crisis that was to lead to the Crimean War was Napoleon's challenge to Russia for the right to be the chief guardian of the holy places (the scenes of the life and death of Christ) in the Ottoman empire. The dispute over the holy places was no mere churchwarden's quarrel or empty issue of national prestige, as it has sometimes been described, but a question of power and influence in the Near East. As protector of the holy places and the sizable Christian population in the Ottoman empire, a state had an excuse to intervene in the internal affairs of that empire and thus gain a valuable means of enhancing its influence in areas under Turkish control.

France already had important economic interests in the Near East, and Napoleon's intervention on behalf of the Latin (Roman Catholic) church as chief protector of the holy places (in opposition to Russia's backing of the Christian Orthodox church) has been interpreted as an effort to foster those interests as well as curry favor with influential clerical groups in France itself. But for the French emperor these were not the main issues: his primary objective was the breakup of the existing international system and the disruption of the alliances designed to defend that system, an objective described with complete candor by Napoleon's foreign minister, Drouyn de Lhuys: "The question of the Holy Places and everything affecting them was of no importance whatever to France," he confided to a friend shortly after the beginning of the war. "All this Eastern Question which provoked so much noise was nothing more for the imperial government than a means of dislocating the continental alliance which had tended to paralyze France for almost half a century. When finally an opportunity presented itself to provoke discord within this powerful coalition, the Emperor Napoleon immediately seized it." Napoleon himself was equally candid. During the final negotiations for peace in March 1856, he informed his ministers that in order to dismantle the treaties concluded after the Napoleonic wars it had been necessary to separate Austria and Russia, "which were always ready to menace us with the European coalition and which deprived us of all our liberty. That was the great objective of the war: to separate the two powers and to regain for France . . . its liberty of action abroad."

Napoleon III launched his campaign in the Near East in May 1850. In a succession of representations to the Ottoman government over the next two and a half years, he demanded the restoration of the rights of the Latin church over the holy places in the Ottoman empire which had been allowed to lapse in the previous century. As both Napoleon and the Turks were well aware, any such concessions to France were certain to generate conflict with Russia because, over the past century, many rights previously conceded to France on behalf of the Latin church had been taken over by default by the Orthodox church, which the tsars had come to regard as being under their special protection. The issue of the Christians in the Ottoman empire was in any case of far greater importance to Russia than to France, for there were approximately thirteen million Orthodox Christians in that empire, well over one-third of the entire population, whereas the size of the Latin population was comparatively insignificant.

The French government set forth its claims in violent and intimidating language, and backed them up with impressive displays of military power and threats to use it if the Turks refused to make the required concessions. Although the Turks professed to be indignant about French demands and threats, they may actually have welcomed France's challenge to Russia over the holy places, especially as the French accompanied their demands with assurances of military support if any concessions to France should involve the Turks in difficulties with Russia. Whether intimidated by French pressure or happy to seize the opportunity to play off France against

Russia in the Near East, the Turks in December 1852 conceded everything the French government demanded.

The Russian response to these concessions to the French was to send what they themselves called a "mission of intimidation" to Constantinople in late February 1853. This mission was led by one of the foremost grandees of the Russian realm, Prince Alexander Menshikov, whose representations to Turkey were backed, as those of France had been, by impressive displays of Russian military might. The mission had been proposed by the Russian chancellor and foreign minister, Count Nesselrode, as the least dangerous means of restoring Russian rights and prestige in the Ottoman empire, and it had been approved by the tsar. "It is fear which drove it [the Turkish government] into the arms of France," Nesselrode said. "It is likewise fear which will bring it back to us."

The Russians demanded a formal treaty with Turkey guaranteeing all rights previously granted the Orthodox church and Russia in the Ottoman empire, including Russia's right to make representations on behalf of the Orthodox church and virtual freedom of that church from the authority of the Turkish government—rights that in fact went far beyond anything the Ottoman government had ever conceded. The Turks protested that these Russian demands were an attempt to reduce the Ottoman empire to the status of a Russian protectorate, they predicted that rejection of those demands would be followed by a Russian attack on Constantinople, and they appealed to the British and French governments to send their fleets to the Near East to protect the Ottoman empire and prevent its falling under Russian dominion.

Napoleon responded to this Turkish appeal, not so much, it would appear, because he actually feared a Russian attack on Constantinople, as because he hoped the British would join in this naval action, thus fostering closer Anglo-French cooperation in international affairs, one of his foremost foreign policy objectives. "If we send our fleet to Salamis [off the coast of Greece]," he said, "England will do the same and the union of our two fleets will initiate the union of our two peoples against Russia." He thereupon gave the order for the French fleet to proceed to Salamis. Contrary to his expectations, however, the British government, still under the control of the pacifically inclined Aberdeen, did not join the French action.

The return of Stratford Canning to Constantinople, at approximately the same time as the dispatch of the French fleet to the Near East, more than compensated for the hesitancy of the British government. Although instructed to do everything in his power to resolve the crisis, Stratford was convinced that Russia was indeed a menace to British interests and the independence of the Ottoman empire. Thus, while advising the Turks to make token concessions over the holy places, he urged them to reject all demands that might give the Russians any excuse whatever for extending their authority in the Ottoman realm.

As the crisis intensified, the Russians saw that it was likely to involve them in far more serious difficulties than they had anticipated and dropped all their demands that might be interpreted as a threat to Turkish independence. They no longer asked for a formal treaty but only for a Turkish note containing assurances that the Orthodox church should continue to enjoy, under the aegis of the sultan, all rights and privileges previously granted by the Ottoman government. Even this was too much for Stratford, who warned the Turks that *any* agreement with Russia would serve as a pretext for Russian interference in Turkish affairs and must therefore be rejected. Thus encouraged and obviously confident that they could count on Anglo-

French support, the Turks turned down a final Russian demand of May 20, 1853, for a Turkish note, whose contents had been so watered down by this time that it represented little more than a Russian effort to save face. On the following day Menshikov left Constantinople, his mission a failure.

Stratford was delighted with the failure of Menshikov's "untoward negotiations," as he called them, and took some pride in the part he had played in the diplomatic defeat of Russia. On the day following Turkey's rejection of Menshikov's final demand, he wrote what has been called a "grim" dispatch to Clarendon, the British foreign secretary, explaining that the Turks had no choice but to reject the Russian demands. "It was not the amputation of a limb, but the infusion of poison into the system that they are summoned to accept." It was now up to Britain to decide how far it was prepared to support the Turks, but Stratford warned that unless Turkey received help it was certain to succumb to Russian domination sooner or later.

In the British cabinet, Stratford's call for a hard line against Russia was most enthusiastically supported by Palmerston. Even before receiving news of Menshikov's failure and Stratford's dire warnings, Palmerston wrote to Clarendon: "The policy and practice of the Russian Government has always been to push forward its encroachments as fast and as far as the apathy or want of firmness of other Governments would allow it to go, but always to stop and retire when it was met with decided resistance, and then to wait for the next favourable opportunity to make another spring on its intended victim."

The tsar reacted to the news of Menshikov's failure with frustrated fury. To show the Turks he could not be trifled with and to secure acceptance of his demands, he sent an ultimatum on May 31 demanding their acceptance of Menshikov's final proposals within eight days; otherwise Russian troops would be ordered to occupy Turkey's Danubian Principalities of Moldavia and Wallachia. His purpose was not to fight a war with the sultan but to obtain material guarantees of Russian rights which the Russian government had attempted in vain to obtain by peaceful means.

The decision for war or peace, however, could not be controlled by the Russians. In London, the Aberdeen government had grown increasingly apprehensive about Russian intentions, bombarded as it was by the alarmist reports of Stratford and British journalists in the Near East. Upon receiving news of the failed Menshikov mission together with reports of massive Russian troop concentrations on the Turkish frontier, Clarendon believed that it was essential to make a dramatic gesture of support on behalf of the Turks. On June 2 the British fleet at Malta was ordered to Besika Bay, just outside the Dardanelles and the passage to Constantinople. Clarendon assured Aberdeen that this was "the least measure that will satisfy public opinion and save the government from shame, if, as I firmly expect, the Russian hordes pour into Turkey on every side." Palmerston immediately and unofficially communicated these decisions of the British government to Musurus, the Turkish ambassador in London, who immediately passed this information on to his own government.

The French, wary of the attitude of the British government, were delighted by the dispatch of the British fleet to Besika Bay and immediately ordered their own fleet at Salamis to join forces with the British. Walewski, Napoleon's ambassador to London, wrote that this union of the French and British fleets was "the most happy event that could happen for France today: a general war in which we would have been alone was the greatest danger for the new government; a war with England against Russia with the rest of Europe remaining neutral can only be considered as an unexpected favor of Providence which is so clearly protecting the Imperial dynasty."

On June 16, buoyed by the presence of the Anglo-French fleets off the Dardanelles and with the encouragement of Stratford, the Turks rejected the tsar's ultimatum of May 31. In response, the tsar proceeded to carry out his threat to occupy Turkey's Danubian Principalities, and early in July 1853 Russian forces crossed the Pruth River into Turkish territory. The crisis in the Near East had now reached a volatile stage, but even at this point vigorous efforts were made to settle it through negotiation.

❏ The Austrian Strategy to Preserve Peace

The statesmen who worked hardest and most persistently for peace were the Austrians, who had most reason to fear a general war, which would expose them to extreme dangers no matter which side they joined or even if they remained neutral. If they sided with Russia, they would disrupt the balance of power in the east and be reduced to the status of a Russian satellite, dependent on Russian support against the hostility of Britain and France, which would seek to undermine their position in Germany and Italy, where they were especially vulnerable. If they sided with Britain and France, they would be compelled to bear the brunt of the fighting because of their geographical position, and even if victorious, they would be obliged to stand guard permanently against a vengeful neighbor. And if they remained neutral, they would be exposed to the pressure, threats, and animosity of both sides. As Count Buol, the Austrian foreign minister, described Austrian policy at the time: "We are seeking to pacify on every side and above all to avoid a European complication, which would be particularly detrimental to us."

The negotiations that now took place on behalf of the preservation of peace were complex in the extreme, but all proposals that represented a sincere effort to mediate between Russia and Turkey relied on essentially the same tactic: that the neutral great powers—Austria, Britain, France, and Prussia—should employ their individual or joint efforts to persuade the Russian and Ottoman governments to agree to an exchange of notes which they had not been able to arrange between themselves and which should satisfy the interests, safeguard the security, and preserve the honor of both sides. The assumption behind all these mediation efforts was that neither Russia nor Turkey would risk rejecting proposals submitted in the name of one or preferably a union of all the four neutral European great powers.

Thanks largely to the diplomatic activity of the Austrians, the Russian desire to escape from the extremely dangerous position in which they now found themselves, and the influence of voices of caution from both London and Paris, the negotiations on behalf of peace were successful—or appeared to be. In late July 1853 the representatives of the four neutral powers reached agreement in Vienna on the text of the document to be exchanged by the Russian and Turkish governments that was to safeguard the interests and honor of both sides. That text, henceforth known as the Vienna Note, was accepted by the tsar (whose government had been consulted in drafting it), and the four neutral governments now instructed their representatives in Constantinople to secure its acceptance by the Turks.

The four-power agreement on the Vienna Note and its acceptance by Russia should have ended the Near Eastern crisis, for it is inconceivable that the Turks, no matter how fanatic or bellicose, should have rejected the demands of the great powers and risked war against a European coalition. The Turks, however, were convinced that the European powers were not united and that they would receive powerful support even if they provoked a break with Russia. This Turkish confidence was based on reports from London of the pro-Turkish attitude of British public opinion and leading British statesmen, most notably Palmerston, and it was powerfully reinforced by Stratford's conduct. Although officially instructed to secure acceptance of the Vienna Note in Constantinople, he denounced it privately in the most violent terms, declaring that war was preferable to such a solution and that a change must take place in the government of England which would bring into power the friends and supporters of his policy in Turkey.

Confident once again that they could afford to be intransigent, the Turks on August 20 refused to accept the Vienna Note unless it was substantially amended, although they had been specifically informed that the note must be accepted without modifications of any kind. The Turks and other opponents of the Vienna Note maintained that amendments were required because the Russians could (and would) interpret the present text in a manner that would give them undue influence over Ottoman affairs. To quash these allegations and put an end to all Turkish excuses, the tsar proposed that the powers again submit the unaltered Vienna Note to Turkey, but accompanied by an unequivocal interpretation of the note to which all the European powers, including Russia, should adhere.

This eminently reasonable proposal was ignored, for by now the governments of the European powers had lost control of the crisis, or more accurately, the Turks were determined to exploit it to their own ends. In early September, in the wake of large-scale popular demonstrations in Constantinople demanding holy war against Russia, the Turks appealed to Britain and France to send their fleets to the Turkish capital to protect foreign lives and property and the Turkish government itself from the mobs. In late September the Anglo-French fleets appeared before Constantinople. On October 4 the Turkish government declared war on Russia with an ultimatum that Russia evacuate the Danubian Principalities; if the Turkish government did not receive a positive reply within fifteen days, Turkey would commence hostilities.

❑ *The Final Plunge into War*

The Turkish declaration of war was greeted with enthusiasm in Britain. That fervent Christian and humanitarian, Charles Kingsley, declared that the Turks were "fighting on God's side," and Karl Marx announced that Britain and France were being driven by the inexorable force of history to take sides with the enemies of the tsar.

Lord Aberdeen, the British prime minister, was considerably less enthusiastic, at last recognizing the position in which the Turks and his own more bellicose colleagues had placed his government. Shortly after the Turkish declaration of war he wrote to Gladstone, the chancellor of the exchequer and one of the few members of his cabinet who still sincerely desired peace: "The Turks, with all their barbarism, are cunning enough, and see clearly the advantages of their situation. Step by step they have drawn us into a position in which we are more or less committed to their support. It would be absurd to suppose that, with the hopes of active assistance from England and France, they should not be desirous of engaging in a conflict with their formidable neighbor. They never had such a favorable opportunity before, and may never have again. They will therefore contrive to elude our proposals and keep us in our present state, from which it will be difficult to escape.''

In contrast to Aberdeen, Palmerston expressed satisfaction that the British government could no longer change course. He reminded the prime minister that Russia had attacked and violated the integrity of the Ottoman empire, and that it must be brought to abandon its aggression ''by fair means or foul.'' ''We passed the Rubicon when we first took part with Turkey and sent our squadrons to support her,'' he said. ''It seems to me, then, that our course is plain, simple, and straight: that we must help Turkey out of her difficulties by negotiation, if possible; and that if negotiation fails, we must, by force of arms, carry her safely through her dangers.''

This is the course the British government actually pursued. Ignoring continuing Austrian mediation efforts and Russian offers to provide any assurances the British or French might require regarding Russian policy toward the Ottoman empire, the British and French governments sought instead to justify sending their fleets into the Black Sea to defend the Turks against superior Russian naval forces, and from the beginning of the conflict they adopted a stance of flagrantly unneutral neutrality.

All mediation efforts were finally doomed on November 30, 1853, when a Russian fleet pursued a Turkish squadron into the Turkish harbor of Sinope on the Black Sea. Within hours the Russians annihilated the Turkish fleet, and in their bombardment of Turkish coastal batteries destroyed a large part of the city of Sinope as well. Accounts differ widely about what this Turkish fleet had been doing in the Black Sea in the face of superior Russian naval strength, and why these and other Turkish vessels had been allowed to expose themselves in this manner. It was strongly suspected at the time, however, that every sortie of the Turkish fleet was a deliberate provocative act to lure the Russians out of their defensive posture and provoke Anglo-French intervention.

If this was indeed the Turkish intention, their stratagem was eminently successful. The Russian naval victory at Sinope was greeted with jubilation in Russia, but the British and French governments denounced the Russian naval action as a violation of the tsar's pledge that Russia would remain on the defensive. The most important result of that action, however, was the moral outrage of British public opinion aroused by the ''massacre of Sinope'' and an outburst of emotional fury against the brutal and inhuman Russians. Napoleon took advantage of the situation to call for the British and French fleets to ''sweep the Russian flag off the Black Sea''—if the British failed to support him he would act alone. On December 22 the Aberdeen government succumbed to the pressure of public opinion and Napoleon's threat to act alone and ordered the British fleet to join the French in the Black Sea. The Russians were informed that any Russian ship caught out of harbor would be seized and sunk; and Anglo-French naval commanders were instructed to sweep Russian shipping from the Black Sea, protect Turkish vessels, and guard the coasts and seaboards of the Ottoman empire from Russian attack.

After protesting repeatedly and in vain against this Anglo-French de facto warfare on his country, the tsar in early February 1854 instructed his diplomatic representatives in London and Paris to demand their passports and to break off diplomatic relations with Britain and France on February 6. The British and French governments responded on February 27 with separate ultimata demanding that Russia refrain from all military activity in its conflict with Turkey, announce the withdrawal of Russian forces from the Principalities, and complete their evacuation by April 15 (the British date was April 30). Refusal to comply with these demands or silence would be regarded as the equivalent of a Russian declaration of war.

The Russians refused to comply and remained silent. "The tsar did not think it proper to make any reply" to the Anglo-French communications. Russia's silence was duly interpreted as the equivalent of a Russian declaration of war on Britain and France, and on March 27-28, 1854, the British and French governments declared war on Russia.

❑ *Allied and Russian War Aims; the Austrian Ultimatum to Russia*

In its public pronouncements, the British government explained that the war was being fought to halt the further aggrandizement of Russia and prevent the destruction of the Ottoman empire, "whose integrity and independence have been so often declared essential to the stability of the system of Europe."

The war aims expressed by Palmerston, which he did not make public, went far beyond these purely defensive objectives. In a memorandum of March 19 to the cabinet, Palmerston spelled out what he called his "beau ideal" of what should be achieved through the war with Russia that was about to begin. "Aaland and Finland restored to Sweden. Some of the German provinces of Russia on the Baltic ceded to Prussia. A substantive Kingdom of Poland re-established as a barrier between Germany and Russia. Wallachia and Moldavia and the mouth of the Danube given to Austria. Lombardy and Venice set free from Austrian rule and either made independent States or incorporated with Piedmont. The Crimea, Circassia and Georgia wrested from Russia, the Crimea and Georgia given to Turkey, and Circassia either independent or connected with the Sultan as Suzerain. Such results it is true could be accomplished only by a combination of Sweden, Prussia and Austria, with England, France, and Turkey, and such results presuppose great defeats of Russia. But such results are not impossible and should not be wholly discarded from our thoughts."

These views of Palmerston were no mere "beau ideal" thrown out in the heat and enthusiasm of the moment, for he was to express the same ideas repeatedly in the course of the war and he remained vigorously opposed to making peace with Russia until at least a substantial portion of these war aims had been achieved. These aims went far beyond anything previously proposed by allied leaders and certainly far beyond anything that could have been achieved through negotiation. Aberdeen commented that the attempt to impose them on Russia would plunge Europe into another Thirty Years War, but Palmerston remained adamant. He thought the war would be pointless if it did no more than halt Russian expansion and failed to eliminate the menace of Russian aggression for the foreseeable future.

Stratford expressed views almost identical with those of Palmerston. Russian power could be effectively curbed only by making a peace that would leave Russia "separated from Turkey by a *cordon* of principalities, or States, no longer dependent upon her." The allies could therefore not afford to hasten peace and stanch the wounds of Europe by a policy of moderation.

The war aims formulated by Russian statesmen were considerably more restrained. "The aim of our war against Turkey," Gorchakov, the Russian ambassador to Vienna, wrote early in April 1854, "is to reaffirm on a solid basis the religious immunities of our brothers of the Orthodox Church." This goal had to be attained and in fact could be attained the moment the other great powers of Europe, equally concerned with the religious and civil rights of Christians, "will endeavor to obtain from the Porte not worthless words but effective guarantees." Once these were obtained, the tsar would allow nothing to stand in the way of making peace.

Such Russian statements were designed to enlist the support of neutral powers, Austria in particular, but this does not mean they were not genuine expressions of Russian intentions. In contrast to the allies, the Russians could afford restraint because of their geographic position and the facts of power politics. Russia was strong; Turkey was weak. All Russia needed to do was sit still and await developments. War with the Ottoman empire was for Russia a great misfortune and a great mistake. Small wonder that the Russians should have been eager to make peace or that their rivals, equally aware of the facts of power politics, should have desired radical amputations of Russian territory to render Russia's geographical position less advantageous and reduce Russia's overall strength.

In comparison with the radical war aims of the more extreme Western leaders, the aims of the Austrians in this crisis were essentially conservative: they wanted little more than the restoration of the prewar status quo. Like the British and the French, they desired to halt the expansion of Russian influence in the Balkans, but they indicated that this would be achieved if Russia withdrew from the Principalities. Instead of seeking that goal through tactful negotiation, however, the Austrians committed the horrendous blunder of presenting Russia with an ultimatum on June 3, 1854, demanding that Russia halt all military operations south of the Danube and fix an early date for evacuating the Principalities.

The Austrian ultimatum came as a shock to the tsar, for until this time he had counted on Austria's neutrality even though he had given up hope of securing Austria's active support. This ultimatum was also a critical turning point in European diplomacy, for it marked the end of friendship and cooperation between the two conservative powers, which, although they were to enter into agreements and even alliances with each other in later years, was never fully restored.

Disillusioned and indignant, the tsar saw no alternative but to yield to the Austrian ultimatum, and in August the Russians withdrew from the Principalities. These were now occupied by the Austrians, a move sanctioned by an Austrian treaty with Turkey of June 14 which provided for joint Austro-Turkish occupation of the Principalities for the duration of the war. It is difficult to see how else the Austrians could have fulfilled the promise they made to Russia to prevent the occupation of the Principalities by the allies, yet their occupation by Austria was regarded as an additional affront, which seemed to emphasize Russia's humiliation and loss of face.

❑ *The Conduct of the War*

Russia's withdrawal and Austria's occupation of the Principalities are frequently considered to have changed the entire course of the war. The most obvious overland route for an allied military offensive against Russia was through the Balkans, a route now cut off by the Austrian occupation of the Principalities so long as Austria remained neutral.

The military significance of the Austrian occupation, however, was not so great as is often assumed. Already the allies had probed the possibility of using their superior sea power to attack Russia in the Baltic, the White Sea, and even the Pacific. They did in fact send a formidable naval force into the Baltic which in August 1854 captured Bomarsund, the principal fortress on the strategic Aaland Islands, but they did not follow up this victory by an attack on the Russian mainland because Russian fortifications daunted all prospects of success. There was no prospect whatever of striking a decisive or even crippling blow against Russia via the White Sea or the Pacific.

But the Black Sea was different. Russia's most important waterways and arteries of commerce flowed into it. On it were located Russia's most important seaports and the great Russian naval base of Sebastopol. Since the Anglo-French entry into the war, their fleets had been in full control of the Black Sea and were therefore in a position to attack Russia anywhere along its extensive Black Sea coast, including the Crimean peninsula where Sebastopol was located. A Black Sea operation was particularly attractive because the destruction of Russian sea power there would accomplish three of the major allied objectives in the war: it would facilitate renewed allied intervention in the event of future Russian threats to their interests in the Near East; it would significantly diminish Russia's ability to mount such threats; and it would make it easier for the allies to ensure freedom of navigation in the Black Sea and Danube areas for their own shipping and commerce.

From the moment the war with Russia seemed likely, British leaders had advocated launching their principal blow against Sebastopol, so that even if a campaign through the Balkans had been feasible, it might never have been more than a sideshow—at least until Sebastopol had fallen. In September 1854 an allied force of sixty thousand men landed in the Crimea, their objective the capture of Sebastopol.

On September 20 the allies defeated a Russian army on the Alma River. If they had pressed home their victory, they might well have captured Sebastopol in their first offensive. Although the allied leaders certainly did not plan it that way, their failure to capture Sebastopol and their subsequent siege of the city was the most effective strategy they could have devised for waging war against Russia. While fighting in the Crimea, the allies could be supplied and reinforced by sea, whereas the Russians, even though fighting on their own territory, were forced to deal with the problems that had so often in the past brought disaster to their invaders: long supply lines, bad roads, and the Russian weather. Men and matériel were sent overland to the Crimea at fearful cost. So severe were the rigors of the long journey, especially in winter, that only one Russian soldier in ten actually reached the front after a three-month march. The Russian army's medical department estimated the country's losses at half a million men. In comparison, the British and French lost about sixty thousand, two-thirds of whom died of disease. The drain on the Russian economy was on a comparable scale. The defense of Sebastopol bled Russia white.

Sebastopol fell in September 1855. In the course of the siege, significant changes took place in the governments of two of the major belligerents. At the end of January 1855, Aberdeen resigned and was replaced as prime minister by Palmerston, the most militant and extreme of leading British statesmen. In March of that same year, Tsar Nicholas I died and was succeeded by his son Alexander II.

These changes in leadership did not bring about significant changes in the policies of Britain or Russia. Neither did the fall of Sebastopol. Alexander II expressed his determination to fight on, and recalled that two years after the burning of Moscow by the French in 1812 the victorious Russian armies had entered Paris. In Britain, Palmerston continued to press not only for a vigorous prosecution of the war but for its extension on a massive scale. For this purpose, he stepped up the pressure on Austria, Prussia, and the German Confederation to participate actively in the war, he concluded an alliance with Sweden, and he proposed to stoke the fires of rebellion among the non-Russian nationalities in the frontier provinces of the tsarist empire, notably the Poles and the peoples of the Caucasus region, who were to be promised their independence in return for supporting the cause of the allies.

Palmerston's efforts to put together a massive anti-Russian coalition failed. Austria and the German states steadfastly resisted active participation in the war, and Palmerston's alliance with Sweden remained a purely defensive agreement. The only allied material diplomatic success, in fact, had been achieved before Palmerston took over the premiership. This was an alliance in January 1855 with the northern Italian state of Piedmont-Sardinia, which promised to supply fifteen thousand men to the allied cause in return for a generous subsidy.

❑ *Austrian Efforts to End the War*

Since the very beginning of the war, as throughout the long period of crisis preceding it, the Austrians remained painfully aware of the perils the conflict posed for the Habsburg empire. The allies' wartime diplomacy only increased their alarm. They saw in the Anglo-French alliance with Sardinia a dangerous threat to their position in Italy. Even more sinister were Palmerston's efforts to stir up rebellion among the non-Russian nationalities of the tsarist empire, a policy which, like Napoleon's program to reorganize the European states system on the basis of nationalities, represented a mortal danger to the very existence of the multinational Habsburg realm. It is not surprising, therefore, that the Austrians played a leading role in promoting peace negotiations so as to escape from their perilous position.

In dealing with Britain and France, the Austrians insisted that they could not consider entering the war on the allied side unless they were given a precise definition of Anglo-French war aims and assurances that the war with Russia was not being fought to promote revolutionary principles. This tactic served several purposes. The first and most important of these was to secure allied guarantees to respect Austria's possessions in Italy and to repudiate Napoleonic and Palmerstonian schemes to stir up nationalist rebellions, whether in Russia or anywhere else. A second purpose was that Austria would then be in a position to demand a reformulation of allied war aims if they did not correspond with Austrian interests as the price for Austria's participation in the war. Finally, with a statement of allied war aims in hand, suitably redefined by Austria, they could present these aims to Russia as a basis for peace negotiations and pressure Russia into agreeing to such negotiations as the price for keeping Austria out of the war.

Eager above all to secure Austria's active participation in the war, the allies responded to the Austrian diplomatic maneuver by formulating four major war aims, henceforth known as the Four Points. These were officially recognized as the allied conditions for the restoration of peace by an exchange of notes between the Austrian, British, and French governments on August 8, 1854.

The Four Points were a far cry from the extravagant war aims proposed by Palmerston and other extremists. They required (1) Russia's renunciation of special rights in Serbia and the Danubian Principalities and their replacement by a collective guarantee of the powers in agreement with the Porte; (2) unrestricted navigation of the Danube for the vessels of all countries; (3) a revision of the Straits Convention of 1841 "in the interests of the Balance of Power in Europe"; and (4) Russia's renunciation of all claims to an official protectorate over Orthodox Christians in the Ottoman empire, and the protection of the rights of all Christians in the empire by a collective guarantee.

With great reluctance and only after suffering a number of military reverses, in late November 1854 the Russians accepted the Four Points as a basis for negotiation. It seemed as though the Austrian tactic had been successful and that no serious obstacle remained to the drawing-up of a peace treaty and the termination of the war.

A peace conference actually convened in Vienna on March 15, 1855, but it was doomed from the start because the Palmerston government had come to a private agreement with the French to insist on a far more punitive interpretation of the Four Points than had been communicated to the Austrians. The British still demanded large-scale amputations of Russian territory, which the Russians could never be expected to concede without suffering truly crippling military reverses, and as yet they had not done so; another six months were to go by before their loss of Sebastopol, and even that was far from being a mortal wound. For the British, therefore, there could as yet be no question of peace, and the Palmerston government agreed to participate in the farce of a peace conference only to avoid alienating the Austrians. Napoleon for his part believed he still needed military victories to bolster the prestige of his regime and therefore avoided any moves that might jeopardize his alliance with Britain. In the course of the Vienna conference, Walewski, the French ambassador to London and a confidant of the French ruler, assured Palmerston that he should "not for a moment suppose that the Emperor wants peace, or would make it on any terms until he has obtained a military success. All he wants is to prolong negotiation in order to satisfy people's minds in France and to keep Austria from breaking with us." Palmerston meanwhile reiterated his own grandiose war aims, calling for the Russian cession of the Crimea to Turkey, the surrender of Bessarabia to Moldavia and Wallachia, which should be granted self-government within the Ottoman empire under the protection of the allied powers, the restoration of the independence of Circassia, and the evacuation of all territory in the Caucasus region conquered or annexed by Russia during the preceding twenty-five years.

Palmerston's program for carrying on the war to the point that the allies could demand Russia's surrender of the greater part of its frontier territories was finally frustrated by Napoleon. Eager as the French ruler was to retain the friendship of Britain, he was confronted with ominous signs of war-weariness in his own country, where the war had never been supported with the same enthusiasm as in Britain. He was also concerned about the immense material costs of the war and the fearful losses in manpower from disease, which were threatening to decimate the French army. For Napoleon, therefore, peace was becoming a military as well as political and financial necessity. The successes of the French army in the final stages of the siege of Sebastopol had given his regime as much military prestige as it was likely to get without perilously large additional investments in the war, so that after the fall of Sebastopol the French emperor was more amenable to proposals for a negotiated peace than at any previous time.

In the negotiations that at last brought the war to an end, the Austrians once again played a central role. They employed essentially the same tactic they had used in all their previous efforts: they persuaded the French, and through them the reluctant British, to agree on yet another formulation of conditions of peace (still based on the Four Points) which they believed the Russians would accept; in return for this Anglo-French agreement, Austria would present these conditions to Russia in the form of an Austrian ultimatum and threaten to enter the war on the side of the allies if the Russians rejected it.

After long and persistent efforts on the part of the Austrians and those French statesmen now eager for peace, the allies reached agreement on peace terms, and in December 1855 the Austrians kept their part of the bargain and submitted their ultimatum to Russia. The Russians yielded unconditionally on January 16. The British still hoped to put forward additional conditions that would prove unacceptable to the Russians, but their maneuvers to sabotage negotiations and the ensuing peace conference at Paris failed because their policies no longer enjoyed support from any quarter.

There were voices in the Russian government that had urged a continuation of the war rather than accepting the humiliation of defeat and submission to an Austrian ultimatum, but a majority of the tsar's advisers opted for peace. They had many sound reasons for doing so. The conditions for peace, as finally arranged and interpreted by the Austrians, were remarkably lenient, and the Russians had received assurances from both the Austrian and French governments that they would support Russia in opposing extravagant demands that might still be raised by Britain. If the Russians rejected the present terms, on the other hand, they would face a continuation of the war, which Austria would now enter on the allied side, and there was a strong possibility that Austria would be joined by the German states and by Sweden, which had been promised Finland as bait for its participation. Moreover, a Russian rejection would force Napoleon, who supported the present allied terms, to return to a policy of full cooperation with Britain and support for the stringent terms desired by Palmerston.

Within Russia itself there were grave dangers and difficulties that would only grow worse if the war were continued. The war had proved a terrible drain on the Russian economy, recruitment for the army had exhausted Russia's manpower resources, supplies of arms and ammunition were running dangerously low, and the finance ministry predicted that a continuation of the war would result in national bankruptcy. Everywhere there were signs of war-weariness and stirrings of revolt that might get out of control if the bulk of Russia's armed forces remained deployed against a foreign foe. In sum, a Russian rejection of the Austrian ultimatum might lead to disasters far greater than any loss of territory or prestige Russia might incur by accepting the relatively mild allied peace terms.

Perhaps the most persuasive argument brought forward by advocates of peace within the Russian government was that the present allied terms would in no way hamper Russia's capacity to develop its resources or otherwise prejudice the country's future. In a few years Russia would again be strong enough to pursue policies rendered impossible by present circumstances. A peace made today would be no more than a truce; if it were postponed for a year or more, the country might be reduced to such a state of weakness that it could require fifty years to recover. Under such conditions, future Russian governments would have no alternative but to adhere strictly to the terms of what would certainly be a far more stringent peace because they could not afford the risk of war to recoup their losses.

Palmerston himself could not have summed up more effectively his own arguments for continuing the war.

❑ *Peacemaking, 1856*

The Congress of Paris that brought the Crimean War to an end convened on February 25, 1856, and officially closed with the signature of the Treaty of Paris on March 30, although the delegates were to remain in the French capital for almost another month to negotiate over problems related to the treaty. Represented at the congress were all the belligerent powers (Britain, France, the Ottoman empire, Russia, and Sardinia) and Austria. Prussia, which had steadfastly refused to join in the war against Russia or to be associated with the Austrian ultimatum, was not invited to participate in the congress until it discussed a revision of the Straits Convention of 1841, to which Prussia was a signatory, and even then the Prussian delegates were received with bad grace.

The final Treaty of Paris confirmed and clarified but did not substantially alter the preliminary agreements concluded among the powers as the basis for peace. Although the controversies over certain points were often bitter, the general desire for peace among the major powers, apart from Britain, was sufficiently great to overcome these obstacles and permit the resolution of all problems through compromise. As usual in all international conferences, much of the work was done in small committees dealing with specific problems, and the most significant agreements and compromises were arranged in confidential meetings among the principal negotiators—the plenipotentiaries of Austria, Britain, and France, who were in fact to settle all major questions between them.

By the terms of the Treaty of Paris, the Russians surrendered only one piece of territory they had not been willing to renounce before the war began—a strategic section of Bessarabia at the mouth of the Danube. They agreed to the internationalization of the Danube and relinquished their claims to protect Christians in the Ottoman empire. They also agreed to leave the Aaland Islands in the Gulf of Bothnia unfortified and to restore to Turkey the fortress city of Kars, south of the Caucasus Mountains, which the Russians had captured in the final weeks of the war. The Danubian Principalities of Moldavia and Wallachia were placed under the protection of the signatory powers, which further promised to respect the independence and integrity of the Ottoman empire.

The question of the rights of Christians in the Ottoman empire, the original cause of (or pretext for) the entire crisis, received comparatively little attention from the Christian powers once the war was under way. To anticipate any discussion of this question at the peace conference and the insertion of any provisions in the peace treaty that would serve as an excuse for *any* foreign interference in the internal affairs of the Ottoman empire, the Turks themselves issued a decree of February 18, before the Congress of Paris convened, guaranteeing all privileges and special immunities previously granted to all Christian and other non-Muslim communities in the Ottoman empire, promising complete freedom of religion, and providing for various political, legal, economic, taxation, and other reforms.

The tsar chose to hail this February 18 Ottoman decree as an act of Providence which had brought to pass the "original and principal aims of this war." In a proclamation to the Russian people he declared that the rights of all Christians in the Orient were now assured and that as a result of this act of justice the Ottoman empire had entered the community of European states: "Russians! Your efforts and sacrifices were not in vain. The great work is accomplished."

The tsar's proclamation represented a face-saving interpretation of Russian accomplishments, but in a literal sense it was also true, for Russia's principal avowed aim throughout the Crimean crisis had been the promulgation of a formal Ottoman decree guaranteeing the rights of Christians. The crucial difference between the February 18 decree and Russia's original demands, of course, was that all specific Russian claims for the protection of Christians had been eliminated.

Quite apart from the question of Christians in the Ottoman empire, the Russians could congratulate themselves on the success of their negotiations in Paris, for the terms of the final treaty were remarkably lenient, especially when compared with the extravagant war aims of Palmerston and Stratford. At the conclusion of the congress, a French statesman complained that anyone reading the treaty would find it impossible to determine who was the victor and who the vanquished.

For Europe as a whole, the Russian cession of the segment of Bessarabia at the mouth of the Danube was a significant gain, for it enabled the powers to ensure the freedom of navigation of the Danube at the entrance to the Black Sea. But, except in terms of prestige, it did not represent a correspondingly critical loss to Russia, which had less at stake in Danubian commerce than many other states and which retained its strategic position in Bessarabia north of the Danube.

The Russians were deprived of their preponderant influence in the Danubian Principalities and Serbia, but they had been prepared to relinquish such influence before the war began. Their troops which had moved into the Principalities in July 1853 had already been withdrawn in July of the following year. And no treaty could sever the close religious, ethnic, and cultural ties between Russia and the peoples of these Principalities, ties which many contemporary observers feared would ensure their ultimate gravitation to Russia.

The Russians were obliged to agree to freedom of navigation and commerce on the Danube and the Black Sea, but these concessions, far from being detrimental, were a positive advantage, for they provided Russia, too, with fresh economic opportunities.

The harshest part of the treaty and the most damaging blow to Russian power, or so it seemed at the time, were the provisions (embodied in a separate Russo-Turkish convention annexed to the final treaty) prohibiting Russia from maintaining a navy or naval bases on the Black Sea. As a blow to Russian prestige these terms were undeniably harsh, but the blow to Russian power was less significant than it appeared or was meant to be. For the Turks were subjected to similar restrictions, and the provision that the Straits remain closed to the warships of foreign powers while the Ottoman empire was at peace meant that Russia was safeguarded from any immediate threat of British or French sea power on their southern flank. The Turks, to be sure, could still retain warships and naval arsenals of their own in the Straits proper, but they too were prohibited from using them to menace Russia's Black Sea coasts.

❏ *The Results of the War*

For all its leniency, the Treaty of Paris, together with the allied coalition formed directly afterward to ensure its observance, might have created a permanent obstacle to further Russian aggression at the expense of Europe and the Ottoman empire had it been permanently enforced. But international settlements are never permanent. The allied coalition had already begun to break apart during the peace negotiations, and Russia was quick to take advantage of the quarrels among its former enemies.

In 1870, while France and Prussia struggled over the fate of Germany, Russia repudiated the Black Sea clauses of the Treaty of Paris; in 1877 Russia was again at war with Turkey; in 1878 Russia regained the greater part of the ceded territory in Bessarabia (to the Pruth River in the west and the northernmost mouth of the Danube in the south), together with Kars and a large section of surrounding territory in the Caucasus area east of the Black Sea. Nor was Russia's behavior unexpected. As the British statesman Lord John Russell observed to the House of Commons shortly after the signature of the Treaty of Paris: "If a treaty be found to be injurious to the interests of a country, and some means of violating it are obvious, I do not know of what country in Europe we could predicate a strict observance of the treaty."

The most permanent result of the Crimean War was the disruption of the Concert of Europe. Forty years of peace were now followed by four wars (1859-1871) that revolutionized the power structure of the continent. Defeated and humiliated, Russia was determined to break the restrictions imposed by the Treaty of Paris, and thus became a revisionist state, although it refrained from active intervention in European affairs during the next two decades while setting its own house in order. Britain, disillusioned by an inglorious war and an inconclusive peace, also concentrated on domestic problems and largely withdrew from European affairs. Austria was isolated. During the Crimean War both sides had confidently anticipated Austrian backing: Russia had expected Austria to support the 1815 peace settlement against France and to repay a debt of gratitude for recent military and diplomatic aid; Britain and France had been certain Austria would recognize the necessity of halting Russian expansion in southeastern Europe, where vital Austrian interests were at stake. Austria's neutrality antagonized all the belligerents, with the result that until 1879 Austria was without friends among the great powers. Prussia's policy during the war was so flaccid and its strength seemed so inconsequential that it was almost dismissed as a major power.

France was the state that seemed to have gained most from the war. French armies had won the most impressive victories at Sebastopol; the international system of 1815 and its restrictions had been swept away; France had ostensibly supplanted Russia as the dominant power in Europe. But France's position was not so strong as it appeared. Britain was apprehensive about the renewed danger of French hegemony on the continent. Russia was alarmed by Napoleon's talk of an independent Polish state, which would deprive Russia of its Polish provinces. Austria and Prussia, with large Polish minorities of their own, were similarly alarmed and also resented Napoleon's interference in German and Italian affairs. France was as isolated among the great powers as Austria, a situation Napoleon never seemed to understand. He pursued an ambitious foreign policy and attempted to reestablish French predominance in Europe by championing the nationalities movement. But his policies were inconsistent and frequently quixotic, and he was unable to control the momentum of the nationalities movement he had hoped to lead. In the end he was to see the establishment of two new national states on France's frontiers, one of which was to destroy his empire and seek European predominance of its own.

Meanwhile, the Russian threat remained as though the Crimean War had never been fought. Because the results of that war had been so meager, it is easy to conclude that Palmerston and Stratford had been right, that the European powers should have recognized the need to join in a great anti-Russian coalition to roll back Russia's frontiers on every front and impose conditions that would permanently diminish its capacity for aggression. But given the sheer size of the Russian empire, it is doubtful whether such conditions could ever have been imposed on Russia, or if imposed, whether they could have been enforced over a significant period of time. Russia was simply too large, its power base too broad; there was no place in Russia where an enemy could strike a mortal blow or even a blow that would substantially reduce Russian strength.

But even if Russian power could have been destroyed and the danger of Russian aggression permanently eliminated, would this have led to a new era of peace and security for the peoples of Europe and Asia? All historical experience indicates that it would not. The belief that security can be achieved through the destruction of the power of the state that seems the greatest menace to such security is based on the supposition that only this state is a threat to international peace and that with its defeat all the world could breathe easily. But this is not the case. The elimination of one threat has always been accompanied by the rise of new threats as other states move to fill the power vacuum. Even before the end of the Crimean War, Palmerston's chief concern for the interests of England had shifted from the threat of Russia to the threat of France, just as after World War II the elimination of the German threat was succeeded almost immediately by a renewed fear of the threat from Russia—or from the Russian viewpoint, the threat from the United States.

EIGHT

❑

The Unification of Italy

❑ The Leadership of Sardinia

The unification of Italy and Germany were the two most significant manifestations of the triumph of the national principle in Europe in the nineteenth century. They were also major revolutions in domestic as well as foreign affairs which swept away centuries-old institutions, transformed the political configuration of Europe, and significantly affected the international balance of power. Although nationalism was the ideological common denominator for the political union of both Italy and Germany, their unification was not the product of irresistible mass movements borne along on a tidal wave of patriotic fervor. On the contrary, the national ideal was fostered by a relatively small number of politically conscious people who differed widely among themselves as to how or even whether their dream of national union should be translated into reality.

The absence of a mass popular base for the nationalist movement was especially evident in Italy, which had not been under a single government for over a millennium and a half, where a large proportion of the population was illiterate, where regional traditions were powerfully entrenched and even language was not a unifying factor, for the dialects spoken in one region were generally incomprehensible to the inhabitants of another. Indeed, local grievances were far more powerful motives for revolution than was nationalism, and on the few occasions when uprisings organized by nationalists were temporarily successful they owed their success to the existence of such grievances and mass discontent. That discontent was deep-seated and widespread, the product of political oppression and economic poverty, resentment of taxes and conscription, of aristocratic and clerical privilege. Throughout Italy, but especially in the south, there were angry masses ready to take part in demonstrations and riots, peasants eager to seize land and wreak vengeance on local landlords, urban workers demanding a more equitable distribution of the products of their labor.

Yet despite the existence of this mass discontent, all popular uprisings in Italy prior to the wars for unification had been successfully suppressed by existing governments, frequently with the aid of foreign powers. And in the end, the Italian

MAP 5 THE UNIFICATION OF ITALY

national revolution triumphed only because the most powerful of the individual Italian states, Sardinia, placed its military power and above all its diplomatic resources at the service of the national movement, securing decisive military and diplomatic support from one of the greatest of the European great powers, France. Even then, many Sardinian leaders were motivated not so much by a desire to serve the Italian national cause as to exploit it, and indeed the unification finally achieved was in many ways largely a victory for Sardinian aggrandizement.

Despite Sardinia's military defeats by Austria in 1848–1849, it had emerged from the turmoil of the 1848 revolutions as the chief standard-bearer of the Italian national cause. It did so because, alone among Italian states, it had dared to take the field against Austria, and because the events of 1848 had exposed the impracticability of the alternatives to Sardinian leadership.

Thoroughly discredited was the idea of unification through a confederation of Italian states under papal leadership. The presence of Austria in Italy had always been a major objection to the confederation idea. Had the 1848 revolutions in Austria's Italian provinces been successful, their enrollment in a national confederation would have presented no problem, but by 1850 those provinces were once again firmly under Austrian control. Elsewhere, the governments of the individual Italian states, with the notable exception of Sardinia, had been more concerned with the suppression of revolution than with the Italian national cause. In the Papal States, the pope's temporal rule in the Romagna (the northernmost papal province) was now directly defended by the Austrians and in the Patrimony of St. Peter (Rome and its surrounding territory) by the French; moreover, it had become evident, as it should have been all along, that the papacy, an international and theoretically universal institution, could never be expected to assume leadership of an exclusively Italian national movement.

Also discredited, though for very different reasons, was the belief that unification could be achieved through a patriotic revolution that would expel the Austrians, overthrow existing dynasties, and establish a democratically elected republican national government. The most eloquent spokesman for this solution to the Italian problem was Giuseppe Mazzini, whose idealistic faith in the people and whose very conception of a free and united Italy exerted a profound influence on the Italian national movement and indeed on nationalists throughout Europe. But his advocacy of a radical political as well as national revolution alarmed the more moderate and conservative Italian nationalists with a stake in the existing system of government and society. They might agree with Mazzini about the need to expel Austria and the desirability of better government in all the Italian states, but they had no desire to release the forces of popular revolution to achieve either goal and they regarded Mazzini as a hopelessly impractical as well as dangerous troublemaker. They saw their fears of revolution confirmed by the popular uprisings of 1848–1849, which had threatened their own interests and seemingly brought nothing but disaster to the Italian national cause. Mazzini, as leader of the short-lived Roman Republic of 1849, had succeeded only in provoking France to intervene, and there seemed good reason to fear that similar radical revolutions would provide the excuse for similar foreign intervention. The ignominious failure of a Mazzini-inspired revolution against Austrian rule in Milan in February 1853 discredited his ideas further, for the mass patriotic uprisings he had confidently predicted had not taken place and the Austrian-supported order in Italy seemed as powerfully entrenched as ever.

For the more conservative and realistic Italian nationalists, the only possibility for achieving national freedom and unity lay in Sardinia, the only Italian state that might once again take the field against Austria with any prospect of success and bring about at least a partial unification of the peninsula by absorbing the former Austrian provinces and the states ruled by Austrian-supported governments.

The need for Italian nationalists to unite behind Sardinia and appeal to that state to assume leadership of the national movement was expressed simply and forcefully in the 1850s by two prominent former republicans, Marquis Giorgio Pallavicino, whose long imprisonment by the Austrians had made him a martyr to the Italian national cause, and Daniele Manin, the heroic leader of the Venetian Republic of 1848–1849. "To defeat cannon and soldiers," Pallavicino said, "cannon and soldiers are needed. Arms are needed, and not Mazzinian pratings. Piedmont [i.e., Piedmont-Sardinia] has soldiers and cannon: *therefore I am Piedmontese.*" Because Piedmont was also a monarchy, it was necessary for republicans to abjure abstract principles and "be Italians." Manin, speaking in the name of all republicans, declared that their party was willing to make this "act of abnegation" of principle for the sake of the national cause. "Convinced that before all else it is necessary to make Italy, that this is the prior and predominant question, it says to the house of Savoy [the rulers of Sardinia]: make Italy and I am with you—if not, no."

Pallavicino and Manin were among the founders in July 1857 of a new National Society dedicated to the unification of Italy under the leadership of Sardinia. Its membership was never large, but it was more effective than similar political organizations because it demanded of its members unquestioning acceptance of its goals and methods and because the members themselves were influential. They included scions of the aristocracy, landlords and industrialists, financiers, shopowners, and bureaucrats, men who were well connected and occupied leading positions in their respective states. Members of the society were to play a critical political role during the wars for Italian unification, assuming positions of leadership in the various Italian states after the ouster of the existing governments and arranging the annexation of these states to Sardinia. Prior to those wars, however, and throughout the period of unification, the society's most notable contribution to the national cause was its propaganda, whereby it did much to convince public opinion, within Italy as well as abroad, of the deep-seated desire of the entire Italian people for national freedom and unification and to persuade Sardinian leaders that their own interests as well as those of Italy required that they act on behalf of the Italian national cause.

Sardinian leadership was to be crucial to the unification movement or at least to the manner in which unification was accomplished. Here one of the most fortunate legacies of 1848 proved to be the constitution King Charles Albert had been obliged to grant his subjects and which his son and successor, Victor Emanuel II, had found it expedient to retain. This Sardinian *statuto* provided for a popularly elected parliament and a system of ministerial responsibility which, no matter how narrow the electoral franchise or how restricted the actual ministerial authority, provided the opportunity for politically concerned individuals to have some voice in the political process. The institutions created by this constitution made possible the rise to leadership of one of the most remarkable statesmen of the nineteenth century, Count Camillo Benso di Cavour.

❑ Cavour

As the younger son of a Sardinian noble family, Cavour was trained to become an army officer, which should have taught him more than it evidently did about his country's armed forces. Finding military life stultifying, he resigned his commission at an early age to manage a part of his family's estates, and, by applying scientific agricultural techniques, he made his farming venture an unusually profitable enterprise. He subsequently enjoyed even greater success as a financier and industrialist, a founder of the Bank of Turin, and an imaginative promoter of shipping and railway construction. He was an avid reader in a wide variety of fields and an observant traveler, learning much, especially from the political and economic systems of Britain and France.

In December 1847, following the liberalization of the Sardinian press laws, he founded a political journal, *Il Risorgimento* (The Resurgence), which was the name eventually given to this entire period of Italian history. By avoiding extremist positions of radical republicans and advocating a program of orderly reform in the direction of greater political and economic freedom, Cavour became an influential journalist and a spokesman for moderate liberalism. Elected to the Sardinian assembly in 1848, he demonstrated outstanding talents as a parliamentary tactitian and debater. In October 1850 he was appointed minister for agriculture, industry and commerce, and the navy; in the following year he became minister of finance; and in November 1852 the king called upon him to assume the office of prime minister, at which time he also took over the portfolio for foreign affairs.

Cavour possessed in abundance those qualities so necessary for a successful career in politics: physical energy, an enormous capacity for hard work, a retentive memory, ambition, self-confidence, and utter ruthlessness when the occasion seemed to require it. A contemporary described him as Byzantine, with his lack of scruple, his sharp logic, and his persuasiveness even when most paradoxical. In his exercise of statecraft, his outstanding quality was flexibility, an ability to adjust his policies to the opportunities of the moment. Supremely confident of his intellectual powers, he could be high-handed and contemptuous in dealing with others. Like Bismarck, his German counterpart, he was intolerant of rivals and liked to keep tight personal control over the conduct of affairs, and again like Bismarck, he failed to train a new generation of statesmen in the exercise of political responsibility and leadership because of his reluctance to delegate authority.

At the time he entered politics, Cavour was more concerned with the welfare and aggrandizement of Sardinia than with the problems of Italy as a whole. Because Austria was the major obstacle to such aggrandizement, he shared the aspirations of Italian nationalists to drive the Austrians from the peninsula, but he was too cautious and practical a statesman to admit to sharing their aspirations for Italian unification. To adopt such a policy openly would have alienated the governments of the individual Italian states and all the great powers with the possible exception of Britain, and the policy itself seemed pointless because for the time being the obstacles to unification were simply too great. As the experience of 1848–1849 had demonstrated, the Catholic powers were determined to defend the temporal power of the papacy in the states of central Italy, and the Bourbon regime in Naples and Sicily enjoyed the support of the conservative powers, Austria and especially Russia. Moreover, even if the states of central and southern Italy could be brought under Sardinian control, absorbing these backward and poverty-stricken regions might do more to drain its energies than contribute to its strength. Cavour, therefore, concentrated on preparing Sardinia to renew the contest with Austria.

As prime minister, Cavour's first concern was to strengthen the country economically and militarily. He reformed the taxation system and borrowed heavily from abroad to stimulate the economy and equip a large modern army. He concluded foreign trade treaties, and he sponsored the construction of highways and railroads, harbors and canals. He encouraged the expansion of credit and stimulated investment in new industrial and agricultural enterprises. The result was a remarkable spurt in the Sardinian economy and a considerable increase in state revenue.

Despite the kingdom's increased power and prosperity, Cavour, unlike many of his countrymen, realized that Sardinia alone was incapable of challenging Austrian supremacy in Italy. Sardinia had failed to defeat Austria in 1848–1849 when the entire Habsburg empire was in revolt; its chances against a stabilized Austria would be considerably worse. Sardinia could expect to engage Austria successfully only with the aid of powerful allies. To secure them, Cavour devoted a large part of his attention to foreign policy.

In his search for allies, Cavour was fortunate to find in Napoleon III a statesman as eager as he to disrupt the existing international order and the Concert of Europe that supported it. Equally fortunate was Napoleon's fondness for Italy, where he had lived in his youth while in exile from France. At that time he had joined a secret Italian revolutionary society, the Carbonari, dedicated to liberating Italy from domestic and foreign despotisms. As ruler of France, Napoleon still professed to be a champion of oppressed nationalities, a particularly potent cause in dealing with that bulwark of the European concert, the multinational Habsburg empire. And nowhere within that empire was there a more convenient or tempting region in which to use the weapon of nationalism than Italy, where his championship of the national cause would enable France to supplant Austrian influence.

❑ *Sardinia and the Crimean War*

In the end Napoleon's objective—to destroy the European concert—was realized not through national revolution but through successfully fostering the international crises that led to the Crimean War (see Chapter 7). It was during this same war that Cavour made his own first significant move in the field of foreign affairs by bringing Sardinia into the conflict as the ally of Britain and France.

Sardinia's entry into the Crimean War was once believed to have been part of a skillful long-range Cavourian plan to win Anglo-French support in his campaign against Austria, but his immediate motive appears to have had nothing to do with foreign policy. His colleagues in the ministry were unanimously opposed to entering the war, which did not directly affect Sardinian interests. King Victor Emanuel, on the other hand, was eager to seize this opportunity to win military glory, and Cavour had learned that the king intended to use the excuse of his ministers' opposition to war to dismiss them and therewith put an end to ministerial restrictions on his personal authority. Cavour's advocacy of war appears to have been, in the first instance, a move to defend ministerial government and preserve his own influence over the conduct of affairs.

Considerations of foreign policy, however, also played a role in Cavour's decision for war. Sardinia was under heavy Anglo-French diplomatic pressure to enter the war. These powers were combing the world for soldiers—despite British popular enthusiasm for the war, British men were singularly reluctant to fight in it— and the Sardinian army was a tempting source of manpower. Their primary interest in Sardinia, however, involved Austria, which had joined the Anglo-French alliance in December 1854 on the condition that these powers guarantee Austria's position in Italy. For Britain and France, the alliance with Sardinia was a convenient way to implement that guarantee while at the same time securing the benefits of Sardinian manpower. It also provided them with a lever for exerting pressure on Austria to go beyond a mere alliance and actually enter the war, for they could now threaten to throw their support to Sardinia in Italian affairs if Austria continued to resist participation.

Cavour's ministerial colleagues opposed joining any alliance that included Austria, but Cavour decided to yield to his sovereign's wishes and Anglo-French pressure. Rejecting the partnership with the Western powers would unquestionably leave Sardinia in a weaker position vis-à-vis Austria, whereas joining the alliance and participating in the war would not only avoid that danger but might improve Sardinia's international status, as King Victor Emanuel confidently expected it would. "Once our soldiers are aligned with yours," he told the French minister to Turin, "I'll snap my fingers at Austria."

In the end, thanks in large part to the intolerable position in which the Austrians found themselves during the Crimean War, the king's confidence proved justified. Despite the Anglo-French guarantee of their position in Italy, the Austrians persistently evaded active participation in the war and thereby provoked the bitter resentment of the Western powers. But by joining the Anglo-French alliance at all and finally submitting the ultimatum that compelled Russia to sue for peace, the Austrians aroused the even greater and far more enduring resentment of the Russians, with the result that after the war they found themselves without friends among the great powers.

Sardinia joined the Anglo-French alliance on January 10, 1855, and through a military convention of January 26 it promised to supply fifteen thousand soldiers in return for a monetary subsidy and a guarantee of its own position in Italy for the duration of the war. It was promised no territorial gains and received none, a matter of some disappointment to Cavour and Italian patriots. Sardinia's entry into the war, however, unquestionably improved its international position. In the eyes of Western governments and public opinion, Sardinia's participation contrasted favorably with the pusillanimous conduct of Austria. At the end of the war, Sardinia was admitted to the peace conference at Paris on an equal footing with the great powers, giving Cavour ample opportunity to exploit the general resentment of Austria to agitate against the Austrian-dominated order in Italy. "We have gained two things," he announced to the Sardinian parliament upon his return from the Paris conference. "In the first place, the unhappy and abnormal condition of Italy has been denounced to Europe, not by demagogues, not by hot-headed revolutionaries or passionate journalists, but by the representatives of the foremost powers of Europe. . . . In the second place, those very powers have declared that it was not only useful to Italy but to Europe to apply some remedy to the ills of Italy. I cannot believe that the judgments expressed, the counsels given, by powers like France and England can long remain sterile."

Cavour grossly exaggerated the Anglo-French pronouncements, perhaps to divert criticism from his failure to reap any territorial rewards for Sardinia, but his evaluation of Anglo-French attitudes toward the Italian problem proved to be more correct than he himself may have dared to hope. For in the years after the Crimean War, the British were generally sympathetic to Sardinian policies, provocative as these might often be; and Napoleon's intervention on the side of Sardinia against

Austria was to be decisive in eventually driving the Austrians from the peninsula. The governments of both Britain and France of course pursued policies in Italy which they conceived to be in line with their own best interests, but Cavour's experience at the Paris conference had provided him with valuable insights as to how those interests might be made to correspond with those of Sardinia.

❑ *The Franco-Sardinian Alliance*

Napoleon is supposed to have been spurred into intervention on behalf of Italy by an Italian revolutionary named Felice Orsini, who on January 14, 1858, made an unsuccessful attempt to assassinate the emperor, allegedly because of Napoleon's failure to do anything on behalf of the Italian national cause, which he had sworn to support in his youth. Although Napoleon felt obliged to have Orsini executed, he encouraged him to write an appeal on behalf of Italy and saw that it was published and given wide publicity. Only a few weeks later, whether as a result of Orsini's gesture or because he had long since decided to intervene in Italy, Napoleon informed Cavour through confidential intermediaries of his desire for an alliance with Sardinia (which, according to an Italian confidant, he conceived as the first step in a grand alliance of the Latin against the Germanic race) for the purpose of waging war against Austria on behalf of the liberation of Italy. To negotiate the terms of that alliance, he arranged to meet Cavour secretly at the French spa of Plombières in the Vosges Mountains.

Cavour traveled to Plombières incognito on July 20, 1858, and met with the French emperor for several hours on the following day. Napoleon came straight to the point. He informed Cavour that he would support Sardinia in a war against Austria provided that war were undertaken for nonrevolutionary ends and could be justified in the eyes of diplomacy and European public opinion. The first objective would be to drive the Austrians out of Italy once and for all "and to leave them without an inch of territory south of the Alps or west of the Isonzo." After that Italy was to be reorganized as a confederation of four states under the presidency of the pope. Sardinia was to become the kingdom of Upper Italy and would annex all former Austrian territory in Italy together with the duchies of Parma and Modena and the Romagna, the northernmost province of the Papal States. In central Italy, a new state was to be formed consisting of the grand duchy of Tuscany plus the Marches and Umbria, two other provinces of the Papal States, which Napoleon envisaged as a kingdom for his cousin, Prince Napoleon Bonaparte. The French alliance with Sardinia and the House of Savoy was to be sealed through the marriage of Prince Napoleon to Clotilde, the daughter of King Victor Emanuel. Evidently the pope was to be satisfied with the honor of being president of the new confederation, for he was to be stripped of most of his territories and left only the city of Rome and its immediate surroundings (the Patrimony of St. Peter). The boundaries of the fourth member of the confederation, the Kingdom of the Two Sicilies, were to remain unchanged.

On the face of it, the Plombières agreement gave Napoleon a variety of means for exercising future control over Italy: he could do so through the pope, the president of the future confederation, who depended on France to maintain what was left of his temporal power; through Sardinia, which would need to hold fast to the

French alliance against a vengeful Austria; through his cousin, who would be king of central Italy; and through the sentiments of the Italian nation, which would be grateful to France for its liberation from Austria and henceforth look to France for leadership. To cap these advantages, Napoleon secured Sardinia's specific promise in their formal alliance treaty of January 19, 1859, to cede to France the Sardinian provinces of Nice and Savoy (a cession discussed but not firmly settled at Plombières) which lay on the French side of the Alps and which the French had long coveted to round out what they regarded as their "natural frontiers": the Alps, the Pyrenees, and the Rhine. The treaty also stipulated that the entire cost of the forthcoming war with Austria would be borne by the kingdom of Upper Italy through annual payments of one-tenth of that state's revenues.

Great as were the apparent advantages of the Plombières agreement for France, the real winner in the negotiations was Cavour. The agreement gave him the alliance he needed against Austria and assured him the support of the strongest military power in western Europe. Nice and Savoy were a small price to pay for the Austrian provinces of the Trentino, Lombardy, and Venetia, the duchies of Parma and Modena, and the large sector of the Papal States that Sardinia would acquire. As Cavour pointed out to his sovereign, such an extension of Sardinian authority would in effect give him predominance over all of Italy.

The marriage of Prince Napoleon and Princess Clotilde, ardently desired by Napoleon to unite his house with one of the most ancient dynasties of Europe, proved to be an unexpectedly serious obstacle to the French alliance, for Victor Emanuel stubbornly opposed the union of his pious fifteen-year-old daughter to a notorious profligate of thirty-six. Cavour finally overcame his sovereign's objections by reminding him of the advantages of the French alliance and warning that Napoleon, "who was after all a Corsican," would regard a rejection of the marriage as a blood insult. Cavour had even greater difficulty with the princess herself, but she was at last persuaded to yield to her father's wishes and thus became, as one of Cavour's aides later expressed it, the first casualty of the Austrian war. The marriage was celebrated on January 30, 1859.

❏ *Diplomatic Preparations for War*

"Now that the wedding has taken place" Cavour wrote jubilantly to his minister in Paris, "we shall think only of war." To ensure French support in the war, however, he had to fulfill Napoleon's condition to justify it in the eyes of European public opinion. To this end, he used all his considerable ingenuity to goad Austria into committing an aggressive act. He engaged in a campaign of vilification, he ostentatiously enlisted Austrian deserters in the Sardinian army, he gave refuge to fugitives from Habsburg rule in the hope that Austria would demand their extradition. Austria was to be made to "dance to our tune in Italy," he said, so that "we may pose as the victims of Austrian menaces."

Besides seeking to provoke Austria in Italy, Cavour was working to stir up rebellion among other nationalities within the Habsburg realm. He devoted his greatest efforts to the Hungarians, but he was also in touch with Serbian and Romanian revolutionaries and was urging the governments of Serbia and the Danubian Principalities (the future Romania) to encourage rebellion of their fellow nationals living under Habsburg rule.

Napoleon himself meanwhile was negotiating with the great powers to ensure Austria's diplomatic isolation in the forthcoming conflict. He was most successful with the Russians, who were still smarting from what they regarded as Austria's perfidious behavior during the Crimean War. Already in September 1858 he had sent Prince Napoleon to Warsaw to negotiate a treaty with Russia to secure its benevolent neutrality in the event of a French war with Austria in Italy and a Russian engagement to prevent Prussia and the other German states from taking Austria's side. In return, Napoleon would support Russia in abrogating the Black Sea clauses of the 1856 Treaty of Paris, which prohibited Russia from maintaining military or naval forces along the coasts or on the waters of the Black Sea—a prohibition which at the time had seemed a major achievement of the Anglo-French victory in the Crimean War. In the end, Napoleon did not have to pay this price. The Franco-Russian treaty concluded on March 3, 1859, made no mention of the Black Sea clauses. The Russians promised to maintain benevolent neutrality in a Franco-Austrian war; they would urge the German states to remain neutral; and they would not oppose the enlargement of Sardinia provided the rights of other Italian rulers who did not participate in the war were respected.

Napoleon was less successful in dealing with Britain and Prussia. He had counted on the pro-Italian sympathies of leading British statesmen and British public opinion to secure assurances of British support against Austria, but Malmesbury, the British foreign secretary, was clearly anxious to prevent war altogether and fearful that Napoleon intended to exploit a crisis in Italy to initiate a wholesale alteration of European frontiers to the benefit of France. He was also annoyed by Sardinia's obvious efforts to provoke war. "I can muster no patience towards that little conceited mischievous State" for which "Europe should be deluged in blood," he wrote to his ambassador in Paris. He warned the Sardinian government that only republicans would benefit from a general conflagration; if Sardinia nevertheless persisted in fomenting a crisis, it would show the world "that a popular Government may be as unwise and grasping as the single mind of an ignorant or despotic ruler." Fearful that Cavour would succeed in goading Austria into an aggressive act, he urged Prussia and other German states to convince Buol, the Austrian foreign minister, not to take steps of any kind in Italy without first consulting France.

Napoleon also failed to secure a promise of neutrality from Prussia. In negotiating with the Prussians, he held out prospects of French support against Austria in their struggle for supremacy in Germany. But the Prussian government refused to make commitments of any kind. Prussian leaders anticipated that German public opinion would favor Austria, and bitter memories of the first Napoleon made them wary of dealing with his present namesake.

On March 9, 1859, the Sardinian government took the most provocative step it had risked so far by mobilizing its army reserves, including a newly formed corps of volunteers composed chiefly of deserters from the Austrian army and fugitives from Austrian conscription. Sardinia's action was allegedly a response to Austria's reinforcement of troops in Italy, but in taking this step it was forcing the pace of events in Italy more rapidly and more crudely than Napoleon desired. The emperor was finding little enthusiasm for his Italian policy in France, and apart from his treaty with Russia his diplomatic campaign to isolate Austria was not going well. To restrain

Sardinia and regain the moral initiative, he arranged with Russia to propose a congress of the great powers to deal with the Italian question. Although he and Sardinia desired the same thing, he told Prince Napoleon, their conduct for the moment was diametrically opposed. To divide his enemies and ensure the neutrality of the rest of Europe, he must display moderation and a desire for conciliation, whereas Sardinia, to maintain its position and prestige in Italy, was eager to precipitate war. He explained his dilemma at greater length to an angry and suspicious Cavour. European public opinion was turning against him, and if forced to declare war under these circumstances he would be compelled to fight not only in Italy but on the Rhine. "Russia . . . has understood the weakness, even the danger of my position. She has proposed the only means that now exists of putting me in the common right without abandoning the cause I wish to serve; it is the convocation of a Congress."

The British government eagerly welcomed the congress proposal and immediately concerted with Russia on an agenda that included the preservation of peace between Austria and Sardinia. Cavour was appalled and instructed his confidential representative in Paris to do everything possible to avoid a congress. For if such an assembly convened, "how the devil could we then start a war? England would never let us raise a *casus belli* against Austria, and would oppose us if we defied her by being belligerent at the conference table." Sardinia could accept a congress only if France and Russia would agree in advance (presumably after consultation with Cavour) about the concessions that should be demanded from Austria.

The Austrians feared that this was precisely what France and Russia intended to do at their proposed congress, and that these powers would be supported by Britain in calling for reforms in Italy that would undermine the Austrian position. The Austrians also suspected, correctly, that Napoleon desired a congress only to gain time to prepare French public opinion for war and secure British diplomatic support. They therefore posed numerous conditions for their participation, the most important of which were that Sardinia should demobilize before the congress convened and engage to respect all existing treaties.

Malmesbury responded to these Austrian conditions with a proposal for general demobilization on the part of all the powers, a proposal accepted immediately by France and eventually by Austria. Walewski, the French foreign minister, who was not in sympathy with Napoleon's Italian policy and appears to have genuinely wished to use the instrument of a congress to preserve peace, now put heavy pressure on a frustrated and furious Cavour to agree as well. "The emperor charges you to engage Piedmont to accept the principle of disarmament," he wrote in a telegram of April 18—an instruction Napoleon himself later disavowed in dealing with the Italians but which certainly corresponded with his desire to appear conciliatory. Cavour was in despair. "There is nothing for me to do now but blow out my brains," he said. He decided instead to yield to French pressure, and on the morning of April 19 wired to Paris that Sardinia was disposed to submit. Believing that his own position was now untenable, he began to burn his private political papers and other compromising documents.

Cavour and his war plan were saved by the Austrians. On the very day he yielded to French pressure and accepted the demand for general demobilization, a courier left Vienna with an ultimatum demanding Sardinia's demobilization and dissolution of its volunteer corps. Sardinia was given three days to reply. This was a blunder of the first magnitude, for it was exactly the kind of action Cavour had endeavored so long to provoke: it made Austria the aggressor, brought the French alliance into play, and allowed Sardinia to appear an innocent victim of Austrian bullying in the eyes of European public opinion. A colleague of Cavour could hardly believe his prime minister's good fortune, calling it "one of those pieces of gambler's luck that happens only once in a century. Whether we are prepared or not, the moral victory is ours and more than half our enemies have become our friends, seeing us now as victims and not as provokers."

It is always difficult to find rational explanations for stupidity, but the Austrian blunder in this case appears to have been due primarily to an arrogant and totally unwarranted overconfidence on the part of Austrian leaders in their empire's military and diplomatic position. Buol interpreted the Franco-Russian proposal for a congress and Britain's mediatory efforts as evidence that Napoleon was losing his nerve and that the other European powers were coming over to the side of Austria on the Italian question. At a meeting of the Austrian council of ministers on April 6 to discuss the problems of the congress and general demobilization, Buol recommended that in view of Sardinia's steadily increasing provocation, Austria should demand the prior demobilization of Sardinia. He was convinced that all the states of Germany with the possible exception of Prussia were on Austria's side, that neither Britain nor Prussia was actually against Austria, and that it was inconceivable that Prussia would not side with Austria in the event of a general war. At the end of the meeting, the Austrian ministers unanimously agreed "that the safety and dignity of the Empire do not permit the continuation of the present conduct of the Sardinian government."

At a ministerial meeting on April 19, Emperor Francis Joseph referred to the decision of April 6 and asked whether the note to Sardinia demanding demobilization had been drafted and whether this was the moment to present it to Turin. Buol replied that the note was ready and should be presented without delay. He believed that France was surprised by the international support building up for Austria, and that France could be expected to persuade Sardinia to yield to Austria's demands.

Buol was in a difficult position. Austria's own mobilization was imposing an intolerable financial burden on the empire that required a speedy resolution of the Italian crisis, and Austrian military leaders were accusing him of being weak and indecisive, a view evidently shared by his youthful emperor, who was also pressing for a resolute policy. It is nevertheless impossible to understand how Buol, an experienced diplomat who had demonstrated considerable resourcefulness and restraint in dealing with international crises in the past, could have deluded himself so completely about Austria's international position and not only consented to but actually recommended sending an ultimatum to Sardinia. The British government had repeatedly warned Austria against making the aggressive move Buol was now proposing, and only a few days before the fateful ministerial meeting of April 19 the Prussian government had rejected an Austrian appeal for support: Austria should seek a peaceful resolution of the crisis with Sardinia; Prussia would support Austria only if *Austria* were the victim of aggression. Buol should have found the attitude of Russia even more discouraging. An Austrian envoy sent to Russia in mid-April to appeal for recognition of their joint conservative principles and interests reported that Russian rancor against Austria was more intense than ever, and his appeal to their joint interests was brutally turned aside by Gorchakov, the Russian foreign minister. There was no chance of reestablishing the former intimacy between the two empires, he said. Russia was no longer disposed to play the role of the watchdog of Europe. "Times have changed, and these old ties have been broken forever."

❑ *The War of 1859 and the Peace of Villafranca*

The Austrian ultimatum, sent by courier rather than by telegraph, was received in Turin on April 23. After the three days given him to respond, Cavour rejected it and Austria was now obliged to declare war. The Austrian declaration activated the French alliance with Sardinia, turned the British government against Austria, and deprived Austria of all immediate prospect of Prussian support. On May 4, in the midst of this debacle of his foreign policy, Buol resigned and was replaced as Austrian foreign minister by Count Bernhard Rechberg, a conservative diplomat of the Metternich school. As Austrian representative to the diet of the German Confederation, Rechberg had skillfully defended Austrian interests in Germany, but he was powerless to alter the fateful course of Austrian policy in Italy.

Austrian military leadership proved to be as inept as its diplomacy. Although Austrian generals had long been alerted to the imminent possibility of war, they did not begin an invasion of Sardinia until the end of April, and even then, delayed by heavy rains, they failed to press their offensive and thus gave the French time to bring a large army into Italy.

French intervention was crucial to the outcome of the war. Although the Sardinians too had long expected war, they were woefully ill-prepared, and to the disgust of the French, they never provided the military or even logistic support Cavour had blithely promised. The French put a far larger and better equipped army into the field and bore the brunt of the fighting. On June 4 the Austrians were defeated at Magenta, east of Milan, and on June 24 they suffered a second serious defeat at Solferino, south of Lake Garda, where some 300,000 men were engaged and which in terms of numbers was one of the greatest battles yet fought on European soil.

The war was ended suddenly and unexpectedly by Napoleon III, who on July 6, barely a fortnight after Solferino and without consulting his Italian allies, asked Emperor Francis Joseph for an armistice. Five days later, the two concluded a preliminary peace treaty at the nearby town of Villafranca.

Napoleon had compelling reasons for wanting peace. In his eagerness to destroy the existing international order, he found that he had made serious miscalculations in his Italy policy and had unleashed forces he was unable to control. The conflict with Austria was proving more difficult and more costly in terms of blood as well as money than he had anticipated, and he feared that French public opinion, already ominously restive, would not support the major and lengthy military effort that would still be required to drive the Austrians out of Italy. Sardinia's military assistance and Italian support for the war in general had fallen far short of what he had been promised and expected. There had been no mass popular uprisings against Austrian rule in northern Italy, where the Lombards had not even managed to keep supplies moving along the railroads. Instead there had been revolutions in central Italy—in Tuscany, Parma, Modena, and the Papal States—where governments had been established under the leadership or with the connivance and support of members of the National Society, which sought annexation of these states to Sardinia.

Napoleon feared that if the war continued, these revolutions might spread to the south, threaten papal rule in Rome, and create further opportunities for Sardinia to extend its authority and become far larger and more powerful than he had envisaged, a rival instead of a satellite of France. Most alarming of all was the growing display of pro-Austrian sentiment among the German states, the mobilization of the Prussian army on June 24, and the prospect of having to fight on the Rhine as well as in Italy. The Russians, who had been expected to keep the German states in check, were manifestly unable to do so and were advising Napoleon to make peace before the war got out of hand.

The Austrians also had compelling reasons for wanting peace, which only underscored their stupidity in allowing themselves to be goaded into war in the first place. Their financial situation, considered desperate before the war began, was inevitably rendered far worse by war itself. The war also increased the danger of national uprisings within the Habsburg empire, which the French as well as the Italians had long been trying to promote and which the French were now encouraging with generous financial assistance. Even the prospect of Prussian support, which Buol had sought in vain before the war, now proved an additional incentive for making peace because the price of that support might be the relinquishment of Austrian supremacy in Germany.

In the preliminary peace of Villafranca of July 11, 1859, the Austrians gave up their rights over Lombardy (apart from the fortresses of Mantua and Peschiera, two of the defensive positions of the Quadrilateral), but to avoid making any concessions to the despised Sardinians, they ceded those rights to the emperor of the French, who would turn them over to King Victor Emanuel. Austria was to retain Venetia, which was to become part of a confederation of Italian states under the presidency of the pope. The Habsburg rulers of Tuscany and Modena, who had been ousted by revolution, were to be restored to power, and Austria and France were to cooperate in persuading the pope to introduce reforms in the Papal States. Thus Austria, far from being driven out of Italy altogether, as Napoleon had promised in his agreements with Sardinia, was left a substantial portion of Italian territory and an influential voice in Italian affairs.

These terms were communicated by Napoleon to Victor Emanuel, who saw no alternative but to accept them, but in doing so he added the significant qualification "only insofar as they concern me" (*pour ce qui me concerne*), thus leaving himself an opening to disregard the terms affecting the other states of Italy. In return for Victor Emanuel's acceptance, Napoleon agreed to drop his claim to Nice and Savoy, but he still demanded substantial payment for the expenses of the war.

Unlike his sovereign, Cavour refused to agree to the terms of Villafranca, he stormed in impotent fury about Napoleon's betrayal, and on the day after the treaty was signed he resigned from the government.

❑ *Sardinian Annexations and the Cession of Nice and Savoy*

Cavour was hardly in a position to complain of betrayal. Sardinia's contribution to the war had fallen far short of what his government had promised, and his own efforts to promote the annexation of the states of central Italy to Sardinia went well beyond, and conflicted with, his treaty agreements with France.

They certainly conflicted with Napoleon's own Italian program. The French emperor had never desired the formation of an Italian state strong enough to be truly independent, much less the unification of the entire peninsula under an Italian national government. "Unity," he confessed frankly, "would stir up dangers for me in France itself because of the Roman question; nor could France be happy to see a great nation established beside her that might diminish her own preponderance." What Napoleon had wanted for Italy, as his agreements with Sardinia made clear, was a confederation of four relatively weak states dependent on France for their security.

Napoleon soon found that, short of going to war against his Italian allies, he could not enforce the terms of Villafranca. Following the signature of that treaty, the provisional governments that had been established in the states of central Italy had held carefully controlled elections to popular assemblies, which could be seen to represent the will of the people. These assemblies proceeded to defy the arrangements made at Villafranca by declaring their former dynasties deposed and demanding annexation to Sardinia—here again the activities of members of the National Society played a critical role. To strengthen their hand in resisting the restoration of those dynasties, Parma, Modena, and the Romagna united to form a new state with the ancient name of Emilia, which entered into a defensive alliance with Tuscany.

Unwilling and unable to use force, which would have represented a repudiation of his nationalities program and the bankruptcy of his Italian policy, Napoleon resorted to his favorite device. He proposed a European congress to arrange a political settlement for Italy; under the cover of a congress he might cooperate with Austria, Prussia, and Russia to control Italian revolutionary movements and thwart Sardinian annexationist ambitions. In the final peace agreement concluded with Austria, the Treaty of Zürich of November 10, 1859, he arranged that the terms of that treaty should form the basis for a European congress to convene in Paris in January. Otherwise the Zürich treaty merely confirmed the principal provisions of the preliminary Peace of Villafranca, with the important difference that it did not require the restoration of the deposed Italian dynasties but merely reserved their rights for the decision of the congress.

That congress never convened because Napoleon soon discovered it would not serve his purposes in Italy, and early in January he announced that it had been postponed indefinitely. The conservative powers might have been willing to support a conservative program for Italy—which would have required the use of force for its implementation—but they left Napoleon in no doubt about their opposition to his own. They were decidedly cool about a Bonaparte prince ruling a central Italian state, and they rejected outright the French claim to Nice and Savoy, which Napoleon now desperately desired to prove to a disgruntled French public opinion that France had gained at least some material advantage from the costly and deadly war with Austria. But the major obstacle to any possible congressional acceptance of his program for Italy was Britain, whose government since mid-June 1859 was once again under the leadership of the ardently pro-Italian Lord Palmerston, with Lord John Russell as his foreign secretary.

Far from wishing to restrain Sardinia, Palmerston favored the greatest possible expansion of its control over Italy so as to create an Italian state capable of maintaining itself independently of Austrian *or* French influence and support. "The larger and stronger Piedmont could be made," he said, "the better it would be for the happiness of the people united to it, and for the peace of Europe depending on the tranquillity of Italy." Following Napoleon's postponement of his congress, Russell proposed that France not only drop its claims to Nice and Savoy but withdraw all its troops from Italy to allow the Italians to work out their own salvation.

Faced with this kind of opposition from Britain and with the hostile German states on his flank, Napoleon decided to seek a direct settlement with Sardinia to obtain Nice and Savoy: in return for Sardinia's cession of the provinces, he would agree to Sardinia's annexations in central Italy. Because Cavour's successors in the Sardinian government refused to make this cession, or felt too weak to deal with Italian patriotic hostility if they attempted to do so, Napoleon urged King Victor Emanuel to reinstate Cavour, who had made the original bargain over Nice and Savoy and was the Sardinian statesman most likely to be able and willing to fulfill it. For Cavour could be expected to understand that Sardinia still needed the French alliance for protection against Austria, and that the French alliance alone offered any hope that Sardinia might yet acquire Venetia and other Austrian-held territory south of the Alps. Ironically, the British also supported the reinstatement of Cavour because they thought he would be capable of resisting French territorial demands, and they were bitterly disillusioned when he eventually agreed to Napoleon's bargain.

Cavour returned to office as head of the Sardinian government on January 20, 1860, and in addition to the prime ministership he took over the ministries of foreign affairs, the interior, and the navy to ensure his control over Sardinian policy. Napoleon was correct in believing that Cavour would negotiate over Nice and Savoy on behalf of preserving the French alliance and to secure France's consent to the Sardinian annexations in central Italy, but in return for this consent he attempted to compel Cavour to settle for less than he had been promised at Plombières. Still anxious to limit Sardinian annexations, he proposed that these be restricted to Parma and Modena, that the Romagna remain a papal state (though ruled by Victor Emanuel as the pope's vicar), and that Tuscany remain independent under "some prince," whereby Prince Napoleon was clearly meant. This proposal was presented to Cavour on February 28 in the form of an ultimatum.

Cavour was saved, or at least given a respite, by the British, who expressed their disapproval of every part of the French proposal. Before Napoleon could come forward with new proposals, Cavour and his political allies again resorted to elections in the states of central Italy to demonstrate the popular will, this time in the form of plebiscites in which every adult male would have the right to vote. In the past Cavour had feared and opposed popular elections, but he had learned from Napoleon's plebiscites in France how easily these could be manipulated and he calculated that the French ruler, who had used this device to demonstrate popular approval of his own policies, could not oppose the holding of plebiscites in Italy or repudiate their results.

On March 1, the pro-Sardinian governments of Tuscany and Emilia (Parma, Modena, and the Romagna) announced that plebiscites would be held in ten days on the proposition "annexation to the constitutional monarchy of King Victor Emanuel II." Voting was in public under the supervision of military and police authorities, free wine was distributed, pro-annexation landlords led their peasants to the polls. Predictably, the plebiscites resulted in immense majorities in favor of annexation with the pro-annexation vote larger in many areas than the number of registered voters. A British observer called the whole procedure a farce, but it served its purpose in dealing with Napoleon. Realizing he could no longer prevent Sardinia's annexation of Tuscany as well as all of Emilia, he agreed to recognize the annexations but now insisted on the immediate cession of Nice and Savoy, a demand which Cavour for his part realized he could not reject without risking a serious crisis with France. The bargain over Nice and Savoy was sealed in a secret treaty signed by Victor Emanuel in Turin on March 12 and by Napoleon in Paris two days later. A public announcement of the cession, which included a provision for plebiscites to determine the wishes of the local population, was not made until March 30, giving French troops and officials time to move into the provinces to ensure proper election results. Once again these produced immense majorities in favor of annexation, this time to France. In seventy-five of eighty villages around Nice, which was still heavily Italian, no negative votes at all were recorded, and once again there were more "yes" votes in many districts than there were registered voters.

Cavour's cession of Nice and Savoy to sustain the French alliance was one of his most dangerous and courageous political gambles, for by assuming responsibility for this action he was risking his career and reputation. His bargain with Napoleon cost him the confidence of Palmerston, who now saw him as a puppet of the French emperor and thoroughly unreliable. But it was in Italy itself that he had become most vulnerable. He managed to secure the consent of the Sardinian parliament to the treaty with Napoleon, but the cession of Nice and Savoy aroused passionate antagonism among Italian patriots and made an implacable enemy of Garibaldi, who never forgave Cavour for the surrender of Nice, the city of his birth. The alienation of Garibaldi proved to be particularly dangerous, for the spectacular gains he was soon to make for the Italian national cause made him one of the most powerful and unquestionably the most popular political figure in Italy and thus a serious threat to Cavour's political authority.

❑ Garibaldi and the Conquest of Southern Italy

In contrast to the devious and politically cunning Cavour, Giuseppe Garibaldi was a single-minded Italian patriot, straightforward, blunt, devoid of guile or selfish ambition. Whereas Cavour prepared the groundwork for his policies with extreme care and understood the risks involved in his political gambles, Garibaldi believed in direct action and courageously took such action no matter how great the odds against him—and with little or no regard for the consequences. A colorful and charismatic military commander, he inspired immense enthusiasm among the men who served under him and the crowds that assembled to hear his speeches, and through his personality and quasi-legendary military exploits he captured the popular imagination as no other Italian leader. He professed to be a radical republican and a believer in the freedom of the individual, but like many men of action he was willing to employ dictatorial methods to achieve his ends. And in the manner of so many nationalists of his own time and since, he was willing to sacrifice his liberal principles on behalf of the success of the national cause.

In 1833, at the age of twenty-six, he fell under the influence of Mazzini and joined the Young Italy movement, taking an oath to fight against injustice and tyranny and for the unification of Italy. Exiled from Sardinia in the following year for revolutionary activity, he became a soldier of fortune in South America, where he acquired exceptional skill as a guerrilla leader. During the revolutions of 1848–1849 he led an army of volunteers against Austria in Lombardy, and in 1849, after the revolution in Rome which expelled the pope, he conducted the defense of the newly established Roman Republic against the French with tenacity and courage.

Back on the battlefield in the 1859 war against Austria, Garibaldi was one of the few commanders on either side to demonstrate initiative and imagination, but he was given little opportunity to exercise significant leadership by a Sardinian government fearful of his political views and anxious to keep him under control. He was disgusted by the Peace of Villafranca, but the cession of Nice and Savoy was more than he could endure and he began to assemble a corps of volunteers to take the field once again on behalf of the Italian national cause. Whether he intended to use this volunteer army to defend Nice and Savoy against the French, drive the French from Rome, or renew the war against Austria—and there was talk of all three possibilities—any one of them would have led to serious international complications.

Cavour's policies in dealing with Garibaldi at this critical time were devious as well as contradictory, for he needed to avoid alienating patriotic opinion at home while at the same time reassuring great power governments abroad. There can be no doubt, however, that he intended to prevent Garibaldi from taking any action that might precipitate a crisis with France or a premature conflict with Austria. It is therefore possible that Cavour himself conceived or at least approved a plan to persuade Garibaldi to take his volunteer corps to Sicily in support of a rebellion that had broken out against the government of Francis II, the Bourbon ruler of the Kingdom of the Two Sicilies.

If this was indeed Cavour's plan, it was a clever move. If the revolution in Sicily were successful, Sardinia might benefit as it had from the revolutions in central Italy; if Garibaldi failed, Sardinia could disavow him. Cavour later assured foreign governments that he had done his best to persuade Garibaldi not to embark on this "mad escapade," but the fact remains that his entire expedition was organized (and with a good deal of publicity at that) on territory under Sardinian control and that the Sardinian fleet did nothing to prevent it from sailing. Because Cavour realized that this fact must also be obvious to foreign powers, he explained in an almost apologetic tone to Paris: "I did not prevent Garibaldi from carrying out his project, because this would have needed force. Moreover the government is in no position to face up to the enormous unpopularity which we should have incurred by arresting Garibaldi. With the elections [to the Sardinian parliament] taking place, and depending as I do upon the votes of every shade of moderate liberal opinion to counter the opposition to get the French treaty [on Nice and Savoy] through, I could not take strong measures to stop him."

Cavour certainly did nothing to help Garibaldi. Shortly before the expedition sailed, the Sardinian government sequestered the modern rifles Garibaldi had captured in the 1859 war and stored in Milan. The only weapons he was finally able to acquire were smooth-bore converted flintlocks, many of them so rusty they could not be fired, and the only transport he could find were old and leaky steamers, which their owners insured for far more than their actual value. Once Garibaldi was at sea, the commander of the Sardinian navy was ordered to arrest him if he decided not to go to Sicily after all and to prevent all efforts to reinforce him. The British minister in Turin may well have been correct that Cavour expected and wanted

Garibaldi's expedition to fail, and "thought the country well rid of him and of the unquiet spirits who went with him."

It is possible, of course, that the entire Sicilian expedition was Garibaldi's own idea, or that the original initiative came from King Victor Emanuel. Garibaldi always claimed to be acting with the authority of the king, who may have given him that authority without consulting or informing Cavour. Garibaldi certainly behaved as though he had received royal authority. When his volunteer army—the famous Thousand Red Shirts—departed for Sicily on May 5, 1860, they took ship at the Sardinian port of Quarto, near Genoa, they sailed and fought under the Sardinian tricolor flag adorned with the arms of Savoy (subsequently the Italian national flag), and after landing at the Sicilian port of Marsala on May 11, Garibaldi proclaimed himself dictator of Sicily in the name of Italy and King Victor Emanuel.

Garibaldi advanced against a professional army that outnumbered his own by twenty to one, but his opponents were poorly led conscripts, whereas his volunteers were inspired to fight and he himself was a daring commander. In his first engagements with the Neapolitans, the uselessness of his muskets as firearms proved to be an actual advantage, for they compelled him to resort to the bayonet charge, which took full advantage of the high morale of his troops. On May 20 he defeated the Neapolitans near the village of Calatafimi, a minor engagement in itself (though Garibaldians were later to describe it as a great and bloody battle) but critical to the success of the entire campaign, for it established the legend of Garibaldi's invincibility. Seven days later he captured the Sicilian capital of Palermo. Success led to success. Thousands of Sicilian peasants, most of whom had no feeling whatever for the Italian nationalist movement (they are said to have cheered for "Italia" in the belief that she was Garibaldi's mistress), were converted into enthusiastic Garibaldians by the dramatic personality of the general himself and by his promises of land and tax reform.

Widespread peasant unrest in Sicily played an important part in Garibaldi's victory. Many of the peasant bands that had terrorized the island and in some areas brought local government to a standstill joined Garibaldi's army. At the same time property owners also supported him because he offered their only hope for reestablishing law and order.

Garibaldi's successes created new dangers, but also new opportunities, for Cavour. The dangers were obvious. Despite the general's professed loyalty to Victor Emanuel, Cavour feared he might be seduced by ambition and popular acclaim to assume supreme authority himself and establish a republican regime in Sicily; if he crossed to the mainland, as he showed every intention of doing, Garibaldian authority might soon be established over all of southern Italy. There was the further danger that if he succeeded in conquering Naples, he might continue his drive up the peninsula into the Papal States, where he would clash with French troops.

But the opportunities were equally obvious. After Garibaldi's first successes in Sicily, Cavour gave up all pretense of opposition to his expedition and sought to exploit the collapse of Bourbon rule as he had the ouster of the dynasties in central Italy. For this purpose he sent an agent to Sicily well equipped with funds for bribes and with secret instructions to take over the government of the island from Garibaldi and prepare its annexation to Sardinia. Cavour's plan failed because his agent's tactless behavior alienated Garibaldi, who on May 7, while still professing loyalty to Victor Emanuel, ordered his expulsion from the island.

Cavour had no better luck in Naples, where he tried to forestall a Garibaldian conquest by stirring up a revolution against the Bourbon regime. The resulting un-rest would give him an excuse to send Sardinian troops into Naples to restore law and order and establish Sardinian authority before Garibaldi could transfer his troops to the mainland. Again his agents were well supplied with funds for bribes, but their efforts were unsuccessful and the speed of Garibaldi's advance soon put an end to any possibility to forestall him.

Cavour then shifted his ground. Instead of Naples, he proposed to provoke a revolution in the Papal States, which would give him the excuse he needed to send a Sardinian army into southern Italy. That army would move into the papal state of Umbria, carefully bypassing the papal territory defended by the French, and thence into Naples, where it would appear to join forces with Garibaldi but in fact be in a position to control him. Any Sardinian advance into the Papal States, however, risked a crisis with France, and to minimize that danger Cavour sought the prior approval of Napoleon for his plan. He drew the emperor's attention to the possibility of a Garibaldian advance against Rome and argued that French interests too would be best served if Sardinian rather than French troops intercepted the impetuous gen-eral. Napoleon warned that the diplomatic complications would be serious and that he himself would be placed in a difficult position, but he ultimately sanctioned Cavour's plan provided that Rome were left inviolate and that the Sardinian invasion be carried out quickly, effectively, and without suggesting any connivance on the part of France.

In the Papal States as in Naples, Cavour's agents failed to provoke a revolution sufficiently impressive to justify intervention, but Cavour was never at a loss for expedients. On September 7, 1860, he sent an ultimatum to the pope demanding that he disband his army of mercenaries, who were accused of perpetrating a num-ber of unspecified massacres of Italian civilians and "who suffocate in blood every expression of the national will." Three days later, upon the papal rejection of this ultimatum, Sardinian forces crossed the frontier of the Papal States. They easily defeated the papal army and advanced into Neapolitan territory, where they joined forces with Garibaldi in the final stages of the campaign against the Bourbon regime. The French government publicly denounced the Sardinian invasion as an act of blatant aggression but did nothing to stop it. Napoleon meanwhile had embarked on a cruise in the Mediterranean and remained at sea—where he could not be reached—for twelve days.

Garibaldi now demonstrated that he was above all an Italian patriot, that his professions of loyalty to Victor Emanuel had been sincere, and that Cavour's fears about his personal ambition had been groundless. On October 15 he signed a decree proclaiming that all his conquests should henceforth become part of Italy under its constitutional monarch, Victor Emanuel II. To prove that Garibaldi's proclamation was in accord with the popular will, the now familiar instrument of a plebiscite was used to allow the people of Naples and Sicily to vote for or against the proposition: an Italy "one and indivisible" under its constitutional sovereign Victor Emanuel. As usual voting was in public, conducted under the supervision of Sardinian and local authorities, and as usual it produced immense favorable majorities. Early in Novem-ber similar plebiscites were held in Umbria and the Marches, the eastern sectors of the Papal States now occupied by Sardinian troops, the only difference here being that the people were asked to opt for outright annexation to Sardinia. The over-whelming majorities of "yes" votes were the same.

The Sardinian government did not act with the same generosity as Garibaldi. Still fearful that his popularity might undercut Sardinian authority, it refused him any significant civil or military position. With his mission in southern Italy accomplished and deprived of any official function, he retired to his island home of Caprera off the coast of Sardinia.

Early in 1861 parliamentary elections to an Italian national parliament were held in all the territories now under Sardinian control, and on March 17 the deputies to that parliament proclaimed the establishment of the Kingdom of Italy with Victor Emanuel as its first king. Just over two months later, on June 6, 1861, Cavour died at the age of fifty-one. His death was a grievous loss to the new state, which badly needed his leadership and political resourcefulness during its period of consolidation.

The Sardinians regarded "Italy" as little more than an extension of their own state. The new king of Italy retained his numerical title as ruler of Sardinia (Victor Emanuel II), the Italian parliament was similarly numbered as part of the succession of Sardinian parliaments, the Sardinian constitution was taken over in its entirety as the constitution of Italy, and Sardinian officials assumed the leadership of the army and administration of the newly annexed territories.

Sardinian rule was intensely resented, and nowhere more than in the south. The influx of Sardinian "foreign" officials, their imposition of a more centralized administration, higher and more efficiently collected taxes, military conscription, and anticlerical legislation aroused widespread unrest, which soon developed into a large-scale civil war. The struggle continued into 1866, but even after all organized resistance had been broken, hatred for Sardinian rule endured and the problems of the south continued to plague the national government.

❑ *Abortive Efforts to Take Over Rome*

Italian patriots were not satisfied with the boundaries of the national state established in 1861. Venetia, the Trentino, and other areas south of the Alps, which they claimed for Italy by reason of nationality, remained under Austrian control, while Rome, which they regarded as the natural capital of Italy, remained under papal authority, defended by French troops.

In the summer of 1862 the Italian government initiated a campaign to gain control of Rome. The plan was to persuade Garibaldi to lead a volunteer army against the city; the Italian government would then use arguments similar to those previously employed by Cavour to convince Napoleon that he could avoid bloodshed and embarrassment by withdrawing his troops from Rome and allowing Italian forces to occupy the city. Garibaldi was easily persuaded. In August he took command of a volunteer army raised in Sicily, and on August 24 he crossed over to the mainland to begin the march on Rome. But Napoleon refused to play this game. Unwilling to face the wrath of clerical opinion in France by abandoning the pope, he announced he would keep his troops in Rome and demanded that the Italian army intercept Garibaldi before he could reach papal territory.

The Italian government now found itself the victim of its own stratagem. Recognizing that it would be less dangerous to defy Italian patriotic opinion than confront France, it disavowed Garibaldi and yielded to Napoleon's demand to stop him.

On August 29 troops of the Italian regular army met Garibaldi's volunteers in the mountains of Aspromonte, deep in southern Italy. Garibaldi refused to fight against fellow Italians, but the Italian regular army commander had no such scruples. Although he had met with no resistance, he ordered his troops to open fire, killed several of Garibaldi's men, and severely wounded the general himself. Garibaldi was captured, charged with treason, but eventually amnestied and allowed to return to Caprera under protective custody.

Although Napoleon had stood firm over Rome in 1862, he was finding it increasingly difficult to defend the French occupation of Rome against Italian nationalist opinion. Eager to regain Italian goodwill, he concluded a treaty with the Italian government on September 15, 1864 (the September Convention), agreeing to withdraw French troops from Rome in return for an Italian pledge not to attack the papal state or allow it to be attacked by others, and to allow the formation of a papal volunteer army to maintain the secular authority of the pope against foreign intervention and domestic revolution. At the same time the Italian government agreed to shift the capital of the new kingdom from Turin to Florence, a move the French emperor was allowed to assume represented the permanent renunciation of Rome as the capital of Italy.

The Italian government, however, never had the slightest intention of renouncing Rome or observing the terms of the September Convention. In December 1866, on the very day the last French troops withdrew from Rome, King Victor Emanuel authorized a revival of the by now familiar plan to stir up revolution in Rome, which would provide an excuse for Italian troops to occupy the city to restore law and order. This plan gave way to a similarly familiar scheme to persuade Garibaldi to lead yet another volunteer army in another march on Rome; the Italian government would then send an army against him as though to live up to the terms of the September Convention but actually to occupy Rome and destroy the threat of Garibaldian radicalism at one blow.

Once again Garibaldi agreed to serve the Italian national cause. Early in October 1867 he was allowed to "escape" from Caprera and take command of a volunteer army that had been recruited in his name for an attack on Rome, now defended only by a papal mercenary force. The Italian government had scheduled its own army's invasion of papal territory for October 8.

This latest Italian plan for the takeover of Rome was also thwarted by Napoleon. Under no illusions about the reliability of the Italian government and well informed about Garibaldi's activities, he sent his own troops back to Italy to intercept Garibaldi and forestall an Italian occupation of Rome. On November 3, 1867, French forces easily defeated Garibaldi at Mentana. Garibaldi was again exiled to Caprera and French troops once again defended papal government in the Patrimony of St. Peter, where they remained until the outbreak of France's war with Prussia in July 1870.

❑ *The Acquisition of Venetia and Rome*

The final steps in the unification of Italy were more the result of Prussian military success than anything done by the Italians. On April 8, 1866, as tension between Austria and Prussia mounted in Germany (see p. 197 ff), Italy concluded a military alliance with Prussia which provided that Italy join Prussia in a war against Austria if that war broke out within three months; in the event of victory, Italy was to receive Venetia. This alliance had been arranged with the help of Napoleon, who hoped that a war between the major German states would so weaken them both as to create a power vacuum in central Europe which he could exploit to the benefit of France. He feared, however, that Austrian military strength, which he had learned to respect during the recent war in Italy, would prove so superior to that of Prussia that Austria would score a quick victory and thus remain sufficiently powerful to frustrate his own designs. Through the Italian alliance with Prussia he hoped to even the sides and thereby give himself greater leverage in dealing with all the belligerents.

The Italians, emboldened by their treaty with Prussia, began to make ostentatious preparations for war. So alarmed were the Austrians that France as well as Italy would take the side of Prussia in the event of war that they concluded a secret convention of their own with Napoleon on June 12, 1866, promising to cede Venetia whether Austria won or lost its war against Prussia. In return, Napoleon promised to observe strict neutrality and to bend every effort to persuade Italy to do the same. In the event of an Austrian victory, the Austrians promised to consult with France before making any changes in Germany that might disturb the European balance of power, and, verbally, they agreed not to oppose Napoleon's creation of a neutral buffer state along the Rhine that would in effect be a French satellite. The Italians, however, refused to back out of the Prussian alliance. They regarded the Austrian offer as a sign of weakness, they wanted the military glory of conquering Venetia, and by going to war they hoped to acquire not only Venetia but all other Austrian-controlled territory between the Alps and the Adriatic.

When the war between Austria and Prussia began in mid-June 1866, Italy entered on the side of Prussia. The Italians gained little by way of military glory, however. Their forces were defeated on land and sea, but thanks to Prussia's victory they acquired Venetia. A plebiscite held in Venetia under the supervision of Italian troops resulted in the customary overwhelming majority favoring incorporation into the kingdom of Italy.

The Franco-Prussian crisis in 1870 (see p. 210) seemed to offer a new opportunity for Italy to acquire the remaining Austrian-held territory south of the Alps. Certain that France would win if it came to war, King Victor Emanuel arranged a secret informal agreement with Napoleon III promising to enter the war on the side of France. In return, France was to support Italy in securing the Trentino and other frontier rectifications at the expense of Austria, which presumably was to be compensated at the expense of Prussia. If Switzerland took the side of Prussia, France was to support Italy's acquisition of the Swiss canton of Ticino as well. Because of the total unpreparedness of the Italian army when the Franco-Prussian war began in July 1870, Italy was unable to join France immediately and was thus spared any share in the French defeat.

As it was, Italy took advantage of the Franco-Prussian war to acquire Rome at last. Upon the outbreak of the war, Napoleon withdrew his troops from Rome. On September 4, 1870, his army was decisively defeated by the Prussians at Sedan, he was taken prisoner, and France was declared a republic. With the collapse of the imperial government, the Italians declared themselves free from all treaties concluded with that government and on September 20, a mere fortnight after Sedan,

Italian troops entered Rome. A plebiscite in October yielded the usual result, and on June 30, 1871, Rome at last became the capital of the new Italian national state.

Italy's acquisition of Rome did not put an end to the international complications arising from the Roman problem. The papacy refused to accept the loss of its temporal power and maintained an uncompromising hostility to the new national state. When in 1871 the Italian government tried to regulate its relations with the papacy by offering the pope and the Roman Catholic church certain guarantees, the pope denounced the proposals and refused to abandon his self-imposed imprisonment in the Vatican. He called upon Catholic powers of the world to help him regain his territories and ordered Italian Catholics to refrain from all participation in the affairs of the secular state. The pope received no direct support from abroad, and politically minded Catholics for the most part disregarded the prohibition on political activity, but the hostility of the papacy remained a constant danger and embarrassment as well as a critical factor in international diplomacy.

The Italian national question itself was not resolved with the acquisition of Venetia and Rome, for hardly had the major work of Italian unification been completed than Italian superpatriots began to clamor for the return of Nice and Savoy from France, for the cession by Austria of the Trentino, Trieste, and the Dalmatian coast, and for southern cantons of Switzerland, all of which they claimed for Italy on the grounds of nationality and which they regarded as territory yet to be redeemed (*Italia irredenta*). Nor were the ambitions of Italian nationalists confined to unredeemed territory, for they were soon to advocate a program of outright expansionism and became busily engaged in the international competition for colonies. Thus the Italians, like so many peoples before and since, had hardly gained their own freedom when they sought to establish their dominion over others.

The unification of Italy and the creation of the Italian national state did not seriously affect the European international equilibrium. Although Italian patriots confidently believed that with unification Italy had joined the ranks of the great powers, Italy did not possess the resources (or did not mobilize them sufficiently effectively) to develop the requisite military capacity. Consequently the established powers never regarded Italy, by itself, as a major threat to their national security or even a dangerous competitor in the colonial field. The British statesman Lord Salisbury expressed a common attitude with his comment that the Italians had such large appetites but such poor teeth. The Italians nevertheless possessed enough teeth to make them desirable as allies and distinctly dangerous as the allies of one's enemies, a position they were to exploit with considerable skill in selling their friendship to the highest bidders among rival greater powers.

Altogether different was the international reaction to the second of the major European national revolutions of the mid-nineteenth century: the unification of Germany and the creation of the German empire, which loomed as a major threat to the security of all the European powers from the moment of its establishment. Before dealing with that revolution, however, and for a fuller understanding of the reasons for its success, it is necessary to examine two quasi-contemporaneous crises in North America that were to have a significant bearing on events in Germany and were to be decisive for the future of the countries concerned: the American Civil War and the French imperialist venture in Mexico.

NINE

❑

The Great Powers and the American Civil War

❑ *The Coming of the War*

While the attention of the European powers focused on the Eastern Question, the problems of Italy, and the maintenance of the balance of power among themselves, the United States was engaged in a prodigious territorial expansion in North America. At the expense of the native Indian population, and through purchase, negotiation, and outright conquest, it acquired a substantial portion of the territorial claims of Britain, France, Spain, and Mexico. This territorial expansion was accompanied by massive economic development that by the mid-nineteenth century had made the United States the dominant power in the Western Hemisphere. Many Americans made no secret of their ambition to use their power to control the entire North American continent, as well as Cuba, the Hawaiian Islands, and other territories in the Caribbean and Pacific areas.

This seemingly inexorable process of American territorial expansion was halted, temporarily at least, not as a result of self-imposed restraint or an effective opposition, but because of profound political and economic differences between the northern and southern sections of the American Union, and of these differences by far the most important involved the question of slavery. Advocates of expansion in the southern slave states wanted to extend the institution of slavery into territories that might someday be annexed to the United States, whereas most expansionists in the northern nonslave states wanted to prevent its extension. This rift over slavery created a political stalemate over territorial expansion, with the result that after the American victory in the war with Mexico in 1848 the United States acquired no more territory before the outbreak of the Civil War with the exception of the Gadsden Purchase, a strip of land at the southern edge of present-day Arizona and New Mexico acquired from Mexico in 1853.

The victory of Abraham Lincoln, the candidate of the newly formed Republican party, in the presidential elections of November 1860 was the event that convinced leaders in the southern slave states that they had no alternative but to secede from the Union. The decisive issue for most southerners was the Republican threat to the institution of slavery, which many Republicans wished to see abolished alto-

147

MAP 6 *AMERICAN EXPANSION, THE CIVIL WAR, AND MEXICO*

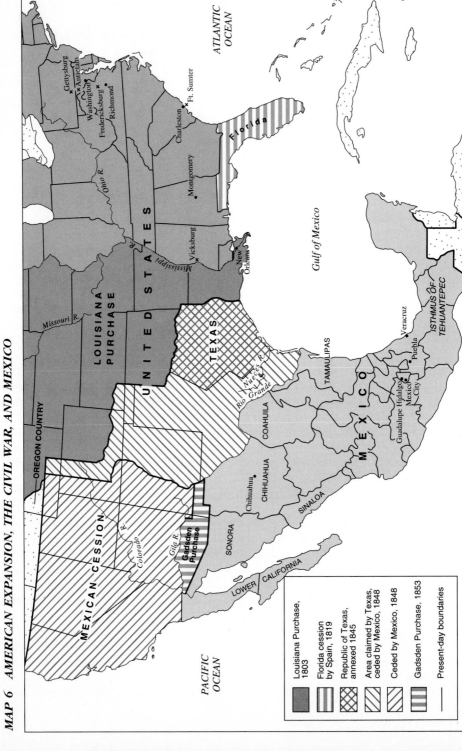

Legend:
- Louisiana Purchase, 1803
- Florida cession by Spain, 1819
- Republic of Texas, annexed 1845
- Area claimed by Texas, ceded by Mexico, 1848
- Ceded by Mexico, 1848
- Gadsden Purchase, 1853
- Present-day boundaries

gether, and the party's opposition to any extension of slavery in the territories. On December 20, 1860, southern delegates to a political convention in South Carolina voted unanimously to secede, and in February of the following year delegates of seven seceding states formed a provisional government for a new federal union they called the Confederate States of America. The secessionist states then proceeded to seize all federal forts, arsenals, and public buildings within their limits and laid siege to fortresses that refused to surrender to Confederate authorities. One of these strongholds was Fort Sumter, on an island in the bay of Charleston, South Carolina.

Lincoln took office in March 1861, and after almost a month of temporizing he finally authorized sending supplies to the beleaguered garrison of Fort Sumter. The Confederate government thereupon decided to attack the fort before federal supplies could arrive. At half past four on the morning of April 12, 1861, Confederate troops opened fire on Fort Sumter and therewith initiated hostilities that proved to be the beginning of four years of civil war.

❏ *The Issue of European Intervention*

Southern leaders had made the decision to secede from the Union in an emotional atmosphere of political passion, but their decision was also based on what they confidently believed to be political realities. They were convinced that southern forces, operating from interior defensive positions, could easily hold their own. They were also convinced that in the event of war Britain, and very probably France as well, would intervene or mediate on behalf of the South because of the dependence of their textile industries on southern cotton.

There can be no doubt that Anglo-French intervention would have affected the outcome of the war in America and might well have been decisive, especially if that intervention had taken place in the early stages of the conflict while northern troops were still inexperienced and northern industries were not yet fully geared to military production. The Anglo-French navies could have broken the northern blockade of southern ports, and the shipment of European supplies to southern armies, even without the active participation of European troops, might well have enabled the South to follow up its numerous early military victories with a decisive thrust into northern territory.

It is noteworthy that at no time during the Civil War was there any serious possibility that a European power would intervene on the side of the North or offer mediation that would have enabled the North to achieve its major war aim: the restoration of the Union. On the contrary, all available evidence indicates that if Britain and France had intervened at all, they would have done so on the side of the South. Even Anglo-French mediation would have favored the South, because any mediation efforts would have involved recognizing the independence of the Confederacy. So the diplomatic game was basically a struggle on the part of the North to persuade the European powers not to meddle in American affairs, and of the South to secure foreign mediation or active intervention.

Britain and France were the only European powers that might have intervened effectively, for they alone possessed fleets capable of breaking the northern blockade; and they alone possessed the industrial and financial resources which, if employed exclusively on behalf of the South, would have given the Confederacy its optimum opportunity for victory. French intervention, however, depended on Britain's attitude, because Napoleon III was convinced that he needed Britain's approval and cooperation to make intervention effective—and safe. The key player in the entire diplomatic game, therefore, was Britain.

Britain seemed to have compelling reasons for intervening on behalf of the South. An independent South would weaken an increasingly dangerous commercial and naval rival and establish a balance of power in North America comparable to the balance in Europe, which had safeguarded British security over the centuries. Such a balance might be presumed to bolster the security of Canada, for the northern states would no longer be able to threaten Canada without risking an Anglo-Confederate coalition and an invasion of their own territories from the south. Strategic considerations apart, a Confederate state that had gained its independence with the aid of Britain might be expected to be favorably disposed to that country and allow for a major extension of British political and economic influence in the Western Hemisphere.

The possibility of British intervention in America seemed all the greater because of the nature of the statesmen conducting British foreign policy in 1861. Lord Palmerston, the prime minister, had built his political reputation as a redoubtable champion of British interests in every part of the world. His foreign secretary was Lord John Russell (from July 1861, Earl Russell), a perennial political rival of Palmerston who could not afford to appear a less ardent advocate of British interests and who in fact saw eye to eye with his prime minister on many foreign policy issues.

Their official and private papers leave no doubt that both Palmerston and Russell saw clearly the potential advantages for Britain of an independent Confederacy, but the experience of the costly and inconclusive Crimean War had made them both far more conscious of the risks involved in bold diplomatic initiatives. Moreover, both understood the need to keep American affairs in European and global perspective, and they realized they could not invest any significant portion of British power in transatlantic enterprises so long as more critical British interests were at stake in areas closer to home. And in the course of the American Civil War British interests did seem threatened by crises in Italy, Poland, and Denmark—crises which Palmerston and Russell regarded as priorities and major motives for a policy of restraint in America.

Palmerston's diplomacy in dealing with the crisis in America was therefore fundamentally cautious, and despite frequent incidents that seemed to call for a more vigorous policy his government adhered to a cautious course. The potential political and economic gains of intervention in America were tempting, but throughout, the essential condition for intervention was a southern military victory so decisive that Britain could venture to mediate without serious risk. Robert Cecil, who as Lord Salisbury was to be several times foreign secretary and prime minister later in the century, summed up the British position succinctly to an American acquaintance: "There is one way to convert us all—win the battles, and we shall come round at once."

It has frequently been assumed that British policy during the American Civil War was strongly influenced by public opinion: that the British aristocracy tended to be sympathetic to the South, but that the working classes, including the textile laborers who suffered most severely from the cotton shortages caused by the Union blockade, resolutely supported the more democratic North and its crusade against slavery and were an important force in preventing intervention.

Scholarly investigations of British wartime opinion have demonstrated that such assumptions have been excessively simplistic. The British aristocracy and so-called upper classes were not necessarily sympathetic to the South and indeed showed little interest in the war as a foreign policy issue. As for the British workers, they exerted little direct political influence because most of them did not yet have the vote, but the belief that their sympathies were solidly with the North has been shown to be a myth deriving from the fact that many prominent political figures who purported to speak for labor were vociferous champions of the northern cause. The evidence about the feelings of the workers themselves shows that many of them, perhaps even a large majority, favored a southern victory, which they believed would best serve their own interests, and so strong did this sentiment appear to be—particularly among textile workers—that the government feared they would resort to violence to compel British intervention on the side of the South in order to obtain cotton.

Public attitudes are always difficult to evaluate, however, especially as they tend to fluctuate with disconcerting speed, and all that can be said with any confidence is that public opinion in Britain was not neatly divided along class lines and that there were broad differences of opinion among people of all classes when they thought about the war at all. There appears to have been widespread agreement on only one point: that Britain should not plunge once again into dubious overseas adventures; there should be no more Crimeas. Whatever influence public opinion did exert, therefore, was on behalf of the government's own policy of caution.

British economic interests, too, did not become the potent force for intervention that southern leaders confidently expected they would be. Virtually all segments of the British economy prospered greatly from the war in America. The war increased demand for British armaments and equipment of every kind, and with much of American industry diverted to military production the British moved into American markets for consumer goods as well. For British shipping the war was a veritable bonanza because it virtually eliminated the rapidly growing American competition, and much of the traffic formerly transported by the Americans was now transferred to British vessels. Even cotton shortages did not prove a serious blow. A bumper crop in 1860 had produced large stockpiles, so that there were no shortages during the critical early stages of the war. Even when acute shortages drove many small textile mills to the wall, the larger manufacturers were not seriously affected and some actually made handsome profits by disposing of their inventories at higher prices. Meanwhile alternative sources of cotton were being developed, notably in India and Egypt, which by 1863 had begun to produce ample yields.

In sum, British economic interests, far from favoring a policy of intervention with all its attendant risks and uncertainties, supported the government's policy of cautious neutrality.

❑ *The Opening Round of the Diplomatic War*

The diplomatic phase of the American Civil War began well before the outbreak of military hostilities. On March 16, 1861, the Confederate government sent three representatives on a diplomatic mission to Britain, France, Russia, and Belgium (whose king was believed to have great influence over Britain's Queen Victoria) to "negotiate treaties of friendship, commerce, and navigation." As an inducement for the European powers to enter into such treaties, they were to be offered almost tariff-free trade with the Confederacy (as compared with the high tariff policies of the North), an uninterrupted supply of cotton, and the prospect of a notable extension of their influence in the Western Hemisphere.

Initially, the British stance with respect to the crisis in America seemed to promise quick success for the Confederate mission. At approximately the same time this mission was sent abroad, Russell instructed the British minister to Washington, Lord Lyons, to warn Seward, the American secretary of state, that if British shipping were excluded from southern ports, Her Majesty's government would come under immense pressure to use all means in its power to open those ports, and "the most simple, if not the only way, would be to recognize the Southern Confederacy."

William Henry Seward, the American statesman primarily responsible for the conduct of Union diplomacy during the Civil War, was in his sixtieth year when he joined Lincoln's cabinet. Trained as a lawyer, he had been governor of New York and a United States senator, and he was a founder as well as leading member of the newly formed Republican party. He had acquired a reputation for social reform, but it was his opposition to slavery that made him an especially prominent, and controversial, political figure. A man of slight build but great physical energy, Seward was a shrewd and tough politician. He was to prove an equally shrewd and tough diplomat. His policies often seemed dangerously reckless, but this recklessness was part of the game of gamble and bluff he believed he must play to compensate for the weak hands he held, especially at the beginning of the war. It was a game he was to play with extraordinary success thanks to his own skill and flair—and a large measure of luck.

When he first took office in the midst of the prewar secession crisis, Seward was painfully aware of how vulnerable America was to foreign intervention, and he understood clearly the significance and danger of British warnings with regard to trade. Instead of adopting a conciliatory stance, however, he responded to British efforts to put diplomatic pressure on the United States by adopting a firm and even threatening posture of his own. The European governments had no legitimate right to intervene in the dispute in America, he told the British minister, and any move on their part to receive the representatives of the Confederacy would risk a severance of diplomatic relations with the United States.

While adopting this uncompromising stance toward Britain, Seward did not give up hope of bringing about a peaceful resolution of the secession crisis. Before the actual outbreak of hostilities, he conceived a daring plan to regain southern loyalty by a dramatic move in the field of foreign affairs that would drown domestic differences in a flood of patriotic fervor. Seward's plan, submitted to the president on April 1, proposed dire measures to deal with a dire political situation. The secretary feared, correctly as it proved, that the shipment of supplies to Sumter would provoke the South and lead to hostilities that would end all possibility of a peaceful settlement. The defense or evacuation of Sumter was not in fact a slavery or party question, Seward said, but it was regarded as such by both sides. He therefore recommended that the fort be abandoned "as a safe means for changing the issue," and that the administration change the question before the public from slavery, *the* major divisive issue, to that of Union or Disunion, "in other words, from what would be regarded as a party question, to one of patriotism." For that purpose Seward proposed diverting American public attention from quarrels at home by playing up the danger from abroad. On March 31 the news arrived in Washington that Spain had invaded its former colony of Santo Domingo, and that the French were preparing to invade Haiti, a former French colony. Seeing in this situation the opportunity he sought to restore American unity on the common denominator of patriotism, Seward advised that the U.S. government now throw down the gauntlet to Spain and France, demand explanations from those powers "categorically, at once," and if satisfactory answers were not received, convene Congress and declare war against them.

Seward's proposals were neither so foolhardy nor so desperate as they appear at first glance. He knew that his compatriots, with southerners prominent among them, had long coveted the island of Cuba, one of Spain's last possessions in the Western Hemisphere, and he therefore saw reason to hope that southerners could be lured back into the Union by the prospect of a war with Spain and the acquisition of Cuba. A war with Spain in the Western Hemisphere could be considered a relatively safe enterprise and a gamble well worth taking if it led to a restoration of the Union. It is doubtful whether Seward seriously considered a war against France as well. The possibility of a French invasion of Haiti was as yet only a rumor, and he may have intended to do no more than exploit the French threat to arouse American patriotic feeling.

Lincoln, however, did not act on his secretary's bold plan. Instead, he authorized the shipment of supplies to Fort Sumter, contrary to Seward's advice, a move that provoked southern leaders to take the fateful step that made war inevitable.

❑ *The Problems of Blockade and Recognition*

One of Lincoln's first acts in response to the South's attack on Fort Sumter was the proclamation of a blockade of southern ports. With that, Seward's most immediate problem in the field of foreign affairs was to deal with the objections the British and other foreign governments were certain to raise and to prevent attempts on the part of foreign powers to break the blockade or otherwise intervene in American affairs.

An international agreement on rules governing wartime naval blockades had been negotiated at the 1856 Paris peace conference that had ended the Crimean War. This so-called Declaration of Paris had been signed by all the powers represented at the conference, and all other states of the world had been invited to accede. The Declaration of Paris abolished privateering (the use by a country at war of privately owned warships to prey on enemy naval and merchant vessels); it provided that all enemy as well as neutral goods transported under a neutral flag were not liable to capture by belligerents unless these goods were contraband of war (contraband was not defined further, an omission that caused much difficulty later); and it required that a naval blockade, in order to be respected by neutral powers, must be effective and maintained by a force sufficient to prevent access to the coast of the enemy.

The United States had refused to accede to this agreement because it did not wish to relinquish the right of privateering, which had proved so valuable to Americans in earlier conflicts, but on April 24, five days after Lincoln's proclamation of a Union blockade of southern ports, Seward announced his government would become a signatory to the declaration. By this move, he hoped to gain international support for Union efforts to suppress privateering, which could now benefit only the Confederacy, and secure international recognition of the Union blockade. At the same time, he expected foreign powers to treat the war in America as a purely domestic conflict, an illegal insurrection against the legitimate government of the United States, and to deny the Confederacy the status of a belligerent. This last point was most important. According to international law, recognition as a belligerent meant recognizing the Confederacy's sovereign powers and its right to raise loans, purchase arms, or issue letters of marque (to private persons to operate as privateers) for purposes of war.

The great weakness of Seward's position was that he wanted international respect for the Union blockade, but at the same time he refused to admit the assumption on which such respect must rest, namely, the existence of a state of war and the recognition of the Confederacy as a belligerent.

It was an untenable position, and Seward was unable to defend it. When news of the declaration of the Union blockade reached London, the British cabinet agreed to adopt a policy of neutrality and to recognize the Confederacy as a belligerent, a decision announced publicly on May 13. Seward's greatest fear was that the recognition of the Confederacy's status as a belligerent might be the prelude to foreign recognition of Confederate independence. His apprehensions on this score were powerfully reinforced by news that the Confederate commissioners who had been sent to Europe to negotiate treaties of friendship and commerce with foreign powers were now in London, and Russell had informed them that he would not be unwilling to see them unofficially.

Seward responded to this information by resorting once again to threats. In a dispatch of May 21 he instructed Charles Francis Adams, the American minister to London, to inform the British government that intercourse of any kind with the so-called commissioners could be construed as recognition of the authority which appointed them, and that if Russell insisted on seeing the southern envoys, Adams was to break off all intercourse, official or unofficial, with the British government. Further, if the British actually accorded official recognition to the Confederacy, the American government would regard such an action as intervention with the intent of overthrowing the Republic and the result would be war with the United States.

Before Seward's dispatch was sent to London, Lincoln made one of his rare moves to intervene in the policy of his secretary of state by expunging some of Seward's offensive phrasing and directing Adams to regard the dispatch as a confidential instruction to himself that was not to be communicated officially to the British government. Evidently Seward recognized the inflammatory nature of his dispatch, and he endorsed the president's directive by marking it confidential, "not to be read or shown to the British secretary of state," and instructing Adams that none of its positions were to be made known "prematurely, unnecessarily, or indiscreetly."

Even so, Adams took a tough enough line when he saw Russell on June 12. He informed the British foreign secretary that his government had adopted a "very decided tone" with regard to Britain's recognition of the Confederacy as a belligerent, and that protracted relations with the "pseudo-commissioners" of the South "could scarcely fail to be viewed by us as hostile in spirit and to require some corresponding action accordingly."

Russell's response was thoroughly conciliatory. He admitted that he had seen the Confederate commissioners "some time ago" and "once more since then," but he assured Adams that he had "no expectation of seeing them any more."

❑ *The* Trent *Affair*

On September 23, 1861, the Confederate government, disappointed by the ineffectiveness of the three commissioners sent to Europe in the previous March, decided to send two new representatives ("special commissioners") to London and Paris with the assignment of securing British and French recognition of the Confederacy and persuading the governments of these countries to repudiate the Union blockade.

The new commissioners were James M. Mason of Virginia, a former chairman of the Senate Foreign Relations Committee, and John Slidell of Louisiana, a prominent New Orleans lawyer. The Confederate government considered the Mason-Slidell mission so important that it chartered a special light and fast steamer to run the Union blockade and take the envoys to Nassau or Havana, where they were to take passage to Europe on the vessel of a neutral country.

On the night of October 12 Mason and Slidell boarded their special steamer at Charleston. It successfully ran the blockade, and in Havana they transferred to the British mail steamer *Trent,* which was to take them to England. On November 8, shortly after leaving port, the *Trent* was stopped by the American warship *San Jacinto* under the command of Captain Charles Wilkes. Taking a broad interpretation of the definition of contraband of war, Wilkes seized the two southern envoys and their secretaries and returned them under arrest to the United States. This action aroused wild exultation in America, but in Britain the incident touched off an explosion of public fury and official indignation. Russell denounced it as "an act of violence . . . an affront to the British flag and a violation of international law," and Palmerston, disgusted with the tepid attitude of some of his colleagues in the cabinet, declared: "You may stand for this but damned if I will."

The incident also aroused the indignation of the French government—or at any rate provided an admirable occasion to exploit British anger for the purpose of initiating joint Anglo-French intervention in America. At a hastily convened cabinet meeting in Compiègne on November 28, Napoleon and his ministers resolved to back up the British in any protests they might make and let them know that France was prepared to recognize the Confederacy if the British government took the lead in doing so.

The British failed to provide that lead. The cabinet met on November 29 and 30 and decided to do no more for the present than address an ultimatum to Washington condemning "the act of violence against a neutral and friendly nation," and demanding the release of the prisoners and an official apology "for the insult offered the British flag." An accompanying letter to Lord Lyons, the British minister to Washington, instructed him to withdraw the British diplomatic mission if the Americans refused to comply. The drafts of both documents were then sent to Windsor to secure the approval of the queen. Here they were reviewed by the queen's consort,

Prince Albert, whose tactful rephrasing of the British demands has been regarded by contemporaries and historians alike as a major contribution to the eventual diffusion of the crisis. This was to be the prince's last official act, for he died of typhoid a fortnight later.

In his commentary on the cabinet drafts, the prince said the queen would like to see hope expressed that Wilkes had not acted under official instructions "or, if he did, that he misapprehended them." Her Majesty's government was unwilling to believe that the American government had intended wantonly to insult Britain and "we are therefore glad to believe that upon full consideration of the circumstances of the undoubted breach of international law committed, they would spontaneously offer such redress as alone could satisfy this country, viz. the restoration of the unfortunate passengers and a suitable apology."

The cabinet inserted the prince's revisions in the final dispatch sent to Washington. Russell, perhaps influenced by the spirit of moderation at Windsor but probably influenced even more by a growing awareness of the dangers of a war with America, was also more conciliatory. He instructed Lyons to prepare the ground tactfully before reading the British dispatch to Seward and to "abstain from anything like menace." He was not to threaten the withdrawal of the British legation, and Seward was to be told that the British government, although inflexible about the restoration of the envoys, was disposed to be "rather easy about the apology."

The British dispatch arrived in Washington on December 19, and in accordance with his instructions Lyons took great care to prepare Seward unofficially before informing him of his government's demands. His care was rewarded, for Seward expressed his gratitude for the minister's "friendly and conciliatory manner," and it was Seward who took the lead in advocating a conciliatory reply to the British demands when the Lincoln cabinet met on Christmas Day of 1861. After almost two days of debate, the cabinet agreed to the course recommended by Seward, and on December 26 the American secretary wrote to Lyons that the prisoners would be "cheerfully liberated." Seward conceded the main point at issue that Wilkes had erred in arresting the prisoners, but he also felt obliged to add that "if the safety of this Union required the detention of captured persons it would be the right and duty of this government to detain them." The British government did not fasten on this argument to revive the crisis and accepted the Seward letter as an adequate response to its demands.

On the afternoon of January 8, 1862, the news arrived in London confirming that Mason and Slidell were to be released. "Thank God," Lady Russell wrote to a friend. "I rejoice with all my heart and soul. John was delighted. He was *very* anxious to the last moment."

So completely did the release of the Confederate envoys close the *Trent* affair that by the end of January, when they finally arrived in Europe, the public had lost almost all interest in them.

❑ *Recognition and Mediation, January–October 1862*

With the arrival of Mason and Slidell in London and Paris, the mission of the Confederate commissioners sent to Europe in the previous March automatically came to an end. The new envoys now attempted to do what their predecessors had failed to accomplish, namely, persuade the British and French governments to grant official recognition to the Confederacy and break the Union blockade.

In Paris, Slidell heard the familiar story that Napoleon was prepared to recognize the Confederacy, but because of the overall situation in Europe he could not act unless Britain took the initiative. Slidell had no better luck with the blockade question. In talking with Thouvenel, Napoleon's foreign minister, he argued that France need not respect the blockade because it was ineffective and therefore did not meet the conditions of the Declaration of Paris. Thouvenel, however, who was far more dubious about the desirability of intervening than his sovereign, replied by posing the awkward question as to why, if the federal blockade were so ineffective, so little cotton had been shipped from southern ports to Europe. A principal reason for this paucity, as Slidell well knew, was that the South itself had held back shipments to cause a cotton famine that would compel European intervention, a policy that had backfired because it made the blockade appear effective and thus undercut the South's principal argument against its legality. Unwilling to admit that the South was deliberately withholding cotton, Slidell could only offer weakly that the mere existence of the blockade intimidated merchant vessels.

Mason was if anything even less successful in London. Russell agreed to see him unofficially (something of a concession in view of the risk of fresh altercations with the Americans), but the foreign secretary's attitude was so discouraging that Mason did not venture to press the question of recognition. He did insist on the illegality of the blockade, but his arguments on this matter were also futile, for shortly after seeing Mason, Russell sent a dispatch to Lyons in Washington reaffirming the British government's resolve to respect it. A blockade could be considered effective, he said, if "a number of ships" were stationed at the entrance to a port sufficient to prevent access to it "or create an evident danger of entering or leaving it." When Mason attempted to contest this interpretation as a violation of the Declaration of Paris, Russell refused to receive him.

As numerous commentators have pointed out, the British government took this position on the blockade question not only to avoid a break with the United States but because the British themselves had used the blockade to such effect in previous wars and did not wish to restrict its future effectiveness by an excessively narrow interpretation of its legality.

William S. Lindsay, a major British shipowner, member of parliament, and ardent supporter of the southern cause, used a different but equally futile tactic to prod his government into repudiating the Union blockade and granting diplomatic recognition to the Confederacy. Learning that Napoleon was sympathetic to such a policy, Lindsay crossed the channel and on April 11 and 13 was granted two interviews with the emperor. Napoleon made it clear that he did indeed favor the Confederacy. He told Lindsay that he had twice asked the British government to join France in repudiating the Union blockade; the British had not only refused but had betrayed his confidence by showing his notes to Seward, the American secretary of state. (Napoleon was to make this charge again, although Thouvenel consistently denied that such notes had ever been sent, and the British denied they had ever been received.) The emperor said he was still prepared to recognize the Confederacy but could do so only after Britain led the way. For the moment all he could do was authorize Lindsay to inform the British government yet again of his willingness to take joint action to break the Union blockade, and to convey this information as well to Lord Derby and Benjamin Disraeli, the leaders of the parliamentary op-position. "I do not want to be embarrassed by the forms and delays of diplomacy," the emperor concluded, "as I feel the necessity of immediate action."

This typical Napoleonic exercise in indirect diplomacy was a total failure. Lindsay was rebuffed not only by Palmerston and Russell but by opposition leaders. In refusing to see him, Russell informed Lindsay in writing, presumably also for the benefit of the French emperor, that the best way for two governments to communicate with each other was through their properly accredited official representatives.

Because Mason and Slidell seemed to be getting nowhere, Judah P. Benjamin, Confederate secretary of state since March 19, 1862, decided that more attractive incentives were required to encourage foreign intervention on behalf of the Confederacy. At his instigation the Confederate senate on April 18 authorized President Davis to arrange treaties with Britain, France, and Spain offering special trade privileges and other inducements to break the Union blockade. Believing that Napoleon would be most amenable to such offers, Benjamin had already instructed Slidell on April 12 to approach the French government with a proposal that amounted to outright economic bribery: the Confederate government would allow France to introduce its goods duty free and would make available approximately 100,000 bales of cotton to French vessels in certain designated ports at a price that would be the equivalent of a monetary subsidy of 12.5 million dollars—a sum sufficient to pay the cost of a French naval force to open the Confederate Atlantic and Gulf ports to French commerce. In other words, the French were to be persuaded to shoot their way into southern ports to break the blockade and obtain cotton.

Slidell, well aware that Thouvenel opposed more active French involvement in America, did not venture to speak to him about Benjamin's offer, and he was to hesitate until mid-July before presenting it to Napoleon. Thouvenel himself, however, although anxious to avoid the dangers of outright intervention, was eager to assist in ending the war in America so as to eliminate all need or temptation to intervene and regain France's access to southern cotton. Already in March he had instructed Mercier, the French minister to Washington, to canvass the prospects for mediation, and early in June he empowered his envoy to make a direct offer of French mediation to the American government as soon as he thought the moment opportune. That moment seemed to have come at the end of June 1862 with the Confederate victory in the Seven Days Battle, when Union forces advancing on Richmond were halted and forced to retreat beyond the Potomac.

On July 1, 1862, Mercier approached Seward to sound him out on the subject of mediation. The American secretary reacted as he had to all previous suggestions of European intervention by issuing dire warnings about the consequences of such a move. "Be assured that the Emperor can commit no graver error than to mix himself in our affairs," he said. "At the rumor alone of intervention all the factions will reunite themselves against you and even in the border states you will meet a resistance unanimous and desperate." Seward's threats were effective with France as with Britain. Mercier advised against offering French mediation for the present, but he remained convinced that the North had shot its bolt and that it would not be long before European intervention could be undertaken safely.

In France, news of the Seven Days Battle prompted advocates of intervention in America to encourage Slidell to make yet another effort to persuade the emperor to recognize the South and break the Union blockade, and they arranged for him to meet with the French ruler in Vichy on July 16. Napoleon told Slidell he believed France's own interests would be best served by keeping America united and powerful as a counterweight to Britain in the Western Hemisphere, but he confessed that his personal sympathies had always been with the South, "whose people are struggling for the principle of self-government, of which I am a firm and consistent advocate." As before, however, he would not act without Britain's cooperation. Britain had a deeper interest in the question than France, and he had no desire to take the lead in drawing Britain's chestnuts out of the fire.

Frustrated by Napoleon's continued procrastination, Slidell presented him with a new proposal, which he said he was making without instructions from his government. This was an offer of Confederate support for Napoleon's military expedition to Mexico to overthrow the republican government of President Benito Juárez and replace it with a conservative monarchical regime (see Chapter 10). Slidell was confident that his government would not regard such a regime with an unfriendly eye, for it too was interested in seeing a "respectable, responsible, and stable government established in that country." As the Lincoln government was the ally and protector of Juárez, Slidell assured Napoleon that "we can have no objection to make common cause with you against the common enemy." With that Slidell renewed the plea for prompt French recognition of the Confederacy. By doing so France would encourage the forces working for peace in the North and secure for itself a faithful ally, bound not only by ties of gratitude but by the more reliable bonds "of a common interest and congenial habits."

It was during this interview of July 16 that Slidell, to stimulate the emperor's interest in the Confederate cause still further, presented him with Benjamin's bribe offer of cotton at a price that would subsidize a French naval expedition to break the northern blockade. Slidell expressed confidence that this would be a simple matter for the French navy, and that the French ironclads could not only break the blockade but pass the fortifications of New York, Boston, and the Chesapeake and lay the northern coastal cities under tribute.

With the consent of the emperor, Slidell on July 24 submitted a formal request for recognition to the French government. It included all the promises of economic gain Slidell had already presented to the emperor but stressed above all the political advantages for France of an independent Confederacy. Such a state would create a balance of power in North America that would put an end to further American annexation of alien territory—an obvious reference to Mexico and a recasting of Slidell's argument that the success of Napoleon's Mexican venture was linked to the fate of the Confederacy.

Meanwhile in Britain, William S. Lindsay, who had talked with Napoleon the previous April on the subject of recognition, introduced in Parliament a motion on behalf of British mediation, which was debated on July 18. Palmerston appealed to the House to leave such a delicate matter in the hands of the cabinet, and Lindsay withdrew his motion. Napoleon, however, read about the debate on the following day and, with the arguments and inducements of Slidell freshly before him, he sent a telegram to his foreign minister Thouvenel, who was briefly in London. "Ask the English government if they don't think the time has come to recognize the South." Unfortunately for the cause of the Confederacy, Napoleon's telegram arrived after

Thouvenel had returned to Paris, but even if the telegram had reached him in London, it is doubtful whether he could or would have done anything to influence British policy. For Thouvenel differed with his sovereign about the desirability of intervention, and the British still adhered to a policy of cautious neutrality. On July 24, just a week after Thouvenel left London, Mason presented the British government with a formal request for recognition (in conjunction with Slidell's formal request to France), which Russell turned aside by simply refusing to see him. The time had not yet come for recognition, Russell explained later, because of the "fluctuating events of the war."

Soon afterward, however, the fortunes of war seemed to be shifting sufficiently in favor of the South to persuade British leaders, too, to give serious thought to mediation. In late July Palmerston confided to Russell his belief that Britain would gain from the separation of North and South (one of his rare expressions of opinion to this effect), and at approximately the same time Gladstone, the chancellor of the exchequer, told his wife that the prime minister had come around to his own view about the desirability of "some early representations of a friendly kind to America, if we can get France *and* Russia to join."

The prospects of Russian participation in any meaningful Anglo-French mediation effort were very slim (in Russia, memories of the Crimean War still rankled, and the Russians remained grateful for America's sympathetic support during that conflict), but the British government nevertheless initiated plans for mediation. The "fluctuating events of the war" seemed to favor an armistice proposal, for in late August the Union army suffered another crushing defeat in the Second Battle of Bull Run, and early in September Confederate forces began an invasion of Maryland. Palmerston commented that the Federals had "got a very complete thrashing," and, with Confederate armies threatening both Washington and Baltimore, he believed the Lincoln government would now be willing to consider an Anglo-French recommendation of "an arrangement upon the basis of separation."

Russell, heretofore reluctant to undertake any kind of intervention, now agreed with Palmerston that the time had come to offer mediation to the U.S. government "with a view to the recognition of the independence of the Confederates." He also agreed that in the event of American rejection Britain should recognize the Confederacy forthwith. Russell proposed that a cabinet meeting be convened on October 23 or 30: "We ought then, if we agree on such a step, propose it first to France, and then on the part of England and France to Russia and the other powers."

Palmerston approved these plans and suggested only that it might be well to secure Russian participation from the start. If the Federals sustained another great defeat, they might be prepared to accept mediation and the European powers should be ready to strike while the iron was hot.

The Federals, however, did not sustain another great defeat, at least not immediately, for on September 17 they stopped the Confederate drive into Maryland at Antietam. The Battle of Antietam has been described as a critical turning point in the diplomatic history of the war, but it is by no means certain that a southern victory would have led to European intervention. Within the British cabinet there was strong opposition to any departure from a policy of strict neutrality. Russia's participation had not been secured and there was little prospect that it would be unless the North suffered a catastrophic military debacle, in which case Russia presumably would act to safeguard northern interests. Even Napoleon III, heretofore willing and even eager to intervene if only Britain would take the initiative, now showed decidedly less interest in doing so. It was not primarily the Battle of Antietam that had dampened his enthusiasm, however, but a new crisis in Italy—Garibaldi's effort in August 1862 to "liberate" Rome, where French troops supported the government of the pope. In addition, the volatile emperor also appears to have been suspicious of Britain's sudden interest in intervention, fearing that the British would leave him in the lurch once they had lured him into an active policy in America. Whatever his reasons for caution, Napoleon did not react to British soundings about joint mediation until the end of October, and by that time the British had all but abandoned their mediation plans.

The Battle of Antietam definitely dimmed Palmerston's interest in intervention: he had always thought that mediation should be offered only when the North was truly crushed, and Antietam had demonstrated that this condition had not yet been fulfilled. On October 22 he wrote to Russell that he had now "very much come back to our original view of the matter, that we must continue to be lookers-on till the war should have taken a more decided turn." By the end of October, when Napoleon at last responded to Britain's mediation proposal, only two members of the cabinet, Russell and Gladstone, still favored mediation, and they found themselves powerless to keep the issue alive.

❑ *The Emancipation Proclamation and the French Mediation Initiative of October 1862*

On September 22, 1862, five days after the Battle of Antietam, Lincoln issued a preliminary proclamation on the question of the emancipation of the slaves in America, declaring that all slaves in states that were still in rebellion by January 1, 1863, should be free as of that date.

Contrary to the assumption that the attitude of European governments toward the war in America was profoundly influenced by the Lincoln proclamation, the reaction of these governments suggests that it had no serious impact on official policy. Palmerston, who for years had promoted international agreements to abolish slavery and the slave trade, dismissed Lincoln's proclamation as "trash" and evidently regarded it as nothing more than a propaganda ploy. Russell was similarly unimpressed. When the final Emancipation Proclamation was issued on January 1, 1863, he observed that it did not emancipate slaves in any areas controlled by Union forces, where it might have been put into effect, and he concluded that "there seems to be no declaration of principle adverse to slavery in this proclamation."

In general, the immediate international effect of Lincoln's proclamation appears to have been negligible, with the exception of one case at least in which it might have proved dangerously counterproductive. Mercier, the French minister in Washington, regarded the proclamation as an act of desperation, "atrocious in the intent it reveals and the consequences it might entail"; he believed it would lead to anarchy, carnage, and crimes too horrible to mention. He therefore urged his government to make a formal mediation proposal that would end the war. If the European governments failed to take such action, Mercier warned, a successful slave uprising in America could be expected to ignite similar uprisings among Europe's own subject populations. Even if no such uprising took place, the abolition of slavery would destroy the southern economic system, and thus render permanent the cotton shortages that were already having such dire effect on the British and French textile industries.

Whether in response to Mercier's warnings or to the British government's soundings about mediation in the previous month, the French government initiated a mediation proposal of its own on October 30, 1862. This was done in the form of two notes to Britain and Russia calling for the three powers to submit a joint proposal to the American belligerents for a six-month truce and the suspension of the Union blockade.

Two days earlier Napoleon had discussed this mediation plan with Slidell. "We can urge it on the high grounds of humanity and the interest of the whole civilized world," the emperor said. "If it be refused by the North, it will afford good reason for recognition, and perhaps more active intervention." At the same time the emperor revealed his anxieties about the dangers of such a move. There were serious complications in Europe involving not only Italy but Greece, where the king had just been deposed following a military revolt, and there was reason to fear that Britain would leave France in the lurch in the event of trouble with the United States. To overcome the emperor's hesitations, Slidell expressed his confidence that the ironclads of the French navy could easily destroy the entire Union blockading fleet, and he reminded Napoleon of the political and economic advantages for France of an independent Confederacy, not the least of which would be Confederate support for France's Mexican venture.

The October 30 notes to Britain and Russia were drawn up by Napoleon's new foreign minister, the veteran statesman Drouyn de Lhuys, who had replaced Thouvenel earlier in the month following differences between the emperor and Thouvenel over France's Italian policy. Drouyn, however, agreed with his predecessor about the desirability of avoiding further French involvement in America. He may therefore have deliberately avoided saying anything in his notes about recognizing the Confederacy or any other steps the three powers might take if their mediation proposal were rejected, as it certainly would be by the North (barring truly catastrophic northern military reverses) because an armistice and suspension of the blockade would operate to the almost exclusive benefit of the South.

In view of Napoleon's own fears about intervention, there is also some reason to wonder whether the French proposal was a serious mediation effort at all, or whether it was primarily an attempt to convince French public opinion of the emperor's humanitarian concern and the seriousness of his endeavors to end the cotton crisis. The theory that the proposal was aimed primarily at French public opinion is supported by the fact that Drouyn published it before receiving a reply from London and that he subsequently published the negative British and Russian replies, which seemed to prove these powers were to blame for the failure of imperial mediation efforts.

Whatever Napoleon's real intentions may have been, and it is probable that they were typically ambiguous, his proposal never had any chance for success. The Russians said they were prepared to give unofficial support to any plan that might restore peace but refused to collaborate in any joint mediation effort. And the British cabinet, although it discussed the French proposal for two days (November 11 and 12), finally decided to inform the French that overtures would best be postponed until better prospects existed for their acceptance.

Drouyn was in no way dismayed and was very probably relieved by the Anglo-Russian rejection of the French proposal. Upon receiving the British reply he informed Mercier in Washington that France too was resuming its previous passive attitude.

❑ *Ships for the Confederate Navy*

Besides the threat to the Union of European mediation or intervention, the most serious diplomatic problem of the American Civil War developed as a result of the efforts on the part of Confederate agents to arrange for the purchase or construction of warships in Britain and France. These efforts had plagued Union relations with those countries since the beginning of the war, and if the South had been successful in securing a substantial number of naval vessels, or even one or more of the most powerful European ironclads, the course of the war might have been significantly altered.

Since the Crimean War, when ironclad warships (little more than floating batteries) were first used, Britain and France had developed screw-propelled ironclads that were much faster, more heavily armed, and with greater firepower than either the *Monitor* or the *Merrimack,* the first ironclads of the Union and Confederate navies, which in any case did not see action until almost a year after the war had begun. Because the Union navy at the beginning of the war consisted entirely of wooden warships, Confederate leaders saw in the European ironclads an ideal instrument to counter the Union's overwhelming naval superiority. Stephen M. Mallory, the Confederate secretary of the navy, believed the possession of an ironclad to be a matter of the first necessity, and very shortly after the attack on Fort Sumter he sent agents to Britain and France to purchase warships of the *Gloire* class, the largest and most powerful French ironclad. "Such a vessel at this time" he said, "could traverse the entire coast of the United States, prevent all blockades, and encounter, with a fair prospect of success, their entire navy." Mallory's estimate of the effectiveness of such vessels was certainly exaggerated, but considering the success of the Confederacy's unwieldy *Merrimack* in sinking Union blockade vessels before being halted by the *Monitor,* there can be little doubt that in the early stages of the war at least a Confederate navy equipped with European ironclads would have been able to wreak havoc on the Union blockade.

Fortunately for the Union, the Confederacy found it impossible to purchase European ironclads that were already built and ready for active duty. The British and French had placed legal restrictions on their sale, and the governments of these countries, deeply suspicious of each other, wanted to retain these vessels for their own navies. Confederate agents were not only interested in ironclads, however, but were eager to acquire vessels of every kind capable of running the Union blockade and preying on Union commerce.

In the end, Confederate agents had remarkably little to show for their efforts thanks in large part to Union diplomatic pressure on Britain and France and their governments' decision not to risk a major breach with the United States while the outcome of the war was still in doubt. In June and August 1861, the Confederacy contracted for the construction of two wooden screw-propelled steamers in Liverpool. They managed to slip out of British waters in the following year, thereby evading the British law forbidding the outfitting on British territory of any vessel intended for use by belligerents against a state with which Britain was at peace. One of these vessels, the *Alabama,* was to terrorize Union shipping over the next two years until it was sunk by a Union warship off Cherbourg in June 1864. The exploits of the *Alabama* set off an ugly Anglo-American diplomatic and legal controversy that was to continue for another ten years, when American claims for damages caused by the Confederate raider were at last settled by international arbitration, which awarded the United States fifteen million dollars in compensation.

Even while the *Alabama* was being built, Confederate agents were negotiating for the construction of warships that were a far greater potential danger to the Union than the *Alabama* could ever be. These included two large ironclads with a steel prong at the bow designed to pierce wooden ships below the water line (the so-called Laird rams), to be produced by the Laird company of Birkenhead, near Liverpool; and an ironclad larger than both Laird rams, which would match in size, speed, and armament the finest ships of the British and French navies and be more powerful than any vessels of the Union, to be produced by the firm of James and George Thompson of Glasgow.

These ironclads never reached the Confederacy. To evade British law, they were sold to a French firm that purported to be acting as agent for the government of Egypt. This transfer of ownership fooled no one, and in September 1863, to avoid a crisis with the United States, Russell, the British foreign secretary, ordered their detention. Confederate agents had no better luck in France, where by this time Napoleon too was anxious to avoid a crisis with the United States. One French-built ironclad, the *Stonewall,* was eventually sold to the Confederacy via Denmark, but the vessel proved unseaworthy and arrived in American waters too late to take part in the war.

Thus the danger to the Union cause that would have resulted had the Confederacy succeeded in acquiring British or French ironclads never materialized. How much greater that danger would have been, however, had Britain and France brought their own navies into the conflict on the side of the South.

❏ *The French Mediation Initiative of January 1863 and the Roebuck Motion*

In January 1863, one month after the serious Union defeat in the Battle of Fredericksburg, Napoleon launched yet another mediation proposal to end the war in America. To circumvent the objections to his previous proposal of a military armistice and suspension of the Union blockade, which so greatly favored the South, he now suggested that peace negotiations be conducted while hostilities continued, an essential condition if the North were to be persuaded to negotiate at all. In making this new proposal, he again appears to have had the additional purpose of currying favor with French public opinion, for his foreign minister, Drouyn de Lhuys, leaked the news of this latest imperial mediation effort to the press before it reached America and then published the details "to dispel false rumors." What Drouyn did not leak to the press was a typically grandiose Napoleonic scheme to resolve the American problem by establishing a confederation of American states consisting of four roughly equal parts—the North, South, West, and Mexico. Creating such a balance of power in North America would curb the imperialist tendencies of both North and South and allow for the expansion of a French-controlled Mexico to include Texas and at least part of the former French colony of Louisiana.

Seward flatly rejected Napoleon's proposal, as he had rejected all previous European interventionist efforts, and with that there was nothing Napoleon could do to further his mediation plan short of throwing all caution aside and joining forces with the Confederacy, as Confederate agents and supporters of his Mexican venture had long been urging him to do. Napoleon, however, still refused to intervene in America unless Britain led the way. And then, almost immediately after launching his mediation proposal of January 1863, his attention was diverted by the outbreak of another revolution against Russian rule in Poland and the resulting international crisis in Europe (see pp. 386–391).

The Polish crisis put an end to any further mediation efforts European governments might have made during the early months of 1863. The only direct consequence of that crisis for America was Russia's decision to send ships of its Baltic and Pacific fleets to New York and San Francisco, where they would be immune to blockade in case of a European war. Although Seward and other northern leaders correctly interpreted the purpose of the Russian "mission" to North America, American public opinion regarded the arrival of Russian ships in September and October 1863 as a gesture of friendship and support for the Union cause, which enhanced the cordial relations that already existed between the United States and Russia.

The Polish crisis did not divert all European attention from America or end efforts of partisans to aid the Confederate cause. Late in May 1863 John Arthur Roebuck, a British member of parliament and something of a political loner, gave notice that he intended to introduce a motion in the House of Commons to accord official recognition to the Confederacy. A discussion of the motion was set for June 30.

The Roebuck motion proved to be of little significance in itself, but at the time the Americans regarded the affair as one of the most serious threats of foreign intervention they had yet faced.

Disturbed by a rumor circulating in Britain that Napoleon no longer favored recognition of the South, Roebuck and another member of parliament went to France to ask the emperor personally about his views on the subject. Napoleon assured them that the rumor was false and, further, that he had instructed his representative in London to sound out the British government on the question of joint recognition. Napoleon's initiative appears to have been sabotaged by his foreign minister, Drouyn de Lhuys, who was dubious about recognition; the emperor's instruction to London has never been found. In any case, Roebuck and his colleague, upon their return to England, informed fellow members of parliament about Napoleon's approach to their own government. When questioned in the House of Commons, however, Russell, the British foreign secretary, denied that a formal recognition proposal had ever been received from Paris. Confronted with this denial, Roebuck was made to look ridiculous, and the debate on his motion was a disaster for him personally and for the Confederate cause.

The Roebuck motion represented the last effort on the part of parliamentary supporters of the South in Britain to secure official recognition for the Confederacy, but by this time their efforts were doomed in any case. For even as the motion was being debated in Parliament, the fortunes of war had turned against the Confederacy. On July 4, 1863, the South suffered defeats at both Gettysburg and Vicksburg, ending all possibility that it might score the decisive military victory that all along had been the prime condition for Anglo-French intervention.

Soon afterward the Confederate government acknowledged that the diplomatic game, at least in Britain, was lost. For early in August, Benjamin, the Confederate secretary of state, wrote to Mason, his representative in London, that the recent parliamentary debates in Britain had convinced him the British government would reject all overtures to recognize the Confederacy, and he authorized Mason to leave London. Two months later the Confederacy severed all relations with Britain when Benjamin expelled the British consuls on Confederate territory (who had never ceased being accredited to the federal government) for challenging the authority of the Confederate government, in particular the right of the Confederacy to conscript British subjects.

The last hope of the Confederacy for obtaining European support now rested in Napoleon and his need for an ally for his Mexican venture.

❑

TEN

The Great Powers and Mexico: Napoleon III's Grand Design

❑ *The Napoleonic Idea*

In retrospect, certainly from the vantage point of the United States, Napoleon III's attempt to establish a monarchy in Mexico under French auspices was the most unrealistic and quixotic of that visionary's many grandiose schemes. But even from the point of view of his own time and country, it remains a cardinal example of a statesman's failure to make a sound evaluation of his country's vital national interests and to concentrate his attention and his country's resources on the defense of those interests.

Napoleon was well aware that France's vital interests lay in Europe, but with an exaggerated conception of the power of France and its imperial mission, he aspired not only to regain France's position as the dominant power in Europe but to recoup its overseas losses and become once again a predominant global power. In Europe, he sought to break up the international treaty system established after the defeat of the first Napoleon to recover France's freedom of action, and for this purpose he encouraged and supported nationalist revolutions in Italy and much of central and eastern Europe. But then, in the midst of European crises he himself had done so much to foment, he turned his attention and a substantial amount of his country's military resources to regain a major French sphere of influence in the Western Hemisphere by setting up a French satellite empire in Mexico.

Napoleon's Grand Design for Mexico was inspired by what was for him a typical mixture of motives: idealistic altruism, materialist calculation, and imperial ambition. And his decision to plunge into this enterprise in particular came of a similarly typical blend of personal characteristics: opportunism, adventurism, wishful thinking, and failure to perceive the difficulties and potential consequences of his policies.

Napoleon had long been fascinated by Mexico as a land of vast natural resources and economic opportunity which, as he saw it, needed only enlightened leadership to become a veritable cornucopia. For years he had also dreamed of building a canal even more ambitious than the one currently being built under French auspices across the Isthmus of Suez—a waterway that would span Mexico's Isthmus of Te-huantepec, connecting the Atlantic and Pacific oceans.

In 1861 the outbreak of civil war in the United States seemed to offer a golden and possibly unique opportunity for France to provide the enlightened leadership Napoleon believed the Mexicans needed, for that war immobilized the United States's capacity to defend the Monroe Doctrine and oppose new European involvement in the Western Hemisphere.

To his credit, Napoleon did not share the general European and American contempt for the Mexicans as a degenerate Indian–Negroid bastardization of the Spaniards. Instead he saw them as a bastion of the Latin race and the Roman Catholic religion in the Western Hemisphere whose nationality and religion were increasingly threatened by the Anglo-Saxon Protestant forces in the north. If the Mexicans were not given strong government soon, they would inevitably fall victim to the expansionist ambitions of the United States. Further, Napoleon believed that France, as the world's greatest Latin power, should be the natural protector not only of the Mexicans but of all the peoples of Latin America. With a French-sponsored government in Mexico capable of resisting Anglo-Saxon imperialism, these peoples too would look to France for leadership. Thus Mexico would serve as a nucleus for the spread of French influence over the entire southern sector of the Western Hemisphere.

Napoleon had considerable reason to feel confident that the French and his own government could provide the guidance and support he believed the Mexicans needed. France itself could offer economic and technical assistance of the highest order. His own government had given France political stability and the country had flourished under the stimulus of his innovative and imaginative economic programs. Napoleonic leadership and French enterprise could be expected to perform similar services for Mexico.

While bestowing the benefits of French government and civilization on the Mexicans, Napoleon would at the same time be giving the French an opportunity to reap bounteous benefits for themselves. Acquiring Mexico would make the resources of that country available to French commerce and industry, create an immense new market for French products, and provide a new source of cotton for French textile manufacturers to compensate for the supplies cut off by the Civil War in the United States.

The economic advantages envisaged by Napoleon were dreams of the future based on exaggerated estimates of Mexico's natural resources and economic potential. As yet French trade with Mexico amounted to only a small fraction of France's total overseas commerce, and Mexican debts to French subjects were a negligible part of French investments abroad. Collecting these debts eventually served as the immediate pretext for French intervention in Mexico and was therefore played up as a big issue at the time. But satisfying French bondholders never figured prominently among Napoleon's motives for intervention and was never a compelling necessity for his government from either a political or economic point of view.

In his thinking about Mexico, Napoleon was unquestionably correct in several major assumptions: the Mexican political situation was unstable, the economic situation chaotic; there could be no doubt that Mexico's political independence and territorial integrity were threatened by the expansionist ambitions of the United States. His great mistakes were his failure to realize that the Mexican people would not necessarily welcome French control or to understand that American opposition to anyone else's expansionist ambitions in the Western Hemisphere was uncompromising.

❑ *The Mexican Political Situation*

In December 1857 the chronic political instability in Mexico developed into an outright civil war between Mexican conservatives and the reform government of Benito Juárez, whose program to secure a more equitable distribution of wealth among the Mexican people had aroused such hostility and fear among conservatives as to drive them into open rebellion. The Mexican civil war (the War of the Reform) ended in December 1860, the eve of the Civil War in America, with the triumph of the Juárez government, which had been accorded official recognition by the United States in April of the previous year.

As is the case with most civil wars, that in Mexico was conducted with vicious brutality on both sides, intensifying the political hatreds among the Mexican people and creating further chaos in an already chaotic economic situation.

Besides the devastation wrought by the conflict in Mexico itself, the civil war had two significant international consequences. The first resulted from the heavy borrowing of both sides from abroad, and although each side warned foreign investors not to purchase bonds issued by the other, foreigners bought them anyway, tempted by high rates of interest and confident that their governments would enforce payment of Mexican debts no matter which side won. The second resulted from the flight abroad of large numbers of conservatives and persons of property, who denounced the atrocities of the liberals in eloquent detail and appealed for European intervention to save their country from political, economic, and religious anarchy. The actual influence of these Mexican refugees may have been exaggerated by contemporaries and historians alike, but there can be no doubt that they contributed to several serious European misconceptions about the Mexican political situation: a belief that the majority of Mexican people opposed the Juárez regime; that his government was as weak as it was tyrannical and godless; and that the mere appearance of European troops in Mexico would be sufficient to inspire a popular uprising among the Mexican people to overthrow Juárez and establish a politically and fiscally responsible government under conservative leadership.

This picture of Mexico produced by the wishful thinking and willful distortions of Mexican refugees was endorsed by the representatives of European governments and business enterprises in Mexico, most of them as eager as the refugees for European intervention to protect their political and economic interests. Their dire predictions about the financial consequences of Juárez's rule seemed confirmed when, on July 17, 1861, the Mexican government issued a decree suspending payment on all foreign debts for a period of two years. This decree was to provoke British, French, and Spanish intervention in Mexico, a tripartite action that set the stage for Napoleon's far more ambitious program to realize his Grand Design.

❑ *The American Threat*

One of the principal arguments put forward by Napoleon and all other advocates of European intervention in Mexico was that such intervention alone could save

Mexico from being absorbed by the United States. In light of the historical record of Mexican–American relations, this was a valid argument indeed.

American expansionists had agitated for the acquisition of Mexican territory while Mexico was still part of the Spanish empire. This agitation did not cease after Mexico became independent. In 1835 American colonists in Texas rebelled against Mexican rule, and on March 1, 1845, Texas was officially annexed to the United States, an annexation delayed by debate over the slavery question. War between the United States and Mexico began just over a year later and ended on February 2, 1848, with the Treaty of Guadalupe Hidalgo, whereby the Mexicans recognized the American annexation of Texas with the Rio Grande as its southern boundary. In addition, the Mexicans relinquished their claims to all territory north of the Rio Grande, which constitutes part of present-day Colorado, New Mexico, and Oklahoma, as well as Texas; and they ceded Upper California and New Mexico, which included not only present-day New Mexico but Arizona, Nevada, Utah, and the western sector of Colorado. In return the United States agreed to pay Mexico $15 million and to assume claims of American citizens amounting to another $3.25 million.

Substantial as were these territorial gains, they were not enough to satisfy the aspirations of many Americans. President Polk, for instance, thought it might have been possible to acquire Lower as well as Upper California together with the Isthmus of Tehuantepec and the provinces north of the Sierra Madre, and he was one of many American expansionists who envisaged an American takeover of all of Mexico. With the exception of the Gadsden Purchase, however (see p. 147), the Americans acquired no more Mexican territory.

The major obstacle to further American expansion at the expense of Mexico was the bitter division among Americans over the issue of slavery: Should new U.S. territories be slave or free? Many Americans were nevertheless confident that they would soon find it possible to acquire more Mexican territory, and they were not unhappy to observe the growing political tension in Mexico developing as a result of the liberal reform program.

In April 1857 John Forsyth, the American minister to Mexico, drew the attention of Lewis Cass, the American secretary of state, to the weakness and apparent instability of the Mexican government. If Mexico could not sustain itself without the support of some friendly power, Forsyth asked, which power should provide this service, a European country or the United States? "I answer unhesitatingly the United States, by every consideration of humanity, good neighborhood, and sound policy." Forsyth acknowledged that he was "of course" a believer in America's manifest destiny. "In other words I believe in the teachings and experience of history, and that our race, I hope our institutions—are to spread over this continent and that the hybrid races of the West, must succumb to, and fade away before the superior energies of the white man."

In February 1857 Forsyth arranged an economic treaty with Mexico which provided for an American loan secured by a mortgage on Mexican land. As Forsyth acknowledged frankly, the treaty was intended to "pave the way" for future American territorial acquisitions. This way-paving was evidently not a fast enough process for Secretary of State Cass, who in July 1857 instructed Forsyth to negotiate the purchase of Lower California, the northern provinces of Sonora and Chihuahua, as well as transit rights across the Isthmus of Tehuantepec—Napoleon III was not alone in perceiving the potential strategic and economic importance of this area.

With the outbreak of outright civil war in Mexico, Forsyth no longer saw any reason to negotiate and instead advocated an even more forthright policy. "You want Sonora?" he wrote to Cass on April 15, 1858.

> The American blood spilled near its line would justify you seizing it. . . . You want other territory? Send me the power to make an ultimate demand for the several millions Mexico owes our people for spoliations and personal wrongs. . . . You want the Tehuantepec transit? Say to Mexico, "Nature has placed that shortest highway between two oceans, so necessary to the commerce of the world, in your keeping. . . . You cannot be permitted to act as the dog in the manger. . . . Give us what we ask for in return for the manifest benefits we propose to confer upon you for it, or we will take it."

The Mexicans were evidently blind to these manifest benefits, and in May 1858, frustrated by the absence of any government with which he thought he could do business, Forsyth broke off diplomatic relations with Mexico on his own initiative.

Although the American government did not endorse his proposals, Forsyth was not alone in his views about U.S. policy toward Mexico. In his message to Congress of December 1858, President Buchanan warned the European powers that the United States owed itself the duty to protect Mexico's territorial integrity against the hostile interference of other countries. Then, with what the Europeans must have seen as a magnificently American disregard for consistency, he asked Congress to allow him to "assume a temporary protectorate over the northern provinces of Chihuahua and Sonora."

Early in 1859 the American government sent Robert M. McLane as minister to Mexico with instructions to recognize any government "which exercises general authority over the country, and is likely to maintain itself." McLane was given discretionary powers, but he was left in no doubt that Washington favored the cause of Benito Juárez. Once diplomatic relations had been established, McLane was to offer ten million dollars for Lower California, double the price suggested by Cass in 1857. Shortly after his arrival in Mexico, McLane recognized the Juárez government, a significant diplomatic success for Juárez because the majority of European states favored the Mexican conservative party.

American recognition did not come cheaply, for on December 14, 1859, Juárez's foreign minister, Melchior Ocampo, found it necessary to agree to a treaty with McLane which in effect reduced Mexico to the status of an American protectorate. By the terms of the McLane–Ocampo treaty, the United States was granted duty-free transit rights across Mexico via three major highways, with the safety of all persons and property transported over these highways to be guaranteed by the Mexican government. If the Mexican government found itself unable to provide such protection, it might request the United States to act on its behalf, and in exceptional cases the United States might take such action without Mexico's consent. A second treaty, also signed on December 14, authorized the United States to exercise police power in Mexico "to enforce treaty stipulations and to maintain order and security," with the costs of such enforcement to be paid by Mexico. The United States for its part agreed to pay Mexico two million dollars for the rights of transit and to assume the Mexican debt to American citizens of an additional two million.

The Juárez government agreed to the McLane–Ocampo treaty because of its desperate need for money and because of an even more desperate need for American support to counter the danger of European intervention on behalf of the conservative cause in Mexico. That treaty never came into effect because antislavery forces in the American Senate prevented its ratification, but the mere news of the treaty provided fuel to the advocates of European intervention in Mexico to save that country from Yankee imperialism. In appealing for French intervention, a Mexican émigré protested that the McLane–Ocampo treaty menaced "the independence and nationality of Mexico" and "adversely affects European commerce and threatens the political equilibrium in America." The Mexican liberals, he said, were giving their country away to the United States, "which by race, education, and political system is the irreconcilable enemy of the Latin race and Catholicism."

❑ *The European Tripartite Intervention*

In the course of the Mexican civil war and even earlier, both the British and French diplomatic representatives added their pleas to those of Mexican refugees calling for intervention in Mexico. They did so not out of any love for the Mexicans (the French representative called them the "most despicable people on earth"), but to safeguard European interests and as the only alternative to the "complete absorption of the Mexican Republic by the United States."

The incident that finally touched off European intervention was the Juárez government's decree of July 17, 1861, suspending payments on all foreign debts for a period of two years. When Juárez refused to rescind his decree in response to Anglo-French protests, the British and French governments consulted to determine what action they should take, if any, to compel the Juárez regime to honor Mexican debts to foreign bondholders and secure compensation for injuries to foreign persons and property in Mexico. Spain joined in these negotiations, which resulted in a tripartite agreement, the Convention of London of October 31, 1861.

By the terms of this convention, the three powers agreed to a joint demand that the Republic of Mexico provide more efficacious protection for the persons and property of their subjects and the fulfillment of its contractual obligations—that is, the payment of its debts. For that purpose the three governments would send naval and military forces to the coasts of Mexico, where the commanders of those forces would decide on the spot how best to secure the fulfillment of their governments' demands. In typically stilted diplomatic language, the three powers engaged "not to seek for themselves, in the employment of the coercive measures contemplated by the present Convention, any acquisition of territory nor any special advantage, and, not to exercise in the internal affairs of Mexico any influence of a nature to prejudice the right of the Mexican nation to choose and to constitute freely the form of its Government." The convention was to be communicated to the United States, which was to be invited to accede to it.

In accordance with the tripartite convention, Spanish troops landed at the Mexican port of Veracruz in December 1861, where they were joined by British and French forces the following January. Napoleon III, however, never had any intention of adhering to the terms of the London convention. Even while that convention was being negotiated he was seeking British cooperation for the realization of his far more ambitious project to establish a monarchical government in Mexico.

❑ *The American Reaction*

The United States government had long feared the possibility of European intervention in Mexico. That danger became far greater with the outbreak of the American Civil War, which immobilized America's capacity to fend off such intervention. Moreover, there was every reason to expect that the Confederate government, in return for diplomatic recognition or foreign support of any kind, would agree to treaties with European powers that would permit European encroachments in Mexico and elsewhere in the Western Hemisphere.

On April 6, 1861, William Henry Seward, the American secretary of state, sent a new American minister to Mexico, Thomas Corwin, with instructions to block every Confederate or foreign plot there. He was to warn Juárez of Confederate and foreign designs on Mexican territory and assure him of America's friendship and opposition to any such designs. After being forced to swallow the McLane–Ocampo treaty, Juárez can hardly have been impressed by such assurances, especially as he learned shortly afterward from Corwin's correspondence (Juárez's agents had no scruples about opening the mail of foreign diplomats) that the American minister was urging his government to seize Lower California to forestall Confederate efforts to do so. Juárez, however, well aware of the danger of European intervention against his regime, realized he could not afford to turn aside American gestures of support, no matter how hollow, and assured Corwin for his part that he regarded the United States as Mexico's only friend.

American fears about European intervention in Mexico increased sharply following the Juárez government's decree of July 17, 1861, suspending payment on all foreign debts and the ensuing Anglo-French breakoff of diplomatic relations. To prevent Europeans from using the debt question as a pretext for intervention, Corwin proposed in a dispatch of July 29 that the American government offer to guarantee the payment of interest due foreign bondholders in return for an equivalent Mexican guarantee to the United States.

The guarantee Corwin had in mind was far from modest and represented quite as great a threat to Mexico's territorial integrity as any posed by the Europeans. "Mexico," he suggested, "would be willing to pledge all her public lands and mineral rights in Lower California, Chihuahua, Sonora, and Sinaloa, as well as her national faith for the payment of this guarantee." If the states of this area could maintain themselves against southern filibusters or European cupidity, Corwin saw no need to meddle in their affairs or add any of their territories to the United States "except, perhaps, Lower California, which may become indispensable to the protection of our Pacific possessions." The United States might depart from this rule, however, if Mexico's present apparent weakness should stimulate southern or European aggression. "The United States are the only safe guardians of the independence and true civilization of this continent," he said. "It is their mission, and they should fulfil it." Europe, he believed, was quite willing to see the Americans humbled "and will not fail to take advantage of our embarrassments to execute purposes of which she would not have dreamed had we remained at peace." Seward replied on September 2 that President Lincoln greatly desired "that the political *status* of Mexico as an independent nation shall be permanently maintained," but he nevertheless authorized Corwin to negotiate the kind of treaty he had suggested.

Palmerston, the British prime minister, was scornful of the U.S. government's chivalrous offer to pay interest on the Mexican debt "taking a mortgage upon all the mineral wealth of Mexico and laying the groundwork for foreclosure," and he suggested that it might be best to invite the United States to join the European powers in putting pressure on Mexico to satisfy their joint claims. Besides, the American proposal made no provision for the satisfaction of numerous other European claims, notably compensation for the damages inflicted on European persons and property. The American proposal was also rejected by the French, who wanted payment of the principal as well as interest of Mexico's debts. In rejecting the American proposal, however, both the British and French governments assured the United States that they had no intention whatever "to obtain any foothold in Mexico or to occupy permanently any portion of its territory."

In a note of December 4, 1861, the Lincoln government declined the invitation to accede to the Anglo-French-Spanish convention for the collection of Mexico's debts. It nevertheless acknowledged the right of the European powers to resort to war against Mexico for the redress of grievances provided they did not seek or obtain territorial acquisitions or any other exclusive advantage and that they did not impair the right of the Mexican people to choose freely their own form of government.

❑ French Unilateral Intervention

In the case of Napoleon III, the assurance of his government to the United States that France had no intention of obtaining a foothold in Mexico was an outright lie. Even as his government was engaged in negotiations that led to the Convention of London, which specifically limited tripartite intervention to the redress of grievances and collection of debts, the French emperor was contemplating a far more ambitious program in Mexico. Although a central purpose of his Grand Design was to halt Anglo-Saxon imperialism at the expense of the Latin race, he nevertheless sought the cooperation of Britain, as he did with all his foreign policy projects. For this purpose he transmitted his ideas about Mexico in some detail (omitting his concern for the Latin race) to Lord Palmerston.

Napoleon assumed that Britain as well as France must desire the reestablishment of a stable government in Mexico, where their interests had been ceaselessly menaced in recent years. Given peaceful conditions, Mexico, a country so richly endowed with all the advantages of nature, would become an important market for British, French, and Spanish goods. Moreover, "by its regeneration, it would form an insurmountable barrier to the encroachments of North America."

For some years, Napoleon continued, important Mexicans had been asking him to help establish a monarchy in Mexico which alone could restore order in a country torn apart by factional strife. Heretofore he had declined to intervene because he was uncertain of Britain's support and had feared falling out with the United States. But the war in America now made it impossible for the United States to challenge European involvement in Mexico. Moreover, the outrages of the Juárez government made it imperative that Britain, France, and Spain now intervene.

The French emperor realized that the convention presently being negotiated among the three powers would speak only of the redress of legitimate grievances "as the ostensible purpose of our intervention," but he thought it desirable to foresee what might happen once this intervention had taken place. He had been informed that as soon as the allied squadrons appeared at Veracruz, a considerable party in Mexico was ready to seize power, call a national assembly, and proclaim a monarchy. Napoleon had been asked confidentially about his choice of candidate and had denied that he had one. But if a candidate were chosen, "he should be a prince animated with the spirit of the times, endowed with enough intelligence and steadfastness to establish a stable order of things in a country stirred by so many revolutions. Finally it was necessary that he must not offend the susceptibilities of the great Maritime Powers, and I put forward the name of Archduke Maximilian [of Austria]." Napoleon concluded by saying he could ask for nothing better than a convention with Britain and Spain whose "ostensible objective" would be the redress of grievances, but given the state of affairs in Mexico he would find it impossible not to support a monarchy "because it is in the interest of civilization in general."

Palmerston commented that he "quite agreed with the Emperor that it would be very desirable to see a settled government established in Mexico, and that a Monarchy is much more stable than a Republic." He also agreed that Maximilian would be a "good and unobjectionable sovereign for Mexico." He greatly doubted the feasibility of any such arrangement, however, and he let Napoleon know, though in carefully guarded diplomatic language, that the British government would have nothing to do with his plan to establish a monarchical regime. But if the Mexicans themselves should establish an orderly government, "be it even a monarchy," the British government "would not probably refuse [to give it] moral support."

Although Palmerston refused to cooperate with Napoleon in carrying out the Grand Design, he was quite prepared to allow the French to go it alone in Mexico and may even have been sincere in expressing his approval of the emperor's scheme to establish a monarchy. "A sound monarchical government would be a blessing for Mexico and a godsend to all countries having anything to do with Mexico," he told Russell in January 1862. "It would also stop the North Americans, whether of the Federal or Confederate States, in their projected absorption of Mexico. If the North and South are definitely disunited, and if at the same time Mexico could be turned into a prosperous Monarchy, I do not know of any arrangement that would be more advantageous for us." Lord Clarendon, who had served under Palmerston as foreign secretary during the Crimean War, expressed similar satisfaction about Napoleon's Mexican project. "It amuses me to see the Emperor cocking up his leg against their Monroe Doctrine which ought long ago to have been *arrosé* [irrigated] in that manner," he said. Palmerston saw yet another reason to take a benign attitude toward Napoleon's Mexican venture: France's activity there "will have a tendency to fetter her actions in Europe . . . for some time to come."

In December 1861 and January 1862, Spanish, British, and French troops landed at the Mexican port of Veracruz in accordance with their tripartite Convention of London of October 31, 1861. Napoleon, of course, never intended to halt at Veracruz; his Grand Design would be realized only when his troops reached Mexico City. His great diplomatic problem now was to find a pretext to justify going beyond the provisions of the convention, and one so convincing that it might even secure the cooperation of his allies.

The strategy he eventually adopted was to make financial claims so exorbitant and set such onerous conditions for their payment that Juárez would be certain to reject them. This rejection would then serve as the pretext for breaking off negotiations and justifying a military advance to the capital.

Napoleon had no difficulty in provoking Mexico's rejection of his claims, but he signally failed to secure British or Spanish support and instead aroused their indignation. By early April 1862 the three powers acknowledged their inability to agree on how to deal with the Mexican problem, and the British and Spanish withdrew their forces from Mexico. "The conduct of the French is everywhere disgraceful," Queen Victoria wrote soon afterward. "Let us . . . have nothing to do with them in the future in any proceedings in other countries."

Although he had hoped to secure Spanish and most especially British support, Napoleon was not discouraged by being left alone in Mexico. From the inception of his Mexican plan, he had been confident that its execution would be a relatively simple matter. He had been assured by Mexican refugees that the French would be welcomed in Mexico as liberators from the Juárez tyranny, and French representatives had expressed confidence that any possible Mexican opposition would melt away at the first appearance of French troops. It therefore came as a nasty shock to the emperor when on May 5, 1862, French troops advancing to Mexico City were defeated at the inland city of Puebla. Instead of seeing in this defeat evidence that the Mexican people looked upon the French not as liberators but as hostile invaders of their country, Napoleon chose to regard it as a blot on France's military honor that had to be avenged. The French army in Mexico was heavily reinforced and a new general sent to replace the commander defeated at Puebla. The Mexicans were to be saved in spite of themselves.

The new French commander was General Elie Frédéric Forey, a professional soldier with long experience in European and colonial wars, who arrived in Veracruz on September 25, 1862. Anxious not to repeat the mistakes of his predecessor, he spent almost six months preparing for the French drive into the interior. Even then it required a siege of two months to subdue Puebla and open the road to Mexico City. He entered the capital on June 10, 1863.

Before his departure for Mexico, Forey was given detailed instructions drawn up by the emperor himself. Once in control of the Mexican capital, he was to cooperate with Mexican notables of every shade of opinion who espoused the French cause in order to set up a strong and stable government in Mexico. With that, Napoleon said, "we shall have erected an insuperable barrier to the encroachments of the United States," and by preventing America's dominion over Mexico— and thence over the Antilles and all of South America—"we shall have maintained the independence of our own colonies in the Antilles as well as those of ungrateful Spain." Instead of an American government in Mexico there would be a government under French influence that "will radiate northward as well as southward, will create immense new markets for our commerce and will procure the materials indispensable to our industry."

If Forey found that the Mexicans desired a monarchical form of government, as

Napoleon confidently expected they would, he was to propose Archduke Maximilian of Austria as the candidate favored by France. Napoleon was perfectly frank about the future role of Maximilian or anyone else who became ruler of Mexico under French auspices. "As for the prince who may ascend the Mexican throne," the emperor explained, "he will always be forced to act in the interests of France, not only out of gratitude but especially because those of his new country will be in accordance with ours and he will not be able to sustain himself without our influence." Meanwhile Forey himself was to act as the actual ruler of Mexico without appearing to do so.

❑ *The Candidacy of Maximilian*

Archduke Ferdinand Maximilian of Habsburg was the brother of Emperor Francis Joseph of Austria. Before the Austro-French war of 1859 he had served as Austrian viceroy of Lombardy, from which the Austrians had been driven by the French and their Italian allies. As so often with Napoleon, it is difficult to determine his reasons for this improbable choice as candidate for the Mexican throne. He told Palmerston he thought it "in good taste" to propose "a prince belonging to a dynasty with which I was recently at war," but his primary motivation appears to have been his desire to fulfill his treaty obligation to Italy to free Venetia as well as Lombardy from Austrian rule. He evidently believed the Austrians might be more amenable to negotiation over Venetia if he obtained an imperial crown for a member of their imperial house.

The Austrians were far from enthusiastic about the dubious as well as dangerous honor of securing the crown of Mexico for a member of the House of Habsburg, but when pressed by high-ranking Mexican political refugees, by important members of Napoleon's entourage, and even by Empress Eugénie, Count Rechberg, the Austrian foreign minister, could not avoid sounding out Maximilian about the French proposal. Rechberg found the archduke remarkably receptive to the idea. After having served as viceroy in Lombardy and Venetia, he resented not having been given another comparable post or any voice in the conduct of Austrian affairs and he was jealous of the power and position of his imperial brother. His own ambitions were spurred by those of his wife, Charlotte, the daughter of the king of the Belgians, who coveted an imperial crown and saw little prospect of obtaining one in Europe.

The Austrian government remained dubious and went to considerable lengths to persuade Maximilian to have nothing to do with the Mexican affair, especially in view of the fact that the entire business was being sponsored by the politically dangerous and unreliable Napoleon III, whose advocacy of nationalist revolution threatened the very existence of the Habsburg empire. In the end, however, Maximilian was allowed to decide for himself, on condition that Austria would be in no way involved. Upon Maximilian's acceptance of the Mexican crown, Austria demanded that he sign a so-called Family Pact renouncing for himself and his heirs all claims to the Austrian crown even if he should leave Mexico, and all claims for himself and his heirs to the private fortune and property of the House of Habsburg.

Maximilian and Charlotte landed in Veracruz on May 25, 1864, and made their formal entry into Mexico City on June 12. Sorely misled by the assurances of Mexican political refugees and the French government about the Mexican people's eagerness for a monarchy and their personal enthusiasm about Maximilian himself, the romantic and incredibly naive Habsburg prince never understood or accepted the fact that his rule depended on French military support, and that in the eyes of patriotic Mexicans his regime was nothing more than a foreign occupation government propped up by foreign bayonets. Nor did he appreciate that the hostility aroused by the French occupation and the conduct of the French army precluded any chance he might have had to win popular support.

French troops had met with unexpectedly fierce resistance, and with their victory over the regular Mexican army this resistance took the form of widespread guerrilla warfare. The French dealt with the guerrilla movement in Mexico as they had with similar opposition in Algeria, and as occupation armies have generally dealt with popular resistance over the centuries. They burned villages and towns suspected of harboring rebels; they took hostages and executed them in reprisal for attacks on their own troops; they declared all guerrillas and even all soldiers still loyal to the Juárez regime to be bandits who were to be shot when captured.

Despite Maximilian's pathetic eagerness to appear a just and benign ruler, he found himself compelled to endorse these Draconian measures by his French military advisers. Even under the best of circumstances, therefore, Maximilian would have had serious difficulty in maintaining his rule over Mexico. With the Union victory in the American Civil War, his government was doomed. Maximilian arrived in Mexico during Grant's final Union offensive, which was to break Confederate resistance and leave the United States free at last to deal with the French and their Mexican satellite regime.

❑ *The Confederacy and Napoleon's Grand Design*

Given the immense French investment of men and money in Mexico, one of the most puzzling questions about French policy is why they failed to adopt the one course that might have given their enterprise some prospect of success: intervention on the side of the Confederacy in the American Civil War.

Secretary of State Seward had devoted much of his diplomatic skill to avoiding French intervention, but he had left the French in no doubt that the United States disapproved of their efforts to set up a monarchy in Mexico. Napoleon therefore should have realized that if the North won the war, his satellite government in Mexico would be in serious danger. If the Confederacy won, on the other hand, especially if its victory were achieved with French support, the French could expect it to be favorably disposed to their government in Mexico, all the more so because the alternative was the Juárez regime, which was recognized and supported by the United States. In any case the Confederate government, with a vengeful neighbor to the north, could not afford to be hostile to France and might even be eager to ally itself with France and its Mexican satellite regime.

Maximilian was far more perceptive than Napoleon about what was at stake in the American Civil War, recognizing that the security and indeed the survival of his regime depended on a Confederate victory. "The creation of this new state, by aid of the support of France and England," he said, "will be, in my opinion, an absolute necessity for the Mexican Empire, and cannot fail greatly to facilitate the task of the power guaranteeing the existence of this Empire." Maximilian therefore urged the

British and French to recognize the Confederacy and believed such recognition should take place before he could accept the Mexican crown. Maximilian's failure to insist on this condition before his departure for Mexico proved to be a fatal sin of omission.

The Confederate government for its part understood how closely its interests were involved with Napoleon's Mexican venture and the government of Maximilian. On January 7, 1864, before Maximilian's final acceptance of the Mexican crown, Judah P. Benjamin, the Confederate secretary of state, issued letters of accreditation to William Preston as Confederate diplomatic representative to Maximilian with authorization to accord his government official recognition. Preston was to make no move until he was certain of receiving a cordial reception, but once received and accredited as Confederate minister to Mexico he was to cultivate the friendship of Montholon, the French minister, and urge a French-Confederate military alliance to check Yankee aggression south of the Rio Grande. Preston was to emphasize that "the future safety of the Mexican Empire is inextricably bound with the safety and independence of the Confederacy. Mexico must indulge in no illusion on this point."

A copy of Benjamin's instruction to Preston was sent to Slidell, the Confederate representative in Paris. But Slidell suffered nothing but disappointment, for Napoleon had decided against an alliance with the Confederacy. This decision was a triumph for the diplomacy of Seward, who somehow convinced the French emperor that if France and France's Mexican satellite government maintained a strict neutrality and refrained from any dealings with the Confederacy, the United States would condone and eventually recognize the Maximilian regime. Under pressure from Napoleon, Maximilian was obliged to agree to this policy of strict neutrality, so that when Slidell attempted to see him before his departure for Mexico, the hapless new emperor did not even grant him an audience.

By 1864 Napoleon may have been correct in believing that France could no longer render effective aid to the Confederacy and that the success of his Mexican enterprise depended on the goodwill of the United States. But in refusing to explore the possibility of military cooperation with the Confederacy, this slim but sole chance for the survival of the Mexican empire was lost.

❑ *American Policy and the End of the Mexican Empire*

On March 3, 1862, shortly after British, French, and Spanish troops arrived in Mexico, the American government expressed its satisfaction about allied assurances that they were seeking no political objectives but only the redress of grievances. The American government nevertheless considered it to be its duty to express the opinion that no monarchical government founded in Mexico with the aid of foreign armies and navies would have any prospect of success, and that in case such a government were formed, the interests and sympathies of the United States would be on the side of the Mexican republic. After the British and Spanish left Mexico, American warnings were addressed exclusively to the French, and these became increasingly explicit after July 1863 as the Union grew confident of ultimate victory.

In September 1863 Seward instructed the American minister to France to urge Napoleon to settle his affairs in Mexico on the basis of the unity and independence of that country as early as possible and to depart, because the American people were "exceedingly desirous that there may not arise out of the war in Mexico any cause of alienation between them and France." This was a definite enough warning, delivered well before Maximilian had even accepted the crown of Mexico, but the French emperor refused to heed it. Throughout his Mexican enterprise he failed to understand the intensity of American objections to a European-sponsored monarchy in the Western Hemisphere and the impossibility of maintaining such a government once the North won the Civil War. Drouyn, the French foreign minister, responded to Seward's warning by repeating the familiar French assurances that they were not meddling in Mexico and were concerned only to see that fair elections were held to give the Mexican people the opportunity to express their opinion. If they voted in favor of a monarchical government with Maximilian as its leader, this would be their free choice.

When it became evident that the French were determined to establish a monarchy in Mexico and that Maximilian would accept the Mexican crown, American warnings became outright threats. On April 4, 1864, the House of Representatives passed a resolution by a vote of 109 to 0 that the Congress of the United States was "unwilling by silence to leave the nations of the world under the impression that they are indifferent spectators of the deplorable events now transpiring in the republic of Mexico, and that they therefore think it fit to declare that it does not accord with the policy of the United States to acknowledge any monarchical Government erected on the ruins of any republican Government in America under the auspices of any European power."

A threatening posture of this kind did not accord with Seward's policy and the congressional resolution was disavowed by the Lincoln government. The South was still far from being defeated, and Seward realized—far more clearly than did Napoleon—that if the French were determined to maintain a satellite regime in Mexico, their best and perhaps only means of doing so would be to join forces with the Confederacy to secure at least a stalemate in the American Civil War. The American secretary therefore continued to play an extremely careful diplomatic game with France to avoid driving Napoleon into an alliance with the Confederacy, allowing him to believe that if France and Maximilian continued to observe a policy of strict neutrality in the American Civil War, the United States would remain similarly neutral over the civil war in Mexico. In response to American pleas for more vigorous protests over French conduct in Mexico, Seward said that "this is not the suitable time we could choose for offering idle menaces to the Emperor of France. We have compromised nothing, surrendered nothing, and I do not propose to surrender anything. But why should we gasconade about Mexico when we are in a struggle for our own life?"

Seward's policy was eminently successful. Napoleon turned aside Maximilian's pleas to recognize the Confederacy and, to reassure the Americans still further, detained all warships being built in France for the Confederacy.

With the North's victory in the Civil War, many Americans believed caution was no longer necessary in dealing with the French over Mexico. On the contrary, many Union leaders were eager to follow up their victory over the South with an invasion of Mexico to drive out the French and establish a government there under American control. One of the more intriguing questions about American policy after the Civil War is why the American expansionist movement, temporarily halted by regional differences over slavery and by war, was not now resumed on an even greater scale, and why the Americans did not in fact use the excuse of the French presence to invade Mexico and establish their own control over that country. The best explanation may be the one provided by Seward, himself an ardent expansionist, who took the lead in advocating a policy of restraint in Mexico. "Those who are most impatient for the defeat of European and monarchical designs in Mexico," he said in April 1864, "might well be content to abide the effects which must result from the ever-increasing expansion of the American people westward and southward."

Seward's policy of restraint did not go unchallenged, most notably by the victorious Union generals, who were not content to "abide the effects" of popular expansion. In May 1865, Ulysses S. Grant, the Union commander in chief, reassigned one of his most capable senior officers, General Philip Sheridan, to the command of an army west of the Mississippi, ostensibly to crush remaining Confederate forces in that area but with the primary task of compelling "the French and Austrian invaders . . . to quit the territory of our sister republic." Grant warned Sheridan to act circumspectly because of Seward's opposition to any American military activities that might involve the United States in a war with European powers.

Grant saw no reason to avoid such a war and may even have desired one. Soon after dispatching Sheridan, he worked out a plan to send the Union general John M. Schofield to Mexico to take command of an army of Union and ex-Confederate soldiers for the purpose of driving out the French. Seward was not informed of this plan, which was approved by President Andrew Johnson (Lincoln had been assassinated on April 14, 1865) and by Seward's bitter rival in the cabinet, Secretary of War Stanton. Seward reacted to this threat to his authority in the field of foreign affairs by sending a circular on July 26 to all foreign diplomatic representatives informing them that they were to carry on their business with the U.S. government exclusively through the American state department. He then neatly undercut Grant's plan by commissioning Schofield to go to France as a special agent of the U.S. government to negotiate the French evacuation of Mexico. Schofield was not sent to Paris until November 1865, long after Seward had begun such negotiations through his regular diplomatic representatives, and even then the general was excluded from all high-level negotiations to minimize the risk that he might disrupt them.

While countering the intrigues of American interventionists, Seward found their agitation useful in dealing with the French because it served to show them how precarious their position in Mexico might soon become and spared Seward himself the need to adopt a threatening posture. Seward's own pressure was polite but firm. He sent no ultimata, he made no overt threats, he did not refer to the Monroe Doctrine. The objective of American policy was to get the French out of Mexico, and Seward's diplomacy was dedicated to accomplishing this without war and if possible even without disrupting America's amicable relations with France. He therefore gave Napoleon every opportunity to save face by making the French withdrawal appear a voluntary move and not a retreat in the face of American intimidation.

Napoleon, who by now obviously recognized that his Mexican project was doomed, took advantage of the opening Seward left him. By January 1866 he had issued orders to begin the repatriation of the French army, a process that was to be completed no later than January of the following year, and he had informed Maximilian of his intention to withdraw French troops from Mexico. His government had also prepared its case to justify its desertion of Maximilian for the benefit of world public opinion: France had not come to Mexico to establish a new government but only to validate the claims of French citizens against the Mexican government; moreover, Maximilian had failed to live up to the terms of his treaties with France, so that France was now justified in renouncing its obligations to its imperial protégé. Maximilian appealed and protested in vain. On August 29, 1866, Napoleon informed him bluntly that he would henceforth be unable to give him another man or another penny. Could Maximilian maintain his position on the basis of his own strength or should he abdicate? In the latter case, before leaving Mexico he should take advantage of the presence of the French army to summon a representative body that could form a government capable of offering the country some degree of stability.

In October 1866 the French informed the American government about the future course of French policy. France was sending General François de Castelnau on a special mission to Mexico to convince Maximilian that he could expect no further aid from France. Castelnau had no authority to compel Maximilian to abdicate, but he was to make it clear that France hoped he would do so. In that event, Castelnau was to take the initiative in providing for elections to create a legitimate government to carry out an orderly transition from empire to republic. The French indicated they would welcome American cooperation in effecting such a transition and invited Washington to come to an agreement about a common course of action.

Seward's response to this overture was to send a mission to Mexico under Lewis D. Campbell, an undistinguished former congressman from Ohio who apparently owed his appointment to his political association with President Johnson. Campbell's military counterpart was the formidable Union general William Tecumseh Sherman, on whom Seward may have counted to make the mission effective. The American envoys were given full discretionary powers, but their orders permitted them to help restore the government of Benito Juárez, to commit American forces to maintain order if requested to do so by Juárez, and to confer officially with Juárez or unofficially with agents of any other political group in Mexico—even with Maximilian and the French if the situation warranted. The American envoys were specifically prohibited from seeking to annex any Mexican territory or from entering into any agreement with the French or Maximilian to support any candidate other than Juárez as leader of the Mexican government. A full copy of these orders was sent to the French, leaving them in no doubt about American policy.

These orders proved to be more important as a statement of American intentions than for the policy the Americans actually pursued in Mexico, for the ineffectual Campbell was preoccupied with the illness of his daughter and never did see Juárez, and Sherman returned to New Orleans rather than remain idle in Mexico.

Maximilian meanwhile refused to recognize or admit the hopelessness of his position. Despite the repeated and urgent appeals of French emissaries in Mexico, he refused to abdicate. In March 1867 the last of the French troops left Mexico. On May 14 Maximilian and the remnants of his Mexican army surrendered to the republican forces of Juárez at Querétaro, about eighty miles northwest of Mexico City. Disregarding appeals from the American as well as European governments, Juárez ordered the execution of Maximilian. He was shot at Querétaro on June 19, 1867.

The long-term significance of the North's victory in the American Civil War and the failure of Napoleon's effort to establish a French satellite government in Mexico was that the United States was left as the sole great power in the Western Hemisphere, free to develop its resources and extend its influence in that hemisphere without serious competition or obstruction from other powers.

The more immediate significance of Napoleon's Mexican venture and its critical importance in the game of great power politics was that it diverted French power from Europe during one of the most decisive periods in European international relations. For in 1864 and 1866, while a substantial number of French troops were tied down in Mexico, Prussia scored decisive military victories over Denmark and Austria that were to pave the way for the Prussian victory over France in 1870–1871 and bring about the collapse of Napoleon's empire. Whether Napoleon could or would have prevented Prussia's fateful victories of 1864 and 1866 if his troops in Mexico had been available in Europe is a question that cannot be answered. But there can be no doubt that his preoccupation with Mexico prevented him from bringing the full weight of French influence to bear in the councils of the great powers during this crucial period of European history.

❑

ELEVEN

The Unification of Germany

In Germany as in Italy, the ideological common denominator for the political union of the German states was nationalism, but the point must be stressed that in Germany, too, national feeling was not an irresistible ideological force sweeping all before it. The aspiration for national unification was confined to a relatively small number of politically conscious individuals, and these nationalists differed sharply among themselves as to how unification was to be achieved, what territories should be included in a German union, and what type of government that union should have. At the same time, throughout the German states there remained powerful and widespread opposition to the unification movement, no matter what form it might take.

As we have seen, during the revolutions of 1848 the German Confederation, long despised by German patriots because of its institutional incapacity to mobilize German power, had been discredited further by its inability to give effective support to the German national cause in a quarrel with Denmark over Schleswig-Holstein. During that same period the attempt to achieve German unity through a popularly elected national parliament had failed. The result was that after 1850 the hopes of German nationalists came to focus on Austria and Prussia, which alone seemed to possess the power to weld the states of Germany into a national union comparable to England or France, a state capable of defending German interests and giving the German people political stature commensurate with what nationalists conceived as their intellectual and moral stature among the peoples of the world.

In the rivalry between Austria and Prussia for supremacy in Germany, Austria had the advantage of a long tradition of supremacy; it held the permanent presidency of the existing confederation; as a Catholic country it appealed to the largely Catholic population of southern Germany. Above all, Austria was believed to possess a stronger army and greater natural resources than Prussia. Austria's weakness lay in the multinational character of its empire; it had barely survived the revolutionary crises of 1848, and most of its subjects were not Germans at all. Further, although Austria's Catholicism was attractive to the Catholics of southern Germany, it alienated the Protestants of the north.

Prussia had the advantage of possessing an almost exclusively German population; its own autocratic tradition had been sufficiently tempered by reform to make its leadership more acceptable to German liberals; and its Protestantism appealed to Germany's Protestant population. Prussia's greatest advantage, however, was its economic strength. By the mid-nineteenth century its Rhineland provinces (given to Prussia in 1815 as a buffer for Germany against future French aggression) had become the heartland of Germany's industrial revolution. During this same period Prussia had gained economic influence over the majority of other German states through a Prussian-controlled German Customs Union (Zollverein), which had its modest beginnings in an 1819 tariff treaty with a small neighboring state and had been extended rapidly to include almost all members of the German Confederation. Notably absent from this economic union was Austria, which had been deliberately excluded to avoid any possible Austrian challenge to Prussian domination.

So important was Prussia's economic strength that some scholars regard it as the decisive factor in the struggle for supremacy in Germany. It is argued, for example, that Prussia's economic policies and its successful defense of the Zollverein against Austrian attacks were far more crucial to Prussia's ultimate triumph than the more spectacular activities of Prussian diplomats and generals, who are generally given major credit for this achievement. Such economic arguments, although a valuable corrective to the usual political emphasis, seriously underestimate the strength and range of the opposition to Prussia and to the German unification movement in general. In the final war for supremacy in Germany, for instance, all members of the Zollverein with any freedom of choice sided with Austria against Prussia. Moreover, it is extremely doubtful whether Prussia could have won this war, or even fought it, if Prussian *diplomacy* had not precluded the intervention of France and Russia, which had compelling reasons to prevent any one state from dominating Germany, for a united Germany would represent a dangerous threat to the security of both. It is not necessary to accept these economic arguments in their entirety, however, to recognize the fundamental importance of the economic and social forces released by the industrial revolution in Germany in breaking down traditional modes of thought and behavior and thus in bringing about conditions conducive to revolutionary political change.

Prussia's rise to great power status prior to the nineteenth century certainly was not based on its economic strength and resources. In fact, as the nucleus of a future great power, few states could have been more unpromising than Brandenburg-Prussia in the seventeenth century, when its rise began. Its territories were scattered, its population sparse; it lacked both natural resources and natural frontiers. These weaknesses, typical of most German states in this period, were overcome in Prussia by a few strong rulers, who with unusual firmness of purpose centralized the government and built a strong army, thereafter devoting a large part of the state's resources to its maintenance. Their success was the result of skillful and often unscrupulous leadership, aided by a bureaucracy that had become proverbial for its honesty, efficiency, and willingness to work hard for little pay. Most obviously significant in Prussia's rise, however, was the army, which was regarded as the central pillar of the state, its main line of defense, its only true frontier. The importance of skilled leadership and the army in Prussia's development makes understandable the subsequent veneration of leadership in Germany and the exalted status of the army in that country.

Kingdom of Prussia, 1866

Acquired by Prussia after Austro-Prussian War, 1866

South German states, 1866

Austria within Confederation, 1815-1866

Austrian possessions outside Confederation, 1815-1866

Boundary of German Confederation, 1866

❑ *The Prussian Constitutional Conflict*

The political history of Prussia after the revolutions of 1848 turned largely on the constitution granted to his people by King Frederick William IV in December 1848, but subjected to several conservative revisions before its final promulgation in 1850. The great importance of that constitution was its provision for a popularly elected parliament with significant legislative and taxation powers. To ensure the election of conservative candidates who would automatically endorse government policies, the government set up a complicated three-class system of voting designed to give maximum representation to the highest taxpayers in the expectation that they would return reliable conservative majorities. This expectation proved to be a serious miscalculation, for the highest taxpayers were no longer conservative landowners but members of the increasingly prosperous middle classes, who were liberals in the sense that they wanted changes in the political system that would give them political power to match their new economic status.

In September 1858 King Frederick William IV suffered a mental breakdown and was declared insane. He was succeeded by his brother William, first as regent, then, upon the death of Frederick William in January 1861, as king. Very shortly after coming to power, William was confronted with one of the bitterest and most critical constitutional conflicts in German history: Would the country be governed by the king or by parliament?

The constitutional conflict in Prussia centered on control of taxation and on army reform, which was deemed essential by the new king and his military advisers if Prussia was to remain in the ranks of the great powers. According to the constitution, parliament's consent was required for the additional taxes needed to pay for the reorganization and equipment of Prussian forces. Besides sharing the usual reluctance of legislative representatives to vote new taxes, liberals in the Prussian parliament feared that the proposed reforms, with their provisions extending the period of compulsory military service, would bolster the authority of the monarchy and strengthen the influence of the conservative-military clique, which might use the reformed army as much against domestic as against foreign foes.

The king could have dealt with the situation most easily by basing his authority squarely on the army, repudiating the constitution, and ordering the parliamentary deputies to go home. But this was a course William could not bring himself to pursue. Although a staunch conservative and certainly no champion of constitutional government, he regarded the constitution granted by the crown as a contract between the king and his people that was as inviolable as any other moral obligation. He seriously considered abdicating in favor of his son, Crown Prince Frederick William, who professed sympathy with the liberal cause and, with the forceful encouragement of his strong-minded English wife (the daughter of Queen Victoria), favored the establishment of English parliamentary institutions in Prussia. But Frederick William was destined not to come to the throne for another twenty-six years; by that time the cause of genuine representative government in Prussia had been lost.

❑ *Bismarck*

It was Albrecht von Roon, the Prussian minister of war, who persuaded William I to remain on the throne and to entrust the government leadership to the conservative statesman apparently offering the last hope for a solution of the constitutional conflict on terms acceptable to the monarchy. On September 23, 1862, Otto von Bismarck was made provisional head of the Prussian government. His official appointment as prime minister followed on October 8.

Bismarck was born in 1815, the son of a dull, unenterprising Prussian Junker, from whom he inherited his massive physique and prodigious strength. His middle-class mother was the daughter of a distinguished Prussian civil servant, whose sponsorship of reform had earned him a reputation for Jacobinism. In contrast to her stolid husband, she was high-strung and often ill-tempered, with a restless, inquisitive mind. It was from his mother that Bismarck inherited his temperament—and his intellect.

Bismarck entered public life in 1847 but was given little opportunity to prove himself until 1851, when the king appointed him Prussian delegate to the diet of the German Confederation in Frankfurt. There he gained his first experience in diplomacy and a detailed knowledge of German affairs. Later, as Prussian ambassador to St. Petersburg, and then to Paris, he had an opportunity to study the political situations in Russia and France and to size up the character of the rulers of these states.

Bismarck has been called a realist in politics, the exponent of a peculiarly modern and amoral realpolitik. But most statesmen, even the most self-consciously idealistic, look upon themselves as realists. The distinctive quality of Bismarck's realism resulted from his ability to recognize the limitations of his own powers and those of the state he governed. In the tradition of Richelieu and Talleyrand, he regarded politics as the art of the possible. His policies were never bound by fixed rules or preconceptions. While remaining aware of long-term goals and broad perspectives, he concentrated on the exigencies of the moment. His plans were resilient, allowing for error, for misinformation, for accident—the "imponderabilia," as Bismarck called them. He took into account not only his opponents' most obvious moves, but their every conceivable move, even the most stupid, which if unanticipated might upset the cleverest calculations. Much of his success depended on patience and timing. He once compared himself to a hunter inching forward through a swamp to shoot a grouse while one false step might cause him to sink into a bog.

Bismarck's outstanding quality, and the one he valued most highly in a statesman, was the ability to choose the most opportune and least dangerous political course. He was keenly aware that politics presents a constant succession of alternatives, that there is rarely a single solution to a specific political problem; and he would explore simultaneously a wide range of possibilities until the moment came for choosing. Even then, except when the choice was war, he left alternatives open and never committed himself irretrievably. Although frequently checked, Bismarck could abandon an unsuccessful policy and embark on some new course by which he might regain the political initiative and recoup his losses.

The absence of doctrinaire rigidity in Bismarck's politics is reflected in the shifts his personal values underwent in the course of his career. He was born a Pomeranian Junker into a society not distinguished for its political sophistication or breadth of vision. Bismarck's fellow squires were loyal to the king, to the kingdom of Prussia, and to the Junker class. Bismarck gradually emancipated himself from the standards of this society, moving from a Prussian, to a German, to a European, and ultimately even to a global point of view. But it would be a mistake to think that Bismarck had no fixed values or loyalties. He was loyal to the Prussian state, which provided the means of his self-realization. At the height of his career, the keystone of his system of values was the German empire, which he regarded as his creation. To maintain and defend that creation became the aim of all his policies and the focus of all his energies.

Bismarck possessed that most rare quality of men of political genius—moderation, the ability to recognize where to draw the line. Unlike Frederick the Great or Napoleon, he was never an impetuous gambler but always remained supremely conscious of the dangers involved in the use of power. Nor did he resort to war, that most hazardous of political gambles, until all other means had been exhausted and all possible odds—military, diplomatic, economic, and moral—were on his side. Each of his wars was fought with a clear, limited purpose. When the advantages to be gained by war no longer justified the risks involved, he became Europe's staunchest defender of peace.

Bismarck's most immediate problem upon becoming head of the Prussian government was the conflict with parliament. His approach to this crisis was characteristic. He first tried to compromise, literally offering parliament an olive branch he had plucked at Avignon. When his various proposals for compromise were rejected, he seized the moral initiative and accused parliament of violating the constitution by claiming exclusive control over the budget. From 1863 to 1866 Bismarck simply ignored parliament. He solved the financial problem by collecting the taxes already voted for 1861 and 1862, from these funds allocating money for military reforms. Meanwhile Bismarck concentrated on foreign affairs, where he believed the crucial questions of Prussia's future would be decided.

Bismarck was well aware that among politically conscious Germans, a substantial number craved some kind of national unification; in his youth he himself had fallen under the influence of romantic nationalism. He therefore could not fail to see the advantage to Prussia of gaining the leadership of the nationalist movement. He also recognized that there were two major obstacles to Prussia's domination of Germany: Austria and France. Neither of these could be expected to concede Prussia the leadership of a united Germany unless compelled to do so, and such compulsion would very probably involve armed conflict.

Unlike many of the German liberals, Bismarck did not eschew the use of force. In one of his first speeches as prime minister—an appeal to the parliamentary finance committee to grant funds for army reforms—Bismarck said: "Germany is not looking to Prussia's liberalism but to her power. . . . The great questions of our time will not be decided by speeches and majority resolutions—that was the mistake of 1848–1849—but by iron and blood." This statement, the most famous of all Bismarck's political pronouncements, disclosed a crucial aspect of his thinking. But it did not mean that Bismarck considered iron and blood the only means of establishing Prussia's leadership in Germany. The speech was primarily an appeal for military appropriations, and necessarily its emphasis fell on the importance of military power. Bismarck was aware of the hazards of war, and of the danger that victories on the battlefield might create military heroes who could become serious political rivals. Moreover, he realized that Prussia needed more than military power. It needed allies and a diplomacy that would undercut the alliances of its opponents and secure the maximum moral advantage in any international controversy. Iron and blood, if used at all, should be employed only under the most favorable possible circumstances. Even then he believed the risks to be so great that he never abandoned his efforts to attain his ends by peaceful means.

❑ *The Polish Revolt*

In January 1863, a little over a month after the disastrous Union defeat at Fredericksburg in the Civil War and while French troops were advancing toward Mexico City, the outbreak of a revolt in Russian Poland once again turned international attention to the Polish question. The Polish struggle for freedom from Russian rule attracted the sympathetic support of liberals and Russophobes throughout Europe, who called on their several governments to come to the aid of the Poles or at least intervene with the tsarist government on their behalf.

The Polish revolt placed Napoleon III in a dilemma. As the professed champion of national liberty in Europe, he found himself obliged to make some gesture on behalf of the Poles, whose cause was enthusiastically supported by French public opinion. On the other hand, in his efforts to dismantle the 1815 treaty system and regain France's freedom of action in Europe, he endeavored to reestablish good relations with Russia. To this end he was prepared to give up some of the most important gains of the Anglo-French victory over Russia in the Crimean War, notably the provisions prohibiting Russia from maintaining military or naval forces on the shores or waters of the Black Sea, and even to allow Russia to resume its advance at the expense of the Ottoman empire.

Influential members of the tsarist government, among them the chancellor and foreign minister, Prince Gorchakov, had long been eager to reestablish full Russian sovereignty in the Black Sea area and were sorely tempted to negotiate a treaty with France for this purpose. They too were placed in a dilemma by the Polish revolt, and to avoid a possible rupture with Napoleon over this issue they urged the tsar to make concessions to the Poles, a policy numerous Russian officials were advocating in any case as the only way to solve the perennial Polish problem.

The Polish revolt created no dilemma for Bismarck. The uprising in Russian Poland posed a threat to Prussian control over its own Polish provinces, and if only for this reason he immediately offered the tsar Prussia's cooperation in crushing it. But in doing so he had a second purpose in mind. He knew that there were influential voices at the tsarist court in favor of an alliance with France and a policy of reconciliation in Poland. Through his offer of Prussian support he hoped to counter the influence of both Francophiles and appeasers in Russia and to encourage the tsar to pursue a conservative and antirevolutionary policy in both foreign and domestic affairs.

Bismarck made his offer through the adjutant-general of the king of Prussia, General Gustav von Alvensleben—the tsar was known to be more impressed by military than by civilian emissaries—who was instructed to explore the situation generally at the tsarist court and beyond that "to prepare the ground for measures that can be taken jointly by both governments to quell the current uprising or any further disturbances of the same kind." Alvensleben was also to stress that "in our view . . . the position of both courts with regard to the Polish revolution is essentially that of two allies threatened by a common enemy." On February 8, 1863,

Alvensleben concluded a treaty with the Russian government (the Alvensleben Convention) providing for Prusso-Russian military cooperation in their respective Polish frontier districts against Polish rebels.

News of the Alvensleben Convention aroused a storm of protest among liberals in Prussia and throughout Germany generally, for German liberals still identified their own political aspirations with the cause of Polish freedom. But the convention also aroused indignation in Russia, where conservatives as well as Francophiles and advocates of conciliation in Poland resented Prussia's unsolicited offer of support and the implication that Russia needed foreign assistance in dealing with its domestic difficulties. The Alvensleben Convention was never ratified, and Bismarck's critics at that time and since have adjudged his precipitate intervention in the Polish affair to have been a mistake, detrimental to his position both at home and abroad.

Bismarck himself, however, professed to have been thoroughly satisfied by the results of the Alvensleben mission, which he considered to have achieved all his objectives with regard to Russia. To his envoy in London he wrote on March 8, 1863, that "through the Alvensleben Convention, which was concluded at the specific order of the tsar despite the strenuous opposition of Gorchakov, we succeeded, insofar as it lay within our power, in giving the upper hand to the anti-Polish and anti-French party in the tsar's cabinet and to transform the previous indecision into a resolute determination to suppress the uprising."

In the long run, Bismarck's estimate of the value of the Alvensleben mission proved to be more accurate than that of his critics, for the tsar himself later acknowledged that gratitude for Prussia's loyal support during the Polish crisis had determined his subsequent benevolent attitude toward Prussia during the wars for German unification. It was not only Prussia's gesture of support, however, that produced the tsar's favorable attitude, but the antagonism aroused in Russia by the reaction of the other European powers to the Polish revolt.

Napoleon III had sought to evade an altercation with Russia over Poland by using the Alvensleben Convention as an excuse to call for an international protest against *Prussian* intervention in the Polish affair, and on February 21, 1863, his foreign minister, Drouyn de Lhuys, proposed to London and Vienna that they send identic notes of protest to Berlin. It was an inept ploy, and Russell, the British foreign secretary, replied naturally enough that the powers should address their notes to St. Petersburg rather than Berlin. He added that if these notes were to have any chance of evoking a favorable response in Russia, they be restricted to recommending more liberal treatment of Poland. The British reaction faced Napoleon with the alternatives of addressing a unilateral note to Prussia, doing nothing whatever on behalf of the Poles, or taking advantage of Russell's proposal to send identic notes to St. Petersburg and thereby run the risk of alienating Russia.

Napoleon chose the last course. In fact, as his enthusiasm for the cause of Polish liberation mounted, he lost all sense of political reality and indulged yet again in grandiose plans for a reorganization of the map of Europe. Confident that he could count on the support of Britain over the Polish question, he now concentrated his diplomatic efforts on securing the support of Austria.

In his overtures to Vienna, Napoleon suggested that if "events" should require Austria to surrender its Polish provinces to an independent Poland, Austria would receive "material compensations" and "exclusive preponderance" in the Balkans;

and if Austria agreed to cede Venetia to Italy, Austria could be assured of similar compensations and preponderance in Germany. With regard to Italy, Napoleon proposed further that if Austria agreed to give up Venetia, France and Austria together could collaborate in breaking up the newly established Kingdom of Italy into three parts—an enlarged Piedmont-Sardinia, which should become the Kingdom of Northern Italy; a state of central Italy under the papacy; and a reestablished Kingdom of the Two Sicilies—a plan that would dispel the danger for both Austria and France of having a united and powerful Italy directly on their frontiers.

These proposals must have seemed alarming enough to the Austrians, but they were relatively innocuous compared to the ideas of Empress Eugénie, who may simply have been letting her own imagination run riot but who must have had some reason to believe she was interpreting the views of her imperial consort. In a three-hour talk with the Austrian ambassador, Prince Richard Metternich, she spoke of Napoleon's eagerness for an entente with Austria and Britain that would lead to the solution of all problems, the consolidation of the Napoleonic dynasty, and the happiness of the world. Russia was to be driven from the Balkans and remunerated for the loss of Poland by compensations in Asiatic Turkey. Poland was to be reconstituted—with a Habsburg archduke as king, if Austria desired, but preferably ruled by the king of Saxony, who would resume his eighteenth-century dynastic rights in Poland in return for the cession of Saxony to Prussia. Prussia in turn should cede its Polish provinces to Poland, restore Silesia (seized from Austria by Frederick the Great) to Austria, and cede the left bank of the Rhine to France. In addition to Saxony, Prussia was to get Hannover and other German states north of the Main River. Austria was to cede Venetia to Italy and its Polish provinces to Poland; in compensation it would receive a stretch of territory in the Balkans from Serbia to the Adriatic, the province of Silesia from Prussia, and all it wanted in Germany south of the Main. Turkey was to be suppressed in the interest of public utility and Christian morality, with its territories divided among Russia, Austria, and Greece, while the Danubian Principalities (Moldavia and Wallachia, the future Romania) were to be set up as an independent state under a native prince. The dispossessed princes and kings of Europe would be sent to the Western Hemisphere to civilize and monarchize the American republics as France was now doing in Mexico.

"This is the plan of the empress" Metternich reported to his foreign minister, and he begged Count Rechberg "not to consider it a joke," for he believed the empress and even the emperor were convinced of the possibility and necessity of fulfilling it someday. While dismissing this "Napoleonic phantasmagoria," Metternich recommended that Vienna take advantage of France's desire for an alliance to end Austria's isolation, but that Austria insist on the inclusion of Britain to moderate French influence and enthusiasms.

Only the desire to end Austria's isolation and perhaps form a connection with Britain by way of France can explain why the Austrians did not reject Napoleon's incredible proposals outright and agreed instead to join Britain and France in addressing a series of identic notes of protest to Russia over Poland. When Russia sidestepped these protests, which in the end called for the establishment of an autonomous Polish state, Napoleon proposed outright intervention in Poland. At this point both Austria and Britain drew the line. With their refusal to join France in threatening Russia with war, Napoleon, with a large part of his army in Mexico, was obliged to abandon the idea of military intervention.

The French ruler made a final effort on behalf of the Poles. In a speech to the French legislature on November 5, 1863, he confessed that the tripartite efforts to obtain concessions for the Poles had failed. But was nothing left except the alternatives of war or silence over the Polish issue? Indeed there was. The Polish cause should be submitted to an international tribunal. Furthermore, the deliberations of this congress should not be confined to Poland; the time had come to reconstruct the entire international order. "The treaties of 1815 have ceased to exist, the march of events has overthrown them or is threatening to overthrow them almost everywhere." What could be more legitimate or sensible than to convene a congress to confront all the problems of Europe, put an end to all discord, and "create a new era of order and peace"?

The only immediate response to Napoleon's proposal for a congress to reorganize the map of Europe was an Anglo-Austrian agreement to oppose any effort to overturn the 1815 treaties. Otherwise this latest display of Napoleonic phantasmagoria served only to revive general European suspicion of the French emperor's motives.

Without foreign aid the Polish insurrection was doomed. It was finally crushed, with brutal ferocity, in March 1864. The sole beneficiary of Napoleon's diplomatic campaign on behalf of the Poles was Prussia. Whatever resentment the tsar and Russian patriots may have felt about Bismarck's unsolicited offer of support at the beginning of the revolt was dissipated in their anger over the interventionist efforts of the three other European great powers.

The revival of European suspicion of Napoleon, the end of any possibility of Franco-Russian rapprochement, the continued isolation of Austria—these problems, together with Britain's preoccupation with the American Civil War and the French involvement in Mexico, constituted the international background of a renewed flare-up of the Schleswig-Holstein question, which was to provide the occasion for Bismarck's first major diplomatic triumph and the first major political step in Prussia's unification of Germany.

❑ *The Schleswig-Holstein Crisis of 1863 and the Danish War*

The 1848 revolution in the duchies of Schleswig, Holstein, and Lauenburg had produced one of the most dangerous international crises in that turbulent era. According to ancient tradition and recent treaties the duchies were inseparably linked with each other, a situation complicated by the statesmen of 1815 who had made Holstein and Lauenburg, with their predominantly German populations, members of the German Confederation, whereas Schleswig, with a substantial Danish minority, had been left out. The status of the duchies was complicated still further by the fact that the duke of Schleswig-Holstein was also king of Denmark, which meant that they were linked by dynastic ties with the Scandinavian kingdom. The revolution in the duchies in 1848 had been the result of efforts of King Frederick VII of Denmark, spurred on by nationalists in his own country, to incorporate the duchies into the state of Denmark in violation of international treaties. That revolution had led to war between Denmark and the German Confederation, which had been brought to an end through the diplomatic intervention of other European powers. An international treaty signed in London in May 1852 reaffirmed the prewar status of the duchies: they were restored to the king of Denmark on a dynastic basis, but the treaty specifically prohibited their incorporation into Denmark.

The crisis over Schleswig-Holstein in 1863 began in exactly the same way as that of 1848. In March King Frederick VII, once again under pressure from Danish nationalists, attempted to take advantage of European preoccupation with Poland to make another attempt to incorporate the duchies into Denmark. He did this by promulgating a common constitution for Denmark and the duchies. This constitution, a de facto act of incorporation and thus a violation of the 1852 Treaty of London, was approved by the Danish parliament on November 13. Two days later King Frederick VII died; having no issue, he was succeeded by the head of a collateral branch of the Danish royal house, who took the title of Christian IX.

This collateral succession introduced yet another complication into the Schleswig-Holstein question because Denmark and the duchies had different laws of succession. In Denmark the throne could be inherited through the female line, whereas in the duchies the succession could only go through males. The new king of Denmark, however, was descended through the female line, and the principal claimant through the male line in 1863 was a German, Frederick, duke of Augustenburg. In 1852 the Augustenburg claim had been relinquished by Frederick's father in return for a monetary payment, and the Treaty of London of that year had recognized the future succession of the Danish claimant despite his hereditary handicap. Upon becoming king of Denmark, therefore, Christian was faced with the question of whether to yield to Danish nationalist pressure and accept the new constitution, which violated the very treaty that provided for his succession to the duchies. The new ruler did not hesitate long. He signed the new constitution on November 18.

Ever since Frederick VII had announced his new constitution in the previous March, the diet of the German Confederation had denounced this violation of the 1852 Treaty of London and supported the claims of the duke of Augustenburg, who maintained that Denmark's treaty violation had invalidated his father's previous renunciation of the succession. In July 1863 the diet resolved that the duchies should be separated from Denmark and placed under the rule of Augustenburg, and in December it voted to send federal troops (contingents from Saxony and Hannover) into Holstein and Lauenburg to forestall any Danish action there.

Bismarck had no intention of allowing Prussian policy to be determined by the diet of the German Confederation, but neither could he afford to alienate German nationalist opinion by remaining aloof from the Schleswig-Holstein question. To secure independent action and gain the political initiative, he pointedly ignored the decision of the German federal diet and came forward in defense of international law as represented by the 1852 Treaty of London. The Austrians, as so often in this age of burgeoning nationalism, found themselves in a quandary. Although tempted to recognize the duke of Augustenburg, whose claims were not only endorsed by the German federal diet but enthusiastically supported by German nationalists, the Austrians hesitated to establish the dangerous precedent of promoting a nationalist cause in Schleswig-Holstein while suppressing similar causes in their own dominions. Unable to resolve this problem, they allowed themselves to be persuaded by Bismarck to join Prussia in the safer course of supporting international law, and on January 16, 1864, Austria and Prussia addressed a joint ultimatum to Denmark demanding the abrogation of the new constitution within forty-eight hours.

The Danes meanwhile had taken a hard line on all proposals for compromise, and, inspired by nationalist fervor of their own, did not hesitate to take up the German challenge. They were confident they could contain an Austro-Prussian invasion behind their island fortifications until foreign powers came to their aid, and they were equally confident that such aid would be forthcoming. In 1848 Britain, Russia, and Sweden had demonstrated that they would not tolerate German control of the base of the strategic Jutland peninsula, and France too might be expected to oppose any threat to European equilibrium in that region.

Bismarck had sounder reasons for confidence. He had taken the firm moral ground of defending international law so that foreign powers would have difficulty finding an excuse for intervention. From the Russians he had received assurances of neutrality, the French were in no better position to intervene in Denmark than in Poland, the British navy could not fight on land, and Sweden would never venture to intervene alone. Bismarck was therefore very much in control of the crisis. If the Danes agreed to withdraw their constitution, there would be ample opportunity to press for further concessions. But because the Danes themselves would surely recognize this danger, they would almost certainly reject the German ultimatum. In that case there would be war in which Austria and Prussia would enjoy an overwhelming military advantage.

The Danes opted for war. On January 21, 1864, Austrian and Prussian troops entered Holstein and Lauenburg, ruthlessly sweeping aside the German federal forces already in occupation of the duchies, and at the beginning of February they crossed the Eider River into Schleswig. The Danes offered only token resistance and retired to their fortifications at Düppel, which guarded the approach to the principal Danish islands. They received no foreign military aid.

The British did their best to save the Danes through diplomacy. They took the lead in garnering the support of neutral powers for an armistice in the Danish war and an international conference to settle the Schleswig-Holstein question, a conference all the belligerents felt obliged to attend rather than flout what amounted to a European mandate.

That conference convened in London on April 25, 1864. Seven days earlier Prussian forces had stormed the Danish fortifications at Düppel, a military success that put Bismarck in a strong bargaining position. He nevertheless took care to maintain his stance as the champion of international law, which, as he did not fail to point out, had been violated by the Danes, and to maneuver them into the position of having to bear responsibility for the failure of compromise proposals based on previous treaties. His own proposal in this regard called for a return to the 1852 Treaty of London and the restoration of the "personal union" of the duchies with Denmark under the rule of King Christian. Because this proposal meant that the duchies would otherwise be completely independent of Denmark, the Danes categorically rejected it, as they rejected a proposal inspired by Napoleon to divide Schleswig along national lines.

The London conference broke up on June 25, the war was resumed, and the Danes, whose continued confidence in receiving foreign support against the German powers proved to be fatally misplaced, were soon defeated. An armistice was arranged on July 18 and a preliminary peace was signed on August 1 in Vienna, where a final peace was signed on October 30, 1864. That peace was designed to minimize the possibility of foreign intervention. It simply called for the king of Denmark's renunciation of all rights to the duchies of Schleswig, Holstein, and Lauenburg in favor of the emperor of Austria and the king of Prussia. The evacuation of allied troops from Jutland (i.e., from Danish territory) was to be carried out in the shortest possible time, at the latest within three weeks of the certification of the final treaty. The treaty made no mention of the final fate of the duchies themselves, which was left to the future decision of the two German powers. During the peace negotiations, the diet of the German Confederation had been bypassed and the claims of the duke of Augustenburg completely ignored.

❑ *From the Danish to the Austrian War*

Throughout the Danish war and the peace negotiations, Bismarck had worked hard and on the whole successfully to keep Austrian policy in line with that of Prussia by emphasizing their joint concern with the defense of international law, conservatism, and the monarchical principle. On July 14, with victory over the Danes assured, he informed the Austrians through his envoy in Vienna that Prussia regarded the conflict with Denmark "as being in essence an episode in the struggle on behalf of the monarchical principle against the European revolution." The future of the duchies should therefore not be allowed to jeopardize "the great conservative interests we are both defending."

In light of later events, Bismarck's appeal for continued Austro-Prussian solidarity has the appearance of crass hypocrisy, a dishonest stratagem to gain time to prepare for a showdown with Austria in the struggle for supremacy in Germany. Perhaps that is really all that it was. But what were Bismarck's objectives in that struggle, and was he convinced that a war would be necessary to achieve them?

To judge from Bismarck's actual policy after the Danish war, these objectives were as yet limited to securing Austria's recognition of Prussian dominance in northern Germany, which would have involved Austria's surrender of its rights in Schleswig-Holstein. (Even after Prussia's military victory over Austria, these were still the principal concessions he sought from the Habsburg monarchy.) Bismarck had ample reason to believe that the Austrians might make these concessions without war on behalf of preserving the alliance with Prussia and in return for assurances of Prussian support for Austrian interests in other parts of Europe. For, apart from Prussia, the Austrians were without friends among the great powers, while within their own empire they faced the ferment of their subject nationalities and a chaotic financial situation.

Bismarck's belief in the possibility of Austria's willingness to make sacrifices to avoid a break with Prussia was not based on mere theoretical speculation, for in August 1864 he learned from Count Rechberg, the Austrian foreign minister, that the Habsburg government was prepared to make the concessions he desired. But in return Rechberg wanted more than vague assurances about mutual support and collaboration. He wanted specific guarantees about shared authority in Germany and the admission of additional Austrian territories into the German Confederation; he wanted a military alliance guaranteeing Prussian support for the preservation and reestablishment of Austrian authority in Italy; and he wanted the fulfillment of earlier Prussian promises regarding Austria's entry into the German Customs Union or at least the negotiation of new tariff agreements to ease Austria's economic difficulties.

Bismarck, while shying away from specific military commitments, was willing to go to some lengths to meet Austria's wishes on economic matters. He informed the heads of Prussia's economic departments that it was "of the greatest importance . . . to secure the goodwill of the Viennese cabinet and to strengthen the position within that cabinet of the ministers who support the Prussian alliance." But at this point he ran into resistance within his own government. Prussian economic officials, with the strong support of the king, refused to give up any part of their considerable economic advantage over Austria. They ruled out any consideration of Austria's entry into the Customs Union and categorically rejected all of Austria's other economic requests.

Having failed to broaden the base of the Prussian alliance, Rechberg was compelled to resign in late October 1864, but his resignation was not followed by Austria's abandonment of the Prussian alliance as Bismarck had feared because, quite simply, Austria had nowhere else to turn. Emperor Francis Joseph admitted ruefully that the Prussian alliance was still necessary under the circumstances, "and we must therefore continue our thankless efforts to keep Prussia on the right lines and within the fold of the law." In the ensuing months the Austrians made a number of unsuccessful efforts to regain the initiative in German affairs through renewed cooperation with the smaller German states and the diet of the German Confederation, but in August 1865 they once again signally turned their backs on the diet by agreeing to Bismarck's proposal to settle the Schleswig-Holstein question by dividing the duchies and selling Lauenburg outright to Prussia.

This arrangement was embodied in the Convention of Gastein of August 14, 1865. To preserve the fiction of the indissolubility of the duchies, their division was restricted to matters of administration, with Prussia assigned the administration of Schleswig and Austria that of Holstein, which lay between Prussia and Schleswig. Austria's authority in Holstein was seriously compromised from the start. To ensure Prussia's access to Schleswig, Prussia was given the right to maintain permanent highway, railroad, and communication links through Holstein; Prussia was to be allowed to build a canal through Holstein connecting the Baltic and North seas; Austria and Prussia together were to recommend to the diet of the German Confederation the creation of a German fleet, based in the Holstein harbor of Kiel, which was to be under Prussian command. Both duchies were to become members of the Prussian-dominated German Customs Union, from which Austria was still excluded. And Lauenburg was to be sold to Prussia for 2.5 million Danish taler. Altogether the terms of Gastein were so favorable to Prussia that foreign powers suspected they had been purchased through secret promises of Prussian support for Austria elsewhere in Europe. But no such promises had been made. Through Gastein, Austria had merely purchased a continuation of the Prussian alliance and acquired administrative rights to Holstein.

The Austrians' acceptance of the terms of Gastein must have led Bismarck to assume that they were still prepared, as Rechberg had been, to surrender both of the Elbe duchies and that they intended to use their rights to Holstein as a bargaining counter. Long before Gastein he had felt reasonably confident that they would not risk war for the sake of territories which, if only because of their geographical position, were bound to fall under Prussian influence sooner or later anyway.

All along, of course, he had never ruled out the possibility of war and had therefore never ceased his efforts to secure for Prussia the most favorable possible international position for waging it.

The international problem was crucial. The national interests of both France and Russia required that they prevent the unification of the German states or any restructuring of Germany that would threaten their own security. This meant that in the event of war between Austria and Prussia, France and Russia could be expected to intervene to prevent a decisive victory of either belligerent. The high probability of Franco-Russian intervention that would deny Prussia the fruits of any victory it might achieve was a compelling reason for Bismarck to have been genuinely eager to achieve his ends without war and argues against the widely held assumption that his policy from the beginning was resolutely set on a collision course. It was nevertheless his task to prepare for such a collision, and for this purpose he concentrated his diplomacy on ensuring the continued isolation of Austria and persuading the French and Russian governments that they would never have cause to intervene against Prussia because Prussia would never pose a threat to their interests.

Bismarck had little difficulty with Russia, where he was able to take advantage of resentment of previous Austrian policies and the tsar's gratitude for Prussian support during the recent Polish crisis. He found, in fact, that the tsarist government did not seem to be worried about Prussia at all in the event of a German war, worrying instead about Austria, for military experts in Russia—like those almost everywhere in Europe—were convinced the Austrian army was far superior to Prussia's. The principal concern of the Russians, therefore, was that Austria would score a decisive victory, and they intimated to Bismarck that they might then intervene to prevent Austria's domination of Germany. In any event, their sympathies would always be on the side of Prussia. Bismarck was thus able to conclude that he could count on the benevolent neutrality of Russia, at least during the early stages of a German war.

After taking soundings in Britain, Bismarck concluded that the British, too, would remain neutral. They had not intervened actively in the war in Denmark, where critical British interests were at stake, and were therefore even less likely to become involved in a war in central Europe. The Civil War in the United States was now over, but the attention of British leaders remained diverted from continental affairs by bitter domestic controversies over franchise reform. As in the case of Russia, the British could be expected to intervene in the event of a threat to the European equilibrium, but for the time being British statesmen did not seem to think any such threat was imminent.

Bismarck's most difficult problem was France, which because of its smaller size and geographical position had even greater reason than Russia to oppose any political change in Germany likely to threaten French security. Napoleon, however, was no defender of the status quo. For years he had called for the dissolution of the 1815 treaty system and a general political reorganization of Europe. After the Danish war he was particularly eager for a reorganization that would give him the opportunity to achieve a dramatic foreign policy success to compensate for the Austro-Prussian victory and divert the attention of French public opinion from the increasingly obvious disaster of his Mexican venture. In sounding the attitude of the French government, Bismarck soon learned that Napoleon would actually welcome a German war that could be expected to drain the resources of all the participants and leave a diplomatic vacuum in central Europe he might exploit to the benefit of France, whether in the Low Countries, the Rhineland, or in territories farther afield.

Bismarck did his best to encourage such expectations and at the same time dissipate any fears the French might have about Prussia. Shortly after Gastein he admitted to the French ambassador in Berlin that Prussia expected to annex both Schleswig and Holstein eventually and to extend its authority over northern Germany. But he assured the French envoy that Prussian interests were strictly confined to the region north of the Main River and that his government had no designs whatever on the states of southern Germany. Consequently Prussia would never pose a threat to French security or even become an obstacle to any territorial ambitions the French might have along their northeastern frontiers. Bismarck even suggested that France, and Italy too, should seek compensation for any future Prussian gains, and that the French government might give its foreign policy greater impetus by seeking increases of territory and influence in regions assigned to France "by similarity of language and race," an unmistakable reference to Belgium.

The French soon made clear that they wanted more than vague suggestions about compensation. When Bismarck visited Paris at the beginning of October 1865, the French foreign minister, Drouyn de Lhuys, frankly acknowledged his fear that Prussia might annex Schleswig-Holstein "without incurring any obligations to France," and he went on to describe in some detail what those obligations might be. Napoleon also expressed apprehensions when Bismarck saw him in the resort of Biarritz a few days later. Surely Prussia had struck a bargain with Austria over Schleswig-Holstein, he said, otherwise it was impossible to explain Austria's acceptance of the terms of Gastein. Had Prussia perhaps promised to support Austria in Venetia? Bismarck admitted that Prussia hoped to purchase Holstein from Austria, but he denied any bargain over Venetia. Moreover, the purchase of Holstein, far from contributing to Prussia's strength, would impose a severe drain on that country's resources and thus make Prussia all the more eager to maintain good relations with France.

Bismarck left France without obtaining commitments of any kind but nevertheless confident that he had assuaged any anxieties Napoleon might have had about Prussian policy. In the event of a crisis in Germany, he believed the French ruler would "dance the cotillion with us," as he expressed it to his own sovereign. Bismarck's confidence seemed justified for early in 1866, as tension between Austria and Prussia mounted, both Napoleon and his foreign minister assured Bismarck that if it came to war, France would remain neutral, but if the struggle assumed larger dimensions, France would be prepared to reach an understanding with Prussia; there could be no question of a similar understanding with Austria. Further, perhaps to improve the chances that there would actually be a war, the French said they would have no objection to Prussia's annexation of Holstein.

With such assurances from France and with his king and the Prussian generals growing increasingly impatient with the lack of progress in negotiations with Austria, Bismarck stepped up his pressure on Vienna for the sale of Holstein. The Austrians, however, instead of agreeing to a sale that would replenish their sadly depleted treasury or bargaining for some other kind of compensation, now chose to make a stand over Holstein: Austria would not allow itself to be ousted from rightfully acquired positions without a struggle.

The Prussian government was not reluctant to take up the challenge. At a meeting of the Prussian Crown Council on February 28, 1866, to discuss the Austrian position and the Schleswig-Holstein question, it was assumed by all those present with the exception of the Prussian crown prince (who was appalled by the prospect of a German civil war) that war was virtually unavoidable and that, without provoking it, the Prussian government should take all necessary political and military measures to prepare for it. Bismarck and the Prussian generals, of course, had long been engaged in such preparations, but now Bismarck took the lead in actually calling for war. He reviewed the record of Austrian efforts to humiliate Prussia and deny it an equal status in German affairs, concluding that the entire historical development of the German question pointed toward war with Austria. Moreover, the moment was propitious for waging it because of Prussia's present superiority in weapons, its friendly relations with France, and the excellent prospect of an alliance with Italy.

The need for an Italian alliance was vigorously pressed by General von Moltke, chief of the Prussian general staff, who declared that securing Italy's active military support was an essential precondition for war, for only if Austria were obliged to maintain a substantial force in the south would Prussia be assured of military superiority in Germany. The council thereupon decided that a diplomatic mission be sent to Italy immediately. It is noteworthy that Bismarck, after all his talk about war, expressed the hope that such a mission would convince the Austrians of the seriousness of the present crisis and make them more amenable to negotiation over the German question. Thus he may still have hoped to settle the relatively minor issue of Holstein peacefully.

Bismarck had long since been negotiating with the Italians, for the desirability of establishing a second front against Austria was obvious. Moreover, that same statesman who had so violently denounced the nationalist revolt in Poland and appealed to Austria in the name of conservative solidarity was also negotiating with nationalist leaders from every part of the Habsburg empire to kindle the fires of national revolution behind the Austrian lines. The irrepressible Garibaldi was to lead a special Italian volunteer force to attack the Italian-claimed Dalmatian coast, veteran commanders of the Hungarian revolutionary army of 1848 were brought to Berlin to plan the formation of a Hungarian legion, and a Slavic corps was being recruited in Serbia to support an uprising of Austria's Slavic population.

Bismarck's negotiations with Italy received providential assistance from Napoleon, who advised the Italians to seek an alliance with Prussia as the only means of applying sufficient pressure on Austria to give up Venetia. The emperor was not giving this advice solely for the benefit of the Italians. He too was convinced of Austria's military superiority and was promoting the Italian alliance to make the sides more even, for a protracted war would afford him the best opportunity to seek compensation for France. With Napoleon acting as midwife, an offensive and defensive alliance between Italy and Prussia was concluded on April 8, 1866: Italy was to join Prussia in a war against Austria if that conflict broke out within three months; both parties promised not to conclude peace or an armistice except by mutual consent; in the event of victory, Italy was to receive Venetia.

In Italy as in Germany, the Austrians refused to cut their losses or make timely concessions in some areas in the interest of maintaining their position in others. In late May 1866 Napoleon, in agreement with Britain and Russia, proposed an international congress to deal with both the German and Italian questions. Napoleon's sudden concern for peace was evidently the product of panic that Austria would score a quick and decisive victory if it came to war in Germany, thus frustrating his efforts to seek compensation. His soldiers were predicting a catastrophic Prussian defeat, despite the Italian alliance, and rumors were rife in Paris of an imminent revolution in Berlin. The Austrians, however, refused to participate in this congress, which might have enabled them to frustrate Prussian ambitions in Germany, because they feared the powers would demand their cession of Venetia or otherwise undermine their position in Italy. At approximately the same time they rejected a compromise solution to their differences with Prussia proposed by two brothers, Anton and Ludwig von Gablenz, the former a senior official in the service of Prussia, the latter the Austrian governor of Holstein, largely because of Prussia's refusal to guarantee their position in Italy.

Yet when the Italians, heartened by their alliance with Prussia, began to make ostentatious preparations for war, the Austrians were so fearful that France as well as Italy would take the side of Prussia that they concluded a secret agreement with Napoleon on June 12, 1866, promising to cede Venetia to Italy whether or not they lost the war. In return they received a guarantee of French neutrality and France's promise to persuade the Italians to remain neutral as well. To compensate for the loss of Venetia, Austria was to be permitted to make territorial gains in Germany, but only after consultation with France and provided those gains did not disturb the European balance of power. The Austrians also promised, orally, to permit the establishment of a new independent state along the Rhine, which Napoleon clearly envisaged as a French satellite. For the Austrians, the agreement to give up Venetia to strengthen their hand in Germany came too late, for by now the Italians hoped to acquire far more than Venetia by joining in the war against Austria, so that the ignominious treaty of June 12 did not even achieve the purpose of keeping Italy neutral.

The Austrians had decided to take a stand against Prussia long before signing their treaty with Napoleon. Although they did not share the confidence of so many foreign observers in their military superiority over Prussia, they were nevertheless confident enough not to fear a military confrontation. They were also encouraged by increasing support from the smaller German states, which were justifiably suspicious of Prussian intentions and looking more and more to Austria as the guardian of their sovereignty and independence.

While still negotiating their treaty of neutrality with Napoleon, the Austrians resolved to take advantage of this pro-Austrian sentiment in Germany to force a showdown with Prussia, which they were convinced could no longer be avoided. On June 1, 1866, they placed a motion before the diet of the German Confederation empowering that body to determine the final status of Schleswig-Holstein. With this move they intended to reestablish their partnership with the confederation, so fatefully abandoned during the Danish crisis in favor of a partnership with Prussia, and to reaffirm their position of leadership in Germany.

The Austrian maneuver frustrated whatever hope Bismarck may have had of avoiding war over Schleswig-Holstein and identifying the cause of Prussia with that of the German nation. Now he could do no more than sound the far from inspiring cry that the Austrians had violated their treaty commitments. "We can see nothing in this action by the Austrian government," he declared in a circular to the governments of Europe, "except a deliberate, direct provocation and a desire to force a rupture of relations and war."

With war now certain, Prussian troops entered Holstein on June 9 to eliminate the possibility of attack from the north, an action the Prussian government justified on the grounds of Austria's treaty violations. The Austrians countered by asking the diet of the German Confederation to mobilize all federal troops "to protect the internal security of Germany and the threatened rights of the members of the confederation." Upon the diet's overwhelming approval of the Austrian motion on June 14, the Prussian delegate denounced its action as a violation of the constitution of the confederation and a de facto declaration of war against Prussia; the Prussian government therefore regarded the German Confederation as dissolved.

The coming of the war revealed that Bismarck's success in dealing with foreign powers was not matched by comparable success in winning confidence and support in Germany itself, for the governments of all the smaller German states with any freedom of choice entered the conflict on the side of Austria. They did so, to be sure, not only because they believed Austria was more likely to respect their sovereignty but because they shared the generally accepted view of Austria's military superiority and thought it crucial to their own future to enter the war on the winning side.

❑ *The Austro-Prussian War*

None of the prophets of Prussian defeat had reckoned with the new Prussian army, which in training and equipment was now far superior to the Austrian. The Prussian breech-loading needle gun, which could be loaded and fired from a prone position, was more accurate and had a higher rate of fire than the Austrian muzzle-loader. In addition, the Prussian network of strategic military railroads gave the army a high degree of mobility.

The Prussians also possessed superior leadership. The nerve center of the Prussian military organization was the army general staff, a body of carefully selected and highly trained experts who applied to the conduct of war a continuous study based on the experience of the past and an analysis of contemporary military developments. General staff officers drew up detailed plans to meet every conceivable military emergency and to ensure rapid mobilization and deployment of their forces, an important consideration in view of Prussia's long and exposed frontiers. The general staff included specialists to coordinate movements of the large armies raised by compulsory conscription and to deal with the technical problems of transportation, communication, and supply. Once the armies were in the field, the general staff provided field commanders with a steady flow of information and advice, readjusting tactics to correspond with the progress of the fighting.

Chief of the army general staff since 1857 was General Helmuth von Moltke, who in manner and appearance seemed far more a scholar than a soldier. In preparing Prussia's campaign plans, Moltke employed bold new conceptions in strategy—among them the use of technical innovations such as the railroad and the telegraph—to solve the problem of military operations with mass armies. Instead of adhering to the traditional strategy of concentrating forces at one point to achieve a military decision, he divided his troops but kept them in a position to converge on a single point at the opportune time. "The main task of good army leadership is to keep the masses separate without losing the possibility of uniting them at the right moment," he said. "If on the day of battle the forces can be brought from separate points and concentrated on the battlefield itself; if the operations are directed in such a way that from different sides a last short march strikes simultaneously against the enemy's front and flank: then strategy has achieved the most that it can achieve, and great results must follow."

With all their plans and preparations made long in advance, the Prussians were able to seize the initiative from the beginning of the war. On June 15, 1866, the day after the diet of the German Confederation voted federal mobilization against Prussia, a Prussian army invaded Hannover, Saxony, and Hesse-Kassel, which had taken the side of Austria. Meanwhile, the bulk of the Prussian forces advanced against the Austrians, who had been forced to divide their armies to meet a simultaneous invasion by Prussia's ally, Italy. On June 29 the Hannoverian army capitulated following its defeat at the Battle of Langensalza. Four days later, on July 3, 1866, the Austrian army was decisively beaten in the Battle of Königgrätz near the northern Bohemian village of Sadowa (another name commonly given the battle). In just over two weeks the Prussians had scored a complete victory. It was one of the shortest and most decisive wars in history.

Bismarck's sense of proportion in international affairs was never more evident than in the period following the Battle of Königgrätz. Before the war, Bismarck had been obliged to overcome the doubts of his king and several military advisers about undertaking a conflict with Austria at all. Now he had to restrain them from exploiting their victory by annexing vast stretches of Austrian territory and staging a triumphal march through Vienna. With Russia on one side and France on the other, Prussia could not afford to prolong the war and thereby give these powers a chance to intervene. Nor could Prussia afford to make Austria and the other defeated German states into bitter and irreconcilable opponents. Bismarck's one aim in the war had been to expel Austria from German affairs. This aim could be realized without annexing Austrian territory and without a victory march through Vienna, which would wound Austrian pride while accomplishing no political purpose. "I have the thankless task of pouring water into the bubbling wine," Bismarck wrote to his wife six days after Königgrätz, "and pointing out that we are not the only inhabitants of Europe but live in it with three other powers that detest and envy us."

❑ *Peacemaking and the Problem of French Intervention*

On July 5, 1866, just two days after Königgrätz, Napoleon made the move Bismarck had most reason to fear: he responded to an Austrian appeal with an offer to mediate. This offer inevitably carried with it the threat of active French military intervention or some form of international diplomatic pressure that would deny Prussia the fruits of its military victory.

Bismarck's greatest asset in his subsequent negotiations with Napoleon was the genuine modesty of his war aims. He assured the French ruler, as he had done repeatedly before the war, that Prussia desired no more than hegemony over northern Germany. The sovereignty and independence of the states of southern Germany, despite their participation in the war on the side of Austria, would be scrupulously respected. French interests would thus not be threatened in any way by the Prussian victory. When Napoleon expressed concern about the nationality problem in Schleswig, Bismarck promised that a plebiscite would be held in the areas of mixed German and Danish nationality. Bismarck also dealt with what he may have regarded as the emperor's greatest concern by holding out the prospect that if the current negotiations with France were successful, Prussia would agree to territorial compensation for France, for example, a restoration of the frontiers of 1814.

Bismarck's negotiations with Napoleon were successful in that they deflected the danger of French military intervention, and the preliminary Peace of Nikolsburg he concluded with Austria on July 26, 1866, corresponded so exactly with the understandings reached with France that it removed all grounds for further French diplomatic intervention as well. According to the terms of Nikolsburg, the German Confederation was dissolved and Prussia was conceded domination over the states of northern Germany, which were to be organized in a North German Confederation under Prussian leadership. Prussia acquired both Schleswig and Holstein, with the reservation that the population in the area of mixed nationalities in northern Schleswig should have the right to decide by plebiscite for union with Denmark—a provision the Prussian-German government subsequently ignored. The Habsburg empire was not to be deprived of any territory apart from the Lombardo-Venetian kingdom (ceded via France to Italy in the final peace treaty with Austria of August 23). Final peace treaties with the other German states involved in the war against Prussia were left to future negotiation.

The speedy conclusion of the Peace of Nikolsburg took Napoleon by surprise, for he had not yet had time to respond to Bismarck's suggestion of territorial compensation for France. On August 4, however, Napoleon's foreign minister, Drouyn de Lhuys, presented formal demands that went far beyond anything Bismarck had proposed. In addition to restoring the boundaries of 1814, which would give France the German territories of Saarbrücken and Landau, France demanded all German territory on the left bank of the Rhine up to and including the city of Mainz (at this time part of the German states of Bavaria and Hesse-Darmstadt). France demanded further that Prussia sever all ties with the duchies of Limburg and Luxemburg. (Although ruled by the king of the Netherlands, both duchies had been former members of the German Confederation and were current members of the German Customs Union; and in Luxemburg, through a treaty with the Netherlands, Prussia had been conceded the right to maintain a military garrison on behalf of the German Confederation.)

Now that Bismarck had made peace with Austria and virtually eliminated the danger of Austria's renewal of the war in alliance with France, he rejected these demands outright with the warning that if the French attempted to force the issue, they would unleash a German national war. Napoleon, suffering from ill health and with much of his army still in Mexico, drew back. It was not he but Drouyn who was the author of these demands, he said, a repudiation on the part of his sovereign that prompted Drouyn's immediate resignation.

While rejecting French demands for territorial compensation in Germany, Bismarck made good use of these demands (in conjunction with veiled threats of punitive peace terms) to persuade the south German states that had sided with Austria in the recent war to enter into offensive and defensive military alliances with Prussia that would give Prussia control of their armies and railway systems in the event of war.

A final peace treaty with Austria, signed in Prague on August 23, 1866, simply confirmed the terms of Nikolsburg. In separate treaties with the south German states

(Baden, Bavaria, and Württemberg), Bismarck kept his promise to Napoleon by leaving them politically independent and their territories intact apart from a few minor boundary revisions. Similar treaties were concluded with most of the states of northern Germany, notably Saxony, the important difference here being that these states, while remaining nominally independent, were enrolled in the Prussian-controlled North German Confederation. In dealing with those north German states that balked at Prussian control, however, Bismarck was ruthless. On August 16, 1866, the king of Prussia, declaring those states to be a threat to national security, submitted a draft law to the Prussian parliament providing for the outright annexation to Prussia of the kingdom of Hannover, the electorate of Hesse-Kassel, the duchy of Nassau, and the free city of Frankfurt. The final decree of annexation was issued September 20.

Prussia's immense gains in terms of both territory and prestige, and the manifest lack of any corresponding gains for France, aroused general consternation in France, where shortly after the Austrian war the cry went up among French patriots of "revenge for Sadowa." With the prestige of his own regime at a low ebb and under heavy pressure from members of his government and French public opinion, Napoleon again bestirred himself to seek compensation. On August 16, 1866, the same day the king of Prussia submitted his annexation draft law, the emperor instructed Count Vincent Benedetti, his ambassador to Berlin, to propose two agreements with Prussia: a public treaty conceding France the frontiers of 1814 and the right to annex Luxemburg; and a secret offensive and defensive alliance which included Prussia's consent to France's eventual annexation of Belgium.

Bismarck refused the request for the 1814 frontiers on the grounds that this would involve the cession of German territory, which would not be tolerated by German public opinion, but he indicated his willingness to allow France a free hand with regard to Belgium and Luxemburg, and at his suggestion Benedetti drew up a draft treaty in his own handwriting incorporating what the French envoy believed to have been the fruits of their negotiation. According to the terms of this draft, dated August 29, 1866, France would recognize Prussia's reorganization of northern Germany and would not even oppose a federal union of the states of southern Germany with the North German Confederation based on a common parliament. In return, the king of Prussia was to help persuade the king of the Netherlands to cede his sovereign rights over Luxemburg to France, and if France should be forced by circumstances to conquer Belgium, Prussia was to provide military and naval support against any power that might declare war on France. To assure the execution of these arrangements, France and Prussia were to enter into an offensive and defensive military alliance.

The Benedetti treaty was an act of almost inconceivable folly, for it required Prussian concessions and guarantees of support, including the high probability of aiding France in a war against Britain over Belgium, in return for gains the Prussians had already made or might hope to make without France's sanction. Worse, it placed in Bismarck's hands evidence of French designs in the Low Countries that could be used to discredit France in the eyes of foreign governments and public opinion—as Bismarck did indeed use it shortly after the outbreak of the Franco-Prussian war. Bismarck, however, did nothing to discourage Benedetti at this time. "The French must retain hope and especially faith in our goodwill without our giving them definite commitments," he said.

❑ *The Luxemburg Crisis*

Early in 1867 France called upon Prussia "in the interest of continued good relations" to make good its promise of support, as stipulated in the Benedetti draft treaty, in persuading the king of the Netherlands to cede Luxemburg to France. Bismarck did not reject this request outright but protested that Prussia could not take the initiative in this matter because the king and his generals were reluctant to give up their garrison in Luxemburg and because any such move would encounter the fierce opposition of German public opinion. He proposed instead that France negotiate directly with the Dutch ruler and allowed Napoleon to assume that he would support such negotiation, for he stipulated only that Prussia should not appear to have been a secret accessory to any Franco-Dutch agreement.

Acting on Bismarck's proposal and with his presumed encouragement, France entered into direct negotiations with the king of the Netherlands on March 16, 1867. After only three days of bargaining the Dutch ruler agreed to sell his rights to Luxemburg for five million gulden, but because Prussian interests were involved, he insisted on obtaining the consent of the king of Prussia to this sale. Instead of readily giving that consent, as the French confidently expected, the Prussian monarch refused to take any responsibility for a treaty over Luxemburg: the king of the Netherlands should decide for himself what he owed to his own position and to Europe. Upon receiving this essentially negative Prussian response, the king of the Netherlands decided in early April not to go through with the sale of Luxemburg. The French government, believing it had been betrayed by Prussia, was infuriated, and when news of the affair leaked out the ensuing outcry on the part of public opinion in both France and Germany produced a serious international crisis.

A good many contemporary observers as well as historians have assumed that Bismarck deliberately fomented the crisis over Luxemburg to provoke a showdown with France, but his entire handling of the affair suggests on the contrary that he was eager to avoid a breach with France, at least at this time, for he played a leading role in arranging a peaceful resolution of the crisis. To circumvent or at any rate deflect the wrath of both French and German public opinion, he cooperated in making use of Napoleon's own favorite device for dealing with international complications, an international congress, which convened in London on May 7, 1867.

A compromise solution, arranged after only three days of deliberation, was embodied in a Treaty of London of May 11. Luxemburg was made a "perpetual" neutral state under a guarantee of the signatory powers (Austria, Belgium, Britain, France, Italy, the Netherlands, Prussia, and Russia). The duchy was to remain under the royal house of the Netherlands, but the fortress of Luxemburg was to be dismantled and the Prussian garrison withdrawn. The London congress also settled the status of the duchy of Limburg, that other former member of the German Confederation Napoleon had coveted, by making it an integral part of the Kingdom of the Netherlands.

The Napoleonic government's failure to obtain Luxemburg was seen by the government itself and French public opinion as yet another blow to the prestige of the imperial regime, a failure blamed not on the congress but on the perfidy of Bismarck, so that Luxemburg became yet another score to settle with Prussia. Yet the affair was anything but a triumph for Bismarck. France had been prevented from acquiring Luxemburg, if this had indeed been Bismarck's intention, but at the cost of disastrous damage to Prussia's relations with France, while among patriots in Germany he was bitterly denounced for the permanent loss of Luxemburg.

The real winners over Luxemburg were the British, for the London treaty denied both France and Prussia this wedge into the Low Countries, and the international guarantee for the permanent neutrality of the duchy created a valuable deterrent to the future aggression of any power in that area.

❑ The Reorganization of North Germany and the Problem of the South

The Luxemburg crisis, and indeed Bismarck's overall policy in dealing with France after the Austrian war, raises virtually the same questions as did his policy toward Austria after the Danish war. What were his objectives? Was he convinced that a war with France was necessary to achieve them? And in that case, was his entire policy dedicated to preparing for such a war?

Bismarck's ultimate objective in Germany was clear. After 1866 he was thinking in terms of extending Prussian control over southern as well as northern Germany, of fulfilling, in fact, the Kleindeutsch program for German unification. As in his policy toward Austria, he always considered the possible necessity for war, but again he had good reason to believe that he could achieve his purpose without a war and even better reason to desire to avoid or at least postpone one. He needed time to deal with domestic problems and consolidate Prussia's gains in northern Germany, and above all he needed time to explore the possibilities for a peaceful integration of the south German states.

His easiest task proved to be bringing the longstanding constitutional conflict in Prussia to what was for him a victorious conclusion. On September 3, 1866, exactly two months after Königgrätz and at the height of his success and prestige, Bismarck came before the Prussian parliament to appeal to the liberal majority for a bill of indemnity to make legal retroactively the taxes whose collection had made possible the reorganization of the Prussian army and the consequent victories over Denmark and Austria. A surprising number of deputies stood by their principles and refused to be swayed by Bismarck's achievements, but the final vote of 230 to 75 in favor of indemnity nevertheless represented a ringing endorsement of Bismarck's authoritarian policies and a triumph of nationalist sentiment over liberal and constitutional principles.

Elsewhere in Germany, the states north of the Main were organized in the North German Confederation. The constitution of that body (which was to become the constitution for the German empire) was largely the work of Bismarck himself. The member states, apart from those annexed outright to Prussia, retained their own governments and bureaucracies, but their armies and foreign policy were to be controlled by Prussia, and the two-chamber parliament established to represent the governments and peoples of the confederation was set up in such a way that the king of Prussia and his ministers retained a large measure of executive authority. Nevertheless, the lower house of that parliament, whose deputies were to be elected by universal manhood suffrage, was conceded surprisingly extensive financial and legislative powers, so that it was anything but a rubber stamp or fig leaf for absolutism, as many critics of the Prussian government chose to call it.

At the time of the organization of the North German Confederation, there seemed a good possibility that the states of southern Germany might enter into some kind of federal union with Prussia immediately and without further ado. During their peace negotiations with Prussia, the south German governments, with the obvious purpose of securing more lenient terms, had expressed their willingness to establish a closer federal relationship or even become associate members of the North German Confederation. Bismarck had not seized on this offer to avoid a breach with France and because there seemed no need to run any risk whatever over this question. By now, after all, a considerable degree of federation with the south German states had already been achieved. They were all enrolled in the Prussian-dominated German Customs Union; the offensive and defensive alliances concluded after Königgrätz, which gave Prussia control of their armies and railways in the event of war, already admitted a good deal of Prussian influence over their military and communication establishments. Surely it was only a matter of time before the south German governments succumbed to nationalist pressures and the forces of circumstance and entered into an outright political union with their northern compatriots.

In southern Germany, nationalist fervor was most evident in Baden, where in October 1866 the parliament voted for unconditional union with the North German Confederation. Bismarck rejected this offer. He was still anxious not to arouse French antagonism, but he also wanted to maintain an independent Baden to serve as a bellwether for bringing the south German states as a block into a German union. By now there was an obvious need for such service on the part of Baden, for the governments of Bavaria and Württemberg, once they had made peace with Prussia and no longer had to fear draconian penalties, reverted into jealous guardians of their countries' sovereignty and independence.

The stratagem Bismarck adopted for the further amalgamation of the south German states was a proposal for reform of the German Customs Union that would include establishing a customs parliament, its delegates to be elected by universal manhood suffrage. The idea behind this proposal was that an all-German parliament for economic affairs would inevitably become involved in politics and thus develop into a de facto all-German political parliament; the provision for universal suffrage was intended to ensure the election of nationalist deputies who would make the customs parliament a national forum and bring the pressure of German nationalism to bear on their respective governments. Through universal suffrage Bismarck also presumed to overtrump middle-class liberalism, for he was convinced that the mass of the German people, the peasants and artisans, even while absorbing the revolutionary cult of nationalism, had remained essentially conservative politically.

Bismarck's calculations about the basic conservatism of the German people proved to be correct—rather more correct, in fact, than he had anticipated, for south Germany gave a conservative answer to the lure of nationalism, or at any rate to Prussianism. In elections in February and March 1868 to the customs parliament in south Germany (the people of northern Germany were to be represented by their previously elected delegates to the parliament of the North German Confederation), nationalist candidates in Bavaria won only 12 of 48 seats, in Württemberg they won no seats at all in a 17-man delegation, and even in Baden, where nationalist sentiment had seemed so strong, nationalists won only a bare majority of the votes. The antinational delegates from the south proceeded to join forces with antinational (or anti-Prussian) delegates from the north—Poles and northern Catholics, delegates from Hannover and other northern states whose populations resented their forcible union with Prussia, and representatives of old-guard Prussian conservatives who felt betrayed by Bismarck's radical restructuring of German politics. As part of this antinational–anti-Prussian alliance, southern delegates could prevent any broadening of authority of the customs parliament or of Prussian authority over their own states.

Bismarck professed not to be disappointed or even surprised by the election results. "To attain with one blow a homogeneous structure for Germany is only possible in the event of war," he wrote to the Prussian representative in Baden. "Aside from this eventuality, which we shall neither predict nor precipitate, the development will have to run through one or more transitional stages." He expected that the elections at the end of each three-year parliamentary term would produce increasingly favorable results for the national cause. All this might take time, perhaps five to ten years or as much as a generation, but the eventual unification of Germany was a certainty.

While acknowledging that the process of unification could be speeded by war, Bismarck steadfastly rejected the pleas of impatient German nationalists to provoke a violent solution to the German problem. An arbitrary, subjectively determined interference in the course of history always resulted in shaking down unripe fruit, he wrote to his minister in Bavaria in February 1869. "That at the present moment German unification is still an unripe fruit is in my opinion obvious." There was the further problem, as there had been earlier in speculating about war with Austria, that foreign powers might intervene to deprive Prussia of the fruits of any victory it might achieve or actually join forces to bring about its defeat. It was not only a question of expediency. War was simply not a method a conscientious government should employ to attain goals that would be realized in any case. Bismarck's fundamental objection to a violent solution of the German problem, however, was that this first national war against France would very likely be the prelude to five or six others. "No one can assume the responsibility for the outbreak of a conflict that would perhaps only be the first of a series of racial wars [*Rassenkriege*]," he said.

Instead of provoking war, Bismarck wanted to accustom European and especially French public opinion gradually to the idea of a unified Germany. When public opinion was sufficiently prepared, the time would have come to absorb part or all of southern Germany. In February 1870 Bismarck turned aside another proposal to incorporate Baden into the North German Confederation. The time for such action was premature, he said. He did not want to alarm the other south German governments, but above all he did not want to provoke a crisis with the recently liberalized Napoleonic regime "as it signifies peace for us." "You know how firmly we have our common goal [of German unification] in mind," Bismarck wrote to his representative in Baden on February 28. "But you also know how carefully considered the motives are by which we choose our course and measure our pace."

❑ *The Hohenzollern Candidacy*

It is one of the paradoxes of history that on the same day Bismarck sent this dispatch to his minister in Baden in which he forcefully restated his views about avoiding war and slowing the pace of German unification, he purposefully took up a campaign which at the very least ran a serious risk of war. The genesis of this campaign was an offer from the Spanish provisional government in February 1870 to confer the crown of Spain on Prince Leopold of Hohenzollern-Sigmaringen, a member of a Catholic branch of the ruling house of Prussia. After only one day of deliberation, Bismarck decided that this offer should be accepted, although he was perfectly aware that the Hohenzollern candidacy would almost certainly provoke a crisis with France. The paradox in Bismarck's policy involved here can be explained most easily by dismissing his statements about a peaceful solution to the German problem as a disguise for his real intentions. It is more difficult to explain why he abandoned the evolutionary policy he had advocated and pursued heretofore, and for so many cogent reasons.

The most obvious explanation is that Bismarck had become genuinely alarmed by the recalcitrant attitude of the south German states, for instead of moving gradually toward union with northern Germany, the people as well as governments of the south were showing more and more signs of opposition to such union and indeed to all forms of Prussianization. So widespread and intense was this hostility that many historians have concluded that by 1870 Bismarck had abandoned hope for a peaceful German unification and deliberately provoked war with France to rekindle the fires of nationalist enthusiasm and weld Germany together at last in the fires of a patriotic war against a foreign foe.

The difficulties over southern Germany undoubtedly figured prominently in Bismarck's calculations, but the crucial problem for him all along was surely the attitude of France. Always clear in his own mind that French national interests required the prevention of a united Germany, he could not help but recognize that the French must fear that such unification would come to pass unless they took decisive measures to prevent it; the French might therefore be expected to intervene in German affairs, and soon, to forestall any further progress in the unification movement. But did Napoleon, with his promotion of nationalism and multifarious plans for reorganizing Europe, clearly perceive where French interests lay—his sponsorship of Italian and Polish nationalism and his Mexican venture left room for doubt on this score— and would his government be prepared to intervene militarily to prevent any strengthening of Prussia's position in Germany and Europe?

The Hohenzollern candidacy provided an opportunity to test a variety of possibilities. The French emperor, beset by ill health and so frequently indecisive in moments of crisis, might passively accept the candidacy of Prince Leopold as preferable to that of a rival French royal house (an Orléans candidate had been considered) and try to make him acceptable to French public opinion by emphasizing his Catholicism and the fact that he was actually more closely related to the Bonapartes than to the Protestant Hohenzollerns. If the Hohenzollern candidacy were indeed allowed to go through, the overall position of Prussia would be strengthened. The prestige of the Prussian ruling house would be enhanced; Germany as a whole would derive substantial political and economic benefits from closer ties with Spain; and the establishment of a pro-German government in Spain would force the French to keep at least part of their army on guard along the Pyrenees. These advantages for Prussia would of course be obvious to the French, so that a Napoleonic policy of passive acceptance might precipitate a revolution or some other domestic crisis that would temporarily immobilize France's capacity to intervene in German affairs.

By far the most likely French reaction, however, would be a demand that the Hohenzollern candidacy be withdrawn, which the Spaniards could deflect as unjustifiable interference in the affairs of another country. If the French turned their wrath against Prussia, the Prussian government could plead ignorance of the entire affair and pose as the innocent victim of French bullying. And if the French chose to go to war with Prussia over the issue, they would appear as the aggressors and find themselves from the start in a morally weak international position.

Bismarck's diplomatic campaign built around the Hohenzollern candidacy broke down by sheer accident—a coding error by a clerk in the Prussian legation in Madrid. Bismarck had counted on keeping the matter secret until Prince Leopold was formally elected by the Spanish parliament so that the cabinets of Europe would be presented with an accomplished fact. Instead, as a result of the coding error, the Spanish parliament was allowed to adjourn June 24, 1870, before the pro forma vote had been held, the news of Prince Leopold's candidacy leaked out, and the French were given ample opportunity to take countermeasures. They at once brought pressure to bear on the leaders of the Spanish government to withdraw the offer and on the Hohenzollern family to decline it. But powerful elements within the French government wanted more than an elimination of the candidacy; they wanted to exploit the incident to humiliate Prussia and thereby bolster the prestige of their own government.

In the beginning, the French were successful in this endeavor. They totally ignored Spain and thrust Prussia to the fore as their chief target. On July 6 the French foreign minister, the duke of Gramont, set the public tone of the campaign with a statement in the chamber of deputies threatening war unless Prussia withdrew Prince Leopold's candidacy. At the same time the French government urged the king of Prussia, as head of the House of Hohenzollern, to order his relative to abandon the Spanish project in the interests of European peace. To Bismarck's chagrin, the king yielded to the French arguments. On July 12, Prince Karl Anton, father of Prince Leopold, withdrew his son's candidacy.

The French had scored a great diplomatic triumph, but Gramont wanted to underline the fact that this victory had been achieved at the expense of Prussia. The French accordingly demanded that the king of Prussia write Napoleon a letter of apology for the trouble his relative had caused. The letter was to state that the king was moved by feelings of respectful friendship for France; it was specifically to disavow the candidacy of the king's relative to the throne of Spain and promise that this candidacy would never be renewed. On July 13, Count Benedetti, the French ambassador to Prussia, tried to present these demands to the king of Prussia, who was at the spa of Ems. When the king understood the nature of the French proposals, he politely dismissed Benedetti and resisted all further efforts by the French ambassador to see him. On the same day the king sent Bismarck an account of what had happened.

Gramont had overplayed his hand, and in so doing he gave Bismarck the opportunity to turn the tables in the Hohenzollern affair. Upon receiving the royal telegram from Ems describing the incident with Benedetti, Bismarck edited it to make the king's dismissal of the French ambassador more brusque than it had been. He then released the edited telegram (the Ems Dispatch) to the press. The French effort to humiliate Prussia now appeared as a humiliation of France.

Bismarck was fully aware of the risk he was taking, but by this time he was evidently convinced that a peaceful settlement was no longer possible. If the French chose to declare war on Prussia, as Bismarck expected, they would appear to be the aggressors, and Prussia might therefore hope to secure the benevolent neutrality of the moralistic Gladstone government in Britain. He had already secured promises of neutrality from Russia, which had also engaged to keep Austria neutral, and he had military alliances with the states of southern Germany. The Prussian generals assured him of the preparedness of the Prussian army. Diplomatically and militarily, Prussia was ready for war. But to the end Bismarck remained cautious, and he waited for the French to make the decisive move.

In France voices of caution were raised against war with Prussia. The emperor vacillated. He lacked confidence in the French army and feared a long, inconclusive struggle. But French public opinion was clamoring for war, Gramont and the Empress Eugénie declared that the empire could not survive if it accepted this latest humiliation from Prussia, and French military leaders were confident of victory. On July 15, 1870, the French government declared war on Prussia. "The army is ready down to the last gaiter-button," said the French minister of war. "We go to war with a light heart," said Emile Ollivier, the French prime minister.

❑ *The Franco-Prussian War*

The ensuing conflict showed that the Prussian political and military calculations had been far more accurate than the French. Napoleon had hoped for support from a vengeful Austria and a grateful Italy, but he had badly misjudged the international situation. The Austrians were still suffering financially from the 1866 war, they were still angry with Napoleon for supporting Italy in 1859, and they were held in check by Russia. Further, the majority of Austrian Germans were enthusiastically on the side of their fellow Germans. The Hungarians, too, who had been reconciled to Habsburg rule by being granted virtual autonomy in their domestic affairs through the so-called Compromise (Ausgleich) of 1867, were opposed to renewing the war in Germany, which if successful would reinforce the German element and correspondingly diminish their own influence in what was now the Austro-Hungarian empire. In Italy, the king was tempted to help Napoleon, but Italian nationalists had been alienated by the French seizure of Nice and Savoy, and they were now eager to take advantage of the crisis with Prussia to occupy Rome, which was still garrisoned by French troops. To counter any effort the Italian sovereign might make to side with France, Bismarck was in touch with republican leaders in Italy to foment an uprising against the monarchical government if this should be necessary. Finally, to deter the Gladstone government from making any move on behalf of France, Bismarck released the Benedetti treaty of August 1866, with its provisions for France's acquisition of Belgium and Luxemburg, to the London *Times,* which published it on July 25, 1870.

In the military sphere, too, Prussian preparations proved far superior to those of the French. The Napoleonic government had undertaken an intelligently conceived reorganization of the French army, but that reorganization had barely begun. A secret weapon on which the French counted for spectacular results, the rapid-firing *mitrailleuse* cannon, had been kept so secret that most of the French troops did not know how to use it. The French *chassepot* rifle was better than the Prussian needle gun, but this advantage was offset by the superiority of the Prussian artillery, which was decisive in a large number of engagements. The Prussian army surpassed the French in organization, mobility, and leadership. As in the war against Austria, the Prussian general staff had prepared careful and detailed plans to ensure the speedy mobilization and deployment of its troops and to make maximum use of the railroad for purposes of transportation and supply. The rapid advance of the Prussian forces through southern Germany prevented the south German governments from even attempting to evade their military commitments and meant that the war was fought on French rather than German territory.

The actual conduct of the war, however, showed that Bismarck had been wise to try to accomplish his purposes by peaceful means. Had the French been better led, had they made full use of their superior weapons, had they taken advantage of Prussian errors, they might have fought the war to a stalemate or at least secured foreign mediation. As it was, the French generals made even more mistakes than the Prussian. Within a fortnight after the outbreak of war the Prussian armies had penetrated deeply into French territory and split the French forces. One French army under General Achille Bazaine was bottled up in the fortress of Metz. While attempting to relieve Bazaine's forces, a second French army, under Marshal Marie Edmé de MacMahon, was surrounded by the Prussians at Sedan. On September 2, 1870, after a day of heavy fighting, MacMahon's entire army surrendered and the emperor was captured. These events were followed almost immediately by the formation of a revolutionary government in Paris, which declared the emperor deposed and proclaimed the establishment of the Third French Republic.

The collapse of the empire did not end the war. Bazaine's army held out in Metz until October 27, and the French continued a dogged resistance from the provinces. They organized new armies that fought effectively despite their lack of training and equipment. The great French hope at this stage was foreign intervention, but Bismarck had laid his diplomatic foundations well and no aid was forthcoming. On January 28, 1871, after a siege of over four months, Paris capitulated. At the end of February representatives of the provisional French government appealed for an armistice. The final peace treaty between France and Germany was signed at Frankfurt on May 10, 1871. France was compelled to give up Alsace and part of Lorraine, to pay an indemnity of five billion francs, and to support a German army of occupation until the indemnity had been paid.

In the course of the war, Bismarck had negotiated treaties with Bavaria, Württemberg, and Baden that achieved what German nationalists had so long desired, the union of these south German states with Prussia and the North German Confederation. The treaties allowed the previously independent south German states to retain their own governments and a certain measure of domestic autonomy, but their chief significance lay in establishing the conditions for unification and the creation of the new German empire. On January 18, 1871, shortly before the war with France came to an end, King William I of Prussia was proclaimed German emperor (kaiser) in the Hall of Mirrors of Louis XIV's palace at Versailles.

❑ *The Problem of Alsace-Lorraine*

The French defeat, the establishment of the German empire, and the loss of Alsace-Lorraine created a hatred between France and Germany that would prevail until well after World War II. Bismarck has been charged with a major political error in aggravating the animosity of the French by annexing territory they regarded as their own, and the question is frequently raised of why he abandoned his restraint in this instance. As in all aspects of Bismarck's statecraft, there is no simple answer. With respect to Alsace-Lorraine, he had German as well as French opinion to consider. To the French the region might be part of their nation's sacred soil, but to the Germans it was a segment of the medieval German empire that France had stolen when Germany was weak and divided. Bismarck did much to incite German national feeling on this issue, for nationalism was his only weapon in overcoming the religious and political particularism of the German people. There was also the cogent military argument that these provinces were strategically essential.

The strategic argument appears to have been the overriding consideration for Bismarck. He realized that the loss of Alsace-Lorraine would arouse bitter hostility in France, but in contrast to his attitude toward Austria in 1866 he assumed from the start that it would be impossible to avoid future French antagonism and that Prussia must therefore annex the strategic territory of the Vosges Mountains in the interest of its future security. During the war his great fear had been that Britain and Russia, perhaps together or in conjunction with Austria, would offer to mediate and prevent Prussia from making the desired annexations.

That this was no idle fear was evident after the first Prussian victories, for on August 7, 1870, the Prussian ambassador to St. Petersburg reported that Gorchakov, the Russian foreign minister, seemed determined to mediate and that the tsar had expressed the hope that Prussia would refrain from any territorial annexations. In reply Bismarck warned the Russians that "a peace settlement unsatisfactory to German interests would pave the way for a republic and socialism," and that only the continued solidarity among the three eastern conservative powers could safeguard order and civilization against the forces of revolution. The actual establishment of a republican government in France provided Bismarck with fresh ammunition for his warnings and for making the case that Prussia, as the conservative state most immediately exposed to the republican contagion, required stronger strategic frontiers.

Besides playing on the tsar's dread of revolution, Bismarck sought to divert Russian attention from western Europe altogether by proposing that Russia take advantage of France's involvement in war and Britain's temporary lack of a continental ally to denounce the clauses of the 1856 Treaty of Paris prohibiting Russia from maintaining military and naval forces on the shores and waters of the Black Sea. The Russians were to act on this proposal in October 1870, thereby becoming involved in altercations with Britain and diverting the attention of both powers from the war in France, which Bismarck had undoubtedly hoped for and intended.

Bismarck saw less reason to fear British than Russian intervention because the British lacked the military capacity to intervene effectively on the continent, but to avoid any British attempt to support the intervention of other powers he tried to convince the British, too, of Prussia's need for better strategic frontiers and hence annexations of French territory. In a dispatch of August 28, 1870, he instructed his ambassador in London to remind the British of the perennial French threat to the peace of Europe and the balance of power. Germany was now being forced to defend itself against the twelfth or thirteenth French invasion in the past two hundred years. French aggressive tendencies had not been curbed in any way by the forbearance of the allies in dealing with France in 1814–1815. "Our protection against this evil will not be served by a fruitless attempt at a temporary regard for French sensibility but by our acquisition of well-fortified frontiers," he said. The French would be hostile to Germany even if they were not obliged to cede territory. "Even our victory at Sadowa aroused bitterness in France; how much more will our victory over themselves." The only correct way to deal with an enemy who *cannot* be won over as a sincere friend was to make him somewhat less dangerous and to improve one's own strategic position. This could not be done simply by demanding the demolition of those French fortresses that posed a threat to German security— the French would rebuild them at the first distraction of international attention— but only through Germany's actual takeover of those fortresses.

Bismarck took up this same theme in a September 13 circular dispatch to all Prussian diplomatic missions abroad. Germany must expect a renewed attack from France no matter how generous its peace terms. "It is the defeat itself . . . which the French will never forgive us." If Germany withdrew from French soil without demanding territorial concessions or indemnities, "the French nation would still harbor the same hatred, the same thirst for revenge, because of its injured vanity and arrogance."

These arguments probably reflect Bismarck's real views and provide a plausible explanation for his annexation of Alsace and Lorraine, mistaken as that policy may appear in retrospect. But no comparable explanation can be found for the proclamation of the German empire in the Hall of Mirrors of Louis XIV's palace at Versailles. This was a symbolic gesture against a monarch who had inflicted so many humiliations on the Germans and was intended to inspire German nationalist enthusiasm for the new empire. It was nevertheless a mean-spirited and unnecessary gesture that rubbed salt in the wounds of the French and was to be bitterly recalled following Germany's defeat in World War I, when the Germans were summoned to sign the peace treaty ending that war in the same hall in the same palace.

Bismarck's dire (and accurate) predictions about future French hostility and his fears for the security of the new German empire point to a tragic irony in the history of that empire and provide a notable example of the paradox of power. Bismarck and German patriots had desired unification in the belief that a national government could mobilize German power most effectively and thus also be most capable of defending German national interests and security. Instead they found that the new empire was in many ways less secure, in the sense that it was more exposed to international dangers than the despised German Confederation. Already during the period of its formation, but especially after 1871, German statesmen were confronted with what Bismarck called the "nightmare of coalitions," the danger that foreign powers, fearful of the new German threat to *their* interests and security, would join forces to destroy the German national state, seize German territory to improve their own strategic positions, and once again divide what was left of Germany into a mosaic of petty states.

German patriots were also obsessed by another fear, a fear which, in retrospect—when one recalls German national cohesiveness during two world wars—seems ridiculous, but one that was nevertheless expressed time and again in the years before 1914: that their new national state would not survive the first serious domestic or international crisis; that Bavaria and other formerly independent states would secede from the union; that particularist forces would find widespread support from other disaffected groups within the empire (Catholics, Poles, Alsatians, socialists); and that these subversive elements would unite or conspire with foreign foes to bring the empire down.

Fears of hostile coalitions abroad and subversive forces at home haunted Bismarck throughout the years of his chancellorship and motivated some of his most ill-conceived and unsuccessful policies, notably his campaign against the Roman Catholic church in Germany, the so-called Kulturkampf, or battle for civilization, as anticlerical supporters of that policy called it. Fears of hostile coalitions developed into a veritable paranoia among Bismarck's successors, especially after the actual formation of such coalitions among states alarmed by the growth of German power and the Germans' own frequent misuse of it. Foreign statesmen regarded these coalitions as essential to the maintenance of the European equilibrium, but to Germans they seemed an invidious policy of encirclement designed to throttle and ultimately destroy their country.

The unification of Germany and establishment of the German empire gave German nationalists a new sense of pride and prestige. It notably failed to give them a sense—or the reality—of security, and in their frantic search for such security and new heights of national greatness, they were to plunge into the most dire catastrophes of their already catastrophic history.

❑

TWELVE

The Search for a New International Stability, 1871-1890

Shortly after Prussia's victory over France in 1871 and the formation of the German empire, the British statesman Benjamin Disraeli declared:

> This war represents the German revolution, a greater political event than the French Revolution of the last century. . . . Not a single principle in the management of our foreign affairs, accepted by all statesmen for guidance up to six months ago, any longer exists. There is not a diplomatic tradition which has not been swept away. You have a new world, new influences at work, new and unknown objects and dangers with which to cope. . . . The balance of power has been entirely destroyed, and the country which suffers most, and feels the effect of this great change most, is England.

Disraeli's statements were somewhat extravagant. As leader of Her Majesty's loyal opposition, he was criticizing the foreign policy of his rival Gladstone, who was in power when the final unification of Germany took place. But he was nevertheless expressing a concern felt by many European statesmen. Prussia now stood at the head of an empire that was unquestionably the greatest military power on the continent. How would Prussia use that power? Would the objective of German unification now be extended to the Netherlands, Belgium, or Switzerland? What was to be the fate of the Germans in the Habsburg empire? In Russia's Baltic provinces?

Bismarck was well aware of Europe's apprehensions, and he also saw the dangers they implied for the new German empire. In their dread of Germany, all the states seeking to restore the European balance of power might join forces with the recently defeated foes of Prussia in a great anti-German coalition. Bismarck's first concern, therefore, was to reassure Europe. The new German empire, he said, was a satiated state whose principal foreign policy objective henceforth would be the preservation of peace and the status quo.

Bismarck was frequently compelled to defend his policy of peace and satiety in dealing with his fellow countrymen and with his allies. The advocates of a more militant policy wanted to take advantage of favorable military or diplomatic situations to wage "preventive" war to crush potential opponents and strengthen their country through new territorial acquisitions. The chancellor's counterarguments differed widely according to the audience he was addressing, but his basic reasoning followed the same general lines. He steadfastly rejected the idea of preventive war. It was easy to start a war but impossible to know how it would end. A war should be fought only for the highest stakes, and then only when all other means of achieving the desired goal had been exhausted. In view of the alarm aroused by the creation of the German empire, it was as good as certain after 1871 that no war involving Germany could be kept localized, and what might be started as a preventive war might end as a life-and-death struggle against an international coalition in which Germany's very existence would be jeopardized.

Even if Germany won a war of this kind, the possible gain would not be worth the risk and cost involved. Large-scale territorial annexations at the expense of Russia would not give Germany a better strategic frontier or important new natural resources, and in population it would only acquire more Poles, whose growing national self-consciousness was causing trouble enough in Germany already. Further German annexations at the expense of France would actually weaken Germany's strategic position, for the frontier Germany had acquired in 1871 was probably the best defensive line that could be established in the west. The permanent German occupation of all of France was hardly a practicable proposition; Germany was finding it difficult enough to integrate the "German" provinces of Alsace and Lorraine. Holland, Switzerland, Denmark, and other states that some German nationalists regarded as Germanic and therefore believed should be absorbed in the German empire were too small a gain to justify a major war and would incorporate additional hostile and resentful populations.

The most likely area for German expansion was Austria, where the process of German unification might have been completed by annexing the Germans of the Habsburg empire. Alone or in alliance with Russia or Italy, Germany might have defeated Austria easily and permanently, and Austria's German population and territories would undoubtedly have strengthened the German empire. With the destruction of the Habsburg empire, however, Germany would be left to deal with the nationality problems of central Europe, unless the non-German nationalities were simply handed over to Russia. Far more important, Germany would be left with Russia as the only great power on its eastern flank, a situation that would put Germany at Russia's mercy diplomatically, for any refusal on the part of Germany to support Russia in the international field would expose it to the threat of a Russian alliance with France. With Austria gone, Germany's only potential ally among the great powers would be Britain, whose navy could not fight on land. As Bismarck saw it, the preservation of the Habsburg empire as a great power was essential for Germany as a balance to Russia in eastern Europe.

The only other area where Germany might have expanded without the risk of dangerous conflict with one or more of the European great powers was overseas, and in the 1880s Bismarck acquired a sizable colonial empire for Germany. But Bismarck was never seriously interested in colonies, which were of dubious economic value and could contribute nothing to Germany's national security because they could always be cut off by a hostile fleet. Because Germany's first line of defense was its army, it could never build a fleet strong enough to defend a colonial empire as could Britain, whose first line of defense was its navy. For Germany to divert resources from the vital army to a luxury navy would be a dangerous act of political frivolity.

By far the most important reason for Bismarck's pacific policy, however, was his conviction that the preservation of peace was the most certain and least costly means of safeguarding and consolidating the state he had created. Bismarck's conception of the future course of German policy was of fundamental importance. As leader of the most powerful state in Europe, and as one of the most talented diplomats of his age, he was to dominate the European international scene until his dismissal in 1890. And because he saw his country's best interests in preserving the peace of Europe, he was one of the few political leaders before 1914 to pursue a European, as opposed to a narrowly national or dynastic, foreign policy.

❑ *The First Three Emperors' League*

Bismarck's first move to stabilize the European states system established in 1871 was an attempt to revive the Metternichian concert among the conservative powers of Europe. He looked upon Russia and Austria as natural allies in this endeavor. In both states the threat of revolution was constant, and both might be expected to join Germany in a policy of preserving the international as well as the domestic status quo because a major war, with all the risks it entailed, could only benefit the forces of revolution. Further, both states had participated with Prussia in the partitions of Poland and thus had a common interest in keeping the Poles under control.

In the course of 1873, several treaties concluded among the three imperial powers resulted in the formation of what came to be known as the first Three Emperors' League. In these treaties the rulers of Austria, Germany, and Russia pledged to combat subversive activities in their respective countries and to consult in the event of disagreement between themselves or in case other powers threatened the peace of Europe. Thus the league, which was joined by Italy in September 1873, was based on little more than a presumed mutual interest in preserving international peace, suppressing revolution at home, and preventing the formation of hostile coalitions against any one of its members. It worked as long as the interests of the conservative powers were in harmony; it cracked the moment their interests began to diverge.

❑ *The War Scare of 1875*

The weakness of the Three Emperors' League was revealed in the course of a German crisis with France that took place in the spring of 1875. The French had paid their war debt to Germany in the remarkably short time of two years, and in accordance with the Treaty of Frankfurt, German troops left French soil when the payment was completed. The speed of the French recovery and the energetic efforts the French were now making to rebuild their army aroused alarm in Germany, especially among military leaders, who now stepped up their agitation for a preventive war against France.

Angered by the irresponsible bellicosity of the German generals, but disturbed even more by the virulence of French hostility and French involvement in anti-German intrigues, Bismarck instructed members of his staff to introduce articles in newspapers with the evident purpose of warning the French not to push their military preparations too far and noting the dangers of their hostile activities. The most provocative of these articles, "Is War in Sight?," published in the Berlin *Post* of April 8, 1875, was a good deal more threatening than the chancellor had intended. "Our friend writes with a broomstock," he commented. The incident that actually ignited the 1875 war scare crisis, however, was an indiscreet remark made at a dinner party by one of Bismarck's diplomats, who told the French ambassador to Berlin that there were influential people in Germany who favored a preventive war against France and that such a war would be justified on political and moral grounds. The diplomat in question later denied the remark, but the French ambassador's report of the incident, coming as it did in the wake of the threatening German newspaper articles, was generally believed and aroused widespread international concern.

The German threats, whatever Bismarck's purpose may have been (and this is still a matter of some controversy), were a diplomatic mistake. The French were able to pose as the hapless victims of a brutal Germany determined to destroy France and subject all of Europe to German militarism, and they appealed to other powers for support. Immediately the cracks in the Three Emperors' League became apparent. Gorchakov, the Russian chancellor and foreign minister, jumped at the chance to deal a blow at Bismarck, his diplomatic rival, and he was seconded by the Conservative government of Disraeli in Britain. Bismarck was forced to provide assurances that Germany had no intention of going to war against France. It was a humiliating incident, but it served to show the advocates of preventive war in Germany the dangers of such a policy. For Bismarck it was a warning of how precarious the position of the new German empire still was, and a demonstration of how unreliable the Three Emperors' League was as an instrument of German security. That league was soon to break apart altogether as the result of a crisis in the Balkans.

❑ *The Balkan Crisis, 1875–1878*

In July 1875 a revolt against Turkish rule broke out in the Balkan provinces of Bosnia and Herzegovina. This revolt was secretly supported by Serbia and Montenegro, both still nominally part of the Ottoman empire, and by Russia. In all three states sympathy for fellow Slavs and Orthodox Christians was conveniently joined with national ambition. Serbia aspired to be the Sardinia of the Balkans and to create a unified Balkan state under Serbian domination. Russia since the days of Peter the Great had hoped to extend its sway over southeastern Europe to Constantinople and the Mediterranean. In May 1876 the revolt against Turkey spread into Bulgaria. With the Ottoman empire seemingly on the verge of disintegration, Serbia boldly declared war on Turkey at the end of June 1876, followed by Montenegro early in July.

In Russia there was widespread popular sympathy for the Balkan rebellions. Thousands of Russian volunteers poured into the Serbian capital of Belgrade, a Russian general assumed command of the Serbian army, and Russian pan-Slavists urged their government to take advantage of the revolts in the Balkans to bring all the Balkan Slavs under Russia's protection. The Russian government, however, held back and continued to stand aside even as the Serbian army was soundly beaten by the Turks in the summer of 1876. There were two major reasons for Russia's restraint:

Austria and Britain, both of which might be expected to intervene against Russia if it threatened their interests in southeastern Europe. In Britain, Disraeli's Conservative government followed the traditional British policy of seeking to keep Russia as far away from Constantinople and the Mediterranean as possible. Disraeli had an added incentive to adhere to this policy, for in November 1875 Britain had acquired controlling shares in the Suez Canal, which the khedive of Egypt had been obliged to sell to pay the interest on his debts to European bondholders. While Disraeli was in power, the Russians could be fairly certain that any direct intervention on their part in the Balkans would encounter British opposition.

In Britain, however, the tide of public opinion turned unexpectedly to Russia's advantage. Following the Turks' victory over the Balkan armies, reports began to reach Britain of their brutality in suppressing the Balkan rebellions. However grim these Turkish atrocities may have been, their horror lost nothing in the telling, for many Western correspondents in southeastern Europe received their news about the Balkans from Russian agents. The Russian government maintained a well-organized and well-subsidized propaganda machine in Constantinople, and the primary target of its campaign was Britain.

The Russian propaganda was thoroughly successful. By the summer of 1876 public opinion in Britain was passionately aroused against Turkey. The most eloquent spokesman for the British conscience was William E. Gladstone, head of the Liberal party, who called upon his fellow countrymen to give up their distrust of the "standing hobgoblin of Russia." Britain should rather seek to emulate Russia by sharing in its good deeds against the Turks, who had been "from the black day when they first entered Europe *the one great anti-human specimen of humanity.* Wherever they went, a broad line of blood marked the track behind them; and as far as their dominion reached, civilization disappeared from view." These sentiments were expressed in Gladstone's famous pamphlet *The Bulgarian Horrors and the Question of the East,* published in September 1876, which did much to put British public opinion squarely in the anti-Turkish camp. The Russians realized that no British government could go to war at this time in support of the Ottoman empire, a situation which freed them, at least temporarily, from the threat of British intervention.

The other major obstacle to Russian intervention against Turkey was Austria, strategically poised to cut Russia's vital supply lines through the Balkans. Russia still depended on these overland routes because the Treaty of Paris of 1856 had forbidden Russia from maintaining military or naval forces on the shores and waters of the Black Sea. Although Russia had denounced the Black Sea provisions in 1871, the Turks retained their naval supremacy over this waterway, so that the Russians were unable to transport their troops and supplies by sea.

To neutralize the potential threat from Austria, the Russians turned to Germany. If Austria attacked Russia while Russia was fighting Turkey in the Balkans, could Russia count on German support? The tsar confidently expected his friend and relative, the German emperor, to render Russia this service in gratitude for Russia's benevolent neutrality during Prussia's wars for German unification; he may even have hoped that Germany would be tempted to engage in a wholesale partition of the Habsburg empire. Bismarck's reply to the Russians at this time supplies the key to his entire Eastern policy: Germany was not averse to a Russian war against Turkey. Bismarck even hoped the problems of the Balkans might be solved by a partition of the Turkish empire. But Germany could not allow the status of either Russia or Austria as great powers to be jeopardized: if Austria attacked Russia, Germany would come to the aid of Russia should that country's status as a great power be threatened; similarly, however, Germany would come to the aid of Austria in the event of a Russian threat to the great power status of the Habsburg empire. Bismarck's response, a bitter blow to the Russians, led to charges of German ingratitude and to a hostility between Germany and Russia over the Eastern Question that was never to be fully overcome.

With their efforts to enlist German support against Austria thwarted, the Russians quite simply bought Austria off. In a convention signed in Budapest on January 15, 1877, supplemented by an agreement of March 18, Austria promised to remain neutral in the event of a Russo-Turkish war. In return, the Austrians were to be allowed to occupy the Turkish provinces of Bosnia and Herzegovina whenever they saw fit to do so. Austria also secured a promise from Russia that no large state would be established in the Balkans that might threaten Austrian security or block the extension of Austrian political or economic influence into the southern Balkans and the Near East.

Disraeli meanwhile was trying to protect the Turks from Russia by diplomacy, since British public opinion prevented him from giving them overt support. After the Turkish military victory over Serbia, Russia had compelled the Turks to grant Serbia an armistice by an ultimatum of October 31, 1876. Disraeli now took the initiative in convoking an international conference at Constantinople "to keep Russia out of Turkey, not to create an ideal existence for Turkish Christians." This conference accomplished exactly what Disraeli intended for protecting British interests. It called for the supervision of Turkey's Balkan provinces by all the European great powers, thereby forestalling the establishment of exclusive Russian influence in this region, and, although it required the Turks to give up some territory, it ensured the preservation of the Ottoman empire.

The terms of the conference agreement were now presented to the Turks, who proceeded to frustrate all British efforts to save them. Inspired by nationalist fanaticism of their own, they denounced the conference terms as a national humiliation; they had won the war against Serbia and Montenegro and saw no reason to surrender territory to Montenegro or to submit to international supervision of their administration in the Balkans. Refusing to see that the alternative to acceptance of the conference terms would be a Russian invasion, they rejected them on January 18, 1877. Three days earlier the Russians had signed their Budapest Convention with Austria. Nothing now stood in Russia's way, and on April 24, 1877, as soon as the snow melted in the Balkan passes, Russia declared war on Turkey.

❑ *The Russo-Turkish War of 1877 and Its Aftermath*

The thoroughness of Russia's diplomatic preparations was not matched by that of the Russian army, and it was not until the end of June that Russian forces crossed the Danube. After that, however, they advanced rapidly through the Balkans as another Russian army moved into Turkey on the Caucasus front. The apparent success of the Russian offensives brought about a decisive change of attitude in Britain. By July 21 Disraeli was able to persuade the cabinet that Britain should declare war if Russia occupied Constantinople. The British even made a loose agreement with Austria about joint action in case of excessive Russian gains—an illustration of the fragility of international agreements when the vital interests of a country are at stake.

A respite for the European cabinets came at the end of July. The Turks made a stand at the strategic fortress-city of Plevna in the Balkan Mountains, which held up the Russian offensive for five months. In view of the desperate state of Turkish finances at the time, Turkey's resistance was regarded as something of a miracle. This miracle was due at least in part to secret loans from Britain, which made possible the Turkish purchase of Krupp steel breech-loading artillery from Germany and, through the American banking house of J.P. Morgan and Co., of breech-loading Peabody-Martini rifles from the United States. By December 1877, however, the Russians had overcome the Turks at Plevna, and in January 1878 Turkey appealed for an armistice.

By this time British public opinion had swung around completely to the side of the underdog Turks. The British fleet was sent to Constantinople, and there was loud clamor in Britain for war against Russia. This was the atmosphere in which the famous music hall song emerged: "We don't want to fight/yet by Jingo! if we do/We've got the ships, we've got the men/And got the money too," a rhyme that gave a new word to the English language, "jingoism," which has since stood for hysterical and militant chauvinism. Before the British could intervene, however, the Russians had made peace with the Turks through the Treaty of San Stefano, signed March 3, 1878.

On the Russian side, the San Stefano agreement was negotiated by General Nicholas Ignatiev, an ardent pan-Slavist, who disregarded his instructions to do everything possible to avoid foreign intervention and instead imposed a peace on Turkey that made such intervention virtually certain. The most important provision of San Stefano was the creation of a large Bulgarian state stretching from the Black Sea to the mountains of Albania in the west, and from the Danube to the Aegean Sea. As the new Bulgaria was clearly intended to be a Russian satellite, the treaty in effect gave the Russians the outlet to the Mediterranean they had so long desired. The treaty was thus a blow to both Britain and France, which had consistently endeavored to keep Russia out of the Mediterranean, and it was a direct violation of Russia's prewar Budapest Convention with Austria, for the new Bulgaria would effectively block Austria's routes to the south and dangerously increase Russian power and influence in southeastern Europe.

By concluding a treaty with Turkey that impinged on the interests of three of the European great powers, the Russians, or more accurately Ignatiev, had made a serious blunder. Only three days after the treaty was signed the Austrian foreign minister issued an invitation to the European powers to attend a conference in Berlin to discuss its revision. The Russians, their resources exhausted by the conflict with Turkey, were obliged to accept the invitation or face a war against a European coalition.

To salvage as many of their gains in the Turkish war as possible, the Russians tried to buy the support of a majority of the great powers before the conference convened. They first tried Austria, but the Austrians were wary of another betrayal and posed too many conditions. They had better luck with Britain. The British could never be sure the three imperial powers might not join forces at the expense of

RUSSIA

AUSTRIA-HUNGARY

Bessarabia

Danube R.

Jassy

Pruth R.

Bosnia
(occupied by
Austria, 1878)

Belgrade

ROMANIA

Bucharest

Danube R.

Sarajevo

SERBIA

Herzegovina

Novi
Pazar

Plevna

Bulgaria
(under Turkish
suzerainty until 1908)

Nish

Sofia

BALKAN MTS.

Varna

MONTE-
NEGRO

Antivari
Dulcigno
(1880)

Scutari

Albania

Eastern Rumelia
(administered by Turkey)

BLACK
SEA

ADRIATIC SEA

Macedonia

Philippopolis

Constantinople

Dedeagach

San Stefano

Salonika

IONIAN
SEA

AEGEAN
SEA

OTTOMAN
EMPIRE

GREECE

Athens

M E D I T E R R A N E A N

Crete

S E A

Gains by Montenegro	
Gains by Serbia	Ottoman boundary, 1878
Gains by Greece	Bulgaria proposed by Treaty of San Stefano, 1878
Gains by Russia	Ottoman Empire after 1878
Gains by Romania	Independent after 1878

Dobruja

British interests and hence seized the opportunity to safeguard them. On May 30, 1878, they concluded a secret treaty with the Russians that pushed the frontier of the new Bulgaria away from the Aegean Sea, thus precluding the danger of having a Russian naval base established on the Mediterranean.

British preconference diplomatic activity did not end with the Russian treaty. To bolster their own position in the Middle East, they concluded a secret treaty with Turkey on June 4, 1878, whereby they guaranteed Turkey's Asiatic territories and therewith gained an excuse to send their troops into Turkey at any time they believed their own interests were threatened. Further, to enable them to implement this guarantee, the British pressured Turkey into giving them the island of Cyprus and with that they acquired a splendid—and strategic—naval base in the eastern Mediterranean, one within striking distance of Constantinople, Asiatic Turkey, the Balkans, and the Suez Canal.

Britain made yet a third preconference agreement. The Austrians had learned from Bismarck of the secret Anglo-Russian negotiations and feared that Russia would indeed gain the support of the majority at the forthcoming conference. They therefore hastened to strike a bargain of their own with Britain. The Austrians wanted above all to keep open an avenue for their economic and political influence in southeastern Europe and to prevent the formation of any large state in the Balkans that would close this avenue or pose a threat to Austrian security. On June 6, 1878, they concluded a treaty with Britain which assured them of British support in securing the breakup of the large Bulgarian state created at San Stefano.

Thus before the Congress of Berlin even met, agreement had been reached among the great powers on the most important revisions of San Stefano. It remained for the congress to set the seal on these preconference decisions and to work out the details.

❑ *The Congress of Berlin*

The Congress of Berlin (June 13–July 13, 1878) was one of the major diplomatic assemblies of the nineteenth century. It differed from the earlier Congress of Vienna, for this time the great powers made no attempt to disguise the fact that they would make all the decisions. The smaller states of Europe were not even invited to participate, nor were representatives of the Balkan states, whose future was to be a major topic of the congress's deliberations. These deliberations were ostensibly conducted in public, but the most critical decisions were reached in secret negotiations. "All questions are publicly introduced," Disraeli wrote frankly to Queen Victoria, "and then privately settled." Bismarck, the head of the government playing host to the congress, was elected its president in accordance with diplomatic custom. But Bismarck was head of the congress in more than name. He dominated the meetings and set the pace and tone of the negotiations.

By the terms of the final Treaty of Berlin of July 13, 1878, the large Bulgarian state created by the Treaty of San Stefano was divided into three parts, all of which remained nominally part of the Turkish empire. The largest of these parts was Bulgaria proper, bounded on the north by the Danube, on the west by an expanded Serbia, and on the south by the Balkan Mountains. Nominally, Bulgaria became a separate principality under Turkish suzerainty; in fact, it was tacitly conceded to

Russia as a satellite. A Russian commission was to "organize" Bulgaria, the new state was to be garrisoned by Russian soldiers, and in April 1879, Alexander of Battenberg, a favorite nephew of Tsar Alexander II, was elected prince of Bulgaria with Russia's approval and support. The second division of the greater Bulgaria was the area south of the Balkan Mountains, which was to be called Eastern Rumelia to avoid associating it even in name with Russia's Bulgaria. Eastern Rumelia was placed under the administration of a Turkish governor general, but its government was to be reformed by a European commission. The rest of San Stefano's Bulgaria, including the critical territory bordering the Aegean Sea, was left directly under Turkish rule.

The three Balkan states of Serbia, Montenegro, and Romania, hitherto still nominally part of the Turkish empire, were recognized as completely independent, but they lost some of the territory assigned to them at San Stefano. Romania, which had been Russia's ally in the recent war against Turkey, was obliged to cede to Russia the Bessarabian territory lost by Russia after the Crimean War; with that Russia once again gained control of the mouth of the Danube. In return Romania received the arid Dobruja region south of the Danube, which was detached from Turkey.

Among the great powers, Austria was given the right to occupy (but not annex) Bosnia and Herzegovina and to garrison the Turkish administrative district (sanjak) of Novi Pazar, a strategic area lying between Serbia and Montenegro. Thus Austria pushed a military wedge between Serbia and Montenegro, frustrated Serbian ambitions to form and dominate a large Balkan state, and kept its own routes to the south open. Russia received Batum, Kars, and Ardahan, strategic strongholds at the eastern end of the Black Sea, and control of what was left of Bulgaria. Britain received the right to occupy Cyprus. France was secretly given permission to take Tunis, also nominally part of the Turkish empire. The Italian delegates came home with clean but empty hands, to be stoned in the streets by compatriots who would clearly have preferred the dirt of territorial gains. The Germans, too, received no territory, but they were relieved of the necessity of choosing between Russia and Austria in eastern Europe or of engaging in a costly and dangerous conflict where vital German interests were not at stake. The preservation of peace was in itself a major gain for Germany.

❑ *The Austro-German Alliance of 1879*

By refusing to allow the balance of power in eastern Europe to be upset by either Russia or Austria, by playing midwife to many of the individual agreements modifying the Treaty of San Stefano, and by assuming the role of "honest broker" at the Congress of Berlin, Bismarck contributed much to the prevention of a general European war during the Near Eastern crisis. But he paid a heavy price for his success. The Russians had expected to receive German support at the congress and bitterly resented German compliance in what they regarded as a severe diplomatic setback. The wrath of the Russians after the congress was turned not against Austria or Britain, their real opponents in the recent crisis, but against Germany, the false friend. Russia was swept by a wave of anti-German sentiment, with the result that Germany now faced the hostility of Russia in addition to that of France. If these powers were to form an anti-German alliance, they might be joined by an Austria eager to regain its lost supremacy in central Europe.

Bismarck's reply to Russian hostility was a defensive alliance with Austria against attack by Russia or by a power supported by Russia. Concluded on October 7, 1879, this alliance served multiple purposes. It assured both powers of support in case of Russian aggression. For Austria it reduced the danger of an agreement among Germany, Russia, and Italy to partition the Habsburg empire; for Germany it lessened the possibility of an Austrian alliance with Russia and France. For Bismarck another advantage of the treaty was the control it gave him over Austrian foreign policy. Any aggressive move by Austria in eastern Europe involved the danger of war with Russia, and Austria did not dare risk a clash with Russia without the certainty of German support. As long as Germany remained in a position to withhold that support, it would be able to exercise a strong if not decisive check on Austrian aggression in eastern Europe.

❑ *The Second Three Emperors' League*

In view of the alliances subsequently concluded by Bismarck, it is safe to assume that he did not intend to restrict his treaty making at this time to Austria, but he hoped to return to some kind of treaty relationship with Russia as well, in order to avoid driving Russia into the arms of France. But he evidently realized that this could not be achieved immediately, for the hysterical anti-German attitude then prevalent in Russia meant that any German effort to establish closer relations would almost certainly be interpreted by the Russians as a sign of fear. A German agreement with Russia, if it could be arranged at all, would have to be purchased at an extremely high price. Bismarck therefore took an indirect approach in dealing with the Russians. The German–Austrian alliance was supposed to be secret, but the secret was badly kept and the Russians learned of its existence even before the treaty was signed. They now found themselves in an awkward position, for the two great central European powers were forming an alliance, with a friendly Britain in the wings.

The next turn of events in Russia may well have been what Bismarck had been counting on. News of the Austrian alliance had a chastening effect on the anti-German agitation. The Russian leaders began to realize that their anti-German attitude was not only pointless but extremely dangerous. Consequently, while negotiations for the German–Austrian treaty were still in progress, the Russians were at Bismarck's door as suppliants to renew the Three Emperors' League in some form. Thus Bismarck's bargaining position was far better than it would have been had he approached Russia directly. "Now I have the best receipt for my Vienna policy," he is reported to have said later. "I knew the Russians would come to us, once we had nailed down the Austrians."

The request to revive the Three Emperors' League was well received in Berlin. Bismarck assured the Russian emissary that his main purpose in making the Austrian alliance was "to dig a ditch between [Austria] and the Western powers," and that he would be glad to reestablish the Three Emperors' League "as the only system offering the maximum stability for the peace of Europe."

Bismarck's chief difficulty in reviving the Three Emperors' League lay in persuading the Austrians to admit Russia into the German–Austrian partnership, which many Austrian statesmen had hoped to exploit against Russia. In his efforts to persuade Austria to accept the Russian alliance, Bismarck was aided by Gladstone's victory in the British elections of March 1880. Gladstone had violently denounced Austria during the election campaign, and his victory temporarily ended Austrian hopes of gaining British support against Russia in eastern Europe. Even so, it was not until Bismarck ostentatiously threw his diplomatic support on the side of Russia and against Austria on every current issue concerning eastern Europe that the Austrians finally yielded.

The second Three Emperors' League, in contrast to the first, was based on an agreement with definite, clear-cut terms. The treaty, which was secret, was signed on June 18, 1881, and was to be in force for three years. Most significant was the stipulation that if one member of the league found itself at war with a fourth power (except Turkey), the other two were to remain neutral, a provision that safeguarded all members from the danger of hostile coalitions. The other articles of the treaty were aimed primarily at removing the major possibilities for friction between the signatory powers in eastern Europe. There were to be no territorial changes in the Ottoman empire without the agreement of all three imperial powers. All three agreed to recognize the principle of the closure of the Turkish Straits in time of war, which meant that Britain and France could not attack Russia via the Black Sea as they had done in the Crimean conflict. Germany and Austria agreed further not to oppose the union of Bulgaria and Eastern Rumelia, therewith reviving the possibility of a larger sphere of influence for Russia in the Balkans. Austria was to be allowed to annex Bosnia and Herzegovina whenever it saw fit to do so, which was a stage beyond the right to occupy those provinces granted Austria by the Treaty of Berlin. By no means did the Three Emperors' Treaty end tension between Austria and Russia or resolve the problems of the Balkans and the Near East. It simply eased those tensions a little and provided a foothold for negotiations between the imperial powers in the event of a crisis.

❑ *Austria's Balkan Policy*

To reduce further the danger of international friction in the Balkans, Bismarck attempted to secure agreement on a partition of the Balkans between Austria and Russia. He reasoned that both powers would then be fully occupied for several years in assimilating their respective spheres. But the partition scheme never materialized. Austrian leaders feared any permanent extension of Russian power in the Balkans, and the Hungarians disliked the prospect of including more Slavs in the Habsburg empire because this would diminish their own importance.

In the meantime, Austrian interests were being advanced successfully without territorial annexations. The rapid construction of railroads in the Balkans permitted Austria to extend its economic influence in southeastern Europe to areas that were not readily accessible to the sea and hence were relatively untouched by British and French economic enterprise. Austria also extended its political influence in the Balkans. Both Serbia and Romania were indignant with Russia for failing to secure them greater territorial gains following their victory over Turkey, with Romania especially disgruntled by being forced to turn over the Bessarabian territory at the mouth of the Danube to Russia in return for the arid Dobruja—hardly a suitable reward, as the Romanians saw it, for their military support of Russia in the recent conflict.

Apart from taking advantage of Serbian annoyance with Russia, the Austrians established their influence by the crude but effective method of bribing the prince of Serbia, Milan Obrenovich, and dangling before him the prospect of recognition as king. Through political and economic treaties concluded with Prince Milan in 1881, they virtually reduced Serbia to the status of an Austrian dependency. Besides their monetary bribes, the Austrians promised to support Serbia in its quest for territorial gains on its southern frontier, a commitment that enraged Bismarck when he eventually learned of it. He denounced it as a "free pass to the most insane and dangerous Serbian undertakings," warning the Austrians that "no lasting bond can be established with the Balkan states. You will suffer the same ingratitude and the same disappointments from Serbia that Russia has suffered in Bulgaria. As soon as King Milan, that unreliable, flighty, and sensual man, has enlarged his country through Austria's aid, he will reveal himself as a pan-Serb and will fearlessly cast his eyes over your frontier."

On October 30, 1883, the Austrians strengthened their diplomatic position in the Balkans still further through a defensive alliance with Romania to which Germany adhered on that same day. The value of the treaty to the Romanians was obvious: it afforded them the protection of two great powers against predatory Balkan neighbors and above all against Russia, which would always be tempted to trespass over Romanian territory to control Bulgaria. For the Austrians, the treaty warded off whatever ambitions the Romanian national state might have to extend its dominion over Transylvania and other parts of the Habsburg empire inhabited by a substantial Romanian population. The treaty with Romania, scheduled to run for five years, was kept secret and renewed periodically until 1916, when Romania deserted its alliance with Austria and Germany and entered World War I on the side of Britain, France—and Russia.

The great mystery about the Romanian treaty is why Germany adhered to it, for it ran counter to the spirit if not the letter of the Three Emperors' Treaty and obligated Germany to defend a country that lay between Russia and Bulgaria and any other ambitions the Russians might have in the southeast. It thus placed Germany in a position Bismarck had always strenuously sought to avoid. Heretofore he had insisted, and he was to continue to insist, that if Russian expansionist ambitions in the southeast were to be halted, this task should be performed by powers with interests in that area—by Austria, Britain, and Turkey itself, but definitely not by Germany, whose interests required the maintenance of friendly relations with Russia and freedom from involvement in eastern Europe so as to have all its strength available to deal with France. The Romanian treaty stands out as a glaring inconsistency in Bismarck's diplomacy, and it is still unclear why he took the enormous risk of alienating Russia, which it certainly would have done if the treaty became known (and how it was kept secret so long is another mystery), for the sake of an agreement that seemingly offered Germany no advantages whatever. The Romanian treaty served as a critical argument for Bismarck's successors in their refusal to renew the secret agreement the chancellor subsequently concluded with Russia (the Reinsurance Treaty of June 18, 1887; see p. 244) because, as they pointed out quite correctly, the terms of the two treaties were contradictory—as though a treaty with a small Balkan state could ever be considered equivalent to one with the tsarist empire.

❏ *The Problem of Bulgaria*

Austria's most spectacular success in the Balkans—more properly, Russia's most spectacular failure—came in Bulgaria. The Russians were tactless in dealing with a people experiencing an awakening of national self-consciousness and highly sensitive about honor and prestige. The Russian choice of Alexander of Battenberg as prince of Bulgaria was also unfortunate. Prince Alexander disliked playing the part of a Russian puppet and wanted to establish himself as the independent ruler of an independent state. Although Bismarck warned the prince in the strongest possible terms that he could expect no help from Germany, Alexander was encouraged to pursue his quest for independence by the Austrians and by Queen Victoria of Great Britain.

In 1883 the prince's ambitions were quickened when he was allowed to become engaged to Princess Victoria of Prussia, the daughter of the heir to the German throne and the granddaughter of Queen Victoria. From a political standpoint the marriage would have been most welcome to the British, who were eager to remove Russian influence from Bulgaria and must have seen in this union a means of using Germany to help them do so. Even if Germany refused to back Prince Alexander against Russia, his marriage to a Prussian princess would arouse serious doubts in Russia about the honesty of Germany's policy in the Balkans and would shake Russia's confidence in the German government, which Bismarck was trying so hard to regain.

These dangers were only too evident to Bismarck, who did everything in his power to prevent the so-called Battenberg marriage from taking place. He pointed out to the Austrian foreign minister that by opposing the establishment of Russian influence in Bulgaria, Austria was disregarding its treaties with Russia and creating an extremely dangerous situation in the Balkans. To compensate for Austria's attitude, Bismarck made every effort to reassure Russia of Germany's good faith. He denounced Prince Alexander and brutally pressured Austria to observe its treaty obligations.

Despite Bismarck's efforts, the Bulgarian problem came very close to involving the European powers in war. In September 1885 a revolution broke out in Eastern Rumelia. The aim of the revolutionaries was to unite their province with Bulgaria, and Prince Alexander found himself compelled by Bulgarian national sentiment to assume leadership of the movement or forfeit his throne.

The union of Bulgaria and Eastern Rumelia, although the three imperial powers had agreed not to oppose it in their secret Three Emperors' treaty of 1881, violated the public Treaty of Berlin, and the Turks prepared to invade Bulgaria to defend that treaty's provisions to keep the two regions separate. To complicate matters, the Serbs, jealous of the potential enlargement of their neighbor, invaded Bulgaria to secure territorial compensation. The Serbian effort to take advantage of what they assumed to be Bulgaria's desperate international position proved to be a serious mistake, for the Bulgarians routed the Serbian army and a Bulgarian invasion of Serbia was halted only by Austria's diplomatic intervention, a move that contributed further to Russian suspicion and hostility.

Peace between Serbia and Bulgaria was finally restored on the basis of the pre-war status quo, and in April 1886 the powers recognized the de facto union of

Bulgaria and Eastern Rumelia, though both were left under the nominal suzerainty of the sultan. Even then international tension did not die down. The Russians, unable to tolerate the rule of Prince Alexander any longer, had him kidnapped and finally secured his abdication in August 1886. Alexander's departure did not improve their position in Bulgaria, however, for the new Bulgarian government proved just as unwilling as Alexander to submit to Russian overlordship.

The Russians seethed with frustration. They were indignant with Austria for violating both the spirit and the letter of the Three Emperors' agreement; many Russians were convinced that Austria would not have dared to act in this way without assurances of support from Germany. Russian pan-Slavists, always hostile to the Teutonic empires of Germany and Austria, proclaimed that Russia could never hope to score solid gains in the Balkans while remaining committed to the Three Emperors' League and should therefore look elsewhere for support.

❑ Germany and France

The surge of anti-German feeling in Russia coincided with a powerful revival of anti-German feeling in France. Since the mid-1870s Bismarck had been working to reduce French animosity toward Germany and to compensate France for the loss of Alsace-Lorraine by helping it acquire an overseas colonial empire. He hoped in this way to divert French attention from Germany and embroil France with other colonial powers. French statesmen were aware of Bismarck's motives, but some thought France should nevertheless take advantage of German support to strengthen its colonial holdings. The colonialists were opposed in France by the continental school, which feared that a colonial policy would lead to disputes with other European powers and delay the reestablishment of French supremacy in Europe.

In 1881, under the leadership of the colonialist prime minister Jules Ferry, the French made their bid for Tunis, which had been promised to them at the Congress of Berlin. They knew that seizing Tunis would anger the Italians, who had large investments in this area and regarded it as a natural sphere for Italian expansion. But the French, too, had large investments in Tunis. Spurred by signs that the Italians were about to take Tunis, the French on May 12 forced the bey of Tunis to sign the Treaty of Bardo, which established a virtual French protectorate over the country.

❑ The Triple Alliance of 1882

Just as the French anticolonialists had feared, seizing Tunis involved France in a bitter dispute with Italy and drove Italy into an alliance with Germany and Austria. The Tunis incident showed the Italians that their old policy of diplomatic independence, which had enabled them to sell their friendship to the highest bidder, was no longer profitable. Within Italy a strong element, primarily republican, advocated friendship with republican France despite Tunis, hoping with French aid to acquire the Italian-speaking territories still under Austrian control. But an even more influential political group favored collaboration with Germany, which because of its superior military power would be a more valuable ally than France and better able to aid Italy in acquiring colonial territory; as a Protestant state, Germany would be of assistance against the papacy, which was still intent on recovering the Papal States; and as a monarchy, it would support the existing Italian government against republicanism and the forces of revolution.

Bismarck had no illusions about Italy's value as a military ally or its political reliability, but he wished to preserve the Italian monarchy, which was less likely than a republic to seek an alliance with republican France. Above all he desired an Italian alliance for the sake of Austria, which remained exposed to Italian irredentist agitation. If Austria were to become involved in war with Russia, it would be useful to have some assurance of Italian neutrality; and if France were to support Russia, it would be preferable to have the Italians, "even one corporal with the Italian flag and a drummer at his side," in the field against France than against Austria.

In the negotiations leading to the alliance of Italy, Austria, and Germany, Bismarck forced the Italians to work through Vienna. He had no intention of acting as a buffer between these old enemies, although he was always available to help the negotiations along. The treaty of May 20, 1882, establishing the Triple Alliance, was a general agreement to support the monarchical principle and the existing political and social order. It also provided for a defensive alliance against France or against "two or more great powers not members of the alliance"—in other words, any combination of France, Great Britain, and Russia. The Triple Alliance improved the prospects for stable government in Italy and assured Germany of Italian neutrality in the event of a German war with France. Austria secured Italian neutrality in the event of a war with Russia and the hope of a diminution of Italian nationalist agitation for "unredeemed" territory still under Austrian control. The Italian monarchy gained badly needed prestige, two powerful defensive allies, support against Vatican efforts to regain the Papal States, and support against revolution.

The newly created Triple Alliance was destined to become a fixture in the international politics of Europe. Intended originally to run for five years, it was renewed periodically and lasted until 1915, when the Italians, like the Romanians a year later, abandoned the Austro-German alliance to enter World War I on the side of Britain and France.

❑ *The British Occupation of Egypt*

Shortly after the treaty establishing the Triple Alliance was signed, an international crisis erupted over Egypt. With the opening of the Suez Canal in 1869, Egypt had become an area of prime strategic importance, but even before the building of the canal it had been a target of European economic imperialism. The khedives of Egypt, nominally under the suzerainty of the sultan of Turkey, had for years behaved as independent rulers and had contracted huge debts with European banking houses, often at usurious rates. It was the need for money to pay the interest on his debts that forced the khedive to sell his Suez Canal stock to Great Britain in 1875. But this sale failed to stabilize Egyptian finances, and in November 1876 the British and French governments established what amounted to joint control over the Egyptian government on behalf of the holders of Egyptian bonds. The Egyptians, who found themselves heavily taxed simply to pay the interest on foreign debts, were infuriated. In February 1882 a group of Egyptian army officers overthrew European control and established an Egyptian nationalist government. The appearance of British and

French gunboats off Alexandria in June provoked antiforeign riots in the city, and the Egyptians began to construct earthworks to defend the city from European naval attack. The British responded in July by bombarding Alexandria and landing troops to protect the Suez Canal. In September 1882 these British forces clashed with an Egyptian army at Tel el-Kebir. The Egyptians were routed, and somewhat to the embarrassment of the anticolonial Gladstone government, the British found themselves in sole control of Egypt.

Gladstone was against colonialism, but he was also a sound financier and a firm believer in law and order. He therefore used the opportunity afforded by Britain's occupation of Egypt to restore order and stabilize Egypt's finances. He assured the other European powers that the occupation was temporary and that the British forces would be withdrawn "as soon as the state of the country and the organization of proper means for the maintenance of khedival authority will admit of it." But to the fury of the French and the Italians, who also had important strategic and economic interests in Egypt, the British were never satisfied that a proper state of order had been established. They retained Egypt in their sphere of influence until they were forced out by a more successful Egyptian nationalist movement after World War II.

During the entire Egyptian crisis, Bismarck urged agreement among the powers to prevent the problem from erupting in a general European war. As the crisis dragged on, however, he encouraged the British to act alone and used his influence to prevent intervention by other states. The consequent tension between Britain, France, and Italy was not unwelcome to him. He feared an entente between the liberal government of Gladstone and republican France, which the volatile Italians might be tempted to join. The Egyptian affair put an end to these possibilities for almost a generation. As one of Bismarck's aides noted with some satisfaction, Egypt had become the Alsace-Lorraine of Anglo-French relations.

❑ Bismarck's Colonial Policy

Bismarck was soon to use Britain's awkward diplomatic position for political purposes of his own. In May 1884 he suggested to the British that in return for Germany's continued diplomatic support in Egypt and elsewhere, Britain should cede Germany the island Heligoland, a strategic base off the German coast in the North Sea, and recognize German claims to a number of overseas colonial territories. This bid for colonies represented a notable change of course on the part of Bismarck, who had previously opposed the acquisition of overseas territories because he did not believe they would contribute in any way to Germany's national security or prosperity. The reason for this change has been the subject of much speculation and controversy, and because Bismarckian diplomacy played such a critical role in the late nineteenth-century European scramble for Africa, the reversal requires consideration in some detail.

As usual Bismarck's motives were mixed and inseparably intertwined. Within Germany he was faced with a growing clamor for colonies on the part of certain interest groups and especially German nationalists, with liberals and progressives prominently among them, who were eager to enhance their country's status as a great power and to extend the benefits of German culture and civilization to as many parts of the world as possible. In the summer of 1884 the British ambassador to Berlin reported to London that the agitation in Germany for colonies had become very vociferous indeed and would have "a great influence on the coming [Reichstag] Elections next Autumn, so that Bismarck must adopt a popular national attitude to secure a majority in the new Parliament. If he cannot shew that he has protected German interests everywhere, the most popular thing he can do will be to throw the blame on England, and leave the Press to do the rest." As the British envoy predicted, Bismarck did indeed adopt a popular stance with regard to colonies, but he was far from enthusiastic about the whole enterprise, remarking cynically to a chancellery official: "All this colonial business is a sham, but we need it for the elections."

There was another domestic political consideration involved in Bismarck's new colonial policy. The imperial succession in Germany, a concern of many years, was looming ever larger. The octogenerian emperor William I was in poor health and his son, Crown Prince Frederick William, who professed liberal opinions, was very much under the influence of his English wife, the daughter of Queen Victoria. The crown princess had long expressed vehement disapproval of Bismarck's policies, resenting him for a host of real and imagined indignities, prominent among them the chancellor's opposition to her daughter's marriage to Prince Alexander of Battenberg; there was widespread expectation that when her husband came to the throne she would persuade him to oust Bismarck. Through a colonial policy, Bismarck might not only bolster his own position but undercut that of the crown prince and especially that of his wife, who had remained an outspoken partisan of her native land and scornfully dismissed the German desire for colonies as a senseless piece of vanity. "I do not see what Germany wants with these places," she wrote to her mother. "When Bismarck begins to play at Germany being a Weltreich I think it is time for us [i.e., England] to let him know where we are, though in perfect friendship." A senior official of the German foreign office summed up the situation succinctly: "No other question is so liable to put the future empress, with her Anglophile tendencies, in a false position vis-à-vis the German nation. For it is precisely the liberals and democrats who want colonies." Bismarck emphasized this same point at a meeting with the tsar in September 1884. The sole purpose of his colonial policy, he said, was to drive a wedge between the crown prince and England. The tsar, deeply concerned about the course of German policy after the death of William I, was much impressed by this reasoning. "Violà qui est intelligent [Now *that* is intelligent]," he remarked.

Bismarck had no desire for an altercation with Britain, and under ordinary circumstances he would probably have dropped the whole colonial business when the British government failed to respond favorably to his bid. But the circumstances in 1884 were far from ordinary. Germany was allied with all the great powers on the continent with the exception of France, and the French were smarting from Britain's unilateral occupation of Egypt as well as British opposition on a variety of other colonial questions. Moreover, the French government at this time was under the leadership of Jules Ferry, who was prepared to cooperate with Bismarck on the colonial issue. The German chancellor was therefore in an admirable position to bring pressure to bear on Britain and all the more willing to do so because the British government was currently under the leadership of Gladstone, whom he despised and would be glad to bring down.

British woes reached a climax in 1884–1885. The French, with the support of Germany and its allies, frustrated British efforts to regulate Egypt's financial problems. A revolt against Anglo-Egyptian rule in the Sudan on the part of a fanatical Muslim sect, the Mahdists, was at its height, and on June 26, 1885, the British general Charles G. Gordon, who had been sent to oversee the withdrawal of Anglo-Egyptian forces from the Sudan, was massacred with all his troops at Khartoum. In central Asia the Russians were advancing with ominous intent toward Persia and Afghanistan, where their victory over Afghan troops at Pendjeh in April 1885 brought Britain and Russia to the verge of war.

By 1885, largely as a result of German diplomatic cooperation with France, much of which was directed against Britain and British colonial governments, Bismarck had succeeded in securing international recognition of Germany's claims to southwest Africa, Togoland, the Cameroons, East Africa, and part of New Guinea (in the Pacific). During this same period, the French acquired the French Congo, part of the Red Sea coast, and predominant influence in Southeast Asia.

In cooperating with France on colonial questions, Bismarck may also have had another purpose in view. He was disturbed by France's uncompromising hostility to Germany and attempted to allay this antagonism in a variety of ways. "I want to persuade you to forgive Sedan as you have forgiven Waterloo," he told the French ambassador. Bismarck was far from sanguine about the possibility of any lasting reconciliation with France. "What the papers are saying about the German-French alliance goes beyond the present and possibly all future reality," he wrote to his emperor in October 1884. "I would never advise Your Majesty to base the future of our policy on such insecure foundations." Nevertheless, as he wrote his ambassador to Paris some time later, although revanchist sentiment would inhibit any French government from a *firm* partnership with Germany, "we should not therefore spurn a *temporary* one."

The partnership with France proved to be very temporary indeed. At the end of March 1885, Ferry's ministry fell as a result of a military setback in Indo-China, and the change in government marked the end of Franco-German cooperation. For Bismarck the short-lived entente had served its purpose. He had proved to himself that genuine reconciliation with France would be impossible for some time to come, he had taught the British that they could not ignore German requests with impunity, and he had acquired a colonial empire for Germany. Throughout the period of his cooperation with France, Bismarck had recognized the probable limitations of French friendship, and for this reason he had never gone so far in putting pressure on the British as to risk alienating them permanently.

For the future, however, Bismarck's policy of bullying and coercion in extracting colonial concessions from Britain proved to be a disastrous political legacy, for subsequent German governments attempted to wrest overseas rights from Britain in the same fashion. Through their crude pressure tactics and insistence on a share of the spoils in virtually every colonial crisis that arose before 1914, they *did* alienate the British permanently, and their colonial policy was second only to the German fleet-building program in persuading the British to seek a rapprochement not only with France but with Russia.

A vigorous argument has recently been advanced that Bismarck's motives in pursuing a colonial policy were primarily economic and social, and thus political in a far more profound and fundamental sense than anything suggested in the preceding paragraphs. Through colonies, so this argument runs, Bismarck sought to ensure a steady growth rate for the expanding system of advanced capitalism, a source of cheap raw materials, and commercial outlets abroad. In social terms, he saw impe-rialism as a means of integrating a state torn by class differences, of diverting do-mestic grievances toward objectives abroad, and of defending the traditional social and power structures of the Prusso-German state. In one respect this argument is absolutely correct: Bismarck never made any secret of the fact that after 1871 *all* his policies were directed toward preserving the existing political and social struc-ture. There is no evidence, however, that Bismarck was ever converted to a colonial policy for its own sake or thought the impoverished African territories he might acquire could make any substantial contribution to Germany's economic or social security. By the later 1880s he was expressing disgust with the entire colonial en-terprise and concentrated, as indeed he had always done, on the problems of the continent, where he believed the real security of Germany was at stake. In response to the arguments of a German colonial enthusiast who pointed out further desirable territorial acquisitions on a map of Africa, Bismarck is supposed to have said: "Your map of Africa is all very well and good, but my map of Africa lies in Europe. Here lies Russia and here lies France, and we are in between: that is my map of Africa."

But to contest the thesis that Bismarck's colonial policy was fundamentally a response to domestic social and economic pressures is not to deny the importance of economic motives in his calculations. Two years after the establishment of the German empire, an economic crash inaugurated a long period of economic depres-sion that was to endure into the 1880s. Already in 1879 the Bismarck government had adopted a protectionist policy to safeguard German economic interests, and there can be no doubt that one of his original purposes in pursuing a colonial policy was to safeguard and extend German economic opportunities. In doing so, however, he had expected German chartered companies and entrepreneurs to assume the risk and costs of laying claim to and administering colonial territories and believed that the role of the German government should be restricted to placing them under the protection of the German flag. Instead, angered by the refusal of Britain and British colonial governments to recognize German claims, and persuaded that those claims were threatened by imminent foreign takeovers, he acted quickly to establish control over colonial territories where German interests seemed at stake and therewith as-sumed the kind of responsibility he had wanted to avoid and about which he sub-sequently complained in typically vehement terms. All along, however, Bismarck's primary and very genuine economic concern with respect to colonies was to keep as much colonial territory as possible open to German economic enterprise. This concern was most clearly demonstrated by his policies in dealing with conflicting European claims to the Congo Basin and the immense region of west and central Africa.

❑ *The Berlin West Africa Conference of 1884–1885*

The predominant European claimants to the Congo and West Africa were Portugal, France, and Leopold II, king of the Belgians, in his capacity as head of a colonial enterprise known as the International Association of the Congo. The British—fearing that if either France or the Association were allowed to make good their claims, they would set up stiff protectionist barriers to keep out foreign commerce—concluded a treaty with Portugal on February 26, 1884, recognizing the claims of Portugal in West Africa. In return, Portugal promised to allow complete freedom of trade in the area, to set a minimal duty on foreign imports, to grant British subjects most favored nation status, and to set up an Anglo-Portuguese commission to regulate traffic on the Congo River. The Portuguese agreed further to cede to Britain their ancient rights to a part of Dahomey, which the British evidently believed could be converted into a major trading station, and to give Britain first refusal should Portugal ever sell or otherwise dispose of the strategic harbor of Lourenço Marques in Mozambique, on the east coast of Africa, the only access of the landlocked Boer republics in South Africa to the sea through territory not controlled by the British. (For the significance of this provision, see pp. 296–297.)

The Anglo-Portuguese treaty, as was apparent to all observers, was intended to block French and Association claims in West Africa, but it was also perceived as a transparent disguise for establishing British paramountcy in that region, for the weak Portuguese government would depend on the British to support its colonial administration, which would perforce become an instrument of British policy. The French and the Association immediately protested, but there was also vigorous opposition to the treaty in Portugal and Britain. Portuguese patriots, still under illusions of former greatness, saw no reason to surrender any colonial claims to the British or grant freedom of trade in their territories. There was even greater opposition to the treaty in Britain, where special interest groups and humanitarians deplored the cession of the Congo region to the Portuguese, who had only recently agreed to abolish slavery in their colonies and whose administrative record held little promise for the future of British trade.

Meanwhile King Leopold and his agents were engaged in a remarkably successful campaign to win international support for the claims of the Congo Association. The French, although bitter rivals of the Association in the field, closed ranks with Leopold in protesting the Anglo-Portuguese treaty, and they subsequently agreed to recognize the majority of Association claims in return for Leopold's promise that those claims should revert to France if the Association should ever find it necessary to dispose of them.

Leopold scored an even more important success in winning Bismarck's support for the Association's position. This he did through Bismarck's banker, Gerson Bleichröder, who was flattered by the attentions of royalty but was also aware of the chancellor's growing concern for German economic interests in the colonial field. Because the Association was willing to promise absolute freedom of trade in areas allotted to its jurisdiction, Bismarck was receptive to Bleichröder's arguments on its behalf, but he insisted again and again that he would settle for nothing less than the most specific guarantees of free trade for Germans for all time to come, even if the Association's rights in Africa should pass to the French.

Confronted with rising opposition to the Anglo-Portuguese treaty at home and abroad, the Portuguese government proposed an international conference on Africa, expecting that Germany and its allies would support the Anglo-Portuguese position against the French and Belgians. This expectation was not to be fulfilled. "We share the fear which . . . has been expressed by merchants of all nations," Bismarck wrote to his ambassador in London on June 7, 1884, "that the actions of Portuguese officials could be prejudicial to trade." Germany, however, was "ready and willing to cooperate in obtaining a mutual agreement by all the powers interested in the question so as to introduce in proper form in this African territory [measures for] the regulation of its commerce [on the basis of] the principles of equality and community of interests."

To obtain the kind of mutual agreement he thought desirable, Bismarck took up the Portuguese proposal for an international conference on African affairs. In cooperation with the French government of Jules Ferry he suggested that such a conference be held in Berlin in November, and invitations were issued to the governments of all the European great powers as well as Belgium, Denmark, the Netherlands, Portugal, Spain, Sweden, Turkey, and the United States. A noteworthy sign of the times was that no representatives of the Africans themselves were invited to attend, nor was such an invitation even considered.

The Berlin Conference on African Affairs, which convened on November 15, 1884, did not become a forum for Franco-German collaboration against Britain, as has often been assumed. Well before that conference met the Franco-German entente had been wearing thin, but the principal reason for the absence of such collaboration was the divergence of French and German interests in Africa. Because Bismarck wanted freedom of trade in Africa, he regarded the British as more promising allies than the traditionally protectionist French in securing international acceptance of a free trade policy. Two days before the conference convened, he invited the British ambassador to call on him, and in an "extraordinarily amiable" discussion they reached agreement about mutual support on behalf of a free trade program. Bismarck did more than discuss free trade. The French had insisted that the question of the actual territorial division of Africa should not be brought before the conference, but the chancellor intimated that this matter might well be decided behind the scenes by the governments of Britain, France, and Germany—a far from subtle suggestion that Britain and Germany might concert in settling territorial issues as well.

In the actual deliberations of the conference, one of the first and most important problems to be decided was the extent of the territory to be covered by any agreement the powers might reach regarding Africa. As defined in the final Treaty of Berlin of February 26, 1885, that territory was far larger than the Congo Basin and included a broad belt across all of central Africa from the Atlantic to the Indian Ocean. Very roughly, the northern boundary of that belt extended from 2°30' south latitude on the Atlantic along the northern rim of the Congo watershed to a point at 5° north latitude on the Indian Ocean; its southern boundary ran eastward from the mouth of the Logé (Ludje) River on the Atlantic along the southern watershed of the Congo and Zambesi rivers to a point just above the junction of the Zambesi and Shire rivers, and thence along the course of the Zambesi to the Indian Ocean. The final treaty, moreover, was not restricted to this immense area but provided for free trade and navigation in the great basin of the Niger River far to the north. (See map, p. 241.)

Freedom of trade and navigation formed the main body of the treaty dealing with the belt across central Africa. All nations were to enjoy complete freedom of trade, they were to have free access to Africa's coasts on the Atlantic and Indian oceans, to the waters of the Congo and all its effluents, including the lakes, to all ports situated on these waters, and to all canals that might be constructed in the future. The products of all nations were to be subject to no other taxes than might be levied to cover the fair cost of expenditures made in the interest of facilitating trade and transport, and all merchandise imported into the region was to be free of import and transit dues. The entire region was declared to be a neutral zone.

All powers exercising sovereign rights or influence in the region bound themselves to protect religious, scientific, and charitable institutions without distinction of creed or nation, and to safeguard all organizations created to instruct the natives and "bring home to them the blessings of civilization." They promised further to watch over the preservation of the native tribes and to seek the improvement of their moral and material well-being. Finally, they bound themselves not to use this territory as a market or means of transit for the trade in slaves, and to employ all means at their disposal for putting an end to slave trade and punishing those who engaged in it.

The controversial problem of the actual distribution of territorial rights among the various European claimants was not raised at the conference itself in deference to French wishes but was dealt with, as Bismarck had envisaged, by the various powers concerned behind the scenes. Once again, King Leopold and his agents did a masterful job of lobbying on behalf of the Congo Association. They played on Anglo-German apprehensions about the protective policies of France and the sorry record of Portuguese colonial administration, and they were lavish with guarantees of their own for freedom of trade and the welfare of the natives in all territories that might be turned over to them. In early December, the famous African explorer and journalist-promoter, Henry M. Stanley, officially an American delegate to the conference but in fact one of Leopold's most effective agents, paid a brief visit to London to persuade the British government to give the Association all it asked; otherwise, it would be thrown into the arms of France. Although the British were warned by one of their own foremost authorities on Africa that the Association's commercial record did not bode well for the future and that its officials treated the natives with barbarous brutality under conditions far worse than slavery, the British were won over by Stanley's arguments, and Bismarck too was obviously convinced that the Association would be preferable to either French or Portuguese administration.

Confronted with Anglo-German support for the claims of the Association, the French made the best territorial bargain they could. In a treaty with the Association of February 5, 1885, they secured recognition of French claims to a large bloc of territory north of the Congo River as far as the Ubanghi River on the east. The northern boundary of this French Congo, which abutted the German-claimed Cameroons, was fixed by a separate treaty with Germany. The Portuguese held out longer, but under heavy Anglo-German pressure they made their own treaty with the Association on February 15 whereby they retained control of both the north and south banks of the Congo at its mouth, and of a substantial area south of the river, which became part of Portuguese Angola. All the rest of the immense region of the Congo Basin went to King Leopold's Association and was subsequently known as the Congo Free State and then, after its annexation by Belgium in 1908, as the Belgian Congo.

MAP 9 THE PARTITION OF AFRICA

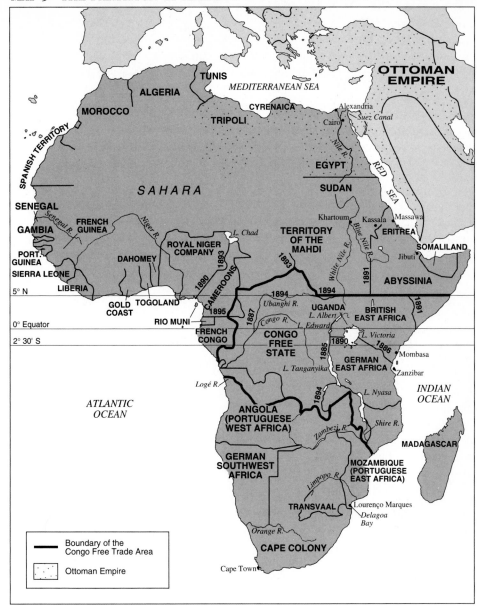

It has been said that the Berlin Conference set off the European scramble for Africa. That scramble, however, had been going on for centuries in one form or another. All the Berlin conference did was lay down a few rules for carrying it on. The most important of these was the provision that any power which henceforth took possession of a tract of land on the *coasts* of Africa beyond its present posses-sions would have to notify all other signatory states of its intentions so as to enable those states to assert any counterclaims they might have to the same territory. Fur-ther, a state taking over such territory was obliged to establish sufficient authority to protect existing rights (presumably those of other Europeans) and to ensure free-dom of trade and the fulfillment of other provisions of the Berlin treaty. In confining its rules for territorial expansion to the coasts of Africa, the conference deliberately bypassed the difficult problem of expansion into the interior, where territorial rights were to remain the subject of much dispute. Even the rules governing coastal ter-ritories were frequently disregarded, as were, far more tragically and flagrantly, the provisions for the humanitarian treatment of African peoples.

In the overall sphere of international relations, the Berlin conference, far from furthering the cause of Franco-German collaboration, paved the way for improved German relations with Britain. In July 1885, with the Conservatives briefly back in power in England, the British prime minister, Lord Salisbury, wrote Bismarck ex-pressing the wish to recover "the good understanding between the two countries which we value as of supreme importance, but which in recent times has been slightly clouded." The German chancellor, faced with a revival of revanchist senti-ment in France since the fall of Ferry the previous March, responded with some enthusiasm to this overture. He ceased pressuring Britain in the colonial field, re-jected the demands of German colonialists to annex Samoa (as distinct from taking measures to protect German interests there), and refused to establish a German protectorate over the Sultanate of Zanzibar on the east coast of Africa because "Brit-ish interests there are more important than our own."

By the later 1880s, in fact, as a result of native insurrections and constant alter-cations with German colonial administrators and entrepreneurs, Bismarck was evi-dently finding the colonies he had already acquired more trouble than they were worth, and on one occasion, perhaps only partly in jest, he offered to sell the whole lot to the Italians. In October 1888 a German foreign office official lamented that "our colonial crises lie upon us like a nightmare; and we need England everywhere. Our relations with the English government [with the Conservatives once again in office] are being most carefully cultivated." The German government was actually urging Salisbury not to make colonial concessions to the Germans that might jeop-ardize his political position at home, where imperialist sentiment was becoming far more vociferous than in Germany. In response to renewed colonialist agitation to appropriate Zanzibar, Bismarck declared that good relations with England were far more important to him than the whole of East Africa. As a means of integrating a state torn by class differences, German imperialism was clearly not doing its job.

❑ The Climax of Bismarck's Alliance System

With the fall of Ferry, there was a sharp reaction in France against his policies. Colonial affairs had involved France in costly conflicts overseas, and to many patri-otic French colonialism appeared to be a German plot to divert French resources and French attention from the recovery of Alsace-Lorraine. Ferry's cooperation with Bismarck was regarded as nothing less than treason. French defeats in Indo-China, along with the agitation of French patriotic societies demanding the return of Alsace-Lorraine, brought about a powerful resurgence of anti-German feeling in France. It was largely this sentiment that thrust General Georges Boulanger into prominence as the man French patriots believed could lead them in a successful war of revenge against Germany. In the end, Boulanger proved to be a man of straw. After a striking victory in a parliamentary by-election in Paris in January 1889 and with detailed preparations made for him to lead a coup d'état against the government, he spent the night with his mistress and then fled to Belgium to escape arrest for treason. But from January 1886, when Boulanger was first appointed minister of war, to the time he fled to Belgium, the possibility that he might establish a military dictatorship in France was a matter of grave concern to the Germans, especially as tsarist Russia might find an authoritarian Boulanger regime more attractive than a radical republic as an ally, and because Russia itself seemed likely to be particularly receptive to French alliance proposals during this period. For the rise of anti-German feeling and Boulangism in France coincided with Russian frustration in Bulgaria and a wave of similar anti-German sentiment in the tsarist empire. The Three Emperors' League was due to lapse in 1887 and the Russians had made clear that they would not renew it. If Russia now actually concluded an alliance with France, hot-headed leaders in either country might decide that the time had come to settle accounts with Germany and Austria. Germany would then be faced with a war on two fronts that would threaten its very existence. Even a German victory in such a war could not possibly yield benefits that would in any way compensate for the costs and hazards it would involve. By far the best policy for Germany would be to keep the peace. How this was to be done posed one of the most difficult problems of Bismarck's career.

Bismarck dealt with this problem through the negotiation of his most complicated and ingenious set of alliances. The Russians did indeed refuse to renew the Three Emperors' League when sounded on the subject in 1886, and it was clear that their present distrust of Austria made an agreement between Russia and Austria as impossible as an agreement between Germany and France. But an agreement between Germany and Russia was not impossible, and indeed seemed the simplest and most obvious way of preventing a Franco-Russian alliance and avoiding the danger for Germany of a two-front war. To secure an agreement with Russia, however, the Germans would have to remove all possible reasons for Russian suspicion of their policy and offer the Russians the prospect of gaining more concrete advantages from cooperation with Germany than they could hope to acquire in association with France.

At the same time, Bismarck had no intention of abandoning Austria or of allowing Russia to dominate eastern Europe and upset the balance of power. If Germany had to throw its weight on the side of Russia, Austria would have to be given additional support for its position in eastern Europe. Austria, in fact, would have to become the nucleus of an anti-Russian coalition, from which Germany would be rigidly excluded so that it could have a free hand to bargain with Russia.

The most obvious ally for Austria among the great powers was Britain, but if British isolationism was to be overcome, they would have to be convinced that unless they assumed their share of the burden in containing Russia, Germany and Austria would allow Russian power to flow into the Mediterranean. Turkey could be counted on as an ally against Russia as long as outside support was assured.

Austria already had defensive alliances with Serbia, Romania, and Italy, and Bulgaria was still hostile to Russia. With the backing of Britain, Italy, Turkey, and the Balkan states, Austria would be in an excellent position. Germany could then make any necessary concessions to Russia, knowing that Russia would be blocked by the Austrian coalition. Such a grouping of alliances would have the further advantage for Germany of leaving France in isolation.

In the last weeks of 1886 and the early part of 1887, Bismarck was engaged in fostering four sets of negotiations: for a renewal of the Triple Alliance, to safeguard Austria from Italy; for an agreement primarily involving Austria and Britain, to preserve the status quo in the Balkans and the Near East; for an agreement centering on Britain, Italy, and Austria, to preserve the status quo in the Mediterranean; and for an agreement between Germany and Russia.

The first tangible result of this complicated network of negotiations was the so-called First Mediterranean Agreement, which was not a full-dress treaty but a confidential exchange of notes between the powers concerned. Central to the agreement was the Anglo-Italian note of February 12, 1887, which called for the maintenance of the status quo in the regions of the Mediterranean, Adriatic, Aegean, and Black seas. Italy was to support British policy in Egypt; Britain was to support Italy in North Africa. Austria adhered to the Anglo-Italian agreement in a note of March 24, which stressed the common interest of Austria and Britain in the Eastern Question. Spain adhered to the same agreement in May through an exchange of notes with Italy. The various notes were somewhat loosely worded and admitted differences of interpretation, but they did provide a basis for cooperation and a definition of the mutual interests of the powers involved.

On February 20, 1887, the Triple Alliance was renewed for another five years. The Italians saw clearly that anti-German agitation in France and Russia had enhanced their value as an ally, and they consequently raised the price of their partnership. The old Triple Alliance treaty was renewed without change, but it was supplemented by separate, secret Austro-Italian and German–Italian notes that met the added Italian demands. The Austro-Italian note provided for maintaining the status quo in the Near East, with the stipulation that if the status quo could not be preserved, Italy would participate in settling the affairs of that region. Thus Italy gained a diplomatic foothold in any future partition of the Balkans or the Ottoman empire. The German–Italian note provided for maintaining the status quo in North Africa, and Germany promised to aid Italy if French activity in that area threatened Italian interests. Because Britain had provided Italy with similar assurances, Bismarck could feel confident that Germany and Britain together could prevent any Italian abuse of these promises of support.

With the conclusion of the First Mediterranean Agreement and the renewal of the Triple Alliance, the decks were clear for Bismarck to make whatever arrangement he could with Russia. As Bismarck had hoped, the tsar, although flatly refusing to renew any kind of treaty relationship with Austria, was not averse to a treaty with Germany. Even so, the negotiations between Germany and Russia proved difficult, for the Russians hesitated to give Bismarck the assurance he most needed, namely, a promise of Russian neutrality in the event of a French attack on Germany.

Finally, on June 18, 1887, a three-year secret treaty between Russia and Germany was signed. In this Reinsurance Treaty, each agreed to remain neutral if the other became involved in war with a third power, but these terms did not apply to an aggressive war by Germany against France, or by Russia against Austria. Both powers promised to support the status quo in the Balkans; Germany specifically recognized Russia's interests in Bulgaria; the principle that the Turkish Straits should be closed in time of war was reaffirmed. The most important part of the treaty was contained in a top-secret protocol. Germany promised to support Russian efforts to regain influence in Bulgaria and to oppose the restoration of Prince Alexander of Battenberg. Germany also promised Russia moral and diplomatic support for any measures the tsar might find necessary to control the "key of his empire"—Constantinople and the Straits. Thus Bismarck offered Russia freedom of action and diplomatic support in areas where German interests were not directly affected, but only after he had helped Austria form a coalition of powers to preserve the status quo in these same areas.

For Germany, the most important aspect of the Reinsurance Treaty was that it reduced the chances of a Franco-Russian alliance, or at least of an aggressive Franco-Russian alliance directed against Germany. As long as France was not certain of Russian support in an aggressive war against Germany, the likelihood of a French attack was greatly diminished.

T he value of the treaty was evident in the months immediately after its ratification. Boulangism reached its peak in France in mid-1887 and 1888, and Russia's frustration in Bulgaria reached new heights with the election in July of an officer in the Austrian army, Prince Ferdinand of Saxe-Coburg-Kohary, as prince of Bulgaria, despite strenuous Russian opposition. Had the Reinsurance Treaty not existed, it is highly probable that a Franco-Russian alliance would have been formed.

Still, with anti-German agitation in both France and Russia intensifying in 1887, Bismarck did not place all his trust in the Reinsurance Treaty but did what he could to strengthen the Mediterranean coalition against these two powers. The cooperation of France and Russia against Britain in colonial affairs during this same period aided Bismarck in this endeavor, for it made British statesmen conscious of the dangerous potentialities of the Franco-Russian combination and receptive to arguments that they should make more definite commitments in the Near East.

The Second Mediterranean Agreement was another exchange of notes between Austria, Britain, and Italy, signed December 12 and 16, 1887. The principle of maintaining the status quo in the Near East was reaffirmed. Above all, the agreement stressed the importance of keeping Turkey free from foreign domination of any kind. Turkey was not to give up any of its rights or to allow occupation by a foreign power of Bulgaria, the Straits, or any part of Asia Minor. The signatory states agreed to help Turkey resist all encroachments on its sovereignty; if Turkey failed to resist such encroachments, the three powers would consider themselves justified in provisionally occupying Turkish territory in order to safeguard Turkish independence.

The terms of the various 1887 treaties were secret, but to increase their effectiveness as instruments of peace, the gist of their contents was allowed to leak out—a warning to potential aggressors.

T he alliances fostered by Bismarck, in contrast to those that would be in force before the outbreak of World War I, did not divide the powers into two hostile camps. Instead, they brought them all into an interlocking network in which no single state, including Germany, could be assured of support in a war of aggression.

On the contrary, an aggressive power would be confronted by an overwhelming defensive coalition, based either upon actual alliance treaties or upon natural alliances that could be expected to form. Because the system would come into operation against any effort to upset the status quo, it served as a deterrent to chauvinist agitators in every country.

The strength of Bismarck's treaties lay in the fact that the advantages they afforded to the powers concerned were great enough to give each participant a vested interest in maintaining them. Also, the formal treaties were sufficiently limited in time to prevent any power from growing restive in the toils of a particular agreement. When the time limit was up, the treaty would lapse; or it could be negotiated anew to accord with changes in the international situation, for no power liked to be left without the assurance of defensive support of some kind.

The greatest weakness of Bismarck's system was its Metternichian emphasis on preserving the territorial and political status quo in Europe. Most European powers were not satisfied with the status quo. Russia and Austria had ambitions in southeastern Europe; France wanted to recover Alsace-Lorraine; Italy coveted Trent, Trieste, and the Dalmatian coast. Among Bismarck's own compatriots there was growing criticism of his conception of Germany as a satiated state and increasing speculation about the nation's future as a great power if it remained restricted to its narrow territorial base in central Europe. German nationalists wanted more territory, either overseas or in eastern Europe; army leaders and diplomats alike wished to stop diplomatic finessing and wage "preventive" war against France and Russia to put an end to the menace of these powers once and for all.

While Bismarck held office, he checked such agitation in his own country and used all his influence and ability to preserve peace and the status quo in Europe. But in 1888 there came to the German throne a new emperor receptive to the most irresponsible proposals for achieving national security and greatness.

❑ *The Accession of William II*

For years, Bismarck had dreaded the prospect of the death of William I. Not only did his son, Crown Prince Frederick William, profess liberal opinions, but his liberal supporters and numerous political opportunists confidently hoped that upon his succession he would dismiss Bismarck and appoint a chancellor with political views more like his own. The Bismarckian fears on this score were never realized, for in the spring of 1887 it was learned that the crown prince was mortally ill with cancer of the throat and was not likely to outlive his aged father. He did, but only barely. Emperor William I died on March 9, 1888. The crown prince took the title of Emperor Frederick III, but in his brief reign of ninety-nine days he was unable to carry out any significant program in either domestic or foreign policy. He died on June 15, 1888, and was succeeded by his son, William II.

Twenty-nine when he came to the throne, William II was still immature in his conduct and thought. The great tragedy for Germany was that he never grew up. An arm crippled at birth may have contributed to a feeling of inadequacy, which he attempted to offset by bombastic self-assertion. He was poorly educated and unable to accept rigorous intellectual discipline or training. He professed interest in the army and navy, but he really cared only for parades and reviews, for galloping over the field in sham battles or cruising at the head of his battle fleet. He never made a serious study of military or naval strategy or of the technological problems of modern warfare. His knowledge of foreign affairs and other aspects of government was similarly superficial.

William has been called clever, but his was the cleverness of the precocious adolescent. He had many bright ideas, but his thoughts lacked continuity. He was unable to formulate a logical course of action and pursue it with consistency and purposefulness. He launched his policies on the inspiration of the moment and might subsequently adopt a totally different or contradictory course in response to some fresh inspiration, leaving his government to deal with the resulting chaos. Disliking contradiction and opposition, he surrounded himself with sycophants and timid mediocrities, yet he could be won over to almost any policy by a person able and willing to cater to his vanity and prejudices. He interfered constantly in the conduct of affairs and thought to provide direction through hasty and ill-considered marginal notes scribbled on official documents, many of them larded with the crudest kind of barrack room vulgarity.

The new emperor was a product of his age. His imagination was stirred by revolutionary developments in industry and technology and by European imperialist ventures in the far corners of the world. He absorbed the most oversimplified concepts of Social Darwinism and pan-Germanism, becoming a spokesman for the strident nationalism and imperialism that aroused the passions of his countrymen as they did the peoples of every other European country at this time. Headstrong, impulsive, inordinately vain, he was resolved to lead his country to a new era of greatness not as a mere European but a world power; he would give Germany its "place in the sun." He insisted on making his voice heard in every international crisis and staked out colonial claims in every part of the world, with little or no concern for how these might conflict with the claims of others or how much damage they might do to Germany's diplomatic position. He proposed to build one of the greatest navies in the world to match the world's greatest army. And he accompanied every move with bombastic pronouncements that added to the alarm caused by his actions.

With his sense of self-importance and dislike of advice and contradiction, William was not the man to submit indefinitely to the authority of a Bismarck. While lavish with professions of admiration for the chancellor, he was determined to rid himself of Bismarck's undesirable tutelage and assume personal direction of the German government. Bismarck nevertheless remained in office for almost two years after William II came to the throne. During that period a major concern of his foreign policy was the continued hostility of Russia.

❑ *The "Lombardverbot" and Search for an English Alliance*

The secret Reinsurance Treaty of June 18, 1887, had done nothing to stem anti-German agitation in Russia or even deter the tsarist government from legislative measures detrimental to German trade and German interests in Russian Poland. The Germans retaliated with attacks on the value of the Russian ruble, but in November Bismarck resolved on a more dramatic step intended, as his son Herbert expressed it, "to make at least some attempt to bludgeon the tsar into seeing where his true interests lay." The bludgeon in this case was an order of November 10 to the Reichsbank (the German National Bank) to stop accepting Russian state bonds as collateral for loans—the so-called Lombardverbot. This action, which immediately lowered the value of Russian bonds, has generally been regarded as one of Bismarck's greatest mistakes because it is seen as the pivotal move that drove the Russians out of the German and into the French financial market and therewith paved the way for the Franco-Russian alliance.

The Lombardverbot came as a nasty shock to the Russians and seemed especially provocative because the interdict was issued in the week before the tsar was scheduled to visit Berlin, but its actual importance has been much exaggerated. In 1887 roughly one-fourth of Germany's entire export of capital was invested in Russia, well over half of Russia's total foreign indebtedness, but the Reichsbank (the only state bank in Europe that even accepted Russian state bonds as collateral) held only a small portion of the Russian securities in German hands. The Lombardverbot in itself, therefore, did not seriously affect Germany's powerful financial ties with Russia. But even if it had done so, the question must be raised as to why these longstanding and powerful financial ties had no appreciable effect in diminishing anti-German sentiment in Russia or creating greater mutual confidence between the two governments. The obvious answer is that economic interests do not necessarily determine popular attitudes or government policies in international affairs. When Bismarck's banker Gerson Bleichröder warned that anti-Russian financial measures would impel the Russians to seek their capital in France, a senior official of Bismarck's chancellery staff pointed out that Germany's experience with Russia had demonstrated that "financial relations do not lead to political intimacies. If this were true, then we should be virtually welded to Russia."

The real importance of the Lombardverbot was the opportunity it offered to Russian Germanophobes to fan the flames of anti-German hostility and bring pressure to bear on their government to establish closer relations with France. Particularly receptive to this pressure was the new Russian finance minister, Ivan Vishnegradski, a fervent nationalist notorious for his anti-German sentiments, who might well have turned from German to French money markets even if there had been no Lombardverbot.

As it was, the Lombardverbot did not prevent German bankers from continuing to compete for Russian loans in the international money market, much to the disgust of anti-Russians in Germany who charged that every penny loaned to Russia would be used to purchase arms for a future attack. Bismarck eventually recognized the ineffectiveness of his economic measures and by the autumn of 1888 Bleichröder was informed that the chancellor wished to "accommodate" Russia. Later that same year, however, a consortium of French financiers succeeded in beating out their long-established German rivals and floated a spectacularly successful 500 million franc loan on the Paris market. This Russian shift from the German to the French money market may have pleased Germanophobes, but it did not lead to an immediate reorientation of Russian foreign policy. It was not until Bismarck's successors refused to renew the Reinsurance Treaty that the Russian government began serious alliance negotiations with France. Even then, another three years were required before those negotiations were successfully concluded.

The Russian antagonism to Germany had its counterpart in German hostility to Russia, especially among German military leaders, and Bismarck was hard pressed to keep that hostility under control. He himself, however, recognized the tenuous nature of Germany's relationship with Russia and, to bolster Germany's international position and his existing network of international alliances, he approached the Conservative government of Lord Salisbury in January 1889 about the possibility of an Anglo-German alliance. Knowing the the difficulties any British government would face in securing parliamentary approval of a formal alliance treaty, he may have hoped for no more than an informal exchange of notes on the order of the 1887 Mediterranean agreements whose substance might be leaked as a deterrent to Russia and also to France, where Boulanger was still riding high early in 1889. But even a negative British reply would serve a useful purpose in demonstrating to Bismarck's own belligerent compatriots that they could not count on British support in a future conflict and that, unless they intended to run the terrible risk of a two-front war, they would have to accept his policy of seeking to remain on good terms with Russia.

Salisbury did not reject Bismarck's alliance proposal outright, but, well aware of the threat Germany faced from both France and Russia at this time, he obviously saw no reason to strengthen Germany's ability to stand up to those countries and thereby risk a diversion of French and Russian energies into areas where they might challenge the interests of Britain. Accordingly, on March 22, 1889, he told Herbert Bismarck, who had come to London primarily to discuss colonial differences, that he wished to leave the matter on the table for the time being without saying yes or no. That, the British prime minister said, was "unfortunately all I can do at present."

While unwilling to strengthen Germany's hand to meet the Franco-Russian threat, Salisbury was acutely conscious of that same threat to British interests, especially in view of the current buildup of the French and Russian fleets. To anticipate this danger, on May 31, 1889, his government secured passage of a Naval Defense Act designed to meet the challenge of Franco-Russian sea power. This act established what became known as the Two-Power Standard and provided that the British fleet should always be as strong as the combined fleets of the next two strongest naval powers.

Although Salisbury refused the German alliance offer, he wanted to remain on good terms with Germany. In the same month that he turned aside the alliance proposal he persuaded a reluctant Queen Victoria to invite her grandson, the new German emperor, to England, a gesture the queen had avoided heretofore because of William II's previous pronounced antipathy to England and his contemptible treatment of his mother, the queen's daughter.

As Salisbury had undoubtedly hoped, the English visit converted the impressionable William into an enthusiastic Anglophile. The British flattered his vanity and catered to his enthusiasm for naval matters by making him an honorary admiral of the British fleet. "Fancy wearing the same uniform as St. Vincent and Nelson," he said. "It is enough to make one giddy." A closer acquaintance with William did not inspire feelings of confidence in Salisbury, however. He took an instant dislike to the young man and told the Prince of Wales he thought him "a little off his head." The prime minister only hoped that the new emperor's excitable nature would not have an adverse effect on Anglo-German relations.

❑ *Bismarck's Dismissal*

It was to be some time before William's excitable nature affected Germany's relations with Britain, but in March 1890 the young man's impatience with Bismarck's efforts to control him led at last to the crisis that resulted in the chancellor's dismissal.

The reign of William II exposed a major flaw in the constitution Bismarck had given the German empire, for it left the supreme decision-making power in the hands of the emperor. Bismarck had long intended to introduce changes in the constitution, and in the months after William came to the throne he attempted to engineer a crisis that would provide the excuse for constitutional changes to curb imperial authority. But in this, perhaps the most fateful campaign of his political career, he failed. William had been warned from many quarters about the chancellor's intentions, and on March 18, 1890, he ordered Bismarck to resign.

The emperor tried to reassure the world that nothing had changed. "The course remains the same," he proclaimed. "Full speed ahead." But the course did not remain the same, and indeed during the coming years it was often impossible to discern whether there was any course at all. The first change, which took place immediately after Bismarck's dismissal, was his successors' decision to dismantle the keystone of Bismarck's alliance system, the Reinsurance Treaty with Russia.

THIRTEEN

◻

The Breakdown of Bismarck's Alliance System

◻ *Dropping the Reinsurance Treaty*

The German government's refusal to renew its Reinsurance Treaty with Russia, which inaugurated the breakdown of Bismarck's alliance system, was a deliberate decision on the part of Bismarck's successors and not a response to any hesitation on the part of Russia. On the contrary, the Russian government had expressed its desire to renew the Reinsurance Treaty some months before it was due to lapse, and it tried vigorously to preserve some kind of diplomatic connection even after being informed of the German government's refusal to renew the existing treaty.

The Russian willingness to continue its treaty relationship with Germany despite the recent acute differences between the two countries and Tsar Alexander III's distrust of Bismarck represented a domestic political victory for the Russian foreign minister, Count Nicholas Giers, over the pro-French and anti-German forces in the Russian government. Like Bismarck, Giers favored a conservative foreign policy designed to preserve peace and the status quo, and he feared the adventurous policies advocated by Russian expansionists and Slavophiles. Giers was also fearful that a Russian refusal to renew the alliance with Germany would force Germany to support Austria on all questions relating to eastern Europe and push Germany into closer relations with Britain. A Russian alliance with France, the alternative to an alliance with Germany, would be dangerous because France might be tempted to take advantage of such an alliance to launch a war of revenge against Germany. Nor did Giers have any confidence in the stability of France's republican government, a prejudice shared by the tsar, who referred to the existing regime in France as "that radical, atheistic French Republic."

The Russian move to renew the alliance with Germany was hastened by rumors of growing tension between Bismarck and Emperor William II and fears that the impressionable young German ruler would fall under the influence of his anti-Russian advisers. Ironically, Bismarck, so long distrusted by the tsar, was now regarded as the sole guarantor of continued amicable relations between Russia and Germany. Bismarck for his part was most receptive to Russian overtures. The Reinsurance Treaty, he declared, "corresponded so exactly to the situation which the two con-

251

tracting parties had both desired to create that even to define its duration would be, strictly speaking, unnecessary, the text of the agreement being, so to speak, the expression of a fixed and unchanging situation."

Bismarck's assessment of the Russo-German alliance was undoubtedly a sincere expression of his political views, but he himself was to be at least in part responsible for Germany's failure to renew the Reinsurance Treaty. For on the day the kaiser ordered Bismarck to resign, March 17, 1890, the Russian ambassador to Berlin informed Bismarck that he had been empowered to negotiate a renewal of the Reinsurance Treaty, and Bismarck now resorted to the dubious tactic of using the treaty as lever to return to power. Through his son Herbert, the head of the German foreign office, he informed the kaiser that the tsar had withdrawn his offer to renew the treaty after hearing of Bismarck's resignation "because such a secret business could not be negotiated with a new chancellor." This was a lie, as the kaiser discovered when he himself talked to the Russian ambassador, but instead of ordering his new chancellor to proceed with the renewal of the treaty, he listened to the opponents of the Russian connection.

Bismarck's successor as German chancellor, General Leo von Caprivi, was a professional soldier, but he was neither so inexperienced in the ways of statecraft nor so readily influenced by the anti-Russian and anti-Bismarck forces in the German government as many of his contemporaries and historians have believed. He took care to consult with longtime associates and supporters of Bismarck, and he was astonished to find almost complete unanimity among Germany's professional diplomats in opposing the renewal of the Reinsurance Treaty. Opponents of the treaty argued that the terms of the treaty with Russia conflicted with Germany's treaties with Austria, Italy, and Romania, as well as with the terms of the Mediterranean agreements with Britain. The treaty thus left Germany in danger of Russian blackmail, for by threatening to reveal those contradictions Russia could expose Germany's bad faith, disrupt its other alliances, and jeopardize its relations with Britain. Further, opponents argued that the treaty gave Germany no advantages to compensate for such grave dangers. It did not eliminate the possibility of a Russian alliance with France or guarantee Russian support for Germany in the event of an attack by France. Even Bismarck had not been able to reap any benefit from the treaty, for during the three years of its existence it had done nothing to reduce Russian hostility. Thanks to his immense prestige, Bismarck had been able to indulge in this dangerous and dishonest policy, but his successors would find it difficult if not impossible to do so. These arguments convinced the kaiser, who on March 28 informed the Russian ambassador that he intended to remain on the best of terms with his country, but that for the time being he intended to avoid all far-reaching commitments and considered it advisable not to renew the Reinsurance Treaty.

Giers was deeply troubled by Germany's repudiation of the Russian alliance and the consequent blow to his own foreign policy. In the following weeks he made every effort to reestablish some kind of treaty connection with Germany, even informing the German ambassador that he was willing to arrange a treaty "entirely according to the wishes of the German government." Receiving no response to this offer, he said that he did not even insist on a formal treaty. "An exchange of notes would suffice—perhaps an exchange of letters between the monarchs."

This Russian persistence only increased the German leaders' suspicion that Russia wanted an agreement with Germany in order to have an instrument to disrupt

Germany's other alliances and its good relations with Britain. If this was not the case, why should Russia offer to make an agreement on any terms? The Germans therefore rejected all further Russian advances. Germany would do everything possible to remain on good terms with Russia, but for that a secret treaty was not necessary.

Whatever the validity of the German reasoning in dropping the Reinsurance Treaty, it was fatally flawed for it totally ignored how severing the Russian connection might affect the policies of other powers. The Germans argued that a German treaty with Russia did not preclude a Russian alliance with France, that the Russians continued to hate Germany, and that, treaty or no, the Russians would attack Germany in the event of a French attack if it suited their purposes to do so. This argument completely failed to appreciate the enormous difference between a Russia tied to Germany, no matter how loosely, and a Russia firmly allied with France, nor did it take into account that Germany's rejection would virtually compel Russia to seek such an alliance. As for France, the certainty of Russian support as compared with the hopeful expectation of such support would greatly increase France's authority in international affairs and the temptation for France to embark on a war of revenge.

The basic reason for Germany's rejection of the Russian alliance, however, was not presented in any of the arguments used against the alliance itself. That reason was that the new German government contemplated a fundamental shift in foreign policy. Instead of Bismarck's complicated system of checks and balances and his interlocking alliances with their apparent contradictions, the Caprivi administration intended to form an alliance of states with interests similar to those of Germany, an alliance system in which Britain would take the place of Russia. As conceived by the kaiser, this would be an alliance of the stable and peace-loving powers (Britain and the Triple Alliance) to hold in check the perennial aggressive powers (France and Russia) and would conform with his desire "above all to pursue a straightforward and honorable policy."

This was an estimable goal, but here again the Germans failed to consider the effect their Russian policy might have on their allies or on the powers they hoped to secure as allies. By casting Russia adrift, the Germans considerably lowered their bargaining power with Austria and Italy, and they lost their most effective lever for prying the British out of their isolationism. With Germany no longer allied with Russia, and especially after Russia concluded an alliance with France, the Austrians and Italians saw that their own value as allies to Germany had greatly increased. Accordingly, over the coming years they were to demand an increasingly high price for their friendship, and that friendship became less reliable.

As for the British, they saw that Germany would now be compelled to support Austria and Italy against Russia and France or risk the disintegration of the Triple Alliance. Consequently, the British had far less reason than in Bismarck's day to make commitments of their own in order to balance the power of Russia in eastern Europe or of France in the Mediterranean. The Germans thus lost their principal leverage for propelling Britain into continental commitments, and in fact the British soon repudiated the various Near Eastern and Mediterranean agreements to which Bismarck had played midwife in the last years of his chancellorship.

Above all, the Germans failed to see (and they never did manage to see) that the British would never enter into the kind of alliance with Germany that the Germans wanted. For if Britain entered into such an alliance, the Germans, assured of the support or even the neutrality of Britain and their partners in the Triple Alliance, would be in a position to dictate terms to France and Russia simply by applying massive diplomatic pressure. This, of course, is precisely the position the Germans hoped to achieve through their new policy, and they probably sincerely believed that they would use it to ensure European peace and stability. But here again the Germans failed to see how other powers would view the situation, or to consider that the British, who had fought for centuries to prevent a single state from establishing a military hegemony over the continent, would hardly be likely to agree to an alliance that would give Germany virtual diplomatic hegemony.

❑ The Triple Alliance and Britain, 1890–1893

The Germans lost no time in making overtures to Britain. On May 13, 1890, more than a month before the Reinsurance Treaty was allowed to lapse, they informed Lord Salisbury, the British prime minister, of their desire to settle all outstanding differences between Britain and Germany over colonial claims, and they encouraged the British prime minister to state his government's terms. These terms were far from modest. In return for Germany's surrender of virtually all disputed claims in Africa, Salisbury offered the Germans the tiny British-held island of Heligoland in the North Sea, which he described (incorrectly) as a mere sandbar that would eventually be swept away and which British naval authorities agreed could not be defended without great expenditure. When the Germans attempted to bargain, Salisbury declared that he would prefer to postpone an agreement indefinitely rather than expose himself to the attacks of British colonial interests by ceding British colonial claims in Africa.

Salisbury's threat to break off negotiations persuaded the Germans to give in all along the line, and on July 1, 1890, an Anglo-German colonial agreement was signed whereby the Germans gave up extensive claims in East Africa in exchange for Heligoland. Heligoland was not a sandbar but a great rock, similar to Gibraltar, which was strategically important to Germany because it dominated the mouths of two of Germany's most important rivers, the Elbe and the Weser, and thus controlled access to Germany's two most important seaports, Hamburg and Bremen. It also lay across the entrance to the prospective North Sea–Baltic canal, which the Germans intended to build across the base of the Jutland peninsula.

Great as was the strategic value of Heligoland, the Anglo-German treaty was so overwhelmingly favorable to Britain that it was generally interpreted as a German move to purchase British friendship and a step toward the formation of an Anglo-German alliance. Its most immediate effect was to make the French and Russians even more conscious of their isolation and spur their efforts to conclude their own agreement. It did nothing to increase Britain's desire for an alliance with Germany.

Very soon after the signature of the colonial treaty, the Germans made an attempt to exploit their relationship with Britain, which can only have reinforced British reluctance to conclude a more general agreement. The Germans proposed that Britain and the Triple Alliance cooperate to curb French pretensions in Africa, something they could do simply by applying "peaceful massive pressure." This German bid for British diplomatic cooperation against France starkly exposed the fundamental British objection to an Anglo-German alliance, for it was precisely to avoid giving the Germans the power to apply this kind of "peaceful massive pressure" that the British consistently refused to be drawn into the kind of alliance that Germans desired and expected.

The Germans never seem to have understood the nature of this objection and remained confident that sooner or later the British, when confronted with sufficiently serious crises in their far-flung empire, would be compelled to seek Germany's support, and when that time came the Germans could dictate the terms of an Anglo-German agreement. Not for many years did the Germans learn how much their bargaining power with Britain had declined, but they were to learn almost immediately how the pretensions of their existing allies had risen with the lapse of the Reinsurance Treaty.

In July 1890 the Italian prime minister, Francesco Crispi, informed the Germans that he had reliable information that the French had just concluded a treaty with the bey of Tunis that would allow France to annex Tunis upon the death of the present bey. Crispi now called for the support of Italy's partners in the Triple Alliance either to prevent the French annexation of Tunis, which would be a severe blow to Italian interests, or to secure appropriate compensation for Italy. If such support were not forthcoming, the Italians would be forced to conclude that the Triple Alliance was worthless. As a result of Crispi's representations, the Germans found themselves obliged to go to considerable trouble in London to persuade the British to agree to compensation for Italy. In the end they were able to inform Crispi that if France annexed Tunis, Italy might count on compensation in Tripoli.

In November 1890, Crispi took advantage of Caprivi's visit to Milan to try to inveigle the inexperienced new chancellor into renewing the Triple Alliance on terms that would oblige Germany to make significant additional commitments to Italy. Crispi's government fell in January 1891 before negotiations with Germany were completed, but his successor, the Marquis di Rudini, clearly expressed his desire for better relations with France and his expectation of greater support from Germany if Italy were to remain in the Triple Alliance.

The Austrians played much the same game. During the autumn and winter of 1890 they made ostentatious advances to Russia with the obvious purpose of securing greater German recognition of their value as allies and firmer commitments of German support for Austrian policy in the Balkans than Bismarck had been willing to provide.

To offset the Franco-Russian rapprochement and the flirtation of Germany's allies with these powers, the kaiser attempted to do some flirting of his own and to use his mother's visit to Paris in February 1891 to improve Germany's relations with France. The visit was a fiasco. With a tactlessness worthy of her son, the Empress Frederick used this goodwill trip to France to inspect battlefields of the recent war with Prussia and to visit St. Cloud and Versailles, the scenes of France's greatest humiliations in that war. Her insensitive behavior so fueled anti-German agitation that the empress needed a police escort to ensure her safe departure.

The French meanwhile were conducting an intensive political and economic campaign to detach Italy from the Triple Alliance. That the alliance did not disintegrate, despite the pro-French inclinations of the new Italian prime minister, Rudini, was due above all to Germany's continued good relations with Britain. For the Italians, good relations with the major European sea power were vitally necessary because of the Italian peninsula's extreme vulnerability to naval attack. Italian statesmen also recognized, however, that they would require British support or at least consent if they hoped to realize Italian colonial ambitions in Africa or any other overseas territory. So long as Germany remained on good terms with Britain, therefore, it was to the Italians' advantage to maintain their own ties with the Germans, who were in a far stronger position to promote Italian interests in London than were the Italians themselves. And the Germans could always be prompted into supporting the Italians in London by threats of Italy's defection from the Triple Alliance.

On March 7, 1891, just after the ignominious flight of the Empress Frederick from Paris, the Italians informed the Germans of new and extremely tempting alliance offers from France and of French threats if these offers were rejected. Two days later Rudini told the Germans he wished to come to an agreement about their own alliance, but on terms considerably more favorable to the Italians. The moment was well chosen to extract maximum concessions from the Germans. "Good," the kaiser commented on the Italian proposal to renew the Triple Alliance. "The sooner the better, as a reply to Paris."

The Italians wanted an extension of Germany's treaty commitments in North Africa and the entire Near East, but above all they wanted assurances of further German and Austrian support in London. The Italians did not even make a gesture to offer the Germans anything in return. The Germans scaled down Italian demands for German support to Cyrenaica, Tripolitania, and Tunisia, but the most important consideration for the Italians—the assurance of German and Austrian support for Italian policies in London—formed an integral part of the new Triple Alliance treaty, which was signed May 6, 1891, and was to run for six years.

What the Italians did not realize, however, was that German leverage in London had declined appreciably since the nonrenewal of the Reinsurance Treaty. German efforts to extend the 1887 Mediterranean agreements and to bring them more into line with Italian desires were unsuccessful. When pressured by the Germans, Salisbury used the excuse that isolationist sentiment in England made it impossible for him to do anything for the Italians, and he asked the Germans to hold up the matter for a while. In mid-July 1892 Salisbury's Conservative party was defeated at the polls and gave way to a Liberal government. The Germans feared that Salisbury's defeat would mark a shift in British foreign policy, for Gladstone, the Liberal leader, was generally believed to prefer France and its republican government to Germany's imperial regime and to regard the autocratic government of Russia as less pernicious than the governments of Austria and Turkey.

Gladstone's election did not result in the drastic change of course in British foreign policy that the Germans had feared, for the political views of the new British foreign secretary, Lord Rosebery, conformed more to those of Salisbury than those of his own party leader. Rosebery's freedom of action was restricted, however, for he could not enter into agreements or make commitments without the consent of his colleagues in the Liberal cabinet.

Paul von Hatzfeldt, the German ambassador in London, understood Rosebery's position, but he was also intent on learning the extent to which the new foreign secretary proposed to follow his predecessor's foreign policy. He was especially eager to discover whether the Gladstone government would consider itself bound by the notes Salisbury had exchanged with the Austrian and Italian governments in 1887 (the Mediterranean agreements). Rosebery was very cautious. He said he was unable to make an official statement about British policy without the consent of his colleagues, and since other members of the cabinet might withhold that consent it would be best to take it for granted that old policies were simply being continued. When pressed for more specific assurances, Rosebery agreed to furnish a statement that in his personal opinion—but only in his personal opinion—the interest and sympathies of Britain would always bring that country to the side of Italy if Italy were attacked.

❑ *The Siam Crisis*

In view of the Gladstone government's refusal to provide any assurance that it intended to honor the 1887 treaties or continue to support Austria and Italy in resisting French or Russian pressures in the Mediterranean and the Near East, the German government observed with some satisfaction Britain's involvement in a serious crisis with France over Siam in the spring and summer of 1893. As the German government saw it, the British, pressured by France, which was now backed by Russia, would at last find themselves compelled to abandon their isolationist policy and seek allies, and the German government intended to take full advantage of this opportunity by forcing the British to make definite treaty commitments.

The Siam crisis developed as a result of French efforts to extend their territory in Indo-China at the expense of Siam (Thailand), which the British wanted to preserve as a buffer state between French Indo-China and British Burma. In May 1893 the French sent two gunboats to Bangkok to put pressure on the Siamese government, and when the Siamese fired on the French warships the French government sent a stiff ultimatum to Siam demanding the cession of all Siamese territory east of the Mekong River and a large monetary indemnity. This ultimatum brought relations between the French and the British, who had also sent a gunboat to Bangkok, to an acute stage.

During this period of Anglo-French tension over Siam, the kaiser arrived in Britain to attend the annual regatta week at Cowes on the Isle of Wight. Late in the evening of July 30, Queen Victoria sent her private secretary, Sir Henry Ponsonby, to the kaiser with a telegram she had just received from Lord Rosebery. "French government demand that we withdraw our gunboat from Bangkok," Rosebery's telegram said. "I have refused to do so. Desire to see Count Hatzfeldt [the German ambassador] in London immediately." Upon this urgent request of her foreign secretary, the queen asked the kaiser to send Hatzfeldt to London at once. The kaiser was jubilant. Clearly the British would now be forced to seek German support, and Germany would at last be able to secure the hard and fast agreement with Britain which it had sought in vain during the past three years. At this point the kaiser grew nervous. He believed war was imminent and gave way to fears that the British navy, even with German support, was not equal to the combined fleets of France and Russia, nor was the German army ready to fight the combined armies of those countries. Might not an alliance with Britain at this time involve Germany in excessive dangers? But all his anxiety did not prevent him from spending the whole of the next day sailing on the Prince of Wales's new yacht. When he returned he found that the entire crisis had been a false alarm and that the news of the French demand for the withdrawal of the British warship had been founded on a misconception. Later the news arrived that the Siamese government had given in to the French ultimatum after the French had reduced their demands somewhat in response to

British protests. The British now expressed themselves satisfied with French assurances that the territorial integrity of Siam would be respected and with that the crisis was over.

The Siam crisis provided the British with further evidence, if further evidence were needed, that Britain could cope with overseas crises without entering into alliances that would tie it to the policies of any continental power. If France and Russia joined forces to challenge Britain's naval supremacy in any part of the world, there would still be time to seek the support of the Triple Alliance. Meanwhile Britain should maintain its freedom of action and seek to strengthen its navy to meet the Franco-Russian menace. In the months following the Siam crisis there was widespread agitation in Britain for a bigger navy, and in March 1894, after Rosebery had succeeded Gladstone as prime minister, the British Parliament passed a bill providing for a large-scale fleet-building program over the next five years.

❑ *The Triple Alliance and Britain, 1893–1894*

For Germany, the British reaction to the Siam crisis was acutely disappointing. The British evidently valued German friendship only in times of peril; as soon as the danger had passed they reverted to their policy of selfish isolation. The Germans expressed their dissatisfaction with British policy in no uncertain terms. The kaiser let Rosebery know he would not put up with this game of hide and seek; if the British were not completely honest with Germany, he would not speak to Rosebery again. Hatzfeldt was slightly more diplomatic. On November 7, 1893, he reminded the permanent undersecretary in the British foreign office of Salisbury's remark upon leaving office: when I return I will probably find you (Germany) in the arms of Russia. "Without stressing the point," Hatzfeldt reported to Berlin, "I let him see a certain anxiety on my part that this prophecy might be fulfilled if they continued to behave as they were doing now."

Hatzfeldt's remark was no idle threat. Toward the end of 1893 the German government attempted to reestablish some kind of treaty relationship with Russia, and Friedrich von Holstein, a senior member of the German foreign office who had been one of the most adamant opponents of a renewal of the Reinsurance Treaty in 1890, was now fearful that the German Reichstag would reject a pending trade treaty with Russia. If this were to happen, Holstein said, "it would mean the collapse of our bridge to Russia, the mere existence of which, whether we use it or not, provides us with strength in all our policy negotiations." With that Holstein unconsciously acknowledged the wisdom of Bismarck's treaty relationship with Russia, but it was too late. The trade treaty Germany finally concluded with Russia on March 16, 1894, proved to be no substitute for the lapsed Reinsurance Treaty. By this time Russia had concluded a formal defensive alliance with France, and all subsequent German efforts for a rapprochement with Russia only enhanced Russia's appreciation of the value of the French connection. Thanks to their treaty with France, the Russians found themselves in a stronger bargaining position with Germany and could subsequently dictate the terms of any cooperation between them.

Germany on the other hand had not succeeded in forming a closer partnership with Britain. On the contrary, the Germans were finding it more difficult to secure commitments from Britain than in the days of the Three Emperors' League and the Reinsurance Treaty, and their bargaining position with their existing allies had also deteriorated.

During Rosebery's term in office, the Germans were given one more opportunity to make an agreement of some kind with Britain—the best opportunity they were to have in the entire period between 1890 and 1914. The Austrians were if anything even more concerned than the Germans about the failure of German diplomacy to secure binding commitments from Britain over the Mediterranean and the Near East, and late in 1893 they took the initiative in dealing with the British government. In February 1894 they extracted an assurance from Rosebery that Britain would oppose any Russian move to secure free passage through the Turkish Straits into the Mediterranean. Rosebery believed the British fleet was strong enough to act alone against Russia, but Britain could not oppose the combined fleets of Russia and France. The question for Britain therefore was whether Austria and the powers friendly to Austria would exert sufficient pressure on France to prevent France from coming to Russia's aid in the Mediterranean. Rosebery desired neither naval nor military assistance from Austria and its allies, but only the promise that they would hold France in check.

Rosebery's statement represented exactly what the German government had always wanted from Britain: the assurance that the British would assume the responsibility for protecting their own interests in the Mediterranean and the Near East. It also met one of the prime conditions the Germans had hitherto required on the question of supporting Britain in war: that Britain should either exchange binding guarantees with the Triple Alliance in peacetime or be actually engaged in war before the Triple Alliance came to its assistance. Rosebery was unable to promise binding guarantees because of the objections of his colleagues in the cabinet, but he did meet the other German condition in that he asked for support only after Britain had actually gone to war.

Rosebery's move might have been expected to open the way for negotiations leading to some kind of firm agreement between Britain and the Triple Alliance, but nothing of the sort happened. Caprivi, the German chancellor, objected that the British proposals obliged the Triple Alliance powers to define their attitude in advance in the event of an Anglo-Russian conflict over the Straits, whereas the British assumed no obligations whatever and reserved complete freedom of decision as to whether and when to oppose the Russians. If the British did take such a decision, the Triple Alliance powers would automatically be forced to carry out their obligation to hold France in check. This could not be done by mere diplomatic pressure in Paris, as the British appeared to assume. If the Russians attacked the Straits at all, they would almost certainly have secured French support beforehand, so that in order to hold France in check the Triple Alliance would be obliged to use force. This would mean that Germany, on which the main burden of controlling France would fall, would be obliged to declare war on France (and thus bear the onus of being the aggressor) whenever it suited British purposes to engage Russia at sea in the eastern Mediterranean. The war with France would inevitably lead Germany into war with Russia, and the result would be the dreaded war on two fronts. This most dangerous of all conflicts for Germany would thus be fought when Britain gave the signal in defense of an area where German interests were not primarily involved and with no guarantee that the British would not withdraw from the conflict whenever it suited their convenience. "Caprivi definitely refuses to explore Rosebery's idea even in a conditional noncommittal manner," the Austrian ambassador in Berlin reported to his government.

In light of Germany's entire policy toward Britain since 1890, the German rejection of Rosebery's proposals in 1894 is almost incomprehensible. Even if those proposals were not entirely acceptable to the Germans, the British negotiations with Austria were moving along the lines on which Germany itself had tried to guide them. As in the case of the rejection of the Reinsurance Treaty, there was some logic in the German objections to the Rosebery proposals, but it was narrow-minded, rigid, and essentially unpolitical logic which failed to take into account the possibility of using those proposals as the basis for further negotiation or the enormous advantage for all Triple Alliance powers of closer ties with Britain.

The only cogent reason for Germany's refusal to negotiate on the basis of the Rosebery proposals would have been that the Germans had concluded or were about to conclude a new political treaty with Russia which secured them the guarantees they needed in eastern Europe and which would have been in conflict with the British proposals. The British may indeed have suspected that this was the case, just as the Russians suspected that a German treaty with Britain was the reason for Germany's refusal to renew the Reinsurance Treaty. But, as in 1890, the Germans had no other treaty. Their rejection of the British, like that of the Russian alignment, was the product of muddle-headed political reasoning alone—dangerous not only in itself but in its capacity to induce totally mistaken conclusions about a government's policies, because stupidity is one of the most difficult factors for both friend and foe to evaluate.

In June 1894 the Austrian negotiations with Britain over a Mediterranean agreement ground to a halt. The Germans made no effort to redeem the situation but allowed their relations with Britain to founder in indecision, suspicion, and a variety of trivial controversies.

❑ *The Franco-Russian Alliance*

Meanwhile, following the German refusal to renew the Reinsurance Treaty, the Russians had entered into alliance negotiations with France.

Although the Anglo-German colonial agreement of 1890 did not lead to an Anglo-German alliance, it was correctly interpreted by foreign statesman as a German gesture of goodwill toward Britain designed to lead to such an alliance. The Russians in fact feared that a secret treaty between Britain and the Triple Alliance had already been concluded, a fear reinforced by the premature renewal of the Triple Alliance in May 1891 and a great visit of state by Kaiser William II to London in July of that year.

Russian fears overcame what remained of the tsar's scruples about negotiating an alliance with republican France. At the very time the German emperor was paying his state visit to Britain, Giers, the Russian foreign minister, suggested to the French that the renewal of the Triple Alliance and Britain's apparent accession to it had created a new situation for France and Russia that might make it desirable for them to take steps toward an entente. Negotiations began immediately, but a final agreement was long delayed because of domestic difficulties in both countries and because both states had very different and indeed contradictory purposes in view: the French wanted support against Germany in western Europe and against Britain in Africa; the Russians wanted support against Austria in eastern Europe and against Britain in Asia.

The negotiations, which were undoubtedly spurred on by enthusiastic expressions of public support in both countries, were finally successful because of continued fear about British and German intentions on the part of both France and Russia. In July 1891 the visit of a French fleet to the Russian naval base of Kronstadt became an occasion for frantic demonstrations of Franco-Russian friendship, completely overshadowing the tepid reception of a British fleet in Italy the previous month. The French visitors were lionized, the French national anthem, "La Marseillaise," was played throughout Russia, and the tsar himself stood bareheaded on a French warship as he listened to this most revolutionary of national hymns. When a Russian fleet paid a return visit to the French naval base of Toulon in October 1893, French demonstrations of pro-Russian sentiment were if anything even more exuberant.

As early as August 21 and 27, 1891, through an exchange of notes, the two governments reached a general agreement "to take counsel together upon every question of a nature to jeopardize the general peace." This vague formula was given effective expression through a military convention of August 1892, which, as it was signed only by military officers, did not have to be ratified by the French parliament. Its terms would therefore not have to be publicized or subjected to public debate. The exchange of notes of December 27, 1893, and January 4, 1894, ratifying the military convention is generally regarded as the true initiation of the Franco-Russian alliance.

This military convention provided that Russia assist France with all available forces if France were attacked by Germany or by Italy supported by Germany, and that France assist Russia in the same manner if Russia were attacked by Germany or by Austria supported by Germany. Should the Triple Alliance or any member of that alliance mobilize, both France and Russia were to mobilize immediately. The treaty was to remain in force as long as the Triple Alliance and was to be kept secret, but the European powers were at once aware that some kind of treaty between France and Russia now existed and that these countries could be expected to cooperate in the event of future international complications.

For France, the alliance meant the end of France's diplomatic isolation. Although the Russians had made it clear that they would not support a French war of revenge against Germany, many French statesmen and a large segment of French public opinion regarded the Russian alliance as a major step toward recovering the lost provinces of Alsace and Lorraine. For Russia, too, the alliance put an end to diplomatic isolation and evoked the prospect of French support for Russian policies in eastern Europe and the Near East. For both, the treaty was above all a security pact against Germany, which each hoped at some time to exploit to its own advantage.

Through a further exchange of notes of August 9, 1899, this time between the French and Russian foreign ministers, the purpose of the Franco-Russian alliance was extended beyond preserving the general peace to maintaining the European balance of power, and the term of the military convention was no longer to be the same as that of the Triple Alliance but "as long as that of the diplomatic agreement," which meant, as there was no time limit to the diplomatic agreement, that the military convention was extended indefinitely. Thus the Franco-Russian alliance, including its provision for immediate mobilization by both powers in the event of the mobilization of any member of the Triple Alliance, was adjusted to deal with virtually any contingency, in particular a threat to the European balance by Germany or Austria. Furthermore, it was now designed to outlast any disintegration of the Triple Alliance that might result from Italy's defection or the breakup of the Habsburg empire.

❑ *Imperialism and the Policies of Germany*

The grave weaknesses in Germany's international position after the lapse of the Reinsurance Treaty and the formation of the Franco-Russian alliance were not to be fully exposed for some years because the attention of the great powers shifted from continental Europe to the rivalry for colonial possessions throughout the rest of the world. In this rivalry Britain, as the greatest colonial power, became the focal point of international tension, and during the first years of its existence the Franco-Russian alliance seemed a greater threat to Britain than to Germany. Indeed, the great British naval rearmament program establishing the so-called Two-Power Standard—that the British fleet should always be at least equal to the combined strength of the two next strongest European navies—was directed in the first instance against France and Russia.

Meanwhile the Germans were lulled into a false sense of the strength and security of their own position, confident that the British would someday be compelled to enter into an alliance with Germany on Germany's terms. To speed the coming of that day, the Germans did everything they could to keep the heat on Britain in the colonial field, a policy candidly described by the German diplomat Holstein in a memorandum of December 30, 1895. Germany had no desire to strike Britain in any vital position; it wanted merely to create difficulties that would force Britain to turn to the Triple Alliance for relief. So long as Britain possessed India and Egypt and had interests in Persia, "she will be obliged eventually to effect a rapprochement with the Triple Alliance."

This policy might have enjoyed a limited success had it been conducted with some measure of subtlety and restraint. Instead, Germany's constant harassment only irritated and alienated the British. Worse, in the mid-1890s the Germans once again joined in the scramble for overseas territories and influence, and though never so great a threat to British interests as France or Russia, they frequently appeared to be an even greater danger because of their bullying behavior and bombastic pronouncements. Worst of all, toward the end of the century, to protect its overseas trade, back up its bid for colonies, and raise itself to the status of a global instead of a mere European power, Germany inaugurated a massive fleet-building program, which the British could only regard as a threat to their national security and which drove them into alliances with France and Russia, the very rivals in the colonial field the Germans had confidently expected would propel the British into the arms of the Triple Alliance.

FOURTEEN

◻

The "New" Imperialism

The precarious position of Germany following the breakdown of Bismarck's alliance system and the formation of the Franco-Russian alliance was not immediately apparent. Indeed, in the decade before Bismarck's dismissal the focus of attention of the European great powers had already begun to shift from Europe to their rivalries for territory and influence in other parts of the world. And in this game of global imperialism the heat was on Britain, the power with the most far-flung and comprehensive global interests.

Imperialism may be defined as the extension of some form of control or influence by one people over other peoples and territories. This definition is necessarily vague because imperialism can be exercised in many ways and assume a wide variety of forms—political, economic, cultural, or any amalgam of these and other methods of control or influence—which defy narrow or precise categorization. The motives for imperialism in any of its many manifestations are similarly varied, but two popular conceptions on the subject can definitely be ruled out: imperialism is not the product of any particular social or economic system, nor is its practice restricted to any particular race, nation, or group of nations. The earliest chronicles of human history contain abundant evidence of imperialist activity, as do the records of virtually every ethnic group and political organization, no matter what their social and economic structure.

The colonial rivalries among European powers in the late nineteenth century have frequently been called the "new" imperialism on the theory that European imperialist activity declined in the earlier part of the century, a marked contrast with its later resurgence. This theory has a certain validity only if imperialism is narrowly defined as the establishment of formal rule over *overseas* territory, but even then it is riddled with exceptions. A great deal of imperialist activity, including the seizure of overseas territory, took place during the first three-quarters of the nineteenth century. The British took over the Cape Colony from the Dutch, they occupied or annexed New Zealand, the Malay states, Hong Kong, Sierra Leone, Gambia, Lagos, and the Gold Coast. From their bases in British India they expanded into the Punjab, Sind, Berar, Oudh, Kashmir, and Lower Burma; from the Cape Colony they expanded into Basutoland, Griqualand, and Natal. During this same period the French annexed

Algeria, the Marquesas, Tahiti, and other islands in the Pacific; they began their conquest of Indo-China; and they attempted to establish an empire in Mexico.

If the definition of imperialism is extended to include expansion into contiguous territories and economic imperialism, then the theory of a decline in European imperialist activity in the first three-quarters of the nineteenth century becomes patently absurd. For during those years the Russians conquered and annexed immense stretches of territory in central and eastern Asia and on the east and west coasts of the Black Sea. In North America, Australia, and New Zealand, the white settlers continued a steady expansion at the expense of the indigenous populations.

Everywhere in the world, with the British leading the way, Europeans extended their influence through various forms of economic imperialism. By gaining a strategic foothold in the trade of another country and a mortgage on its revenues, Europeans established their influence in the countries of Central and South America recently liberated from formal Spanish and Portuguese rule; in the Ottoman empire and its quasi-independent vassal states in the Balkans and North Africa; and in many parts of Asia. Where their influence was resisted, Europeans did not hesitate to use political or military measures to push their way into foreign markets. The British and the French forced the opening of several Chinese ports to gain entry into the China market, and the Americans did the same in Japan. This extension of economic interests came to be known as the imperialism of free trade, and because it was cheaper and less dangerous than direct rule it was the preferred system of control so long as it remained effective. It was only when informal means failed to provide sufficient security for economic enterprises—for example, when the economic interests of an imperialist state were threatened by civil strife, refusal to honor debts, and above all the competition of rival powers—that the establishment of formal rule or at least a stricter form of control was considered necessary. "British interests in China are strictly commercial," the British foreign secretary, Lord Clarendon, declared in 1870, "or at all events only so far political as they may be for the protection of commerce." This was still the attitude of the British government, and of Bismarck too, at the time of the Berlin Conference on African Affairs of 1884–1885, which set up the greater part of central Africa as a free trade area (see pp. 237–242).

What was "new" about European imperialism in the final years of the nineteenth century was the marked increase in the establishment of formal rule over non-European territories and an intensified interest in imperialist enterprises on the part of all European governments and peoples.

This change in the nature of European imperialism was a reflection of changes in the political and economic situation in Europe itself: the growth of nationalist sentiment that accompanied the national revolutions and an increased awareness of the need for economic resources and markets that accompanied the spread of the industrial revolution. Before 1871, especially in the period of flux following the revolutions of 1848, the attention of the continental powers had been focused on Europe. After 1871, as it gradually became clear that no major adjustments of the western European boundaries were imminent, national ambitions were diverted to the territories beyond Europe. The British, who had enjoyed a virtual monopoly on overseas expansion earlier in the century, were faced with serious competition from France and Russia. Two new European powers, Germany and Italy, entered the field, as did two non-European powers, the United States and Japan, which had achieved their great power status through the large-scale adoption of European military, economic, and administrative systems.

Political imperialism was reinforced by economic imperialism. During the long economic slump following the worldwide financial crash of 1873, all the world's major economic powers with the exception of Britain had abandoned free trade and put up tariff barriers to ward off foreign competition. Foreign observers were confident that Britain too would resort to tariffs as soon as British industrialists, with their enormous head start in the world's markets, began to feel the hot breath of foreign competition. The only way to counter the pernicious effect of foreign protectionism on one's own economy, so the economic argument ran, was to acquire a colonial empire, which would ensure free and permanent access to the raw materials required by the new industrial economy for the manufacture of goods and weapons, markets for the products of industry, and investment opportunities for surplus capital.

A steadily growing and, at times, almost pathological concern about national security was nourished by theories that a nation's survival as a great power (which was assumed to be an essential condition for its survival as a free and sovereign state) depended on the extent of its territorial possessions and on the strategic advantages and economic resources such territories would provide. Moreover, the need to acquire such territories was growing more pressing with each passing day. Because the total amount of land in the world was limited, a state had to acquire as much territory as possible as quickly as possible while there was still territory left to take, if only to prevent it from falling into the hands of rival powers. Colonization, said the eminent French political economist Paul Leroy-Beaulieu, had become for France "a matter of life and death: either France will become a great African power, or in a century or two she will be no more than a secondary European power and will count for about as much in the world as Greece or Romania in Europe." Similar arguments were advanced by the historian Sir John Seeley in England, who predicted that within fifty years the power of states like France and Germany would be dwarfed by Russia and the United States, and who warned that a similar fate would befall England if it failed to maintain and expand its empire. What was involved here, in the words of the British statesman Lord Rosebery, was a process of "pegging out claims for the future."

Not to be overlooked or cynically dismissed as motives for imperialism were religious and humanitarian idealism. Missionaries by the thousands journeyed to every part of the world, often at the risk of their health or their lives, to convert the heathen to Christianity and to found schools and hospitals. Many colonial administrators were imbued with a missionary zeal of their own and genuinely sought to abolish the slave trade, introduce what they believed to be higher standards of law and government in areas under their jurisdiction, and in general bring the benefits of European civilization to those who had not yet had the good fortune to share in them.

By the end of the nineteenth century, imperialism, like nationalism, had developed into a mass cult. Colonies became symbols of national greatness and prestige, desired by nationalists of every economic and social class. The imperial idea, like nationalism itself, had been stirred into flame by visionaries, theorists, and prophets; it was subsequently nourished by the systematic propaganda of interest groups, patriotic and colonial societies, and the nationalist press. But, again like nationalism, imperialism appears to have met some profound psychological need for vicarious excitement, to feel oneself the member of a national team that was making its mark in the world and proving its superiority over other peoples and races. For millions of Europeans, the need for empire became a matter of faith, and no European government, democratic or otherwise, could afford to ignore the clamor of its public opinion—not isolated individuals or small interest groups, but the masses with no immediate political or economic stake in imperialism—for a vigorous expansionist policy.

The prime ingredient in European imperialism, however, and certainly the most important reason for its vigorous growth, was power—a feature stressed from the beginning of this study. For several centuries Europeans had enjoyed a power advantage over other peoples of the world, which had enabled them to undertake large-scale and successful imperialist enterprises, and that advantage had increased immeasurably with the coming of the industrial and technological revolutions. Never before in history had any group of people possessed such a superiority of power as did the nineteenth-century Europeans—power not only in the form of superior weaponry, but power stemming from the political, economic, and military machinery of the modern European state.

Armed with repeating rifles, machine guns, and artillery, conveyed to foreign shores in ironclad gunboats, a small number of Europeans could easily defeat large armies of Asians and Africans equipped with primitive weapons. So formidable was European power that the use of force was sometimes not even necessary. The mere presence of a gunboat, or a European emissary backed up by European guns, was often sufficient to persuade a local potentate to sign a treaty or yield to an ultimatum giving Europeans complete or partial control over his peoples and territories.

As Europeans demonstrated in the nineteenth century, there were many ways of using power and many different means of establishing control over another people or territory: by outright conquest, as in Russia's seizure of the khanates of central Asia and parts of the Ottoman empire; by setting up a "protectorate" over a native government, as the British did in Egypt and the French in Tunis; by establishing an outright colonial government, as the British, French, and Germans did in central Africa; by governing through a commercial enterprise, as the British did until 1858 in India and the Belgians until 1908 in the Congo; by dominating the economy of a region, as the British did in South America; by large-scale immigration, as the white settlers did in North America, Australia, and Siberia; by establishing a "sphere of influence" in a country, usually after treaty agreements with other European powers, as several European states and Japan did in China.

During the heydey of European imperialist activity, imperialism not only reflected European power; it made a major contribution to that power. This does not mean that all European colonial ventures were profitable. Most of the overseas colonies acquired in the era of the "new" imperialism were losing propositions. Although a small number of traders and investors extracted profits from them, they generally cost the mother country and its citizens a great deal more to pacify and administer than they brought in by way of revenue. Trade with these new colonies was minimal (Germany's trade with its colonies, for example, amounted to only 0.5 percent of its total foreign trade), they did not attract investments, and most of them were unsuitable for large-scale European immigration.

For Europe as a whole, however, imperialism in all its forms was unquestionably enormously profitable. Europe became the foremost supplier of manufactured goods and capital to the world, the foremost shipper and insurer, and from its visible and invisible exports it derived immense revenues. Far more important, Europe drew on the resources of the world and received the benefit of the cheap labor that produced those resources. Meat and grain, coffee and tea, sugar, tin, rubber, cotton, and petroleum poured into Europe from every corner of the world to feed and clothe its burgeoning population and stoke its ever-expanding industrial economy.

In terms of national security, the benefit of overseas colonies in wartime was restricted to those states with navies powerful enough to keep open the routes of access to them, which in the event proved to be only Britain and its allies. Britain's ability to draw on the resources of its colonial empire (formal and informal) was a major factor in the Allied victory in World War I. Overseas colonies were useless to Germany during that war, and the international ill-will Germany aroused in the process of acquiring them was diplomatically disastrous.

The most significant and permanent form of European imperialism, whether in terms of economic profitability or national security, was the acquisition of territories that were not only conquered but *settled* by Europeans. The Russian empire, acquired through expansion into contiguous territories, is the only European empire that is still intact and the only European state that remains one of the world's great powers, though the Russian empire too is now threatened by the ferment of nationalism that undermined the empires of its European rivals. Europeanized countries such as the United States and Australia are not even regarded as empires by the majority of their inhabitants, but in the eyes of the people from whom these lands were conquered they stand out as particularly vicious examples of European imperialism, for their conquest and settlement were accompanied by the large-scale extermination of the existing population.

For the world as a whole the most important result of European expansion has been Europe's cultural imperialism, which non-European peoples will never shake off. Europeans brought the industrial revolution to the rest of the world: they built factories and railroads; they opened mines; they introduced new methods of agriculture. To administer colonies effectively they introduced European methods of government, bureaucratic centralization, efficient systems of taxation. They trained native soldiers in the use of European arms and military methods. Above all, they brought with them their ideologies, and of these the most influential were not the Christian faith or the principles of law or self-government which European missionaries, religious and secular, tried to impart, but nationalism and Marxian socialism, which had an automatic appeal to people living under foreign political or economic domination.

The next five chapters deal largely with the diversion of the great powers' attention to problems of imperialism, a game now joined with considerable enthusiasm by the newly united states of Italy and Germany and by the major non-European powers, Japan and the United States. The great power rivalries over Africa and Asia, over the Balkans, Asia Minor, North Africa, the Pacific, and the Caribbean, intensified international antagonisms and led to a succession of diplomatic crises in the years before 1914, an imperialist competition that many contemporary observers as well as historians have regarded as a fundamental cause of World War I. An equally strong case could be made, however, that imperialist rivalries served as a lightning rod for the energy and ambitions of the major powers. With the notable exception of the Russo-Japanese War of 1904–1905, which the Japanese at least regarded as crucial to the defense of their national security, none of the imperialist wars before 1914 was waged between the great powers themselves. (Spain, the victim of war with the United States in 1898, had long since dropped from their ranks.) Moreover, by 1914 some of the most serious problems in the imperialist field, such as the Bagdad Railway and the Russo-Japanese rivalry over Manchuria, had been settled by diplomacy, insofar as international problems are ever settled.

Ironically, it was Germany's entry into the imperialist race and its construction of a major battle fleet to acquire and defend an overseas empire that once again focused the attention of the European great powers on Europe; and it was in Europe that the great clash between them at last took place.

The chapters focusing on imperialism and imperialist rivalries continue to concentrate on the policies of the great powers because these policies were the primary agents of imperialist activity. But the most significant and enduring consequences of imperialism, as every student of international affairs must recognize, has been its impact on the subjects and victims of imperialist enterprise, a topic that has only begun to receive the attention it deserves.

◻

FIFTEEN

The Competition for Control of the Nile

◻ Egypt and the Importance of the Upper Nile

As interest in colonies and imperialist rivalries intensified in the final decades of the nineteenth century, so did resentment of Britain, which had staked out claims to a large part of the world beyond Europe and was perceived by rival powers as the major obstacle to their own ambitions.

The British takeover of Egypt in 1882 (see pp. 233–234) had infuriated the Turks, for Egypt was still part (even if only a nominal part) of the Ottoman empire. But it had aroused even fiercer anger among the French, who had a comparable economic stake in Egypt and who were already smarting from Britain's coup in 1875 in acquiring controlling shares in the Suez Canal, which the French had built. Gladstone, the British prime minister, who regarded himself as an anti-imperialist, had assured the world that the British occupation of Egypt was only temporary and that the British would withdraw as soon as order had been restored in the country, but no one seems to have taken these assurances seriously except the British voters, many of whom were antagonized by Gladstone's apparent willingness to abandon British interests on behalf of a specious sense of morality. Subsequent British governments, however, including Gladstone's own, did not withdraw from Egypt, so that Egypt remained a bone of contention between Britain and all other states with interests in that country, France in particular.

Earlier in the century during the regime of Mehemet Ali, Egyptian rule in Africa had been extended far to the south along the valley of the Nile into the region known as the Sudan. At the time of the British takeover, Egyptian control over the Sudan was being challenged by the armies of a fanatical religious movement known as Mahdism, which by the end of 1883 had succeeded in expelling most of the Egyptian forces from the Sudan and establishing control over the region. Because the Sudan was not considered sufficiently valuable or important to justify the costs of its reconquest, the Gladstone government ordered the withdrawal of the remaining Egyptian forces from the area, and early in 1884 a British general, Charles George Gordon, was sent to the Sudan to supervise their evacuation. Instead of speeding the Egyptian evacuation, Gordon assembled the Egyptian forces at the fortress city

MAP 10 NORTHERN AFRICA AND THE NILE WATERSHED

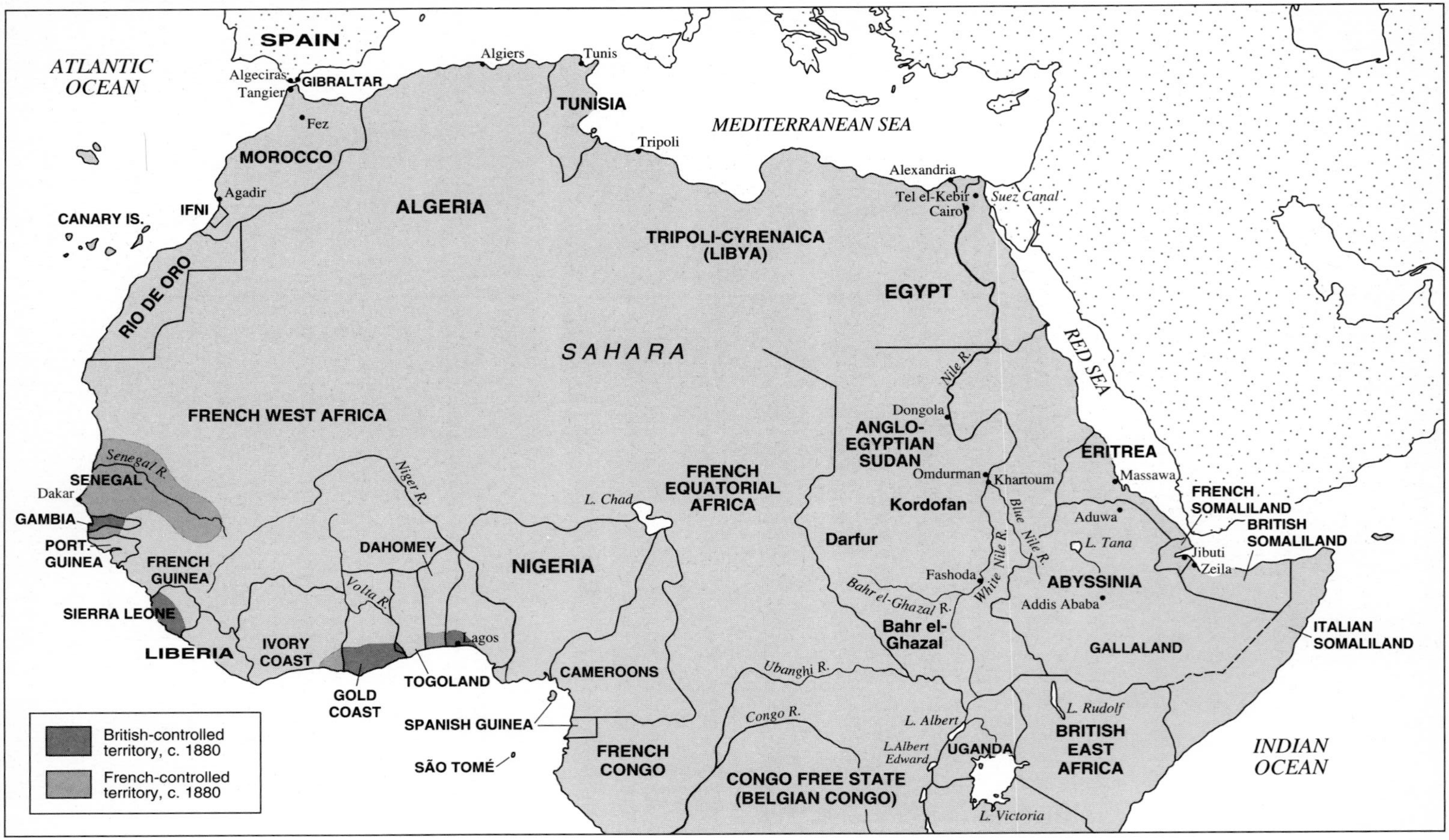

SPAIN

GIBRALTAR

Algeciras • Tangier

MOROCCO

Fez •

Agadir

IFNI

RIO DE ORO

CANARY IS.

ATLANTIC OCEAN

Algiers

Tunis

TUNISIA

Tripoli •

ALGERIA

TRIPOLI-CYRENAICA (LIBYA)

MEDITERRANEAN SEA

Alexandria
Tel el-Kebir •
Cairo •

Suez Canal

RED SEA

EGYPT

SAHARA

Dongola •

ANGLO-EGYPTIAN SUDAN

Omdurman • Khartoum

Kordofan

Darfur

Nile R.

White Nile R.

Blue Nile R.

Fashoda •

Bahr el-Ghazal R.

Bahr el-Ghazal

ERITREA

Massawa •

Aduwa •

Adduwa

L. Tana

ABYSSINIA

Addis Ababa •

FRENCH SOMALILAND

BRITISH SOMALILAND

ITALIAN SOMALILAND

Djibouti
Zeila

GALLALAND

INDIAN OCEAN

L. Rudolf

BRITISH EAST AFRICA

L. Victoria

UGANDA

L. Albert

L. Albert Edward

CONGO FREE STATE (BELGIAN CONGO)

Ubangi R.

Congo R.

FRENCH EQUATORIAL AFRICA

FRENCH CONGO

CAMEROONS

SÃO TOMÉ

SPANISH GUINEA

L. Chad

NIGERIA

TOGOLAND

GOLD COAST

Lagos

DAHOMEY

Volta R.

Niger R.

IVORY COAST

LIBERIA

SIERRA LEONE

FRENCH GUINEA

PORT. GUINEA

GAMBIA

SENEGAL

Dakar

Senegal R.

FRENCH WEST AFRICA

British-controlled territory, c. 1880

French-controlled territory, c. 1880

of Khartoum at the confluence of the Blue and White branches of the Nile and appealed for reinforcements, confident that the Gladstone government would find itself compelled by British public opinion to respond to this appeal and thereby enable him to hold at least part of the Sudan. A rescue mission was indeed sent, but it arrived too late to prevent the massacre of Gordon and his troops at Khartoum in January 1885, an incident that seriously damaged the prestige of the Gladstone ministry.

The British government's conception of the importance of the Sudan was to change radically in the next decade. In studying the critical problem of the flow of the Nile River, European hydraulic engineers confirmed a popular theory (later proved incorrect) that a technologically advanced state in control of the headwaters of the upper Nile would be able to divert the course of the Nile or otherwise regulate its flow. This state would thereby acquire a stranglehold over Egypt, whose economy could be ruined and lands devastated by cutting off the flow of the Nile or releasing its waters in time of flood. Even the longtime principal representative of British interests in Egypt, Lord Cromer, who had never thought the Sudan important enough to warrant its reconquest, was sufficiently impressed by this theory to write to Prime Minister Rosebery in 1895: "It is obvious that if any civilized Power holds the waters of the Upper Nile, it may in the end be in a position to exercise a predominating influence on the future of Egypt."

Gladstone himself refused to consider the reconquest of the Sudan (he described the Mahdists as "a people struggling to be free, and rightly struggling to be free," although the freedom fighters in this case were Muslim fanatics struggling to maintain the slave trade), and subsequent British governments were too much occupied with other problems, notably Ireland, to pursue a vigorous policy in Africa. Besides, with the technically backward Mahdists in control of the headwaters of the Nile, the threat to Egypt seemed remote. The main problem for British statesmen concerned with the upper Nile, therefore, was to make certain that this area did not come under the control of a technically advanced state.

The British appeared to have checked any threat that might have been posed by Germany in this region through the Anglo-German colonial agreement of July 1, 1890, whereby the Germans gave up extensive claims to territories at the southern headwaters of the Nile. Following this settlement, Salisbury wrote with some satisfaction to the queen: "The whole country outside the confines of Abyssinia and Gallaland territory to the south and east of Abyssinia will be under British influence up to Khartoum, so far as any European competitor is concerned."

❑ *The Role of Abyssinia; the Italian Debacle*

Abyssinia itself, however, threatened the control of the headwaters of the Nile. French agents were working methodically to increase French influence in Abyssinia, and it was widely believed that the ultimate French objective was to create a belt of French-controlled territory across central Africa from the Indian Ocean in the east to the French Congo and the Atlantic Ocean in the west. To counter the French threat in Abyssinia, the British were receptive to German and Austrian pleas to support the efforts of their Italian allies to extend Italian influence in Abyssinia. Italy, to be sure, was a technologically advanced state, but a far weaker power than France and thus a correspondingly lesser threat to British interests.

Italian claims in Abyssinia were based on the so-called Treaty of Uccialli, which the Italians had concluded on May 2, 1889, with Menelik, at that time still a pretender to the throne of Abyssinia, who became emperor (king of kings) in November of that year. According to the Italian interpretation of the treaty, which the Abyssinian government subsequently denounced as a faulty translation of the Amharic text (the only text that had actually been signed), the treaty gave them a virtual protectorate over the entire country, and thus also over Abyssinian-claimed territory extending all the way to the Nile. By two treaties with the Italians of March 24 and April 15, 1891, the British agreed to support the Italian interpretation of the Treaty of Uccialli, but with the condition that the Italians recognize the British delimitation of the Abyssinian frontier one hundred miles east of the Nile and promise not to interfere in any way with the course of the Atbara River, an important Nile tributary that flowed through Abyssinia.

Because of the extent of Italian claims at the expense of his country, Menelik, at one time a protégé of the Italians, now looked to France for support. The French were eager to provide it. Not only could they establish their own influence in Abyssinia through Menelik, but by supporting him against the Italians they could strike a blow at the Triple Alliance and their archenemy, Germany. Moreover, in pursuing this policy in Abyssinia, they would have the vigorous support of their new ally, Russia.

With the encouragement of France, Menelik repudiated the Treaty of Uccialli in February 1893, and in the following year he granted the French a concession to build a railway from the port of Jibuti, on the east coast, to the new Abyssinian capital of Addis Ababa, and thence westward as far as the Nile. To enable Menelik to withstand Italian pressure, the French and Russians supplied him with technically advanced weapons, particularly rifles and the kind of artillery that could be effectively deployed in Abyssinia's mountainous terrain. By 1895 he is supposed to have had 100,000 rifles, a substantial number of mountain guns, and appropriate supplies of ammunition; in the summer of that year he was waging a large-scale undeclared war against the Italians. In September he formally declared war, and in March 1896 he decisively defeated the Italians in the mountains near Aduwa. This defeat put an end to Italian pretensions in Abyssinia, which were not to be revived until the era of Mussolini. By the Treaty of Addis Ababa of October 26, 1896, the Italians recognized the independence of Abyssinia and restricted themselves to their coastal possessions.

With the demise of Italian influence in Abyssinia and the surprising strength demonstrated by Menelik's army, the Abyssinians now loomed as a threat to British interests in the Nile valley, a threat all the more serious because, as the British were well aware, behind the Abyssinians stood the French and the Russians.

❑ *The Approach from the Congo; France, Belgium, and the Policy of Germany*

Just as disquieting to the British as the problem of Abyssinia was the news of French efforts to penetrate to the Nile valley from the French Congo on the west coast of

Africa. To block this French threat, the British adopted tactics similar to those they had used in Abyssinia, only here they sought to make use of Germany instead of Italy. Because the Germans had given up a substantial portion of their colonial claims in Africa in the Anglo-German colonial agreement of 1890, the British were led to believe that the Germans were not seriously interested in African territory. They therefore saw no danger in concluding a new colonial agreement with Germany in November 1893 conceding a large tract of disputed territory in western Africa, which, if held by Germany, would establish a barrier between the French Congo and the Nile valley and therewith block the French advance into this area from the west.

The British calculations were correct insofar as German colonial ambitions at this time were concerned. What they had not counted on was that the German government would now begin to implement its new strategy of exacerbating British difficulties in the colonial field in order to force the British to recognize their need for a general political agreement with the Triple Alliance. For instead of holding onto the territory conceded them by the British, the Germans in March 1894 surrendered much of it, including the crucial avenue to the Nile, to the French.

Frustrated in their attempt to use Germany to block the French, the British turned to Leopold II, king of the Belgians, in his capacity as ruler of the Congo Free State—that immense bloc of territory east of the French Congo and Portuguese Angola which had been established as an independent state at the Berlin Conference on African Affairs in 1885 (see pp. 237–242). By a treaty of May 12, 1895, the British leased to Leopold and the Congo Free State further tracts of British-claimed (but disputed) territory west of the Nile, thereby interposing Leopold and his Congo state between the French Congo and the Nile. In return Leopold leased the British a corridor twenty-five kilometers wide between Lake Tanganyika in the south and Lake Albert Edward in the north, which the British needed as a link in a future Cape to Cairo railroad, a project dear to the heart of British imperialists.

The French immediately protested, contending that Britain's treaty with Leopold violated treaties of their own with the Congo Free State and that the British were leasing territory to which they had no legitimate claim. The British appear to have been prepared to ignore French protests, but once again the Germans moved to demonstrate to the British their need for German friendship. They did this by joining the French in protesting Britain's treaty with Leopold on the grounds that much of the corridor leased by the Congo Free State to Britain for the Cape to Cairo railroad was territory that rightfully belonged to German East Africa. Even after the British and Leopold agreed to drop that portion of the treaty to which Germany objected, the Germans continued to support French protests. As a result of combined Franco-German pressure, the British were forced to abandon the crucial part of their treaty with Leopold, namely, the cession of territory that would have blocked France's access to the Nile from the west.

In September 1894, the French mounted an expedition from the French Congo in the west to establish French claims to the region of the upper Nile. And despite British warnings that they would regard any French expedition to the upper Nile as an "unfriendly act," the French continued to make well-publicized plans to send further expeditions into this area.

The British hoped they could exert sufficient pressure on the French and the Belgians to keep the African problem under control until the railway they were building in Uganda was far enough along to allow them to send a military contingent to the upper Nile from the south to establish British claims to that region once and for all. With the Italian military defeat at Aduwa on March 1, 1896, however, the British were faced with a renewed and far more pressing threat from Abyssinia, where the French and Russians were attempting to move into the upper Nile from the east. To counter this danger, the British decided to allow the Egyptian government to begin a military advance up the Nile as far as Dongola, below Khartoum, a move that seemed to presage an Anglo-Egyptian effort to reconquer the Sudan from the Mahdists and establish control over the upper Nile from the north.

The kaiser was delighted by the news of the Dongola expedition. Upon learning of the Italian disaster at Aduwa, he had approached the British in great alarm to alert them to the threat this Italian defeat posed to their own position in Africa and warn them of the nefarious schemes of the French and the Russians in Abyssinia. The British would now have to act, the kaiser declared, and he informed them that he expected "that England would join the Triple Alliance or at any rate come to the assistance of the Italians in their difficult situation." When he heard about the Dongola expedition, the kaiser was convinced the British had made this move in response to his warnings. "My purpose has been attained," he said. "England has proceeded to take action and has compromised herself; the flirtation with Gallo-Russia is ended, and that is all I wanted." He was certain the Egyptians would be thoroughly trounced by the Mahdists, and that the British themselves would then have to intervene. "The English will yet come to us crawling on their knees if only we let them struggle long enough."

The kaiser's predictions proved wrong on both counts. An Anglo-Egyptian army under General Herbert Kitchener advanced cautiously but steadily up the Nile. It captured Dongola on September 21, 1896, and two years later it thoroughly trounced the Mahdists. Meanwhile, although the Germans gave them ample time to struggle, the British signally failed to come crawling.

❑ *The Fashoda Crisis*

At approximately the same time as the Anglo-Egyptian expedition was moving toward Dongola, a small French military mission, which had left France in May 1896 under the command of Major Jean-Baptiste Marchand, was moving up the Congo River from the west with instructions to go to Fashoda, a tiny fortress town on the upper Nile. Marchand's mission was not to conquer the area—his force was too small for that purpose—but to stake out a French claim to the upper Nile to serve as a bargaining counter in future negotiations with the British over Egypt. Marchand's progress was delayed by native risings in the lower Congo and transportation difficulties, but on July 10, 1898, his mission arrived at Fashoda, where he proceeded to raise the French flag over the ruined Egyptian fort.

Marchand's was only one of several military missions sent into the upper Nile region at this time. In 1896 the Belgians had organized two large expeditions in the Congo Free State which were also instructed to go to Fashoda, and between 1896 and 1898 four such expeditions were organized in Abyssinia, where French, Russian, and Belgian agents had stirred the ambitions of Emperor Menelik and therewith secured the support of Abyssinia's formidable military power to challenge the British in the upper Nile.

The activities of rival Europeans in Africa once again spurred the British into action. In June 1897 a force under Colonel James MacDonald left England with secret instructions to head off the Marchand mission. MacDonald was to advance from the south through Uganda even though the railway there, once thought essential to the success of such an enterprise, was far from completion. MacDonald, however, was prevented from carrying out his mission by an uprising in Uganda, so that the British government at last decided to order Kitchener to move into the upper Nile region from the north. The decision to order Kitchener to continue his advance up the Nile from Dongola had been delayed because such an expedition would require the destruction of the Mahdists, who were not only a formidable foe but whose presence in the Sudan had served British purposes well by keeping other European powers out of the region of the upper Nile. Now, however, it seemed that the only Europeans they were keeping out were the British.

Kitchener again advanced cautiously. On September 2, 1898, he defeated the principal Mahdist forces on the plains of Kerreri outside Omdurman, a victory so complete it broke the Mahdists' military power and in effect crushed the Mahdist movement.

Kitchener had been ordered to follow up his victory over the Mahdists by pressing on into the upper Nile region to head off the expeditions of rival powers. He found it necessary to act on these instructions almost immediately, for on September 7 he learned that Europeans had fired on a Mahdist steamer at Fashoda. Three days later he himself set out for Fashoda. On finding that the Marchand expedition had established itself there, he addressed a letter to Marchand on September 18 demanding the French withdraw and claiming the entire territory of the upper Nile as a part of Egypt. Marchand refused despite the inferiority of his forces compared with those of the Anglo-Egyptians, and Kitchener, filled with admiration for so gallant an enemy, decided against taking military action. Instead he invited Marchand to join him in a whiskey and soda, and both men agreed to refer the entire problem to their respective governments.

The Marchand–Kitchener confrontation marked the beginning of the so-called Fashoda crisis and a period of acute Anglo-French tension. The British, well aware of the strength of their position, were brutally firm. They refused to negotiate until Marchand evacuated the disputed territory, which the British now claimed for Egypt by right of conquest. The French foreign minister at this time, Théophile Delcassé, was not anti-British. On the contrary, he was eager to establish good relations with Britain in order to strengthen France's position vis-à-vis Germany, and it was only Britain's refusal to make face-saving concessions of any kind that prevented Delcassé from arranging a quick settlement of the crisis. As it was, he knew France had no choice but to give in. The British navy prevented any kind of effective French military action in Africa. France was occupied with a domestic crisis: the Dreyfus affair, which for a time seemed likely to explode into civil war and had left French society so bitterly divided that it was in no condition to face a conflict with a foreign foe. The French position was no stronger on the diplomatic front, because the Russians had given no sign of willingness to support their ally in standing up to the British in Africa.

On November 3, 1898, the French government ordered Marchand to evacuate Fashoda so that negotiations with Britain could begin. Owing largely to British recalcitrance these negotiations dragged on until March 21, 1899, when the British and French at last signed a convention excluding France from the entire Nile basin as well as from the region surrounding the Bahr el Ghazal river area to the west of the upper Nile. All the French were allowed to retain were their claims to large tracts of the Sahara desert, from Darfur in the east to Lake Chad in the west.

❑ *Britain Victorious; the Failure of Germany's Policy*

Three years later, on May 15, 1902, the British succeeded in arranging a treaty with Abyssinia that excluded Abyssinia from the Nile basin and protected the flow of waters into the Nile. By the terms of this treaty, the Abyssinian government accepted a boundary between Abyssinia and the Sudan well to the east of the Nile and agreed not to allow the construction of any work that would arrest the waters flowing into the Nile from Abyssinia except in agreement with the governments of Britain and the Sudan.

Negotiations with the king of the Belgians to exclude the Congo Free State from the Nile were more difficult. By the time of the Fashoda crisis, Congo-Belgian forces had established themselves in the basin of the upper Nile well to the south of Fashoda. Since these forces were far removed from any British troops that might have dislodged them, Leopold was in a position to reject British demands that they be withdrawn. Not until May 9, 1906, after the British had cut off all his communications by way of the Nile, did Leopold agree to a treaty giving up most of his claims on behalf of the Congo Free State in the Nile basin. He managed to retain a block of territory along the east bank of the Nile north of Lake Albert, but only for his own lifetime. Thus after Leopold's death the Congo Free State, like France and Abyssinia, would be completely excluded from the Nile basin. In this treaty, too, the British arranged that no works be constructed in the territories left to Leopold and the Congo Free State that would restrict the flow of the Nile or of waters flowing into the Nile.

With these treaties the great international struggle for the control of the headwaters of the Nile came to an end. Thanks largely to British naval superiority and the lack of any real unity among rival powers, that struggle had concluded with complete victory for Britain. German policy, on the other hand, designed to exploit British colonial difficulties in Africa to pressure Britain into an agreement with the Triple Alliance, had been a complete failure. The Germans nevertheless saw no reason to change that policy. They believed Britain's relations with both France and Russia had been severely strained during the recent crisis and that those powers would seek revenge in other parts of the world. Convinced that international animosity was building up everywhere against Britain, they remained confident that it was only a matter of time before the British government found itself compelled to seek the support of the Triple Alliance and that Germany had only to keep the heat on and wait.

As they did so often during this period, the Germans miscalculated. The Fashoda crisis had indeed contributed to French animosity against Britain, but France's defeat had not alienated Delcassé. The French defeat in fact provided him with an irrefutable argument in dealing with his colleagues: France could not afford two mortal enemies, Britain and Germany; if French foreign policy were to have any success in the future, the French government must overlook its grievances and seek the friendship of one or the other. For Delcassé there was never any question of which choice

France should make. Imbued with a deep hatred for Germany, he had long advocated reconciliation with Britain, and after Fashoda he persuaded his government to allow him to pursue a policy with this end in view. Thus Fashoda, instead of permanently poisoning Anglo-French relations, proved to be a turning point in their improvement.

❑

SIXTEEN

The Struggle for Supremacy in South Africa

❑ *Boers and British*

Among the many critical colonial problems with which the British government had to deal in the late nineteenth century, none provoked more international controversy than South Africa. Here, a crisis developed not as a result of competition with another great power but because of friction between the British and the Boers, the Dutch settlers who had been migrating to South Africa since the mid-seventeenth century. The great danger for Britain in the South African crisis was not the Boers themselves, though they proved to be a far more difficult problem than had been expected, but the possibility that one or more rival powers, frustrated by Britain in so many other parts of the world, would exploit the situation in South Africa by threatening to come to the aid of the Boers in order to compel the British to make concessions in other areas or, most dangerous of all, that rival powers would actually join forces in an anti-British coalition.

The Cape Colony, the first European settlement in South Africa, had been established by the Dutch East India Company in 1652 as a station on the route from the Netherlands to the Indies. Encouraged by the company, a small number of Dutch farmers migrated to the Cape Colony to raise crops and make wine to supply the company's ships.

In 1795, acting at the request of the Netherlands after it had been overrun by the French, the British took over the government of the Cape Colony to prevent this strategic territory from falling under the control of France. By the Treaty of Paris of May 30, 1814, the British secured permanent possession of the Cape Colony for nominal monetary compensation to the Dutch.

In considering the development of the conflict between British and Boers, it should be noted, especially in view of the importance this problem has assumed in our own era, that the descendants of the first European settlers in South Africa maintain that their forefathers had moved into a virtually uninhabited country, that they were the "native" inhabitants of that country. They thus had a legitimate claim to ownership of land by right of original settlement, and that landownership conferred on them the right to govern the country as they saw fit while excluding others from the rights of citizenship.

The claims of the European settlers in South Africa to landownership and political supremacy also derive from the fact that the customs and laws of native Africans differed from those of Europe. Much of the territory of southern Africa was sparsely inhabited upon the arrival of the Europeans because the native Africans were nomadic and had not established territorial claims—defined, of course, by Europeans, as permanent fixed settlements. In the nineteenth century, however, the right of Europeans to take over the lands of non-Europeans, through either outright seizure or token purchases, was not an issue. Most Europeans took this right for granted, as they took for granted their right to govern these territories in their own interest. The European takeover in North America is a notable case in point.

Among the Boers in South Africa, the European assumption of superiority over non-Europeans was powerfully buttressed by their version of Christianity. Most of these Dutch settlers were Calvinists, firm believers in John Calvin's doctrine of predestination, the idea that God had determined the worldly and ultimate destiny of all creatures and that the status they occupied in the world was an indication of God's grace, or lack of it. Thus people who prospered in this world were considered to be in a state of grace, an attitude that did not lead to passive acquiescence in one's status but, on the contrary, stimulated Calvinist believers to make every effort to prosper in order to demonstrate their worthiness. In racial terms, this belief in predestination had the unfortunate result of allowing whites to assume that their color and way of life were indications of their superiority over black people, who had been condemned by God to an inferior status on this earth and thus very probably to eternal damnation as well.

Almost from the beginning the Dutch in the Cape Colony were unhappy about British rule. In 1807 the British government abolished the slave trade throughout the British empire, a blow to the economy of the Dutch farmers, who depended on slaves for cheap labor. British rule had also brought many British settlers to South Africa, including substantial numbers of missionaries who did not share the Calvinist view of the natural inferiority of the black population and who strove to protect blacks from white exploitation while trying to convert them to Christianity.

In 1820, spurred on by the missionaries, the Cape government decreed the equality of all free persons of color with the whites, and in December 1834 the British government abolished the institution of slavery throughout the British empire, bringing freedom to some thirty-nine thousand slaves in South Africa. The act of abolition provided for monetary compensation to slaveholders, but because this compensation was made payable only in London most South African slaveholders were forced to sell their claims to collection agents, who paid far less for them than their nominal value, which most owners had considered ridiculously low in the first place. The loss of slave labor and of much of the value that that labor represented brought ruin to a large number of South African farmers and aroused further resentment against the British government.

The abolition of slavery in 1834 was followed two years later by the Cape of Good Hope Punishment Act, which was designed to protect African natives from white aggression and to check European seizure of their lands. It empowered co-

MAP 11 SOUTHERN AFRICA AND THE ANGLO–GERMAN PARTITION AGREEMENT

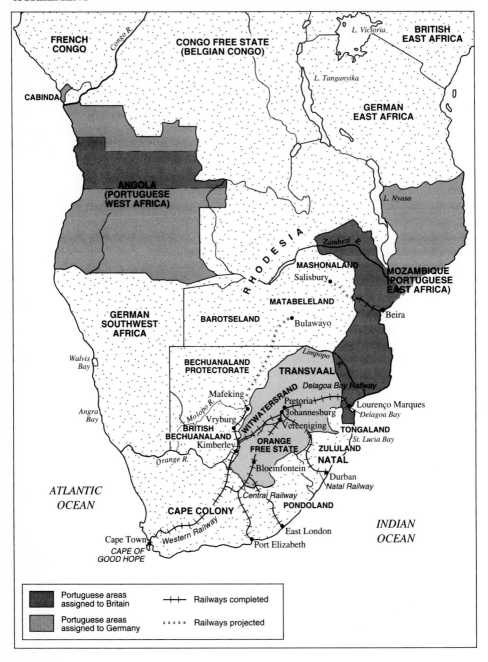

FRENCH CONGO

Congo R.

CONGO FREE STATE (BELGIAN CONGO)

L. Victoria

BRITISH EAST AFRICA

CABINDA

L. Tanganyika

GERMAN EAST AFRICA

ANGOLA (PORTUGUESE WEST AFRICA)

L. Nyasa

R H O D E S I A

Zambezi R.

MASHONALAND

Salisbury

MOZAMBIQUE (PORTUGUESE EAST AFRICA)

GERMAN SOUTHWEST AFRICA

BAROTSELAND

MATABELELAND

Bulawayo

Beira

Walvis Bay

BECHUANALAND PROTECTORATE

Limpopo R.

TRANSVAAL

Delagoa Bay Railway

Angra Bay

Mafeking

Molopo R.

Vryburg

Pretoria

WITWATERSRAND

Johannesburg

Vereeniging

Lourenço Marques

Delagoa Bay

BRITISH BECHUANALAND

Kimberley

ORANGE FREE STATE

TONGALAND

St. Lucia Bay

ZULULAND

NATAL

Orange R.

Bloemfontein

Durban

Natal Railway

ATLANTIC OCEAN

CAPE COLONY

Central Railway

PONDOLAND

INDIAN OCEAN

Cape Town

Western Railway

East London

Port Elizabeth

CAPE OF GOOD HOPE

▮ Portuguese areas assigned to Britain	+++ Railways completed
▨ Portuguese areas assigned to Germany	×××× Railways projected

lonial courts to deal with offenses committed by British subjects in any part of South Africa up to twenty-five degrees south latitude, and thus represented an assertion of British authority over regions far beyond the previously acknowledged frontiers of the Cape Colony.

These British measures on behalf of the native Africans provoked large numbers of Boers to undertake what came to be known as the Great Trek, a migration between 1836 and 1840 of ten thousand Boers and their families from the Cape Colony into the lands beyond the Orange and Vaal rivers. Many of these Boers settled in Natal, on the eastern coast of Africa north of the Cape Colony, but in 1842 the British, motivated at least in part by a desire to protect the native Africans from exploitation, went to war with the Natal Boers and in April of the following year Natal was made a British colony. Most of the Natal Boers thereupon trekked yet again to join those who had settled in the territory north of the Vaal River (the Transvaal.)

Distracted by a war with the native Kaffir tribesmen on the eastern frontier of the Cape Colony, the British recognized the independence of the Transvaal Boers by the Sand River Convention of January 17, 1852, and two years later, by the Convention of Bloemfontein, the British abandoned their claims to the territory north of the Orange River. In that same year, 1854, the Boer settlers in the region between the Orange and Vaal rivers established the Orange Free State with its capital at Bloemfontein, and in December 1856, after a good deal of bitter dissension among themselves, the Boers in the Transvaal established the South African Republic with its capital at Pretoria.

The Boers were not left long to manage their own affairs and exploit the natives as they saw fit, for in 1867 diamonds were discovered near Hopetown on the Orange River, an event that led to decisive changes in British South African policy. In October 1871 the British annexed the diamond region claimed by the Orange Free State, and in April 1877 they violated the Sand River Convention by annexing the South African Republic.

Infuriated by these treaty violations and renewed interference in their affairs, the Transvaal Boers rose up against British rule in 1880. After only a few minor British military reverses the British government, now under the leadership of Gladstone, once again recognized the independence of the South African Republic by the Convention of Pretoria of August 3, 1881, but with the critical reservation that the state was to remain under British suzerainty and subject to British control of its foreign relations. The British government had yielded so easily because Gladstone and some of the members of his Liberal cabinet believed the Boers had a legitimate right to seek their independence and were reluctant to wage war against a people struggling to be free, although in this case, as in many others of its kind, freedom for the Boers meant giving them a free hand in restricting the freedom of others.

British imperialists in South Africa were dismayed by the Gladstone government's failure to press the campaign against the Transvaal and its renewed recognition of Transvaal independence. Even more dismaying, indeed alarming, was the British government's recognition in 1885 of a German protectorate over a large area on the west coast of Africa north of the Cape Colony, a territory taken under the direct control of the German government in 1892 as German Southwest Africa.

❑ *Cecil Rhodes and the Advancement of British Interests*

Foremost among British imperialists in the Cape Colony was Cecil John Rhodes, an Englishman who had come to South Africa for his health in 1870 and had subsequently made a fortune in the diamond mines and other business ventures. Called the most visionary of businessmen and the most businesslike of visionaries, Rhodes did not regard the acquisition of wealth as an end in itself but as a means for acquiring power and influence, which in turn were to be used to realize his vision of opening up Africa and the world to British imperial and commercial enterprise. Steeped in contemporary imperialist and Social Darwinist theory, he was convinced that a people must prove its fitness and worthiness to survive, and that to ensure its ability to survive a people must acquire a territorial empire. As he saw it, the great conflicts of the future for supremacy and survival would not be between the white and colored races—he took the superiority of whites over blacks for granted—but between various branches of the white race, and among the white competitors for supremacy he feared the Germans the most.

It was above all this fear of the Germans that alarmed Rhodes and other British imperialists when the British government recognized an independent Transvaal and a German protectorate over southwest Africa. They were convinced the Boers and Germans would now advance into the unclaimed (by Europeans) territories between them and therewith not only extend the German foothold in southern Africa but cut off the avenues for future British expansion from the Cape Colony to the north, thus ending as well Rhodes's dream of eventually constructing a British-controlled railway from the Cape to Cairo. A lesser but nonetheless real danger was that the Portuguese, or foreign adventurers condoned by the Portuguese government, would push eastward from Portuguese Angola or westward from Portuguese Mozambique into the interior of Africa. To counter the German and Portuguese threat, contain the Boer republics, and leave open a broad avenue to the north for British enterprise, Rhodes considered it essential that the British establish clear claims to the territories north of the Cape Colony. He was also convinced that there was every need for haste in establishing those claims, for he had long been receiving reports that Boers, Germans, and other foreigners were already engaged in trying to secure concessions from native chieftains in this area.

From the time he first entered politics as a member of the Cape assembly in 1881, Rhodes urged the vigorous advancement of British claims in the north and the appointment of an official boundary commission to determine the exact frontiers of the German protectorate and the Boer republics so as to acquire some form of legal documentation to frustrate Boer and German claims. At Rhodes's instigation, the British government concluded treaties in May 1884 with the native chiefs of Bechuanaland, the region north of the Orange River between German Southwest Africa and the Boer republics, promising them British protection in return for the formal cession of all their territories to the British government of the Cape. Meanwhile, using the evidence provided by the Cape boundary commission, the British government had taken an important step to end all Boer claims to Bechuanaland. In a convention signed in London on February 27, 1884, Britain secured the South African Republic's acceptance of the Cape boundary commission's delimitation of the frontier of the Transvaal which excluded it entirely from Bechuanaland in return for

Britain's agreement to delete the reference to British suzerainty over the Transvaal embodied in the 1881 Convention of Pretoria. This agreement, however, retained the critical reservation that the foreign relations of the South African Republic were to remain subject to British control, which meant the Boers could not conclude treaties or any other agreements with foreign powers without British consent.

In August 1884 Rhodes was appointed Britain's resident commissioner in Bechuanaland, and he at once invoked the London convention to compel the Transvaal government to order the withdrawal of all Boer "freebooters" from the area. Just over a year later, in September 1885, the British government declared southern Bechuanaland (between the Orange and Molopo rivers) a British possession and established a British protectorate over all Bechuana territory north of the Molopo as far as twenty-two degrees south latitude. Rhodes's ambitions extended far beyond the twenty-second parallel, however, and soon his belief in the need for haste in establishing British claims in the north was to be powerfully reinforced. For in 1886 it was discovered that the gold deposits which had long been known to exist in the Witwatersrand region of the Transvaal were among the richest in the world, a source of wealth and power that gave the Boer South African Republic an entirely new dimension of importance.

To establish British claims to the territory north of the twenty-second parallel and at the same time shut off Boer, German, and Portuguese claims, Rhodes conceived of forming a chartered company that would occupy the entire region north of the Transvaal and which, with all its possessions, would be under the protection of the British government. His methods in gaining control of this territory were those he had used in Bechuanaland. On February 11, 1888, Rhodes and representatives of the British government arranged a treaty with Lobengula, chief of the Metabele tribe, which claimed dominion over a large part of the northern territories, promising British protection in return for a Metabele promise not to enter into any kind of agreement with any foreign state without British consent. On October 30 of that same year Rhodes's emissaries arranged a second and far more valuable treaty with Lobengula which turned over to a Rhodes-directed syndicate complete control of all metals and minerals in the Metabele territory together with the authority to exclude from Lobengula's dominions "all persons seeking land, metals, minerals, or mining rights therein." In return for these concessions, Lobengula was promised 100 pounds a month, 1,000 Martini-Henry rifles, and 100,000 rounds of ammunition.

After concluding these treaties with Lobengula, Rhodes moved to buy out the claims of other Europeans who had secured earlier concessions in Metabele territory. He then rounded out his project by securing a charter from the British government for his British South Africa Company on October 28, 1889. This charter conferred virtually unlimited rights and powers of government in the region north of the Transvaal between German Southwest Africa and Portuguese Angola on the west and Portuguese Mozambique on the east, without northern limits. With that, Rhodes achieved his goal to build the largest possible wedge between Germans and Boers in South Africa and to establish an immense avenue for the advancement of British enterprise to the north.

Meanwhile Rhodes had not neglected to nourish his influence in his home base in South Africa, and in July 1890 he became prime minister of the Cape Colony.

The extension of British authority and the establishment of British settlements in the territory north of the twenty-second parallel soon led to trouble with the

Metabeles, which erupted into open warfare in July 1893. The Metabeles, although bold warriors greatly outnumbering the forces of the South Africa Company, were no match for troops equipped with machine guns, which the Europeans used with terrible effect. Upon the death of Lobengula in January 1894, his followers submitted to British authority. Troubles continued with the Metabeles, the neighboring Mashonas, and other African tribes, but the Europeans with their superior weaponry had little difficulty in dealing with them and steadily extended their control. On May 3, 1895, the British government officially recognized Rhodes's contribution to this remarkable enterprise by giving the enormous territory he had brought under the administration of the British South Africa Company the name of Rhodesia.

The very extent of Rhodes's success seems to have clouded his judgment, however, and early in 1896 he was obliged to resign as prime minister of the Cape Colony because of his association with the disastrous Jameson raid into the Transvaal (see pp. 286–288), a key incident in the mounting tension between British and Boers in South Africa that eventually led to the Boer War.

Rhodes had never considered a conflict with the Boers inevitable or desirable. He had managed to gain the support of the large Boer population that had remained in the Cape Colony by pursuing policies that contributed to their prosperity and by abandoning or modifying previous British policies designed to protect the native Africans from European exploitation. By offering generous political and economic inducements, he hoped to lure the Boers in the independent Boer republics into closer partnership with the Cape government and his own enterprises and eventually bring them into some kind of all-embracing South African federation. His desire for closer relations with the Boer republics increased greatly with the discovery of the extent of the gold deposits in the Transvaal in 1886 and the consequent growth in that country's wealth and importance.

Eager to establish better relations with the Boers, Rhodes nevertheless remained acutely aware of the threat they represented to British interests in South Africa, a threat that might become very serious indeed if they were to receive support from one or more of the European great powers, notably Germany. To anticipate this danger, Rhodes had pursued a policy of encirclement to cut the Boers off from any possibility of establishing direct contact with the Germans in the north and west. It was even more important, however, to encircle them in the south and east, cutting them off from all outlets to the sea and thus from immediate access to foreign military and naval support, foreign supplies of arms, and foreign markets in general. This policy of encirclement had the additional and enormously significant advantage that it would put Rhodes in a position to throttle the Boers economically and force them into some kind of British and Rhodes-controlled federation.

To complete the most important part of his policy of encirclement—that is, to cut the Boers off from access to the sea—Rhodes had long advocated an extension of British control over the entire east coast of southern Africa. The British had already acquired control over a large bloc of this territory through their annexation of Natal in 1843; in 1884 and 1887 they annexed Santa Lucia Bay and Zululand. Now, with considerable prodding from Rhodes, they extended their control over the remaining coastal territory not yet annexed by Europeans (which meant everything south of Portuguese Mozambique) by annexing Pondoland in 1894 and Tongaland in 1895, therewith closing the ring around the Boer republics. Thus after

1895 the Boers' only access to the sea through non-British territory was through Mozambique, which made that country and its harbor of Lourenço Marques on Delagoa Bay the focus of intense international attention as the tension between Boers and British mounted in the last years of the nineteenth century.

❑ *The Stumbling Block of Paul Kruger*

Rhodes might have been successful in bringing the Boers into a southern African federation had it not been for the opposition of Paul Kruger, a leader in the Boer rebellion against British rule in 1880 who became president of the South African Republic in 1883. A devout Calvinist, convinced that all his actions were taken in response to divine guidance, he was suspicious of foreigners and fearful of modern economic and social developments, which he regarded as threats to the traditional values, religion, and political independence of his people. He was therefore neither impressed nor enticed by prospects of material progress and economic prosperity that might be achieved in partnership with Rhodes, and he adamantly opposed any form of political or economic federation with the British.

Kruger might have been able to preserve his country's independence and its population's relative isolation from foreign influences had it not been for the discovery in 1886 of the extent of the gold deposits in the Transvaal. The lure of gold attracted fortune hunters from every part of the world, and soon the city of Johannesburg, laid out near the gold fields in September 1886, had a population of 100,000, half of them black workers, the rest largely foreigners, or Uitlanders, as the Boers called them, a large proportion of whom were British.

Kruger and his conservative supporters recognized at once the threat this foreign population posed to the political supremacy of the Boers in the Transvaal, and the additional threat the country's newfound wealth posed to its political independence. For Rhodes and other foreign interests would now be more tempted than ever to extend their influence and control over the South African Republic. To deal with the threat of the Uitlanders, the Kruger government severely restricted their political and civil rights. To counter the threat to the Transvaal's political independence, Kruger sought to increase his country's economic independence. For this purpose, he sought control over a seaport to gain free access to foreign markets, but his efforts were anticipated and successfully blocked by the British. Even before the British had completed their encirclement of the Boers, however, Kruger had begun to explore the possibility of building a railway to connect the Transvaal with the Portuguese harbor of Lourenço Marques on Delagoa Bay, and in 1887 his government gave the Transvaal-controlled Netherlands South Africa Company a charter to undertake its construction. By this time the Cape and Natal governments had also recognized the desirability of building railways to the Transvaal to take advantage of the country's new wealth, and a Cape line to the Transvaal frontier was completed well before Kruger's Delagoa Bay project.

In 1891, despite the substantial increase in national income derived from his country's new prosperity, Kruger found it necessary to borrow money from the Cape government to finance his Delagoa Bay line. The Cape government was willing to make this loan because, although it could build a railway to the frontier of the Transvaal, it still needed lines to transport goods from the frontier to the interior of the country. In return for its loan, therefore, the Cape government demanded that the Netherlands South Africa Company build a railway bridge across the Vaal River and a line from that bridge to Johannesburg, with the Cape government to set the rates for all traffic on its portion of the line. So profitable was this traffic that income from the railway soon became an important factor in the Cape Colony's economy. It was clear from the beginning, however, that this lucrative situation would only be temporary, for with the completion of the Natal and Transvaal lines the monopoly of the Cape railway would be broken, and there was every reason to expect that the Transvaal government would do everything possible to funnel traffic over its Delagoa Bay line. Even more important, the line to Lourenço Marques would bolster the political as well as economic independence of the Transvaal.

Rhodes saw the danger clearly. "If the Delagoa Bay Railway is carried out, the real union of South Africa will be indefinitely deferred," he said. He nevertheless allowed the loan to Kruger to go through because he believed the British government would find means to persuade the Portuguese government to restrict foreign use of the harbor of Lourenço Marques. Rhodes was correct, but to his dismay the British did not exert their powers of persuasion for some time.

The Transvaal's Delagoa Bay railway was opened in July 1895 and immediately began to divert traffic from the Cape railway, for the distance to the Portuguese seaport was shorter than to the ports of the Cape and the shipping rate correspondingly lower. Worse, the Transvaal government imposed prohibitive rates on traffic using the link across Transvaal territory connecting the Cape line with the cities of the interior. The resulting plunge in the income of the Cape railway created a financial crisis in the Cape Colony and acute tension with the government of the Transvaal.

From a political point of view, an even more serious threat to the interests of Britain and the Cape Colony was the apparent influence of the Germans over the Kruger government and Transvaal affairs in general. Germans had been streaming into the country since the opening of the gold fields in 1886; a large proportion of Transvaal imports, including arms and ammunition, now came from Germany; it was estimated that one-fifth of all foreign investments in the Transvaal were German; and in the 1890s the Germans had acquired a controlling interest in the Transvaal National Bank. Rhodes, therefore, had good reason to believe Kruger would turn to Germany for support in opposing Rhodes's political and economic policies in southern Africa, and that the Germans would respond positively to a Boer appeal, perhaps with the eventual aim of making the South African Republic a German protectorate.

❏ *The Jameson Raid*

These accumulated political and economic circumstances led Rhodes and others with a stake in the affairs of southern Africa to explore seriously the possibility of exploiting the grievances of the Uitlanders in the Transvaal to overthrow the government of Paul Kruger. Throughout the summer and autumn of 1895 Rhodes and his associates paid for large stores of arms and ammunition to be smuggled into Johannesburg for the use of Uitlander revolutionaries, and they arranged that a substantial force of the South African Company's police should be stationed at the Transvaal frontier to come to the support of the uprising that was being planned.

These troops were to be under the command of the company's administrator for Rhodesia and a close friend of Rhodes, Dr. Leander Starr Jameson.

Political changes in Britain gave Rhodes reason to hope that his plans might be supported or at least condoned in London. The British government was no longer under Gladstone and those among his Liberal colleagues who had sympathized with the efforts of the Boers to retain their independence. In March 1894 Gladstone had resigned following the defeat of his efforts to secure home rule for Ireland, and in July of the following year the Liberals gave way to a Conservative government under Lord Salisbury.

The colonial secretary in the new British government was Joseph Chamberlain, who had left the Liberal party in opposition to Gladstone's Irish home rule policy and had helped form a new Liberal Unionist party, which stood for preserving the union of Ireland and Britain and had joined forces with the Conservatives in opposing the Liberal party's home rule program.

Chamberlain, the son of a London shoemaker, had entered politics after making a fortune in manufacturing in Birmingham, where he had served as lord mayor and gained a reputation as a political radical and social reformer. Like many radicals of his era, Chamberlain was also an ardent imperialist, convinced that a great territorial empire was necessary to provide markets for British industry, which would in turn ensure the employment and prosperity of the British working-class population. Chamberlain was convinced too that the preservation and maximum extension of the British empire was a great good in itself, for it conferred on the backward peoples of the world the inestimable benefits of British government and civilization.

Political pundits were surprised that the ambitious Chamberlain, who was thought to have been able to choose almost any position in the cabinet, had selected the colonial office, at that time still a comparatively humble bureau. But he did so deliberately and brought to that office an immense energy combined with a passionate missionary zeal. Upon taking over as colonial secretary, he claimed to have two important qualifications for the position: first, his faith in the British people, "the greatest of governing races that the world has ever seen"; and second, his belief "that there are no limits to its future."

For all his own imperialist enthusiasm, Chamberlain had serious reservations about Cecil Rhodes, who seemed to have become altogether too powerful and independent and who might well be tempted to pursue policies that diverged from Britain's overall interests. Nevertheless, when informed by one of Rhodes's agents shortly after taking office about the Cape prime minister's plans for organizing an Uitlander revolution in the Transvaal, Chamberlain evidently saw no alternative to allowing these plans to go forward. If he opposed them and the revolution succeeded, a new Uitlander government might be as adamant as the Boers in rejecting closer association with Britain; if the revolution failed, the British government could always disown it and disclaim all knowledge of Rhodes's plot; and if the revolution succeeded with Britain's blessing, "it might," as Chamberlain wrote later to Salisbury, "turn to our advantage." Chamberlain therefore pursued a policy of keeping in close touch with Rhodes to preserve the possibility of maintaining some control over his activities—and of reaping the benefits for Britain of any successes Rhodes might achieve.

In August 1895 Rhodes's agent in London informed him, perhaps with excessive optimism, that Chamberlain was "heartily in sympathy" with Rhodes's designs, and that he would "do anything to assist, except hand over administration of the [Bechuanaland] Protectorate [to the South Africa Company; it was from this territory that Rhodes proposed to launch an invasion of the Transvaal] provided he does not know officially of your plans." In October Chamberlain abandoned even this reservation and agreed to turn over a strip of the Bechuanaland Protectorate along the Transvaal frontier to the South Africa Company in response to Rhodes's plea that this strip was needed for a railway the company proposed to build to Rhodesia.

Chamberlain, however, remained suspicious of both Rhodes and the Uitlanders, fearful that they might yet set up a government in the Transvaal independent of or even hostile to Britain. To counter this danger, he repeatedly sought assurances from Rhodes that the British flag be hoisted upon the success of the revolution in the Transvaal, thus symbolically recognizing British authority over the country and the new revolutionary government.

By December 1895 preparations for the revolution in Johannesburg were in their final stages, and Jameson was provided with an undated Uitlander appeal, prepared weeks in advance, to come to the aid of the unarmed and oppressed "men, women and children of our race." The uprising did not take place as planned, however, because of differences among the conspirators, including disagreement on the critical question of which flag should be raised in Johannesburg following their victory. Altogether, to the disgust of the outside instigators of the plot, the Uitlanders seemed apathetic about the revolution—far more concerned about preserving their opportunities to make money than with risking their lives to secure political rights.

Because the situation in Johannesburg seemed so uncertain, Jameson was instructed to delay action, but with a confidence derived from easy victories over ill-equipped native Africans and evidently certain he could similarly crush any force of Boer peasants mobilized against him, he ignored these instructions, cut the telegraph wires to prevent further instructions from reaching him, and on the evening of Sunday, December 29, crossed the Transvaal frontier at the head of five hundred horsemen. The Boers, fully informed of Jameson's movements by their own agents, allowed him to get within ten miles of Johannesburg, caught his troops in ambush, and secured his surrender on January 2, 1896.

The Jameson raid gravely embarrassed both the Cape and British governments. Rhodes, deeply implicated in the revolutionary plot, was obliged to resign as prime minister of the Cape Colony, and in London awkward questions were raised about the involvement of the British government. An official commission of inquiry subsequently whitewashed Chamberlain and found the British government ignorant of the entire revolutionary scheme, but even at the time it was widely recognized that the government was probably covering up many unsavory aspects of the affair, and among skeptics the official inquiry commission became known as the "lying in state in Westminster."

❑ *The Kruger Telegram*

Chamberlain and the British government were rescued from prolonged embarrassment over the Jameson raid by an even more colossal blunder on the part of the kaiser. On January 3, 1896, almost immediately after receiving news of the raid's failure, William II sent a telegram to President Kruger congratulating him on the fact that, with the support of his people and "without appealing for the help of friendly powers," he had succeeded in defeating "armed bands which invaded your country as disturbers of the peace, and have thus been enabled to restore peace and safeguard the independence of your country against attacks from without."

This brief message managed to embody a policy position on virtually every aspect of the South African crisis that was most certain to outrage the British. The kaiser's reference to the help of friendly powers implied that such help would have been available, at any rate from Germany. His description of Jameson's raiders as armed bands and disturbers of the peace insulted the honor of the British soldiers involved, and the fact that the description was justified made it even more distasteful. Worst of all from a political point of view was the kaiser's reference to the Transvaal's independence, which seemed an explicit German recognition of that independence and thus also a rejection of Britain's claim to suzerainty over the Transvaal and control over its foreign relations.

The moment the Kruger telegram was published in Britain, all the shame and frustration the British public had felt over the failure of the Jameson raid and the overall situation in South Africa was diverted from Jameson, Rhodes, and their own government and concentrated instead on the German emperor. No single incident in the years before 1914 did more to inflame British public opinion against Germany or make the British conscious of a German menace.

How did the German emperor come to commit such an outrageous blunder? The most obvious and probably the most correct explanation is that the kaiser had not bothered to consider the implications and possible repercussions of his telegram, for it was only one of a long succession of politically ill-considered gestures on the part of this exceptionally thoughtless and impulsive ruler. At the time of the Jameson raid he was in an angry frame of mind because of a domestic political setback, and he had long felt annoyed with Britain for failing to respond as he would have liked to Germany's efforts to establish closer diplomatic relations. He also appears to have felt he had a score to settle with the British prime minister, Lord Salisbury. In the previous August during his visit to England to attend the Cowes sailing regatta, he believed Salisbury had deliberately snubbed him, and his unfortunate telegram may have been motivated by a desire to humiliate the British statesman in retribution.

News of the Jameson raid aroused the kaiser to a state of high excitement, and he went so far as to speak to his chancellor, Prince Hohenlohe, about whether to declare war. On January 2 he wrote to his cousin the tsar lamenting crises in the Middle East and South America stirred up by England. "And now suddenly the Transvaal Republic has been attacked in a most foul way as it seems not without England's knowledge. I have used very severe language in London, and have opened communications with Paris for common defense of our endangered interests." He now asked the tsar for Russia's support. "I hope that all will come right, but come what may, I never shall allow England to stamp out the Transvaal!"

The news of Jameson's defeat reached Berlin on the evening of January 2, and on the following morning the kaiser hurried to the chancellor's palace for an emergency conference accompanied by his principal naval advisers and Colonel Schele, the former governor of German East Africa. Marschall, the head of the German foreign office, was summoned later. The kaiser, clearly determined to make a dramatic gesture, first proposed a protectorate over the Transvaal but was persuaded by Marschall to drop this idea. He then proposed sending troops to the Transvaal.

When Chancellor Hohenlohe objected that this would mean war with England and that any transport of German troops would be intercepted by the British navy, the kaiser responded that this would be a colonial war and that therefore the question of British sea power did not arise. It was then decided to send Colonel Schele, disguised as a lion hunter, on an advisory mission to President Kruger. Finally, at Marschall's suggestion, the kaiser agreed to drop these preposterous ideas and satisfy himself with a telegram congratulating Kruger. When Marschall emerged briefly from the conference to instruct an aide to draft the telegram and tell him what to put in it, a senior foreign office official was horrified and tried to protest, but Marschall urged him not to interfere. "You've no idea of the suggestions made in there. Everything else is much worse." And so the telegram was drafted, sharpened at the kaiser's orders, and sent off over the imperial signature at 11:20 that same morning.

There is evidence to suggest that the kaiser's telegram was more than an impulsive gesture, and that it was part of his campaign to arouse the German public to the need for a major increase in the size of the German navy. The composition of the conference at which the Kruger telegram was conceived would seem to support this theory, for the only advisers the kaiser assembled initially to consult with the chancellor were the commander-in-chief of the navy, the heads of the imperial naval offices, and a former colonial official. But the evidence we have of the course of that conference does not indicate the naval issue dominated the kaiser's thinking or that it provided the motivation for the unfortunate telegram. Moreover, it was to be another two years before the expansion of the German navy became a dominant theme of imperial policy.

And so one falls back on the explanation that the telegram, for all its political importance, was not designed to serve any serious political purpose whatever but was simply an act of stupidity. A German official who had first-hand accounts of the origin of the telegram from both Hohenlohe and Marschall concluded that it was "only a naive expression of bad temper," and "typical of that lack of seriousness and breadth of view, not to say sound common sense, which brought about the fateful switching of our foreign policy in the direction of hostility to England. The driving force was not reflection but only the kaiser's whim."

❏ *The Road to War*

In the Boers' camp, the Jameson raid had two significant results. One was to transform Kruger, whose policies had been coming under increasing attack from more moderate Boers and who had barely survived the reelection campaign of 1893, into a national hero with more authority than ever before. The other was to make Kruger himself aware of the deplorable state of his armed forces. After the raid the Boer burgher armies were reorganized for more effective mobilization and deployment, and the most modern weaponry was purchased in large quantities from France and Germany as well as from Britain itself, so that when war finally came the Boer artillery had British-manufactured weapons that were not yet in use by the British army. Moreover, in this era of the gospel of free trade, much of this weaponry was shipped to the Transvaal in British ships via British-controlled ports and railways.

In 1896 Martinus Steyn, who was well known to favor closer relations with the Transvaal, was elected president of the Orange Free State. Already in 1889 the two

Boer republics had been linked by a customs union and a defensive alliance. To establish even firmer ties, Steyn negotiated a new treaty early in 1897 reiterating the terms of the earlier alliance and envisaging the formation of a Transvaal–Free State federal union. In February 1898 Kruger was again reelected president of the South African Republic, not by the narrowest of margins as in 1893 but by a large majority, a victory that represented a decisive defeat for the Boer moderates and a popular endorsement of Kruger's intransigent policies toward the British and the Uitlanders. Among the Uitlanders themselves, his victory regenerated agitation against the Boer-dominated government and renewed appeals to the British to intervene in the Transvaal.

The raid also had a powerful impact on British policy. With Rhodes now removed from the center of the political scene, Chamberlain himself assumed prime responsibility for defending British interests in South Africa. Early in 1897, he secured the appointment of Alfred Milner as high commissioner for the Cape Colony.

Milner was an obvious choice to act as Chamberlain's principal agent in South Africa. They had cooperated in forming the Liberal Unionist party, dedicated to preserving the union of Britain and Ireland. They were both ardent believers in British imperialism and the benefits the empire bestowed on the working class at home and the untutored savage abroad. In a public speech delivered on the eve of his departure for the Cape Colony, Milner expressed his belief in the desirability of a British-controlled union of all the states of South Africa, and he concluded with a ringing confession of nationalist-ethnic faith: "It is the British race which built the Empire, and it is the undivided British race which alone can uphold it. . . . Deeper, stronger, more primordial than material ties is the bond of common blood, a common language, common history and traditions."

Milner arrived in the Cape Colony in May 1897. Kruger's reelection early in the following year convinced him that Britain's previous policy of watchful waiting in South Africa had failed and that the Boers were not only determined to resist closer association with the British colonies but were plotting to establish their own control over them. Shortly after the Kruger election he wrote to Chamberlain and to Lord Selbourne, the undersecretary for colonies and Salisbury's son-in-law, that there was now "no ultimate way out of the political troubles of South Africa except reform in the Transvaal or war; and at present the chances for reform in the Transvaal are worse than ever." Kruger had returned to office even more autocratic and reactionary than before. Milner confessed that Kruger himself would not provoke a fight, and suggested that it should be the objective of British policy "to work up a crisis." This might be done by keeping up British pressure for reforms in the Transvaal, in particular on behalf of the political and civil rights of the Uitlanders. It was not that Milner, or Chamberlain either, was particularly concerned about protecting the Uitlanders. Both regarded them as being for the most part contemptible rabble interested almost exclusively in making money, and both feared that if the Uitlanders ever did gain control of the Transvaal government, they would turn their backs on the British and convert Kruger's republic into a republic of their own. The issue of Uitlander rights, however, was the best they could find to put pressure on Kruger and secure the support of British public opinion for their policies.

In November 1898, Milner returned to England to confer with Chamberlain and other leaders of the British government. He returned to the Cape in February of the following year assured of Chamberlain's support for forcing a showdown with the

Boers, and with instructions to draw up a memorandum on the situation in South Africa that would justify British intervention in the Transvaal if this should be necessary.

Meanwhile, the Uitlanders were doing their best to aid Milner in working up a crisis. The shooting of an Englishman by a Boer policeman the previous December and the dilatory handling of the case by the Transvaal courts were exploited to the full to expose the brutality and injustice of the Boer government. In March 1898, the Uitlanders handed Milner a petition addressed to the queen with over twenty-one thousand signatures that recited their grievances and appealed for British intervention on their behalf.

Two months after receiving this petition, Milner responded to Chamberlain's request for a memorandum to justify British intervention. This was done in a telegram of May 4, subsequently known as the "helot despatch." "The case for intervention is overwhelming," Milner said. The spectacle of thousands of British subjects kept permanently in a position of helots and calling in vain for redress was undermining the influence and reputation of Great Britain and respect for its government. The situation was one of extreme danger, for the Boers were moving toward establishing a Boer-controlled and republican union embracing all of South Africa. The only way to stop this movement and the mischievous anti-British propaganda exploiting the British failure to intervene on behalf of their oppressed fellow citizens would be to give some striking proof that Britain did not intend to be ousted from its position in South Africa.

Chamberlain did not immediately release Milner's helot despatch to the press. That was reserved for the moment it seemed desirable or necessary to arouse British public opinion in support of intervention. He did, however, make effective use of Milner's document in dealing with members of his own government, and at a critical cabinet meeting on May 9 he secured his colleagues' support for Milner's (and his own) policy of using the issue of Uitlander reform to "turn the screw" on Kruger until he "climbed down." What most members of the cabinet evidently believed was meant by a "climb down" was that Kruger, confronted with inexorable British pressure, would make concessions that would allow for the peaceful but steady extension of British influence and control over the Boer republics, for it was impossible to believe that he would be so foolish as actually to risk war with the mighty British empire.

This was not Milner's view, nor does it appear to have been Chamberlain's, though his attitude is not quite so clear. Milner at any rate was convinced that the only way the Boers could be compelled to climb down in such a way as to ensure British paramountcy in South Africa was through war. To this end, he pursued a policy deliberately designed to provoke a break in diplomatic relations that would force his government to go to war and at the same time provide it with a justification for doing so.

The negotiations between the Boers and British through the spring and summer of 1899 were complex. Throughout, Milner used the strategy, as defined by himself, of keeping up the pressure on Kruger through demands for reform, and of responding to every Boer concession by making further demands so as to ensure the failure of all negotiations and goad Kruger into making some kind of desperate move that would give Britain its justification for war.

Milner's strategy had the wholehearted backing of Chamberlain, who was quite candid about what was involved. "The question at issue is greater than any particular grievance or special act of oppression and . . . if we have to go further, it will not be for the franchise [or other specific issues] but for the maintenance of our position in South Africa," by which Chamberlain meant, as he made explicit in a later dispatch to Milner, "our supremacy in South Africa and our existence as a great power." Chamberlain's only warning was that Milner should bear in mind that it was "of the utmost importance to put the President of the South African Republic clearly in the wrong."

Kruger, or some of his advisers, saw through this game, and on August 13 he authorized a representative of his government to make an offer of concessions to the Uitlanders that went beyond anything Milner had so far demanded. But in return he wanted Britain to renounce all claims to suzerainty over the Transvaal and control over its foreign policy. In other words, he wanted Britain's formal recognition of the Transvaal's sovereignty and independence.

This offer placed Chamberlain and Milner in an awkward position, for if they rejected it they would be acknowledging that political reform was not the issue at all but rather the establishment of a British paramountcy in South Africa that would not admit a recognition of Transvaal sovereignty. To evade such a confession, Milner proposed to Chamberlain that they insist on a joint inquiry on the franchise question, which Kruger had previously rejected, and that in addition they demand the Transvaal disarm.

The blatant unacceptability of this demand was too much even for Chamberlain, who warned Milner to "avoid any language which would lead the South African Republic to think we are determined to pick a quarrel." Chamberlain, therefore, instructed Milner to concentrate on Kruger's demand for British recognition of Transvaal sovereignty, which was to be rejected as inadmissible because the provision for British suzerainty over the Transvaal embodied in the Anglo-Boer treaty of Pretoria of April 5, 1881, had never lapsed. Chamberlain dropped the British demand for a joint inquiry, but apart from that he expected the Transvaal government to concede everything offered in its proposal of August 13 unconditionally. Milner was to add the warning that if Kruger insisted on conditions in return for his concessions, the British government would in all probability issue an ultimatum and support it by dispatching further troop reinforcements to South Africa.

In dealing with his colleagues in the cabinet, too, Chamberlain concentrated on Kruger's "inadmissible" demand for British recognition of Transvaal sovereignty to explain the failure of all negotiations with the Boers. In doing so, he not only managed to convince them that the Boers alone were responsible for this failure but that the reason was their determination to attain paramountcy in South Africa. On September 8 he secured cabinet approval to reject the Transvaal claim to sovereignty and to respond to Milner's plea for a show of force by increasing the number of British troops in South Africa to twenty-two thousand, still far weaker numerically than the armies the Boers were thought capable of putting into the field. He subsequently secured the approval for additional sharp increases to bring the number of British troops in South Africa up to seventy thousand and instructed his representatives to prolong negotiations with the Boers in order to gain time for these troops to arrive.

A letter from Salisbury to the queen on September 23 is probably an accurate reflection of how Chamberlain was portraying the situation in South Africa. "It is impossible to avoid believing that the Boers really aim at setting up a South African Republic, consisting of the Transvaal, the Orange Free State, and Your Majesty's Colony. It is impossible to account in any other manner for their rejection of our most moderate demands.''

Having persuaded the cabinet of the Boer menace, Chamberlain on September 29 secured agreement on the text of an ultimatum to the Transvaal government demanding that it repeal all legislation affecting the rights of Uitlanders passed since 1881 (when almost all such legislation had been enacted); that it grant home rule to the inhabitants of the Rand (the region of Johannesburg and the gold fields where the majority of Uitlanders lived); that it surrender its right to import arms through Mozambique; and, to make absolutely certain that the ultimatum would be rejected, that the Transvaal disarm.

Kruger spared the British the need to make use of this ultimatum by at last responding to the goading as Milner had hoped he would. By early September 1899 Kruger no longer doubted that the British were determined to control his country, and he developed a war plan to strike through Natal and capture the harbor of Durban before British reinforcements could arrive, a stroke that would secure the Transvaal's access to the sea and encourage Britain's rivals among the great powers—France, Germany, and Russia—to intervene. The news of the dispatch of British reinforcements to South Africa finally evoked the sense of desperation in Kruger that Milner had clearly intended when he appealed for a show of force. Convinced that he could delay no longer if the Boers were to have any chance of preserving their independence, Kruger sent an ultimatum of his own to the British accusing them of violating the London Convention of 1884 (in which the British had dropped the specific reference to their claim to suzerainty over the Transvaal) by interfering in the Transvaal's domestic affairs, and of provocative behavior by stationing troops along the Transvaal's frontiers. The ultimatum demanded impartial arbitration on all points of mutual difference; the immediate withdrawal of British troops from the Transvaal frontiers; the withdrawal of all British reinforcements that had arrived in South Africa after June 4; and a British promise that all reinforcements now on the high seas not be landed at any South African ports. The British were given forty-eight hours to comply. Failure to do so would be regarded by the South African Republic as a British declaration of war.

Kruger's ultimatum was greeted with jubilation in Britain. Chamberlain positively exulted. "They have done it!" he said. Lansdowne, the secretary for war, hastened to send his congratulations. "Accept my felicitations. I don't think Kruger could have played our cards better than he has. . . . My soldiers are in ecstasies.''

By sending his ultimatum, Kruger had unquestionably played into the hands of the British, but it is difficult to see what else he could have done given his belief that the British were determined to control his country and his own determination to resist, no matter how great the odds. Not to be underestimated as a factor in his decision to risk war was Kruger's faith in God, his belief in the righteousness of the Boer cause, and his consequent confidence that his people could rely on divine guidance and support. On a more mundane level, he may still have hoped that the British, when squarely confronted with the Boer resolve to fight, would soften their position rather than incur the expenses and risks of war. Among those risks, the most dangerous was the intervention of one or more of Britain's rivals among the great powers, a possibility Kruger had reason to believe might well be realized. Whatever expectations he may have had in this regard were not to be fulfilled.

The country to which Kruger had reason to look most confidently for support was Germany, whose leadership had expressed sympathy for the Boer cause on so many occasions in the past. But throughout the prewar crisis and the war itself, Germany signally failed to intervene in any way on behalf of the Boers. The most cogent explanation for Germany's behavior was that its principal foreign policy objective was still an alliance with England, and that the Germans hoped the crisis in South Africa, together with Britain's complications with other powers in almost every other part of the world, would at last persuade the British to agree to the kind of alliance the Germans desired.

The more immediate reason Germany abandoned the Boers, however, was that the Germans had allowed themselves to be bought off. Indeed, the Germans themselves had initiated the buying-off process. With the German government's refusal to take any action over South Africa, the governments of the other great powers also held aloof. Deprived of any kind of foreign support, the Boer cause was doomed from the start.

❑ *The Portuguese Colonies Payoff*

In dealing with the crisis in South Africa, the British were keenly aware of their global difficulties, and a number of British leaders, justifiably alarmed by the accumulation of foreign hostility they were facing, advocated negotiating alliances with one or more great powers to end Britain's diplomatic isolation. One of the strongest advocates of an alliance policy was the colonial secretary, Joseph Chamberlain, who in a comprehensive search for diplomatic partners approached Germany in March 1898. The negotiations with Germany conducted over the next three years finally ended in failure (see pp. 388–389), but the very fact that the British had initiated them rekindled the hope among German statesmen that a satisfactory partnership with Britain might yet be arranged and helps explain the Germans' desire to avoid a confrontation with Britain over South Africa or any other major issue while these negotiations were in progress.

In contrast to Chamberlain and other alarmists in his government, Lord Salisbury maintained his patrician calm throughout the diplomatic crises of his administration, confident that the British navy could cope with any existing dangers and that Britain could always buy off one or more of the rival great powers to prevent the formation of an anti-British coalition, which alone could pose a serious threat to British security and interests.

The subsequent course of events proved that Salisbury's confidence was justified, and the power the British succeeded in buying off when war seemed imminent in South Africa was none other than Germany, whose government had been most vociferous in supporting the Boers. The payment in question concerned the colonies of Portugal, a state that no longer possessed the resources to defend them. It was therefore widely assumed that these colonies would soon be taken over by one or more of the world's stronger powers.

The focal point of British interest in the Portuguese colonies was Mozambique, with its harbor of Lourenço Marques on Delagoa Bay. In their struggle with the Boers in South Africa the British had succeeded by 1895 in extending their dominion over all the territories surrounding the landlocked Boer republics with the exception of Mozambique, which was the sole remaining Boer outlet to the sea through territory not controlled by the British.

Since 1891 Cecil Rhodes and the Cape government had tried on various occasions to purchase the southern part of Mozambique or at least the Delagoa Bay area to complete the encirclement of the Boers. The Portuguese government, however, had turned down all financial offers because the colonies, even though they did not pay for themselves and were a drain on the economy, were objects of national pride, the last remnants of former greatness. In his bid for Mozambique, Rhodes had also encountered opposition from the Germans, whose ambassador to London had warned that if the British attempted to interfere in Portuguese East Africa, "Germany would make its power felt elsewhere," a warning that may explain the British government's reluctance to give Rhodes greater support in his financial negotiations with Portugal.

As the crisis in South Africa mounted in the years following the Jameson raid, the British government showed increasing interest in establishing control over Mozambique, and in the spring of 1898 it was presented with the best opportunity it had yet been offered for doing so. The Portuguese government was in chronic financial difficulties, and in June the Portuguese ambassador to London approached Salisbury with a request for a loan. The Portuguese had frequently turned to the British for loans in the past, but now for the first time they were offering to connect a loan to the possibility of British control over Lourenço Marques. What the Portuguese proposed was that part of the loan be used to develop the harbor and railway of Lourenço Marques under the aegis of an Anglo-Portuguese company, and that the interest on this part of the loan be guaranteed by the customs revenues of the province of Mozambique. This guarantee, as both the British and Portuguese realized, would give the British the leverage they needed to control traffic through Lourenço Marques and thereby achieve what Rhodes had hoped to accomplish: the final encirclement of the Boer republics, which would give the British a stranglehold over the Boer economy and ensure British supremacy in South Africa. What the Portuguese wanted in return for this enormously valuable concession, apart from the loan itself, was British reaffirmation of earlier treaties with Portugal promising British protection for all the possessions of the Portuguese crown. This was a promise the British were not only happy but eager to provide in order, as they expressed it themselves, to prevent Portugal and its colonies from "falling under the influence, if not the power, of other nations—that is, France and Germany."

The British cannot have been surprised that the Germans soon heard of the Anglo-Portuguese financial negotiations and that they should seek to intervene, but they may have wondered that the Germans did not raise objections over Lourenço Marques as they had done heretofore. They quickly learned that the Germans expected to be paid, and to be paid handsomely, for what amounted to their sellout of the Boers, and that the Germans evidently assumed, given Britain's desire for an alliance with Germany, that the British would be prepared to make the payment they wanted, especially as this could be done with someone else's property. To this end the Germans proposed that they be allowed to participate in the loan to Portugal, and that the security given to Germany should be the greater part of the Portuguese colonial empire not already earmarked for security to Britain. The entire arrangement was based on the expectation that the Portuguese government would not be able to meet its interest payments, and that Germany would thus acquire a substantial addition to its colonial empire.

Salisbury showed no interest in making concessions to the Germans for something he believed the British were perfectly able to acquire without Germany's blessing or consent; he may even have had scruples about allowing the Germans to believe they would ever acquire any part of the Portuguese empire, which the British were bound by treaty to protect. It was only after the Germans had applied the heaviest kind of diplomatic pressure, including threats to cooperate with France and Russia to thwart British enterprises in other areas, that the British government at last agreed to enter into negotiations. Even then the British negotiated with stubborn tenacity, perhaps to preserve the German illusion that they were actually achieving something, and it required two months of hard bargaining before the British finally agreed to a treaty that seemed to promise the Germans at least part of the compensation they desired.

The Anglo-German treaty over the Portuguese colonies of August 30, 1898, provided for joint British and German participation in future loans to Portugal, for which the colonies were to serve as securities. At the heart of the treaty was the division of these securities. Those assigned to Britain included southern Mozambique, with Lourenço Marques and Delagoa Bay, and a strip through central Angola that would connect Rhodesia to the sea; those assigned to Germany, northern Mozambique and the northern and southern sectors of Angola. Britain and Germany were to divide Portuguese Timor in the East Indies.

The British, however, never had any intention of allowing this treaty to go into effect. On October 14, 1899, three days after the outbreak of the Boer War and just over a year after signing their treaty with Germany, the British concluded a secret agreement with Portugal promising to protect all colonies belonging to the crown of Portugal—a simple reaffirmation of previous treaties. In return the Portuguese promised to prohibit the shipment of all war materials to the Boers through Portuguese territory. This was all the British had ever desired of Portugal, a point the German diplomats had somehow never understood. For it stood to reason that the British would have no desire to replace Portuguese weakness with German strength along the frontiers of Britain's own colonial possessions in Africa.

The Anglo-Portuguese agreement put an end to all German prospects of cashing in their own treaty with Britain, but it was some time before the Germans suspected the extent of their miscalculations.

Following their successful buying off of the Germans in Africa, the British had no hesitation about standing firm against the French during the Fashoda crisis in the autumn of 1898 or accepting the military challenge of the Boers a year later.

The kaiser, who in 1896 had assured the tsar that, come what may, he would never allow the British to stamp out the Transvaal, even took a certain pride in his government's behavior over South Africa. Early in 1900, when the tide of war had clearly shifted in favor of the British, he congratulated the British ambassador to Berlin but expressed the hope that this military success would not blind the British government to the need for a thorough reorganization of its army; he himself was working on a plan for that purpose, which he presumably intended to submit to the British war office. Meanwhile he, the kaiser, was having great difficulty combating anti-British sentiment in Germany and the forces at home and abroad calling for German intervention on behalf of the Boers. He took great credit for having prevented hostile action on the part of France and Russia: "I have kept those two tigers quiet," he said, and thought it only fair that his attitude be known and recognized in England.

❑ *The Boer War and Its Aftermath*

When the Boers sent their ultimatum to Britain on October 9, 1899, they did not know of the German bargain with England that virtually put an end to any prospect of their receiving foreign support. Even if they had known, it is doubtful whether they would have yielded peacefully to British pressure given the nature of the ultimatum the British had been prepared to submit to the Transvaal.

At five in the afternoon of October 11, upon the refusal of the British to respond favorably to the terms of the Boer ultimatum, the South African Republic went to war with Great Britain. It was joined in the conflict by its ally, the Orange Free State.

Because of their initial numerical superiority and excellent equipment, the Boers won a number of early victories, and some military historians believe that if they had advanced rapidly to secure the seaports of South Africa they might have prevented the arrival of British reinforcements and therewith gained an opportunity to win the war. The Boers, however, lacking the manpower for so vast an enterprise, could not have held the ports against British sea power even if they had been able to capture them. In any event, the seaports were not taken, the British were soon heavily reinforced, and by the spring of 1900 they had defeated the principal Boer armies in the field. The Boers resorted to guerrilla warfare, which the British countered with a scorched earth policy—a ruthless destruction of Boer farms and crops, and the herding of the Boer civilian population into concentration camps. Of the 120,000 women and children assembled in these camps, approximately one-fifth died of disease and exposure in the first year.

The Boer War came to an end with the signature on March 31, 1902, of articles of peace at Pretoria. The Boer decision to come to terms was undoubtedly facilitated by unusually generous British peace conditions motivated by the British desire to reconcile the two white races in South Africa. All burghers who accepted British sovereignty and declared themselves subject to the British crown were to be repatriated; all who surrendered were assured that they would not be deprived of their liberty or property. The Boers were promised a grant of three million pounds to enable them to rebuild their farms. The Dutch language was to be allowed in courts of law and would be taught in public schools at the request of parents. Most important of all, the Boers were promised representative institutions that would guarantee them a powerful voice in the future government of their countries, and they were assured that the question of the franchise for native Africans would not even be considered until after the introduction of self-government (for whites), which meant that when the question was considered the Boers would be in a position to quash it.

The British kept their word about granting representative institutions and about the franchise. A constitution providing for representative government was given to the Transvaal in 1906 and to the Orange Free State in 1907. In both countries the vote was restricted to adult male British subjects of European descent. The results of the first elections held in the former Boer republics in 1907 showed that the Boers' fears about the Uitlander franchise had been groundless. For although the Uitlanders now had the vote, the parties representing predominantly Boer interests won decisive victories.

With the establishment of the Union of South Africa in 1910, the franchise remained restricted to male citizens of European descent in the former Boer republics, and in Natal voting was made sufficiently difficult for "colored" people so that they were disenfranchised in practice. There was no franchise color bar in the Cape Colony, and many colored people there actually exercised their right to vote. But thanks to the franchise restrictions in effect elsewhere and the large number of Boer voters, parties representing Boer interests were also victorious in the first all-union elections held in September 1910, and Boer political leaders continued to play a major role in South African politics in general.

So it was that the Boers, thanks to the British government's commitment to representative institutions for persons of European descent, emerged as the eventual victors in South Africa, and under British auspices achieved the very goal the British had fought the war to prevent: Boer domination of a union of the states of southern Africa. In 1961, just fifty-one years after the formation of the Union of South Africa, the Boer-dominated political parties took the step the British believed they had been plotting at the end of the nineteenth century: they severed all connection with Britain and the British Commonwealth and declared South Africa to be a republic.

❑

SEVENTEEN

The Great Power Competition over China

❑ The Opium Wars and the First of the Unequal Treaties

In East Asia as in Africa, Britain played a leading role among the European powers in the competition for territory and influence. In Asia, however, Britain's principal rival was not France but Russia. And in the late nineteenth century a non-European state, Japan, appeared unexpectedly on the scene to become a major factor in East Asian affairs.

At the beginning of the nineteenth century, the Chinese empire, the largest of the countries of East Asia, was virtually closed to foreigners. The Chinese government, alarmed by increasing numbers of Europeans coming to China since the seventeenth century, gradually restricted Christian missionary activity and foreign trade. By 1757 legal seaborne trade with China was confined to the single southern port of Canton (the name given to the city by the Europeans; the Chinese name, in its present-day transliteration, is Guangzhou) and to Macao, the Portuguese trading post just below Canton. Even this trade was rigidly controlled by the Chinese authorities, who supervised all trading operations and fixed the rates of all tariffs and service charges, which were generally set as high as the traffic would bear. Foreigners were forced to live and conduct their business in a small area outside Canton, and then only for a few months of every year. They were not allowed to enter the city or otherwise "go out and ramble about," they could not bring "foreign" wives to China, and they were subject to Chinese laws and statutes, including Chinese criminal law, which might involve torture and arbitrary punishment. Because they regarded foreigners as "barbarians," altogether inferior to themselves in terms of culture and civilization, the Chinese refused to deal with foreign traders or the representatives of foreign governments on a basis of equality. Foreign delegations were considered tribute-bearing missions, expected to perform the ritual kowtow to Chinese authorities, who contemptuously turned aside all efforts to ease trade and residence restrictions. When King George III sent an emissary to China in 1793 in an attempt to improve and expand commercial relations, the Chinese emperor commended the British monarch for his "respectful spirit of submission" but pointed out that "our celestial empire possesses all things in prolific abundance."

The opening up of the Chinese empire to European commerce and influence may be said to have begun with a clash between the British and Chinese in November 1839. The immediate cause for these hostilities was the Chinese government's effort to end the lucrative (and under Chinese law, illegal) British–Indian opium trade with China, which by the first decades of the nineteenth century had become the principal means of payment for imports from China, in particular tea, already well established as the British national beverage. For the British, however, the opium trade, though extremely important, especially to the economy of the Indian province of Bengal, was not the fundamental reason for the quarrel with China. The British chafed under the restrictions the Chinese imposed on foreign trade in general, the humiliating conditions under which this trade had to be conducted, and the lack of legal protection afforded British citizens in China.

Unable to obtain the trading rights and assurances the British considered essential to their commercial interests in China through negotiation, Palmerston, the British foreign secretary and ever a redoubtable champion of British interests abroad, decided "to put British relations with China on a proper footing" and followed up the initial British clash with the Chinese by sending an expeditionary force that arrived in China in March 1840. In this so-called First Opium War, the British easily defeated the Chinese, who were still equipped with relatively primitive weapons, and in August 1842 Britain imposed on China the Treaty of Nanking, the first of those agreements with foreign powers the Chinese were to label the "unequal treaties." By the terms of the Nanking treaty, China ceded to Britain in perpetuity the island of Hong Kong opposite the approaches to the Canton harbor. Besides ceding Hong Kong, which rapidly became one of Britain's most important commercial bases in Asia, the Chinese were obliged to open five Chinese port cities, Canton among them, to foreign residence as well as trade, to standardize—and lower—all tariffs, and to pay a sizable monetary indemnity covering losses suffered by British merchants (including China's destruction of contraband opium) and the cost of the war. The British were to be allowed to maintain official representatives in each of the five newly opened ports to serve as the "medium of communication" with Chinese authorities and ensure that the provisions of the treaty were carried out. The treaty also specifically stipulated that British officials should henceforth communicate on terms of equality with Chinese authorities. The Treaty of Nanking was supplemented in October 1843 by a treaty providing that the Chinese government give the British all rights and privileges it might subsequently grant to other foreign governments. This so-called most favored nation provision was subsequently to be included in the treaties of almost all other foreign powers with China, so that the rights obtained by one were automatically secured by the others.

The importance of this provision was seen almost immediately, for on July 3, 1844, the Chinese concluded a treaty with the United States granting Americans a privilege known as extraterritoriality—the right of American citizens who committed crimes in China to be tried and punished by American authorities in accordance with American laws. Thanks to Britain's most favored nation status, this enormously important right, a major objective of British policy in China, was now extended to British citizens and subsequently to the citizens of all foreign powers that secured a similar treaty relationship with China.

During the following decade, the British were occupied with international crises in the West and the Crimean War (1853–1856), but they continued to press for

MAP 12   IMPERIALISM IN ASIA

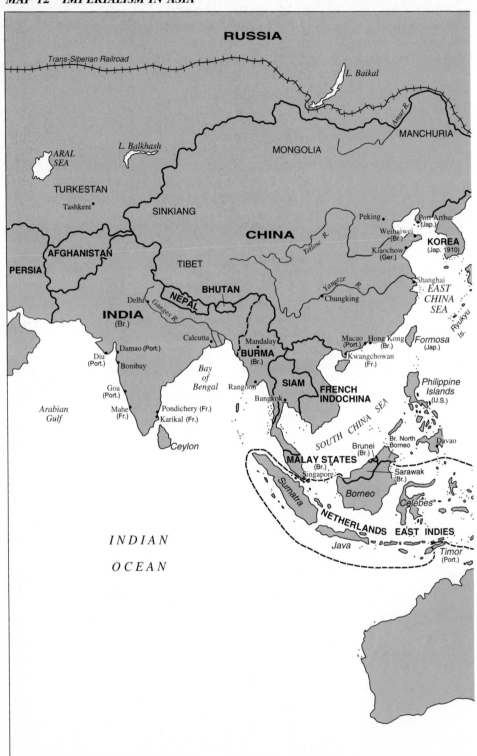

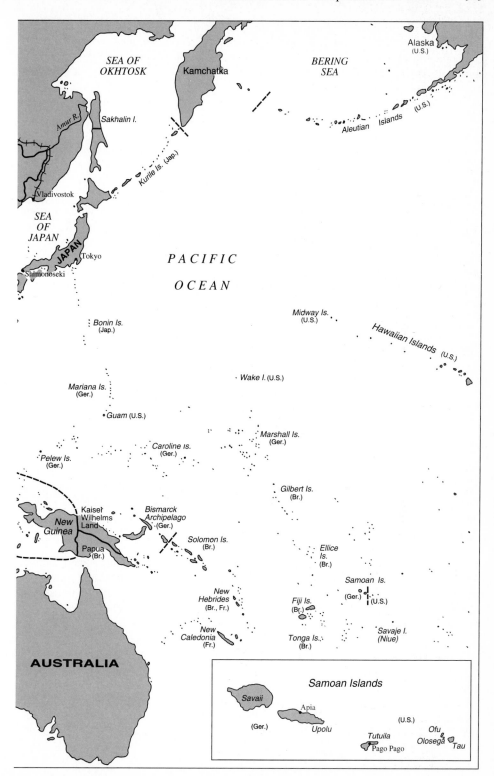

SEA OF OKHTOSK

Kamchatka

BERING SEA

Alaska (U.S.)

Amur R.

Sakhalin I.

Aleutian Islands (U.S.)

Kurile Is. (Jap.)

Vladivostok

SEA OF JAPAN

JAPAN

Tokyo

Shimonoseki

PACIFIC OCEAN

Bonin Is. (Jap.)

Midway Is. (U.S.)

Hawaiian Islands (U.S.)

Wake I. (U.S.)

Mariana Is. (Ger.)

Guam (U.S.)

Marshall Is. (Ger.)

Caroline Is. (Ger.)

Pelew Is. (Ger.)

Gilbert Is. (Br.)

Kaiser Wilhelms Land

New Guinea

Bismarck Archipelago (Ger.)

Solomon Is. (Br.)

Ellice Is. (Br.)

Papua (Br.)

Samoan Is. (Ger.) (U.S.)

New Hebrides (Br., Fr.)

Fiji Is. (Br.)

New Caledonia (Fr.)

Tonga Is. (Br.)

Savaje I. (Niue)

AUSTRALIA

Samoan Islands

Savaii

Apia

(Ger.)

Upolu

(U.S.)

Tutuila

Pago Pago

Ofu

Olosega

Tau

removal of the remaining restrictions on their trade with China. In the autumn of 1856, shortly after the conclusion of the Crimean War, the British government under the leadership of Palmerston, now Britain's prime minister, once again went to war with China, this time over an alleged Chinese insult to the British flag being flown by the lorcha *Arrow*, a Chinese-owned sailing vessel registered in Hong Kong. In this conflict, the Second Opium War, the British were joined by Napoleon III, their ally in the Crimean War, who seems to have been motivated largely by reasons of prestige, for French commercial interests in China were as yet negligible. The American and Russian governments did not join in the military operations against China but sent diplomats to accompany the Anglo-French forces so as to be represented at future peace negotiations and to share in the spoils of war, an endeavor in which the Russians proved particularly successful.

In June 1858 the Chinese government, its forces defeated on land and sea, negotiated a succession of treaties at Tientsin with the British, French, American, and Russian governments whereby China made additional large-scale concessions to the foreign powers. The Chinese government, however, refused to ratify the Tientsin treaties, and it was only after another two years of warfare, culminating in October 1860 with the entry of Anglo-French forces in the Chinese capital of Peking and the burning of the imperial summer palace northeast of the city, that the Second Opium War at last came to an end.

A set of new treaties concluded in Peking in October 1860 confirmed and considerably extended the Tientsin agreements. The Chinese government was to permit the establishment of foreign diplomatic missions in the capital of Peking, thereby recognizing the equal status of Chinese and foreign officials. The treaties provided further that China open an additional eleven Chinese ports to foreign trade, allow foreign governments to maintain consular representatives in those ports, and allow their citizens to reside there. Foreign merchant ships were to be permitted on the Yangtze River, China's greatest commercial waterway, and foreigners with passports were to be allowed to travel anywhere in the empire. The treaties with all four powers specifically confirmed the principle of extraterritoriality. Besides opening up China to foreign travel, which meant that Christian missionaries would be able to move freely throughout the empire, the treaties obligated the Chinese government to protect Christian missionaries and their converts. A special treaty with France secured the right for Roman Catholic missions to hold property in the interior of China and provided for the restitution of all property of the Catholic church previously confiscated by Chinese authorities. Finally, China was once again obliged to pay a large monetary indemnity to compensate the allies for their losses and expenses incurred in the war, a reparations debt that compelled the Chinese government to borrow heavily from the West and thus gave the Western powers additional economic leverage in China.

A series of subsequent agreements regulated tariffs and rules of trade with China and arranged for the establishment of an Imperial Maritime Customs Service under the direction of a foreign inspector-general assisted by a partially foreign staff. A special treaty with Britain gave British ships of war the right to visit "all the ports within the dominion of the Emperor of China," thus giving Britain and all other powers enjoying most favored nation status legal sanction to use force to protect their treaty rights and commercial interests. Altogether, the Treaties of Tientsin and

Peking, with their later supplements, provided for a sweeping extension of foreign control over trade and residence in China and opened the entire country to Western influence.

❑ China's Domestic Difficulties

In view of the immense superiority of Western armaments and military organizations over those of China, there can be little doubt that even under the best of circumstances the Chinese government could not have resisted Western pressures to open the empire to foreign trade or Western demands for extensive political, legal, and commercial privileges. But the success of Western powers in extracting these concessions (in particular territorial concessions, to be discussed later) was facilitated by an epidemic of rebellions against the imperial government in the mid-nineteenth century and by natural catastrophes that brought economic ruin to some of the empire's most productive regions.

The greatest of these domestic upheavals was the Taiping rebellion (1850–1864), whose leaders established their power base in the Yangtze valley with their capital at Nanking. At the same time, however, organized leagues of bandits terrorized the provinces of central and eastern China (1853–1868), and the Muslim populations in the provinces of Yunnan, Kansu, and Turkestan rebelled (1855–1868), as did the Miao tribesmen in the south central province of Kweichow, just east of Yunnan (1855–1881). The causes of these rebellions differed from province to province. The existing imperial dynasty, the Ching, had originally come from Manchuria, and antagonism to this foreign Manchu regime may have played a part in arousing latent antigovernment feeling among native Chinese. But the most profound and obvious reason for all these uprisings was widespread discontent with the incompetence, economic exactions, and corruption of the imperial government and its officials. And a major reason for the early successes of the rebellions appears to have been this same official incompetence.

In addition to these political upheavals, the imperial government was confronted with a succession of natural catastrophes, the most dire being the shift in the course of the Yellow River, which in 1852 broke out of its channel and began changing its route to the sea from the southern to the northern side of the Shantung peninsula. The diversion of this major waterway brought about massive economic dislocation in east central China and caused wholesale destruction of the intricate system of dikes, irrigation canals, and other installations essential to agricultural production and transport.

In the end the imperial government surmounted these natural disasters and managed to crush all the political rebellions mounted against it. The failure of the rebellions may be explained in part by the lack of administrative and military competence of their own leaders, but the defeat of the Taiping movement in particular was due in large measure to the ruthless fanaticism of its leaders and the destructive fury of its armies.

Taiping means the Great or Perfect Peace, a singularly inappropriate name in view of the ideological precepts of the movement and the conduct of its followers. The Taiping faith was an extreme and intolerant puritanical monotheism based on a Chinese interpretation of Old Testament Protestant Christianity that not only called for the overthrow of the imperial government but the destruction of the greater part of China's existing social, intellectual, and religious institutions. The Taipings and their armies indulged in a wholesale and willful destruction of cities and religious monuments and indeed virtually everything that represented the existing political and social fabric. They devastated agricultural installations, slaughtered livestock, and cut down orchards and mulberry trees essential to silk production. This destruction of property was accompanied by an immense loss of life: it has been estimated that as many as twenty million people fell victim, directly or indirectly, to the revolutionary fervor of the Taiping movement.

On the imperial side, a major factor in the defeat of the rebellions was the initiative shown by two unusually able imperial officials, Tseng Kuo-fan and Li Hung-chang. Bypassing the existing cumbersome bureaucratic procedures and the ineffective imperial military organizations, they recruited, organized, and trained entirely new armies that were far superior to the regular imperial forces. Tseng died in 1872 soon after the suppression of the most serious rebellions, but Li Hung-chang lived on until 1901 and played a critical role in Chinese government and diplomacy for the rest of the century.

In its efforts to deal with domestic rebellions, the imperial regime was supported by foreigners living in China and by their governments, though the significance of that support is still a matter of debate. After some initial hesitation, foreigners generally came to recognize that the existing regime was a far better guarantor of their interests in China than the quasi-anarchic rebels, many of them intensely antiforeign and dedicated to ousting the barbarians and canceling all concessions granted to them.

Among the private militias recruited and organized by foreigners that took part in the campaigns against the rebels, the most famous was commanded by an American, Frederick Townsend Ward, whose steady succession of victories earned his troops the name of the Ever-Victorious Army, an honorary title officially bestowed by imperial decree in March 1862. Ward was killed in combat in September of that year, and his successor, after quarrels with Chinese authorities, went over to the side of the rebels. Early in 1863, at the request of Li Hung-chang, the command of this army went to a British officer, Major Charles George Gordon, whose participation in the eventual defeat of the Taipings in 1864 won him international fame as "Chinese Gordon." He was to gain even greater, if more dubious, fame as the commander of the Anglo-Egyptian forces massacred at Khartoum in the Sudan in 1885.

In comparison with the fratricidal slaughter and the wholesale destruction of the cities and countryside carried out by the Chinese themselves, the destruction and loss of life wrought by the Western armies in China seem insignificant. But for the Chinese these mid-nineteenth–century encounters with Western imperialism—the two opium wars, the "unequal treaties" imposed on their government, the right of extraterritoriality that made foreigners immune to Chinese law, and the commercial concessions and monetary indemnities that left China in thrall to foreign economic interests—together with other real or assumed violations of Chinese honor and dignity loomed far larger in the Chinese consciousness and historical memory than the horrors they had inflicted on each other.

❑ *Foreign Territorial Encroachments*

In the eyes of many Chinese, the greatest humiliation of all suffered by their country, and certainly one that has endured the longest, was the foreign encroachment on or actual seizure of territories which the Chinese regarded as part of their empire. Most of these seizures took place in peripheral areas where the Chinese government exercised little or no actual authority or control, but for patriotic Chinese this foreign territorial spoliation provided particularly substantial evidence of Western disregard of Chinese rights and the helplessness of the imperial government to defend them.

The most substantial of these territorial gains was made by Russia. Prior to the nineteenth century, Russian settlers had moved into Chinese-claimed territory in Mongolia and the Amur River region. This migration was halted by two Russian agreements with China, the treaties of Nerchinsk (1689) and Kiakhta (1727), which laid down conditions for Sino-Russian trade and established the boundaries between the two empires. In assigning the Amur valley and the greater part of Mongolia to China, these treaties diverted Russian expansion to other parts of Asia and to North America. In the course of the eighteenth century Russian settlers advanced in central Asia into the region that was to become known as Russian Turkestan; in the north they pushed ahead steadily through Siberia to the Pacific and into the Kamchatka peninsula; crossing the sea, they established posts on the island of Sakhalin, on the Kurile and Aleutian islands, in Alaska, and along the Pacific coast of North America to a point not far north of San Francisco.

The Russians eventually withdrew from North America because their colonies on that continent had not proved profitable and because the Russian government recognized that it lacked the means to defend them. By treaties with the United States (1824) and Britain (1825), Russia relinquished all territorial claims south and east of present-day Alaska, and in 1867 Russia sold Alaska together with the Aleutian Islands to the United States. The sale of Alaska was motivated in part by the Russian belief that the Americans, in acquiring boundaries to the northwest as well as to the south of British Canada, would find themselves in a situation that was "bound to increase the opportunities for disagreement between the United States and England," thus establishing a rivalry that would be "the best guarantee against the ambitious projects and political egotism of the Anglo-Saxon race."

The Russo-American treaty over Alaska was bitterly denounced by antiexpansionists in the United States and by economy-minded members of the American Congress. The Senate nevertheless ratified it by a vote of twenty-seven to twelve, a decision that may have been influenced by generous bribes provided by the Russian minister to Washington, who spent $200,000 on "secret expenses" during the final vote on the Russian treaty.

During the same period that they pulled out of North America, the Russians resumed and accelerated their territorial advance in East Asia. Following the British successes at the expense of China in the 1840s, the Russians once again pushed forward in the region of the Amur River. In the 1850s Nicholas Muraviev, the ambitious and adventurous governor of Eastern Siberia, sent a succession of Russian expeditions down the Amur to establish posts along its northern bank.

In June 1858 Russia joined Britain, France, and the United States in imposing

MAP 13   THE SINO–RUSSIAN BORDER PROBLEM

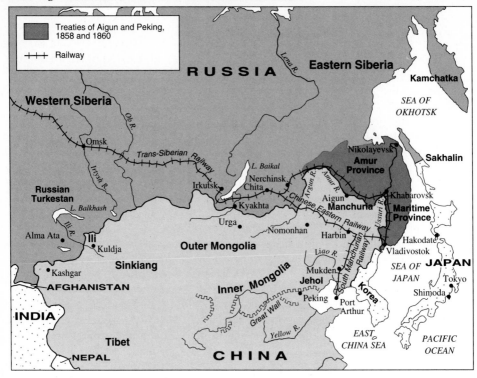

the Treaties of Tientsin on China, thereby securing for Russia all the rights and privileges these treaties conferred on the three other Western powers. Even before the signature of the Treaties of Tientsin, however, Muraviev had taken advantage of China's preoccupation with the Taiping rebellion and the Second Opium War to browbeat the representative of the Chinese government in the Amur region into accepting a treaty signed at Aigun, on the middle course of the Amur, on May 28, 1858. By the terms of this agreement, China ceded to Russia the immense region north and west of the Amur and gave Russia joint sovereignty with China over the territory between the Amur and Ussuri rivers and the Pacific.

The Chinese government refused to ratify this treaty, as it refused to ratify the Treaties of Tientsin, but following the renewal of the Anglo-French war with China and the allied capture of Peking in October 1860, the Russians again joined with Britain, France, and the United States in securing the ratification (and broad extension) of the Treaties of Tientsin.

The Russian envoy to Peking, General Nicholas Ignatiev, played a clever if unscrupulous game. While acting as "never-failing counselor" to the commander of the British forces in China, who later testified that Ignatiev's advice had been of great value in the capture of Peking, he offered his services to the Chinese government as mediator to save China from the wrath of Britain and France. The price he exacted for this service was the ratification and broad extension of the 1858 Treaty of Aigun. Through a separate Treaty of Peking with Russia (November 14, 1860), China not only confirmed its recognition of Russian sovereignty over the territories north and west of the Amur, but gave Russia sole sovereignty over the region between the Amur and Ussuri rivers, a region now incorporated into Russia's newly established Maritime Province. By June 1860, even before the formal Chinese cession of this territory, the Russians had already founded a city at the southern end of the Maritime Province; they called it Vladivostok, Ruler over the East, a name that suggests the nature and extent of Russian ambitions.

Elsewhere along the frontiers of the Chinese empire, the Russians took advantage of a Muslim insurrection in Chinese Turkestan to send an army into the strategic Ili River valley, which for centuries had been one of the main trade and invasion routes into eastern China, and in 1871 this region was declared to be a permanent part of the Russian empire by the local Russian military commander. Here, however, the Chinese government moved vigorously and effectively to regain control. Flanked by Mongolia in the north and Tibet in the south, Chinese Turkestan had been a focus of Chinese concern for centuries, more so than Korea or Vietnam or other frontier territories facing the sea, because it was from inner Asia that the great invasions of China had been launched in the past, whereas prior to the nineteenth century no serious threat to Chinese security had come from the sea.

The Chinese response to the revolution in Chinese Turkestan and the Russian invasion of the Ili valley showed that the Peking government still regarded the frontier territories of inner Asia of greater importance to Chinese security than the frontier coastal provinces. For although faced with threats along the coast during this period, the Chinese government concentrated its resources on reconquering Chinese Turkestan. After nearly a decade of warfare, Chinese forces recovered most of the province and expelled the Russians, the latter success due at least in part to Russia's involvement in war with Turkey in 1877–1878 and the consequent international complications. By a treaty with Russia concluded in St. Petersburg in 1881, China regained most of the Ili region and its strategic passes in return for a large indemnity. Three years later China made Chinese Turkestan an integral part of the Chinese empire as the province of Sinkiang (New Dominion).

The Chinese were less successful in holding Mongolia and Tibet. Early in the twentieth century Mongolia was divided into spheres of influence between Russia and the new great power in East Asia, Japan, with Outer Mongolia going to Russia and Inner Mongolia to the Japanese.

The Chinese also lost all real control over Tibet. In the late nineteenth century that mountainous buffer zone between British India, the Chinese empire, and Russia had become an object of intense Anglo-Russian rivalry that ended in a de facto stalemate. In a convention of 1907, Britain and Russia agreed to recognize the sovereignty and independence of Tibet and to refrain from seeking special political and economic advantages for themselves in that country. In that same convention they acknowledged China's suzerainty over Tibet, a face-saving provision only, for when the Chinese attempted to exercise their authority they were sternly warned by the British to respect Tibet's sovereignty and independence.

While the Russians advanced into territories claimed by China in the west and north, the British and French advanced in similar fashion in the south.

Since the early nineteenth century the British had been pushing from India into

MAP 14 SOUTHERN CHINA AND SOUTHEAST ASIA

Burma, a country over which China claimed suzerainty and whose government paid a decennial tribute to the Chinese emperor, although it had never been under effective Chinese control. In a succession of wars with Burma, the British gradually extended their control and by 1886 they had taken over the entire country. By a treaty of July 24 of that year, the Chinese government recognized a British protectorate over Burma in return for a face-saving provision that Burma would continue to send its decennial tribute-bearing mission to Peking.

The French were most active in the easternmost part of southeast Asia. Most of the territory the French were to acquire in this region had come under the rule of the emperor of Annam (the name by which Vietnam was known at that time in the West) in the early nineteenth century. Like the rulers of Burma, the emperors of Annam recognized the suzerainty of the emperor of China and paid regular tribute to Peking. The Annamese empire included Annam itself; Tonkin, the northernmost region bordering on China proper; and Cochin China, the southernmost region. Annam was also engaged in a protracted struggle with Siam (Thailand) for control over Cambodia, on its southwestern flank.

The French first became seriously involved in the affairs of southeast Asia in the late eighteenth century when the government of Louis XVI, eager to regain some of the prestige lost to the British in North America and India, responded to an appeal for support from a claimant to the Annamese throne. In return for their aid, the French were awarded trading bases in Tourane (Da Nang) on Annam's eastern coast and the offshore island of Pulo Condore. The French-supported claimant triumphed in Annam, but his government subsequently turned against the French and Western influences in general, and the French were soon too preoccupied with their own revolution to pursue their interests in Asia.

French ambitions in Asia were revived under the government of Napoleon III, who joined Britain in 1856 in the Second Opium War against China. News of the persecution of Christian missionaries and their converts in Annam gave Napoleon an excuse to send a fleet to Tourane in 1858, and in the following year his troops captured Saigon, the capital of Cochin China, and made it their base of operations in southeast Asia. In 1861, upon the successful conclusion of the Opium War with China, the French sent reinforcements to Annam and by 1867 they had gained control over all of Cochin China and annexed it to France. In that same decade they also intervened in the affairs of neighboring Cambodia, the perennial object of contention between Annam and Siam, making it a French protectorate.

The French gains at the expense of the Annamese empire inevitably involved them in war with Annam, which for the French proved to be an unexpectedly long and costly conflict. It was nevertheless carried on by successive governments of the third French republic, as eager for prestige and imperial dominion as Napoleon III. By treaties with Annam of 1883 and 1884, France secured recognition of a French protectorate over both Annam and Tonkin. By this time, however, China, which still claimed suzerainty over Annam, had become alarmed by the French incursion into Tonkin, on the very borders of China proper, and in 1883 the Chinese government sent troops to aid the Annamese and guerrilla forces still fighting the French. As a result France again found itself at war with China, a conflict that now merged with the overall struggle for supremacy in southeast Asia. A French military debacle in that conflict brought down the government of Jules Ferry, the most ardent colonialist among France's republican prime ministers, but his successors carried on the war as his predecessors had done. Eventually, thanks largely to their superior sea power, the French prevailed, although the territories thus brought under French dominion were far from pacified.

In a treaty signed at Tiensin on June 27, 1885, the Chinese recognized French suzerainty over Tonkin and Annam, thereby ending their own ancient claim to suzerainty, and agreed to permit French trade with China from Tonkin. In return the

French restored to China the Pescadores Islands and Formosa (Taiwan), occupied in the course of the war, and promised to respect China's frontiers bordering on Tonkin.

Two years later, in 1887, the French united all the provinces of the former Annamese empire—Cochin China, Annam, and Tonkin—together with Cambodia into a single administrative unit, French Indo-China, under a French governor-general whose capital was at Saigon. Of these provinces, only Cochin China was designated a colony and placed under French rule. The others retained the status of French protectorates under their own, though largely symbolic, rulers.

In 1893, following a period of acute tension with Siam that precipitated a serious crisis with Britain (see pp. 257–258), the French extended their dominion in southeast Asia by compelling the Siamese to surrender their claims to Laos, west of Annam, which was also designated a French protectorate and made part of the administrative unit of French Indo-China.

Finally, in 1900, the French forced the Chinese to give them a ninety-nine–year lease to territory surrounding the Bay of Kwangchowan, about halfway between the Tonkin frontier and Hong Kong, which despite its geographical separation from Indo-China was also made part of that administrative unit.

❑ *The Emergence of Japan as a World Power*

In the 1870s Japan joined in the game of encroaching on territories over which China claimed suzerainty by taking over the Ryukyu Islands, an archipelago between the southernmost islands of Japan and the Chinese island of Taiwan (Formosa). In 1876 the Japanese concluded a treaty of friendship and commerce with Korea, which they declared to be an independent state, thereby challenging China's claim to suzerainty over that country.

The Japanese entry into the game of European imperialism began remarkably soon after the first successful efforts on the part of Western powers to impose on Japan political and commercial treaties that would open it to Western imperial penetration in the same way as the treaties they had imposed on China.

In the mid-nineteenth century, Japan was even more closed to foreign contact than China had been. During the past three centuries the Japanese government had observed a policy of rigid isolationism. Japanese citizens were not allowed to go abroad, those who had done so were not allowed to return, shipbuilders were forbidden to construct vessels large enough to undertake voyages on the open sea, and all Japanese were forbidden any kind of political or commercial contact with foreign governments or their subjects. The only foreigners who had been permitted to continue any kind of trade with Japan were the Dutch, who did so under rigid restrictions from a tiny island in the harbor of Nagasaki, at the easternmost end of the Japanese archipelago.

Until 1854 the Japanese government had successfully warded off all attempts of Western powers to arrange commercial treaties or even secure the right to purchase supplies or seek refuge in Japanese ports in heavy weather. This isolation was abruptly ended when the American commodore Matthew C. Perry, at the head of a fleet of modern naval vessels, persuaded the Japanese government to conclude a commercial agreement on March 31, 1854, which opened two Japanese ports to

American ships for refueling, provisioning, refitting, and limited trade. An American consul was to reside in each of these newly opened ports, both clearly chosen by the Japanese government because of their remoteness from the centers of Japanese political and commercial life: Shimoda, at the end of the mountainous Izu peninsula; and Hakodate, on the northern island of Hokkaido. The agreement provided further that sailors shipwrecked on Japanese shores should be treated well, something the Japanese had not always done heretofore. Of more general significance, the agreement contained a provision common to most Western treaties with China: a most favored nation clause stipulating that additional treaty privileges accorded to other countries should automatically also be extended to the United States.

Perry's treaty proved to be the wedge for similar treaties with the British, the Dutch, and the Russians. The treaty with the Dutch removed many of the previous restrictions on trade with Japan. That with the Russians of February 7, 1855, opened Japan to limited Russian trade, but in addition it regulated the claims of both countries to suzerainty over the islands north of Japan: Sakhalin, off the coast of the Maritime Province, where Russia and Japan were to exercise joint sovereignty; and the Kurile archipelago, between the northernmost islands of Japan and the Kamchatka peninsula, where the Russians were to exercise sovereignty over the northern sector, the Japanese over the southern sector. Of particular importance for Japanese foreign relations in general was the provision in the Russian treaty granting Russians the right of extraterritoriality. Because all Japanese treaties with foreign countries at this time contained most favored nation clauses, the citizens of these countries were automatically also accorded the right of extraterritoriality, which the Japanese, like the Chinese before them, considered a humiliation.

Although these first treaties opened Japan to foreign trade, such trade was rigidly restricted and closely supervised by the Japanese government. It was not until July 29, 1858, that the first American consul to Japan, Townsend Harris, secured a treaty that removed many of the restrictions as well as Japanese government supervision. The July 29 treaty opened four additional Japanese ports to foreign trade, permitted foreigners permanent residence in those ports as well as in the cities of Edo (Tokyo) and Osaka, and contained a schedule of import and export duties fixed at moderate rates (whereby the Japanese government gave up its right to fix its own rates). The treaty specifically conceded to the Americans the right of extraterritoriality, while the Americans agreed to make ships, armaments, and technical experts available to Japan.

The Townsend Harris treaty, like that of Matthew Perry, paved the way for similar treaties with other Western countries. The resulting new commercial contacts with the West and the influx of foreign residents ignorant of Japanese customs and immune to Japanese laws through the right of extraterritoriality did not dispel traditional Japanese fear and suspicion of foreigners. On the contrary, the presence of foreign merchants, missionaries, and diplomats in Japan nourished Japanese xenophobia and provoked antiforeign riots and assassinations. Antiforeign demonstrations in turn provoked European and American reprisals—the bombardment of Japanese ports and demands for more concessions—which the Japanese lacked the power to resist. This evidence of helplessness convinced the more realistic Japanese leaders that to avoid becoming another victim of European imperialism, the Japanese had to adopt those features of European society that had given the European peoples such overwhelmingly superior power in relation to the rest of the world.

In 1868 a political revolution took place in Japan. Known as the Meiji Restoration, it was alleged to have restored supreme power to the emperor, though in fact, especially after the death of the Meiji emperor in 1912, the emperor was relegated to an almost purely symbolic role in government. The real significance of this revolution was that it marked the triumph in Japanese political life of the advocates of westernization, a remarkable group of statesmen who were to carry out the westernization process with incredible speed. In just over a decade, they transformed Japan from a feudal, predominantly agricultural society into one of the world's most formidable industrial and military powers.

❑ *Japanese Imperialism: Korea, the Sino-Japanese War, and the Treaty of Shimonoseki*

The Japanese were quick to adopt yet another aspect of westernization, namely, intervention in the affairs of other countries to promote their own interests. The initial object of such Japanese concern was Korea, still a tributary of the Chinese empire though a kingdom in its own right.

Like Japan, Korea had attempted to exclude foreign influences, but by a treaty of February 26, 1876, the Japanese opened Korea to Japanese trade just as Japan had been opened by the Americans some twenty-two years earlier. In that same treaty Japan recognized the independence of Korea, a provision the Chinese government evidently did not consider sufficiently significant to protest.

The 1876 treaty marked the beginning of Japanese involvement in Korean affairs, which very soon brought them into conflict with China. In this rivalry, both China and Japan sent troops into Korea. These were withdrawn following the conclusion of a Sino-Japanese agreement in 1885, but that agreement was violated when rebellion broke out in Korea in 1894 and the rival factions appealed to China and Japan for aid. Both countries responded to these appeals, and on August 1, 1894, China and Japan went to war over Korea.

Contrary to the expectations of most European observers, who believed that China, with its vastly superior resources, would defeat Japan, the Japanese scored easy and impressive victories over the Chinese on both land and sea. Japan's victories were a striking demonstration of its eminently successful westernization, but at the same time they were a glaring revelation of Chinese weakness.

The Sino-Japanese war came to an end with the signature on April 17, 1895, of the Treaty of Shimonoseki, a Japanese city opposite the southeastern tip of Korea. By the terms of that treaty, China was compelled to recognize the independence of Korea, which now became an exclusively Japanese protectorate, and to cede to Japan outright the island of Formosa, the Pescadores Islands (just west of Formosa), and the strategic Liaotung peninsula, with its important harbor of Port Arthur. China was required to pay a large war indemnity, to open additional ports to foreign commerce, and to conclude a commercial treaty that gave the Japanese significant advantages in their trade with China.

The Treaty of Shimonoseki was immensely profitable for Japan, but the Japanese soon discovered that it was easier to gain a victory in war over a nonwesternized opponent than to retain the full fruits of that victory if it impinged on the interests of European powers.

MAP 15 *NORTHERN CHINA, MANCHURIA, KOREA, AND JAPAN*

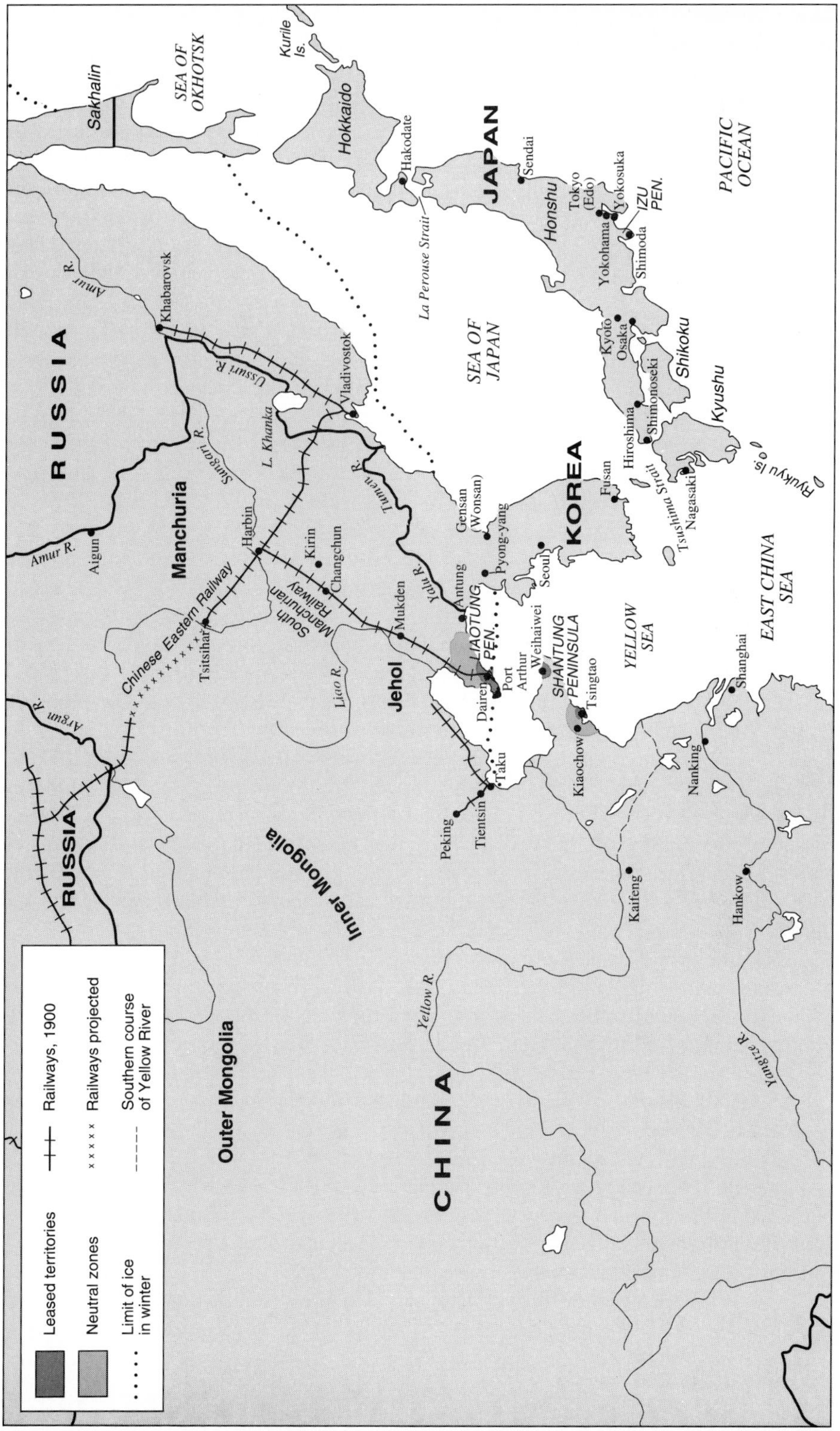

❑ *The Reaction of the European Powers and the Revision of the Treaty of Shimonoseki*

Among the European great powers with interests in East Asia, Britain alone saw no reason to object to the Treaty of Shimonoseki. The treaty opened additional commercial opportunities in China, which the British could only welcome. Nor were the British unhappy about seeing Japan installed in Korea and the Liaotung peninsula, for Japan would now become something of a buffer between Russia and the British spheres of interest in China, which lay farther to the south. Japan itself, whose strength continued to be underestimated in the West, seemed far less of a threat to British interests than Russia. On the contrary, it seemed likely that Japan, which had intruded into areas the Russians had regarded as potential Russian spheres of influence, would henceforth be obliged to look to Britain for support against Russia and thus become something of a natural ally for Britain in East Asia.

There was ample reason for this expectation, for Russia was the European state most adversely affected by Shimonoseki. The acquisition of the territory east of the Ussuri River in 1860 had brought Russia to the border of Korea, and from that time Russian imperialists with interests in East Asia had called for the extension of Russian control over that country. The harbor of Vladivostok, which the Russians had founded at the southern tip of the Maritime Province, was ice-bound four months of the year, so that Korea, with its many excellent ice-free ports farther to the south, was an obvious temptation. That the Russians had not taken over Korea after acquiring the Maritime Province was due in large measure to opposition of the British, whose naval supremacy enabled them to block all Russians attempts to seize a Korean harbor or otherwise establish themselves on the Korean coast. The Russians refrained from actually invading Korea because of the obvious transportation problems that would be involved (the Trans-Siberian Railway was not begun until 1891) and because they feared an invasion would encounter opposition not only from China and the Koreans themselves, but also from Britain, Japan, and the United States. They had therefore played a very cautious game in Korea and sought to preserve Korean independence until such time as they were in a better position to extend their own dominion over the country. This game had now been wrecked by Japan.

The Japanese had dealt Russian interests another damaging blow by taking over the Liaotung peninsula and its harbor of Port Arthur. In planning the Trans-Siberian Railway the Russians had considered shortening the line by several hundred kilometers by running it through Manchuria instead of following the long northward bend of the Amur River, and by placing a principal terminus of the railway at ice-free Port Arthur instead of Vladivostok. This possibility too had been frustrated by the Japanese.

Confronted with these blows to their prospects in East Asia, the Russians sought to compel the Japanese to give up those gains from their war with China that were most damaging to Russian interests. Rather than risk war with Japan, however, they sought the diplomatic support of other powers in demanding a revision of the Treaty of Shimonoseki. Somewhat surprisingly, the first country to respond to this appeal was Germany, the only great power that as yet had no significant interests in East Asia.

Germany's action was motivated in part by the pressure of political and economic leaders who favored greater German participation in European colonial enterprise and were urging their government to acquire a German stake in East Asia. These Germans were convinced, as were many other Western imperialists, that China's defeat by Japan was the prelude to the collapse of the Chinese empire and its partition among the great powers, and when such partition took place they wanted Germany to be in a position to claim a share. A more immediate reason for Germany's support of Russia, however, was the German government's decision to exploit the situation in Asia to score a victory for German foreign policy.

The Germans badly needed a foreign policy success. Following their refusal to renew the Reinsurance Treaty with Russia in 1890, they had been obliged to witness the formation of a Franco-Russian alliance while they themselves had been signally unsuccessful in securing an alliance with England. By responding positively to the Russian appeal for support in East Asia, the Germans believed they would accomplish several purposes simultaneously: they would ensure Russia's continued involvement in Asia, which relieved Russian pressure on German and Austrian interests in the West; they would be promoting the likelihood of a Russian conflict with Britain in which both powers would look to Germany for support; they would pave the way to regaining Russian friendship and take some of the luster out of the French alliance; and, finally, they would compel the French, who were eager above all to redirect Russian attention to the West, to join Germany in supporting Russian policy in East Asia or risk the disintegration of their Russian alliance.

The German calculations with respect to France were correct. The French reluctantly joined Germany and Russia in what became known in diplomatic parlance as the Far Eastern Triplice. On April 23, 1895, just six days after Shimonoseki, France, Germany, and Russia notified Japan that its possession of the Liaotung peninsula "would be a constant menace to the capital of China, would at the same time render illusory the independence of Korea, and would henceforth be a perpetual obstacle to the peace of the Far East." The Japanese capitulated on May 5, agreeing to retrocede the Liaotung peninsula in return for an increased monetary indemnity.

In all other respects German calculations went awry, for once again they had failed to appreciate the impression their policy would make on others. Instead of discrediting the French alliance in the eyes of Russia, they enhanced its value for the Russians, who saw that the Germans' apprehension over the Franco-Russian alliance made them far more amenable to Russian requests for diplomatic support than in the days of Russia's partnership with Germany. The Germans also failed to see that the Russians would do nothing to jeopardize their valuable new alliance with France by accepting German support in Asia, and that even in Asia the French had sufficient financial and diplomatic clout to prevent a closer Russian rapprochement with Germany. The result of Germany's Asian policy, in fact, proved to be exactly the opposite of what the Germans had intended and hoped: the Russians, instead of establishing closer relations with Germany at the expense of France, proceeded to conclude a financial agreement with France over Asia to the complete exclusion of Germany.

The circumstances were these. The Far Eastern Triplice had compelled Japan to retrocede the Liaotung peninsula to China in return for an increased monetary indemnity, a provision welcomed by all the European powers, for the greater the indemnity, the more the Chinese would have to turn to European money markets for loans to pay it. The European powers were eager to be involved in such loans because in making them they could demand additional political and economic concessions as security. Following the revision of the Treaty of Shimonoseki, the French and Russians persuaded the Chinese government to turn to the members of the Far Eastern Triplice for loans in return for its services in securing China more lenient treaty terms. At the same time, the French made the necessary financial arrangements to allow their ally Russia, which had no money to lend, to participate in the first major postwar loan to China. In return for arranging Russian participation, however, they secured Russia's agreement to exclude the Germans. Thus Germany was successfully kept out of the Franco-Russian partnership.

The Russians played their cards even more shrewdly than the French. To ensure that Russia would gain preponderant influence in China without interference from France, they threatened to allow Germany to participate in future loans to China. They thus persuaded the French to allow the Russian government *alone* to guarantee the Franco-Russian loan, an exclusive engagement that would enable the Russians to gain even greater influence in China. For in the event of any Chinese default on interest payments, Russia alone would have the right to exact further concessions.

The Germans soon realized that they had been thoroughly outmaneuvered. As a dejected German diplomat acknowledged in summing up the failure of German policy: "The experiment of the present regime in collaborating with Russia for the first time in several years has not turned out very well."

❑ *The Late Nineteenth-Century Scramble for Concessions in China*

The Franco-Russian loan to China proved to be only the first step in the renewed European scramble for Chinese territorial and economic concessions set off by the Japanese victory in 1895.

In two conventions with China, signed June 20, 1895, the French secured a highly favorable delimitation of the boundaries between China and French Indo-China and valuable economic privileges, including the right to extend a railway they proposed to build in Indo-China into China itself. The British, claiming that these Chinese concessions to France contravened previous agreements with Britain, demanded compensation, and by a treaty of February 1897 they secured concessions similar to those awarded to France: a favorable rectification of the frontier between China and British Burma, and the right to extend into China a railway they proposed to build in Burma.

The greatest concessions, however, were secured by the Russians thanks to the provisions of the Franco-Russian loan, the financial support of their French allies, and Russia's uniquely favorable location.

A prime Russian objective was the right to build the final leg of the Trans-Siberian Railway across Manchuria. But to ensure and enhance the strategic and economic value of that railway, the Russians also needed controlling rights over all other railways that might be built in Manchuria and northern China and control over one or more ice-free ports to serve as terminal stations for the Trans-Siberian and Chinese railways.

In the first stage of their operations, the Russians established a bank in China to make themselves independent of British, French, or German institutions in conducting financial negotiations with the Chinese. With the aid of the French, who feared to refuse any request that might jeopardize their Russian alliance, they secured the necessary funds, and in December 1895 the charter of a Russo-Chinese bank was granted to the Committee of the Siberian Railway.

In April 1896 the Chinese statesman Li Hung-chang went to St. Petersburg to represent China at the coronation of Tsar Nicholas II. There he was offered an immense bribe to secure his government's agreement to a treaty giving Russia the right to build and operate a railway across northern Manchuria to Vladivostok with a branch line to the Yellow Sea. Li refused to commit himself on the branch line, but he agreed to the Manchurian concession, insisting only that this be granted to the Russo-Chinese bank, not to the Russian government, and that the Chinese government have the right to repurchase the line after thirty-six years. As the conditions for repurchase were exceedingly severe, Li's stipulation on that score can have been little more than a face-saving maneuver. His stipulation with regard to the Russo-Chinese bank was completely futile because before agreeing to this condition, the Russians had made an agreement with the bank guaranteeing the Russian government full control over the railway concession. In return for the Manchurian concession, the Russians offered China a fifteen-year defensive alliance against Japan in the event of a Japanese attack on Chinese, Russian, or Korean territory in East Asia. Li successfully secured his government's agreement to this treaty, which was signed in Moscow on June 3, 1896.

The inclusion of Korea in the Russo-Chinese treaty of June 3 reflected not only the Russians' continued interest in that country but their success in challenging Japanese influence there since the signature of the Treaty of Shimonoseki. The Japanese, still uncertain about their military capacity and apprehensive about the strength Russia might be able to bring to bear in East Asia after the completion of the Trans-Siberian Railway, had offered Russia a compromise proposal with respect to Korea that would divide the country into Russian and Japanese spheres of influence at the thirty-eighth parallel. The Russians rejected this proposal on the grounds that they recognized the independence and territorial integrity of Korea as a whole, but the real reason for their rejection may have been the same as Japan's reason for making the proposal: they expected that they would soon be in a position to oust the Japanese from Korea and bring the entire country under Russian dominion. That this was indeed Russia's intention was frankly stated in a memorandum drawn up by the Russian foreign minister Count Lamsdorff some time later: "The fate of Korea, as a future integral part of the Russian Empire by force of geographical and political conditions, has been determined by us."

Following the rejection of their proposal, the Japanese, still fearful of challenging Russia, accepted a Russian compromise proposal over Korea. By the terms of a treaty signed June 9, 1896, Japan and Russia agreed to withdraw all their troops from Korea except a thousand-man security force which both powers would retain there. Japan and Russia agreed further to cooperate to maintain Korea's independence, to preserve order, and to reform that country's government, army, and finances. In effect, the treaty of June 9 provided for a joint Russo-Japanese protectorate.

The establishment of a Russo-Japanese condominium over Korea did not contribute to improved relations between these two powers. It may even have harmed them, for it created a situation that made for constant conflict and did nothing whatever to halt Russian endeavors to extend their influence in Korea at the expense of Japan.

The Russian government's principal interest in East Asia was not Korea, however, but the concession for constructing the Manchurian link of the Trans-Siberian Railway, which would allow the Russians to bring more effective power to bear not only in Korea but elsewhere in the Pacific area. The details of the desired concession were finally worked out and embodied in a treaty between the Chinese government and the Russo-Chinese bank of September 8, 1896. The link of the Trans-Siberian Railway through Manchuria, to be called the Chinese Eastern Railway, was to be under the nominal control of the Russo-Chinese bank, although as we have seen the actual control was to be exercised by the Russian government. All lands necessary for the construction of the railway were to be provided free of charge if they were state property or were to be sold or rented if they were private. The Chinese Eastern Railway Company (and thus the Russian government) was to have absolute and exclusive administrative rights in these lands, the railway was to be free of all taxes or imposts, goods carried on the line from either direction were to pay only two-thirds of the usual Chinese customs duties, the company was to be allowed to fix its own rates and have the exclusive right to operate the line for eighty years. Finally, to safeguard the railway and its installations, the Russians could maintain an army in the railway zone. The broad right of way of the Chinese Eastern Railway was thus nothing less than a Russian colonial administration that became a base for extending Russian political and economic influence throughout Manchuria.

The Russians continued their efforts to secure a concession for a branch line from a junction on the Chinese Eastern Railway to a harbor on the Yellow Sea and thence to Peking. But despite offers of immense new bribes, Li Hung-chang refused to grant concessions that would have allowed the Russians to extend their influence so far to the south. The Russians might have submitted to these rebuffs, especially as it would be some time before they could build the projected lines through China, but the activity of other European powers in East Asia evidently convinced them of the need to take immediate action to secure the desired concessions. Abandoning bribery and diplomacy, they resorted to military threats to extort two treaties from the Chinese government of March 27 and May 7, 1898, giving Russia a twenty-five-year lease to the Liaotung peninsula, including Dairen and Port Arthur, and giving the Chinese Eastern Railway the right to build a railway from Harbin, on the projected Chinese Eastern line, to these ports on the Yellow Sea—the future South Manchurian Railway. The Liaotung peninsula, it will be recalled, was one of the territories the Russians and their allies had compelled the Japanese to retrocede to China in the revised Treaty of Shimonoseki on the grounds of preserving China's territorial integrity. Russia's seizure of this same strategic peninsula therefore hardly eased Russo-Japanese relations, already sorely strained over Korea.

The Russians had ample precedent for extorting concessions from the Chinese government by force or the threat of force, but the incident that triggered the

Russian action in this instance was the German occupation on November 14, 1897, of the territory surrounding the Bay of Kiaochow on China's Shantung peninsula. The German move aroused such intense Russian concern because the Shantung peninsula jutted into the Yellow Sea just south of the Liaotung peninsula, where the Russians hoped to locate a principal terminus of the Trans-Siberian Railway.

The German seizure of Kiaochow has been regarded as the incident that set off the European scramble for territory in China, but as we have seen European territorial encroachments had already been going on for a long time. What the Kiaochow incident did do was precipitate a rash of new European territorial demands, including the Russian demand for the Liaotung peninsula.

The excuse given by the German government for seizing Kiaochow was the murder of two German Roman Catholic missionaries in Shantung, but in fact the Germans had decided much earlier that they needed a coaling station and naval base in East Asia, and by the summer of 1897 they had settled on Kiaochow. The murder of the German missionaries in November therefore came at a most opportune time. The German government, however, was less concerned with finding an appropriate pretext for taking Kiaochow than with Russia's potential opposition. Russia's interest in all the territories bordering the Yellow Sea was well known, and the Germans feared that Russia had already acquired treaty rights to the Shantung peninsula. The kaiser was therefore persuaded by his advisers to ask the tsar's approval to send a German squadron to Kiaochow.

Nicholas II's response was most gratifying: he could neither approve nor disapprove, he said, because the harbor had only been temporarily occupied by Russia, by which he seemed to imply that Russia did not have a prior claim to the area. The German government thereupon ordered its fleet to proceed. The tsar's reply took the wind out of the sails of the German officials who opposed the takeover of Kiaochow because of the potential damage to Germany's relations with Russia. Their fears on this score were soon confirmed. The tsar had acted without consulting his advisers, and his reply was followed almost immediately by a telegram from the Russian foreign minister brutally rejecting Germany's request to occupy Kiaochow. The kaiser was determined to stand firm, however, and after a period of acute diplomatic tension the Russians gave way and advised China to submit to Germany's demands. By a treaty with China of March 6, 1898, Germany acquired a ninety-nine-year lease to the Bay of Kiaochow and surrounding territory together with political and economic concessions that gave Germany preponderant influence over the entire Shantung province.

Why did the Russians finally condone this German incursion in China? The obvious answer is that they were not prepared to run the risk of war with Germany. Their French allies were in the throes of a domestic crisis (the Dreyfus affair) and at loggerheads with Britain over Africa, and they had reason to fear the Japanese might enter the conflict on the side of Germany to oust the Russians from Korea. The Germans for their part, in persuading the Russians to yield on Kiaochow, were lavish with assurances of support should the Russians decide to take Port Arthur. This was the course the Russians finally adopted.

The Sino-German treaty over Kiaochow of March 6, 1898, was followed almost immediately by a spate of similar treaties: the aforementioned treaties of March 27 and May 7 giving Russia a twenty-five–year lease to the Liaotung peninsula and railway construction rights; a treaty of August 10 giving France a ninety-nine–year lease to the peninsula of Kwangchowan, east of Tonkin, together with further economic concessions in southern China; a treaty of June 9, 1899, giving Britain a ninety-nine-year lease to the Kowloon peninsula on the Chinese mainland opposite Hong Kong; and a second treaty of July 1 giving Britain a lease to Weihaiwei, a harbor city on the northeastern shore of the Shantung peninsula opposite Port Arthur, which was to run as long as the Russian lease to Port Arthur.

Through their takeover of Kiaochow, the Germans acquired a valuable naval base in East Asia, but in terms of international politics this move was yet another terrible German mistake. For it inserted Germany into an area where the interests of three great powers (Britain, Japan, and Russia) clashed or were about to clash and drew upon Germany the anger of all three, thereby doing serious injury to Germany's overall diplomatic position.

❑ *The Wrath of China: The Boxer Movement*

The Chinese themselves soon produced new international crises in East Asia. Resentment over foreign violations of Chinese territory and economic exploitation had fostered an intense antiforeign sentiment that erupted in violence in north China in the summer of 1900. This antiforeign movement was led by a secret society whose name was crudely translated by Westerners as the "Righteous and Harmonious Fists," from which the movement got the name "Boxers."

On June 13 a Boxer army entered Peking, massacred Chinese Christians, pillaged and burned foreign property, and laid siege to the foreign diplomatic legations where the majority of foreigners, their dependents, and Christian converts in the Chinese capital had sought refuge. On June 20 the German minister was shot on his way to discuss the situation with officials of the Chinese government, and on the following day the Chinese government, under pressure from the Boxer leaders, declared war on all foreign powers. It is noteworthy that these powers, still concerned with preserving the imperial Chinese government, which had granted the concessions, contracted the loans, and provided the guarantees for their interests in China, chose to ignore the fact that that government had made common cause with the Boxers in its declaration of war. Instead, they persisted in calling the movement the Boxer "rebellion"—a label that was correct only in that this was a rebellion against foreign encroachments in China.

In response to the Boxer siege of the Peking legations, the foreign powers, acting with unusual unanimity and speed, agreed to send an international expeditionary force to the relief of the legations, and the kaiser, after a good deal of diplomatic maneuvering, secured the grudging agreement of the other European governments to the appointment of a German general as supreme commander of this international army. It was on the occasion of the departure of the German troops to China that the kaiser made one of the most unfortunate of his many speeches that contributed so much to blacken Germany's reputation in the international world in the years before 1914. "If you meet the enemy, you will beat him! There will be no pardon! Prisoners will not be taken! . . . A thousand years ago the Huns under King Attila made a name for themselves which in history and legend still stands for power. May your actions ensure that the word German is similarly looked upon in China for a thousand years so that never again will a Chinaman even dare to look askance at a German."

In fact, long before the German general arrived in China the legations had been relieved by European forces closer to the scene of the action, the Boxer armies were defeated, and the Boxer movement was effectively suppressed. The sole immediate accomplishment of this unfortunate movement was that it provided foreign governments with new excuses to subject China to further humiliation, extract more concessions, and demand an immense additional monetary indemnity.

❑ *The American "Open Door" Notes*

The late nineteenth-century European and Japanese scramble for Chinese territory and concessions alarmed the Americans, who were involved in war with Spain during this period. That war ended with Spain's cession of the Philippine Islands to the United States, a territorial acquisition that brought the Americans directly into East Asian affairs. The principal American concern with respect to China at this time, however, was the threat to present and future economic interests of the United States that might result from China's concessions to foreign powers. This concern was shared by others with vested interests in the existing treaty system with China, notably the British and Robert Hart, the British inspector-general of the Chinese Imperial Maritime Customs Service, which supervised and regulated the tariffs on Chinese exports and imports.

It was partly in response to the prompting of the British and Hart that on September 6, 1899, John Hay, the American secretary of state, addressed the first of a series of notes to the governments of the states that had recently acquired (or were expected to acquire) spheres of influence in China. He called upon them for formal assurances that the commerce of all nations in China should enjoy perfect equality of treatment within such spheres and that there should be no interference with the tariffs and other commercial regulations established by the existing treaty system. All governments addressed by Hay responded positively to the American appeal, although all were evasive to some degree, especially Russia. But the American statesman expressed himself satisfied and described the replies as "final and definitive." This first American attempt to keep the door of the China trade open to foreign enterprise is generally regarded as the inauguration of America's "open door" policy toward China, although Hay did not use these words in his initial notes.

In the course of the Boxer war, when it seemed likely that the foreign powers would be tempted to extend their spheres of influence in China or partition the Chinese empire outright, Hay addressed a second round of open door notes to the powers. These notes did not call for a reply but instead defined American policy toward China. Once again Hay stressed his country's resolve to protect all legitimate American interests in China and all rights guaranteed to friendly powers by international law, and to safeguard for the world the principle of equal and impartial trade with all parts of the Chinese empire. But these second notes went far beyond a statement of concern over commercial interests, for in addition Hay now declared it was America's policy to seek a solution "which may bring about permanent safety and peace to China" and to "preserve China's territorial and administrative entity." With that the United States government expressed its opposition in principle to the very establishment of foreign spheres of influence in China and its resolve to prevent the further partition of the Chinese empire.

This pious expression of America's disinterested concern for China did not prevent Hay himself from investigating the possibility of acquiring exclusive American use of Samsah Bay, on the Chinese coast opposite Formosa. Unfortunately for Hay's project, Samsah Bay lay in the Fukien province, and China had recently concluded a treaty with Japan promising not to alienate any part of that province to a third power. Upon learning of this treaty, Hay approached Tokyo with regard to Samsah Bay. The Japanese responded by drawing attention to their agreement with China over the Fukien province, but at the same time they reminded Hay of his own note on behalf of preserving China's territorial integrity. This objective, the Japanese suggested, could best be achieved if all nations exercised restraint. With that the matter ended.

Most Americans remained ignorant of the Samsah Bay episode and chose to regard Hay's second open door notes as a fundamental statement of American policy toward China and a monument to America's unique moral position in dealing with that country. In fact, the open door notes were of no practical importance whatever except as an expression of a political ideal and a precedent for future American policy that sought to achieve its objectives in Asia through mere declarations. Theodore Roosevelt, who had been America's vice president when the open door notes were drafted, was more realistic about them than many of his countrymen. In discussing the open door policy with President Taft in December 1910, he endorsed the policy in principle but pointed out that in fact it served no practical purpose and would be rendered completely meaningless "as soon as a powerful nation determines to disregard it, and is willing to run the risk of war rather than forego its intention."

The truth of Roosevelt's observation was obvious long before 1910. The open door notes did not prevent foreign powers from imposing a new indemnity on China following the Boxer war, which gave them additional leverage in China's internal affairs, nor did the notes prevent further foreign encroachments on China's "territorial and administrative entity."

❑ *The Persistent Threat of Russia: Britain, Germany, and the Formation of the Anglo-Japanese Alliance of 1902*

The country that profited most from the Boxer upheaval was Russia, which used attacks on the Chinese Eastern Railway as an excuse to send an army into Manchuria in July 1900 and rapidly extended its control over the entire region. The Russians subsequently remained in Manchuria, strategically poised to expand even farther into China.

Alarmed by the Russian threat to their own interests in China, the British sought the support of other powers, including Germany, to halt the Russian advance in East Asia. The British negotiations with Germany at this time might have led to the overall Anglo-German alliance the Germans so much desired had the Germans been willing to promise Britain support against Russia in East Asia. But this was precisely what the Germans did not want to do. On the contrary, as in 1895 they wanted to encourage Russian involvement in Asia to ease Russian pressure on German and Austrian interests in the West.

On October 16, 1900, Britain and Germany concluded a treaty known as the

Yangtze Agreement, which seemed nothing less than an endorsement of American policy in China, for it disclaimed all Anglo-German territorial designs and called for the maintenance of the open door in all Chinese territory as far as the contracting parties could exercise influence. For the British, the primary purpose of this treaty was to enlist German support against further Russian encroachments in China. For the Germans, however, who continued to favor Russian expansion in East Asia, the treaty represented a step toward their desired overall alliance with Britain. As soon as the Germans were called upon to act in concert with Britain against Russia in Asia, Bülow, the German chancellor, publicly repudiated what the British regarded as the major objective of the treaty. In a speech to the Reichstag on March 15, 1901, he declared that the Yangtze Agreement did not apply to Manchuria, the principal avenue for Russian expansion in China.

The British found willing partners for an anti-Russian coalition in Asia in the Japanese, who were if anything even more eager than they to halt the Russian advance into China. Negotiations resulted in an Anglo-Japanese alliance on January 20, 1902, in which Britain and Japan expressed their desire to maintain the independence and territorial integrity of the empires of China and Korea but recognized the special interests of Britain in China and of Japan in both China and Korea. If either ally should become involved in war with another power in defending those interests, the other would maintain strict neutrality and work to prevent other powers from entering the war against its ally; but if another power joined in the hostilities, the neutral ally would come to the assistance of its partner and they would wage war in common. The treaty provided further that the British and Japanese navies would cooperate in time of peace and that they would maintain naval strength in the "extreme east" superior to that of any third power. Neither ally was to enter into separate agreements with another power without consulting its alliance partner. The treaty was to run for five years.

❑ *Russo-Japanese Tensions; the Russo-Japanese War of 1904–1905 and Its Aftermath*

Even after concluding their alliance with Britain, the Japanese remained cautious in dealing with the Russians and continued to seek compromise agreements that would safeguard Japanese interests in East Asia, particularly in Korea, without war. The Russians' response to Japanese proposals was not reassuring, however, and they continued to show a disconcerting interest in Korea. The dismissal in 1903 of Count Sergei Witte, the Russian finance minister who had always advocated peaceful penetration in East Asia, seemed to signal the triumph of proponents of a more aggressive Asian policy in the Russian government. An even stronger signal was the administrative reorganization of Russia's Amur and Kwantung provinces into a single Russian viceroyalty. Since these provinces were separated by an immense expanse of Manchurian and North Korean territory (the Kwantung province was at the southern tip of the Liaotung peninsula), their administrative unification was naturally interpreted as a notice of Russian intentions to take over these intervening areas as well.

It is easy to see in retrospect that the Russians would have been wise to pursue a more cautious policy in East Asia in their own right, and to respond positively to

Japanese attempts to secure mutual recognition of their respective interests, at least until the entire Trans-Siberian Railway and Russian military installations in Port Arthur and other strategic positions in East Asia had been completed. The formulators of Russia's Asian policy, however, shared the confidence of most Europeans in their superiority over all non-Europeans. Their records make abundantly clear that they looked down on the Japanese, who would be crushed like insects if they were foolish enough to challenge the Russian colossus.

Many Japanese obviously shared the general belief in Russian military superiority, as is evident from their hesitation to challenge Russia militarily and their persistent search for a compromise agreement. This Japanese attitude gradually changed following their 1902 alliance with Britain and as a result of their own fearful awareness that within a few years the Russian position in East Asia would be immeasurably strengthened with the completion of the Trans-Siberian Railway and its branch lines to Port Arthur and Peking.

By 1904 the Japanese had decided that they could not afford to give the Russians time to build up their military and economic power in East Asia, and that if they hoped to ensure the safety of their own islands and their interests on the Asiatic mainland they would have to strike while their own military position vis-à-vis Russia was still relatively favorable. Dispensing with a declaration of war, the Japanese launched a surprise attack on Port Arthur in February 1904. Their objective was skillfully chosen. Not only was Port Arthur the most strategic naval base from which the Russians might have attacked Japan, but the greater part of the Russian Pacific fleet, including all the Russian battleships, was stationed there. In their initial attack, the Japanese severely damaged seven Russian naval vessels, and by blocking the narrow entrance to the harbor they effectively bottled up the entire Port Arthur squadron. Japan's bold and successful surprise attack was greeted with admiration by many Americans, including Theodore Roosevelt. The American reaction was rather different when the Japanese did the same thing to them thirty-seven years later.

With their success at Port Arthur, the Japanese gained what for them was the indispensable condition for fighting on the Asian mainland: naval supremacy in the Pacific, which allowed them to transport their forces to the mainland and keep them reinforced and supplied. When in August 1904 the undamaged Russian naval vessels attempted to break out of Port Arthur, they were intercepted by a Japanese fleet and almost totally destroyed. The few Russian ships not sent to the bottom fled to neutral ports where they were interned; the rest returned to Port Arthur, never to put to sea again.

The Russians made a valiant attempt to regain supremacy at sea by sending their Baltic fleet to the Pacific. But before it could join forces with what was left of the Russian Pacific fleet at Vladivostok, it was met by Japanese ships in the Straits of Tsushima (between Japan and Korea), where on May 28, 1905, the Japanese destroyed this second Russian fleet as completely as they had destroyed the first.

The Russians fared little better on land. In April 1904 the Japanese won a major military victory on the Yalu River in North Korea. In May they captured the Russian fortifications guarding the communications to the Kwantung area on the southern tip of the Liaotung peninsula and laid siege to Port Arthur, which surrendered in December. The bulk of the Russian forces had meanwhile retreated northward where, although heavily reinforced, they continued to suffer defeats whenever they made a stand. In the Battle of Mukden in February 1905, the greatest in terms of numbers until World War I (approximately 300,000 men were engaged on either side), the Russians lost 90,000 men, including 25,000 prisoners and immense quantities of supplies and equipment. The Russians managed to stabilize their front north of Mukden, but with the destruction of their Baltic fleet in the Tsushima Straits in May and the rapid spread of revolutionary activity in Russia itself, the Russian government accepted the invitation of the American president Theodore Roosevelt to mediate and to enter into peace negotiations. The Japanese, although victorious on land and sea, also accepted the American offer and agreed to peace negotiations because the war was imposing a catastrophic burden on Japan's human and economic resources. Already the Japanese had suffered almost a quarter of a million casualties and the cost of the war was approaching a billion dollars.

The peace conference that ended the Russo-Japanese War convened in Portsmouth, New Hampshire, on August 5, 1905, with Witte, the former Russian finance minister, and Komura, the Japanese foreign minister, as the principal negotiators for their respective countries. The negotiations were conducted with dispatch, and after only twelve negotiating sessions the draft of a final peace treaty had been drawn up. President Roosevelt proved to be a skillful and forceful mediator, and both belligerent powers were under great pressure from their allies to reach agreement: in 1904 Britain, the ally of Japan, had concluded an agreement with France, the ally of Russia, and both partners in this new entente had found themselves in a most uncomfortable diplomatic position during the war between their respective allies. But the rapid success of the peace conference was due above all to the Japanese and Russian negotiators' recognition that their countries needed peace.

By the terms of the Treaty of Portsmouth of September 5, 1905, Russia recognized Japan's paramount political, military, and economic interests in Korea and agreed not to oppose any steps Japan might take in that country, thus preparing the way for Japan's eventual annexation of Korea. Russia ceded to Japan the southern half of the island of Sakhalin and transferred to Japan its lease on the Liaotung peninsula, including the harbor cities of Port Arthur and Dairen, as well as Russian rights to the section of the South Manchurian Railway between Port Arthur and Changchun (about halfway between Mukden and Harbin). Both powers agreed to withdraw their troops from Manchuria and to restore that region to the exclusive administration of China. The Russians were not obliged to pay a monetary indemnity, but the Japanese received the equivalent of a substantial indemnity by acquiring all Russian installations and properties in the Liaotung peninsula and "all rights, privileges, and properties appertaining to the Southern Manchurian Railway, which include all coal mines belonging to or worked for the benefit of that railway."

The Treaty of Portsmouth aroused inevitable bitterness on both sides: the Russians believed they had given up too much, the Japanese that they had received too little. That treaty nevertheless inaugurated an era of better relations between Russia and Japan, a reconciliation eagerly sponsored by their British and French allies. Russo-Japanese reconciliation was also fostered by their joint opposition to the efforts of American financiers to acquire control of the railways of northern China, including the extensions of the Trans-Siberian line through Manchuria.

To counter the American threat, Japan and Russia concluded a treaty of navigation and commerce on July 28, 1907, providing for mutual economic cooperation, and two days later they signed a convention promising to respect each other's territorial integrity and to uphold the principle of the open door in Manchuria. The most important provisions of this second treaty were secret articles whereby Russia again conceded Japan a free hand in Korea and recognized southern Manchuria and Inner Mongolia as Japanese spheres of influence, while Japan recognized northern Manchuria and Outer Mongolia as Russian spheres of influence.

Three years later, on July 4, 1910, Japan and Russia concluded another treaty which omitted all mention of the integrity of China and the open door but included secret articles providing for common action to safeguard and defend their respective spheres of influence as defined in their treaty of 1907. On August 22, 1910, the Japanese took advantage of the free hand Russia had conceded them in Korea and formally annexed that country. In November 1912, while China was in the grip of revolution, the Russians established a de facto protectorate over Outer Mongolia.

The great period of Russian expansion in East Asia, however, had come to an end with Russia's defeat by Japan in 1905. In global perspective the major significance of that defeat for all the great powers was that the Russians, their expansionist ambitions temporarily halted in East Asia, once again directed their attention to the West.

❑

EIGHTEEN

The Reemergence of the Eastern Question

❑ *The Armenian Problem*

In the Near East, that perennial breeding ground of international crises, a new threat to regional stability and to the peace of Europe emerged in the late nineteenth century with the rise of yet another nationalist movement, this time within the Armenian population of the Ottoman empire. The development of national self-consciousness among the Armenians was similar to that of other nationalities during this period. For centuries the Armenians in the Ottoman empire had lived as a Christian and ethnic minority within a predominantly Muslim population of Turks and Kurds. Most of these Armenians (approximately one million) lived in the provinces of eastern Anatolia, but a substantial number (another half million) had migrated over the years to the larger cities where they became prominent in urban commercial life. During the nineteenth century, inspired by the success of Christian nationalities in the Balkans in winning their independence from Turkish Muslim rule, the Armenians began to agitate for their own freedom.

The great difference between the Armenian and Balkan nationalist movements was that the Armenians did not constitute a solid block of the population of any one area but were widely scattered in three different countries: the Ottoman empire, Russia, and Persia (Iran). Even in the Ottoman empire, where the largest number of Armenians was located, they did not constitute a majority of the population in any one of the empire's provinces or larger cities. Nor were the Armenians solidly united in their religion. Most Armenians were members of the Armenian Apostolic (Christian) church, but over the years many had converted to Islam, while others had joined other Christian sects. Thus there was no territorial, ethnic, or any other basis for an independent Armenian national state; the most the Armenians in the Ottoman empire could hope for was an improved legal status that would afford better protection for their lives and property. Unfortunately, the more fanatic Armenian nationalists persisted in their unrealistic demands for an independent state and thereby not only failed to achieve their goal but brought disaster to the Armenian people as a whole.

In the aftermath of the Russo-Turkish war of 1877–1878, when the claims of several Balkan nationalities to freedom from Turkish rule were recognized by the great powers, Armenian nationalists attempted to secure similar recognition for themselves. Their efforts were a total failure. The Russians, with a sizable Armenian population of their own, could not afford to encourage an Armenian independence movement in neighboring Turkey, and the other European great powers were more concerned with shoring up what was left of the Ottoman empire as a bulwark against Russia than with the aspirations of the Armenians. All the European powers would or indeed could do, short of instituting a massive population transfer, was demand that the Ottoman government institute reforms on behalf of its Christian subjects, a demand which they were unable to enforce and which the Ottoman government largely ignored.

In the summer of 1890 Armenian nationalists formed the Armenian Revolutionary Federation to unite the various Armenian political groups into a single body with the immediate aim of securing independence for Turkish Armenia and the formation of an Armenian national state, which would eventually include Russian and Persian Armenia as well. The federation was committed to permanent revolution against Ottoman overlordship, but its leaders were realistic enough to recognize that the Armenians themselves lacked the power to achieve national independence without the intervention of one or more of the European powers on their behalf. To secure such intervention they began a terrorist campaign with the deliberate, frankly acknowledged purpose of provoking brutal Turkish reprisals, which they expected would arouse European public opinion, as such incidents had done in the case of the Greeks and Bulgars. The resultant public pressure would compel the European governments to come to the aid of the Christian Armenians as they had aided other Christian nationalities in the Balkans.

The Armenian revolutionaries had no difficulty provoking Turkish reprisals, and reports of Turkish atrocities had the anticipated effect on European and especially British public opinion. When the news arrived in Britain of the brutal massacre of Armenians in the Sassun region of east central Anatolia in August 1894, the Liberal government of Lord Rosebery, who had succeeded Gladstone as prime minister in the previous March, came under intense pressure to compel the Ottoman government to institute reforms that would prevent such outrages in the future. Rosebery was less easily moved by humanitarian pleas than Gladstone had been, and he believed in Britain's traditional policy of preserving the Ottoman empire as a bulwurk against Russia, but public opinion was too insistent to be ignored. Recognizing the danger as well as the futility of unilateral British intervention, he appealed to the continental powers for support in pressuring the Ottoman government to accept a reform program.

Rosebery's appeal gave the German government yet another opportunity to demonstrate to the British the high diplomatic cost of their refusal to join the Triple Alliance. Still annoyed by what they regarded as Rosebery's spineless and dishonest conduct during the recent Siam crisis (see pp. 257–258), the Germans rejected his appeal and called upon their partners in the Triple Alliance to do the same. Rosebery thus was compelled to look to France and Russia. These powers, long fearful that Britain was indeed preparing to join the Triple Alliance, saw in Rosebery's appeal an opportunity to improve their own relations with London and at the same time demonstrate their traditional concern for the Christian subjects of the sultan. They accordingly joined Britain in recommending a reform program to the Ottoman government, thereby forming what became known in diplomatic parlance as the Near Eastern Triplice.

There never was any likelihood that the Near Eastern Triplice would be effective because all three members were far more concerned with protecting their own interests than those of the Armenians. The Russians, with their own large Armenian population, were fundamentally opposed to any action on behalf of the Armenians in Turkey, and with their attention focused on East Asia at this time they wanted to avoid disturbing the status quo in the Near East. The French followed the lead of their Russian allies on the Armenian question, but they had compelling reasons of their own to oppose any policy likely to undermine the Ottoman government. Nine percent of France's total capital abroad was invested in the Ottoman empire, and France held sixty percent of the Ottoman government's bonds. Neither the French nor the Russians were therefore prepared to give Rosebery's reform efforts more than token support. This they did by instructing their representatives in Constantinople to cooperate with the British in working out a reform program to protect the Armenians.

By May 1895 the ambassadors of the Triplice had drafted such a program, but their governments were unable to agree on the crucial question of how to persuade the sultan to accept it. The most obvious way of doing so—a show of force—was ruled out by the Russians, who opposed any establishment of international (and thus also British) control over Constantinople and the Turkish Straits, and on this issue they had the backing of the French. The manifest failure of Lord Rosebery to accomplish anything on behalf of the Armenians accelerated the erosion of his government's popular support, and in June 1895 he resigned. He was succeeded by the Conservative leader, Lord Salisbury, who took over the leadership of the British government for the third and last time.

In contributing to the ouster of Rosebery, the Germans believed they had taught the British government a lesson, and that they need only keep up the pressure on Britain in international affairs until its leaders recognized the necessity of joining the Triple Alliance.

They were especially hopeful that this necessity would be recognized by Salisbury, who had negotiated the 1887 agreements over the Near East with Austria and Italy (see pp. 244-245) and whose previous relations with Germany had been relatively harmonious. Salisbury for his part hoped to resume his good relationship with the Triple Alliance powers and was therefore surprised as well as annoyed to find that he was no more successful than his predecessor in securing their cooperation on the Armenian question. Unable to secure more than token support from France and Russia, and failing to get even that from Germany and its allies, he resorted to vigorous public denunciations of the Ottoman government and dire warnings of the consequences of its failure to respond to demands for reform, while in private conversations with foreign diplomats he spoke of the possibility of abandoning Britain's traditional policy of preserving the Ottoman empire and its peaceful partition among the powers, including the assignment of Constantinople and the Straits to Russia. In putting forward such revolutionary proposals (in terms of traditional British foreign policy), Salisbury may have intended to frighten the sultan into accepting a reform program and provoke the Austrians, who had always dreaded the prospect of Russian dominion over Constantinople and the southern Balkans, into defying Germany and supporting Britain over the Armenian question.

The mere suggestion of partition, however, which had given rise to such suspicion when proposed by Tsar Nicholas I prior to the Crimean War, was met with equal suspicion when proposed by a British prime minister scarcely half a century later. Nowhere was this suspicion greater than among the Germans, who believed Salisbury had at least three objectives in view with his partition proposals: to sow the seeds of a continental war that would leave the British a free hand to advance their imperial interests; to divert the Russians' attention from East Asia and back to their rivalry with Austria in the Balkans; and, by declaring Britain's own disinterestedness in the Balkans and Constantinople, to force Germany to take sole responsibility for protecting the interests of Austria in the Near East.

As so often in dealing with questions of foreign policy, the German emperor William II was out of step with the leaders of his own government. While visiting England early in August 1895, he had been warned by his advisers not to be drawn into a discussion of partition with the British prime minister. William was obviously intrigued by the subject, however, and toward the end of the month, without consulting anyone, he presented Salisbury with ideas of his own regarding the Ottoman empire through the British military attaché in Berlin, Colonel Leopold Swaine. He advised the use of force, and asked only that Germany be consulted in advance and that Germany's allies, Austria and Italy, be offered adequate compensation should the use of force lead to the collapse and partition of the Ottoman empire.

In holding out the prospect of German support for a policy of force, the kaiser undoubtedly intended to exact the price of Britain's adherence to the Triple Alliance. Salisbury, however, had no desire to enter into negotiations on so critical a subject with so volatile a ruler or to bind Britain more closely to Germany. He replied evasively to the kaiser's proposals, avoiding all specific reference to Turkey beyond stating in a general way that Britain's policy in the Near East had not changed. The kaiser, infuriated by Salisbury's bland rejection of his overture (for there was no other way to interpret the prime minister's response), was now convinced that his officials were correct after all: Salisbury's sole purpose was to sow discord among the continental powers. To frustrate that nefarious scheme the kaiser began to talk of making common cause with France and Russia. At the same time, however, with typical inconsistency, he predicted that sooner or later the British would be forced to abandon their isolation and choose for or against the Triple Alliance. Blithely confident that when that time came the British would come crawling to Berlin, he made no effort to make the German connection more palatable in London.

Renewed Armenian agitation at the end of September 1895 was followed by further Turkish massacres, this time in the Turkish capital itself directly under the eyes of European diplomats and journalists. This blatant display of savagery forged a temporary alliance among the ambassadors of all the powers in Constantinople, who now joined together in demanding that the sultan accept the reform program drawn up in the previous May by the Near Eastern Triplice. But the usual problem remained: How was the Turkish government to be persuaded to accept and implement that program?

To demonstrate its own seriousness of purpose, the British government sent a fleet to the entrance of the Dardanelles. This British initiative prompted Goluchowski, the Austrian foreign minister, acting contrary to the wishes of his German allies, to propose that all the European powers join Britain in sending fleets to the Levant to back up their demands for reform; if these should be rejected, the international fleet should breach the Straits and impose their demands on the sultan. In making this proposal, Goluchowski, well aware that Russia and thus Russia's ally France would oppose any move that might put an international force in control of the Straits, clearly intended to reactivate Austria's 1887 entente with Britain in Near Eastern affairs and secure specific commitments of mutual support, something the Germans had so signally failed to accomplish over the past five years. The Germans, however, still suspicious of British motives and resolved to keep up their diplomatic pressure on the British government, promptly undercut Goluchowski's proposal by alleging that they had no warships available for service in the Levant. With this repudiation by Germany and Russia's declaration that it would oppose the use of force "by any or all the powers," Goluchowski abandoned his proposal. In view of the attitude of the continental governments, he explained to the British ambassador, any attempt at international intervention in Constantinople "was likely to lead to a catastrophe far greater than the extermination of the entire Armenian race."

Even after learning of this Austrian decision, Salisbury continued to explore the possibility of unilateral British action. The Admiralty, however, warned that any effort to force the Straits in the face of French and Russian opposition might prove disastrous, and the cabinet thereupon resolved that no action should be taken. Salisbury professed to be disappointed. "In Armenia I have been told by the Cabinet practically to sit still," he said.

It was fortunate for the peace of Europe that Salisbury was obliged to sit still, for Nelidov, the Russian ambassador to Constantinople, was urging his government to anticipate any British or international attempt to force the Straits by seizing the Bosporus and establishing sole Russian control over the Turkish capital, a plan the Russian government was actually to endorse in December of the following year when international intervention in Constantinople again seemed likely. For the moment, however, the governments of the powers recognized that they had reached a stalemate over the Armenian question, and in the last days of 1895 British concern for the Armenians was eclipsed by the crisis in South Africa, the Jameson raid, and the kaiser's Kruger telegram.

The Armenian question was dramatically recalled to international attention in August 1896 when Armenian revolutionaries seized the Ottoman Bank in Constantinople. This act of terrorism produced the grimmest Turkish reprisals thus far—a three-day slaughter of Armenians in the capital, once again in full view of European observers. There followed a repetition of the events of the previous year, as an aroused European public opinion once again put pressure on their various governments to intervene on behalf of the Armenians.

In late September 1896 Salisbury took advantage of a visit of Tsar Nicholas II to Britain to sound the impressionable Russian ruler as to whether his government would now be prepared to support an international reform program for the Ottoman empire and, if necessary, back it up with the use of force. The tsar did not respond as positively as Salisbury may have hoped. Although not ruling out the use of force, he was concerned primarily about the fate of the Straits in the event of international action: the Straits were the door to the room in which he lived and "he must have the key to that door." Salisbury went a long way to reassure the tsar on this score. He himself still desired to maintain the status quo in the Near East, he said, but Britain's former rigidity on this matter had been replaced by a more realistic flexibility, and if international action should lead to the disintegration of the Ottoman empire, he would be prepared to allow Russia to have the Straits. Britain could defend its interests in the Near East adequately by consolidating its control over Egypt, and Austria would be given compensation elsewhere. Although Nicholas refused to commit himself, Salisbury was evidently sufficiently encouraged to address a circular note to the powers on October 20 embodying the proposal he had presented to the tsar: the ambassadors of the powers should work out another reform program, and their governments should agree in advance to impose it on the sultan, by force if necessary.

To avoid being accused of a lack of humanitarian concern, all the European governments responded favorably to the Salisbury circular, but the new reform program worked out by their representatives was doomed from the start, and for the same reason that all similar programs had failed in the past: the European powers disagreed fundamentally about how to enforce it. So alarmed was the Russian government about the prospect of international intervention in Constantinople that on December 5, 1896, it empowered Nelidov, its ambassador in Constantinople, to carry out his plan to seize the Bosporus before other powers could do so. As in the previous year, however, the European governments recognized that active intervention in Turkey without prior agreements among themselves would involve risks they were not prepared to take.

In the end the reform program formulated in response to the Salisbury circular was not even presented to the sultan, for once again the plight of the Armenians was overshadowed by other international crises: a resumption in February 1897 of the revolution of Greek Christians against Turkish rule in Crete, which led to war between Greece and Turkey two months later; and the German seizure of Kiaochow in November, which again focused European attention on East Asia. Well before the Kiaochow incident, however, Salisbury confessed to his ambassador in Constantinople that the question of Armenian reform was a dead letter: ever since the cabinet had refused to allow him to send the fleet into the Dardanelles two years earlier, "I have regarded the Eastern Question as having little serious interest for England." Britain should now concentrate on strengthening its position on the Nile "and to withdraw as much as possible from all responsibilities at Constantinople."

The Armenian revolutionaries continued to provoke Turkish reprisals to revive European interest in the Armenian question, but in the last years of the nineteenth century the European governments were increasingly absorbed by more immediate problems. Gradually the revolutionaries abandoned their agitation, having accomplished nothing but the slaughter of thousands of their hapless compatriots. More tragic still, the hatred and suspicion engendered by this revolutionary activity provided the Turks and Kurds with a motive and excuse to continue the persecution and expropriation of their Armenian neighbors. With the outbreak of World War I this persecution was developed into a program of outright genocide, which Turkish authorities justified on the grounds that this was their only recourse in dealing with the traitorous Armenian population.

❑ *The End of the Anglo-Austrian Entente; the Austro-Russian Agreement of 1897*

The most significant international consequences of the Armenian crises were a widening of the rift between Britain and Germany and the final breakdown of the Anglo-Austrian agreements of 1887. Upon returning to office in June 1895, Salisbury had informed the Austrians that he regarded these agreements as being still in force, but in the ensuing Near Eastern crises the Austrians had asked the British government to go beyond the mere "agreement to agree" of 1887 and to pledge to fight in the event of a Russian threat to the Straits and Constantinople. Salisbury refused, explaining that constitutional limitations prevented him from making such specific commitments, but as we have seen he had gradually come to the conclusion that British interests no longer required the defense of Constantinople, which he described in January 1897 as "an antiquated standpoint." Unable to secure concrete commitments from Britain, Goluchowski, the Austrian foreign minister, declared that Austria would henceforth keep a free hand to make other arrangements in the Near East to safeguard its interests.

This de facto Austrian repudiation of the 1887 agreements was a serious diplomatic blunder, for vague though they might be, these agreements to agree at least provided a basis for some kind of cooperation with Britain, which now no longer existed. But Goluchowski was lucky. The Russians, still concerned primarily with the problems of East Asia, were as eager as the Austrians to avoid further crises in the Near East at this time. In the course of a visit of Francis Joseph and his foreign minister to St. Petersburg in late April 1897, the Austrian and Russian governments concluded an agreement recognizing "the necessity of maintaining the present status quo in the Balkan Peninsula as long as circumstances will permit." If this proved impossible, Austria and Russia would reach a separate agreement over the Balkans, but they renounced in advance all idea of conquest in that region and were resolved to make this principle respected by other powers. The Austro-Russian treaty specifically excluded the problems of Constantinople and the Straits because these were a pan-European concern and could not be the subject of a bilateral agreement, but at Russia's insistence the treaty nevertheless stipulated that there should be no change in the existing principle which closed the Straits to foreign warships because this was essential to Russian security. In return for their agreement on the Straits question, the Austrians sought Russia's consent to Austria's outright annexation of the Ottoman empire's Balkan provinces of Bosnia, Herzegovina, and the sanjak of Novi Pazar, a step beyond the mere right to occupy these territories as provided by the 1878 Treaty of Berlin. Further, the Austrians wanted an independent Albanian state established in the region south of Montenegro as a counterweight to the Slavic states in the southern Balkans. But here Russia drew the line. These matters raised more extensive questions and would require special scrutiny when the occasion arose to deal with them.

Despite these Russian reservations and the fact that the Austrian and Russian governments continued to vie for political and economic influence among the Balkan states in a manner that violated both the spirit and letter of the 1897 agreement, that agreement nevertheless helped to preserve a relative calm in this volatile area for almost a decade. But with Russia's defeat in East Asia in 1905, Russian attention again reverted to the West and Austro-Russian cooperation in the Balkans gave way to an increasingly bitter rivalry that was to climax in 1914.

❑ *The Cretan Revolution*

The Austro-Russian Balkan agreement of 1897 was intended to avoid the perils that had arisen during the recent Armenian crises, but it was also a direct response to yet another crisis in the Near East: a flare-up of the long-simmering rebellion in Crete of Greek Christians against Turkish Muslim rule, an uprising enthusiastically supported by Greek nationalists on the mainland with the avowed aim of annexing the island. The great danger to the peace of Europe in this situation was that a successful Cretan revolution would inspire further rebellion in other parts of the Ottoman empire and elsewhere, and that Greece's acquisition of Crete would give rise to demands on the part of other Balkan states for compensation. Moreover, the ambitions of Greek nationalists were not confined to Crete but extended to the greater part of what was left of the Ottoman empire in the Balkans, in particular Thessaly, Epirus, and Macedonia, all of which the Greeks claimed should be part of a Greek national state on ethnic, religious, and historical grounds.

On February 6, 1897, Cretan revolutionaries proclaimed the union of their island with Greece. Shortly afterwards the Greek government, swept along on a wave of nationalist fervor, sent troops to Crete to support the revolution, therewith beginning an undeclared war against Turkey.

To control the Cretan revolution and prevent a general conflagration in the Balkans, the European great powers sent identic notes to Greece and Turkey demanding the withdrawal of troops of both states from the island. Crete would be made autonomous, though with the face-saving provision for Turkey that it would remain under the nominal suzerainty of the sultan. To back up their demands, the powers agreed to send an international force to Crete to hold the island "in deposit" pending the outcome of negotiations with the Greek and Turkish governments. The fact that Turkey was being called upon to withdraw its troops from territory that was still part of the Ottoman empire and grant autonomy to Crete made it obvious to the Turks that the European powers were far from neutral on the Cretan question, but they saw no alternative to accepting these conditions. The Greeks, however, did not. The Greek government held out for the right to annex Crete outright, while Greek nationalists attempted to exploit the Cretan imbroglio to begin the takeover of Greek-claimed territory on the Balkan mainland.

The Greeks were evidently convinced, as were most European leaders, that the Ottoman empire was on the verge of disintegration, and they were confident of European support no matter what they did, for the powers had already revealed their pro-Greek position on Crete and throughout Europe there was pro-Hellenic sentiment. Finally, the Greek royal house was closely related to the major ruling families of Europe: King George of Greece was the son of Christian IX of Denmark; his sister Alexandra was married to the future King Edward VII of England; another sister, Dagmar, was the dowager empress of Russia; George himself was married to a sister of Tsar Nicholas II; and his eldest son Constantine was married to Princess Sophie of Prussia, a sister of Emperor William II of Germany and a granddaughter of Queen Victoria.

The very factors that encouraged the Greeks made the Turks cautious, so it was not until April 17, following blatant aggression on Turkish territory by troops of the regular Greek army, that the Ottoman government at last severed relations with Greece and declared war. The Turkish army soon demonstrated that the Ottoman empire was a long way from disintegration, defeating the Greeks quickly and decisively. On May 10 the Greeks appealed to the European powers to mediate; however, it was only on May 19, after the Greeks saw they could not hope for active European military intervention, that they agreed to an armistice.

Although the Greeks received no military aid, their expectations of European support were amply fulfilled on the diplomatic front. By the terms of the preliminary peace settlement between Greece and Turkey of September 18, 1897 (confirmed in the final treaty signed December 4), the Turks were denied the major fruits of their military victory and were conceded only minor border rectifications at Greece's expense together with a nominal indemnity. The fate of Crete was left undecided.

Throughout the Greek–Turkish war Crete was under the control of the international force sent to the island in the previous February. Following the signature of the preliminary peace of September 18, the powers again agreed to make Crete autonomous, and in November the Russians put forward the candidacy of Prince George of Greece, the second son of the Greek sovereign King George I, as governor of the island. Prince George was a favorite cousin of the tsar, whose life he had saved from an assassin during a visit to Japan in 1891. As the prince was also known to be a fervent advocate of the union of Crete with Greece—he had led a naval squadron to Crete earlier in the year in an unsuccessful attempt to establish a de facto union—his nomination by the Russians was interpreted as a sign of Russian support for annexation and a move to promote Russian influence in Greece.

Prince George's candidacy was opposed by the Germans and Austrians—by the Austrians because they feared annexation would set off a general revolutionary conflagration that would spread to their own empire, and because they resented this Russian violation of their 1897 agreement to preserve the status quo in the Balkans; by the Germans because they were already embarking on a campaign to build German influence in Constantinople. Both Austria and Germany now withdrew their contingents from the international occupation army in Crete. British, French, Italian, and Russian contingents remained, and under their auspices Prince George of Greece was named governor of the island in November 1898. In July 1909 the European international army was withdrawn from Crete on the understanding that the island would remain autonomous, but just three months later Greek Cretans proclaimed their union with Greece. The Greek government, having learned the dangers of precipitate action, delayed formally annexing Crete until after the Second Balkan War in 1913.

❑ *The Macedonian Problem*

In their war against Turkey in 1897, Greek ambitions had extended beyond Crete to liberating and annexing Thessaly, Epirus, and Macedonia, the greater part of what was left of the Ottoman empire in the Balkans. Although the Greeks claimed these territories on the basis of the ethnic and religious composition of their populations, these populations consisted in fact of an inextricable jumble of nationalities and religions. This was especially true of Macedonia, the ancient homeland of Alexander the Great, an ill-defined region in the southern Balkans consisting roughly of the Ottoman administrative districts of Kossovo, Monastir (Bitolj), and Salonika. Lying as it did between Greece, Bulgaria, and Serbia, Macedonia was a natural objective for the expansionist ambitions of all three of these recently established national states, and all laid claim on similar ethnic, religious, and historical grounds. To complicate matters further, within Macedonia itself a nationalist movement had developed dedicated to achieving autonomy from all foreign control.

The inflammatory nature of the Macedonian problem had been another important motive for the 1897 Austro-Russian agreement to preserve the status quo in the Balkans, and during the Greek–Turkish war only the rapid defeat of the Greeks and diplomatic pressure from Austria and Russia had prevented Bulgaria and Serbia from entering the conflict to establish their own claims to Macedonia. The Austro-Russian agreement did not put an end to revolutionary agitation in Macedonia, however, nor did it prevent the governments and agents of neighboring Balkan states from contributing to this agitation in support of their own interests. In an attempt to deal with this increasingly dangerous situation, Austria and Russia drew up a reform program for Macedonia in February 1903 (the Mürzsteg agreement), which, with the approval of other great powers, they proceeded to impose on the Turkish administration. The Mürzsteg program called for greater Austro-Russian supervision of the Turkish administration together with a variety of administrative, judicial, and financial reforms, and for the establishment of a police force composed of Christians and Muslims, according to population, under the command of a foreign (and thus presumably neutral) general. Further, in an ill-conceived effort to appease nationalist interests, the program provided for a new administrative division of the region on the basis of "ethnic realities." This provision was to have disastrous consequences, as the Austrian and Russian governments should have been the first to appreciate, for it encouraged the various nationalities in Macedonia to adjust the ethnic realities in their favor, so that after 1903 the Macedonian problem was no longer largely a question of protecting Christians against Turkish Muslims but of keeping the various Christian nationalities from slaughtering each other.

Over the ensuing years national revolutions and conflicts in Macedonia continued to fester, and the region was to be a major bone of contention during the Balkan wars of 1912–1913 (see pp. 425–431). These wars were to result in the expulsion of the Turks from Macedonia and its division among the various Balkan claimants, none of whom felt their ambitions fulfilled, let alone the Macedonian nationalists themselves, so that Macedonia remained a dangerous repository in the notorious Balkan powderkeg.

❑ The Bagdad Railway

The various national and territorial problems that developed in the Near East around the turn of the century were all threats to the peace of Europe, because a spark from any of them might have set off a general conflagration—as one such spark was to do in 1914. But so long as the great powers exercised restraint and cooperated in imposing similar restraint on the minor powers in this region, problems were kept under control.

Meanwhile, however, a longer range but potentially more fundamental threat to the international equilibrium in the Near East was developing as a result of growing German political and economic influence in the Ottoman empire. After Turkey's defeat by Russia in the war of 1877–1878, the Turks appealed to Germany for political and military advisers to assist in reforming and reorganizing their government and army. The Turks were impressed by the efficiency of Germany's own administration and the achievements of its army, but in the eyes of Turkish leaders Germany enjoyed the additional advantage of being the only European power that had not engaged in the spoliation of their empire. Moreover, because of its geographical position, Germany even now represented no direct threat to the Ottoman empire or its territories. It is therefore understandable that the Turks regarded the Germans as safer partners in rebuilding their empire than other European powers, and equally understandable that within Germany there were political and economic entrepreneurs who found the opportunities that came their way in the Near East impossible to resist.

In 1876 Bismarck made his famous remark in the Reichstag advising against an active German policy in the Near East because German interests there were not worth the bones of a Pomeranian grenadier. Nevertheless, when the Turks appealed for German aid two years later he saw no reason to prohibit German advisers from going to Constantinople provided they did so in a purely private capacity and severed any official connections they might have with the German government. It was thus with the consent of the Bismarck regime, but without any kind of official support, that a group of German political advisers went to Constantinople in the autumn of 1880, to be followed a year later by a similar group of military advisers. From that time retired German officers regularly entered the Turkish service, and Turkey's victory over Greece in 1897 was widely credited to the effectiveness of German military tutelage. Bismarck himself, however, remained inexorably opposed to any official involvement in the Near East, where vital German interests were not at stake; any attempt to establish German influence there would convert Germany's position from that of aloof arbiter, able to exercise some control over the policies of other powers, into that of abrasive buffer between traditional rivals in this most strategically critical of international arenas, therewith exposing Germany to the wrath of them all.

Somewhat surprisingly, it was not the German military presence in Turkey that aroused greatest alarm among foreign powers (at least not until the Liman von Sanders military mission of 1913; see pp. 432–434), but Germany's economic involvement in the Ottoman empire, notably the Turkish government's award of concessions to German firms to build a railway through Asiatic Turkey from Constantinople via Bagdad to the Persian Gulf. As the project developed, it came to be seen as a vehicle for massive penetration of German influence throughout the Near East and beyond, and as the "Berlin to Bagdad Railway" it became a symbol of Germany's sinister involvement in the Eastern Question. As if to make German interest in this region as obtrusive and offensive as possible, Emperor William II, on a visit to the Holy Land in 1898, proclaimed in a speech in Damascus that the world's 300 million Muslims could count on him as their friend, a pronouncement hardly reassuring to the governments of Britain, France, and Russia, with their own immense Muslim subject populations.

The Turkish government's interest in railway construction in the late nineteenth

MAP 16   *THE OTTOMAN EMPIRE IN ASIA AND THE BAGDAD RAILWAY*

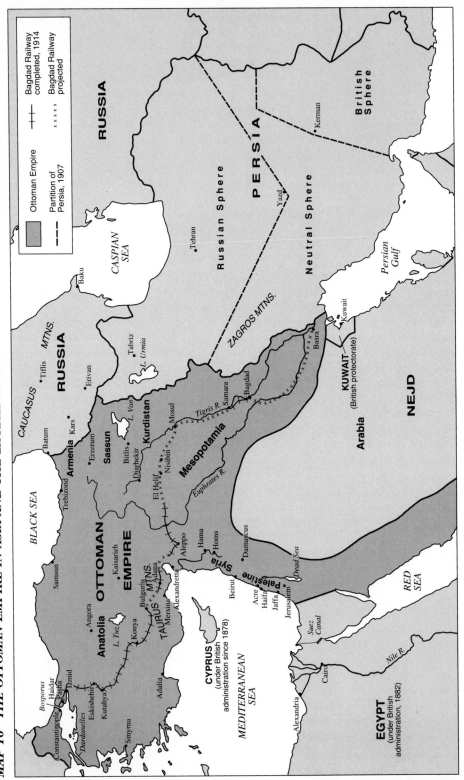

century derived from the obvious contribution of railways to the economic and military strength of the European powers. The decision to construct an Ottoman railway network was made following the completion in 1888 of a line through Hungary and the Balkans that linked Constantinople with the railways of western and central Europe (the route of the legendary Orient Express). What the Turks now proposed was to extend this railway connection with Europe through lines radiating from Constantinople to all the cities and provinces of Asiatic Turkey. Such a railway network would allow for greater administrative centralization and control, facilitate the transport of troops to deal with domestic as well as foreign foes, and provide the sinews for the empire's economic development. It was with these objectives in view that Sultan Abdul Hamid, besides turning to Germany for political and military advisers, sought out German entrepreneurs to assist in constructing Turkish railways.

The prospect of an Ottoman railway network aroused most alarm in Russia, which opposed Turkish railway construction for the very reasons the Turks desired it. The Russians favored the preservation of the Ottoman empire so as to exclude rival powers from this strategic area, but they wanted to keep that empire weak and divided to prevent its becoming a threat to Russian security in its own right and to leave it vulnerable for their eventual takeover. They also feared the competition of Turkish grain and other agricultural products if the provinces of Asiatic Turkey gained access to world markets. But above all they disliked the prospect of Turkish railways along the Black Sea coast and their own frontiers, which would allow for the rapid transport of not only Turkish troops but those of rival powers, a serious threat to Russian security.

The British, with their extensive economic interests in the Near East and their traditional policy of shoring up the Ottoman empire against Russia, generally looked with favor on any projects likely to strengthen that empire, but from the beginning there were British political, military, and economic leaders who regarded a railway through Asiatic Turkey to the Persian Gulf as a threat to British strategic as well as commercial interests, especially because of the German association. Swift and inexpensive overland transport to the Persian Gulf and the waterways to the Pacific would compete with the Suez Canal and do incalculable damage to British shipping and commercial interests in the Mediterranean, the Near East, and the entire Pacific area. The most serious objection to the railway, however, was the same as that of the Russians: rail lines through Asiatic Turkey would make possible the rapid transport of foreign (German) as well as Turkish troops to strategic points throughout the Near East to threaten vital British bases and avenues of communication.

In view of the international clamor eventually raised by German involvement in the Bagdad Railway, it is noteworthy that German entrepreneurs showed scant interest in Turkish railways or any other kind of investment in the Ottoman empire when first approached by the sultan's agents. The German involvement appears to have been initiated by Alfred Kaulla, a German banker who had negotiated munitions contracts in Constantinople; he was sufficiently intrigued by the Turkish government's proposed concessions to bring them to the attention of Georg von Siemens, founder and director of the powerful Deutsche Bank.

In October 1888 the Deutsche Bank accepted a concession to purchase the existing railway from Constantinople to Izmid, some fifty miles to the southeast, and to construct and operate a line from Izmid to Angora, three hundred miles farther east, with the understanding that this line should eventually be extended via Bagdad to the Persian Gulf. The costs of this initial sector of the railway would be guaranteed by taxes from the Turkish provinces through which the line was to pass.

If Bismarck had been fully informed about the Turkish concession and its ultimate scope, he would very probably have opposed its acceptance on political grounds. As it was, he saw no more reason to object to private German investment in the Ottoman empire than to private German advisory missions, but he specifically refused to accept any government responsibility for German money invested in "speculative" enterprises in Turkey.

At first even the political implications of the railroad seemed inconsequential, for neither Kaulla nor Siemens regarded it as an exclusively German enterprise. Having accepted the concession for the Izmid–Angora line, the Deutsche Bank organized a company to build and operate it, the Société du chemin de fer Ottoman d'Anatolie (the Anatolian Railway Company), which the Germans expected would attract a substantial amount of foreign capital. British financiers actually purchased shares to the value of one million pounds but sold them the following year to cover losses in Argentina (banking at least was becoming truly international); and the French, who may have hoped the Germans would not be able to raise the necessary capital and therewith get an opportunity to secure the concession for themselves, refrained from investing altogether. Thus the Anatolian Railway Company was left by default under predominantly German control.

The Izmid–Angora line was completed in 1892, but already two years earlier the sultan was urging the Germans to accept a concession to continue the line eastward to Kaiserieh and beyond. The Deutsche Bank, in a financial crisis of its own, was reluctant to take on this additional responsibility, finally doing so only after the sultan had solicited the personal intervention of the kaiser, who had just begun to get the taste of personal authority after his dismissal of Bismarck. Under pressure from the kaiser, and with new guarantees from the Turkish government, the Deutsche Bank accepted a concession in February 1893 for the Anatolian Railway Company to build two extensions of the existing line en route to Bagdad and the Persian Gulf: one to extend eastward from Angora to Kaiserieh and central Anatolia; the other to run more directly south from a junction on the Angora line to Konya, the ancient Seljuk capital. The Anatolian Railway Company never made use of the Angora–Kaiserieh concession because its directors decided the line via Konya would be cheaper to build and more profitable. Construction on that sector, delayed by the world financial crisis of 1893, was finally completed in 1896.

Foreign interest in Turkish economic enterprises flagged considerably in the mid-1890s, the period of the Armenian massacres and the Cretan crisis, but in October 1898 the kaiser paid his flamboyant visit to the Holy Land proclaiming his friendship for the Muslim peoples. The following January a German syndicate secured a concession to develop the harbor works of Haidar Pasha on the Asiatic shore opposite Constantinople, the point of departure for all major railway lines into Asiatic Turkey. And in November the Anatolian Railway Company was awarded a preliminary concession to continue the Bagdad Railway from Konya all the way to the Persian Gulf.

The award of this concession to a German-controlled company was not so great a threat, either immediate or long range, to the interests of rival powers in the Near East as foreign statesmen and publicists believed it to be. German financiers proved singularly reluctant to take advantage of the apparent economic opportunities open-ing up to them in the Ottoman empire because they doubted the ultimate profita-bility of railways in Anatolia and the security of investments there. As a result, Ger-man concessionaires found it impossible to raise the large funds needed for building the Bagdad Railway in their own country. But even if the German money market had made ample sums available, the concessionaires recognized that they needed to relieve foreign apprehensions about a German-controlled line by securing foreign involvement in its financing, construction, and operation.

Accordingly, well before receiving the preliminary concession of November 1899 to extend the line to the Persian Gulf, the Germans sought British, French, and other foreign participation in the project. The British were too preoccupied with South Africa to be interested in Turkish railways at this time, but in May 1899 the Deutsche Bank concluded an agreement with a French consortium that was to take forty percent of the shares in the Konya–Gulf line.

By January 1902 the surveys for the line were completed, and on January 21 the Turkish government gave the Anatolian Railway Company a definitive concession (to replace the preliminary concession of November 1899) to build it, which in-cluded a guarantee of 16,500 francs per kilometer. The problems of raising funds for so vast an enterprise remained formidable, however, and in February 1903 the French and German firms revised their original agreement and sought changes in the terms of the Turkish concession in order to attract British investors. The resulting new Franco-German-Turkish agreement of March 3, 1903, set up a new company chartered under Turkish law, the Société impériale du chemin de fer de Bagdad (the Bagdad Railway Company), with provisions for equal British, French, and German participation in the construction, management, and control of the Konya–Gulf line. British, French, and German firms were each to be allotted twenty-five percent of the shares of the new company, with the remaining twenty-five percent divided between the Anatolian Railway Company (ten percent) and various other financial groups. Membership on the thirty-man board of directors was to be apportioned on a similar basis, with eight seats each assigned to representatives of British, French, and German interests, and the other six divided among the Anatolian Railway Com-pany (three), Switzerland (two), and Austria (one).

Up to this time the British government had favored the involvement of British investors in the railway as a means of strengthening Turkey and ensuring a British voice in its operation. "It would be a great mistake to oppose the project, which we ought, on the contrary, to encourage to the best of our power," the director of British military intelligence advised in November 1902. When informed of the con-ditions for British participation formulated the following March, the British govern-ment remained favorably disposed to the project but objected to the role assigned the German-controlled Anatolian Railway Company and to the possibility that mem-bership on the board of directors of the Bagdad Railway would be affected by changes in the ownership of its shares. The British therefore demanded that the Anatolian Railway Company be included in arrangements for the Bagdad Railway, thereby ensuring international control of the line all the way from the Bosporus to the Persian Gulf, and that membership on the board of directors not be affected even though ownership of shares should pass to subjects of other countries. Arthur Gwinner, who had succeeded Georg von Siemens as director of the Deutsche Bank upon the latter's death in October 1901, was willing to negotiate with the British on these terms provided they make three concessions of their own: allow the Turks to raise their customs duties and pledge part of the increased revenues as additional guarantees for the Bagdad Railway; assign to the railway as large a share as possible of the Indian mail and passenger service that heretofore went by ship; and provide terminal facilities for the railway at British-controlled Kuwait on the Persian Gulf.

These were very significant demands indeed, for their acceptance would imperil British commercial as well as strategic interests in the Persian Gulf, but the British government was still sufficiently interested in participating to continue negotiations. On April 7, 1903, in reply to questions raised in the House of Commons, Prime Minister Balfour declared that proposals regarding British participation were being considered, and on the following day he argued vigorously in favor of the railway's internationalization. Balfour was obviously influenced by a memorandum from his foreign secretary, Lord Lansdowne, who thought it would be a serious mistake to allow the railway to be built without securing for England "a full share of its development and control, as well as the advantages to be derived from its construction"; the entire question should be treated "as one of common and international interest."

All along, however, there had been opposition in Britain to the entire Bagdad Railway project because the mere existence of such a railway was seen as a threat to British interests, and several articles sharply critical of British participation had already appeared in influential journals when Balfour was first questioned on the subject. Opponents of the railway exploited the intense anti-German sentiment that had developed in Britain at this time to represent the project as an essentially German enterprise from which Germany alone would reap the prestige and profits. Within the cabinet the railway's opponents had a powerful ally in the colonial secretary, Joseph Chamberlain, who had joined the ranks of the Germanophobes after recent unfortunate experiences in negotiating with the Germans (see p. 386). The cabinet quickly gave in to the arguments of Chamberlain and public pressure, and on April 23 Balfour announced in the Commons, to loud cheers, that the government had decided that the terms offered by the Bagdad Railway Company did not guarantee equality of control after all and was therefore rejecting all requests regarding Turkish customs duties, the Indian mails, and the facilities at Kuwait.

In a private letter of April 24 to Lord Curzon, governor-general of India, who had been among the most vigorous opponents of British participation, Lansdowne explained, belatedly and now without any hope of reversing the government's decision, why he considered that decision to have been mistaken. "I believe we had the game very much in our own hands and that we might have done a great stroke by getting rid of the existing Anatolian Railway as a German enterprise, and substituting for it an international line from sea to sea upon conditions that would have permanently secured for it and for its terminus on the Persian Gulf an international character." He predicted that with the opening of every new sector of the railway it would "acquire a more distinctly German complexion" and feared that "in the long run our attitude will be somewhat difficult to explain."

With the British government's refusal to participate in the Bagdad Railway, the Russians increased their pressure on France to refuse as well and to compel the withdrawal of French investments from the project. The French government lacked the power to control French investments but made its opposition clear by prohibiting the listing of its shares on the French stock exchange and warning French investors against participation.

Rebuffed by both the British and French governments, the Bagdad Railway Company was left under predominantly German control. The French government's opposition did not prevent French investments in the railway, however, and bonds for the construction of the first sector of the line beyond Konya were sold by a syndicate headed by the Deutsche Bank that included Austrian and Swiss as well as French representatives, with the French finally taking thirty percent of the total offering.

The first sector beyond Konya, to Bulgurlu, was completed in the autumn of 1904, but even with a substantial infusion of non-German capital the company lacked the funds to push construction through the difficult mountainous terrain of southeastern Anatolia, and it was not until the spring of 1908 that the Ottoman government could provide the financial guarantees the company required to resume construction. Through an agreement of June 2 of that year, the Bagdad Railway Company was empowered to build two extensions of the line beyond Bulgurlu: the first over the Taurus range to Aleppo (Haleb); the second from Aleppo to El Helif and thus to the frontier of Mesopotamia, about four hundred kilometers above Bagdad. Only one month after the conclusion of that agreement, however, construction was delayed again and all German contracts with the Ottoman government seemed threatened as a result of the Bosnian crisis and the Young Turk revolution (see pp. 411–415), whose leaders, at least at first, looked to Britain rather than Germany for support.

German fortunes in Constantinople revived unexpectedly rapidly, however, because of the triumph of pro-German leaders within the Young Turk movement, who recognized the importance of the Bagdad Railway for strengthening their country. By the autumn of 1909 the Young Turk government had given de facto endorsement to the previous government's agreements with the Bagdad Railway Company, and therewith construction of the line through the Taurus Mountains was at last begun.

Up to this time, despite tempting offers from the Germans, the French government had stood firmly behind its Russian ally in opposing the Bagdad Railway, as had the British government since the conclusion of its entente with Russia in 1907 (see pp. 405–407). It was therefore with some consternation that London and Paris received the news that during a visit of the tsar and his foreign minister, Sazonov, to Potsdam in early November 1910 the Russians had negotiated an agreement with Germany abandoning their opposition to the Bagdad Railway in return for German recognition of Russia's preponderant position in northern Persia. A final Russo-German treaty confirming this bargain was not signed until August of the following year, but Potsdam had already broken the united front of Triple Entente opposition to the Bagdad Railway, and the British and French governments now hastened to make bargains of their own with Germany to safeguard their interests.

German negotiations with Britain and France proceeded relatively rapidly, and by the eve of World War I the entire Bagdad Railway business was apparently settled by compromise agreements with these powers as well as with Russia, which in effect divided the Ottoman empire into economic spheres of interest and safeguarded their strategic interests as well. But by this time the suspicion and ill-will generated by the project had contributed significantly to poisoning Germany's relations with all three powers.

In the Ottoman empire itself, however, the Germans had achieved exactly what their opponents had sought to prevent. Through their leading role in the Bagdad Railway and the loans and bribes involved in the concessions for its construction, the Germans had substantially enhanced their prestige and influence in Constantinople. That influence survived the Young Turk revolution and the Bosnian crisis, and was to be powerfully reinforced with the arrival in November 1913 of a German military mission under General Liman von Sanders in response to a Turkish request for help in reorganizing the Turkish army.

With the Germans as with all foreign powers, the Turks played their traditional game of setting the European states off against each other, but the influence gained by the Germans through the Bagdad Railway and their various military missions undoubtedly played a part—though how important a part will never be accurately determined—in Turkey's decision to enter World War I on the German side.

❑

NINETEEN

The United States Enters the Great Power Arena

The rise of the United States to great power status came as no surprise to knowledgeable Europeans, who had long predicted that the United States, with its vast resources and technologically conditioned population, would inevitably take its place among the world's economic giants and that it was only a matter of time before it would play a corresponding role in the world's power politics. The only surprising thing about America's emergence as a great power is how long it took most European governments to appreciate the present and future importance of the United States and how long they persisted in regarding Washington as an insignificant diplomatic outpost where they could unload their mediocrities.

By the end of the nineteenth century the United States had become the world's leading economic power. It surpassed all other nations in the production of coal, oil, and steel. The value of its manufactured products was almost as great as that of Britain, France, and Germany combined; the value of its exports was second only to those of Britain. America's 35,000 miles of railway at the end of the Civil War had grown to 250,000 by 1899; its total exports had risen from 281 million dollars to 1,394 million.

The emergence of the United States as a major factor in global affairs was delayed by the Civil War and the subsequent problems of reconstruction and westward expansion. All along, however, it had been involved in international affairs in one form or another, especially in the Western Hemisphere, and all along there were American leaders who clung to the ambitions of earlier generations to extend American dominion over Canada, Mexico, the Caribbean, and the islands of the Pacific. In 1867 the United States had compelled the French to withdraw from Mexico; in that same year it had purchased Alaska from Russia, an acquisition which for a time seemed to have achieved little more than add to America's chronic disputes with Britain and Canada over boundaries and fishing rights; also in 1867, almost unnoticed, the United States laid claim to the Midway Islands, a harbinger of American interest in the Pacific.

In the decades after the Civil War there was a strong body of opinion in the United States opposed to acquiring overseas or noncontiguous territories. It was only with some difficulty that Secretary of State Seward secured Senate ratification of his treaty with Russia for the purchase of Alaska, which critics scornfully referred to as Seward's ice box. His treaty for the purchase of the Danish West Indies (the Virgin Islands) was rejected, as was a treaty negotiated by the Grant administration in 1870 for the annexation of the Caribbean island of Santo Domingo.

Although its importance was not generally recognized at the time, one of the most significant developments of American foreign policy in the post–Civil War era was a treaty providing for settlement through arbitration of America's major differences with Britain and Canada—disputes over boundaries and fishing rights, and America's demand for compensation for the damage caused by British-built Confederate raiders to Union shipping during the Civil War (the so-called *Alabama* claims). This was the Treaty of Washington of May 8, 1871, negotiated by President Grant's secretary of state Hamilton Fish with the Gladstone government of England. On August 25, 1872, an international tribunal sitting in Geneva awarded the United States 15.5 million dollars in settlement of its *Alabama* claims, more than double the price paid for Alaska. In October of that year the dispute over northwestern boundaries with Canada, which had been submitted for arbitration to the German emperor, was also decided in favor of the United States. The differences over fishing rights were only partly resolved, but all three cases set precedents for similar settlements through arbitration. Still more important, they cleared the way for the diplomatic rapprochement between the two English-speaking peoples that was to be so crucial in international affairs in the next century.

❑ *The Revival of the American Navy and Mahan's Theories*

American attitudes about territorial expansion shifted rapidly toward the end of the century, as large numbers of Americans became enthusiastic converts to a policy of imperialism and the United States joined in the great power scramble for empire. The most obvious evidence of American concern for overseas interests was the revival of its navy, which had been allowed to decline to practical insignificance after the Civil War. That revival owed much to the appointment by President James A. Garfield and his successors of secretaries of the navy who believed in the need for radical improvements and secured appropriations from Congress for the construction of new ships.

Of major importance in the development of the American navy was the founding in 1884 of a Naval War College in Newport, Rhode Island, and the appointment to its faculty in the following year of Captain Alfred Thayer Mahan, who lectured on tactics and naval history. Out of these lectures grew a remarkable book, *The Influence of Sea Power upon History, 1660-1783*. Published in 1890, Mahan's work transformed conventional theories about naval strategy and profoundly affected civilian thinking and public policy.

Drawing largely on the lessons of British history, Mahan developed a thesis that a nation's power and prosperity depended on its commerce, a flourishing domestic economy, and foreign trade, which required a substantial merchant marine and a powerful navy capable of keeping its sea lanes open to the markets of the world. A nation's greatness was therefore directly related to its sea power, but durable sea power in turn depended on a steadily expanding commerce.

Mahan's theories of sea power were integral to his views on empire and imperialism. Essential to both a merchant fleet and navy were secure ports of call for refueling and repairs, but in addition a great commercial nation and steady economic growth required overseas colonies as markets and sources of raw materials. Great as were the resources of the United States, it could not remain an isolated continental power but must follow the example of Britain and seek new outlets for its commercial enterprise. Indeed, it was imperative that it do so, for, as Mahan reviewed the lessons of history, a nation was in the process of either expansion or decline. Permeating his writings were currently fashionable theories of Social Darwinism, the concept of the "survival of the fittest" applied to nations, and a strident nationalism that positively gloried in competition and conflict. The martial spirit alone was capable of coping with "the destructive forces that from outside and within threaten to submerge all that the centuries have gained," and that martial spirit could be preserved only "in the rivalries of nations, in the accentuation of difficulties, in the conflict of ambitions." The best hopes of the world resided "not in universal harmony, nor in any fond dream of unbroken peace," but rather "in the competition of interest, in that reviving sense of nationality, . . . in the jealous determination of each people to provide first for its own."

Mahan's theories of imperialism were very much part of his era's climate of opinion. Far more original were his ideas about the kind of navy the United States needed for the protection of its coasts and commerce and to carry out its national mission. He dismissed as useless the kind of fleet currently in vogue consisting of cruisers and lightly armed vessels capable of carrying out raids on enemy commerce. Instead Mahan called for a navy built around a nucleus of capital ships, a fleet powerful enough to ensure battle supremacy through a wide zone contiguous to America's coasts. Mahan's naval theories had an immediate impact on American naval policy. The 1889 report on the state of the navy by Benjamin Tracy, President Harrison's naval secretary, was pure Mahan. America required a fleet of armored battleships capable of defending its coasts from blockade or attack by posing so great a threat to a blockading fleet that it could not remain in place and by being able to inflict such losses on an enemy that it could not risk an attack "for a war, though defensive in principle, may be conducted most effectively by being offensive in its operations." Specifically the secretary called for the construction of two fleets of battleships, twelve for the Atlantic, eight for the Pacific, each vessel to be equal to the best in existence with respect to armament, firepower, and speed. In addition he wanted sixty fast cruisers, "essential adjuncts to an armored fleet," and at least twenty "floating fortresses" for coastal and harbor defense.

At the same time that he was making recommendations for a navy to meet America's immediate defensive requirements, Mahan was looking beyond the continental United States to a global expansion of American commerce to Latin America and especially to China, and for this purpose an even larger navy would be required, as would far-flung naval bases. Crucial for America's future competition in global markets would be an isthmian canal across Central America. An artificial waterway between the Atlantic and Pacific oceans would increase enormously the mobility of the American navy and America's capacity for commercial competition. It would enable the Atlantic coast "to compete with Europe, on equal terms as to distance, for the markets of eastern Asia, . . . shorten by two-thirds the sea route from New York to San Francisco, and by one-half to Valparaiso." So important a waterway would "become a strategic center of . . . vital importance," its security a paramount objective of national policy that would require establishing indisputable American naval supremacy in the Caribbean as well as the eastern Pacific, the exclusion so far as possible of European powers from these areas, and the acquisition of naval bases at strategic points, in particular Cuba and the Hawaiian Islands. Besides being essential to the defense of the canal and America's coasts, control over Cuba and the Hawaiian Islands would support American commercial expansion in Asia, where Mahan already saw reason to fear the rising power of Japan. The world was entering a period when the question would be decided as to whether the Eastern or Western civilization was to dominate the earth. The mission of Christian civilization, "which it must fulfil or perish," was to overspread and assimilate to its ideals those ancient and different civilizations at the head of which stood China, India, and Japan.

❑ *The Venezuelan Crisis*

Since the promulgation of the Monroe Doctrine in 1823, Americans had come to regard the entire Western Hemisphere as an American protectorate. After the Civil War, they reaffirmed this conception of their role in hemispheric affairs by pressuring the French to leave Mexico; in 1895 they forcefully restated this idea in connection with a boundary dispute between Britain and Venezuela.

At the time Venezuela declared its independence from Spain in 1811, no clear line of demarcation had been established between Venezuela and Dutch Guiana, whose western sector bordering Venezuela was ceded to the British in 1814. In 1840 Palmerston, the British foreign secretary, sent a commission under an engineer named Robert Schomburgk to determine the exact boundary between Venezuela and what was now British Guiana, the most important issue being the disputed territory at the mouth of the Orinoco River, whose possession was considered decisive for controlling trade and the economic resources of the great Orinoco watershed. Schomburgk placed the south bank of the Orinoco within the boundaries of British Guiana, but the Schomburgk line was never accepted by Venezuela and the dispute dragged on. With the discovery of gold in the disputed territory, including the largest single nugget ever found, the boundary controversy became increasingly intense, and in 1888 Venezuela broke off diplomatic relations with Britain.

Long before this diplomatic rupture, the Venezuelan government had appealed to the United States to arbitrate on the grounds that British incursions into territory claimed by Venezuela violated the Monroe Doctrine. To press its case in Washington, it engaged a former American minister to Caracas, William L. Scruggs, who in 1894 published a pamphlet, *British Aggressions in Venezuela, or The Monroe Doctrine on Trial.* So effective were his lobbying efforts that early in 1895 the U.S. Congress passed a joint resolution by unanimous vote urging President Cleveland to "recommend" arbitration "most earnestly" to both sides.

Despite serious criticism of his conduct of foreign affairs, Cleveland did not hurry to respond to the congressional resolution, and it was not until July that his secretary of state, Richard Olney, presented him with the draft of a note to Britain calling for arbitration of the Venezuela boundary issue. Cleveland subsequently referred to that note as "Olney's twenty-inch gun," but he approved and even praised it—"the best thing of the kind I have ever read"—and on July 20 it was sent off, with minor modifications, to Ambassador Thomas Bayard in London.

The Olney note was a remarkable document. With ponderous pedantry, and in terms that were as self-righteous as they were pompous, the secretary of state reviewed the history of American interest in the Western Hemisphere, quoted the Monroe Doctrine at length, and declared that any European disregard of that doctrine would be deemed an act of unfriendliness toward the United States. "Today the United States is practically sovereign in this continent, and its fiat is law upon the subjects to which it confines its interposition." This was so not only because of America's pure friendship and goodwill, not because of "its high character as a civilized state," not even "because wisdom and justice and equity" were "the invariable characteristics of the dealings of the United States." This was so because, in addition to all else—and here Olney resorted to outright threats—America's "infinite resources combined with its isolated position render it master of the situation and practically invulnerable as against any or all other powers." The British government was warned that if it persisted in refusing to have its title to the disputed territory investigated, this refusal would be regarded as "injurious to the interests of the people of the United States." Ambassador Bayard was instructed to read this note (more than seventeen pages long in its printed form) aloud to Lord Salisbury and to demand a decision as to whether the British government would consent or decline to submit to arbitration; the president wanted Britain's answer before he delivered his annual message to Congress in December.

On August 8 Bayard presented Olney's note to Salisbury, who "expressed regret, and surprise that it had been considered necessary to present so far reaching and important a principle and such wide and profound policies of international action, in relation to a subject so comparatively small." He informed the American envoy that so long and elaborate a statement could not be answered quickly, nor did he hasten to do so. Preoccupied with the Armenian question and vexing problems in Africa and East Asia, he did not submit Olney's note to the cabinet until November, at which time the decision was made to deflate American claims and pretensions. This was done in two separate documents, dated November 26. The first stated that the Monroe Doctrine was not recognized as international law and had no application whatever to the dispute with Venezuela; the second maintained that Venezuela's claims were baseless and in effect rejected the American demand for arbitration: Britain could not risk arbitration over any territory that might result in the transfer of "large numbers of British subjects . . . to a nation of different race and language, and whose institutions as yet too often afford very inadequate protection to life and property."

On December 6 Sir Julian Pauncefote, the British ambassador to Washington, presented the British reply to Cleveland, who on December 17 informed Congress of Britain's refusal to arbitrate. Cleveland now asked to be empowered to appoint a boundary commission to investigate the claims of both parties, warning that when the commission's report had been made and accepted the United States must be prepared to uphold it, by force if necessary. The president assured Congress that he was "fully alive" to "all the consequences that may follow," but a great nation could invite no worse calamity than "supine submission to wrong and injustice." A bill embodying the president's request was passed unanimously by both the House and Senate, and on January 4, 1896, Cleveland named the members of the commission. Theodore Roosevelt, ever a passionate defender of his country's honor and interests, expressed the belligerent sentiments shared by many of his compatriots.

"Let the fight come if it must," he said. "I don't care whether our sea coast cities are bombarded or not; we would take Canada."

The imperturbable Salisbury appears to have been prepared to stand firm, but any resentment the British might have felt toward the United States was almost immediately drowned out by the flood of fury and frustration in Britain caused by news of the Jameson raid in South Africa and the kaiser's telegram of congratulation to President Kruger. After a meeting of the cabinet on January 11, Salisbury informed the queen that with respect to Venezuela, "the general impression was that a widespread wish for an honourable arrangement existed, and that every effort should be made to attain it." At the end of the month he wrote to his colonial secretary Joseph Chamberlain, who had previously favored a firm line against the United States, that as their colleagues in the cabinet refused to take any step that might lead to war, Britain might well be compelled to agree to arbitration. He nevertheless saw reason to hope that Cleveland's boundary commission might meanwhile "commit some folly which will prejudice the facts before the ultimate tribunal of arbitration whatever it may be."

Salisbury's cabinet colleagues not only declined any step that might lead to war. They were effusively eager to heal the breach with the United States. In a speech in Manchester on January 15, Arthur Balfour, Salisbury's nephew, chancellor of the exchequer, and leader of the Conservative party in the House of Commons, welcomed the time when "some statesmen of authority, more fortunate even than President Monroe, will lay down a doctrine that between English-speaking peoples war is impossible." And Chamberlain, speaking a few days later in Birmingham, looked forward with pleasure "to the possibility of the Stars and Stripes and the Union Jack floating together in defence of a common cause sanctioned by humanity and by justice."

Notwithstanding their desire to improve relations with the United States, the British still did not hurry matters and almost an entire year of negotiation passed before the British and Americans agreed on the terms of an arbitration treaty to be concluded between Britain and Venezuela—a treaty arranged, it is interesting to observe, without the participation of the Venezuelans. That treaty, dated November 12, 1896, provided for an arbitration tribunal of five members, two to be nominated by the United States, two by Britain, and one by the king of Sweden.

The Venezuelans, who had been informed of the terms of the Anglo-American agreement only on the eve of its signature, were naturally outraged, but under heavy American pressure they at last accepted the treaty that had been drawn up for them. The only concession made in response to Venezuelan protest was that they should be allowed to nominate one member of the boundary commission. That commission, as the Venezuelans had feared, decided substantially in favor of the British position, and the boundary finally established corresponded closely to the Schomburgk line with one significant exception: Venezuela was conceded control over the southern bank of the mouth of the Orinoco River, a concession the British had been prepared to make long since but which the Venezuelans had rejected because they claimed far more.

The Venezuelan boundary crisis, which in itself was of marginal concern to Britain and no concern at all of the United States, was nevertheless a critical turning point in modern diplomatic history, for it marked Britain's recognition of America's supremacy in the Western Hemisphere and, although numerous differences remained to be settled, the transformation of the Anglo-American relationship from one of suspicion and hostility into one of mutual respect and friendship. (See also pp. 380–381.)

□ *Cuba and the Spanish–American War*

The island of Cuba, under Spanish rule since the early sixteenth century, had remained loyal to Spain during the Latin American revolutions of the early nineteenth century and many Spanish loyalists had settled there following the overthrow of Spanish rule on the mainland. In the course of the nineteenth century, however, the population of Cuba had grown increasingly restive. A rebellion in 1868 was only brought under control with great difficulty after ten years of conflict, and in 1895 rebellion flared up anew. To deal with the rebels' guerrilla warfare, the Spanish administration divided the island into military districts and herded much of the civilian population into concentration (*reconcentrado*) camps to deprive the guerrillas of local support. These stringent measures stirred up greater resentment in Cuba and aroused widespread sympathy for the rebel cause in the United States, where reports of Spanish atrocities lost nothing in the telling when related to the sensationalist press by Cuban refugees and well-organized Cuban lobbying groups.

The rebels meanwhile were systematically devastating property on the island to force Spain to pull out or compel the United States to intervene. American intervention had long been urged by humanitarians and Americans with property in Cuba, and in April 1896 Secretary of State Olney warned Spain that intervention was probable unless conditions on the island were stabilized through a program of far-reaching reforms and concessions, for the United States could not "contemplate with complacency another ten years of Cuban insurrection."

In the summer of 1896 the American government sounded out Salisbury as to what Britain's reaction might be in the event of American intervention in Cuba. The British prime minister's reply made it clear that Britain now regarded the Caribbean as an American sphere of influence: Britain was friendly to Spain and would be sorry to see her humiliated, "but we do not consider that we have anything to say in the matter whatever may be the course the United States may decide to pursue."

In October 1897 the Conservative administration in Spain gave way to the Liberals, who had been quite as critical of their government's policies in Cuba as the Americans and who introduced a comprehensive reform program that gave the Cubans a large measure of self-government, though the island was to remain under Spanish sovereignty. But by this time the rebel leaders would settle for nothing short of complete independence.

The Cubans loyal to Spain did not help matters. In January 1898 they staged riots in the Cuban capital of Havana to protest the Spanish government's concessions to the rebels, creating sufficient turmoil to raise doubts about the Spanish administration's ability to deal with the situation. Using the familiar pretext of protecting American lives and property, the United States government sent the gunboat *Maine* to Havana, where on February 15 it was blown up with the loss of 260 American lives. The cause of the disaster was never discovered, but the American press, which for months had padded its circulation with detailed reports of Spanish atrocities in Cuba, left no doubt in its readers' minds that the tragedy was the work of the

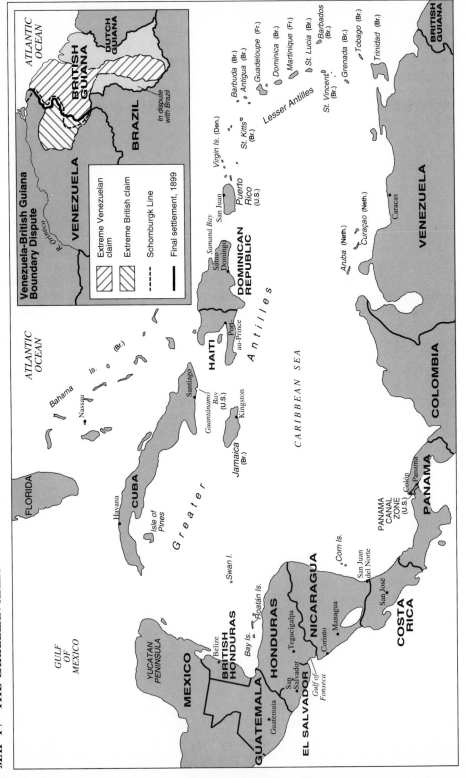

MAP 17 *THE CARIBBEAN AREA*

treacherous Spaniards. Meanwhile American relations with Spain had been damaged still further by the publication of a stolen letter written by the Spanish ambassador to Washington, Dupuy de Lôme, complaining of American hostility to Spain and describing President McKinley as "weak" and a "bidder for the admiration of the crowds."

On March 26 the United States addressed a note to Spain which amounted to an ultimatum: make peace within a month and offer Cuba "full self-government, with reasonable indemnity." When the American ambassador to Madrid asked whether "full self-government, with reasonable indemnity" meant Cuban independence, Acting Secretary of State Day replied that it did.

This American ultimatum led to what amounted to Spain's complete capitulation. On April 5 the American ambassador to Madrid telegraphed McKinley that the queen-regent, at the request of the pope, proposed to proclaim an unconditional suspension of hostilities in Cuba effective as soon as it was accepted by the insurgents. The armistice was to last for six months, by which time she hoped passions would have cooled and a permanent and honorable peace obtained between Spain and the Cuban rebels. If the queen did issue such a proclamation, would President McKinley sustain her and could he prevent hostile action by Congress?

With increasingly alarming reports of the belligerent mood in the United States, the Spanish government decided not to wait for McKinley's response and on April 4 proclaimed an unconditional armistice. The Cubans were promised a constitution "as liberal as that of Canada," and Spain agreed to an investigation of the sinking of the *Maine*. At the same time Spain called upon other powers to use their good offices on behalf of a mediated settlement.

Although European public opinion was generally sympathetic to Spain, the response of the European powers to this request could hardly have been more cautious. On April 6 representatives of the six European great powers, led by Sir Julian Pauncefote, the British ambassador and senior member of the group, presented a joint note to McKinley appealing to his humanity and moderation and expressing the hope that America's differences with Spain could be settled peacefully. It was an appeal the Americans knew they could ignore. In London, the British government had assured the American ambassador that Britain did not propose to take any steps that would not be acceptable to the government of the United States; in Washington, Pauncefote had actually cleared the European note with the acting American secretary of state before submitting it to the president.

By this time the Spaniards had conceded essentially everything the American government had demanded. All they hoped to do now was save face. They were not to be allowed to do so. McKinley's response to the European appeal and the Spanish armistice was a message to Congress on April 11 stating that all the expedients of diplomacy had been exhausted and requesting authority "to take measures to secure a full and final termination of hostilities between the Government of Spain and the people of Cuba, and to secure in the island the establishment of a stable government capable of maintaining order and observing international obligations, insuring peace and tranquility and the security of its citizens as well as our own, and to use the military and naval forces of the United States as may be necessary for these purposes. . . . The issue is now with the Congress." Only at the end of his (very long) message did McKinley inform Congress that on the preceding day, after the preparation of his message, he had received official word that the queen-regent had ordered a suspension of hostilities, "the duration and details of which have not yet been communicated to me." The president expressed his confidence that this fact, together with every other pertinent consideration, would "have your just and careful attention. . . . If this measure [presumably the armistice] attains a successful result, then our aspirations as a Christian, peace-loving people will be realized. If it fails, it will only be another justification for our contemplated action."

McKinley's blatantly false statement that all diplomatic expedients had been exhausted and his offhand treatment of the Spanish armistice and other concessions were too much even for the pro-American Pauncefote, who on April 14 again summoned the ambassadors of the major European powers to the British embassy. Here they drew up similarly worded telegrams to their respective governments to urge the United States to agree to a peaceful settlement: Spanish offers for a settlement eliminated all justification for war. According to the French and German envoys, Pauncefote took a leading part in drawing up these telegrams, and Jules Cambon, the French ambassador, quoted Pauncefote as saying that the United States could not be allowed to engage in this "act of brigandage" without expressions of protest in the name of the public conscience of Europe. From London, Balfour, the acting foreign secretary, replied the next day that Britain was "ready to join in any response that is agreed upon by the other Powers in favour of peace," but it seemed very doubtful "whether we ought to commit ourselves to any judgement adverse to the United States, and whether in the interests of peace anything can be gained by doing so." After consultation with Chamberlain, the colonial secretary, Balfour sent a second and more precise instruction to Pauncefote: "Do nothing." The reaction of the kaiser, who at an earlier stage of the crisis had vigorously advocated a joint European note, was similar to that of the British. "I think it absolutely mistaken, pointless, and therefore harmful. We should put ourselves in the wrong with the Americans." With both Britain and Germany abstaining from any kind of protest, the note drawn up by the European ambassadors was never presented to the American government.

The American Congress gave short shrift to McKinley's appeal to give "just and careful attention" to the Spanish armistice. On April 20 a joint resolution was passed by unanimous vote recognizing the freedom and independence of the people of Cuba, demanding that Spain evacuate the island, and directing the president to use force to ensure these results. In an amendment to this resolution, accepted without debate or a vote, the United States disclaimed all intention of imposing its own authority on Cuba "except for the pacification thereof, and . . . when that is accomplished, to leave the government and control of the island to its people."

In response to this American ultimatum, Spain broke off diplomatic relations with the United States on April 21 and declared war three days later. On April 25 Congress declared that a state of war with Spain had existed since April 21.

Although Cuba was the issue that set off the American war with Spain, the first major engagement in that war took place in Manila Bay in the Philippines on the other side of the world. As early as February 25, 1898, Theodore Roosevelt, the assistant secretary of the navy, had instructed Commodore George Dewey, the commander of American naval forces in the Pacific, to concentrate every effective unit at the British base of Hong Kong; if war came he was to prevent the Spanish flotilla from leaving the Pacific and to undertake an offensive against the Philippine Islands. On April 24, a full day before America's official declaration of war, Dewey was instructed to "proceed at once to the Philippine Islands. Commence operations at once, particularly against the Spanish fleet. You must capture vessels or destroy. Use utmost endeavors."

On May 1 Dewey arrived at Manila Bay, where the greater part of Spain's antiquated and ill-equipped Pacific fleet was conveniently concentrated, and within hours it was destroyed. Up to that time the American government had no plans for the future of the Philippines. After his victory at Manila Bay, Dewey asked that troops be sent to the islands to secure naval bases that would be indispensable if an American fleet were to remain in Philippine waters, and he made it clear that only the presence of that fleet could prevent a takeover of the islands by rival powers.

The American government responded quickly to Dewey's request, but the army was ill-prepared for so distant a campaign and it was not until June 30 that American troops arrived in the Philippines. With the support of local insurgents, however, they had little difficulty overcoming Spanish resistance. Despite Filipino moves to set up their own independent government, the Americans refused to relinquish their newly established authority and at the end of the war the islands were still under American military occupation.

In the Caribbean as in the Pacific, Spanish naval forces were no match for those of the United States, although rumors of a Spanish naval attack set off a brief panic on America's eastern seaboard. The Spanish, however, had no such capabilities. Their naval vessels sought refuge in the Cuban harbor of Santiago, and when they ventured forth to do battle for the honor of Spain they were destroyed as quickly as their Pacific fleet had been in Manila Bay. In Cuba as in the Philippines, the American army received support from local insurgents so that despite incredible disorganization it easily defeated the Spanish forces, now totally cut off from outside support.

On July 19 the Spanish government appealed to France to arrange an armistice, which was concluded on August 12. The American terms were stringent: Spain was to renounce all claims to Cuba, Puerto Rico, and all other Spanish islands in the West Indies, and to cede one island, to be named later, in the Ladrones (Marianas) group in the Pacific. As to the Philippines, the victor would "hold the city, bay, and harbor of Manila" until a final settlement had been determined as to its "control, disposition, and government." Commissioners representing Spain and the United States, not exceeding five in number, were to meet in Paris no later than October 1 to negotiate a final settlement.

In his instructions to the American commissioners of September 16, 1898, McKinley asked that the concessions made in the armistice be confirmed in the final treaty and informed them that the United States had selected Guam as the island to be ceded in the Ladrones. "The Philippines stand upon a different basis," but the fact remained that "without any original thought of complete or even partial acquisition, the presence and success of our arms at Manila imposes on us obligations which we cannot disregard." Besides, "incidental to our tenure in the Philippines is the commercial opportunity to which American statesmanship can not be indifferent."

The final peace treaty between Spain and the United States, signed in Paris on December 10, 1898, confirmed the terms of the armistice of August 12 but secured for the United States even more than McKinley had envisaged. While forcing Spain to relinquish all sovereign rights over Cuba, the United States simply took over from Spain sovereign rights over Puerto Rico and all other Spanish-held islands in the Caribbean, the island of Guam in the Pacific, and the entire Philippine archipelago. In taking possession of the Philippines, the United States ignored the pleas of native Filipino leaders to be treated as the Cubans and be granted freedom and independence.

In deciding to annex the Philippines, McKinley subsequently told a group of clergymen that he had turned to God for guidance. God had duly provided it: to give the islands back to Spain would have been cowardly and dishonorable and "opposed to the interests of humanity"; to turn them over to France or Germany, America's commercial rivals in the Orient, would have been bad for business and therefore discreditable (it is indicative of America's new relationship with Britain that McKinley made no mention of that country, which had actually offered to receive them); nor could he leave the Filipinos to themselves, for they were unfit for self-government. So there was nothing left to do but take them all, "to educate the Filipinos, and uplift and civilize and Christianize them [McKinley had conveniently forgotten that the Spaniards had been engaged in this endeavor since they first took over the islands] and by God's grace to do the very best we could by them."

The Filipinos themselves did not share American views about their fitness for self-government or welcome America's civilizing and Christianizing mission. The Filipino leader Emilio Aguinaldo, who had taken part in a rebellion against Spain in 1896, returned from exile in 1898 to help overthrow Spanish rule, promptly issuing a Filipino declaration of independence, which the Americans refused to recognize. In February 1899 open warfare broke out between Filipinos and American occupation forces, and for the next three years as many as 125,000 American troops were engaged in the islands before Filipino resistance was finally crushed. In the course of that conflict some 200,000 Filipinos lost their lives, and critics of American policy observed that the American response to guerrilla warfare was not significantly different from that of the Spaniards in Cuba, whose atrocities they had so vigorously and virtuously denounced.

In Cuba, the Americans were restricted by their promise to grant complete independence to the Cuban people. American forces nevertheless remained on the island after the war and a native Cuban administration was organized under the auspices of American military government. On February 21, 1901, a Cuban constituent assembly, elected under American supervision, adopted a constitution establishing a government modeled on that of the United States. Later, at American insistence, the Cubans were obliged to incorporate into their constitution the so-called Platt amendment (to the American arms appropriations bill of 1901–1902), which reduced Cuba to the status of an American dependency. That amendment prohibited Cuba from concluding any treaty with a foreign power that might endanger Cuban sovereignty or from contracting similarly endangering debts to foreign powers; it provided that the United States might intervene to protect Cuban independence or to maintain a government in Cuba capable of preserving life, property, and personal liberty; finally, to enable the United States to carry out its supervisory commitments, Cuba was obliged to lease territory to the United States for naval bases and coaling stations. Two years later, to make certain the Cubans could not expunge the Platt amendment from their constitution, the Americans made it part of a formal treaty with Cuba.

With its takeover of Puerto Rico and agreements with Cuba, the United States acquired bases ensuring its supremacy in the Caribbean and protection for the eastern access to a future isthmian canal. Long before Dewey's victory in Manila Bay the Americans had also begun to acquire bases in the Pacific, though at first in a seemingly haphazard manner. Several islands south of the Hawaiian group were acquired in 1857–1858, the Midway Islands in 1867, and in the 1880s the United States became involved in altercations with Britain and Germany over the Samoan Islands, which in 1889 came under joint Anglo-American-German supervisory control. In the Hawaiian Islands, where American missionaries and traders first arrived in the 1820s, American interests carried out a revolution in 1893 against the native government and arranged for the islands to be annexed to the United States. President Cleveland, however, withdrew the annexation treaty from the Senate and demanded an investigation of the affair, and for the next five years Hawaii was the subject of bitter partisan debate.

The war in the Philippines revived American interest in Pacific bases. On May 10, 1898, an American naval vessel en route to the Philippines was ordered to seize Guam, which was surrendered by its weak Spanish garrison on June 22 and formally ceded to the United States after the war. In July Congress finally settled the problem of Hawaii by passing a resolution for the annexation of the islands. In that same month an American force landed on Wake Island, which was formally claimed for the United States the following January. The final disposition of the Samoan Islands was arranged in November 1899 when Britain concluded a treaty with Germany relinquishing its rights to the Samoan group in return for concessions elsewhere and providing for the division of the islands between Germany and the United States. The final division was arranged through a tripartite treaty of December 2 which awarded Germany the islands of Upolu and Savaii and the United States the island of Tutuila, whose harbor of Pago Pago was to become an important American naval base.

There were two significant international repercussions of the Spanish–American War. One of these was a further strengthening of Anglo-American friendship, a process considerably aided by Britain's renewed recognition of American supremacy in the Caribbean and its encouragement of American annexations in the Caribbean and the Pacific: if America was to be a friend and ally, Britain could only desire that this ally should be in the best possible position to protect its own, and British, interests.

The second repercussion was a corresponding worsening of German–American relations. In contrast to the British press, that of Germany had generally been pro-Spain, but a far more serious American grievance was Germany's behavior in the Philippines. After Dewey's victory at Manila Bay, the British, French, German, and Japanese governments had sent warships into Philippine waters to protect the lives and property of their citizens. It was the arrival of these foreign squadrons that had prompted Dewey to request the dispatch of American troops to the islands to prevent their takeover by foreign powers, a possibility that figured prominently in the American decision to retain them. In the American view, the German squadron in the Philippines was far larger than necessary and its presence especially resented because of the Germans' alleged disregard for the rules of identification and anchorage. On May 7 a German warship in Subic Bay was reported to have openly supported the Spaniards against the Filipino insurgents. Far greater indignation was aroused by the story, which gained widespread credence, that the Germans were prevented from intervening against the Americans during their final assault on Manila only by the friendly interposition of the British, whose warships lay, quite by accident, between the German and American squadrons. Again in contrast to the British, the Germans made no attempt to hide their displeasure over the American takeover of the entire Philippine archipelago or of their own desire for a share of the Spanish spoils.

❑ *The Panama Canal*

From their very arrival in Central America, the Spaniards had dreamed, as others must have before them, of cutting a canal across the narrow isthmus that separated the Atlantic and Pacific oceans, but it was not until the technological developments of the nineteenth century that the dream became practicable.

The first country to undertake construction of a canal in Central America was France. Encouraged by their success in building the Suez Canal, French entrepreneurs organized a company which in May 1878 negotiated a treaty with Colombia granting exclusive rights to construct a canal across the Isthmus of Panama, at that time still part of Colombia. In the following year a Panama Canal Company was organized under the nominal leadership of Ferdinand de Lesseps, the chief engineer of the Suez project, and in 1880 work began. The engineering difficulties encountered in Panama were far different and far greater than those of Suez, and the yellow fever endemic in the region proved fatal to large numbers of technicians sent to direct operations. Besides these natural problems, the directorship of the company proved to be both incompetent and corrupt. French citizens from all walks of life had eagerly invested in the enterprise, motivated in many cases as much by patriotism as by prospects of financial gain. As disasters mounted in Panama, the company directors bribed legislators and journalists to hide the facts from the public, and when the company went into bankruptcy in February 1889 the resulting scandal shook the very foundations of the Third Republic. Five years later a second company was organized which resumed work on the canal until 1899, but even by that time little actual construction had been accomplished.

The United States, too, had long been interested in an isthmian canal, an interest quickened by Mahan's writings and the war with Spain, which had revealed the pressing need for faster passage of naval vessels between the two oceans. Before anything could be done about the actual construction of a canal, however, the United States faced a critical policy decision and a number of diplomatic difficulties.

The policy decision concerned the route the canal was to take: Should it run through Panama, the shorter route where there were major engineering difficulties to be overcome, as the French experience showed, or through Nicaragua, which though a longer route had the advantage of numerous natural waterways including Lake Nicaragua in the southeastern part of the country? Although a commission appointed by the president reported in favor of the Nicaragua route, the French

Panama Canal Company, eager to salvage something from its investments, lobbied successfully in favor of the Panama route, which was the one ultimately selected by President Theodore Roosevelt in 1903.

Once the decision was made in favor of the Panama route, the United States had to obtain construction rights previously conceded to the French Panama Canal Company. But there was an additional and more delicate diplomatic difficulty to be overcome. As long ago as April 19, 1850, the United States had concluded an agreement with Britain (the Clayton–Bulwer Treaty) which provided that neither power should seek exclusive control over a future isthmian canal and that such a canal should be neutralized, meaning that no power should be allowed to garrison or fortify it in a manner that might prejudice the rights of others.

By the time the Americans began to think seriously about actually constructing a canal, they decided it was essential to have exclusive control as well as the right to defend it, and they therefore sought the amendment or outright abrogation of the Clayton–Bulwer Treaty. Negotiations with the British were initiated soon after the war with Spain, and by December 1898 Secretary of State Hay and Pauncefote, the British ambassador, had worked out amendments to the original treaty which Hay believed met all American requirements. These amendments met with objections on both sides of the Atlantic. The British believed that in return for the concessions they were being asked to make the Americans should agree to a "benevolent settlement" of differences over boundary questions, fishing rights, and other matters of mutual concern, whereas the Americans complained that the concessions secured by Hay were inadequate.

British resistance crumbled in 1899 with the outbreak of the Boer War and the prospect of foreign intervention in that conflict, and by the end of the year the British government gave up its demands for reciprocity and sacrificed Canadian interests on behalf of American friendship. With British objections removed, Hay proceeded to conclude an agreement with Britain (the first Hay–Pauncefote Treaty) in February 1900, but the American Senate was still dissatisfied and refused to ratify the treaty without additional amendments, which totally altered its meaning. Now it was the turn of the British to balk. The treaty as amended by the Americans was decisively rejected in Parliament, and Lord Lansdowne, who had taken over as foreign secretary from Lord Salisbury in January 1901, complained bitterly about the Americans' one-sided conditions. He nevertheless assured them that his government "would sincerely regret a failure to come to an amicable understanding in regard to this important subject." Negotiations therefore continued, and once again the British saw no alternative but to yield on every significant point. A second Hay–Pauncefote Treaty, signed November 18, 1901, specifically suspended the Clayton–Bulwer Treaty of 1850, granting the United States the exclusive right to construct, maintain, and control the canal, and, although the treaty omitted any mention of fortification, the British conceded this right in a separate memorandum.

The second Hay–Pauncefote Treaty reaffirmed yet again Britain's recognition of American supremacy in the Western Hemisphere. Quite as significantly, it demonstrated anew the British government's determination to remain on good terms with the United States.

Having concluded its negotiations with Britain, the United States faced a second diplomatic problem: securing from the government of Colombia the construction rights previously conceded to the French. This was done through the negotiation of an agreement with Tomas Herrán, the Colombian envoy to Washington (the Hay–Herrán Treaty of January 23, 1903), which transferred to the United States the right to build, operate, and control a ship canal across the Isthmus of Panama, together with control over a three-mile strip of territory on either side of that waterway. The treaty was to run for 100 years and was to be renewable for similar periods. In exchange, the United States agreed to pay Colombia 10 million dollars immediately, and an annuity of 250,000 dollars beginning in 1912. The Hay–Herrán Treaty was approved by the United States Senate on March 23. It was rejected by the Colombian senate, by unanimous vote, on August 12. The Colombians thought they should be paid far more for the canal rights and were justifiably fearful that the treaty would jeopardize their sovereignty over the rest of Panama.

The Colombians soon learned that America's fiat was indeed law upon this continent. On November 3, 1903, a group of Panamanians, with the support and encouragement of officials of the French Panama Canal Company (who did not wish to lose America's payment for *their* rights), carried out a revolution against the Colombian government and on the following day proclaimed Panama's independence. Within forty-eight hours Secretary of State Hay had instructed his consul in Panama to enter into diplomatic relations with the new government, on November 13 the United States extended full diplomatic recognition to the new Republic of Panama, and two days later the United States began negotiations with the Panamanian government for a canal treaty.

These negotiations did not take long. On November 18 the United States and Panama signed a treaty giving the Americans even more generous terms than those obtained in their previous treaty with Colombia. The United States was conceded the canal zone in perpetuity, not just for 100 years, and a strip of territory on either side of five instead of three miles, as well as four small but strategically located islands in Panama Bay guarding the Atlantic end of the proposed canal. Within that zone the United States would have the authority to act "as if it were sovereign" with the right to build, maintain, and operate the canal, to fortify and defend it. Instead of Colombia, it was Panama that was now to receive 10 million dollars immediately and 250,000 dollars annually starting in 1912. The only new obligation assumed by the United States was to guarantee the independence of the Panamanian state.

Although no evidence has been found establishing a direct connection between the American government and the Panamanian revolution, President Theodore Roosevelt took considerable pride in his speed and determination in taking advantage of it. He responded to criticism of the whole unsavory episode with customary vigor. "Have I defended myself?" he asked his secretary of war Elihu Root. "You certainly have, Mr. President. You have shown that you were accused of seduction and you have conclusively proved that you were guilty of rape."

The Roosevelt government made sure that it should control not only the canal but the state of Panama itself. To be able to honor its guarantee of Panama's independence the United States demanded the right to intervene in that country to maintain order, a right embodied in the text of the constitution of the new republic adopted on February 13, 1904. On April 3, 1904, the United States purchased the property of the French canal company for forty million dollars, a transaction negotiated long since but delayed by the need to secure the prior consent of the governments of Colombia/Panama. The construction of the canal was authorized by an act of Congress of June 29, 1906. It was opened to traffic in 1914.

To leave the rest of the world no doubt about America's interpretation of the Monroe Doctrine or the fact that America regarded itself as supreme in the Western Hemisphere, President Roosevelt in his annual message to Congress of December 6, 1904, set forth what became known at the Roosevelt Corollary of the Monroe Doctrine. This proclamation was prompted by the efforts of certain European powers to collect debts owed by the Dominican Republic, the kind of problem that had provoked European interference in Latin American affairs in the past.

In the first place, Roosevelt called for the permanent maintenance of a powerful army and navy to enable the United States to back up its policies, by force if necessary. But while remaining strong, the steady aim of the United States, as of all enlightened nations, should be to create a world of peace and justice. To this end he proposed to lay before the Senate arbitration treaties with all powers willing to enter into them, and he called upon the powers to join with the United States in a second Hague conference to carry on the work already begun there (see pp. 366–369).

At the same time Roosevelt recognized that at this stage of the world's development it was not yet possible to settle all international differences through arbitration, and that "chronic wrong-doing" might "ultimately require intervention by some civilized nation." In the Western Hemisphere, however, the Monroe Doctrine precluded the intervention by non-American powers. It was therefore the responsibility of the United States to exercise, "however reluctantly," an international police power in cases of "flagrant wrong-doing" on the part of the states in the Western Hemisphere. While those states obeyed the primary laws of civilized society, they could be assured of American sympathy. "We would interfere with them only in the last resort, and then only if it became evident that their inability or unwillingness to do justice at home and abroad had violated the rights of the United States or had invited foreign aggression to the detriment of the entire body of American nations."

To Americans who shared Roosevelt's confidence in the superiority of their own country's civilization, the Roosevelt Corollary was a self-evident and even altruistic statement of principle, but this bland assumption of American superiority and the United States's frequent use of its self-assigned right to intervene in hemispheric affairs—so often in causes of dubious propriety—was destined to stir up a cauldron of resentment, which continues to boil.

TWENTY

❑

Attention Reverts to Europe

As the imperial rivalries among the European powers extended to the remotest regions of Asia and Africa, and with the entry of Japan and the United States into the international arena, great power diplomacy had become truly global in scope. Yet only a few years after the turn of the century, with imperialism seemingly still in its heyday, the European powers turned their attention back to relations with each other and renewed concern about the European balance of power. Ironically, a major reason for this shift from global to more parochial concerns was Germany's embarkation on a global policy.

Bismarck had worked hard and not altogether successfully to calm international apprehensions about the threat to the European equilibrium posed by Germany's immense increase in strength following its unification. Although Bismarck did embark on a colonial policy in the mid-1880s, his conduct of foreign affairs after 1871 was fundamentally conservative and dedicated to preserving peace and the status quo, the surest and certainly the cheapest way to maintain the state he had created. This conservative policy was abandoned by William II. His frenetic and heavy-handed efforts to ensure Germany's status as a world power by acquiring a global empire and building a world-class navy made the other European powers increasingly aware of what they came to regard as the German menace and obliged them to adjust their policies accordingly. But even before William II had made Germany the focal point of European concern, the policies of other major European powers had taken significant new directions.

The British had been jolted into recognizing their need to settle differences with rival powers during the Transvaal crisis and by the outbreak of the Boer War in 1899, when the surge of hostility toward Britain throughout continental Europe seemed likely to result in the formation of an anti-British continental coalition. To eliminate or at least reduce this danger, the British saw that they could no longer afford to adhere to their policy of diplomatic isolation and must enter into coalitions of their own. Their various bids for foreign alliances included lengthy negotiations with Germany, which broke down as the British began to perceive Germany itself as the major threat to their interests and security. They had greater success with Japan, but the primary purpose of their 1902 alliance with that country was still the

364

protection of British imperial interests. Very different were their 1904 and 1907 ententes with France and Russia, which involved comprehensive compromises over colonial differences and were negotiated for the primary purpose of defending the European balance of power against Germany—in other words, for the protection of Britain itself.

The French had long regarded Germany as the major threat to *their* interests and security, and bitterly though they might resent past humiliations at the hands of Britain in their imperial rivalries, the loss of Alsace and Lorraine to Germany always loomed larger in their national consciousness. The French therefore welcomed the opportunity to arrange a compromise colonial settlement with Britain, especially as the British were offering generous territorial compensations in North Africa. But, as French statesmen acknowledged frankly at the time, the principal attraction of an entente with Britain, like that of their earlier alliance with Russia, was that it offered new hope for recovering their lost provinces in Europe. To strengthen their international position still further, the French vigorously and ultimately successfully promoted an entente between Britain and Russia to round out their own agreements with those powers.

The timing of these French diplomatic efforts was propitious. Following their defeat by Japan in 1905, the Russians made the best settlement they could in East Asia and once again directed their attention to the West. Their catastrophic postwar financial position also left them more dependent, politically and economically, on their French allies and therefore more amenable to French diplomatic and financial pressure to reach a settlement with Britain, pressure that bore fruit with the conclusion of the Anglo-Russian entente of 1907.

With Italy too the French waged a successful diplomatic campaign. Although Italy remained a nominal member of the Triple Alliance until 1915, the Italians concluded agreements with France early in the century which in effect nullified their treaty obligations to Germany and Austria. The Italians were lured into the French camp by promises of territorial gain at the expense of the Ottoman empire in North Africa. But for many patriotic Italians, who in any case had never been comfortable in alliance with their former Austrian overlords, the principal attraction of the French connection (as the entente with Britain had been for patriots in France) was the prospect of French support to acquire what they regarded as unredeemed Italian territory in Europe still held by Austria—*Italia irredenta.*

Alone among the European powers, Austria had not embarked on a global policy. Beset by economic and ethnic difficulties, surrounded by states great and small eager to promote and profit from the disintegration of the Habsburg realm, Austria was in no condition to engage in global competition and confined its foreign policy operations to the Balkans. While Russia was occupied primarily in East Asia, Austria and Russia cooperated to maintain a certain stability in southeastern Europe, but after Russia's defeat by Japan and the reversion of its attention to the West, the Austro-Russian rivalry in the Balkans revived. As in the 1870s the Russians sought to exploit their ethnic and religious relationship with the Slavic and Christian Orthodox populations of the Balkans to strengthen their own position, and they encouraged nationalist agitation among Austria's neighbors and within the Habsburg realm to weaken their Austrian rivals. In what had by now become a struggle for sheer survival, Austria turned with increasing desperation to Germany for support.

And Germany, with Austria as its only remaining ally, saw no alternative but to provide it.

In considering the problems of Austria and the Near East in general, two critical changes in Britain's conduct of foreign policy around the turn of the century require attention. The first is Britain's quasi-abandonment of its traditional role of shoring up the Ottoman empire, which had long stood in the way of good relations with Russia, and where Germany, with its military missions and Bagdad Railway, was inserting itself as a buffer between these two ancient antagonists.

The second change is a comparable British abandonment of Austria. In one sense this was natural enough because Austria was Germany's ally and Russia's principal rival in the Balkans, but this change involved dangers which the British failed to perceive or refused to acknowledge. They emphatically declared their determination to maintain the European balance of power and reminded Germany repeatedly that they would be obliged to intervene should the integrity of France be threatened, but they did not take a similarly firm position on behalf of Austria, which was also part of the European balance. Nor did they seem to appreciate that Germany was bound to take as strong a stand against any threat to the integrity of Austria as Britain was with respect to France.

For the Ottoman empire, the Bagdad Railway proved no substitute for the British navy or Britain's overall diplomatic support, and by 1912 a coalition of Balkan states formed under Russian auspices conquered almost all of what was left of the Turkish empire in Europe. Austria's struggle to avoid a similar fate was to be a key factor in the July crisis of 1914.

❑ *The First and Second Hague Peace Conferences*

Before turning to a detailed discussion of Germany's global policy and the shifts in the policies of Germany's European rivals, mention should be made of the first efforts of the great powers since 1815 to set up political machinery for the peaceful settlement of international disputes. In August 1898, while Russia was still pursuing a vigorous imperialist policy in East Asia, Tsar Nicholas II appealed to the states of the world to meet in conference to study "the most effective means of ensuring for all peoples the benefits of a real and lasting peace, and in particular to put an end to the progressive development of existing armaments."

The tsar's appeal, like that of his ancestor Alexander I on behalf of a Holy Alliance, was greeted with cynical amusement not unmixed with resentment by many leaders of the great powers. Industrial and technological developments of the past century had contributed to an immense proliferation of more effective—and expensive—weaponry, resulting in an arms race that imposed ever greater burdens on the economies of all the powers but was most difficult to sustain by those states with the least developed industrial bases. Since Russia was a prime example of a country whose industrial economy was lagging behind that of other major powers, cynics among foreign observers saw in the tsar's appeal nothing more than a ploy disguised as humanitarian concern to escape the consequences of his country's economic backwardness.

The tsar's appeal evoked a far more sympathetic response among the peoples of the world than among their governments. Taxpayers everywhere were feeling the burden of the increasing costs of armaments, but even more important was a growing and even passionate concern among humanitarians about the destructive power of the new weaponry, which promised to make future wars even more grim than those of the past in terms of human and material destruction.

Despite whatever cynicism they may have felt, twenty-six states, including all the countries of Europe along with the United States and Japan, responded positively to the tsar's appeal and agreed to send representatives to the conference he proposed. Their most obvious reason for doing so was to avoid offending Russia, but the world's smaller states and powers with economic difficulties comparable to those of Russia, notably Austria and Italy, had a genuine interest in arms limitation. Further, not a single government could ignore the rising tide of humanitarian concern and expose itself to the world as being opposed to peace.

Muraviev, the Russian foreign minister, described the objectives of the proposed conference in a circular of January 11, 1899. These should include the negotiation of an international agreement to limit and reduce armaments and military armaments budgets; to prevent the use of destructive weapons such as new explosives, submarines, and projectiles dropped from the air; to devise more stringent laws and controls for the conduct of war; and, finally, to promote peaceful resolution of international conflicts through mediation and arbitration.

The conference proposed by the tsar convened in the Dutch capital of The Hague on May 18, 1899, the tsar's birthday. Most of the delegations were headed by experienced diplomats and included military, naval, and legal experts, but the mood among them was anything but optimistic and many delegates were indignant at being called upon to participate in what they regarded as a hypocritical farce. The atmosphere was described by Andrew D. White, the head of the American delegation, which included the president of Columbia University and Alfred Thayer Mahan, the world's most celebrated naval theorist. "Probably since the world began," White wrote in his diary on the day before the opening session, "never has so large a body come together in a spirit of more hopeless skepticism as to any good results."

The Germans took the lead in pointing out the practical difficulties of arms control and opposing any limitation, much less reduction, of weaponry. Though they were doing no more than expressing the views of other leading industrial powers, their scornful and adamant attitude gratuitously drew upon themselves the blame for the conference's failure to make meaningful progress and conjured up before the world, yet again, the image of a saber-rattling Reich. The American secretary of state John Hay, for example, also thought the tsar's proposals were "lacking in credibility" and that to discuss them would do more harm than good. The British War Office agreed that it would not be desirable to accept "any restrictions upon the employment of further developments in destructive agencies," or "to assent to an international code on the laws and evolution of war."

The French were very guarded in their public statements, but they too opposed arms control and actually encouraged the Germans to take the initiative in dealing with the question. "We have quite the same interests in this conference as you," Delcassé, the French foreign minister, told Count Münster, the head of the German delegation, who was also ambassador to Paris. "You do not wish to limit your power of defense at this moment nor to have anything to do with proposals for disarmament. We are entirely in the same position. We mutually wish to spare the tsar and to seek a formula to circumvent the question." But it was also necessary to consider European public opinion, which had been greatly excited "by this ill-considered initiative on the part of Russia."

In the end a resolution was adopted unanimously that "the Conference is of the opinion that the restriction of military budgets . . . is extremely desirable for the increase of the material and moral welfare of mankind." The various resolutions on the use of weaponry and conduct of war were similarly innocuous.

The Germans were also in the forefront in opposing the proposal for compulsory arbitration of international disputes. They argued that much of their strength lay in their army's ability to mobilize and strike quickly, and that a long period of arbitration would deprive them of this advantage. They also objected to an Anglo-American proposal to set up a permanent court of arbitration on the grounds that such a tribunal would be composed of representatives of sovereign states and therefore could never be impartial. The kaiser was infuriated by the idea of a permanent court and arbitration in general. He had promised the tsar to help secure a satisfactory result of the conference. "I have agreed to this nonsense to prevent him from making a fool of himself before all Europe. But in practice I will continue as before to trust only in God and my sharp sword! And will shit on all the resolutions!"

The American Andrew White warned the Germans about the consequences of their emperor's attitude. The tsar would now become the hero of the "plain people" of the world, the kaiser their villain. "The ministers of the German Emperor ought to tell him that, should he oppose arbitration, there will be concentrated upon him an amount of hatred which no minister ought to allow a sovereign to incur," he told Münster. According to White, Münster could only reply: "That is true, but there is not a minister in Germany who dares to tell him." In fact it was Münster who finally persuaded his government to agree to a permanent court in order to avoid incurring still more international opprobrium.

The Convention for the Pacific Settlement of International Disputes finally accepted by the conference contained three main provisions: it entitled any signatory state not party to a dispute to extend its good offices for mediation; it recommended that commissions of inquiry be set up for investigating any situation that threatened the peace, but their findings would not be binding on the disputants; and it established a permanent court of arbitration, which again would have no authority but serve as a mere board of appeal. The article defining the role of the court stated that "the signatory powers consider it a duty in the event of an acute conflict threatening to break out between two or more of them to remind these latter that the permanent court is open to them. This action is only to be considered as an exercise of good offices."

A more innocuous statement could hardly have been formulated. Yet the permanent court created to serve as an instrument for international arbitration was actually to be employed in settling international disputes, and though its decisions were ignored by states powerful enough to do so, the principle of arbitration had been given material form and endorsed by the world's major powers.

The Hague conference adjourned on July 29, 1899. Three months later the Boer War began in South Africa. Neither the British nor the Boers submitted their case to the Hague court or to arbitration of any kind. Moreover, only a few days after the conference adjourned, the French and Russian foreign ministers exchanged notes extending indefinitely their 1893–1894 military convention, which provided for the immediate mobilization of both powers in the event of the mobilization of any member of the Triple Alliance (see pp. 261–262).

A second international peace conference, originally proposed by Theodore Roosevelt (see p. 363), met in the Hague on June 15, 1907, but all prospects that it might achieve something meaningful on behalf of the preservation of peace were clouded from the start. As in 1899 the tsar was conceded the honor of convening the conference, but, with his own country so recently defeated in war and engulfed in revolution, he now objected to any discussion of arms limitation. On this question he had the support of all other major powers apart from Britain, but once again it was Germany that took the lead in opposing not only arms limitation but the compulsory arbitration of international disputes. In the end the "principle" of compulsory arbitration was accepted unanimously, but only after the article was so watered down as to render it meaningless. It stated only that international disputes *"may* [author's emphasis] be submitted to compulsory arbitration without restriction," which of course meant that such disputes might *not* be so submitted. All other substantive issues, including the question of convening a third conference, were left as a "recommendation" for the future consideration of participating states.

Despite the apparent futility of the Hague conferences, the point must be reiterated that at least the principle of international arbitration had been accepted by the world's major powers and rules of procedure laid down which could serve as guidelines for arbitration whether or not conducted by the Hague court, which in fact settled a number of international disputes submitted to it over the next years. Most important, the very establishment of the Hague court set a precedent for the creation of similar organizations to deal with international problems—the International Court of Justice, the International Labor Office, and the more ambitious League of Nations and United Nations. Futile as these organizations have generally been when confronted with major problems, their very existence nourishes the hope that states will turn to them rather than resort to war to settle their differences.

❑

TWENTY-ONE

Germany's Weltpolitik

With Bismarck's dismissal in 1890, Kaiser William II had proclaimed "the course remains the same; full speed ahead." But the course did not remain the same, for in the late 1890s his government embarked on what the Germans themselves called a global policy (*Weltpolitik*), though neither the kaiser nor most of his advisers were clear in their own minds as to what they meant by global policy or what the objectives of a German *Weltpolitik* should be, while the most vigorous advocates of this policy among his subjects held widely divergent views on the subject. The imperial government nevertheless embarked with much fanfare on a major fleet-building program to back up Germany's global interests and claims, and, again with much rhetoric and bombast, sought to intervene (and profit from) every global complication, with the result that the Germans aroused global suspicion and hostility.

During Bismarck's chancellorship, many German patriots and representatives of various vested interests had bitterly criticized the old statesman's conception of the new German empire as a satiated state and had become increasingly vociferous in calling for Germany to demonstrate its status as a great power by acquiring a global empire comparable to Britain's. Bismarck had endeavored to divert this criticism and strengthen his own political position by acquiring a modest colonial empire for Germany in the mid-1880s, but he never believed that overseas colonies could contribute in any significant way to Germany's future political or economic security. Situated as it was in central Europe between rival powers, Germany could safeguard its security effectively only by keeping itself strong and preventing the formation of hostile foreign coalitions. Further, and far more important in view of later developments, he recognized the limitations of German power and the restrictions imposed on German policy by the European states system. He consequently opposed every suggestion of preventive war and the idea that Germany seek to achieve security by destroying its continental rivals.

Bismarck's immediate successors adhered to this general line of thought in their foreign policy. Although they dropped Germany's Reinsurance Treaty with Russia, they did so in the confident expectation that they could arrange an alliance with Britain to take the place of what they regarded as the dangerous and unreliable

Russian connection. Their 1890 treaty with Britain, whereby they abandoned substantial German colonial claims, was clearly intended to lead to a more comprehensive Anglo-German agreement. That treaty was bitterly resented by German imperialists, who launched a vigorous propaganda campaign to oppose any further renunciation of German claims and to agitate for a renewed quest for overseas empire.

Given its failure to establish closer ties with Britain and Russia's entry into an alliance with France in 1894, the German government would have been wise, or so it seems in retrospect, to have done everything possible to avoid international complications, to maintain cordial relations (even if not treaty relationships) with all major powers, and to concentrate on economic production and trade to maintain and extend German power and influence. The desirability of such a policy was in fact recognized by Bismarck's immediate successors and by many other politically conscious Germans, but there were others—and not only emotionally charged patriots or the self-seeking representatives of vested interests, but thoughtful and level-headed political analysts—who asked whether other powers would sit idly by and allow Germany to harvest the fruits of its economic enterprise. Would these powers condone indefinitely Germany's intrusion into world markets or its extension of economic (and thus also political) influence in areas where their own interests would be adversely affected? Was it not just a question of time before these powers closed their homelands and overseas empires or spheres of influence to German commerce, or resorted to the more drastic step of using their superior sea power to sweep German commerce from the seas?

To prevent such dire eventualities, Germans who regarded themselves as political realists argued that Germany must acquire overseas territories of its own, and not only as markets and sources of raw materials, but also as settlements for Germany's surplus population so that the valuable workers lost each year through emigration could be retained for the German fatherland instead of contributing to the strength of foreign countries. Indispensable for acquiring and defending a German colonial empire was a strong German fleet, impressive enough to compel respect for German colonial claims and so powerful that no rival sea power could risk attacking Germany's overseas territories or interfering with German trade. The arguments of German proponents of empire and sea power were similar to and often identical with those of imperialists of other countries, but in Germany, as in Japan, the need for overseas empire seemed particularly compelling. Both had entered late into the competition for overseas territory and both were restricted to a narrow territorial base, Germany by its geographical position between three major powers, Japan by its island location. Britain and France, with similarly narrow territorial bases, had long ago acquired large overseas empires; Russia and the United States, which had been able to expand on an immense scale into contiguous territories, represented self-contained empires that were nevertheless seeking to expand still further. Germany must acquire a global empire on the model of Britain or France, so the imperialist argument ran, or it would inevitably become another Holland or Sweden, its security and interests constantly at the mercy of stronger powers. German imperialists invoked America's Admiral Mahan, who had demonstrated by the lessons of history that a great nation's prosperity depends on a constantly expanding foreign commerce, and that this commerce in turn requires empire and sea power.

That Germany's overseas trade had become crucial to the country's strength and prosperity was amply demonstrated statistically. Germany's merchant fleet tonnage had increased 150 percent between 1873 and 1895, the value of its maritime exports had increased more than 200 percent, and the country's burgeoning population had become critically dependent on overseas imports for its food supply. Germany's total overseas trade was second only to that of Britain; its fleet on the other hand had actually declined in relation to that of all other great powers and in 1895 was inferior to that of Italy in terms of total tonnage.

❑ *William II and Sea Power*

In Germany, Emperor William II was an early convert to theories that his country needed empire and sea power. In 1894 his mother, the Empress Frederick, had written to her own mother, Queen Victoria of England, that "William's one idea is to have a Navy which shall be larger and stronger than the British Navy, but this is really pure madness and folly and he will see how impossible and needless it is." This prophecy could not have been wider off the mark, for William, far from recognizing the folly and danger of building a navy to rival and surpass Britain's, became increasingly convinced of its necessity.

William's belief in the need for sea power was confirmed by Germany's failure to extract colonial concessions from Britain and by his own inability to intervene effectively in South Africa during the Transvaal crisis. Upon receiving news of the Boers' defeat of the Jameson raid in early January 1896, he could do no more than send his provocative congratulatory telegram to President Kruger (see pp. 288–290), which was of no material use to the Boers and converted Britain's own frustrations over the Transvaal into a storm of rage against Germany. To overcome Germany's inability to cope with overseas problems, the kaiser urged his government to exploit the public furor aroused over the Jameson raid to obtain appropriations from the Reichstag for massive increases in the German fleet, and on January 18, on the occasion of the twenty-fifth anniversary of the founding of the German empire, he addressed an appeal to his subjects to recognize their country's need for sea power and empire. Germany could no longer afford to take a parochial view of the world, for German interests were now global in scope. "German merchandise, German science, German energy sail the oceans. The value of our sea trade amounts to thousands of millions. It is your duty to aid me in creating firm links between this greater Germany and our Fatherland." These links were a fleet and colonies, essential for the protection of Germany's commerce and future economic prosperity and thus also essential to the security of the German homeland.

Under the kaiser's prodding, the German government submitted a modest naval appropriations bill to the Reichstag, but even the popular furor over the Transvaal was not enough to convince German parliamentarians of the need for a larger German fleet, and in March 1897 the naval appropriations bill was defeated. This setback, together with numerous other political frustrations, propelled the kaiser to make sweeping changes in the government to give himself greater control and to bring in more determined promoters of imperial legislation. The most significant of these changes was the appointment of Bernhard von Bülow as state secretary of the

German foreign office and Admiral Alfred von Tirpitz as state secretary of the imperial naval office (Reichsmarineamt).

❑ *The Role of Bülow*

Bülow, whose father had served as state secretary of the foreign office under Bismarck, was one of Germany's most experienced diplomats, with a record of service in the Balkans and all the major European capitals with the exception of London. Bülow did not owe his appointment in Berlin primarily to his experience or other political qualifications, however, but to the fact that he had managed to convince the kaiser of his personal devotion and total commitment to imperial policies. Bülow's appointment as head of the foreign office was envisaged by the kaiser from the beginning as a mere steppingstone to succeeding the elderly Prince Hohenlohe as German chancellor. "Bülow shall be my Bismarck," he said, "and just as he and my grandfather hammered Germany together externally, so will we two clean up the filth of parliamentary party machinery internally"—whereby William did not mean a reform of parliamentary institutions but the augmentation of his own authority at the expense of the Reichstag. It was Bülow's task to set German foreign policy on a course of *Weltpolitik* in line with the kaiser's aspirations and to represent government policy in the Reichstag, where he was to employ his oratorical talent and considerable skill in personal manipulation to secure the passage of appropriations bills and any other measures that *Weltpolitik* would require.

From the kaiser's point of view, Bülow proved to be an admirable choice. Bülow reveled in the exercise and trappings of power, and, fully conscious that his power depended entirely on the will of the kaiser, his conduct of policy was determined almost exclusively by his desire to retain imperial approval. To this end, he deluged his sovereign with flattery that knew no bounds or shame. To the kaiser's friend Philipp Eulenburg he wrote, confident that his letter would be passed along, about his ever-increasing faith in their imperial master. "In a manner I have never seen before, he combines genius—the most genuine and original genius—with the clearest good sense. He possesses the kind of fantasy that lifts me on eagle's pinions above all triviality and, at the same time, the shrewdest appreciation of the possible and the attainable. And with all that, what energy! What reflectiveness! What swiftness and sureness of conception!" The kaiser wallowed with delight in such adulation. "Bernhard—superb fellow! He has proven himself magnificently and I adore him. . . . What a joy to deal with someone who is devoted to one body and soul and who will and can understand one!"

Bülow's colleagues in the foreign office were more critical of their new head. He was known there as "the eel," and a senior colleague who knew him well described him as "beardless and pasty, with a shifty look and an almost perpetual smile. Intellectually plausible rather than profound." Not until after World War I, however, did Bülow reveal to the world the degree of his intellectual superficiality and meanness of spirit. This he did in four thick volumes of memoirs, published after his death. Far too late, the kaiser, now in exile in Holland, recognized the true nature of his former minister, and upon reading his memoirs he is said to have remarked that Bülow was surely the only figure in history to have committed suicide posthumously.

❑ *The Role of Tirpitz*

Tirpitz was an obvious choice to head the Reich naval office, for he was an administrator of proven competence and energy as well as the country's foremost advocate of the need for sea power. "In the economic struggle which the nations must wage in the coming century, it will become increasingly necessary to defend the maritime interests of Germany by armed force," he said. As matters stood at present, however, Germany's maritime trade was at the mercy of every rival. Because the German economy now depended so heavily on that trade, the very survival of the German nation required a German fleet equal to the task of defending the country's economic interests.

Although his own first major assignment had been the command of the torpedo squadron, Tirpitz came around to the view, apparently quite independently of Mahan, that the current emphasis of German naval strategists on swift cruisers and torpedo boats was misplaced. Such a fleet might have considerable nuisance value for raids on an enemy's coasts and commerce, but in any major conflict it would be swept from the seas by vessels with heavier armor and superior firepower. Worse still, a fleet of this kind would be virtually useless in defending Germany's commerce and might not even be up to the task of preventing enemy landings on Germany's coasts.

As Britain was the world's greatest sea power and Germany was Britain's most serious as well as most vulnerable commercial rival, Tirpitz focused almost exclusively on the problem of Britain, which he perceived as the power most likely to seek the destruction of German commerce. He was under no illusion that Germany could build a fleet equal to Britain's, at least not for many years, but he was not thinking in terms of equality. What he advocated was a fleet of heavy battleships capable of standing up to the most formidable warships of other powers, a fleet that Britain could neither challenge nor destroy except at the risk of so weakening its own fleet as to leave the country and its overseas interests perilously vulnerable to the navies of other powers. This was the fundamental idea behind Tirpitz's "risk" navy. Tirpitz proposed that most of the new German battle fleet should remain in home waters where it would pose the greatest threat to Britain and thus exercise a maximum deterrent effect. "Germany's geographical position would make the new fleet particularly dangerous to Britain," he said, "because, to protect its own security, it would have to withdraw its forces from the Mediterranean and elsewhere in the world, and thus be far more vulnerable to pressure from France and Russia."

But Tirpitz's ambitions were not limited to building a risk navy, which he acknowledged in 1911 had been no more than a slogan that could be understood by the masses. By 1918–1920 he hoped to have a battle fleet of no fewer than sixty ships, which, if concentrated in the North Sea while at least a third of Britain's navy was deployed to protect its global interests, would give Germany naval equality if not superiority in northern waters. This was the ultimate goal, for if the fleet was to be an effective lever in dealing with Britain, as he intended it should, Germany had to be capable of actually defeating the British navy—a fleet so powerful "that in case of war we must at least have a promising chance of a defensive victory [*Defensivchance*]."

Tirpitz's greatest fear was that Britain would launch an attack on the German navy and major seaports before his battle fleet could be completed. During the

Napoleonic wars, the British had boldly entered the harbor of Copenhagen and destroyed the Danish fleet while it lay at anchor to prevent its use by the French. The possibility that Britain would "Copenhagen" the German fleet became something of an obsession among German navalists; this was not an altogether idle fear, for as the German fleet grew, Sir John Fisher, Britain's first sea lord, actually considered a Copenhagen operation, which was openly advocated by a number of reputable British journalists.

Tirpitz professed to believe that his great battle fleet would not pose a serious obstacle to amicable Anglo-German relations. On the contrary, he predicted that the existence of a powerful German fleet would achieve what German diplomacy had failed to accomplish: an Anglo-German alliance. He reasoned that the British could not withdraw their squadrons from the oceans of the world and leave their overseas interests at the mercy of France and Russia, nor would any British government dare to ask Parliament for the vast sums that would be necessary to meet the German challenge. The British could therefore be expected to recognize at last the desirability of a closer political alignment with Germany as well as to be more amenable to German requests for colonial concessions. "Even the greatest seapower would act more accommodatingly towards us if we were able to throw into the scales of international politics, or if necessary into the scales of conflict, two or three well-schooled squadrons," he said. Thus the battle fleet would be another, and indeed the most effective, instrument to bully Britain into a German alliance.

As seen from an exclusively German point of view, Tirpitz's theories were sufficiently convincing to win widespread approval among parliamentarians and other German leaders who had originally opposed his fleet-building program, but as so often happened during this period the Germans failed to consider or totally misconstrued how other powers, above all Britain in this case, would interpret their policies. The fleet was for Britain what the army was for Germany, *the* main line of national defense. Tirpitz might convince his compatriots that the German fleet he desired was intended for defensive and deterrent purposes only and that it was essential for the protection of Germany's coasts and commerce, but to the British a great German battle fleet stationed permanently in home waters within striking distance of their islands could have only one meaning: such a fleet was being built to challenge British naval supremacy and prepare the way for an eventual German invasion. Any threat to British naval superiority was therefore a threat to British national security and absolutely decisive in determining British foreign policy. The Tirpitz fleet, far from making Britain more amenable to a political accommodation with Germany, touched off a massive new British fleet-building program and drove the British to seek diplomatic alignments with other sea powers, including their greatest competitors in the colonial field, France and Russia, to enable them to concentrate their own forces against the German menace.

The Germans themselves provided abundant fuel to feed the flames of British fears. To secure from the Reichstag the immense appropriations that would be needed to build a battle fleet, the public had to be convinced of its necessity. Germans had traditionally looked to the army as the principal guardian of their national interests and security. Being essentially a continentally minded people, they found it difficult to comprehend how their security could be threatened at sea, especially if Germany remained on friendly terms with Britain. The only way navalists could deal with this attitude was to persuade the German public, as they had persuaded themselves, that vital German interests were at stake at sea as well as on land, and that Britain was not friendly but on the contrary the major threat to those interests. The German government's campaign to convince the public of the need for a great battle fleet thus had to be launched on a wave of anti-British propaganda—and this at a time when German diplomats were still hoping for a British alliance.

Tirpitz proved to be a masterful propagandist. Under his leadership the Reich naval office became a major propaganda agency, the center of a news and information network that brought the government's arguments on behalf of a great battle fleet to all sectors of the German public through newspapers and journals, business and labor organizations, and other important molders of public opinion. Of particular significance was his use of Germany's system of compulsory education to convey his message to the nation's schoolchildren, while at the upper levels, he paid court to *Gymnasium* instructors and university professors to preach the doctrine of sea power from their prestigious rostrums. Under Tirpitz's auspices a German Navy League was founded and rapidly became a second major center of naval propaganda and the foremost political lobbying organization on behalf of naval appropriations bills.

The Tirpitz propaganda campaign was an immense success. On March 28, 1898, barely eight months after the Reichstag's rejection of the government's relatively modest naval appropriations bill, that same body approved Tirpitz's far more ambitious bill by a voice vote. The kaiser was delighted, and with typical exuberance he exulted that Tirpitz, in less than a year and singlehandedly, had converted fifty million "obstinate, ill-informed, and ill-willed Germans" into enthusiastic supporters of his naval program.

❑ *Domestic Factors in the Success of Tirpitz's Program*

Tirpitz's success was far from singlehanded. From the beginning he had the support of most patriotic organizations, notably the German Colonial Society, the principal lobby for an imperialist foreign policy. More significantly, he had the backing of the immense political and economic power wielded by the captains of German industry, who stood to profit mightily from the sale of guns and armor plate required in constructing a battle fleet and who contributed lavishly to the Navy League and other beaters of the navy drum. Most important of all, perhaps, Tirpitz was playing to a receptive audience, for in Germany as in all Europeanized countries of this era, the masses as well as the leadership were enveloped in a cultural climate of strident nationalism, and public opinion could be aroused to hysterical and totally unreasonable frenzy by appeals to patriotism and nationalist paranoia.

Far more difficult to explain than Tirpitz's success is his opponents' failure to mount a more effective campaign against his fleet program. Those politically conscious Germans who anticipated correctly the disastrous consequences of German navalism on their country's foreign relations, particularly with Britain, may have lacked the power or authority to oppose the kaiser and an aroused public opinion on this issue. But what of the leaders of the German army, that so-called state within a state, so often described, and decried, by historians? Army officers were aware of their country's limited resources and saw that all resources devoted to the navy would mean correspondingly fewer available to the army, which they correctly re-

garded as the true bastion of German security. Yet in dealing with their government's naval expansion program, where the vaunted influence of the army might
have been most salutary in focusing attention on Germany's fundamental interests,
that influence was conspicuously absent.

The German army did not step up its demands for funds until 1912, when a
modest military appropriations bill was submitted to the Reichstag. After that, however, army demands rose dramatically, and in 1913 the Reichstag passed the largest
military appropriations bill in German history (see p. 436).

A frequent explanation for the remarkable restraint on the part of Germany's
military leaders is their fear that increases in the size of the army would dilute the
aristocratic composition of the officer corps. The importance of the snobbery factor
seems questionable, however, considering the increasingly frequent marriages of the
old aristocracy into wealthy middle-class families and the ease with which wealthy
commoners could purchase patents of nobility.

A more convincing though even less edifying explanation for the army leaders'
restraint may be a selfish concern for their own careers. They knew of the kaiser's
enthusiasm for the fleet, and they had ample occasion to observe that their supreme
war lord did not take kindly to advice or opposition. To any suggestion of criticism
he was heard to remark: "You surprise me; I thought you valued your position."
Military leaders therefore recognized that any attempt to undercut the kaiser's most
cherished project would very likely put an end to all prospects of a major command
or to any influence they might already possess—a situation that did not encourage
independence of thought or make for the promotion of men of intellectual integrity
or moral courage, and one that does much to explain the mediocre quality of Germany's top military leadership, as revealed in 1914.

Many army officers, it is only fair to point out, appear to have been honestly
convinced by Tirpitz's arguments, as were senior members of the German government including Chancellor Hohenlohe, although his conversion to navalism appears
to have been due far more to the lessons of the Spanish–American War. Shortly after
that conflict he acknowledged that the kaiser was correct: Germany's commerce
was at the mercy of Britain and the naval imbalance between the two powers must
be corrected. "We must not expose ourselves to the danger of suffering the fate
from England that Spain has suffered from the United States," he said. "That the
English are merely waiting for an opportunity to fall upon us is clear."

Tirpitz's first naval appropriations bill was passed in the Reichstag on March 28,
1898. At almost exactly the same time the British made their first serious bid for a
German alliance. This British approach had nothing to do with Tirpitz and his fleet,
however, but was rather the result of Britain's overall international position. German
leaders, expecting that Britain's international difficulties would force it to seek German support sooner or later, greeted the British approach with high but, as it
proved, ill-founded and unrealistic expectations.

TWENTY-TWO

❏

Britain's Defensive Strategy

Because of the sheer size of its empire and the extent of its overseas interests, Britain was confronted with a steady succession of colonial and international crises. The more significant of these were discussed in earlier chapters: the confrontations with France in Egypt and central Africa, with the Boers in South Africa, with the United States in the Western Hemisphere, and with the Russians in East Asia and along almost every sector of that vast empire's southern and eastern frontiers.

The venerable Lord Salisbury, who formed his third and final ministry in June 1895 and who also held the office of foreign secretary until November 1900, maintained a patrician calm in the face of all these difficulties, coolly confident that the British navy would be up to the task of defending the home islands and Britain's overseas interests, and that British diplomacy could prevent the formation of a hostile great power coalition—the only threat he saw reason to fear—by buying off or otherwise conciliating one or more of its potential members.

❏ *Maintaining Naval Superiority*

Salisbury's appreciation of the key role of the British navy in protecting Britain's security and interests was fully shared by the leaders of both major political parties and the British public. As one of Britain's foremost naval authorities wrote in October 1893: "To all other Powers a strong navy is more or less of a luxury. . . . To England alone it is from the very nature of the case an absolute and primordial necessity."

Already in Salisbury's second ministry, national alarm about the growth of the French and Russian fleets had led to the passage in 1889 of a Naval Defense Act, which provided not only for major increased spending on the British fleet but for the adoption of the so-called Two-Power Standard: that the British fleet should always be at least equal to the combined strength of its two closest naval rivals. In 1894 a British Navy League was founded to disseminate naval propaganda and lobby for larger appropriations in the same manner as the German Navy League, founded four years later, for which it was clearly the model. Naval estimates, which stood at roughly 13 million pounds for 1888-1889, rose to 17.5 million pounds for 1894-1895 and to more than 26.5 million for 1899-1900.

These increases were in response to Britain's international difficulties. In 1896, as foreign hostility toward British policy in South Africa intensified and the kaiser's Kruger telegram raised the specter of German collaboration with France and Russia, the Salisbury government proposed large additional increases in fleet appropriations. Instead of criticizing these increases as extravagant, the Liberal opposition complained that they were not large enough and called for a Three- rather than a Two-Power Standard—and this a full two years before the passage of Tirpitz's first bill. This should have warned the Germans that even the most economy-minded British administration would be prepared to devote whatever funds seemed necessary to maintain not mere naval superiority but a superiority capable of coping with the challenge of a hostile coalition.

The British were slow to recognize the import of the German naval bill of 1898 and the even more ambitious bill passed in 1900, but by the following year the Admiralty came to regard the German fleet as a direct and indeed the major threat to British security. British fears aroused by German naval development quite naturally grew with the passage of each new German naval appropriations bill, and the British reacted, as was only to be expected (although not, incredibly, by Tirpitz), with massive naval increases of their own.

The British not only increased the size of their navy to keep well ahead of their rivals but initiated major reforms in recruitment, training, and strategy. Rates of pay for officers and men were increased and conditions improved to attract a higher standard of recruit, instruction in the use of rope and canvas gave way to increased technological training, and nucleus crews were maintained for every vessel to ensure that each would always be ready to go into action. Older and slower vessels were scrapped and the newer vessels concentrated into battle squadrons in accordance with Mahan's ideas. On February 10, 1906, the first battleship of the Dreadnought class was launched, not the largest ship ever built, but the fastest (driven by turbine engines) and the most maneuverable, with the heaviest armor and the greatest firepower. With the Dreadnought, the British had rendered all other navies, including their own, obsolete. They therewith gave up much of their head start in naval construction from the previous decades, but in doing so they hoped they were making the stakes so high that the Germans could not compete.

This hope proved illusory. Tirpitz immediately began a German Dreadnought-building program, which required enlarging, at immense expense, the recently completed Kaiser Wilhelm (Kiel) Canal across the base of the Jutland peninsula to accommodate the larger vessels. For the Germans it was a futile race. Britain remained well ahead in naval construction and by 1914 had twenty Dreadnoughts to Germany's thirteen, along with a substantial lead in every other type of naval vessel including the submarine.

Quite as important as ship construction in maintaining Britain's naval superiority was British diplomacy, which was to make it possible to withdraw capital ships from the oceans of the world and concentrate them in the North Sea to meet the German challenge.

❑ *The Case for an Alliance Policy*

Whereas virtually all British leaders agreed with Salisbury about the British navy, there were marked differences of opinion about his foreign policy, even among members of his own cabinet. Prominent among the dissenters were his own nephew, Arthur Balfour, deputy foreign secretary, first lord of the treasury, and leader of the Conservative party in the House of Commons; and Joseph Chamberlain, the powerful colonial secretary who played such an important role in the Transvaal crisis. These men did not share Salisbury's confidence that Britain could cope single-handedly with its multitude of colonial problems as well as with the competition and hostility of foreign rivals; they proposed instead abandoning an isolationist policy in favor of diplomatic alignment with one or more foreign powers. Their objective was twofold: to anticipate and prevent the formation of hostile great power coalitions; and to secure treaty guarantees and protection for the British empire and overseas interests.

❑ *The Special Relationship with the United States*

The most significant political component of Britain's defensive strategy was not any kind of formal diplomatic alignment, but a cultivated friendship with the United States. Germans at that time and since have wondered why the British so feared the German fleet and so resented Germany's commercial competition, and why they seemed so comparatively unconcerned about the potentially far more serious naval challenge and commercial rivalry of the United States.

The reason for Britain's fear of the German naval buildup was, or should have been, obvious. Lying in the North Sea directly opposite the British home islands, the German fleet represented a direct threat to British security. The reason for Britain's accommodating attitude toward the United States was equally obvious. Great power and global empire though it might be, Britain was not powerful enough or in a position to challenge the power of the United States—and had every reason to avoid doing so. In the event of conflict, Britain could not defend Canada; unlike Britain's European rivals, the United States was not constrained by any balance of power in its own hemisphere; and finally, the United States possessed the resources to challenge, and ultimately defeat, Britain at sea.

The safest and indeed the only way Britain could deal with the threat posed by the United States was to remain on the best possible terms with it, and by the late nineteenth century this was the policy Britain pursued with considerable consistency. The British recognized sooner and more clearly than their continental counterparts that the United States was potentially the greatest of the great powers and adjusted their policies accordingly. Inevitably there were crises in Anglo-American relations, but at any danger signal, the British were quick to arbitrate, compromise, or surrender.

In retrospect this policy can be seen as having begun, perhaps not altogether consciously, with the Treaty of Washington of 1871 and the settlement in the following year of the *Alabama* claims. In the course of the Venezuelan crisis it developed into a deliberate diplomatic strategy, becoming a principle of British diplomacy by the time of the Cuban crisis. As we have seen, the British remained benevolently aloof while America settled accounts with Spain, they made no claim to compensation and even encouraged America's takeover of the Hawaiian and Philippine islands, they surrendered their own claims to equality of control over a future isthmian canal, and they lodged no protest to the American claim to exclusive authority over the affairs of the entire Western Hemisphere. The more perceptive American statesmen appreciated the advantages derived from Britain's accommodating attitude, but it was not until the Spanish–American War that the American public in general became conscious of how much British support and friendship had contributed to their own successes, and with all the bluster about their own achievements Americans by and large were grateful. By 1898, in fact, the British had succeeded in establishing that "special relationship" with the United States that was to endure, with inevitable vicissitudes, to the present day.

In a speech at the Lord Mayor's banquet on November 9, 1898, Lord Salisbury spoke of that year as "the first year in which the mighty force of the American republic has been introduced among the nations whose dominion is spent." Never optimistic about human behavior, Salisbury was uncertain whether America's intrusion into Asiatic or even European affairs would necessarily be conducive to the interests of peace, "though I think in any event they are likely to be conducive to the interests of Great Britain."

Britain's defensive strategy through diplomacy expanded early in the twentieth century through alliances and alignments with Japan, France, and Russia. But Britain's first step in that direction was the search for some kind of agreement with Germany.

❑ *The Anglo-German Alliance Negotiations*

The special relationship with the United States was to be of incalculable value to Britain in the future, but it contributed little to solving that country's more immediate diplomatic requirements: the prevention of a hostile European great power coalition and the defense of the British empire and overseas interests. It was to deal with these requirements that on March 25, 1898, Arthur Balfour, acting director of the Foreign Office while his uncle, Lord Salisbury, was on holiday, arranged to meet with Paul von Hatzfeldt, the German ambassador, therewith initiating a succession of Anglo-German alliance negotiations that were to continue intermittently over the next three years.

An Anglo-German alliance had long been considered "natural" by contemporary observers. According to theories prevalent at that time the two countries shared a common racial and political heritage, and there were no points at issue between them comparable to Britain's differences with France and Russia—in the late 1890s the German fleet was not yet a critical factor. Moreover, although Germany was rapidly becoming a formidable commercial competitor, it was also Britain's best customer.

The belief that such a natural alliance had been possible at the time was fostered by the publication after World War I of two volumes of memoirs, replete with supporting documentary evidence, by a German nobleman named Hermann von Eckardstein, who had had close connections to leaders of both the British and German governments. In these memoirs he described his own efforts on behalf of an Anglo-German agreement and ascribed their failure to the machinations of Germany's professional diplomats, who, blinded by suspicion and prejudice, frittered away a golden opportunity to establish a partnership with Britain that might have changed the course of history.

Largely on the basis of Eckardstein's evidence, historians who first dealt with the subject regarded the failure of these Anglo-German negotiations as a turning point in pre-1914 history. It was not until some years later, when scholars gained access to the official and private papers of the major figures involved, that it became clear that Eckardstein's memoirs were seriously misleading and many of his supporting documents falsified or outright forgeries. The evidence now available makes clear that the possibility of an Anglo-German alliance was never so great as many contemporary and later analysts had assumed because neither side was able or willing to offer terms that were desired or considered essential by the other. Indeed, the very absence of colonial differences between Britain and Germany made negotiations more difficult, for while the Germans wanted colonial concessions from Britain, they had no comparable concessions to offer in return.

What the British were primarily interested in at this time, apart from preventing the formation of a hostile great power coalition, was protection of British interests in East Asia, which seemed menaced by the steady advance of Russia in that region. As can now be seen from British documents covering this period, British leaders were far from enthusiastic about seeking Germany's cooperation for this purpose; their approach to Germany in the spring of 1898 was, in fact, virtually a last resort. After Germany seized Kiaochow in November 1897, the Salisbury government had tried unsuccessfully to reach a direct agreement with Russia over China. It had then tried, again without success, to make an agreement with the United States and Japan. But the Americans were involved in their troubles with Spain, and the Japanese, still uncertain about their own strength, decided it would be safer and easier to reach agreement with Russia to protect their interests.

❑ Mutual Misconceptions

On March 24, 1898, the news reached London that Russia intended to take over Port Arthur and Dairen (Talienwan) on China's Liaotung peninsula. It was this news that evidently decided British leaders to seek agreement with Germany, for on the following day they made their first approach to the German ambassador. They did so in the evident expectation that Germany, now that it was established in Kiaochow, would share Britain's concern about holding the line against Russia in China, but here the British made their first serious miscalculation. For despite Kiaochow, the Germans had no interest whatever in checking the Russians in this area. Quite the contrary: the more deeply the Russians became involved in East Asia, the less likely they would be to impinge on German and Austrian interests in the west.

The Germans entered the negotiations with equally serious misconceptions about Britain. Well aware of Britain's troubles in every part of the world, they believed Britain was at last turning to Germany for support, as they had always believed it would, and that they could now dictate their terms. These terms would necessarily be stiff, because in an alliance with Britain, Germany would assume by far the greatest dangers: if British troubles with France or Russia led to war, Germany would assume the brunt of the conflict. Still vivid in German historical memory was Frederick the Great's alliance with England in the mid-eighteenth century, when Prussia had to fight for its very existence against a coalition of Austria, France, and Russia, while the British, secure behind the Channel, used their superior sea power to pick up Canada and India. If the Germans were to assume risks of this kind, they would require a formal treaty with Britain, approved by Parliament, providing guarantees of British support or at least neutrality should Germany become involved in a continental war, guarantees of Germany's existing frontiers (and thus of Germany's possession of Alsace and Lorraine), and generous colonial concessions.

These were conditions the British would not and could not accept. In 1890 they had shied away from a diplomatic partnership with Germany because they feared it would give the Germans de facto diplomatic hegemony in Europe. Eight years later their fears on this score had steadily increased as a result of the German government's forays in international affairs. In any case, however, they had no intention of giving Germany guarantees that would in effect overturn the European balance of power: if Germany threatened the great power status of either France or Russia, Britain must retain its freedom to intervene. No German assurances that their alliance would be strictly defensive or that they had no hostile designs on France or Russia could alter this British standpoint. Britain's adherence to the Triple Alliance or the mere existence of a formal Anglo-German alignment would alter the balance of power in Germany's favor, and this the British could not afford to tolerate. Thus fundamental differences between British and German interests and conceptions doomed the Anglo-German alliance negotiations from the beginning, as they were to doom all subsequent efforts to revive them. These fundamental differences were never understood by the Germans, or for that matter by some of the British negotiators, Chamberlain in particular. This failure of perception explains how the negotiations went on for so long and the bitterness on both sides when they failed.

❑ *German Blackmail; the Portuguese and Samoan Payments*

Bülow, the head of the German foreign office, did not help matters. He refused to be lured into cooperation with Britain against Russia in East Asia; on the contrary, Germany encouraged Russia's involvement in this region, and for this purpose Bülow responded to the first British approach with proposals as alarming as they were impolitic: Britain should make concessions to Russia in Asia and settle accounts with France before the Russians had completed their military preparations along the frontiers of India, as thereafter it would be more difficult to keep Russia neutral in an Anglo-French war; at the same time, Britain should not jeopardize the chances for a future agreement with Germany by excessive recalcitrance over minor issues—a broad hint that Britain should be more accommodating about colonial concessions.

Salisbury was in no way surprised by the incredible crudity of this German response. The kaiser's one objective since coming to the throne was to push Britain into a war with France, he said, and unfortunately the French seemed to be doing everything possible to drive Britain into Germany's arms, "which I look to with some dismay, for Germany will blackmail us heavily." Whereas Balfour and Chamberlain thought it prudent to make concessions on behalf of a German agreement,

Salisbury did not believe such an agreement was either desirable or necessary, and he had no intention whatever of paying blackmail. "You demand too much for your friendship," he told the German ambassador, and in a public speech of May 4 he declared: "We know that we shall maintain against all comers that which we possess, and we know in spite of all the jargon about isolation that we are amply competent to do so."

The kaiser nevertheless remained confident that the British would and should pay handsomely for German friendship. When Hatzfeldt, his ambassador in London, telegraphed on May 22 that according to certain British sources the British were thinking of making concessions to Germany in Borneo in return for compensation in Africa, the kaiser retorted: "Not enough! Samoa, the Carolines, one of the Philippine islands (if possible)." Nor was the kaiser content to see what he could extract from Britain, for he made use of what he chose to interpret as Britain's alliance offer to blackmail Russia. With a crudity that matched Bülow's, he wrote to the tsar on May 30 of enormous British offers to be taken into the Triple Alliance and of negotiations to extend that alliance to include Japan and the United States. "Now as my old and trusted friend, I beg you to tell me what you can offer me and will do if I refuse?" The response of the old and trusted friend was masterful. The British had made similar tempting offers to Russia three months ago, he said, but he had rejected them without a second thought. He found it impossible to say whether or not it would be useful to Germany to accept the English proposals, for he had no idea of their value. "You must of course decide what is best and most necessary for your country."

Bülow fumed with righteous indignation. "Here we have the proof," he wrote to Hatzfeldt in London on June 8, that the kaiser had been correct in believing "that England, if she had been able, would long ago have reached agreement with Russia at the expense of third parties." Hatzfeldt was nevertheless to continue negotiations with Britain and to demand payment in the event of any British move to extend their own territories, for instance at the expense of the Portuguese empire in Africa.

As Britain's differences with France over Africa became steadily more bitter and the problems of South Africa continued to fester, the British government did at least pay blackmail to keep Germany friendly, or appeared to do so, through a treaty of August 30, 1898, providing for a future partition of Portugal's colonial empire between Britain and Germany. The long and acrimonious negotiations required to produce that treaty were discussed earlier, as was Britain's maneuver to deprive Germany of any benefit from it. For at the time of its signature, Balfour informed the Portuguese ambassador to London confidentially of its existence but assured him that nothing would be done to curtail the sovereign rights of Portugal so long as the interest on the Anglo-German loans to Portugal (for which the colonies served as security) was paid—and that Britain intended to make sure Portugal would always be able to make its payments (see pp. 295–297).

From the British point of view the treaty with Germany over Portugal was a splendid bargain. At no cost to themselves, or to Portugal, they had purchased German neutrality in South Africa, and it was with understandable satisfaction that Balfour reported to the cabinet that with this agreement Germany had renounced all interest in the Transvaal. He was not so crass as to spell out how Germany was to be cheated, but, as a senior official of the foreign office expressed it, Germany had "waged and won a fight for the shadows."

The Germans did not restrict their demands for colonial concessions to the Portuguese colonies. Just a few days after signing the treaty on that subject, Hatzfeldt was instructed to ask whether Britain would be prepared to join Germany in sounding out the United States about a final partition of the Samoan Islands, which had been the subject of rival American, British, and German claims since the 1880s. Salisbury was not interested. Nothing could be done about changing the status of Samoa owing to Australia's opposition, he said. Early in 1899, however, a rulership crisis in the islands themselves brought the problem to the fore, and to the fury of the Germans, the Americans and British used their superior sea power in the Pacific to ensure their candidate's victory. "The Samoan incident is renewed proof that overseas policy can only be conducted with an adequate fleet," Bülow concluded in reporting the situation to his sovereign, to which the kaiser commented: "What I have preached every day for the last ten years to those blockheads in the Reichstag." He now instructed Bülow to threaten to break off diplomatic relations with Britain if the Samoan question was not settled to Germany's satisfaction.

Once again Salisbury pleaded that neither Australia nor public opinion at home would allow him to give up British claims to Samoa, and it was not until the actual outbreak of war in South Africa that the British government agreed to negotiate over the islands. As in their negotiations over the Portuguese colonies, the British bargained with stubborn tenacity even though they believed that in the case of Samoa, too, any concessions to Germany would be meaningless. Australian forces would soon oust both Germany and France from any possessions they might have in the Pacific, Chamberlain predicted in writing to Salisbury shortly before the negotiations over Samoa began. "If, therefore, you think it necessary or desirable to pay the price for the German Emperor's support—or neutrality—I shall make no objection on my account, and we must face colonial indignation as best we can."

To avoid a colonial outcry over Samoa, Chamberlain offered the Germans concessions in Africa (the Volta delta) and the Solomon and Savage islands in the Pacific, urging them to accept because it would "settle at one blow all outstanding colonial differences between us." To the consternation of Hatzfeldt, who saw in Chamberlain's proposal an opportunity to arrange the kind of more general colonial treaty with Britain he had always desired, the kaiser and his naval advisers, with Tirpitz in the lead, adhered stubbornly to their demands for Samoa "for national and strategic reasons." "If our foreign policy depends on the views of Herr Tirpitz, we will not go very far in this world," Hatzfeldt commented. This was not a matter of strategic, commercial, or even colonial interests, he said, "but above all a question of greatest political importance, which will have decisive influence on our whole future." Hatzfeldt's hopes that Germany's acceptance of Chamberlain's offer would pave the way to a genuine rapprochement with Britain were undoubtedly excessively sanguine, but his government's point blank refusal to take up that offer ended all chance of testing its possibilities.

After weeks of dreary and often acrimonious negotiation, an Anglo-German treaty over the Samoan Islands was finally signed on November 14, 1899. Britain relinquished its claims to Upolu and Savaii to Germany and its claims to Tutuila and other islands in the Samoan group to the United States. In return Britain received Tonga and the Savage Islands, some minor islands in the Solomon group, and a disputed area of Togoland in Africa. The kaiser was jubilant and, as in the case of the Kiaochow acquisition, he gave all credit for this dubious success to Bülow. "Bravo. Am most pleased and delighted. You are a real magician granted to me quite undeservedly by Heaven in its goodness."

Toward the end of November 1899, the kaiser put the seal on the new Anglo-German accord by paying a visit to Britain accompanied by Bülow. This visit had more than ordinary political significance, for it announced to the world that Germany would not intervene against Britain in the Boer War, thus narrowing the chances that France or Russia would attempt to do so. Upolu and Savaii, which did not belong to Britain in the first place, were a small price to pay for such advantages.

❑ *Germany's Alienation of Chamberlain*

Bülow took advantage of the imperial visit to Britain to confront Chamberlain about Anglo-German relations, going so far as to ask the colonial secretary for a public statement regarding the mutual interests of Britain, Germany, and the United States. Bülow's purpose in making this request is unclear—perhaps he wanted fresh material for blackmailing Russia—but Chamberlain went much further than Bülow had expected or desired. In a speech at Leicester on November 30, delivered without consulting Salisbury or his colleagues in the cabinet, he called for the formation of "a new Triple Alliance" between the Anglo-Saxon and Teutonic powers, clearly revealing his own lack of understanding of the implications for Britain of a German alliance.

Chamberlain's public advocacy of an alliance with Germany came at a bad time for Bülow, who upon his return faced the formidable task of securing passage of a second great naval appropriations bill in the Reichstag. For opponents of that bill might well ask why, if Germany had an alliance with Britain, it needed a great fleet for defense against that country. Bülow's response to Chamberlain's proposal, however, was a dreadful malapropism and a slap in the face to Chamberlain, one of the few British statesmen sincerely eager for an agreement with Germany—now transformed into an infuriated Germanophobe. In a speech to the Reichstag on December 11, Bülow acknowledged Germany's desire to live in peace and harmony with Britain, but no one could know for certain whether their future relations would in fact be peaceful. Germany must therefore be made secure against surprises on land and sea. "We must build a fleet strong enough to prevent an attack—I underscore the word *attack,* for with the absolutely peaceful nature of our policy there can be no talk of anything but defense—from any power."

❑ *The* **Bundesrath** *Affair and the Russian Intervention Proposal*

As if the Bülow speech and the propagandistic fanfare on behalf of the naval appropriations bill had not done enough damage, Anglo-German relations were further embittered when Britain stopped the German mail steamer *Bundesrath* in December 1899 on suspicion that it was carrying contraband to the Boers via the Portuguese harbor of Lourenço Marques, in Mozambique. Britain admitted in January that no contraband had been found and promised to release the steamer, but the incident added new fuel to mutual hostility on both sides of the channel. Tirpitz was delighted when he received news of the affair. "Now we have the wind we need to bring our ship into harbor," he said. "The naval law will pass." It did, on June 12, 1900, by a margin of 201 to 103.

Meanwhile, by late February 1900 the tide of war had turned decisively against the Boer republics. Faced with the imminent collapse of these anti-British bastions in South Africa, Muraviev, the Russian foreign minister, explored the possibility of joint mediation with both the French and German governments. "To put an end to the further shedding of blood," Muraviev proposed that the continental powers exercise "amicable pressure" on Britain on behalf of the Boers.

Bülow replied that Germany was obliged to avoid all complications with other powers, especially sea powers, unless it could be certain of France's attitude, and that this certainty could be achieved only through a treaty guaranteeing the present territorial status quo in Europe for a fixed number of years—in other words, France would have to guarantee Germany's possession of Alsace and Lorraine before Germany would consider joining a continental coalition. The German ambassador in Paris assured his government informally that this was a condition no French government could accept. To this the kaiser commented: "What cheek. Just wait! Once I get out of the woods with John Bull, there'll be a thrashing for Johnny Crapaud!"

Because of the conditions set by Germany nothing came of the Russian proposal, but the kaiser could not resist informing his uncle, the Prince of Wales (the future Edward VII), about the Russian intervention initiative and his own rejection of it. The prince, who detested his imperial nephew, replied with the fulsome gratitude he knew William expected and which at this time may have been sincerely meant. He was not surprised by Muraviev's conduct, he said, and believed there was nothing Russia and France would not do to annoy England. "You have no idea, my dear William, how all of us in England appreciate the loyal friendship which you manifest towards us on every possible occasion."

❑ The Anglo-German Treaty over China

One manifestation of German goodwill the British still desired, and the prime objective of their original diplomatic initiative in March 1898, was Germany's cooperation in halting the Russian advance in East Asia. "Both in China and elsewhere," Chamberlain wrote in a memorandum for the cabinet, "it is in our interest that Germany throw herself in the path of Russia," and for this purpose "our policy clearly is to encourage good relations with Germany . . . and to emphasize the breach between Germany and Russia."

On October 16, 1900, the British concluded a treaty with Germany that seemed to give them what they desired: a promise of mutual support in maintaining the territorial integrity of China and the principle of the Open Door, which the British believed should apply to all provinces nominally part of the Chinese empire, including Manchuria. However, the Germans still had no intention of throwing themselves in the path of Russia, certainly not in East Asia, and Bülow promptly undercut any expectations the British may have had on that score by assuring the Reichstag shortly after the signing of the October 16 treaty that "Germany would take care not to do other peoples' business in China." Some time later, in response to a Reichstag question, he stated bluntly that the Anglo-German treaty "was in no sense concerned with Manchuria" and that "the fate of that province was a matter of absolute indifference to Germany." Salisbury had never harbored any illusions about the China treaty or any other agreement with Germany. Germany lives in mortal terror of Russia because of its long eastern frontier, he said. "I have no wish to quarrel with her but my faith in her is infinitesimal."

❑ *The Final Breakdown of the Anglo-German Negotiations*

On October 17, 1900, one day after the signing of the Anglo-German treaty over China, Hohenlohe resigned as German chancellor. He was succeeded by Bülow, who had been groomed for the post since his appointment as head of the German foreign office three years earlier.

One month later Salisbury relinquished the post of foreign secretary he had held along with the prime ministership since the beginning of his third term in office in June 1895. His successor at the Foreign Office was Lord Lansdowne, who had served as governor-general of Canada, viceroy of India, and most recently as Salisbury's secretary for war.

Lansdowne's appointment did not lead to any significant change in the course of British foreign policy. In May 1901, once again badly misled by Eckardstein about Britain's desire and need for an alliance, the Germans made their most grandiose bid for an agreement: a defensive alliance, to be ratified by Parliament, that would apply to the Triple Alliance as a whole and the British empire as a whole and would come into effect when one or more of the contracting parties was attacked by two or more great powers. The Germans wanted the agreement to cover all members of the Triple Alliance because, if Austria or Italy were attacked and Germany came to their aid in accordance with the provisions of the Triple Alliance, the British, if they had a defensive pact with Germany alone, could always claim that Germany itself had not been attacked and thus would stay out of the conflict. A defensive pact restricted to Germany alone would actually be dangerous, the Germans reasoned, for the moment such a treaty was submitted to Parliament Germany's foes would know how to begin a conflict to avoid Britain's involvement: they could attack Austria or Italy.

Hatzfeldt did his best to impress on Lansdowne the benefits of the proposed treaty: it would ensure Britain enormous and effective aid against attack by a great power coalition in every part of the British empire, the probable preservation of peace for at least another decade, and the undisturbed development of British commerce throughout the world. The British were not impressed or even interested. Lansdowne delegated the analysis of the German proposal to an undersecretary who hardly seems to have read it. "However the Convention may be worded," he concluded, "it seems to me that it might practically amount to a guarantee to Germany of the provinces conquered from France. . . . I do not see exactly what Germany will guarantee to us." As the Germans were offering to guarantee the entire British empire, this analysis reveals an almost willful lack of comprehension of the German offer.

Salisbury, who had never wanted an alliance with Germany, exhibited a similar lack of comprehension, and in a memorandum of May 29, 1901, he sounded the death knell of the Anglo-German negotiations. "The liability of having to defend the German and Austrian frontiers against Russia is heavier than that of having to defend the British Isles against France," he said. "Even, therefore, in its most naked aspect, the bargain would be a bad one for this country. Count Hatzfeldt speaks of our *'isolation'* as constituting a serious danger for us. *Have we ever felt that danger practically?* . . . It would hardly be wise to incur novel and most onerous obligations in order to guard against *a danger whose existence we have no historical reason for believing.*" Quite apart from the fact that Britain did not need or want a German alliance, Salisbury did not think either the British or German government was in a position to make commitments to the other because of the mutual hostility of public opinion, which might well prevent the governments from honoring any agreements they might make.

❑ *The Anglo-Japanese Alliance*

Having failed to secure guarantees of German support to halt the Russian advance in East Asia, the British made renewed but futile efforts to reach direct agreement with the Russians to achieve the same purpose (see p. 382). Rebuffed by Russia, they redirected their attention to Japan, which had turned aside previous British advances in favor of a direct agreement of their own with Russia. That treaty—the Nishi–Rosen agreement of April 25, 1898—proved far from satisfactory from the Japanese point of view, for from the time of its signature the Russians persistently and flagrantly violated it. The Japanese therefore decided to let the British understand they would now be more receptive to joining an anti-Russian alignment.

The advantage to Britain of an alliance with Japan was obvious. "Such an agreement would, I believe, add materially to the naval strength of this country," the first lord of the Admiralty, Lord Selbourne, wrote on September 4, 1901, "and effectively diminish the probability of a naval war with France or Russia, singly or in combination." Further, a Japanese alliance would give the British the support against Russia in East Asia they had sought in vain from Germany and, perhaps even more important, forestall the possibility of a Russo-Japanese agreement at Britain's expense.

The advantage of a British alliance to Japan was equally obvious, but the Japanese hesitated to take a step so challenging to Russia. It was only after they failed to secure new commitments from Russia and a conflict with that power seemed unavoidable that they decided, and then with fearful misgivings and after bitter controversy within the Japanese government itself, to opt for an agreement with Britain.

The terms of the Anglo-Japanese alliance of January 20, 1902, were summarized earlier (see p. 325). That alliance was not a direct prelude to the Japanese war with Russia in 1904. On the contrary, both the British and Japanese hoped their alliance would make the Russians more amenable to striking a compromise agreement over their respective spheres of interest in East Asia.

Russia's reaction was not encouraging. Immediately after the signing of the Anglo-Japanese alliance, Lamsdorff, who had succeeded Muraviev as Russian foreign minister in 1900, attempted to revive the Far Eastern Triplice of 1895 (see pp. 317–

318) by proposing that France and Germany join Russia in a joint declaration of their determination to safeguard *their* interests in China. The Germans, not to be lured again into an unprofitable partnership, responded as they had to Russia's proposal for joint intervention in the Boer War: they could cooperate with France and Russia in East Asia only if France would guarantee the territorial status quo in Europe, that is, Germany's possession of Alsace-Lorraine—a condition they knew France would not accept.

As in 1895, the French were not at all eager to support Russia in China, but, as on that earlier occasion, they believed they could not afford to alienate their Russian allies. Accordingly, on March 20, 1902, they joined Russia in declaring that "in case the aggressive action of third powers or new troubles in China endangering the integrity and free development of that power [China] become a threat to their interests, the two allied governments would consult on means for safeguarding them." With that the French found themselves committed to supporting Russia in its disputes with Japan and Britain in a part of East Asia where no major French interests were at stake, and this at a time when the French government had at last decided to seek a settlement of its own differences with Britain in order to concentrate on the problem of Germany. The French therefore gave what support they could to Anglo-Japanese efforts to reach a compromise agreement with Russia.

Within the Russian government there were broad and bitter differences of opinion about the future course of Russian policy. The advocates of a continued extension of Russian influence in East Asia won. They were contemptuous of the Japanese and saw nothing to fear from their military or naval forces; the British navy could not fight on land; the French were allies; and the Germans, although they had refused outright support of Russia in China, had made it abundantly clear that they looked with favor on Russia's involvement in East Asia. The Russians were therefore convinced that they could pursue an aggressive Asian policy with impunity.

In Japan, Russian obduracy was decisive in securing a victory for the militants over the cautious moderates in government councils. The uncompromising attitude of the Russians had demonstrated clearly, so the militants argued, that Russian ambitions in East Asia were insatiable; Russia's capacity to realize those ambitions would be vastly increased with the completion of the Trans-Siberian Railway and military and naval installations in the Liaotung peninsula and Manchuria; if Russian expansion were to be halted at all, Japan must act decisively and soon. The alliance with Britain assured Japan the support of the world's greatest sea power, an invaluable asset to the island empire, and minimized the danger of joint action by the Russian and French fleets to cut off Japan's access to the Asiatic mainland.

Japan did act decisively. The great international importance of its subsequent defeat of Russia, however, was that it redirected Russian attention to the West. Thus in the end the most enduring consequences of the Anglo-Japanese alliance were to be experienced in Europe.

The alliance with Japan was the first formal diplomatic move in Britain's defensive strategy. The next two important steps, the entente with France in 1904 and that with Russia in 1907, are best examined in the context of French and above all German policy.

❑

TWENTY-THREE

The Franco-German Duel

❑ The French Diplomatic Offensive

The Anglo-Japanese alliance was a serious embarrassment to France, and as tension between Japan and Russia mounted in East Asia the French government worked vigorously to avoid being drawn into a conflict with Britain as a result of the altercation of their respective allies by seeking a peaceful resolution of all outstanding Anglo-French differences.

After France's humiliating defeat at the hands of Britain in the Fashoda crisis, Théophile Delcassé, the French foreign minister, recognized that his country could not afford the luxury of two mortal enemies, Britain and Germany. There was never any question as to which enemy Delcassé would choose. Although the French passion for revenge against Germany might ebb and flow, patriotic Frenchmen had never become reconciled to the loss of Alsace and Lorraine and, as all French governments demonstrated in their conduct of diplomacy, they did not dare face the wrath of public opinion to reach a settlement with Germany confirming this loss.

On the other hand, although France's rivalry with Britain might be far older, the only serious bones of contention were overseas territorial interests, Egypt in particular, and for the sake of a rapprochement, Delcassé was prepared to sacrifice French claims to Egypt and allow Britain a free hand there. But to make concessions over Egypt palatable to French public opinion and his own ministerial colleagues, Delcassé thought it prudent to seek compensation in some other part of North Africa. The obvious choice was Morocco, a still independent state adjacent to French-controlled Algeria and a country the French had long sought to include in their North African empire.

Morocco's sovereignty and independence had been recognized by the major European powers and the United States through an international convention signed in Madrid on July 3, 1880. The Madrid Convention was primarily the product of a British initiative to ensure that this strategic territory, which dominated the southern entrance to the Straits of Gibraltar, did not fall under the control of a rival power capable of contesting Britain's control over the Straits, exercised through its possession of Gibraltar, the rock that dominates the Straits' northern entrance.

Well aware of Britain's sensitivity regarding the Straits, Delcassé contemplated some arrangement whereby the critical area opposite Gibraltar could be neutralized, internationalized, or given to Spain, which was no longer regarded as a major power. But Delcassé also recognized that both Spain and Italy were concerned about Morocco, and he inaugurated careful negotiations with both to overcome any objection they might have to a French takeover. His negotiations with these countries, particularly those with Italy, were designed to serve yet another and even more important purpose: to undermine their relations with Germany and bring them into France's diplomatic orbit.

❑ *The Neutralization of Italy*

In November 1898 France concluded a commercial treaty with Italy, ending a long and costly tariff war and marking the beginning of a determined French diplomatic effort to detach Italy from the Triple Alliance. Earlier French efforts to accomplish this purpose had foundered over economic differences and enduring Italian bitterness over the French seizure in 1881 of Tunis, which the Italians had hoped to acquire for themselves. The Italians also had reason to remain loyal to Germany so long as Germany maintained cordial relations with Britain, for the Germans were more effective advocates of Italian interests in London than the Italians themselves and they could always be pressured into championing Italian policies for the sake of preserving the Triple Alliance. Britain, in fact, was the keystone of that alliance so far as Italy was concerned, for Italy, with its long and exposed coastlines, needed to remain on good terms with the world's greatest sea power. Furthermore, because of British naval supremacy in the Mediterranean, the Italians depended on British goodwill to realize their colonial ambitions in Africa.

Italian aspirations for overseas empire cooled perceptibly following their defeat by the Ethiopians in May 1896, and at approximately the same time growing Anglo-German antagonism lowered Germany's value as a champion of Italian interests in London. By the late 1890s, therefore, the Italians were more receptive than previously to offers of support and cooperation from France. Further, there had always been an influential body of public opinion in Italy that opposed the alliance with its former Austrian overlord and whose priority in foreign policy was the recovery of territory still held by Austria—*Italia irredenta,* unredeemed Italy—which they claimed should be part of Italy by reason of nationality. Colonial and irredentist ambitions were by no means mutually exclusive, however, and the Italians eagerly seized the colonial bait the French now dangled before them. In exchange for Italy's recognition of French claims to Morocco, France offered to recognize Italian claims to Tripolitania and Cyrenaica, territories in North Africa that were still part of the Ottoman empire. This bargain was sealed by an exchange of notes with Italy of December 14 and 16, 1900, which served a threefold purpose for the French: to strengthen their diplomatic ties with Italy, undermine Italy's ties with the Triple Alliance, and pave the way for France's acquisition of Morocco.

At the same time, the Italians exercised caution with Germany and Austria, for they recognized that membership in the Triple Alliance strengthened their bargaining position with France and their international position generally. They agreed readily enough to renegotiate the Triple Alliance treaties when these came up for renewal in 1902, but they sought to exploit the situation by demanding firmer assurances of Austrian and German support for their interests in North Africa and the Balkans. Further, to escape any danger to themselves from the Triple Alliance treaties, they demanded the insertion of specific provisions that these treaties were not directed against France. This was too much for the Germans, who were not blind to Italy's flirtations with France, and at Germany's insistence the Triple Alliance treaties were renewed without change on June 28, 1902.

The Italians yielded to the Germans because they were prepared to give France more specific assurances of their own. On June 30, only two days after the renewal of the Triple Alliance, Italy engaged in another exchange of notes with France to clarify the earlier notes regarding Morocco and Tripoli and to eliminate any possible French misunderstanding of Italy's treaty obligations to Austria and Germany. In these notes the Italians declared they would maintain strict neutrality in the event of a direct or indirect attack on France by one or more powers; that they would also remain neutral "in the event that France, as the result of direct provocation, should find herself compelled to take the initiative in a declaration of war for the defense of her honor and security"; and that they had no treaty obligations, nor would they contract any, that conflicted with the present declarations. With these notes of June 30, the Italians in effect repudiated their treaty obligations to Austria and Germany. The notes were subsequently postdated to November 1 to make their virtual overlap with the renewal of the Triple Alliance less obvious. Their purpose, however, remained the same.

❑ *The Wooing of Spain*

While negotiating with Italy, Delcassé was also negotiating with Spain over Morocco. By November 1902 he was able to submit a draft treaty to the Spanish government providing for a Franco-Spanish partition of Morocco. Spain was to receive northern Morocco, including the capital city of Fez, and the all-important coast opposite Gibraltar; all the rest of the country, including its Atlantic coast, was to go to France. Conceding the coast opposite Gibraltar to Spain was obviously done in the expectation that Britain would not object to Spain's possessing this strategic area, but the Spaniards were less sanguine on this score. Fearful that Britain would deprive them of the most valuable fruit of their bargain with France, they refused to sign the treaty offered by Delcassé unless Britain became a party to it. Uncertain himself about Britain's reaction, Delcassé did not press the issue, and it was only after the French agreement with Britain over Morocco was concluded in April 1904 that a Franco-Spanish treaty was finally signed on October 3 of that year. The published portion of this treaty proclaimed the intention of both states to maintain the independence and territorial integrity of Morocco, but this pious intention was contradicted in secret articles providing for the country's eventual partition. Once again Spain was assigned the coastal area opposite Gibraltar, but with far less hinterland than had been offered in the draft treaty of 1902, and in deference to Britain's wishes the coast opposite Gibraltar was to remain unfortified.

❑ *The Anglo-French Entente*

The crux of Delcassé's diplomatic campaign was an agreement with Britain, which he regarded as particularly necessary and urgent after the formation of the Anglo-

Japanese alliance and the growing possibility of a Russo-Japanese war in which Britain and France would find themselves in opposite camps. The political situation in Morocco also gave reason for haste, for widespread revolutionary agitation against the regime of Sultan Abdul Aziz seemed likely to develop into an outright civil war before Delcassé could complete diplomatic preparations for France's takeover of the country.

Delcassé's efforts to seek an accord with London came at a fortunate time, for Anglo-German negotiations had ground to a halt and the British were coming to regard Germany, with its ambitious naval program, as their most serious foreign threat. They were therefore as anxious as the French to avoid being drawn into a European conflict as a result of their Asian commitments.

Anglo-French negotiations began in the summer of 1902, and in the following year a spirit of reconciliation among the people of both countries was fostered by a visit of King Edward VII to Paris in May (Queen Victoria had died in January 1901) and a return visit on the part of President Loubet and Delcassé himself in June. But the decisive impetus for the successful conclusion of an Anglo-French agreement was provided by the Japanese attack on Russia in February 1904, which set off the Russo-Japanese War. According to Lansdowne, the British foreign secretary, from that time "the French negotiations, after sticking in all sorts of ignoble ruts, suddenly began to travel at the rate of an express train."

The Anglo-French *entente cordiale,* signed April 4, 1904, marked the end of the oldest national rivalry in European history. The entente was not an alliance, but simply an overall settlement of outstanding economic and colonial differences. It provided for an adjustment of disputed claims in Newfoundland, the New Hebrides, and spheres of influence along the frontiers of Siam (Thailand) in southeast Asia. But the heart of the treaty was the bargain over Morocco and Egypt, which had embittered Anglo-French relations for over two decades. The French promised not to obstruct British policies in Egypt in any way or oppose financial reforms the British administration in Egypt considered necessary. In return the British agreed to "recognize that it appertains to France, more particularly as a power whose dominions are coterminous with those of Morocco, to preserve order in that country, and to provide assistance for the purpose of all administrative, economic, financial and military reforms which it may require." At Britain's insistence, the two governments agreed not to permit the construction of any fortifications or strategic works along the Mediterranean coast of Morocco, and to give special consideration to the interests of Spain. These interests were spelled out in a secret article providing that a narrow strip of northern Morocco, including the (demilitarized) Mediterranean coast, was to go to Spain when the sultan ceased to exercise authority—provisions subsequently embodied in France's treaty with Spain over Morocco of October 3, 1904. To execute the provisions of the Anglo-French treaty, the two governments pledged reciprocal diplomatic support, a commitment that proved to be crucial in the diplomatic crisis that erupted over Morocco in the following year.

❑ *The German Counteroffensive*

Although the Germans knew that Anglo-French negotiations were in progress, the actual conclusion of the entente came as a terrible shock, for they had come to regard Anglo-French antagonism as a permanent fixture on the international chess-board. Bülow might tell the Reichstag that Germany welcomed the entente as a contribution to peace, but behind this public appearance of confidence the Germans worried about the broader implications of the entente for their own international position.

❑ *The Abortive Approach to Russia*

The outlook for Germany was not entirely bleak, however, for the Russo-Japanese War seemed likely to open up new diplomatic opportunities for Germany and create situations that might disrupt the alliances between Germany's rivals. The kaiser, now thoroughly disillusioned with Britain, thought the war offered a golden opportunity to displace France as Russia's principal ally in Europe, because the Russians would feel betrayed by the French entente with Britain, the ally of Japan. The French, fearing precisely what the kaiser had in mind, made strenuous efforts to reassure the Russians of their loyalty. Thus the Russians, despite catastrophic defeats on land and sea in Asia and revolution at home, found themselves in an exceptionally strong diplomatic position throughout the war and beyond.

Just how strong that position was became evident in the aftermath of an incident that took place on October 21, 1904, when the Russian Baltic fleet en route to the Pacific fired on British fishing boats on the Dogger Bank in the mistaken belief that they were Japanese torpedo boats. (It will be recalled that Russia's Pacific fleet had been sunk or immobilized by the Japanese in the first days of the war, and that the Straits Convention forbade the passage of Russia's Black Sea fleet into the Mediter-ranean.) The Dogger Bank episode provoked angry protests in Britain and created the kind of situation the Germans hoped to exploit to lure or pressure Russia into a German alliance.

As part of their campaign to win Russia's friendship, the Germans were supply-ing coal to the Russian fleet, and they let the Russians know that in doing so they too had incurred the wrath of Britain. The Germans therefore asked, for the sake of their mutual protection, for definite Russian commitments to Germany. The tsar agreed and asked the kaiser to send him a draft treaty embodying the commitments Germany desired. That draft, dated October 30, called for a defensive alliance for mutual support against one or more *European* aggressors because, as the kaiser told the tsar in a private letter, it was essential that the United States, which was friendly to Japan and suspicious of Russian activities in Manchuria, should not feel threatened by their agreement.

For over a fortnight—in fact, until the crisis with Britain over the Dogger Bank incident had been resolved, largely through the mediation efforts of Delcassé—the Russians allowed the Germans to believe they were on the point of agreeing to the German alliance. Then on November 23 the tsar telegraphed that he thought it desirable to consult France before signing the treaty with Germany. With that the treaty was doomed, as the kaiser sadly acknowledged at the end of December. The tsar had proved himself spineless in dealing with France, he said, and his ministers had "spat into the German soup." "A completely negative result after two months of honest work and negotiation. The first failure I have personally experienced."

The kaiser now sought to reverse his policy. "We must now do everything possible to cultivate our relations with America and Japan," he said. "We must treat Russia with very definite coolness, and keep America and Japan friendly." The Russians, however, skillfully kept the kaiser's hopes for a rapprochement alive so that he continued to woo Russia throughout the years that Russia was immobilized in the west by defeat in Asia and domestic revolution. The kaiser's Russian policy during this period was an important and perhaps the principal reason why Germany failed to take advantage of this uniquely favorable opportunity to improve its international position.

❏ *The First Morocco Crisis*

Germany's failure to destroy or dilute the Franco-Russian partnership through an alliance of its own with Russia coincided with the first French move to begin the takeover of Morocco, which had been conceded to them by their treaties with Britain, Italy, and Spain. The French had hoped to delay this move until Russian support would again be available to them in the West, but their hand was forced by events in Morocco, where it appeared the existing government would soon be overthrown and France's carefully prepared plans disrupted.

On January 25, 1905, after much hesitation, a French mission arrived in Fez to open negotiations with the sultan designed to lead to the establishment of a de facto French protectorate over the country. The Germans had repeatedly stressed their lack of interest in Morocco, but they were decidedly interested in the Anglo-French entente, which had been arranged through a division of spheres of influence in countries that did not belong to Britain or France in the first place—and all this without consulting or offering compensation of any kind to Germany. They therefore determined to block the French takeover of Morocco, and by thus depriving the French of their chief reward for relinquishing their rights in Egypt, knock the keystone out of the Anglo-French entente and sow suspicion and discord between the entente partners.

Germany's Morocco campaign was largely the conception of Friedrich von Holstein, a senior official of the German foreign office, who convinced Chancellor Bülow of its feasibility and necessity. Holstein's policy was based on the expectation that the British and French, if faced with international opposition over Morocco and the prospect of a serious crisis, would each have doubts about the reliability of the other and would seek to evade entente commitments through separate bargains of maximum advantage to itself.

The Germans were in a strong legal and seemingly strong diplomatic position to block a French takeover of Morocco. The Madrid Convention of July 3, 1880, signed by all the European countries with an interest in Morocco and by the United States, guaranteed the sovereignty and territorial integrity of Morocco and guaranteed all the signatory states a most favored nation status in the country. Thus, according to an international treaty the French themselves had signed, they could do nothing in Morocco that would infringe on the rights of other signatory states without their consent.

To initiate its Morocco campaign and proclaim to the world its intention to defend Morocco's sovereignty as established by the Madrid Convention, the German government decided to make use of the kaiser's forthcoming cruise to the Mediter-

MAP 18   THE MOROCCO QUESTION

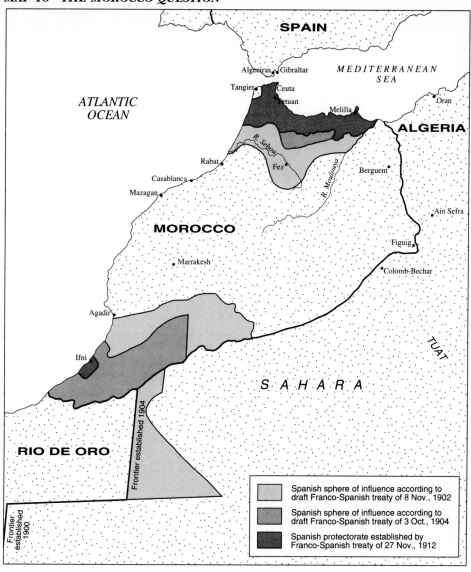

SPAIN

ATLANTIC
OCEAN

MEDITERRANEAN
SEA

Algeciras　Gibraltar

Tangier　Ceuta

Tetuan

Melilla

Oran

ALGERIA

R. Sebou

Rabat

Fez

R. Moulouya

Berguent

Casablanca

Mazagan

Ain Sefra

MOROCCO

Figuig

Marrakesh

Colomb-Bechar

Agadir

Ifni

TUAT

SAHARA

Frontier established 1904

RIO DE ORO

Frontier
established
1900

	Spanish sphere of influence according to draft Franco-Spanish treaty of 8 Nov., 1902
	Spanish sphere of influence according to draft Franco-Spanish treaty of 3 Oct., 1904
	Spanish protectorate established by Franco-Spanish treaty of 27 Nov., 1912

ranean. He was to land at Tangier, on the Moroccan coast opposite Gibraltar, where he was to ignore the French altogether and deal solely with the government of the sultan, which was to be assured that the preservation of Moroccan independence was in the interest of all trading nations. It was with some difficulty that the kaiser was persuaded to land at Tangier, where reports of civic disturbances gave him reason to fear for his personal safety, but he finally disembarked at the Moroccan seaport on March 31, 1905.

Once he had made his formal entry into the city, the dramatic possibilities of the occasion excited his imagination and his representation of the German position on Morocco was a good deal more vigorous and provocative than his government had intended. Instead of ignoring the French, the kaiser pointedly informed the French representative in Tangier that he intended to deal with the sultan as a free and equal ruler of an independent state, that he would know how to safeguard Germany's interests in Morocco, and that he would expect these to be recognized by France.

With the kaiser's landing in Tangier, the Germans threw down the gauntlet to France and set off what became known as the First Morocco Crisis. There has been much speculation about the fundamental purpose of Holstein's Morocco policy. A strong case can be made that his ultimate purpose was to provoke war with France, and from a cold-blooded point of view war would certainly have been in Germany's interest in 1905. France was allied with Russia and had recently arranged diplomatic alignments with Britain, Italy, and Spain. Germany was thus encircled by a ring of hostile powers and left with only one ally, Austria-Hungary, and even that ally might be wooed successfully if the encircling powers offered Austria the prospect of regaining its former dominant position in central Europe.

Quite the simplest way for Germany to have abolished the danger of encirclement would have been to smash the parts of the circle, and in 1905 its chances for doing so were exceptionally good. Russia, France's most formidable continental ally, was immobilized by defeat in Asia and revolution at home; Britain was reorganizing its armed forces, but that process had barely begun and British sea power would be of no use in defending Paris. German military leaders had great respect for the French army, which they considered far superior to that of 1870, but France itself had been weakened by domestic conflict, the legacy of the Dreyfus case, and a bitter controversy between church and state. The Germans thus had a unique opportunity, and one they themselves realized would be of short duration, to fight France without having to face the prospect of a war on two fronts. After that they would be free to deal with Russia, drill Italy back into line, and ensure the loyalty of Austria. In short, they had an opportunity to establish their hegemony over Europe, a prospect the British justifiably dreaded.

It was with full awareness of this opportunity that General Alfred von Schlieffen, chief of the German general staff, perfected his famous Schlieffen plan, which depended for its success on Germany's concentrating its forces in the west to achieve a quick and decisive victory over France before Russia could intervene. (For a fuller discussion of the Schlieffen plan, see pp. 455–457.) As Holstein and Schlieffen were in frequent touch with each other throughout the Morocco crisis, there can be no doubt that they discussed the possibility—and desirability—of war against France at this time.

The most obvious objection to the theory that Holstein's Morocco campaign was designed to provoke war with France is that Germany did not go to war. But the war theory is also undercut, and very convincingly so, by the documentary record of Germany's diplomatic strategy and its overall conduct of policy. Here the important difference must be borne in mind between a diplomatic campaign conducted with the deliberate purpose of provoking war, and one that is based on the threat or possibility of war.

The immediate purpose of German policy was to prevent France from gaining any benefit from its entente with Britain and to make both powers realize that they could conclude no far-reaching colonial settlement without the participation and consent of Germany. "We don't want to achieve anything in particular," Holstein wrote to his cousin and confidante. "Our action was intended to demonstrate 'that things can't be done without us.'" France was to be taught a lesson, but far from desiring a rupture with France, Holstein wanted this lesson to be administered in such a way as to avoid a Franco-German confrontation, and for this purpose he proposed to make use of that familiar instrument of the European concert: an international conference attended by representatives of all the states that had signed the 1880 Madrid Convention. "Contractual collectivity," he wrote to Bülow on April 5, "is a principle on which we can take a firm stand without ourselves appearing to harbor aggressive intentions. Moreover, this idea has the advantage that while affecting French interests it does not affect French pride, just as the collective victories of 1814 were less of an insult to France than the German victory, gained alone, of 1870. . . . If the conference is held it will, whatever the result, definitely not hand Morocco over to the French."

An international conference had the further merit of opening the way for an eventual settlement between Germany and France, for arrangements could be made behind the scenes to give Germany as well as France an international mandate for restoring order in certain parts of Morocco. In this way, Germany would be eased out of its commitments to Morocco, France would have been taught its lesson, and Germany would receive a share of the spoils of Morocco or suitable compensation elsewhere. Before the conference met at which such arrangements could be made, however, Germany could not appear willing to bargain over Morocco, for this would undercut the very principle on which its international support would be based.

That Germany would receive such support Holstein did not doubt for a moment. The United States would automatically champion the principle of the Open Door in Morocco as it had in China. Britain could not afford to back France actively for fear of offending the Americans, and in any case influential interest groups in Britain would welcome the opportunity to evade their government's commitments to France under the umbrella of an international agreement. "We will surely be able to hold Italy in line," Holstein said, "if necessary by a gentle hint that while we settle [i.e., reach a compromise agreement] with France, Austria might make a settlement about the *irredenta*." Moreover, Italy would be unwilling to see Morocco reduced to the status of Tunis, where French political ascendancy had already been accompanied by the gradual exclusion of Italian interests. Spain, which had long coveted Morocco for itself, would certainly oppose a French takeover, and the smaller signatory states would vote readily enough for the principle of the Open Door when they saw they were in good company. Finally, Russia, in defeat and revolution, would not dare oppose an international mandate or run the risk of an altercation with Germany.

Holstein's assessment of the foreign powers' positions on Morocco proved to be totally wrong in almost every respect, but the important point insofar as his motives are concerned is that the diplomatic victory he so confidently expected eliminated any reason for war. Foreign powers, of course, had no way of knowing the limited nature of Holstein's objectives, which he failed to clarify with any precision for the benefit of his own government—or for himself for that matter. "We don't want to achieve anything in particular" is a ludicrously inadequate guideline for the conduct of a diplomatic campaign, and this very lack of a clear perception of purposes and goals among the Germans themselves was certainly a major reason for Germany's ultimate diplomatic debacle.

In the first weeks of the Morocco crisis, however, Holstein's policy seemed to be working beautifully. On June 6, 1905, Delcassé, the principal architect of the Anglo-French entente and the statesman Germans regarded as their most formidable foe, resigned under pressure from ministerial colleagues who feared that his determination to stand firm over Morocco would play into Germany's hands by offering an excuse for war.

In bringing about Delcassé's fall, the Germans appeared to have scored a great diplomatic triumph, but that triumph was illusory at best. They had achieved nothing concrete: the Anglo-French entente was still intact; they had secured no concessions. All they had achieved in fact was to alarm the world over their intentions and confirm their reputation abroad as saber-rattling bullies. As if to emphasize Germany's insensitivity to its appearance, the kaiser chose the day Delcassé resigned to elevate Bülow, to whom he gave sole credit for this diplomatic success, to the rank of prince.

The fall of Delcassé did not lead to a relaxation of German pressure on France. On the contrary, now that Delcassé was gone the Germans expected the French government to agree at last to their proposal for an international conference, which Holstein at least believed would provide the forum for an amicable settlement. "Basically, the problem between ourselves and France is now a matter of form," he wrote to his friend Radolin, the German ambassador to Paris, "for we don't want to upset France's future." Holstein's "vision of the future," as he himself termed it, was that an honest effort should be made to introduce reforms in Morocco, presumably under international mandate. In all likelihood these reforms would fail. In this situation Germany would be free from commitments to the sultan and in a position to reach a direct understanding with France to the exclusion of third parties, specifically Spain, whereby Germany might be conceded a sphere of influence in Morocco while all the rest went to France.

But Rouvier, the French prime minister, who upon Delcassé's fall took over the portfolio for foreign affairs as well, proved to be no more yielding than Delcassé to German demands. He had received what the French interpreted to be unequivocal assurances of support from Britain; Italy and Spain were already enrolled on France's side over Morocco; and from the United States he had received word from President Roosevelt that his government would decline to participate in a conference if France so desired. The most encouraging assurances of all, however, came from Germany itself, where the kaiser, quite as baffled as were foreign powers by his government's insistence on a conference and elated by the fall of Delcassé, informed the French of his desire to extend the hand of friendship. On the occasion of the wedding of his son, the German crown prince, on June 6, 1905, William expressed his disgust about the uproar his own government was causing. "I haven't the slightest intention of waging war with France over Morocco," he told General de Lacroix, the leader of the French delegation at the ceremony, an assurance he authorized the general to report to his government. Thus the French knew they had nothing to fear by standing firm. Germany's negotiators were dismayed by the Rouvier government's rigidity, which differed not at all from Delcassé's policy, and though they suspected imperial indiscretions had something to do with it, they had no idea to what extent their own emperor had sold them out.

On July 8, 1905, the French at last agreed to a conference over Morocco, but their acceptance hardly represented a victory for the Germans, for the French only did so after making certain the majority of states represented at the conference sided with them. Even then, as the price for their acceptance they compelled the Germans to agree in advance to onerous conditions, in particular to secure French consent to all items on the conference agenda. This meant in effect that the Germans would be obliged to yield on all differences over the agenda or accept the blame for the breakdown of negotiations in setting up a conference they themselves had demanded.

❑ *The Kaiser's Diplomatic Initiative: The Björkö Treaty*

On July 20, 1905, just a fortnight after France agreed to attend the Morocco conference, Bülow received a message from the kaiser that shifted the focus of German policy. The tsar had agreed to meet the kaiser on board his yacht in the Bay of Björkö (off the coast of Finland), and he asked Bülow to telegraph him *"at once and directly"* the text of the draft defensive alliance treaty Germany had proposed to Russia the previous November (see p. 395). The kaiser was evidently convinced, following Russia's most recent military and naval disasters in Asia, that the time was ripe to renew his bid for a Russian alliance, and he announced his intention to push this through "no matter what the cost."

The meeting of the imperial cousins at Björkö took place on July 24. When presented with the German treaty, the tsar protested that he could not possibly agree because of Germany's strained relations with France over Morocco. The kaiser brushed this objection aside. He regarded Morocco as a "steppingstone" to better relations with France, and he assured the tsar that he intended to adopt a conciliatory attitude on this question. With that the tsar was won over. "Treaty just signed by the tsar and me," the kaiser telegraphed triumphantly to Bülow that same day. ". . . Tsar immediately willing *because we were now on good terms with France,* which especially pleased him. He regards this as the permanent settlement of the Alsace-Lorraine question. It is to remain secret until peace [with Japan] is concluded."

Bülow was effusive with his praise. "For this success Your Majesty alone is to be congratulated, for Your Majesty alone has made it possible and realized this turn of events." The kaiser declined all personal credit. "God arranged and willed it so," he said. ". . . That which Russia dismissed in her pride last winter, and in her passion for intrigue tried to exploit to our harm, she has now accepted with thanks and pleasure as a lovely gift after being humiliated by the terrible, hard, and humbling hand of the Lord."

Bülow, although disturbed by changes the kaiser had introduced in the original draft of the treaty making it, he thought, more favorable to Germany, recognized that even in its present form it would free Germany from the Franco-Russian vise, and like the kaiser he believed Morocco could be used as a steppingstone to better relations with France, an ideal bribe to secure France's agreement and perhaps adherence to the Russo-German treaty. "Morocco could not serve a better purpose for us," he said, "and would be far and away the best outcome of our Morocco campaign."

Holstein did his best to convince Bülow that a policy of bribery and concessions would be disastrous. If Germany now retreated over Morocco, no matter for what reason, "it would put an end to any doubts as to the usefulness of the entente [with Britain] for France, and France would not be drawn closer to Germany but driven further away." It was not up to Germany to conciliate France for the purpose of luring France into the Russo-German alliance. Rather it was the task of Russia to persuade France to take a more conciliatory attitude toward Germany. Moreover, Russia had every reason to prevent France from scoring a resounding diplomatic victory in partnership with Britain, because a victory for the Anglo-French entente would lower the value of the Russian alliance for France.

❑ *The Aftermath of Björkö; Germany's Diplomatic Defeat*

After Björkö, however, Holstein's Morocco policy was totally bankrupt, a victim of the kaiser's (and now Bülow's) willingness to sell out what remained of the German position on behalf of the Russian alliance. Instead of persuading the French to be more conciliatory to the Germans, the tsar and his ministers did everything they could to persuade the Germans to yield to France over Morocco. They received significant support from Count Witte, the president of the Russian council of ministers and leader of the Russian delegation to the peace conference with Japan at Portsmouth, New Hampshire. After signing the peace treaty with Japan on September 5, 1905, Witte returned to Russia by way of Paris, where he was entrusted with the task of securing a major loan for Russia, in desperate financial straits following the disastrous war in Asia and confronted with revolution at home. In Paris he was informed by Rouvier that a loan was out of the question until the Morocco affair was settled, and he asked Witte to persuade the Germans to be more amenable. "In return for my services," Witte wrote in his memoirs, "he promised to give me full assistance in the matter of the loan." Witte immediately called on the German ambassador to urge that Germany settle its differences with France at all costs, for never again would there be a French cabinet so favorably disposed to Germany or so immune to the blandishments of Britain. Witte made a number of specific proposals as to how such a settlement could be reached, all of them along the lines recommended to him by Rouvier.

Upon receiving Witte's reports from Paris, his government instructed him to go to Berlin to talk directly with the kaiser and his ministers in the sense desired by the French. Witte did his work well. To Bülow he held out the prospect of an alignment of Germany, France, and Russia to put an end to Britain's prospering at the expense of others; but to win over France, it would be necessary to make further concessions over Morocco. Bülow promised that this would be done, as did the kaiser. He wanted the "disgusting bickering" with France over Morocco to end. "Gaul must now be accorded conciliatory treatment," he said, ". . . so that she can make the necessary shift that will take her into our alliance." Witte promptly informed the French of his success. The kaiser had told him "that he did not intend to make difficulties for the French government and that he would give imperial orders to this effect." These orders were transmitted through Bülow and conceded virtually everything the French wanted on the agenda of the forthcoming conference over Morocco.

These concessions gained the Germans nothing except a broad hint to make more concessions. Persuading the French to join their alliance was going to be difficult, the tsar wrote the kaiser on October 7, and it might be a good idea to postpone ratification of the Björkö treaty "until we know how the French will look at it." Witte made the case for further concessions more specific. Because the French government could not act against the sentiment of French public opinion, Germany should cultivate French opinion through friendly gestures to prepare the way for France to join the Russo-German alliance.

Although discouraged, the kaiser pressed on. The Russians were having great difficulty persuading the French to enter into an alliance with Germany, he told Bülow on November 26. "We must therefore do this ourselves, and try to resolve the great problem of winning over Gaul supported by our clear conscience and the good cause." Bülow saw the situation more clearly and realized that the tsar's decision to await the consent of France before ratifying the Björkö treaty was equivalent to its repudiation by the Russian government. With Germany's Russian policy in shambles, Bülow now advocated returning to a firm line on Morocco, but in a letter written on New Year's Eve of 1905 the kaiser ordered him to preserve peace, virtually at any price. A firm stand on Morocco would run the risk of war. Before Germany could even consider a foreign war, it would be necessary to conclude a firm alliance with Turkey, equip the German army with new weapons, and above all eliminate the socialist menace at home. "First the Socialists, cut off their heads and make them harmless, if necessary by a blood bath, and then a foreign war. But not before and not *a tempo!*" German foreign policy should be conducted to avoid war "so far as at all possible, and *certainly for the present.*" Such hysteria over the Socialists, or indeed any person or group opposing his policies, was typical, but it is noteworthy that the kaiser rejected war as a "solution" to the Socialist problem, at least at this time, because some historians believe a major motive of the German government's decision to go to war in 1914 was to divert domestic discontent to foreign battlefields.

Bülow was careful not to comment on his sovereign's domestic program, but he fully agreed with the kaiser in rejecting a military solution to the Morocco problem. Instead he opted for what he called a "well managed and graceful retreat," which he believed would preserve Germany's prestige and save face for its government.

Bülow's policy achieved neither objective. The international conference on Morocco finally convened in the Spanish city of Algeciras, directly opposite Gibraltar, on January 16, 1906. By March it was evident to the Germans that they did not have majority support at the conference and were doomed to defeat, but they were bound to accept the decisions of a conference they themselves had demanded at the cost of so much international tension.

The final Act of Algeciras reaffirmed the independence and territorial integrity of Morocco, but France and Spain were given control of the Moroccan police and France predominant control over a Moroccan state bank. These provisions were generally understood to give France and Spain the necessary footholds for gradually establishing their respective spheres of influence in Morocco as agreed in their treaty of October 3, 1904. In the final voting over the crucial issue—control over the police and finances—the Germans were supported only by Austria and Morocco itself. Rarely has a state not previously defeated in war suffered so complete and humiliating a diplomatic defeat as Germany at Algeciras.

Germany's opponents had played a skillful game, but the Germans themselves were chiefly responsible for their diplomatic debacle. Their leadership was divided, their policies ill-conceived, ill-executed, and inconsistent. The Holstein plan to use Morocco as a wedge to break up the Anglo-French entente was based on thoroughly unrealistic assumptions, as were his expectations of international support at an international conference on Morocco. His hope that French disillusionment with Britain and an amicable settlement with Germany under international auspices might actually pave the way to a French–German rapprochement ignored the fundamental difference between France's attitude toward Britain and Germany. "France has only one enemy and that is Germany," Baron Courcel, the former French ambassador to Berlin, told Salisbury at the time of the Kruger telegram crisis. "You can adjust your policy accordingly."

The kaiser's effort to use Morocco as a steppingstone to agreements with both France and Russia doomed whatever chances the Germans might have had of getting colonial concessions through a bargain over Morocco, but his policy too was thoroughly unrealistic. France, now so favorably aligned with Britain as well as Russia, would never have agreed to abandon Britain in favor of Germany or admit Germany into its partnership with Russia. And the Russians depended far too much on Anglo-French financial markets to risk concluding a treaty of their own with Germany, although they made good use of German offers to ensure a benevolent attitude on the part of Paris and London.

Throughout the Morocco crisis the one policy Germany could have adopted with any real prospect of success was the threat or actual use of force: force to compel Britain and France to allot them a share of Morocco or significant colonial concessions elsewhere; force to browbeat Russia into an alliance, although the value of such a partnership would have been dubious at best; or, finally, force to achieve German hegemony over Europe by going to war, which most military authorities and certainly Germany's military leadership at that time believed Germany could have won. That Germany did not go to war in 1905–1906, and the actual conduct of German policy during the crisis, argues against the widely accepted belief that the war in 1914, which Germany waged under incomparably worse circumstances, was deliberately provoked by the Germans as part of a carefully conceived plan to conquer the world. Theodore Roosevelt was nearer the mark when he wrote to the British ambassador in Washington in May of 1905: "If the Kaiser ever causes trouble, it will be from jumpiness and not because of long-thought-out and deliberate purpose."

The long-range importance of the Morocco crisis was not Germany's defeat but the crystallization of the anti-German alignments that were to prevail in World War I. The British and French governments entered into military and naval talks to convert their entente into an outright alliance; the first serious moves were made toward the Anglo-Russian entente of 1907; and Italy's unreliability as a partner in the Triple Alliance was clearly exposed. Left with only the dubious support of Austria, Germany from this time forward was compelled to cater to the Habsburg empire, which was rendered increasingly desperate by the threat of national revolutions at home and abroad. The stage was set for the Bosnian crisis of 1908 and the events of July 1914.

❑ *The Anglo-Russian Entente*

On August 12, 1905, while the Russo-Japanese War was still in progress, the British renewed their defensive alliance with Japan, which was now extended to include India. This treaty was obviously intended to discourage Russian advances in East Asia after the tsarist empire's recovery from defeat, but the British also hoped this reaffirmation of their ties with Japan would secure milder peace terms for Russia and thereby lessen the danger of a Russian turn to Germany. The situation was delicate in the extreme because of Japan's sensitivity to any form of foreign pressure. The British were therefore as relieved as they were delighted to find that America's President Roosevelt was willing to mediate between Russia and Japan, and it was in America that peace negotiations were conducted and a final peace treaty signed on September 5, 1905.

To further stabilize Russo-Japanese relations and the situation in East Asia, the British and French extended loans to Japan as well as Russia and encouraged negotiations between the two recent antagonists, which led to the Russo-Japanese agreement of July 30, 1907 (see pp. 327–328). Ostensibly this agreement was a mutual guarantee for the preservation of the status quo in East Asia, but secret articles provided for dividing Manchuria into spheres of influence between Russia and Japan, which were henceforth to cooperate in consolidating their positions and keeping other powers out of that region.

The policies of Britain and France in dealing with Russia at this time were designed primarily to block Germany's ostentatious efforts to lure Russia into the German camp: hence their mediation on behalf of Russia in dealing with Japan, their immense loans to a bankrupt Russian government, and their contribution to stabilizing Russia's position in East Asia. For the French, preserving the Russian alliance undiluted by Germany was critical to their national security, but for France as for Britain it was also important to discourage Russian ambitions in East Asia and focus Russian attention once again on the problems of the West, where Russian support would be of greatest value to them.

It was also critical to the French to settle differences between their old and new allies, and even while negotiating their own entente with Britain, they were promoting a comparable entente between Britain and Russia. For a time the obstacles to such a settlement seemed insuperable, but Russia's defeat in East Asia and Britain's fears of Germany made both governments increasingly receptive to rapprochement. Britain's willingness to consider a settlement with Russia was not affected by a change of government in December 1905, when the Conservative administration of Arthur Balfour gave way to a Liberal ministry under the leadership of Sir Henry Campbell-Bannerman and Sir Edward Grey replaced Lansdowne as foreign secretary.

Grey had served as parliamentary undersecretary for foreign affairs under Rosebery, and like Rosebery his conception of British interests abroad was closer to that of the Conservatives than to the more radical and anti-imperial members of his own party. He adhered closely to the diplomatic course set by his predecessor, and it was he who guided British policy through the difficult final weeks of the Morocco crisis and the conference of Algeciras.

In his overall conception of British national interests, Grey was a staunch believer that maintaining the European balance of power was crucial for British security, and long before he took office he had come to regard Germany as the principal threat to that balance. Writing in 1903 he described Germany as "our worst enemy and greatest danger," and it was largely because of his concern over the German menace that he became an early advocate of diplomatic alignments with foreign powers to strengthen Britain's international position. He welcomed the Japanese alliance as well as the entente with France, and he needed no prompting from Paris to see the desirability of an entente with Russia.

In February 1906, to anticipate the possibility that Germany might yet go to war over Morocco, Grey wrote that "the door is being kept open by us for a rapprochement with Russia" and that this could be arranged "if it is necessary to check Germany." After Algeciras, Grey's suspicions of Germany's sinister intentions were kept alive by reports of German activities in Persia and Asia Minor, but it was evidently his fear that Russia might still be lured into some kind of agreement with Germany that prompted him to initiate talks designed to lead to a Russian agreement with Britain. In the last week of April 1906 a new British ambassador to St. Petersburg, Sir Arthur Nicolson, was dispatched to negotiate an entente with Russia.

Britain's motives in seeking an entente with Russia were clearly if somewhat ponderously spelled out by the chief of European intelligence of the British War Office. "By detaching her [Russia] from Germany we should have her on our side if and when Germany reaches the Persian Gulf—a contingency which is far less to be desired than Russia's presence there. It would also tend to weaken Germany's military position in Europe, and therefore to strengthen our own as well as that of France, the ally of Russia, and the Power which, like Great Britain, has much to fear from German preponderance in Europe."

The British treaty with Russia finally concluded on August 31, 1907, resembled the earlier entente with France in that its primary purpose was to eliminate outstanding differences between the two countries. The treaty did not cover China, where the interests of both powers seemed adequately safeguarded by their agreements with Japan, but it did deal with Tibet, over which China still claimed suzerainty and which both Britain and Russia sought to include in their respective spheres of influence. Both powers now agreed to stay out of Tibet, which was to be preserved as a neutral buffer state independent of China. Of special significance for Britain was Russia's renunciation of all direct contact with Afghanistan, which removed the Russian threat from that quarter to British India.

But the most important provisions of the treaty for both powers concerned Persia (Iran), heretofore a focal point of Anglo-Russian rivalry now being threatened with German inroads. The treaty divided Persia into British and Russian spheres of influence, with the northern sector adjacent to Russia's frontiers in the Caucasus and east of the Caspian Sea going to Russia, while a smaller southern sector dominating the entrance to the Persian Gulf and the overland routes to Afghanistan and India went to Britain. A large sector between the British and Russian spheres, including the greater part of the Persian Gulf littoral, was declared a neutral zone.

Each power promised not to seek special privileges in the sphere of influence of the other, and although it was not stated in the treaty, it was tacitly understood that both powers would cooperate to keep Germany out of Persia altogether. Since the magnitude of Persia's oil fields was as yet unknown, oil was not mentioned in the treaty.

The most critical issue plaguing Anglo-Russian relations during the past century—the control of the Turkish Straits—inevitably came up for discussion during the entente negotiations. In the 1890s Salisbury had suggested, perhaps chiefly for bargaining purposes, that the Straits were no longer a crucial question for Britain, but when the Russians raised the subject in 1907 Grey objected that any changes in the status of the Straits would make public opinion uneasy. He nevertheless assured the Russians that "if the negotiations now in progress between the two Governments with regard to the Asiatic question had a satisfactory result, the effect upon British public opinion would be such as to very much facilitate a discussion of the Straits question if it came up later on." This formula evidently satisfied Isvolsky, the Russian foreign minister, who believed that once the Anglo-Russian treaty was signed the British would be amenable to changes in the existing agreement regarding the Straits, an assumption that contributed to Isvolsky's frustration when the Straits again became a major international issue just a few months later.

❑

TWENTY-FOUR

Confrontational Diplomacy

The British entente with Russia completed the formation of what became known as the Triple Entente, which now stood opposed to the German-dominated Triple Alliance, more accurately called a Dual Alliance since Italy had long since been neutralized by its agreements with France. In contrast to Bismarck's alliance system, which had enmeshed all the European powers in a network of defensive agreements that made unilateral aggressive action on the part of any one of them impossible or at any rate extremely dangerous, the alliances in existence in 1907 were confrontational and the members of each group soon realized that they could blackmail their alliance partners by threatening to defect to the opposite camp. The result was a new succession of crises that threatened the peace of Europe as a whole.

❑ *The Renewal of the Austro-Russian Rivalry*

The two powers that first sought to take advantage of their bargaining position within their respective diplomatic alignments were Austria and Russia. Both empires were faced with revolutionary challenges to their political and social systems, and both were eager to enhance their prestige and divert domestic discontent through successes in foreign policy. Fatefully, both, after Austria's exclusion from Italy and Germany and Russia's containment in East Asia, could achieve such successes only in the Near East at the expense of the Ottoman empire, the Balkan states—or each other.

The 1897 Austro-Russian agreement to preserve the status quo in the Balkans had put the problems of this troubled region "on ice" for a brief period. The particularly dangerous problem of Macedonia, which was still under direct Ottoman rule, was covered by a second Austro-Russian treaty of February 1903, providing for their joint supervision of the Turkish administration and a wide-ranging program of reform (the Mürzsteg agreement; see p. 338). These treaties had restrained but by no means quelled the ambitions of the independent Balkan states and the revolutionary ferment among the subject nationalities of the Ottoman and Habsburg empires.

Austro-Russian cooperation in maintaining the status quo in the Balkans continued during the years when Russia was preoccupied in East Asia, but that cooperation gradually broke down as Russian attention shifted back to the West, where the revolutionary activity of the predominantly Slavic nationalities in the Balkans once again tempted the Russians, as on so many occasions in the nineteenth century, to support their Slavic brothers and thereby extend their own influence in the Balkan region.

During the decade after 1897 the Austrians failed to use the respite from competition with Russia in the Balkans to initiate reform programs to deal with their own nationality problems, and they observed with increasing anger and frustration how their allies, the Italians and the Romanians, were encouraging nationalist agitation among their compatriots living under Habsburg rule. But the nationalist agitation they saw most reason to fear emanated from Serbia, once their subservient satellite, which had now moved into Russia's political orbit.

❏ *The Serbian Factor*

Serbia's political orientation had shifted abruptly with the assassination in June 1903 of King Alexander, the leader of the Obrenovich dynasty, which had maintained close ties with Austria, and his succession by Peter, the head of the rival Karageorgevich dynasty. Both Alexander's assassination and Peter's election by the Serbian national assembly had been engineered by an intensely nationalistic faction of Serbian leaders who henceforth dominated the Serbian government, and who, even without the Slavic connection, could have been expected to look to Austria's principal rival, Russia, for support. Most prominent among the new Serbian nationalist leaders was Nicholas Pashich, twice prime minister between 1904 and 1908, who returned to power in 1912 and was leader of the Serbian government during the crisis that culminated in the outbreak of World War I.

To pressure Serbia into adopting a more conciliatory policy toward Austria and stop supporting nationalist revolutionaries, the Austrian government in 1906 imposed an embargo on Serbian exports to the monarchy, heretofore approximately eighty percent of Serbia's foreign trade. These exports consisted primarily of agricultural products and livestock, chiefly pigs, which explains how the Austrian embargo became known as the "pig war." Although at first a serious blow to the Serbian economy, the pig war ultimately proved beneficial because it forced the Serbs to find new markets and develop their own manufacturing and food-processing plants. After one year Serbia's foreign trade had actually increased, with the result that Serbia was emancipated from Austria economically as well as politically.

As was only natural, the pig war intensified the Serbs' hostility toward the Austrians, but it also made them extremely sensitive to keeping open and developing new outlets for their foreign trade: if Serbia was to maintain its economic independence from Austria, it needed its own ports on the Aegean and Adriatic seas and its own railways with access to the major eastern and western European lines. Its heightened awareness of the importance of trade routes explains Serbia's extreme reaction to the announcement in January 1908 by Count Aehrenthal, the Austrian foreign minister, of Austria's intention to build a railway through the sanjak (administrative province) of Novi Pazar. This sanjak was a narrow strip of territory through the Balkan Mountains between the Slavic states of Serbia and Montenegro, which, though still nominally part of the Ottoman empire, had been placed under Austrian military occupation by the 1878 Treaty of Berlin (see p. 227). The Austrians had two principal reasons for wanting control over the sanjak: to maintain a wedge between Serbia and Montenegro to prevent the political union of these ethnically related nations, and to preserve a route of their own to Ottoman Macedonia and thence to the Aegean. The Serbs interpreted this railway project, quite correctly, as an attempt to solidify Austrian control over the sanjak and extend Austrian political and economic influence throughout the southern Balkans. The Serbs' indignation was shared by the Russians, who protested that constructing a railway through Novi Pazar violated the spirit of the 1897 agreement with Austria to preserve the status quo in the Balkans. The British were quick to take advantage of the Austro-Russian rift to reinforce their own good relations with Russia, and in May 1908 Grey, the British foreign secretary, proposed a new reform program for Macedonia that clearly encouraged greater Russian involvement in the Balkans and would enable Britain to supplant Austria as Russia's principal partner there. The announcement of Austria's proposed railway through Novi Pazar was greeted with frank delight by a senior official of the British foreign office: "The struggle between Austria and Russia in the Balkans is evidently now beginning, and we shall not be bothered by Russia in Asia. The action of Austria will make Russia lean on us more and more in the future. In my opinion this will not be a bad thing."

❑ *Austria, Russia, and the Young Turk Revolution*

The Russians, however, still reeling from the shock of defeat and revolution, re-mained cautious, and though they endorsed the British reform scheme for Mace-donia, they were clearly eager to avoid trouble in the Balkans and still hoped to safeguard and promote their interests in the Near East through agreements with Austria.

Russia's most immediate objective in this region was to change the provision in the Straits Convention prohibiting the passage of Russian warships through the Turk-ish Straits—the rule that had kept Russia's Black Sea fleet bottled up during the recent war with Japan. But the Russians also retained grim memories of the Crimean War, when the British and French fleets had passed through the Straits to launch their attack on Russian soil. What the Russians wanted, therefore, was a one-sided agreement that would allow their own warships to pass through the Straits but deny a similar right to other powers. At the conclusion of his entente negotiations with Britain, Isvolsky had been led to believe, or allowed himself to believe, that Britain would agree to the changes over the Straits that Russia desired, an impression bol-stered by his meeting with King Edward at the spa of Marienbad in September 1907 and by a second meeting with the king in Reval in June 1908, this time in the company of the tsar.

Confident of Britain's approval, and confident too of the support of Russia's ally, France, Isvolsky now sought the agreement of Austria, whose interests would also be affected by changes in the Straits Convention. Shortly after his meeting with King Edward at Marienbad, Isvolsky sounded Aehrenthal on the question and evidently proposed that in return for its support, Austria should be allowed to annex Bosnia and Herzegovina. These Balkan provinces, like the sanjak of Novi Pazar, were still nominally part of the Ottoman empire, but they too had been placed under Austrian military occupation by the 1878 Treaty of Berlin. The annexation proposed by the Russians was thus a significant constitutional step beyond Austria's existing status in the provinces.

The furor over Austria's proposed sanjak railway temporarily put an end to further Austro-Russian negotiations, and in July 1908 the entire situation in the Near East was changed by the Young Turk revolution. This was an uprising of politically conscious Turks, initiated by army officers stationed in Macedonia, against the repressive regime of Sultan Abdul Hamid. Its most immediate result was the sultan's restoration of a constitution promulgated in 1876 by an earlier generation of reformers. That document proclaimed the indivisibility of the Ottoman empire, guaranteed political and religious freedom and equality, and provided for the establishment of parliamentary government with equality of representation for all the peoples of the empire regardless of nationality or religion.

The British warmly welcomed the Young Turk revolution and the prospect of a constitutional government in Constantinople, which they confidently expected would look to Britain for support and advice and abandon the previous regime's misguided employment of German military advisers and concessions to German entrepreneurs, in particular those involved in the construction of the Bagdad Railway. British pleasure in the triumph of the Young Turks was not shared in the other capitals of Europe. The French and Germans feared for their investments and concessions, the Austrians and Bulgarians for the Young Turk program of imperial reform. In accordance with the provisions of the restored constitution of 1876, which declared the Ottoman empire to be indivisible and promised equal political representation to all its peoples, the Young Turk government announced plans to summon representatives to Constantinople from all its provinces, including those over which the government at Constantinople had long since lost all but nominal authority. The Young Turks were, in effect, challenging Austrian control of the sanjak of Novi Pazar and Bosnia and Herzegovina; threatening the very existence of Bulgaria, which the 1878 Treaty of Berlin had left under Ottoman suzerainty; and threatening Bulgarian, Greek, and Serbian claims to Macedonia as well as Macedonia's own national independence movement. The Russians for their part feared that the Young Turk regime would be less likely to agree to changing the Straits Convention, and that the British might revert to their traditional opposition to Russia on this question to reestablish their influence in Constantinople.

Mutual concern about the Young Turks reactivated Austrian and Russian efforts to cooperate. The possibility that the Turks might seek to reassert their authority over Bosnia and Herzegovina seemed to make Austria's annexation of these provinces, as suggested by Isvolsky in the summer of 1907, not only desirable but necessary. Aehrenthal was therefore most receptive when Isvolsky renewed that proposal a year later, and on September 16, 1908, he and the Russian minister concluded an informal agreement at Buchlau in Moravia: Austria would not oppose changes in the Straits Convention desired by Russia; Russia would not oppose the Austrian annexation of Bosnia and Herzegovina.

Having cleared the decks with Austria, Isvolsky set off to the capitals of Europe to secure or, as he thought, confirm the agreement of the other great powers. Before he embarked, however, he was confronted by an announcement from Aehrenthal that Austria intended to proceed immediately with the annexation of Bosnia and Herzegovina. Aehrenthal realized this move would have international repercussions, for it violated the terms of the 1878 Treaty of Berlin, and to divert attention from Austria he arranged with Bulgaria, which was even more seriously threatened by the Young Turk program, to proclaim its complete independence from Turkey on October 5, 1908, one day before Austria's annexation announcement. Annexation would forestall any Turkish attempt to reclaim authority over these provinces, and it was also the kind of bold stroke in foreign policy Aehrenthal considered necessary to refurbish the Habsburg monarchy's prestige. To soften the blow for Turkey, he proposed to withdraw Austrian troops from Novi Pazar and restore that province to Ottoman authority.

❑ *The Bosnian Crisis*

The Bulgarian declaration of independence and Austria's annexation announcement duly took place on October 5 and 6, but contrary to Aehrenthal's expectations the Bulgarian declaration was almost totally eclipsed by Austria's action, which was greeted with howls of outrage from almost every part of Europe and set off what became known as the Bosnian crisis. The British denounced this move by "reactionary" Austria as a plot to undermine the liberal Young Turk regime "which is really pure and honest." The Germans were angry that Austria had not consulted them in advance, for the Austrian move would make it more difficult for Germany to maintain its influence in Turkey, although the Germans were nevertheless obliged to assure Austria of their support to avoid losing their one remaining ally. Agonized protests came from Serbia, which aspired to make these predominantly Slavic provinces part of a great south Slav state under Serbian control and saw in Austria's annexation a decisive setback to its ambitions. But the most vigorous protests came from Isvolsky, who was evidently surprised by the intensity of public indignation in Russia as well as Serbia. To fend off the criticism that would certainly be aimed at him when Aehrenthal revealed the bargain made at Buchlau (which Aehrenthal was certain to do in reply to criticism of Austrian policy), Isvolsky took the lead in denouncing the Austrian action and maintained that Aehrenthal had promised to submit the Bosnian–Straits dispute to an international conference, which alone would have the authority to alter existing international treaties. As no formal record had been made of the Buchlau negotiations, the Austrians could not provide documentary refutation of Isvolsky's version of the agreement. Isvolsky now stepped forward as the champion of the Serbs and demanded that the Austrians honor their commitment to submit the Bosnian question to an international tribunal.

Aehrenthal staunchly denied that he had agreed to an international conference and staunchly refused to attend one. The Austrians as well as their German allies had learned the lesson of the 1906 conference of Algeciras, where they were hopelessly outvoted, and Aehrenthal had no intention of submitting to a similar diplomatic defeat. As was to be expected, Britain and France supported Russia's demand for a conference, while Germany supported Austria's rejection of any kind of international meeting that was not restricted to a mere ratification of the Austrian annexation. German support was unequivocal. "I shall regard whatever decision you come to as the appropriate one," Bülow informed Aehrenthal on October 30, 1908.

In Serbia and Russia public demonstrations called for war against Austria, a challenge a number of Austrian as well as German leaders were eager to take on. In the forefront of Austrian warmongers was Count Francis Conrad von Hötzendorf, the Austrian chief of staff, who saw an opportunity to put an end once and for all to the Serbian menace while Russia was still weakened by defeat and revolution. If Serbia were allowed to survive, the Serbian threat would become steadily greater as Russia recovered its strength, by which time Austria might no longer be equal to the challenge.

To Conrad's enduring regret, the Bosnian crisis was settled not by war but by diplomacy. In January 1909 Aehrenthal strengthened Austria's diplomatic position through an agreement with Turkey whereby the Ottoman government recognized Austria's annexation of Bosnia and Herzegovina in return for monetary compensation. With this Turkish treaty in hand and guarantees of German support, Aehrenthal submitted what amounted to an ultimatum to Serbia to join Turkey in recognizing the Austrian annexation, drop its demands for compensation, and henceforth pursue "a correct and peaceful policy" in its relations with Austria. If these demands were not met by the end of March, he told the Germans on February 26, he proposed to follow them up with an outright ultimatum and to invade Serbia should this be rejected.

In vain Isvolsky sought assurances of military support from Britain and France, but Britain's Liberal government was preoccupied with social legislation and in France the Clemenceau government, although bitterly anti-German, was beset by labor strikes. Moreover, neither was willing to face the very real possibility of war at the side of a still weakened Russia to oppose an annexation of Ottoman provinces which the Ottoman government itself recognized. Both Britain and France therefore urged Russia to arrange a peaceful settlement of the crisis, and at the end of February Isvolsky informed the Serbs that they could not expect Russian military intervention on their behalf.

In accordance with the advice of his entente partners, Isvolsky now appealed for German cooperation in resolving the crisis. The Germans were thus presented with a splendid opportunity to work out an arrangement that would allow Isvolsky to save face and at the same time reassure Europe of Germany's peaceful intentions. Instead, although they agreed to mediate, the mediation they offered was a demand for Russia's complete surrender. On March 21, 1908, they sent a dispatch to St. Petersburg telling the Russians that they would advise Austria to send a circular note to the signatories of the 1878 Treaty of Berlin asking their consent to nullify the article in that treaty dealing with Bosnia and Herzegovina. But first the Germans wanted to be sure that Russia would accept the Austrian note. The German ambassador to St. Petersburg was therefore instructed to inform Isvolsky "in a definite manner that we await a precise answer—yes or no; we shall be obliged to consider an evasive, ambiguous, or unclear answer as a refusal." At the same time Russia must abandon its support of Serbia and persuade Serbia to recognize the Austrian annexation without further ado.

Had the Germans actually been seeking to provoke Russia into a declaration of war, their demands and the manner in which they were presented could hardly have been more insulting. But, although some German military leaders agreed with Conrad that this might be the last opportunity for war before Russia should again be at full strength, Bülow and his state secretary for foreign affairs, Alfred von Kiderlen-Wächter, were not bent on war; otherwise they would have formulated demands that Russia would have been compelled to reject and made certain beforehand of Austria's involvement. The Germans aspired to no more than a diplomatic triumph to recoup the prestige lost at Algeciras, and when Russia yielded to their de facto ultimatum they thought they had achieved it.

Abandoned by Russia, the Serbs also yielded. On the last day of March 1909 the Serbian government addressed a note to Austria embodying everything the Austrians demanded. Serbia would "abandon the attitude of protest and opposition" to the annexation and "change the direction of its present policy towards Austria-Hungary in order to live henceforth on terms of good neighborliness with the latter." Further, Serbia would reduce the size of its army and prevent the formation in Serbian territory of anti-Austrian revolutionary terrorist organizations.

With the submission of Russia and Serbia, Austria and Germany ostensibly scored the diplomatic triumph they desired, but at terrible cost to their international reputation and even at some loss so far as their own interests were concerned. In annexing Bosnia and Herzegovina, the Austrians fended off a potential but unlikely challenge to their control over provinces they already occupied under the authority of an international treaty, but at the same time they relinquished the strategic sanjak of Novi Pazar, which actually worsened their overall position in the Balkans. Further, incorporating another large body of discontented south Slavs only added to their existing surplus of nationality problems.

The Germans gained nothing at all but international ill-will and an intensification of foreign fears that Germany aspired to nothing less than European hegemony. As at the time of the Morocco crisis, however, Germany made no move to take advantage of Russia's temporary weakness to make the bid for European dominion their rivals so greatly feared. Helmuth von Moltke, chief of the German general staff (a nephew of the Moltke of 1866 and 1870), shared Conrad's regret that the crisis had not resulted in war. He was convinced that a war between Austria and Serbia could have been kept localized, Serbia would have been crushed, and Austria could have established its preponderance in the Balkans. But even if a full-blown European war had developed, the opportunity to wage it under such favorable circumstances was not likely to recur.

What did occur was a further aggravation of Russian and Serbian hostility toward Austria and Germany and a growing sense of Slavic solidarity. From Belgrade the Austrian minister reported that "everyone here is thinking of revenge, which can only be achieved with the help of Russia," while from St. Petersburg the German ambassador described similar sentiments on the part of the Russians. Russian Slavophiles were advocating closer relations with the Slavic nations of the Balkans and the Western powers to prepare for the final struggle between the Slavic and Teutonic races; Germany had inflicted a humiliation on the tsarist empire the Russians would never forgive or forget.

These sentiments were translated into practical politics as Russia and Serbia accelerated the buildup of their armed forces and sought to strengthen their international diplomatic positions. Far from honoring their promises, made under duress, to maintain good neighborly relations with Austria, the Serbs stepped up their anti-

Austrian agitation and abetted the formation of revolutionary terrorist organizations in Serbia and in the Slavic provinces of the Habsburg empire, with particular success in newly annexed Bosnia and Herzegovina.

❑ *The Aftermath of Bosnia: Turkey, Persia, and the Russo-German Potsdam Agreement*

The Bosnian crisis could have had unfortunate repercussions for Germany's relations with Turkey, for German support of Austria's annexation of the Ottoman provinces of Bosnia and Herzegovina might have destroyed whatever influence the Germans had acquired in Constantinople through their military missions and involvement with the Bagdad Railway. But the Germans were lucky. In April 1909 Sultan Abdul Hamid, who was accused of sympathizing with a conservative counterrevolution, was deposed and replaced by his ineffective brother, Mehmed V, and the constitution of 1876 was revised to deprive the sultan of his power to dissolve parliament and to make the cabinet responsible to parliament rather than the sultan. By this time the Young Turk movement was increasingly dominated by Turkish nationalists and the liberal idealism of the first phase of the revolution, with its program of freedom and equality for all the empire's nationalities and religions, had given way to a renewed Turkish Muslim zealotry. Providentially for the Germans, some of the more influential Turkish military leaders in the new government had been trained in Germany or by Germans, and under their auspices German influence in Turkey gradually revived.

In promoting their interests in Turkey, the Germans received unexpected help from Russia, where Isvolsky, now a bitter foe of Germany, had been happy to leave the foreign ministry after his Bosnian debacle to take the post of ambassador to Paris. His successor was Serge Sazonov, who had seen diplomatic service as embassy counselor in London and agent to the Vatican but was otherwise relatively inexperienced in foreign affairs. As described by a Russian diplomat serving in the Balkans, and one clearly not favorably disposed toward the new foreign minister, Sazonov was "modest, well-meaning, sensitive, and touchy," as well as "lacking in talent and experience," without energy, character, or initiative, and "totally ignorant about the Balkans."

Perhaps because of his inexperience, Sazonov was tempted to take advantage of temporarily favorable international situations to advance Russian interests without considering sufficiently the long-term implications of his policies—though succumbing to short-sighted temptation is a common failing among diplomats. Stalled in the Balkans, Sazonov endeavored to exploit Russia's geographical position to score successes in Persia, which Britain and Russia had divided into spheres of influence between themselves in their entente treaty of August 31, 1907. Ever since the signature of that agreement the British had complained of Russian treaty violations, but after Sazonov became foreign minister their complaints became increasingly frequent and angry.

The Germans were quick to exploit the Anglo-Russian rift over Persia. When the tsar and Sazonov paid an official visit to Potsdam in November 1910, the Germans arranged a tentative agreement with their Russian guests promising to recognize Russia's preponderance in northern Persia if Russia abandoned its opposition to the Bagdad Railway—a bargain that aroused consternation in Britain and France, which up to this time had turned aside German offers to participate in the Bagdad Railway in deference to the wishes of Russia (see pp. 344–345).

Germany's principal objective in negotiating with Russia at Potsdam, however, was not removing Russian objections to the Bagdad Railway but breaking up the Triple Entente. For this purpose Germany proposed a second agreement: a German guarantee to restrain Austria in the Balkans in return for a Russian declaration not to support a British policy of hostility toward Germany. The Germans did not attach great importance to such a declaration for its own sake; what they wanted was a document that could be used to sow suspicion between London and St. Petersburg. "The Russian assurance concerning relations with England is the alpha and omega of the whole agreement," Kiderlen said. "It must be drafted in such a way that it will compromise the Russians the day the English learn of it." The Russians, however, saw through this far from subtle game and would have nothing to do with the second agreement, although the tsar assured the kaiser personally that he would not pursue an anti-German policy. Even the agreement over the Bagdad Railway was treated with extreme wariness by the Russians, and almost a full year of further negotiation was required before an acceptable text was drafted.

❑ *Anglo-German Relations, the* Daily Telegraph *Affair, and Bülow's Fall*

Germany's relations with Britain were meanwhile growing steadily worse. Early in August 1908, prior to the Bosnian crisis, Wolff-Metternich, the German ambassador to London, had reported on a meeting with David Lloyd George, the chancellor of the exchequer. The British statesman spoke of negotiating an agreement between Britain and Germany to slow the naval arms race while a pacific and economy-minded Liberal government was still in power. Metternich had passed along this message in the evident hope that his government would discuss a naval agreement during the forthcoming visit to Germany of King Edward VII and Sir Charles Hardinge, permanent undersecretary for foreign affairs. The kaiser's reaction was typically forthright. On the margin of Metternich's report he wrote "No! Three times no!" Metternich's entire conversation with Lloyd George was "shameful and provocative for Germany," and the kaiser insisted that in the future his ambassador should "categorically reject such expectorations" with the reply "you can lick my ass." Metternich himself deserved "a strong kick in the ass" for being so flabby. The kaiser was scarcely more polite when he received the king and Hardinge on August 11, firmly refusing to consider any reduction in his naval program.

But in Britain too there was skepticism about economizing on Britain's naval construction, a point of view forcefully expressed by Sir Eyre Crowe, one of the senior Foreign Office officials most apprehensive about the German menace. "The more we talk of the necessity of economizing on our armaments," he said, "the more firmly will Germans believe we are tiring of the struggle, and that they will win by going on."

Anglo-German relations deteriorated still further during the Bosnian crisis, nor did they benefit from the kaiser's efforts to improve them. On October 28 an interview with the German sovereign was published in the London newspaper *The Daily*

Telegraph. The kaiser expressed dismay at the persistent British hostility toward him; unlike most of his subjects, he had always desired friendship with Britain and pursued pro-British policies. During the Boer War, for instance, he had firmly resisted French and Russian appeals to join in saving the Boer republics "to humble England to the dust," and he had sent the British a campaign plan to defeat the Boers that was remarkably similar to the one they had actually adopted.

The kaiser's *Daily Telegraph* interview did little more than create a certain amusement in Britain. In Germany, however, public opinion and the leaders of all major political parties were incensed at this latest display of imperial irresponsibility, and the *Daily Telegraph* affair developed into a domestic crisis of major proportions. But nothing came of the crisis except a break between Bülow and the kaiser, who believed his chancellor had not defended him with sufficient fervor against criticism in the Reichstag.

Bülow was already in deep political trouble. In 1908 the Reich naval office secured passage of a new naval bill providing that capital ships be replaced every twenty instead of twenty-five years by Dreadnought-type vessels, which accelerated the tempo of German fleet construction to four ships a year and enormously increased costs, for the new battleships were far more expensive to build than those of the pre-Dreadnought class.

Britain's reaction to news of the new German navy bill was what might have been expected: an outburst of public indignation, a demand for immediate and immense British naval increases ("we want eight and we won't wait"), and a proclamation that the Liberal government was determined to maintain the Two-Power Standard no matter what the cost. Early in 1909 Parliament duly authorized funds for eight new British battleships, with the construction of four to begin in March 1909 and a contingency plan for four more that was implemented in July.

Meanwhile the German government was having ever greater difficulty financing its naval program; between 1896 and 1908 German expenditure on armaments had almost doubled, with the greatest part of the increase going to the navy. When it became evident that Britain was determined to maintain its naval superiority by stepping up its fleet construction program at a pace beyond anything Germany could match, Bülow at last approached London to discuss a naval arms limitation agreement. Given the suspicion and hostility that Tirpitz's fleet building had aroused in Britain, however, it is little wonder that Bülow's soundings met with a frigid reception in London, especially as they were linked to a request for some kind of assurance that Britain would remain neutral if Germany became involved in war with other powers. Grey dismissed Bülow's proposal with the observation that such an entente with Germany "would serve to establish German hegemony in Europe and would not last long after it had served that purpose."

Although Bülow failed to negotiate a naval agreement with Britain, his mere attempt aroused the wrath of Tirpitz, who threatened to resign if there was any modification of his current fleet-building program. At this same time Bülow needed to raise the necessary funds for fleet construction and cope with Germany's increasingly perilous overall financial situation. For this purpose he introduced a finance bill in the Reichstag calling for a sharp increase in taxes, including a sharp rise in death duties, a provision that infuriated Germany's powerful monied interests and owners of large landed estates. The finance bill was defeated on June 24, 1909. Rebuffed by the British, rejected by the Reichstag, unable to counter Tirpitz's influence, and with his own influence with the kaiser eroded, Bülow resigned on July 14, 1909. He was succeeded by his minister of the interior, Theobald von Bethmann-Hollweg.

Bethmann, who lacked Bülow's diplomatic experience, perceived far more clearly the need for a naval agreement with Britain, but his efforts too ended in failure and for virtually the same reasons. The British were interested only in establishing a fixed ratio for the naval strength of the two powers that would guarantee Britain's continued naval superiority, a condition the kaiser and Tirpitz angrily rejected. Moreover, Bethmann, like Bülow, wanted some kind of assurance that Britain would not engage in or support a war against Germany, which the British in turn refused to consider. "We cannot enter into a political understanding with Germany which would separate us from Russia and France and leave us isolated while the rest of Europe would be obligated to look to Germany," Grey wrote to Goschen, the British ambassador in Berlin, in the last days of 1910. "No understanding with Germany would be appreciated here unless it meant an arrest of the increase of naval expenditure."

Two years after Bethmann took over the chancellorship, the only result of Anglo-German naval talks was increased mutual suspicion: the British were convinced that Germany only desired a free hand to establish hegemony in Europe and challenge British supremacy at sea; the Germans, that Britain was drawing together the cords of an anti-German coalition to encircle and ultimately destroy their country.

The British were indeed doing everything possible to preserve the Triple Entente, which they regarded as essential to the preservation of the European balance of power. They not only rejected all German requests for promises of neutrality in the event of a continental war but, to reassure Russia of Britain's loyalty, they steadfastly supported Russia in opposing railway building in Turkey. They were therefore understandably angry about Russia's Potsdam bargain with Germany over the Bagdad Railway (see p. 345) and fearful that Russia might betray them even more flagrantly if offered sufficiently alluring conditions—which, as we have seen, was exactly what the Germans were attempting to do.

❑ *The Second Morocco Crisis*

The Triple Entente was saved, or more accurately the danger of its disintegration was averted, by a new crisis over Morocco that developed, ironically enough, as a result of another German effort to undermine the Triple Entente, this time through a separate bargain with France. On February 8, 1909, at the height of the Bosnian crisis, France and Germany concluded an agreement over Morocco which the Germans evidently hoped would not only improve their relations with France but would sow further suspicion between France and Russia, whose relations had been embittered by France's refusal of support over Bosnia. The Franco-German agreement reaffirmed Morocco's independence and territorial integrity, but in addition Germany specifically recognized France's "special political interests" in that country in return for France's recognition of Germany's economic interests.

In the months that followed the German government came under increasing public criticism for failing to gain any concrete concessions in Morocco or anywhere else in the colonial field. This criticism grew more intense in April 1911 when the French took advantage of antiforeign demonstrations in the Moroccan capital of Fez to send troops into the country with the familiar excuse that such action was necessary to restore order. Although the French move violated the Act of Algeciras, as the Germans hastened to remind them, a French military occupation of Morocco had been expected by the powers ever since that same act had assigned France supervision of Morocco's police and finances. The Germans therefore knew they could expect little international support in protesting the French violation, but they believed they could and should receive compensation. Accordingly, after the French occupation of Fez, they made it very clear to Paris that they were waiting for French offers. When such offers failed to arrive (a ministerial crisis in June and the formation of a new ministry under Joseph Caillaux on June 28 delayed any decision the French might have made on the matter), the German government sent the gunboat *Panther* to Morocco's Atlantic seaport of Agadir, allegedly to protect German economic interests, and a German businessman was dispatched hastily to Agadir to establish that such interests existed. This tactic was inspired by Alfred von Kiderlen-Wächter, the head of the German foreign office, whose de facto ultimatum to Russia of March 21, 1909, had given Germany its "victory" in the Bosnian crisis. "It is necessary to thump the table," Kiderlen said, "but the only object of all this is to make the French negotiate."

Yet again the Germans failed to take into account how foreign governments and public opinion would interpret their table-thumping. For many years now they had thumped too much and too ineptly, and the "*Panther*'s leap" only served to rekindle foreign fears about Germany's intentions and convince the British and French governments that they must consolidate their ties with each other and with Russia. For the Germans, the timing of the Agadir demonstration was particularly unfortunate because Caillaux, the new French premier, was one of the few French leaders who sincerely desired better relations with Germany. A policy of reconciliation was now ruled out by a surge of anti-German sentiment in France and by the exorbitance of Germany's compensatory claims. After waiting in vain for French offers, the Germans finally set their own terms: in return for abandoning all German rights and interests in Morocco, they demanded the entire French Congo be ceded to Germany.

The British were if anything even more alarmed than the French by Germany's behavior: for the British a German gunboat at Agadir conjured up the specter of a German naval base on the Atlantic coast within striking distance of Gibraltar, and the British navy now prepared for war. Officials of the foreign office, on the other hand, believed the Germans were interested less in territorial gain than in disrupting the entente, which would give them the chance to establish hegemony over Europe. "The French game in Morocco has been stupid and dishonest," Grey's private secretary, Sir William Tyrell, told Hardinge, the permanent undersecretary, on July 21, "but it is a vital interest for us to support her on this occasion in the same way in which the Germans supported the Austrian policy in 1908 in Bosnia." In a speech on that same day, Lloyd George, generally regarded as the most conciliatory among Britain's Liberal leaders, issued an emphatic warning addressed to France even more than to Germany (though neither country was mentioned by name) that Britain would not tolerate any kind of international settlement that ignored Britain or British interests, by which he was generally understood to mean a separate wide-ranging settlement of Franco-German differences.

Now, as at the time of the first Morocco and Bosnian crises, the Germans had yet another opportunity to adopt that policy of the mailed fist (i.e., resort to force) about which the kaiser had declaimed so often and which inspired such international apprehension. But again the Germans did nothing. They allowed the French to spin out negotiations that kept their own hopes for compensation alive, and in the end they settled for a mere fraction of their original demand. In a convention signed November 4, 1911, the Germans gave France a free hand to establish a protectorate in Morocco; in return France ceded to Germany two strips of territory in Africa connecting the German Cameroons with the Congo and Ubanghi rivers, which the Germans desired as outlets for their colony's exports.

With that the Morocco problem, insofar as it was an international problem, was finally resolved, but instead of leading to a Franco-German reconciliation the November 4 treaty was met with howls of indignation in both countries. In France, public outrage over *any* compensation to Germany was a major factor in the overthrow of the Caillaux ministry in January 1912 and his succession by the foremost representative of French patriotic fervor, Raymond Poincaré, who was to lead what French patriots proudly hailed as a national revival (*réveil national*) and who professed that his generation had "no other reason for existence than the hope of recovering the lost provinces [Alsace and Lorraine]." In Germany, Tirpitz was delighted with the attacks of German patriots on Bethmann and Kiderlen for having settled for so little. "The more we are humiliated the more uproar there will be," he said. "The chances for a new naval law become steadily greater."

❑ *The Haldane Mission*

The Second Morocco Crisis reinforced British fears about the German menace, but it also raised questions about Britain's entente policies. Why should Britain allow itself to become embroiled in a European war for the sake of French colonial ambitions or take such pains to preserve its entente with Russia, which, as the British saw it, was consistently violating its treaty commitments in Persia? The behavior of France and Russia gave rise to sharp criticism in Parliament and the press and made the British government receptive to renewed domestic appeals for an agreement with Germany to limit the naval arms race, which imposed such financial burdens on the British economy. The actual initiative for the renewed Anglo-German negotiations appears to have come from Bethmann-Hollweg, who had sought an understanding with Britain since taking over the German chancellorship. Informed by Metternich, his ambassador to Britain, of the more receptive mood of the British government and public opinion, he turned for assistance to Albert Ballin, the head of the Hamburg-America steamship line and a friend of both the kaiser and Tirpitz. For some years Ballin had tried to convince his august compatriots of the political as well as economic necessity to limit Germany's fleet construction, and at Bethmann's request he approached Sir Ernest Cassel, a German-born British financial magnate, who enjoyed a status in British political and financial circles comparable to that of Ballin in Germany and who was similarly convinced of the need for a naval treaty. Cassel agreed to act as intermediary in Britain and brought the German request for arms negotiations to the attention of Winston Churchill, the first lord of the Admiralty.

Churchill welcomed the prospect of a naval treaty, as did Lloyd George, the chancellor of the exchequer, who since 1908 had desired an agreement with Germany to cut expenditures. With the approval of Prime Minister Asquith and Grey, Churchill and Lloyd George prepared a memorandum as a basis for negotiation: Germany should recognize Britain's need to maintain its superiority at sea and should agree not to increase or better still to slow the pace of its naval construction program; in return Britain would give favorable consideration to German colonial wishes and welcome reciprocal assurances debarring "either Power from joining in aggressive designs or combinations against the other."

This memorandum was communicated to Berlin on January 29, 1912, where it was accepted by Bethmann as a basis for negotiation. The only problem (and it proved to be insuperable) was that the kaiser had already approved the draft of a supplementary naval bill desired by Tirpitz. (To secure Reichstag approval of earlier bills, the rate of construction was scheduled to drop to two ships a year from 1912 to 1917, and Tirpitz now wanted appropriations for six additional battleships during those years to keep up the pace of German fleet building.) In response to the protests of Bethmann and Adolf Wermuth, the head of the Reich treasury, and chastened by the results of recent parliamentary elections in which the Socialists polled 4.25 million votes and therewith became the largest single party in the Reichstag, Tirpitz eventually agreed to pare down his demands from six to three, but the critical significance of this supplementary bill was that it provided for an increase in Germany's existing construction program.

To Bethmann's surprise, especially in view of the kaiser's previous refusal even to consider any treaty limitation on naval construction, William was positively enthusiastic about the prospect of negotiating with Britain, perhaps because he had exaggerated expectations of what Britain was prepared to offer. He had always been confident that his fleet-building program would bring Britain to the bargaining table, and he may well have thought that that time had come. As the British government memorandum specifically required that an Anglo-German agreement include Germany's engagement not to increase its naval armament, both Bethmann and Cassel naturally assumed that the kaiser was prepared to negotiate about the supplementary bill—the so-called Novelle—a copy of which Bethmann gave Cassel to take to London. And it was certainly on the basis of this assumption that the British government embarked on negotiations and sent an emissary to Berlin.

The man chosen for this mission was Lord Haldane, the minister of war, who had studied philosophy at a German university and who, besides being the foremost authority in the British government on German military and naval affairs, had a genuine sympathy for Germany that might make him a more successful negotiator in Berlin than his colleagues. The Haldane mission began under unfavorable auspices, for on February 7, the day he arrived in Berlin, the kaiser addressed the opening session of the Reichstag and announced in general terms the military and naval bills to be brought in during the current session, thus appearing to commit himself to the Novelle. Bethmann cannot have believed that this was his sovereign's intention, however, for at the same time the kaiser made his announcement to the Reichstag he was saying that the fate of Germany and the world hinged on the talks with

Haldane and he hoped Tirpitz would not let any "petty" objections stand in the way of their success. Moreover, if they proved successful, the kaiser would see to it "that the world was told that it was to Tirpitz that Germany and the world owed peace and a large chunk of colonial territory besides." To strengthen the lure of this appeal to Tirpitz, the kaiser appended a list of the large colonial concessions he expected the British to make.

Tirpitz's objections proved to be anything but petty, and his efforts to disguise the actual import of his Novelle were futile, for Haldane saw clearly enough that it would violate Britain's basic condition for an agreement, namely, that there be no increase whatsoever in Germany's fleet construction. "The world would scoff at such an agreement," Haldane said, "and our people would think we had been hood-winked." Although negotiations continued after Haldane left Berlin on February 11, Tirpitz, with the kaiser's backing, refused to accept Britain's conditions despite Beth-mann's pleas. All possibility for an agreement with Britain was thereby eliminated. On March 5 the kaiser declared his patience was at an end and ordered Bethmann to publish the Novelle as it was originally drafted. Bethmann resigned the next day but was persuaded to remain when the kaiser agreed to postpone publication. There-upon Tirpitz threatened to resign, and once again it was Tirpitz who prevailed. The supplementary bill was published on March 22 and subsequently passed by the Reichstag by a wide margin. The hapless Bethmann stayed on.

The kaiser was jubilant; he seemed to regard the collapse of the negotiations with Britain—on which the fate of Germany and the world may indeed have hinged—as something of a personal triumph. He hoped his diplomats would listen more attentively than in the past to their master, "especially when anything is to be accomplished with the British, with whom they do not know how to deal, whereas I understand them well! . . . Thank God no part of the bill had been sacrificed. . . . I saw through Haldane and his fine fellows in time and thoroughly spoiled their game. I have saved the German people their right to sea power and self-determination in arms matters and I have shown the British that they bite into granite when they touch our armaments. Perhaps I have fed their hatred, but I have also won their respect, which may at the proper time persuade them to continue negotiations, let us hope in a more modest tone and with a favorable issue."

Instead the British concluded an agreement with France providing for greater mutual naval support. In July the British withdrew their fleet from the Mediterra-nean, where their interests were henceforth to be protected by France, in order to concentrate their naval strength in the North Sea against the German menace. At the same time they stepped up their own fleet construction program so that, despite all of Germany's efforts, its navy was left far behind.

❑

TWENTY-FIVE

The Collapse of the Sick Man of Europe

❑ *The Tripolitanian War*

The Germans were not alone in seeking compensation for the French takeover of Morocco. While the Moroccan crisis still absorbed the attention of the great powers, the Italians decided that the agreement they had made with France in December 1900 had come due. In return for conceding France a free hand in Morocco, Italy now claimed a similar privilege in the North African provinces of Tripolitania and Cyrenaica, which were still part of the Ottoman empire. Italy was confident, justifiably as it proved, that to avoid a breakup of the Triple Alliance, Austria and Germany would not object. In October 1909 Italy further strengthened its diplomatic position by securing Russia's consent to an Italian takeover of Tripolitania in return for Italian support of changes Russia desired in the Straits Convention (the Racconigi Agreement).

On the afternoon of September 28, 1911, the Italians abruptly presented an ultimatum to Constantinople demanding that the Ottoman government agree within twenty-four hours to an immediate Italian occupation of Tripolitania–Cyrenaica, a demand they justified on the familiar grounds of the need to restore law and order. Twenty-four hours later, ignoring the conciliatory Turkish response, Italy declared war on Turkey. The Italians soon found that subjugating the fiercely independent nomadic Muslim Senussi population of Tripolitania–Cyrenaica was far more difficult and costly than they had anticipated, but to forestall any attempt on the part of the powers to mediate and deprive them of their prize, on November 5 they proclaimed their annexation of these provinces, which they subsequently called Libya, the ancient Greco-Roman name for this region of North Africa.

In fact the powers were not particularly concerned about the fate of these comparatively barren North African tracts, which most of them had already conceded to the Italians, but they were concerned that any blow to the Ottoman empire might stir up the Eastern Question. The Germans feared a further destabilization of the Constantinople government, where their own interests were now so heavily engaged. Far more worried were the Austrians, who believed the Italian attack would encourage similar aggression against the Ottoman empire by Russia or the

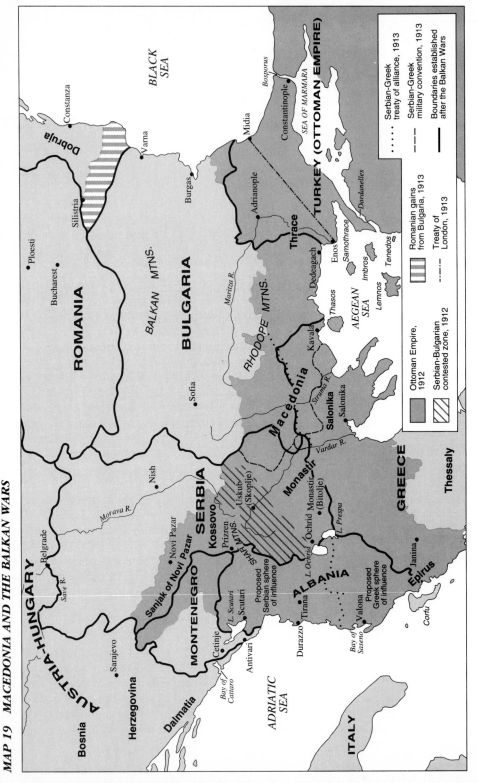

MAP 19 MACEDONIA AND THE BALKAN WARS

Balkan states (as it did just over a year later), and that such attacks would then be directed against them.

The Austrians were in any case thoroughly disgusted with the Italians. Not only had they proved to be unreliable as allies, but they had stepped up their agitation for the cession of Habsburg territories they claimed for Italy on the basis of their large Italian population (*Italia irredenta*). Seeing in such agitation a threat to the very existence of the Habsburg monarchy, the fiery chief of the Austrian general staff, Conrad von Hötzendorf, urged his government to take advantage of Italy's involvement in North Africa to wage a preventive war that would quash Italian irredentism permanently and at the same time regain the lost provinces of Lombardy and Venetia—the same sort of policy he had advocated against Serbia during the Bosnian crisis and was to propose on several more occasions. But the aged emperor Francis Joseph responded to Conrad's call to arms by dismissing him. "My policy is a policy of peace," he said. "It is possible, even probable, that such a war may come about but it will not be waged until Italy attacks us."

Austria's fears about Italy's aggression were matched by the Russians, who believed Italy might seek a decision in its war in North Africa by attacking some other part of the Ottoman empire where Russian interests would be affected. These fears proved justified, for on April 8, 1912, the Italians bombarded the Dardanelles in an effort to compel the Turks to come to terms. Thinking this bombardment might be a prelude to an attack on Constantinople, the Turks promptly closed the Straits to all shipping. The Italians, however, realized they lacked the capacity to force the Straits and that any attempt to do so would ignite a major international crisis. They settled instead for seizing Rhodes and other Turkish-held islands in the eastern Mediterranean, which they retained after the war. Closure of the Straits was exactly the development the Russians most feared, for the Straits had become not only strategically but economically crucial to them. Fully ninety percent of Russia's grain exports and fifty percent of all other exports went through the Straits, and Russia depended on those exports to pay interest on foreign debts as well as purchase machinery and other technological equipment to build its rapidly expanding economy, purchases which in turn were imported via the Straits. In response to vigorous international protest, the Turks reopened the Straits on May 4, but their brief closure showed the Russians yet again their vulnerability in this area and reinforced their determination to establish control over this vital waterway.

By a treaty of October 18, 1912, signed in Lausanne, Switzerland, the Turks made peace with Italy and agreed to withdraw their troops from Tripolitania–Cyrenaica. This decision was forced on them not by Italian successes in the field but by a new attack on the Ottoman empire, this time from a coalition of Balkan states formed under the sponsorship of Russia.

❑ *The First Balkan War*

In the overall international picture, the greatest significance of the Tripolitanian war was its impact on the Balkans. All the Balkan states with the exception of Romania bordered on the Ottoman empire, and all were eager to seize the lands adjacent to their own. Serbia and Montenegro wanted the sanjak of Novi Pazar, that wedge of territory between them that Austria had restored to Ottoman control in 1909; Serbia,

Montenegro, and Greece aspired to Albania; Bulgaria, Greece, and Serbia all had designs on that large, ill-defined region known as Macedonia; and Bulgaria coveted Ottoman territory to the south and east that would give it access to the Aegean Sea and possibly control over Constantinople itself.

The Russians had long sought to form a coalition of Balkan states, which they expected to use to extend their own influence in the Near East at the expense of both the Ottoman and Habsburg empires. All such efforts had foundered because of the suspicions and rivalries among the Balkan states themselves and because, although these states were happy to receive Russian support, they had no desire to become pawns or mere satrapies of the northern colossus.

The Italian attack on Tripolitania achieved what Russian diplomacy had so far failed to accomplish. With a substantial part of the Ottoman army in North Africa, the Balkan states saw an unusually favorable opportunity to realize their own ambitions at the expense of the Ottoman empire. Encouraged by Russian diplomats and agents, they all (except Romania) entered into negotiations resulting in the formation of what amounted to an anti-Turkish coalition.

The first link in this coalition was an alliance treaty between Bulgaria and Serbia, signed March 13, 1912. "Well, this is perfect," Sazonov, the Russian foreign minister, said when he heard of the alliance: "500,000 bayonets to defend the Balkans. This should bar the road forever to German penetration and Austrian invasion." Such a barrier against Germany and Austria may well have been what Sazonov most desired from a Balkan alliance, but he knew perfectly well that this was not its principal purpose. For although ostensibly a defensive alliance, the Serbo-Bulgarian treaty was nothing less than a pact for war against Turkey, with detailed provisions (in a secret annex) for dividing the spoils. Serbia would receive all territory north and west of the Shar Mountains, which meant the sanjak of Novi Pazar and the northwestern part of Macedonia; Bulgaria's share would be the territory east of the Rhodope Mountains and the Sturma River; the territory between these areas would be left to the tsar to arbitrate.

Quite apart from the territory designated for arbitration, the Serbo-Bulgarian treaty left open many other territorial questions. It made no specific mention of the fate of Albania and the Adriatic coast, of the territory east of Bulgaria, including Constantinople, and even its detailed provisions were so vague as to leave much to interpretation.

On May 28, 1912, the Serbo-Bulgarian alliance was extended by an alliance between Bulgaria and Greece, which again envisaged common action against Turkey but did not include specific territorial provisions. There followed oral agreements between Greece and Serbia, Greece and Montenegro, and Bulgaria and Montenegro (which promised the Montenegrins "all the Turkish territory they could conquer"). These alliances and oral agreements were buttressed by a succession of military conventions, so that by late summer 1912 all the Balkan states with frontiers on Ottoman territory were joined in a coalition to plunder the Ottoman empire in Europe.

Unlike Sazonov, who outwardly clung to the fiction that the Balkan alliances were defensive measures directed against Germany and Austria, Poincaré, the French prime minister, declared immediately "this is an agreement for war" when shown the text of the Serbo-Bulgarian treaty while on a visit to St. Petersburg in mid-August 1912. But far from trying to persuade the Russians to restrain their Balkan friends, he assured Sazonov that should they become involved in a conflict with Austria, and Germany intervened, "France will fulfill her [treaty] obligations [to Russia]." Further, he expressed confidence that Britain would support its entente partners and urged Russia to conclude a naval agreement with London.

On August 14, 1912, Bulgaria lit the fuse to ignite the war against Turkey by addressing an ultimatum to Constantinople demanding autonomy for Macedonia. On that same day the Austrians, fearfully aware of the implications for their own empire of a liquidation of the Ottoman empire by the Balkan national states, appealed for the cooperation of the great powers to restrain the Balkan governments and persuade Constantinople to introduce reforms in Macedonia to eliminate any excuse for foreign intervention there. This Austrian appeal was endorsed by all the powers including Russia, which had begun to realize that a Balkan war might unleash a European war for which it was still unprepared or that the Balkan states might seek gains that would conflict with Russian interests. Russia therefore agreed to accept a commission of the European powers to act jointly with Austria to preserve peace and the status quo in the Balkans.

After receiving so many assurances of support from Russian diplomats and agents, the Balkan governments saw no reason to take Russia's warnings seriously, for on October 8, the very day they received an Austro-Russian note adjuring them to keep the peace and respect the status quo, Montenegro declared war on Turkey, as did Bulgaria, Greece, and Serbia a few days later. The Turks hastened to make peace with Italy (the Treaty of Lausanne of October 18), but being extricated from North Africa availed them nothing, for the Balkan armies triumphed on every front. By the end of October the Bulgarians had overrun Thrace and were preparing to move against Constantinople; the Serbs had advanced to the Adriatic; and the Greeks had conquered Thessaly and much of southern Macedonia including the important Aegean port of Salonika.

The speed and decisiveness of the Balkan victories took the European powers by surprise, but one thing was now clear. Turkey, the perennial Sick Man of Europe, was now dead, at least in Europe, and the prewar status quo in the Balkans could never be restored. There remained the problems of how to deal with the Ottoman heritage and the rival claims of the victorious Balkan states while safeguarding their own interests.

Russia's overriding concern was that the Bulgarians might capture Constantinople, and Sazonov was obliged to warn them that Russia would intervene to prevent their takeover of the Ottoman capital. So alarmed were the Russians that they initiated preparations for war against Bulgaria and set about wooing Romania (since 1883 the ally of Austria and Germany) to secure transit rights through Romanian territory.

The French appreciated Russia's concern about Constantinople, but they as well as the British feared the Russians themselves would seize the city. Consequently, Poincaré, with Britain's backing, proposed that the powers mediate between Bulgaria and Turkey to ensure that the Ottoman capital remain in Turkish hands. Poincaré's other principal worry was that Austria, with Germany's support, would take advantage of the Balkan crisis to settle accounts with Serbia, and he impressed on the Russians that this time they must back Serbia to the limit. As on the occasion of his visit to St. Petersburg the previous August, but even more emphatically, he assured the Russians that they could count on French support. "If Russia goes to war," he said, "France will also, for we know that in this question Germany is behind Austria."

Fearing that war might indeed be imminent, Poincaré initiated talks with Britain that led to an exchange of notes in late November 1912 between Grey, the British foreign secretary, and Paul Cambon, the French ambassador in London, which provided that if the general peace were threatened, Britain and France would take immediate steps to decide on joint measures to deal with the crisis. The British government followed up this exchange of notes with a stern warning to the Germans early in December that if an Austrian invasion of Serbia led to a general European war, Britain could hardly remain a silent spectator; Britain could not tolerate the defeat of France and the destruction of the balance of power that would leave all of Europe under the control of a single state. Enraged by this warning, the kaiser hastily convened a conference of his principal military and naval advisers on December 8, 1912, and announced that in view of the British attitude Germany must declare war at once against France and Russia. Tirpitz protested that the navy would not be ready for war for another eighteen months (an estimate he subsequently extended to four years), but Moltke, the chief of the army general staff, supported the kaiser's call for action. He believed a war was unavoidable and urged that it be waged "the sooner the better." He was alarmed by the steady large-scale increase in Russia's military might, which if unchecked would invalidate all assumptions on which Germany's military planning was based.

This conference of December 8 has been seen as convincing evidence of Germany's determination to launch a war for European and ultimately world domination, but nothing whatsoever came of the conference. Bethmann, the German chancellor, was not even informed about it until almost a week later, the German army made no preparations for war, and the German and Austrian governments did nothing to coordinate their policies or military plans. Admiral von Müller, chief of the naval cabinet, whose notes are a principal source of what went on at the conference, concluded that "the result was pretty well zero."

Conrad von Hötzendorf, who had been reinstated as chief of the Austrian general staff on December 12, once again advocated war against Serbia. And once again he was firmly rebuffed by Emperor Francis Joseph, who on this issue had the support of Archduke Francis Ferdinand, the heir to the throne, Foreign Minister Berchthold, and the Hungarians. Austria not only refrained from intervening against Serbia but made no move when Serbia and Montenegro occupied the sanjak of Novi Pazar, thereby substantially increasing the possibility of an outright union between these two south Slav states, which the Austrians had always dreaded.

The Austrians, in fact, took a firm stand on only one issue in the Balkans at this time. They wanted the former Turkish territory between the Albanian mountains and the Adriatic coast, which the Greeks, Serbs, and Montenegrins had occupied in the course of the war, to be made an independent Albanian national state as a counterweight to the south Slavs and to deny them this further territorial aggrandizement. Most affected by this proposal were the Serbs, whose control of central Albania gave them a much-coveted independent outlet to the sea. In the end the Austrians secured the agreement of the powers to establish an independent Albania, but at the cost of further international crises.

❑ *The Treaty of London and the Genesis of Future Conflict*

The First Balkan War came to an end with the Treaty of London of May 30, 1913, which compelled the Turks to surrender all their territory in Europe with the exception of a narrow strip around Constantinople and to abandon all claims to Crete. The final disposition of Albania and the Aegean islands, most of them occupied by Greece in the course of the war, were left to the later decision of the great powers. Long before the Treaty of London, however, it was obvious that peace with Turkey would not bring peace to the Balkans and that new crises in that region were certain to develop over the division of the spoils.

One such problem was Albania, where the three Balkan states that had taken over Albanian territory refused to recognize the boundaries the powers assigned to an independent Albanian state. Only after Austria threatened war did the Montenegrins in early May 1913 relinquish their claim to Scutari (Shkodër) in northern Albania and the Serbs evacuate the port city of Durazzo (Durrës). In the south, however, the Greeks stubbornly held on to the territory they had occupied during the war and, as we shall see, managed to retain most of it.

An even more serious problem was Bulgaria's frustration over the division of the spoils. The Bulgarians had borne the brunt of the fighting against the Turkish forces operating out of Constantinople, but their hopes for establishing control over the Turkish capital had been firmly blocked by Russia. In Macedonia they felt cheated on a major scale by their erstwhile allies, Serbia and Greece. The Greeks, who had captured the port city of Salonika just hours before the Bulgarian army arrived, not only retained this prize but took a long strip of the Aegean coast to the east of the city as well. Meanwhile the Serbs had taken over the greater part of Macedonia that had been assigned to Bulgaria in their treaty of March 13, 1912, as well as the region assigned to the tsar for arbitration, which they claimed as compensation for being deprived of Albania and the Adriatic coast. As if these indignities were not enough, the Russians were now pressuring the Bulgarians to give territorial compensation to Romania, which had not even taken part in the war against the Turks.

This Russian move on behalf of Romania derived from its efforts to secure transit rights through Romania to prevent a Bulgarian takeover of Constantinople. The Romanians' price was the Bulgarian frontier fortress of Silistria and its surrounding territory on the Danube, and they held the Russians to their promise even though military action against Bulgaria had not been necessary. On May 7, 1913, an international conference held under Russian auspices in St. Petersburg awarded Romania the town of Silistria, though without its fortifications—a compensation the Romanians by this time considered grossly inadequate and the Bulgarians grossly unfair.

For mutual protection against a vengeful Bulgaria and to safeguard their wartime territorial gains, Greece and Serbia concluded an alliance with each other on June 1, 1913, one day after the signing of the Treaty of London ending the First Balkan War. Their alliance, a defensive pact, was at the same time a staking out of territorial claims. In Macedonia as in Albania they would observe the "principle of effective occupation," which meant that they intended to retain most of Macedonia and simply ignore the intention of the great powers to establish Albania as an independent state.

Besides concluding the alliance between themselves, Greece and Serbia cast about for other allies in the event of trouble with Bulgaria. They received specific assurances of support from Montenegro. They failed to obtain similar guarantees from Romania and Turkey, but both states indicated they would not be reluctant to make gains, or in the case of Turkey recoup losses, at Bulgaria's expense.

❑ *The Second Balkan War*

The Bulgarians made no secret of their dissatisfaction with the results of the First Balkan War so far as their own territorial ambitions were concerned. What they most wanted at this juncture was Russian diplomatic intervention on their behalf to compel their erstwhile allies to agree to arbitration. For, despite Russia's role in coercing Bulgaria to give compensation to Romania, the Bulgarians were confident Russia would take their side in this situation, especially since the Russians had played so prominent a role in arranging the Serbo-Bulgarian alliance of March 13, 1912, including its territorial provisions.

It was primarily to force Russia's hand on the question of arbitration that General Savov, the commander-in-chief of the Bulgarian army, at the orders of his king, launched a surprise attack on Greek and Serbian occupation forces in Macedonia on June 29 and 30, 1913, and therewith started the Second Balkan War. The attack had a threefold purpose, Savov informed his generals: "To compel Russia, by the threat of a declaration of war [presumably against Greece and Serbia], to arrange a speedy settlement"; "to force our allies to take a more conciliatory attitude"; and "to occupy by force the territories claimed by us and held by them, until foreign intervention stops further military action."

The Bulgarian attack was incredibly foolish, the product of military overconfidence and totally unjustifiable expectations of Russia, whose pointed evasions of Bulgarian appeals should have been ample warning that they would receive no help from that quarter. Any sympathy the Russians felt for Bulgaria was overshadowed by concern over Bulgarian ambitions toward Constantinople and the Straits, and far from siding with Bulgaria the Russians supported Greek and Serbian efforts to enroll Romania in their anti-Bulgarian coalition. For Greece and Serbia, the Bulgarian attack was a most welcome development, because the Bulgarians had therewith taken upon themselves the moral stigma of aggression. On July 5 and 6 they declared war on Bulgaria, as did Romania on July 10 and Turkey two days later. The Bulgarians were defeated quickly and decisively. A mere seven days after starting the war they appealed to Russia to arrange an armistice with their Balkan antagonists, and after the Turkish reconquest of Adrianople they appealed for an armistice with Turkey as well.

The one country that might have been expected to intervene on Bulgaria's side in the Second Balkan War, diplomatically or even militarily, was Austria in order to curb the pretensions of Serbia. On the day Bulgaria launched its war against Greece and Serbia, the Austrian government approached Germany about some kind of diplomatic intervention, but the Austrian initiative was thwarted by the almost immediate military collapse of Bulgaria and Germany's firm veto. The kaiser feared jeopardizing his alliance with Romania and was working to foster better relations with Greece, policies evidently influenced by his personal dislike for Bulgaria's ruler and family considerations: the king of Romania was a Hohenzollern and King Constantine of Greece was his brother-in-law. Germany's strongest motive in denying support to Bulgaria, however, was Turkey, where the Germans still sought to regain the influence lost during the Young Turk revolution and subsequent deposition of Sultan Abdul Hamid.

In Austria, Emperor Francis Joseph had consistently opposed intervention and instructed Berchthold, his foreign minister, not to let himself be influenced by Conrad, who was again urging that Austria take advantage of this opportunity to settle accounts with Serbia. "For naturally," the emperor said, "Conrad will again be for all kinds of wars and a great hurrah policy, to conquer the Serbs and God knows what." Berchthold should keep cool and watch from the sidelines while the Balkan rabble broke each other's heads; under no circumstances should Austria itself attack Serbia or otherwise intervene, as Conrad was advocating.

Peace negotiations between Bulgaria and its Balkan foes were conducted for the most part in the Romanian capital of Bucharest. In the Treaty of Bucharest, signed August 10, 1913, the Bulgarians ceded a large bloc of territory between the Danube and the Black Sea to Romania, and the greater part of their Macedonian claims to Serbia and Greece, whose territory along the Aegean coast was extended to include the important harbor city of Kavala. Six weeks later the Bulgarians made peace with Turkey. Through the Treaty of Constantinople of September 29, the Turks regained the city of Adrianople, and their new boundary with Bulgaria was established west of the city along a line extending almost due north from the mouth of the Maritza River.

❑ *Austria, Serbia, and the Problem of Albania*

The crisis in the Balkans did not end with the treaties of Bucharest and Constantinople. The future status of Albania and the Aegean islands had been left to the decision of the great powers by the Treaty of London ending the First Balkan War. After much palaver, the powers finally did nothing at all about the Aegean islands, almost all of which were eventually awarded to Greece following Turkey's defeat in World War I.

The problem of Albania presented more immediate difficulties. In late September 1913, Serbia again invaded Albania, allegedly in retaliation for Albanian raids into Serbian territory, therewith provoking yet another crisis with Austria. Conrad sounded his by now familiar call for decisive diplomatic or military action to eliminate the Serbian menace: Serbia should accept peaceful integration into the Habsburg empire with a status similar to that of Bavaria or Saxony in the German empire; or, if Serbia refused, Austria should go to war, annex part of Serbia, and divide the rest among its Balkan neighbors, thereby winning their gratitude and bringing them into Austria's diplomatic orbit. In Germany, the kaiser, who had turned a blind eye to Austrian concern about Serbia earlier in the year, now made a typical turnabout and was all for war. "Now or never! We must finally have order and quiet down there!" If Serbia did not give way, Belgrade should be bombarded and occupied. "And of this you can be certain," he told the Austrians, "that I stand by you and am ready to draw the sabre whenever your action makes it necessary." (By the spring of 1914 the kaiser had veered round yet again. When Austria called for support to prevent Serbia from gaining access to the Adriatic through union with Montenegro, William declared that a war for such a purpose would leave Berlin "completely cold" and the Austrians were "crazy" even to consider such a thing.)

In the autumn of 1913, however, firm German assurances of support encouraged the Austrians to address an ultimatum to Belgrade on October 17 demanding that Serbia respect Albanian territory and withdraw its troops within eight days. "Otherwise Austria would be compelled, with regret, to have recourse to the proper measures to secure the fulfillment of her demands."

Since the powers had agreed earlier to the establishment of an independent state of Albania, Serbia received no support and was obliged to accede. As in the Bosnian and earlier crises over Albania, Austria had scored a diplomatic victory, but again it was a victory achieved through drastic and humiliating means that left Serbia and its friends among the great powers furious. Far worse, Austria had learned the lesson yet again that drastic measures worked in dealing with Serbia, and that Russia had not dared to intervene. Indeed, Sazonov had actually advised the Serbs to yield and rest content for the present to consolidate their existing territorial gains, in order to be ready "when the time comes to lance the Austro-Hungarian abscess, which had not yet come to a head as had the Turkish one."

In southern Albania the Austrians did not even score a diplomatic victory. On October 30, 1913, four days after Serbia had yielded to the ultimatum over northern Albania, the Austrians, this time in conjunction with the Italians (who had designs of their own on Albania), addressed a similar ultimatum to Greece. Greece, however, was in a far stronger geographic as well as diplomatic position than Serbia. Greece was separated from Austria by ranges of rugged mountains, and it was still being courted by both Germany and the entente powers. The Greeks were therefore able to procrastinate, finally agreeing to a compromise settlement that left them the lion's share of the disputed territory. Even in the region they evacuated, Greek irregular forces continued to support a pro-Greek government, which later declared its independence from Albania.

❑ *The Liman von Sanders Mission*

Germany's courtship of Greece achieved little more than winning an excellent international bargaining position for the Greeks. The Germans had greater success in reestablishing their influence in the Ottoman empire. The idealism of the first phase of the Young Turk revolution had long since given way to an increasingly intolerant spirit of Turkish nationalism. After Turkey's disastrous defeats in the First Balkan War, a group of ultranationalists carried out a coup d'état on January 23, 1913, and formed a government dedicated to carrying on the war to a victorious conclusion. These nationalists were no more successful than their predecessors, but they enjoyed one decisive political advantage: they controlled and had the support of the army, and were therefore able to retain power even after Turkey's final military defeat.

On June 11, 1913, less than a fortnight after the signature of the Treaty of London ending the First Balkan War, Mahmud Shevket Pasha, the grand vizier and nominal leader of the Turkish nationalist government, was assassinated under mysterious circumstances. This act of terrorism provided a pretext for the nationalist leadership to conduct a reign of terror against its opponents. From that time until well into World War I the Turkish government was dominated by a nationalist triumverate: Enver Pasha, the minister of war; Djemal Pasha, the minister of the navy; and Talaat Pasha, the minister of the interior.

The leaders of the Young Turk revolution, whether liberal, moderate, or ultranationalist, all shared a common goal: to strengthen Turkey and prevent further spoliation of its territories. They went to greater lengths than prerevolutionary regimes in recruiting foreign advisers to help reform and westernize their government and institutions and, in particular, reorganize their armed forces. British experts were brought in to supervise the reform of the navy and civil service; French for the reform of the financial administration, taxation system, police, and judiciary; and despite their army's poor showing in the First Balkan War, the Turks continued to look to Germany to restructure their armed forces, a choice undoubtedly influenced by the fact that so many of their own officers, including the powerful Enver Pasha, had received military training in Germany and returned with a high opinion of the German military establishment.

During the debacle of the First Balkan War, the Turkish government had sounded Berlin about sending a new military mission to Constantinople when General Kolmar von der Goltz, the foremost German officer previously associated with a training mission, resigned, allegedly because he was not given sufficient authority and his advice was ignored. The German government, eager to regain its influence in Turkey, responded favorably, although it took five months to negotiate an agreement embodying conditions the Germans considered essential for success. Their advisory mission was to consist of forty-two officers under the command of General Otto Liman von Sanders. His appointment was to run for five years, and this time there was to be no question about his authority. He was to be a member of the Turkish war council in charge of all Turkish military training establishments, with full disciplinary powers and responsibility for the promotion of all senior Turkish officers, and he was to have direct command of the First Turkish Army stationed in Constantinople. The Liman mission arrived in the Turkish capital in December 1913.

In a manner typical of German policy during this period, the German government negotiated the Liman contract without considering the interests and sensibilities of other powers. The kaiser did not improve the situation when he called upon the Liman mission to Germanize the Turkish army and ensure paramount German influence over Turkish foreign policy. The Russians were naturally infuriated. "You know what interest we have at the Bosporus, how sensitive we are at that point," Sazonov complained to a German journalist. "All southern Russia depends on it, and now you stick a Prussian garrison under our noses." Liman's command of the Turkish army in Constantinople was tantamount to handing the Straits over to Germany, "and the state which possesses the Straits will hold in its hands not only the key to the Black Sea and the Mediterranean, but also that for the penetration of Asia Minor and the sure means to establish its hegemony over the Balkans."

The Russians took the lead in protesting the Liman mission and called upon their allies, Britain and France, for support. "This matter would be a test of the value of the Triple Entente," Sazonov told the British representative in St. Petersburg. The French responded immediately, but the British hesitated when the Germans pointed out that Liman's position with the Turkish army was analogous to that of the British admiral in command of the Turkish navy.

The most serious Russian objection to Liman's appointment was removed or at least deflected by his promotion in the German army, which allowed him to assume a higher rank in the Turkish army with headquarters in Adrianople. He was thus removed from direct command of the army that controlled the Straits. The mere shift of Liman's headquarters, however, did nothing to quell Russian fears of German designs in the Near East and only impelled them to step up their military and diplomatic preparations so they could deal more effectively with future German or Austrian provocations.

As Sazonov was to write in his memoirs: "The appearance of German officers on the Bosporus, armed with unusual powers, was the decisive moment which prompted Russia to seek an understanding with England, more definite than the vague sense of common danger." Sazonov was referring to Russia's attempt to negotiate a naval convention with Britain, a step long advocated by France, with definite commitments on both sides for coordinated naval action to confront crises that would inevitably arise in the future. The British, however, remained wary of definite naval or military commitments, and both France and Russia were left in doubt about the extent of Britain's commitment to its entente partners until Britain actually entered the war in 1914.

The Russians had better luck reinforcing their treaties with the Balkan states in the wake of the Liman mission. In February 1914, the crown prince of Serbia and Nicholas Pashich, the Serbian prime minister, paid a visit to the tsar in St. Petersburg, where the idea of a new Balkan league was discussed. Though stressing their desire for peace, the Serbs spoke of policies that were anything but peaceful. They wanted Russia to arrange for an international army to be installed in Albania to protect that country from the Austrians and Italians; they suggested greater territorial concessions to Bulgaria in return for a guarantee of Bulgarian assistance in solving the Serbo-Croat problem, by which they meant detaching Bosnia and Herzegovina and other Slavic provinces from the Habsburg empire and incorporating them into Serbia; and they wanted arms. In reply to a question from the tsar, Pashich assured him that Serbia could mobilize half a million men. "That is a lot," the tsar said, "and much can be done with them." To seal their friendship with Russia, the Serbs proposed marriage between their crown prince and one of the tsar's daughters, but at this the tsar balked: his daughters should be free to follow the dictates of their hearts, he said, but otherwise "we shall do anything for Serbia."

Besides consolidating their relations with Serbia, the Russians continued to woo Romania from the Austro-German camp, where it had moved following Russia's takeover in 1878 of the Romanian province of Bessarabia—even though Romania had fought on Russia's side in the recent war against Turkey. The loss of Bessarabia still rankled, but the Russians offered very attractive bait to regain Romanian friendship and detach that country from the Triple Alliance. This bait was the Habsburg province of Transylvania, long coveted by Romanian nationalists because of its predominantly Romanian population and one they could only hope to acquire by helping to break up the Habsburg realm.

The Russians made no attempt to disguise their courtship of Romania. They conferred a Russian field marshal's baton on King Carol, they invited a Romanian delegation to St. Petersburg to commemorate their joint victory over the Turks in 1878, and on June 14, 1914, the tsar and tsarina, accompanied by Foreign Minister Sazonov, visited King Carol at the Romanian resort of Constanza on the Black Sea.

On this occasion Sazonov failed to get a definite promise of Romanian support or neutrality in the event of a Russian war with Austria, but his hosts assured him that they were not bound by any treaty to take part in a conflict in which their own interests were not at stake—the Russians could hardly have asked for more. The Austrians were under no illusion about what was happening: the Romanian alliance was now a dead letter, the Austrian minister to Bucharest reported to his government. "Rumania's swing to the Triple Entente, which had been expected for a year, took place in full view of the public today at Constanza."

❑ *The Burgeoning Arms Race*

Throughout the Liman crisis, and indeed on all important international issues since the blowup over Bosnia, the Russians had received repeated assurances from Paris about the solidity of the Franco-Russian alliance and that "France will go as far as Russia wishes." What worried the Russians about France in the spring of 1914 was not that France would leave Russia in the lurch but whether the French could supply sufficient military assistance. There was a possibility that the three-year compulsory military service in France, put into effect the previous year, would be reduced back to two years because of pressure from the radicals. An article in a Russian journal of June 12, 1914, reputedly inspired by the Russian minister of war, compared the sizes of the various European armies and stated bluntly that the size of the army Russia expected from France could be maintained only by keeping the three-year service. "Russia and France want no war," the article concluded, "but Russia is ready and France must be ready too."

Russia was indeed ready, or at least vigorously trying to be so. At the end of 1913 the government adopted a military program providing for vast increases in the Russian army. Annual recruitment was raised from 450,000 to 580,000 for a three-year period of service, which would give Russia a peacetime army of well over 2,000,000 men, three times the size of Germany's; the number of infantry divisions was to be substantially increased, as was the supply of heavy and light artillery, and a new and much enlarged network of strategic railways was to be constructed to permit the swiftest possible concentration of Russian forces in case of war. The entire program was expected to be in place in 1917. Of particular concern to Germany were the provisions for improving Russia's strategic railways, lavishly funded by French loans, for Germany's plans to cope with a two-front war hinged on the slow pace of Russian mobilization, which would certainly be accelerated with improved railway facilities.

These increases in the French and Russian armies, like the buildup of the British navy, took place at the same time and in response to Germany's large-scale buildup of its armed forces. In contrast to the German navy, the army for almost twenty years had been remarkably modest in its demands for military appropriations (see p. 377). A bill of June 1912 calling for an increase in the size of the army of 27,000 men was still comparatively moderate, but the army sharply stepped up its demands as Germany's diplomatic situation deteriorated and its military leaders estimated the strength of their forces against those of their prospective adversaries. The discrepancies shocked Bethmann. "One must have a good deal of faith in God and count on a revolution in Russia to be able to sleep at all," he said. "Because of the navy we have neglected the army, and our 'naval policy' has created enemies on every side."

On July 13, 1913, the Reichstag approved the largest military bill in German history, providing for an immediate increase in the peacetime strength of the German army from 663,000 to 761,000 men, not including officers; the number was to rise to 810,000 by October 1914. In Austria a law of March 1914 increased the annual peacetime levy from 175,000 to 200,000, giving Austria a standing army of approximately 480,000, larger, but not much larger, than Serbia's.

German military leaders knew that numbers alone were not an accurate measure of an army's fighting capacity, but Russia's prospective increases were alarming and they feared Germany might ultimately be overwhelmed by manpower alone. Already in 1914, even after the German and Austrian military increases, the French and Russian standing armies were roughly twice as big as Germany's and Austria's, and the new Russian army bill would leave them even further behind in the arms race.

❑ *The Deteriorating Position of Austria*

Austria and Germany were also losing ground, or rather had already lost it, on the diplomatic front. Italy and Romania were still their nominal allies, but neither Berlin nor Vienna had any illusions that they would receive effective support from either in the event of a crisis. On the contrary, it seemed that both had already been lured into the camp of the enemy by the prospect of dismembering the Habsburg empire. This meant that Austria, besides confronting a conflict with Serbia backed by Russia, had to reckon with an attack from Italy and Romania as well (both of which did in fact take the field against Austria in World War I) and thus faced the prospect of a war on four fronts.

In Vienna, alarm over comparative military strength and a deteriorating diplomatic position was compounded by the empire's nationality problems and by the Germans' failure to understand just how perilous Austria's situation was, especially with respect to Serbia. In the spring of 1914 Berchthold, the Austrian foreign minister, complained to his ambassador in Berlin that the Germans were still urging Austria to reestablish good relations with Serbia, seemingly oblivious to the fact that this was a hopeless endeavor "in view of the animosity towards Austria-Hungary in the Serbian national consciousness and the hopes—cherished everywhere in Serbia and brazenly paraded—of incorporating component parts of the Monarchy." So long as the Germans had no clear conception of Serbian feelings and aspirations, they could hardly appreciate the importance of that question in the formulation of Austrian policy.

In mid-June 1914 the Austrian foreign ministry drew up a balance sheet of the Habsburg empire's international position to convey to Germany the scope of Austria's problems. In nearly every regard, the situation in the Near East after the Balkan wars was unfavorable to Austria and the Triple Alliance. Albania, as an independent state, was a barrier to the advance of Serbia, and Bulgaria was no longer hypnotized by Russia, but everywhere else the situation had changed for the worse. Turkey, heretofore a counterweight to Russia and the Balkan states, had been pushed out of Europe almost completely and its power disastrously eroded. Serbia, aggressively hostile to Austria and entirely under Russian influence, had substantially increased its territory and population and seemed on the verge of becoming even larger and stronger through union with Montenegro. Austria's erstwhile ally Romania had swung over to Russia and might at any moment announce itself as an outright enemy of the Triple Alliance. Russia and France meanwhile were using all their political and economic influence to create a Balkan union, which, now that Turkey had been eliminated, could be directed only against Austria. To lure Bulgaria into such a union, Serbia, under Russian pressure, would no doubt agree to pay a fair price in Macedonia.

The principal purpose of this grim survey was to shock the Germans into comprehending the seriousness of Austria's plight and to remind them that the fate of their own country was inexorably linked to the Habsburg monarchy. There could no longer be any doubt, the Austrian memorandum said, that Russian policy was dedicated to encircling and destroying Austria, but destroying Austria was only the first step toward realizing Russia's ultimate goal: destroying Germany and establishing Russian hegemony over Europe. In supporting Austria, therefore, Germany was not merely being loyal to an ally or defending purely Austrian interests but preserving a partner essential to its own survival.

This document was submitted for final revision to Berchthold. Before it could be sent to Berlin, Archduke Francis Ferdinand, the heir to the Habsburg crown, and his wife, Sophie, were assassinated in the Bosnian capital of Sarajevo on June 28, 1914.

❑ *The Sarajevo Assassinations*

The assassin was a nineteen-year-old Bosnian named Gavrilo Princip, a fanatic south Slav nationalist who had gone to Serbia and joined or was at least associated with an organization there called Union or Death, better known by its enemies as the Black Hand. The founder and leader of Union or Death was a Serbian army officer, Colonel Dragutin Dimitrievich (code name Apis), who had taken part in the revolution of June 1903 and the grisly murder of King Alexander and his entourage. According to its statutes, the purpose of the organization was the union of all south Slavs in a single state, and its preferred methods were terrorist action and revolutionary agitation in all south Slav territories still under foreign control. Apart from representatives from Serbia itself, the society's central committee was composed of representatives from all "unredeemed" south Slav territories including Macedonia and the Habsburg lands of Croatia, Dalmatia, Slovenia, the Voivodina, and of course Bosnia and Herzegovina. It was of necessity a secret society, its members carefully recruited for their demonstrated dedication to the cause of a south Slav union. Members were assigned numbers and were not known to each other, only to the central committee, which directed all their operations.

Prime Minister Pashich and many of his colleagues feared the radical extremism of Union or Death but did not dare suppress the organization, fearing it might carry out a coup against the government that would call for their own assassination. They therefore condoned its operations and even allowed it to set up a training school for guerrillas and saboteurs near the Serbian city of Nish.

In the summer of 1914 Dimitrievich and his central committee initiated plans to assassinate Francis Ferdinand, the heir to the Habsburg crown, who was selected as a target, ironically enough, because he sympathized with the south Slavs and desired to improve their constitutional position in the empire. Students of Austrian history differ about the character and political abilities of the archduke, but as heir to the throne he advanced some of the most imaginative and promising ideas for reforming and reconstructing his polyglot empire. He conceived of a federal solution along the lines of the Swiss Confederation, which had so successfully reconciled its various nationalities. As the first step in that direction, he proposed the formation within the empire of a third state made up of territories inhabited by south Slavs (Croatians, Serbs, and Slovenes), which would be given a status comparable to the Hungarians' (i.e., virtually complete independence in their domestic affairs), and converting the empire from a Dual into a Trialist Monarchy. "I live and die for federalism," he said in the summer of 1913 (a fatefully prophetic pronouncement). "It is the sole salvation of the Monarchy, if anything at all can save it."

The possibility that Francis Ferdinand might actually reconcile the empire's south Slavs to Habsburg rule was what Serbian nationalists dreaded above all. The assassin Princip admitted frankly at his trial that the archduke had to be killed because "as future sovereign he would have prevented our union through reforms that would clearly have gone against our interests." One of Princip's accomplices stated the case even more bluntly. "Trialism would without doubt have been fatal [to our program], . . . our hopes of liberation, the union of all south Slavs, and the destruction of Austria."

The unfortunate Francis Ferdinand was almost as much hated by his own government and empire as by Serbian nationalists, especially by the Hungarians and others whose vested interests were threatened by his proposed constitutional changes and reforms. So great was this hostility that rumors circulated at the time, and persist to the present day, that there were Austrian officials who, if not actively associated with the assassination plot, may have been informed of it and did nothing to warn the archduke. Certainly they failed to warn him urgently enough against his visit to Sarajevo on June 28, a date that could not have been more ineptly chosen, for this was the anniversary of the Battle of Kossovo of 1389, when the Ottoman Turks annihilated the allied forces of Serbs and Bosnians, destroyed the Serbo-Bosnian state, and established Turkish rule over the southern Balkans, which endured until the nineteenth century. Besides allowing the archduke to go to the capital of Bosnia on this day of national mourning for all south Slavs, security arrangements for his visit were sloppy in the extreme. So far, however, no evidence of complicity on the part of Austro-Hungarian officials has been found.

The question of Serbian complicity is another matter. The Serbian government was more involved with the plot than was known at the time. Nothing was known then, for example, of the responsibility of Colonel Dimitrievich, who was not only the leader of Union or Death but the chief of Serbian military intelligence. The corpus of evidence about the assassination plot is immense, but it is also complex and contradictory, revealing many bitter feuds and jealousies among the Serbs themselves so that despite years of meticulous research many questions remain unanswered or at least controversial.

The Austrians in any case did not need concrete evidence of Serbian complicity.

For years they had observed the operations of Serbian terrorists within their own borders and the anti-Austrian agitation condoned and encouraged by the Serbian government within Serbia. For the Austrians, the assassinations dramatically confirmed that the Serbs would stop at nothing to achieve their goals and gave them an excuse (or a final prod) to delay no longer in taking drastic action to eliminate the Serbian menace.

TWENTY-SIX

☐

The Coming of World War I

☐ *The Austrian Appeal for German Support and Germany's "Blank Check"*

There is no doubt that Austria wanted to exploit the general horror aroused by the assassination of Francis Ferdinand and Sophie throughout Europe to take punitive action against Serbia. An essential precondition for doing so, however, was to secure ironclad assurances of German support should action against Serbia provoke the intervention of other powers. Another condition, whose importance the Austrians never seemed to appreciate fully, was swift and decisive action before the shock of the events of Sarajevo was dissipated by time and other concerns. They set up an elaborate trial for the assassins, which by its very nature would be a long-drawn-out process, and almost a full week went by before they addressed their appeal to the German government.

This appeal took the form of two documents: the memorandum prepared before the assassinations analyzing the overall situation in the Balkans and the dangers threatening both Austria and Germany (see pp. 436–437), and a personal letter, drafted by Berchthold, from Emperor Francis Joseph to Kaiser William II.

The original purpose of the Austrian memorandum had been to secure German cooperation for a diplomatic offensive in the Balkans to frustrate Franco-Russian designs there. Following the assassinations, however, the central thesis was decisively altered by a postscript added by Berchthold: the Sarajevo murders provided irrefutable evidence, if any was still needed, of the irreconcilable nature of Serbian antagonism. Austrian efforts to establish a tolerable relationship with Serbia as recommended by the Germans had been quite useless, and it was now obvious that Austria would always have to reckon with Serbia's "tenacious, implacable, and aggressive" hostility. In view of this situation, it was necessary, indeed imperative, that Austria break the threads of the net in which its opponents were seeking to bind it.

The personal letter from Francis Joseph to the kaiser, dated July 2, stressed the same themes. His nephew's murder was "the direct consequence of the agitation carried on by the Russian and Serbian pan-Slavs, whose sole aim is the weakening

440

MAP 20 EUROPE IN 1914

of the Triple Alliance and the destruction of my empire." It would probably be impossible to prove the direct complicity of the Serbian government, but there could be no doubt that Serbia's avowed aim of unifying all south Slavs under the Serbian flag encouraged such crimes and that the continuation of this situation represented a lasting danger to "my House and my lands." Henceforth the Austrian government would seek the isolation and diminution of Serbia. This policy called for an alliance with Bulgaria, which might eventually include Greece and Turkey, the recovery of Romania's allegiance, and the formation of a Balkan league under the aegis of the Triple Alliance as a barrier to the pan-Slav tide—whereby the emperor, or rather Berchthold, conveniently overlooked the fact that Bulgaria was a Slavic state. "This will only be possible if Serbia, which at the present is the pivot of pan-Slav policy, is eliminated as a political power factor in the Balkans." The emperor hoped that the kaiser too would see that a friendly settlement of differences between Austria and Serbia was no longer possible, and that the pacific policy of all European monarchs was at risk so long as the incubator of criminal action in Belgrade was allowed to go unpunished.

The two documents were taken to Germany personally by Count Hoyos, Berchthold's confidential secretary, and presented to William II in Potsdam by the Austrian ambassador, Count Szögyény, at noon on July 5. The Austrian envoy found the kaiser in an emotionally receptive mood. Two days after the Sarajevo murders, Tschirschky, his ambassador to Vienna, had reported that everything pointed to the fact that the threads of the conspiracy ran through Belgrade, and he was now hearing the opinion expressed "even among thoughtful people" that the time had come for a final reckoning with Serbia. (Marginal comment by the kaiser: "now or never.") Tschirschky himself was taking the opportunity whenever such views were aired to warn "calmly but firmly" against excessively hasty steps. The kaiser was infuriated by this attitude on the part of his ambassador. "It is none of his business as it is solely the affair of Austria," he commented on Tschirschky's report. ". . . Let Tschirschky be good enough to stop this nonsense! It is essential to clean house in Serbia, and that soon."

The kaiser's reaction to the Austrian documents presented to him on July 5 was similarly impulsive and thoughtless, but fully in line with his reaction to previous crises. Without waiting to consult his chancellor or any other senior political or military leaders, he authorized Szögyény to inform his imperial master that he might rely in this case as in all others on Germany's full support. This was especially true with respect to Serbia, where he believed Austria should act immediately. Even if it came to war with Russia, Austria could be assured that Germany would stand by its ally, but he did not think Russia was in any way prepared for war and would certainly think twice before resorting to arms. The kaiser understood how hard it would be for the peace-loving Austrian ruler to invade Serbia, but if Austria decided military action against Serbia was necessary, he, the kaiser, would be sorry if Austria did not take advantage of the present favorable opportunity. He would see to it that King Carol of Romania observed a correct attitude, but could not endorse an alliance with Bulgaria for he had never trusted King Ferdinand or his advisers. Still, he would make no objection to a treaty between the Monarchy and Bulgaria provided it contained nothing to offend the Romanians and was promptly communicated to them.

Only after giving the Austrians these assurances did the kaiser discuss the situation with the few political and military advisers who could be assembled at short notice—Chancellor Bethmann; Zimmermann, the undersecretary for foreign affairs; Falkenhayn, the minister of war; Lyncker, chief of the military cabinet; and Plessen, an imperial aide-de-camp. Even then he did so hastily and superficially, reading the Austrian documents aloud so rapidly that his listeners had trouble following their argument. In the end, according to Plessen's diary entry, "the opinion prevailed among us that the sooner the Austrians made their move against Serbia the better, and that the Russians, although friends of Serbia, will not join in." The kaiser was confident that the tsar "would not take the part of regicides in this case," and besides neither Russia nor France was prepared for war. Therefore, "he did not believe there would be any further military development," by which he clearly meant any development beyond whatever moves Austria decided to make against Serbia. In response to a question from Falkenhayn, the kaiser saw no reason for Germany to make any special military preparations, nor did he bother to recall from leave the chiefs of his military and naval staffs or the chief of military intelligence. On July 6 he himself went off on his annual three-week cruise to Scandinavia. During the next three weeks there was no change in the regular routine of the German army and navy, nor was there any coordination of plans among German and Austrian military leaders.

On the afternoon of July 5, almost immediately after his conference with the kaiser, Falkenhayn wrote a letter to Moltke, the chief of the army general staff, who was taking the waters at Karlsbad, informing him about the Austrian appeal and the German reaction. Falkenhayn shared Bethmann's doubts that the Austrians, for all their talk, were in earnest. Their documents did not speak of the need for war but rather of some "energetic" political step, for example, a treaty with Bulgaria, for which they wanted German support. Bethmann did not object to the kaiser departing on his northern cruise and had even advised it, and Falkenhayn for his part saw no reason for Moltke to curtail his stay in Karlsbad. "It will be a long time before the treaty with Bulgaria is signed," Falkenhayn said, but he thought Moltke should be informed of the strained situation in case events took a sudden turn.

Bethmann spoke with the Austrian envoys on the following day, July 6. According to his own account, he assured them the kaiser was not blind to the dangers threatening Austria, and although he had no great confidence in Bulgaria he would instruct his minister to Sofia to support Austrian efforts to negotiate a Bulgarian alliance if requested to do so. He would also use his influence with King Carol to bring Romania into line. Finally, concerning Serbia, the kaiser naturally could take no stand on questions between Austria and that country, for they were beyond his competence, but Francis Joseph could be assured the kaiser would be true to Austria in accordance with his treaty obligations and old friendship.

Szögyény's report of this conversation differs significantly from Falkenhayn's description of the chancellor's attitude or, for that matter, from Bethmann's own. According to Szögyény the Germans not only promised Austria their support but positively urged them to take action. "I made certain," the Austrian envoy informed Berchthold, "that the imperial chancellor as well as his imperial master considers immediate action on our part as the best solution to our Balkan difficulties. From an international point of view, he regards the present moment as more favorable than some later time."

Despite the discrepancies between the German and Austrian records of their conversations of July 5 and 6, all confirm the essential point: Germany was prepared to support Austria no matter what action Austria might take. These assurances on the part of the kaiser and Bethmann constituted what was later to be called Germany's "blank check" to Austria. In fact the check was not blank at all but had already been filled in: Germany would back up, and was even urging, Austrian punitive measures against Serbia—even if they involved the risk of war against Russia.

❑ *The Austrian Decision for War and the Ultimatum to Serbia*

The guarantee of German support was decisive for Austrian policy, for even Conrad, the most ardent and persistent advocate of a military solution to the Serbian problem, had advised that nothing be done until Austria was certain of Germany's attitude. Berchtold reported the results of the Austrian appeal to Berlin to a meeting of the Austro-Hungarian ministerial council on July 7. The kaiser and chancellor had given emphatic assurance of their unconditional support in case of military complications with Serbia. Berchtold was well aware that attacking Serbia might result in war with Russia, but Russia was seeking to form a coalition of Balkan states to use against the Monarchy when the time seemed opportune and he believed that unless Austria took energetic countermeasures its position was bound to get steadily worse, especially since Serbia and Romania would interpret Austrian passivity as a sign of weakness. The logical conclusion was that Austria should get ahead of its enemies by a timely reckoning with Serbia to eliminate the south Slav menace, something that might not be possible later.

Berchtold's call for military action against Serbia was vehemently opposed by Tisza, the Hungarian prime minister, who believed military measures should be taken only after all diplomatic efforts to secure satisfaction from Serbia had been exhausted. In any event war would be extremely dangerous, for Austria could not rely on the support of its allies, Italy and Romania, and any attempt to crush Serbia would involve a life and death struggle against Russia. Moreover, as Hungarian premier Tisza could never permit the Dual Monarchy to annex any part of Serbia—a consistent attitude on the part of the Hungarians, who feared that incorporating more Slavs into the empire would dilute their own influence.

All other ministers at the July 7 conference agreed with Berchtold that a purely diplomatic campaign, as advocated by Tisza, even if it resulted in a striking humiliation of Serbia, would be nugatory, for the Serbs would promptly disregard any promises they might make, as they had after the Bosnian crisis in 1909. Consequently the demands made to Serbia must be so onerous as to make their rejection certain and thus prepare the way for a radical solution through military action.

Tisza resisted the pressure for military action until July 14, when he too was convinced by belligerent demonstrations on the part of the Serbs and pan-Slavs generally that Austria must act now to avoid being throttled in the future. Heretofore he had always urged caution, he told the German ambassador, but he had come to the conclusion that the Monarchy must demonstrate its ability to survive and put an end to the intolerable conditions in the southeast. "I have found it hard to decide to advise in favor of war," he said, "but I am now firmly convinced of its necessity." Tisza's one condition in sanctioning war was that the ministerial council agree unanimously that there should be no annexation of Serbian territory apart from minor frontier rectifications, a condition the council accepted although with significant mental reservations on the part of some members.

By July 19 the Austrian government had drafted its ultimatum to Serbia, which was euphemistically called a "note with a time limit," and submitted it to the Dual Monarchy's ministerial council. The ultimatum began by quoting the Serbian declaration to Austria of March 31, 1909, which was supposed to have resolved the Bosnian crisis, whereby Serbia renounced its opposition to Austria's annexation of Bosnia and Herzegovina and promised to maintain friendly relations with Austria. Far from carrying out these agreements, the Serbian government had permitted and even encouraged subversive activities of every kind against the Monarchy and its institutions. To ensure that the promises made in the declaration of 1909 were at last fulfilled, Austria was presenting a new set of conditions to Serbia including demands that all anti-Austrian propaganda and revolutionary activity be suppressed and, most importantly, that Serbia accept the collaboration of Austrian officials for this purpose. Austria expected a reply within forty-eight hours. The Austrians fully expected their ultimatum to be rejected, but if accepted, the provision for Austrian supervision of Serbian domestic affairs would make it impossible for Serbia to evade its commitments.

The Austro-Hungarian ministerial council accepted the government's draft ultimatum at its July 19 meeting, but three full weeks had now gone by since the Sarajevo murders. The council then decided that delivery of the ultimatum should be delayed still further because of the impending visit to Russia of President Poincaré of France and René Viviani, the premier and foreign minister, who were to be accompanied by Alexander Isvolsky, now Russia's ambassador to Paris and bitterly anti-Austrian since his unhappy experiences during the Bosnian crisis. The Austrian council believed it would be unwise to threaten Belgrade while the impressionable tsar was enveloped in the "champagne mood" of Franco-Russian toasts and under the influence of Isvolsky and the powerful personality of Poincaré, who might persuade him to support Belgrade and thus thwart Austrian hopes of keeping their conflict with Serbia localized. This new delay meant that the Austrian ultimatum would not be submitted to Belgrade until the evening of July 23, by which time whatever sympathy the Sarajevo murders had generated for Austria would surely have eroded still further.

❏ *The Policy of Russia*

The Austrian decision to delay presenting their ultimatum until the French leaders had left Russia was futile, for the Russians had broken the Austrian diplomatic code and knew the main points of the ultimatum soon after it was formulated. The Russians therefore had ample opportunity to discuss countermeasures with their French guests. In any case the Austrians should have realized that their policy decisions, discussed by so many officials over so long a time, could not be kept secret. On July 18—before the final text of the Austrian ultimatum had been approved by the ministerial council—Sazonov had already been informed by his ambassador to Vienna that Austria intended to make "certain demands" on Serbia, and that same day he warned the Austrian ambassador to St. Petersburg "in a most decided manner" of Russia's determination "on no account to permit any attempts against the independence of Serbia."

The French visitors—Poincaré, Viviani, and Bruno Jacquin de Margerie, the director of the French foreign ministry—arrived on July 20. No record of any discussions of the Serbian crisis between the French and Russian leaders has been found in French or Russian archives, which is curious, but the British archives contain a summary of the Franco-Russian talks by Sir George Buchanan, the British ambassador to St. Petersburg, who was informed of them confidentially by Sazonov and by the French ambassador, Maurice Paléologue, the day after the French departed. According to Buchanan's report to his own government, the following points had been established: (1) complete agreement that peace and the existing balance of power should be maintained; (2) diplomatic action would be taken in Vienna to prevent demands for explanations from Serbia that would serve as an excuse for intervention in Serbian domestic affairs and impinge on Serbian sovereignty and independence; and (3) obligations imposed by the Franco-Russian alliance were solemnly affirmed.

The French and Russian leaders appear to have reached agreement with respect to Serbia at a very early stage of the French visit, for on the morning of July 21, the day after the French arrived, Sazonov summoned the German ambassador to warn Germany, as he had previously warned Austria, that Russia would not condone any infringement on Serbia's sovereignty and independence. His warning also reveals how accurately he was informed about Austria's intentions. There were people in Austria who would apparently not be satisfied merely with making representations in Belgrade, he said, but were bent on annihilating Serbia. (Marginal comment by the kaiser: "would be the best thing, too!") If the Austrians were absolutely determined to disturb the peace, they would *have to reckon with Europe.* (The kaiser: "No! Russia, yes, as the perpetrator and advocate of regicide!") Russia could not remain indifferent to any demands on Belgrade whose objective was the humiliation of Serbia. Moreover, the situation was causing serious concern in Paris and London, where Austria's attitude was meeting with strong disapproval. (The kaiser: "he is wrong!") Sazonov concluded by repeating his warning: "Russia *would not be able to allow* Austria-Hungary to *make any threats* against Serbia or to *take any military measures.*" The policy of Russia was "pacific but not passive," a warning the kaiser breezily dismissed with the comment *"qui vivra verra!"* (He who lives shall see). In the afternoon of that same day, July 21, Poincaré reinforced Russia's previous warning to Austria. "Serbia has a very warm friend in the Russian people," he told the Austrian ambassador, "and Russia has an ally, France."

Disregarding these warnings, the Austrians presented their ultimatum to Serbia as planned at six in the evening of July 23 after the departure of the French visitors from St. Petersburg. Sazonov received news of the delivery of the ultimatum the next morning. "This means war," he said. He immediately telephoned the news to the tsar, who commented "this is most disturbing" and requested to be kept informed of further developments. Left without orders from the tsar, Sazonov consulted with Yanushkevich, the chief of the army general staff, proposing that he prepare for the partial mobilization of the Russian army, meaning mobilization of the military districts opposite Austria but not those opposite Germany to avoid provoking German military intervention. Sazonov also took the initiative in summoning all government ministers in the St. Petersburg area to a ministerial meeting that same afternoon and in recalling all other senior government officials from leave.

Later that same morning of July 24 Sazonov received Szápáry, the Austrian ambassador, who had been instructed to read Sazonov the text of the Austrian ultimatum. According to Szápáry's account of their meeting, Sazonov listened in comparative quiet, but from time to time he interrupted by saying: "I know what it is. You want to go to war with Serbia! . . . You are setting fire to Europe! It is a great responsibility you are assuming, you will see what kind of impression you will make in London and Paris and perhaps elsewhere. It will be considered unjustified aggression." He protested most vigorously against Austria's demand to take an active part in suppressing subversive movements in Serbia. Serbia would no longer be master in its own house. "You will always be wanting to interfere, and what sort of life will you make Europe lead?" Sazonov dismissed Szápáry's repeated warnings that the interests of all monarchical governments were at stake in suppressing subversion. "What you want is war," Sazonov said, "and you have burned your bridges behind you."

A curious lapse on the part of Austrian statesmen at this time was their failure to inform Russia and all other powers that Austria did not intend to make any territorial acquisitions at Serbia's expense. Sazonov was not informed of this decision until the evening of July 24, and even then not by the Austrians but by Pourtalès, the German ambassador. A similar assurance was not provided by the Austrian envoy until July 26.

After talking with the Austrian ambassador on the morning of July 24, Sazonov met for lunch with the British and French ambassadors and urged them to ask their governments to join Russia immediately in preparing a plan of action. It was at this luncheon meeting that Sazonov and Paléologue informed Buchanan confidentially of the points of agreement reached between the French and Russian leadership during the recent French visit (see p. 446). "The French ambassador gave me to understand," Buchanan reported to London, "that France would not only give Russia strong diplomatic support, but would, if necessary, fulfil all the obligations imposed on her by the alliance. From the French ambassador's language it looked as if France and Russia were determined to make a strong stand even if we declined to join them." In response to the plea of Sazonov and Paléologue that Britain proclaim its solidarity with France and Russia, Buchanan replied that he would inform London of all that had been said, but that he personally could hold out no hope for a British declaration that would entail force of arms.

The Romanian minister arrived toward the end of this luncheon meeting, at the invitation of Sazonov, and was asked to join with the entente powers in making representations to Vienna. Russia considered it a matter of the greatest importance to draw Romania in on the side of the entente, Buchanan reported to London, and the Romanian envoy was obviously flattered that his country had been asked to participate as an equal with the great powers.

It was a busy day for Sazonov. At three that afternoon he presided over the meeting of the ministerial council he had arranged in the morning to discuss the Serbian crisis. The Austrian ultimatum had undoubtedly been drawn up with Germany's connivance, he said, and if accepted would turn Serbia into a de facto protectorate of the central powers. He spoke of the immense sacrifices Russia had made in the past to secure the independence of the Slavic peoples; if Russia now abandoned this "historic mission," it would be dismissed as a decadent state, a second-class power, and the result would be the total collapse of Russian prestige in the Balkans. But even if Russia agreed to concessions, such a policy would not ensure peace now or in the future because Germany would only be encouraged to mount further challenges to Russian interests. A firm stand, on the other hand, would involve a serious risk of immediate war.

Krivoshein, the minister of agriculture, although eager to avoid war, observed that the conciliatory policy Russia had pursued hitherto had not succeeded in placating Austria and Germany. Russia should therefore return to a "firmer and more energetic policy in dealing with the unreasonable claims of the central European powers." Such a policy would involve serious risks, but "the only hope of influencing Germany was to show them, by taking a firm stand, that we were no longer prepared to make concessions." According to Back, the minister of finance, Krivoshein's comments were "the most persuasive in influencing our decisions." Sukhomlinov, the minister of war, and Admiral Grigorovich, the navy minister, agreed with Krivoshein that "hesitation was no longer appropriate" and they "saw no objection to a display of greater firmness in our diplomatic negotiations," although Russia's rearmament program was still far from completion.

The ministerial council's opinion was summed up by its chairman, Goremykin: "It was the imperial government's duty to decide definitely in favor of Serbia." A policy of firmness was more likely to ensure peace than conciliation, but if it failed to do so, "Russia should be prepared to make the sacrifices required of her." The council thereupon resolved that Vienna be asked to extend the time limit of its ultimatum; that Belgrade be urged to show a desire for conciliation insofar as this would not "jeopardize the independence of the Serbian state"; and that the service ministers request permission from the tsar for partial mobilization, that is, of the military districts opposite Austria, as well as the Baltic and Black sea fleets.

After the council meeting Sazonov met with Spalaikovich, the Serbian minister to Russia, and advised the utmost moderation in replying to the Austrian note, but, as Spalaikovich reported to his government, Sazonov had also assured him that Russia would permit no infringement on Serbian sovereignty or independence.

At seven that evening, still on July 24, Sazonov had a long talk with Pourtalès, the German ambassador, who had been instructed to warn the Russian statesman, as the Austrian ambassador had attempted earlier, that the monarchical powers must stand solidly behind Austria in this crisis, otherwise they would deal a mortal blow to the monarchical principle. Sazonov would have none of it. "Russia *knew* what it *owed to the monarchical principle,* with which this case has nothing to do," he said. *"Very much excited,"* he virulently criticized Austria. The Austrian note to Serbia was totally unacceptable. The obligations Serbia had assumed after the Bosnian crisis to which the note referred had been assumed toward *Europe,* consequently it was up to *Europe* to determine whether Serbia had lived up to those obligations. Once again Sazonov issued a blunt warning: "If Austria-Hungary devours Serbia, we will go to war with her," to which the kaiser commented: "well then, go to it." Pourtalès's reaction to Sazonov's warning was less frivolous but revealed a fatal misunderstanding of Russian intentions. "From this it may be concluded that Russia will only take up arms in the event of Austria's attempting to acquire territory at the expense of Serbia." (The kaiser: "That it does not want to do, it seems"—a point the Austrians had not yet bothered to make clear to Russia for some inexplicable reason.) "The expressed desire to Europeanize the question also seems to point to the fact that immediate intervention on the part of Russia is not to be anticipated." (The kaiser: "Correct.")

At a ministerial council meeting the following morning, July 25, the tsar authorized partial mobilization as requested by his service ministers. That afternoon Sazonov met again with the British and French ambassadors. As reported by Ambassador Buchanan, Sazonov informed them of the tsar's decision, taken that morning, to authorize the mobilization of 1.1 million men, but the decree would not be issued until Sazonov decided it was essential to implement it. The preparations for mobilization were to begin at once, however. When Buchanan expressed the hope that Russia would not precipitate war by mobilizing before the British government had time to use its influence in favor of peace, Sazonov assured him that Russia had no aggressive intentions and would take no action until forced to do so.

At this point Paléologue said he had received several telegrams from the officials in charge of the ministry of foreign affairs in Paris (Poincaré, Viviani, and de Margerie were still at sea) and was in a position to give Sazonov "formal assurance that France placed herself unreservedly on Russia's side." Sazonov reiterated that Russia did not wish to precipitate a conflict, but unless Germany could restrain Austria he could only regard the situation as desperate. "Russia cannot allow Austria to crush Serbia and become [the] preponderant power in [the] Balkans," he said, and "secure of [the] support of France she will face all the risks of war." Buchanan too evidently regarded the situation as desperate, and he warned his government that Britain would have to choose between giving Russia active support or renouncing its friendship. "If we fail her now we cannot hope to maintain that friendly cooperation with her in Asia that is of such vital importance for us."

Poincaré and Viviani, en route to France, learned of the delivery of the Austrian ultimatum and Russia's decisions through garbled radio messages, but Poincaré's policy was in full accord with that of Russia: Serbia should accept as many of Austria's conditions "as honor would allow"; it should seek to prolong the Austrian deadline, a request France would support in Vienna; and the Triple Entente should try to arrange an international inquest into the Sarajevo murders.

❑ *The Serbian Reply and the Austrian Declaration of War*

In their ultimatum to Serbia, the Austrians had stated that they would be satisfied only with total and unconditional Serbian acceptance of all their demands, which they evidently expected (and hoped) would be indignantly rejected. Instead the Serbs, buoyed by assurances of Russian support, responded in effusively conciliatory terms shrouded in verbiage to disguise their de facto rejection of Austria's most critical demands. The Serbian government was "pained and surprised" by Austria's accusations. It agreed to suppress all anti-Austrian propaganda and organizations and to dismiss all persons engaged in undermining Austrian authority, but it expected Austria to supply the names of all people and organizations it was accusing of such behavior and evidence of their guilt. Serbia felt obliged to confess that it did not clearly understand the Austrian demand to accept the collaboration of Austrian officials in Serbian territory, but it would "admit such collaboration that conformed with the principles of international law, criminal procedure, and good neighborly relations." Serbia also agreed, "it goes without saying," to open an inquiry against all persons implicated in the Sarajevo murders who happened to be in Serbian territory, but it could not accept the participation of Austrian authorities "as this would be a violation of the constitution," though in concrete cases Serbia might communicate the results of its own investigations to Austrian agents. Finally, if Austria were not satisfied with the Serbian reply, Serbia was ready "as always" to accept a pacific mediation of all points at issue by referring them to the international tribunal at The Hague or to the great powers that had taken part in drawing up the Serbian promises of good behavior presented to Austria on March 31, 1909.

The Serbian reply was a masterpiece of public relations. If the Austrians rejected it, as they were virtually certain to do because Serbia had not agreed unequivocally to all their demands, they would be exposed as the villains responsible for a continuation of the crisis, whereas the Serbs would emerge as eminently reasonable and sincerely eager for a peaceful settlement. So certain were the Serbs that Austria would reject their reply that they ordered full mobilization of their army three hours before they delivered it.

The Serbian reply certainly evoked the desired reaction in Britain, where Grey told the German ambassador that "Serbia had agreed to Austrian demands to an extent such as he would never have believed possible." Should Austria fail to be satisfied with this reply, "it would then be absolutely evident that Austria was only seeking an excuse for crushing Serbia."

Grey was quite right. The Austrians *were* only seeking an excuse for crushing Serbia, whether through gaining control of Serbia's domestic affairs as demanded in their ultimatum or through conquest, the course they were now obliged to pursue. At 6:10 P.M. on July 25, only minutes after receiving the Serbian reply, the Austrian government broke off diplomatic relations, and at 8:30 that evening Emperor Francis Joseph ordered Austrian mobilization—but against Serbia alone to avoid provoking Russia, another futile gesture, for Russia had already begun preliminary preparations for mobilization that same morning.

The ensuing events reveal an incredible lack of coordination between Austrian and German political and military authorities and an incongruous degree of nonchalance on the part of the Austrians in general.

From the Austrians' first appeals to Berlin for German support, the German government had not only provided them with the desired assurances but had urged them to strike swiftly while they still enjoyed the European sympathy evoked by the Sarajevo murders. As the weeks passed, the Germans continued to urge action and made very clear to Vienna their disgust with Austrian delay and indecisiveness. When Austria finally presented its ultimatum to Serbia, the Germans advised that a negative reply from Serbia should be followed immediately by an Austrian declaration of war. "Every delay in beginning military operations regarded here as increasing danger of intervention by other powers," Szögyény, the Austrian ambassador to Berlin, telegraphed Berchthold in Vienna. "We are urgently advised to proceed without delay so as to confront the world with a *fait accompli.*"

Berchthold received Szögyény's telegram from Berlin on the evening of July 25, shortly after Austria had broken off diplomatic relations with Serbia, but he waited until the afternoon of the following day to ask Conrad, the chief of the Austrian general staff, when he should issue a declaration of war. According to Conrad's diary, he had replied that war should be declared only after Austrian mobilization had been completed and military operations could begin; that would be about August 12. In other words, after almost a full month of diplomatic crisis, which the Austrian government had intended all along to exploit to take military action against Serbia (as Conrad himself had been advocating for years), the Austrian army would not be ready to go into action for over two more weeks. Berchthold objected that "the diplomatic situation will not hold as long as that." Conrad was firm and apparently for the first time impressed on Berchthold the imperative need to find out what Russia would do: if it became clear that Russia would intervene, then Austria should proceed from the start against Russia; if Austria moved against Serbia, on the other hand, and *then* Russia intervened, Austria would be dangerously weakened in dealing with a Russian invasion—which should have been obvious from the start to everyone concerned.

Berchthold, however, accused so long of flabbiness and delay in his conduct of affairs, decided to take Germany's advice, and at eleven in the morning of July 28 Austria declared war on Serbia. The Austrian army was no more ready to march than before, but it was now mobilized to attack Serbia. It was thus seriously weakened, as Conrad had foreseen, to face a Russian offensive in the northeast, where the Germans counted on effective Austrian holding operations while they deployed the bulk of their forces against France in the west.

This was exactly the situation the Serbs and Russians had hoped for. On July 28 the British chargé d'affaires in Belgrade telegraphed Grey that the Serbian government expected an immediate attack on Belgrade. "Plan of campaign is now to draw into the interior as large a portion as possible of Austrian army so as to weaken Austria elsewhere. [Serbian] under secretary of state tells me that Russian support is assured."

This was exactly the situation the Germans had wanted to avoid. On May 12, 1914, well before the beginning of the crisis, Conrad had met with Moltke, his German counterpart, who told him Germany must unconditionally seek success in the west and would have few troops to spare for the east. Austria would therefore have to bear the brunt of the fighting in that sector. Asked what would happen if Germany lost in the west, Moltke replied: "Well, I'll do what I can. We are not superior to the French." Their exchange on this occasion hardly suggests either military leader was confident of victory in a war, but what is most striking is the lack of coordination between the Austrian and German armies and their total failure to plan for emergencies they had known for years might develop.

❑ *Germany's Efforts to Draw Back*

On the morning of July 28, at almost exactly the same time as the Austrian declaration of war, the kaiser, who had just returned from his Scandinavian trip, saw the Serbian reply to the Austrian ultimatum for the first time. His reaction was almost the same as that of Grey in London: the Serbs had essentially agreed to all of Austria's demands and the few remaining reservations could be clarified through negotiation. "A capitulation of the most humiliating kind . . . and with that *every reason for war* is eliminated," he said. He nevertheless saw that Austria must secure a pledge to make certain the Serbs would honor their promises this time, and for this purpose he proposed that Austria occupy Belgrade and remain there until its demands were fulfilled. This would also give the Austrian army a badly needed sense of achievement by actually standing on foreign soil.

Bethmann was still cautious about pressuring Vienna, so cautious in fact that in presenting the pledge plan to the Austrian government he did not even reveal it had been conceived, or at any rate endorsed, by the kaiser himself. "You will have to avoid very carefully giving rise to the impression that we wish to hold Austria back," he told his ambassador to Vienna. "The case is solely one of finding a way to realize Austria's desired aim, that of cutting the vital chord of Greater Serbia propaganda, without at the same time bringing on a world war, and, if the latter cannot be avoided in the end, of improving the conditions under which we have to wage it in so far as possible."

Bethmann was obviously appalled to learn that the Austrian army would not be ready to move against Serbia until August 12. This would allow time for all kinds of mediation and conference proposals, and if Austria continued to reject them, it would be Austria that would incur the odium of causing a world war. If the war could not be kept localized, it was imperative that the blame fall on Russia. Austria should therefore emphatically repeat its declaration that it did not intend to make territorial acquisitions of any sort at the expense of Serbia, and most seriously consider accepting the pledge plan.

About the same time the kaiser put forward his pledge plan, Grey, the British foreign secretary, came up with an almost identical proposal: Austria should occupy Belgrade as a pledge that Serbia fulfill its promises, but should take no further military action. Lichnowsky, the German ambassador to London, telegraphed Grey's proposal to Berlin on the evening of July 29 urging that Germany join Britain, France, and Russia in mediating the Austro-Serb dispute. "It would seem to him [Grey] to be a suitable basis for mediation if Austria, after occupying Belgrade, for example, or other places, should announce her conditions . . . *mediation* now seemed to him to be urgently necessary *if a European catastrophe were not to result.*" At the same time Grey warned, as he had already on several occasions, that if the conflict spread beyond Austria and Serbia, Britain could not stand aside for long. The kaiser took this warning to heart. "This means they will attack us," he wrote on the margin of Lichnowsky's report.

The Germans were at last beginning to comprehend the magnitude of the crisis in which they were involved and the very high probability that, if it came to war, the conflict could not be kept localized as they had so blithely assumed. In response to Grey's warning, received in Berlin the evening of July 29, Bethmann dispatched a telegram to Tschirschky in Vienna later that same night in a state of near panic. "In case Austria refuses all mediation, we stand before a conflagration in which England will be against us; Italy and Romania to all appearances will not go with us; and we two shall be opposed to four great powers. On Germany, thanks to England's opposition, the principal burden of the fight will fall." Austria's honor and interests could be amply satisfied by the occupation of Belgrade and other places. "Under the circumstances we must urgently and impressively suggest to the consideration of the Vienna cabinet the acceptance of mediation on the above-mentioned honorable conditions. The responsibility for the consequences that would otherwise follow would be an uncommonly heavy one both for Austria and for us."

When Vienna categorically refused to enter into direct negotiations, Bethmann sent another plea: Germany did not expect Austria to enter into such negotiations with Serbia, with which it was at war, but Austria should not refuse to negotiate with Russia in order to avoid provoking Russian military intervention, "which Austria-Hungary is beyond all else interested in preventing." Germany was of course ready to fulfill its alliance obligations, "but must decline to be drawn wantonly into a world conflagration by Vienna, without having any regard paid to our counsel"—whereby Bethmann conveniently forgot that Vienna had paid all too much regard to Germany's counsel in hastening its declaration of war.

Bethmann returned to the charge the next day. If Vienna refused to compromise in any way, especially along the lines of Grey's proposal, it would hardly be possible to blame the outbreak of a European conflagration on Russia. Germany had urged Britain to propose that France and Russia halt military preparations. "If England's efforts succeed while Vienna declines everything, Vienna will be giving documentary evidence that it absolutely wants war, into which we shall be drawn, while Russia remains free of responsibility." Bethmann's efforts were seconded by the kaiser, who sent a personal telegram to Francis Joseph asking for a quick decision about Grey's mediation proposal, which the German ambassador had twice submitted to the Austrian government.

The German warnings were discussed in Vienna at a meeting of the ministerial council for joint Austro-Hungarian affairs on the morning of July 31. Berchthold, who presided over the meeting, reported that the emperor had declared that a cessation of hostilities against Serbia was impossible, as was Austrian acceptance of the British offer of mediation; as Austria had learned from bitter experience, mediation would mean that Britain, France, and Italy too would take Russia's part, while Austria would be left with the support of Germany, and even that was now doubtful. If Austria's present action against Serbia achieved no more than a gain in prestige (i.e., a diplomatic victory that left Serbia intact), the entire business would have been undertaken in vain. "From a mere occupation of Belgrade we should gain absolutely nothing, even if Russia should give her consent to it. All this would be mere tinsel [*Flitterwerk*]. Russia would come forward as the savior of Serbia, and especially of the Serbian army. The latter would remain intact, and in two or three years we should again have to look forward to the attack of Serbia under far more unfavorable conditions."

The members of the council accepted their emperor's estimate of the situation but decided to make a gesture for the sake of their own public image. They agreed unanimously to accept the British offer of mediation on principle, but without informing the powers of the actual conditions Austria intended to impose on Serbia as the British had stipulated. Even then, Austria would agree to international mediation only if it were allowed to continue military operations against Serbia and if Russia stopped its mobilization.

Although the Austrians reached this decision on the morning of July 31, they did not reply to Germany's plea to accept mediation until 3:45 in the morning of the following day. By that time, even if Russia had agreed to Austria's conditions, which it certainly would not have done, diplomacy had been engulfed by military considerations.

❑ *Russia's Mobilization*

On the morning of July 25 Russia initiated preliminary preparations for mobilization with the understanding that partial mobilization (of the military districts opposite Austria) would begin the moment Austria moved against Serbia.

Early mobilization was imperative for the Russians because their immense territory and inadequate transport system meant they required considerably more time to mobilize than other powers. There was another, more complicated problem. To avoid forming military units with a high concentration of non-Russian nationalities, who might prove unreliable, the Russian army had a rule that units should be three-quarter Slav and if possible one-half Great Russian. This meant that recruits were not drawn solely from the military districts in which they were stationed but from every part of Russia, a system that not only made for slower mobilization but made partial mobilization virtually impossible.

Because the Russian army needed to mobilize early, the government did not wait for an actual Austrian invasion of Serbia but issued orders for partial mobilization immediately after receiving word of the Austrian declaration of war, that is, on the afternoon of July 28. It was only at this late stage that the army high command informed the government that partial mobilization would throw the entire mobilization procedure into confusion, a problem General Dobrorolsky, the chief of the mobilization section of the Russian general staff, had explained several days earlier to General Yanushkevich, the chief of the general staff. Yanushkevich, however, had raised no objection to the ministerial council's decision on the morning of July 25 for partial mobilization, perhaps because he intended to force the government's hand for full mobilization if military action became necessary at all. Whatever his intentions, he prepared two decrees for the tsar's signature, one for partial, the other for full mobilization, and it was the decree for partial mobilization that went into effect on the afternoon of July 28. The next day, upon receiving news that the Austrians were bombarding Belgrade, the tsar allowed the decree for full mobilization to go into effect. That same evening, however, in response to an appeal from the kaiser, he changed his mind again and reinstituted the order for partial mobilization. In great agitation Sukhomlinov, the minister of war, and Yanushkevich explained to Sazonov on the morning of July 30 why partial mobilization was impossible and they begged him to persuade the tsar, whom he was to see that afternoon, to renew the order for full mobilization. If Sazonov succeeded, Yanushkevich asked to be informed immediately by telephone. "After that," he said, "I will go away, smash my telephone, and generally make sure that no one can find me to give contrary orders."

Sazonov found the tsar tense and fully aware of the gravity of the decision required of him, but he finally agreed that it was impossible to delay full mobilization. Sazonov immediately informed Yanushkevich of the tsar's decision. "Now you can smash your telephone. Give your orders, general, and then disappear for the rest of the day."

❑ *Germany's Reaction to Russia's Mobilization;* *the Schlieffen Plan*

Russian mobilization was decisive for Germany policy. Ever since the formation of the German empire, but especially since the Franco-Russian alliance, German military leaders had considered having to wage a war on two fronts and had made plans for that dreaded possibility.

Moltke, the chief architect of Prussia's victories in 1866 and 1870, planned a holding operation against France along the strategic Alsace-Lorraine frontier, while deploying the bulk of Germany's forces in the east for limited operations against Russia. He proposed to overrun Russia's Polish provinces, but, well aware of the perils of a more ambitious campaign, he intended to call a halt there. "To follow up a victory in the kingdom of Poland by a pursuit into the Russian interior would be of no interest to us," he said. His plan, based as much on political as military calculations, hinged on the expectation that Russia, beset by economic difficulties and the perennial threat of revolution, could not sustain a long war, and after being expelled from Poland could be persuaded to sue for peace if offered generous terms. If France then refused to make peace at the same time, Germany could shift its armies to the west to wage war on only a single front.

Moltke's strategy was reversed by General Alfred von Schlieffen, who became chief of the army general staff in 1891; his strategy for a two-front war was still in place, though with significant modifications, in 1914. The Schlieffen plan called for holding operations or even a strategic retreat in the east, while launching the major German offensive against France in the west. A French campaign, in contrast to any that could be waged against Russia, offered the possibility of a quick and decisive victory. Schlieffen was a diligent student of military history, and his plan was based on a detailed study of Napoleonic battles and especially on Hannibal's great victory over the Romans at Cannae in 215 B.C., which he had analyzed in a scholarly two-volume monograph—neglecting to consider the implications of the fact that although Hannibal had won this battle he lost the war.

In Schlieffen's campaign against France, Germany would launch its major offensive through the flatlands of Holland and Belgium, which alone offered the kind of terrain that would permit rapid advance and deployment of modern mass armies. The objective would be to outflank and envelop the bulk of the French forces and drive them against the German fortifications of Alsace and Lorraine where they would be destroyed or compelled to surrender. The entire operation was carefully timed so that it could be completed before Russia could mobilize for a major offensive in the east, where the Austrians and a small German covering force were expected to hold up the Russians until France was defeated. The slow pace of Russian mobilization was therefore crucial to the success of the Schlieffen plan.

It was a bold and imaginative plan that still fascinates students of military history, but it was a fatally flawed plan from a military and above all from a political point of view. Militarily it depended far too much on timing: the slow Russian mobilization, a speedy German advance through the Low Countries, and rapid envelopment of the French armies. It took far too little consideration of the inevitable accidents and errors in every military campaign. It also failed to take into sufficient account the difficulties of the campaign itself: the tenacity of enemy resistance and the fact that the German armies would be advancing on foot through terrain intersected by networks of rivers and canals, where the bridges and railways would have been destroyed by retreating armies and the highways clogged by refugees. The French, on the other hand, operating on interior lines, their railways and highways intact, would thus be better able to transport troops and supplies to any part of the fighting front.

But the truly disastrous features of the Schlieffen plan were political. It required violating the neutrality of three states (Belgium, Holland, and Luxemburg—though by 1914 the plan had been revised to exclude Holland) whose sovereignty and independence were guaranteed by international treaties signed by all the great powers, including Prussia-Germany. Such treaty violations would destroy Germany's moral position at the very start of the war and almost certainly bring Britain into the conflict against Germany. Schlieffen, however, did not think British intervention merited serious consideration—it was a military axiom that the British navy would be of no use in defending Paris—and like so many military leaders he failed to appreciate the full importance of the moral factor.

By far the worst feature of his plan, however, was its rigidity, which failed to allow for the multitude of circumstances that might make war necessary. Nor did it take into account that all Germany's alliances were defensive and would come into effect only if Germany were attacked. Instead, the plan simply took for granted that a future war would have to be waged against France and Russia simultaneously, it required that Germany launch immediate offensive operations against France, and it required that Germany respond to Russian mobilization by immediate mobilization of its own. These features of the Schlieffen plan proved disastrous in 1914, for they did not allow time for mediation, which the German government was desperately seeking in the final days of the crisis, or for any other peaceful resolution of the problems.

To be fair to Schlieffen, it should be pointed out that his plan was not fully developed until 1905, when Russia was largely immobilized by defeat in Asia and revolution at home, and that he was aware that such a favorable situation could last only two to three more years. Hence his desire to take advantage of the First Morocco Crisis to wage a "preventive" war against France before Russia had a chance to recover.

After Schlieffen retired in 1906 his successor, Helmuth von Moltke (a nephew of the Moltke of 1866 and 1870) revised his plan to take into account Russia's revived power and an anticipated French drive through Alsace and Lorraine. This meant assigning larger forces to the eastern front and leaving more troops in Alsace to withstand a French offensive. He also restricted Germany's deployment in the Low Countries to Belgium and Luxemburg so as to leave Holland neutral and its ports thus available for overseas trade—a hopelessly naive calculation. Some military historians believe that when Moltke narrowed the corridor for the German offensive in the west and diverted forces to the eastern front and Alsace, he fatally restricted Germany's sphere of operations and weakened the armies required for the great enveloping operation in the west, thereby destroying the Schlieffen plan's chances for success. Whether that plan might have succeeded under the best of circumstances can never be determined; as it was, it proved to be a political and military disaster. When the kaiser in the last days of the 1914 crisis called for mobilization against Russia alone, he was informed, as the tsar had been when he called for partial mobilization against Austria, that this was impossible because it would throw the entire mobilization procedure into confusion. Thus the fabled German general staff, which is still admired by military experts for the quality of its training and its intellectual caliber, compounded the errors of Germany's political leadership and brought Germany into World War I under the worst possible political, military, and moral circumstances.

❑ *The Policy of France*

The French were as careful to safeguard their moral image as the Austrians and Germans were profligate in destroying theirs. Poincaré and Viviani returned to Paris from their trip to Russia and Scandinavia on July 29, the Scandinavian leg cut short by the Serbian crisis. At a cabinet meeting the following morning, July 30, it was agreed that war was imminent and the minister of war urged that precautionary military measures, which had been initiated five days earlier, be sharply accelerated. Joffre, chief of the French army general staff, insisted—and the cabinet agreed—that *couverture,* a disguised form of mobilization, must begin at once, but the army would not call up reservists for the present and the government would ostentatiously announce that French covering troops along the German border were being withdrawn ten kilometers from the frontier to avoid any kind of incident. The French vividly remembered the moral opprobrium they had brought down upon themselves by being the first to declare war in 1870 and they were not about to make the same mistake. Prime Minister Viviani telegraphed Paul Cambon, the French ambassador to London, to draw attention to the ten-kilometer withdrawal. "We have not done this for any other reason than to show the British government and public opinion that France, like Russia, will not be the first to fire." Paul's brother, Jules Cambon, the ambassador to Berlin, also emphasized the moral factor. "What matters," he advised, "is to take public mobilization measures in France only after they have been definitely decided upon in Germany, so that British public opinion, which plays such an important role in what is happening, cannot attribute to us any initiative that led to war."

France nevertheless had supported Russia throughout the crisis in exactly the same way Germany had supported Austria, even to giving Russia the same kind of blank check. The big difference was that Germany (until too late) actively supported an Austrian policy of aggression against Serbia, whereas the French cautioned Russia to wait for overt action on the part of Austria and Germany. At the same time, the French took care that the Russians should not misinterpret their cautionary advice. During their visit to St. Petersburg, Poincaré and Viviani assured them of France's absolute loyalty to the Russian alliance and of French support for Russian policy even if it came to war. They repeated these assurances while at sea on the way home to France. Viviani telegraphed Sazonov on July 27 that "in the interests of the general peace" France was "ready to second wholeheartedly the action of the imperial government." This renewed confirmation of French support was sent because of Poincaré's belief that Russia must be constantly reassured of France's loyalty if France were to influence Russian policy. If Russia ever felt abandoned, the tsarist government might turn once again to Germany to reestablish the traditional monarchical solidarity between those two conservative powers.

Following Poincaré's and Viviani's return to Paris, Schilling, the head of chancery in the Russian foreign ministry, recorded in his diary on July 28: "The French ambassador, upon instructions from his government, informed the Russian minister of foreign affairs of the complete readiness of France to fulfill her obligations as an ally in case of necessity." This French assurance arrived just at the time that Russia, in response to Austria's declaration of war on Serbia, had ordered partial mobilization, and Sazonov was preparing instructions to Isvolsky in Paris to explain Russia's action. Austria, Sazonov said, was evidently unwilling to agree to a peaceful settlement with Serbia, forcing Russia to assume that war was inevitable and hastening its own mobilization. Isvolsky was also instructed to "express to the French government our sincere gratitude for this declaration, which has been made to me officially in its name by the French ambassador, that we can count fully upon the assistance of our ally, France. In the existing circumstances, this declaration is especially valuable to us." Finally, Sazonov hoped Britain would align itself immediately with France and Russia, because that was the only way to avoid a dangerous disruption of the European balance of power.

Poincaré did his best. If there were a general war, he warned the British ambassador, Britain would inevitably be involved to protect its own interests. A British declaration now of its intention to support France, which desired to remain at peace, "would almost certainly prevent Germany from embarking on a war."

The question here is whether Poincaré was being altogether candid about his desire to preserve peace. In July 1914 France was in an incomparably favorable diplomatic position with respect to Germany. France had a firm military alliance with Russia, and although still without guarantees of military support from Britain, France had military and naval agreements that virtually assured British support if it came to war. Italy and Romania, nominal allies of Austria and Germany, had concluded agreements with France and Russia that assured their neutrality in the event of war and might very well bring them into the conflict on the French side. But how long would this uniquely favorable international constellation endure?

With good reason Poincaré feared that the weak-willed tsar, who had been lured into a German alliance during the First Morocco Crisis, might fall under the influence of advisers who believed Russia's interests would be best served by restoring the conservative coalition with Germany and Austria, if only to play Germany off against the Western powers. Increasing tension between Russia and Britain over Persia threatened to weaken if not disrupt altogether the Anglo-Russian entente. Italy and Romania were unreliable, and with sufficient inducement might betray their agreements with France and Russia as they had betrayed those with Austria and Germany. Finally, there were ominous signs of improved relations between Germany and Britain, which were on the verge of settling their differences over the Bagdad Railway and about to conclude a new agreement over the Portuguese colonies. Were these the prelude to a more far-reaching rapprochement?

For the moment, however, France's diplomatic alignments were intact. Meanwhile, in the enemy camp, Austria had committed itself to a policy of aggression through its ultimatum and declaration of war against Serbia, and if Germany supported Austria, as it was certain to do, Germany would be branded with the same moral stigma. If war were to come between France and Germany, as most observers were certain it would, what better time to wage it than the present, even though Russia's ambitious rearmament program was still far from completion? It strains credulity to believe that Poincaré, native of Lorraine, passionate patriot, and fierce foe of Germany, was not tempted to take advantage of this uniquely favorable opportunity, if only to the extent of offering unconditional support to Russia and allowing the bungling Teutons to stumble to their doom.

□ *The Policy of Britain*

The British did not give France and Russia the guarantees of military support they desired, but Britain was clearly preparing for trouble. On July 26 Winston Churchill, the first lord of the Admiralty, ordered that the fleet, which had been concentrated for maneuvers, not disperse, and two days later he ordered that it proceed during the night, at high speed and without lights, through the Straits of Dover from Portland to its fighting base at Scapa Flow off the northeastern tip of Scotland. Nor did the British leave the Germans in any doubt about their attitude. From London, Lichnowsky, the German ambassador, addressed a steady stream of warnings that Germany could not count on British neutrality in the event of a general European war but should on the contrary reckon with the almost certain prospect of British intervention. The British government saw the entire Serbian crisis as a test of strength between the Triple Alliance and the Triple Entente. On the eve of the Austrian declaration of war against Serbia, Lichnowsky again sounded the alarm. Should Austria attack Serbia, "I am certain that England will place itself unconditionally on the side of France and Russia. . . . If it comes to war under these circumstances, we shall have England against us."

The British government meanwhile was prepared to go to remarkable lengths to persuade Austria to agree to mediation. On the evening of July 29 Lichnowsky communicated to Berlin Grey's pledge proposal that Austria occupy Belgrade and other Serbian territory as hostages for Serbia's good behavior. Grey believed that if mediation were accepted, he could secure every possible satisfaction for Austria. Thus Austria could obtain guarantees for the future without a war that would jeopardize the peace of Europe. It was this offer that prompted Bethmann's belated desperate appeals to Austria to accept Grey's proposal. If Austria rejected all offers of mediation, the result would be a European conflagration in which Austria and Germany would have all of Europe, including Britain, against them. In London, Grey endeavored to make this point unmistakably clear. He did not want Lichnowsky or his government to be misled by the friendly tone of their conversations into supposing that Britain would not take action.

British efforts to keep the peace did fail, but even before Austria's de facto rejection of the British mediation proposal all prospects for peace were eliminated by Russia's mobilization and the inexorable requirements of Germany's Schlieffen plan. Bethmann was therefore obliged to shift his policy toward Britain from supporting mediation to persuading Britain to remain neutral in the forthcoming conflict.

It was a hopeless task, as Bethmann must have realized from the start, but his tactics could hardly have been more inept. He informed Goschen, the British ambassador, that if Russia attacked Austria, Germany's obligations to Austria might, to his great regret, make a European conflagration inevitable. In that case he hoped Britain would remain neutral. He realized that Britain could not allow France to be crushed, but Germany had no intention of doing so. Therefore, if Britain would promise to remain neutral, Germany would promise that in the event of a victorious war it would seek no territorial acquisitions at France's expense—a promise that did not extend to France's colonies, as Bethmann confessed in response to Goschen's query on that point. Germany also promised to respect the sovereignty and territorial integrity of Holland so long as these were respected by Germany's adversaries, but he could not promise the same about Belgium because Germany might be forced to undertake operations there in response to French actions. What he could promise, however, was that Belgium's integrity would be respected after the war provided it did not take sides against Germany.

Grey's response was clear and unambiguous. "You must inform the German chancellor," he told Lichnowsky, "that his proposal that we should bind ourselves to neutrality on such terms cannot for a moment be entertained. . . . My answer is that we must preserve our full freedom to act as circumstances seem to us to require." Sir Eyre Crowe, a senior official of the Foreign Office, expressed what must have been the general British reaction. "The only comment that need be made on these astounding proposals is that they reflect discredit on the statesman who makes them."

Bethmann got the message. "Hopes of England precisely nil," he informed his ministerial colleagues, yet the virtual certainty that Britain would intervene against Germany did not deter the German government from mobilizing. This certainty may even have removed any doubts the Germans might have had about invading Belgium.

❑ *Into the Abyss*

The final events on the road to war are quickly told. In the late afternoon of July 30 the tsar authorized full Russian mobilization. At half past three in the afternoon of the following day, Bethmann dispatched two ultimata from Berlin, one to St. Petersburg, the other to Paris. Russia and France were informed that Russia's mobilization compelled Germany to declare a state of threatening danger of war, which did not yet mean mobilization. Full German mobilization would follow, however, if Russia did not suspend every military measure against Austria and Germany within twelve hours and make a specific declaration to that effect. The ultimatum to France asked if the French intended to remain neutral in the event of a Russo-German war, and a reply was demanded within eighteen hours. In a secret addendum to this ultimatum, the German ambassador was instructed to demand, in the unlikely event that France agreed to remain neutral, that it turn over the fortresses of Toul and Verdun to Germany as a pledge; these would be returned at the end of the war against Russia.

In St. Petersburg, Sazonov attempted to convince the German ambassador that Germany overestimated the significance of Russian mobilization, but he refused to halt that mobilization as Germany demanded. "In that case," Pourtalès replied, "nobody can blame us for our unwillingness to allow Russia a longer start in mobilization." The French response was briefer. "France will act in accordance with her interests."

On the afternoon of August 1, both the French and German governments ordered full mobilization. At seven that evening Germany declared war on Russia. Upon delivering that declaration to Sazonov, Pourtalès is said to have burst into tears.

At eight in the evening of August 2 the German government addressed an ultimatum to Belgium, a document drafted a full week earlier by the German general staff, anticipating the need for an offensive against France. The ultimatum stated (falsely) that Germany had reliable information that France intended to advance against Germany through Belgium; Germany did not believe Belgium could repel a French invasion; therefore Germany considered it necessary to enter Belgian territory itself in the interests of self-defense. If Belgium did not resist, Germany undertook to guarantee its independence and possessions upon the conclusion of peace and would pay for all damage incurred through Germany's military action; if Belgium resisted, Germany would have to consider it an enemy and leave the relations between the two states to the decision of the battlefield. A reply was demanded within twelve hours. The Belgian government rejected the German demands. On August 3 Germany declared war on France. At eight in the morning of August 4 German troops invaded Belgium.

The German attack on Belgium was followed by a British ultimatum demanding that Germany respect Belgian neutrality. This ultimatum was rejected, and at midnight on August 4 Britain declared war on Germany. Bethmann's reaction was in keeping with the diplomatic ineptness Germany had displayed throughout the crisis. "Just for a word 'neutrality,'" he lamented to the British ambassador, "a word which in wartime has so often been disregarded—just for a scrap of paper, Great Britain was going to make war on a kindred nation who desired nothing better than to be friends with her."

❏ *Austria, Germany, and the Question of War Guilt*

In the peace treaties ending World War I, Germany and its allies were obliged to accept full responsibility for starting the war, and since that time the question of war guilt has been a dominant theme in virtually all studies of the war's origins. Austria's decision to submit an ultimatum to Serbia deliberately designed to provoke war or subject Serbia to Austrian control and Germany's decision to support and actually encourage a militant Austrian policy leave no doubt whatever about the question of responsibility both for the outbreak and proliferation of the conflict.

The question of war guilt in history is a subject unto itself, but until absolute standards of international behavior are universally accepted, all judgments about war guilt depend very much on the point of view of the observer. Although it is tempting to assume the role of judge and jury, the primary responsibility of a historian is to explain how and why a country's leaders decided to go to war, or believed that that decision had been thrust upon them. These decisions are generally made on the basis of what the leaders regard as their own or their country's best interests, and they involve problems that cannot be evaluated in simplistic terms of right or wrong, guilt or innocence.

This was the case with the Austro-Serbian conflict, which was not a confrontation of right and wrong but of two kinds of right, or at least of two principles their protagonists conceived to be right, with Serbia representing the principle of nationalism, Austria the ancient principle of multinational or supranational empire. As the realization of the one principle could not be achieved without the destruction of the other, the battleground was clearly established. Austrian leaders such as Archduke Francis Ferdinand might seek to amalgamate the national principle within the imperial framework, as the empire had absorbed or broken down so many ideological challenges in the past, but there was never any question that he or any other Austrian leader would sit idly by and do nothing to prevent the dissolution of their realm.

In the controversy over war guilt in 1914, the case of Austria was almost completely overshadowed from the beginning by that of Germany. The Germans were held responsible for a far more heinous crime than supporting the Austrians and urging them to strike while the Sarajevo iron was hot. In fact, so their accusers argue, they were not primarily concerned about Austria at all, but cynically exploited the Sarajevo incident to unleash a general European war with the aim of establishing German hegemony over Europe and thence the world.

This war guilt thesis was powerfully supported by the record of German policy before and during World War II and with the capture of the bulk of Germany's official and private archives, which included abundant new information about its pre-1914 policies. The evidence found in files of German military and civil government departments, industrial and commercial enterprises, patriotic societies and labor organizations, as well as in the private papers of hundreds of German leaders from every walk of life provides a damning indictment of Germany's policies and its imperialist ambitions. German policy, however, was not being conducted in a vacuum, but rather in competition with and reaction to the policies of other states and within a climate of opinion of fervent nationalism that accepted imperialist enterprise as a condition for a nation's survival as a great power. And whereas the kaiser and his compatriots might harbor extravagant imperialist ambitions and talk about world power, rival states—notably Britain, Russia, and the United States—had already achieved it, and they had done so by methods which, as seen by their rivals and victims, were in many cases far from moral.

But quite apart from the fact that so much attention has been focused exclusively on Germany, there are two major objections to the thesis that Germany in 1914 deliberately initiated what has been called a "grab for world power." The first is the quality of German leadership; the second, the evidence of the actual course of the 1914 crisis. The deliberate provocation of a major war requires a rare degree of foresight, daring, and nerve, but it was the very absence of these qualities that characterized German policy since 1890. There is no evidence that the situation suddenly changed in 1914. The only German organization with anything like a long-range program was the army with its preposterous Schlieffen plan, but this was to come into effect only in the event of war. It was in no sense a war plot.

Bethmann-Hollweg, who soon after the outbreak of war formulated ambitious war aims to justify the sacrifices demanded of the German people, has been seen as bearing particular responsibility for unleashing the conflict. The German chancellor certainly played a sorry role in the July crisis. Yet Bethmann was a man of decency and integrity, and in calmer moments he had a solid sense of political responsibility and even a certain amount of moral courage. In the autumn of 1913, for example, William, the German crown prince, a man even more foolish than his father, submitted to the chancellor the bitter criticisms of a group of German chauvinists about the flabby conduct of German foreign policy, criticisms with which the crown prince obviously agreed.

Bethmann replied on November 15:

> Our foreign policy is accused of striving to preserve peace at *any price,* of compromising the honor and dignity of the German Reich. . . . In no instance so far has the honor and dignity of the German nation been violated by another nation. Whoever wants war without such provocation must have vital national tasks in view which cannot be achieved without war. It was to accomplish such tasks and reach such goals that Bismarck desired and launched the wars of 1864, 1866, and 1870. After they were fought and won, he believed that "the most important political interest was the preservation of peace." This was stated by him so often and so clearly, this was so obviously the guiding principle of his entire policy after 1870, that one can only accuse today's warmongers of a consummate lack of political judgment or bad faith when they constantly appeal to the example of Bismarck and actually gain credence for such falsification of history. Every policy for the sake of prestige was condemned by Bismarck as basically un-German. Whither such policy leads he could, and we can, see from the example of Napoleon III. In a future war undertaken without compelling reason, not only the Hohenzollern crown but the future of Germany will be at stake. Our policy must of course be conducted boldly. But to rattle our sabers in every diplomatic complication when the honor, security, and future of Germany are not threatened is not only foolhardy but criminal.

These are not the words of a man who is thinking of launching precisely the kind of war his critics seemed to desire. Bethmann's views on this occasion do not in themselves refute theories about his government's responsibility for war in 1914, but once again we must return to the question of why, if Germany was indeed determined to wage war to win hegemony over Europe, it did not take advantage of earlier crises which offered far better prospects of success.

An alternative theory to explain (or justify) German policy in 1914 is that the decision for war was an act of desperation, that Germany's leaders, obsessed by fears of encirclement and the growing strength of hostile powers, were convinced Germany's only chance for survival was to break the ring by going to war and that this was their last chance to wage it on anything like even terms. This was certainly the view of Moltke and Conrad. Yet this theory too presupposes long-range thinking and a sense of purpose that were notably lacking among German as well as Austrian leaders. Even as the Austrian government finally decided to move against Serbia, which both the Austrians and Germans knew might well cause other great powers to intervene, the most striking feature about the activity of the two chiefs of staff was their lack of planning: their quite incomprehensible failure to take emergency measures or coordinate their military plans to deal with the imminent repercussions.

The course of the 1914 crisis suggests yet another theory, however, which fits far better with what we know of the nature of Germany's leaders, their handling of previous crises, and their conduct of policy since the Sarajevo murders. The most consistent feature of that policy was their support for Austria to "clean house" in Serbia, but scarcely less consistent was their often-expressed confidence that an Austro-Serbian conflict could be kept localized. This confidence was ludicrously unrealistic, a characteristic of German policy over the past years, but this belief in localization is crucial in considering the question of German motivation, for it suggests that German leaders did not expect and certainly did not want the crisis with Serbia to escalate into a general European conflict.

Bethmann and his colleagues were well aware that supporting Austria was dangerous, but they decided to take what Americans would later call a calculated risk, believing that failure to do so would be more dangerous still. Bethmann was not at all happy about supporting Austria, and he complained to his secretary that Germany was faced with the usual dilemma whenever Austria contemplated action in the Balkans. "If we urge them ahead, then they will say we pushed them in; if we dissuade them, then it will be a matter of our leaving them in the lurch. Then they will turn to the western powers, whose arms are wide open, and we will lose our last ally, such as it is."

Germany's dilemma with respect to Austria was spelled out in far greater detail by Gottlieb von Jagow, the head of the German foreign office, in a letter of July 18 to Lichnowsky, the German ambassador to Britain, to explain to him, and through him to the British government, why the Germans considered it essential to support Austria. If the Austrians did not take action now, they would lose their last chance for political rehabilitation and their standing in the Balkans would be destroyed forever. The result would be the establishment of Russian hegemony over the Balkans, an intolerable extension of Russian power and influence for Germany as well as Austria.

Maintaining Austria—the strongest possible Austria—was therefore absolutely essential for Germany. Jagow realized that Austria could not be maintained forever, but preserving it for the present would give Germany time to arrange for other combinations. The immediate task of German policy was to keep the Austro-Serbian conflict localized. "Whether we succeed will depend in the first instance on Russia and secondly on the moderating influence of Russia's allies. The more determined Austria shows herself to be and the more energetically we support her, so much the more quiet will Russia remain." There would be agitation in St. Petersburg, but Russia, with its military buildup still far from complete, was not ready to strike and therefore both France and England would also want to avoid war at this time. All observers agreed, however, that Russia would be far better prepared for war in a few years and would then be able to crush Germany with the sheer weight of numbers. Meanwhile the German group would have grown steadily weaker. It followed that Austria would have to act now.

Even at this time, Jagow continued, the great danger for Germany would be the intervention of other great powers, for in that case Germany would be obliged to support Austria actively and would find itself "in the midst of an isolation that could scarcely be called 'splendid.'" Lichnowsky's major task should therefore be to secure British support for localization. Grey, the British foreign secretary, was always talking about the balance of power, but it should be perfectly obvious to him that this balance would be utterly destroyed if Germany abandoned Austria and Austria were demolished by Russia. "Therefore, if he is honest and logical, he must stand by us in attempting to localize the conflict."

Localization remained a central theme and principal concern of German leaders throughout the crisis, and when they finally woke to the fact that localization would not be possible they made their last-minute and futile efforts to draw back from the brink. The final blow came when Russia refused Germany's demand to halt mobi-

The Revolutions of 1848 and Their Aftermath

In addition to Langer, *Political and Social Upheaval,* cited previously, Peter N. Stearns, *1848: The Revolutionary Tide in Europe* (New York, 1974), with an excellent bibliography; George Fasel, *Europe in Upheaval: the Revolutions of 1848* (Chicago, 1970); L. C. Jennings, *France and Europe in 1848: A Study of French Foreign Affairs in Time of Crisis* (Oxford, 1973); F. Fejtö, ed., *The Opening of an Era: 1848, An Historical Symposium* (New York, 1948) includes an excellent short summary by J. P. T. Bury of the diplomatic problems raised by the revolutions; L. Namier, *1848: The Revolution of the Intellectuals* (London, 1946) concentrates on the nationalism of German intellectual leaders; I. Déak, *The Lawful Revolution: Louis Kossuth and the Hungarians, 1848-1849* (1979); Frank Eyck, *The Frankfurt Parliament, 1848-1849* (New York, 1968), an excellent study.

The revolutions produced two important new leaders, Emperor Francis Joseph of Austria and Louis Napoleon, who was to become Emperor Napoleon III of France. Among the many excellent studies of Napoleon, J. P. T. Bury, *Napoleon III and the Second Empire* (London, 1964), and the works of J. M. Thompson, A. Guérard, T. A. B. Cowley, and the brilliant earlier studies of F. A. Simpson. On Napoleon's consort, Nancy N. Barker, *Distaff Diplomacy: The Empress Eugénie and the Foreign Policy of the Second Empire* (Austin, Tex., 1967); and Harold Kurtz, *The Empress Eugénie, 1826-1920* (Boston, 1964), a sympathetic reevaluation of her character and influence; further, Jasper Ridley, *Napoleon III and Eugénie* (London, 1979). On the Austrian emperor, Joseph Redlich, *Emperor Francis Joseph of Austria* (New York, 1929) stands up well, but see also the works of K. Tschuppik and O. Janetschek.

Also of interest, A. Schwarzenberg, *Prince Felix zu Schwarzenberg, Prime Minister of Austria, 1848-1852* (New York, 1946); G. E. Rothenberg, *The Army of Francis Joseph* (West Lafayette, Ind., 1976); and for foreign policy, especially C. W. Hallberg, *Franz Joseph and Napoleon III, 1852-1864: A Study of Austro-French Relations* (New York, 1955).

The Crimean War

N. Rich, *Why the Crimean War? A Cautionary Tale* (Hanover, N.H., 1985), a synthesis of the diplomacy of the war, includes bibliography; G. B. Henderson, *Crimean War Diplomacy and Other Historical Essays* (Glasgow, 1947), valuable analyses of critical problems; H. W. Temperley, *England and the Near East: The Crimea* (London, 1936), staunchly pro-British. S. Lane-Poole, *The Life of the Right Honourable Stratford Canning, Viscount Stratford de Redcliffe. From His Memoirs and Private and Official Papers,* 2 vols. (London, 1888), admiringly uncritical, but quotes extensively from Stratford's revealing private papers, all of them now apparently destroyed.

Five outstanding monographs deserve special mention: P. W. Schroeder, *Austria, Great Britain, and the Crimean War: The Destruction of the European Concert* (Ithaca, N.Y., 1972), sympathetic to Austria, critical of Britain, with a brilliant final chapter examining the principles of nineteenth-century European diplomatic relations; Ann Pottinger Saab, *The Origins of the Crimean Alliance* (Charlottesville, Va., 1977), especially valuable for its attention to the Turkish side of the story; J. S. Curtiss, *Russia's Crimean War* (Durham, N.C., 1979); W. Baumgart, *The Peace of Paris, 1856: Studies in War, Diplomacy, and Peacemaking* (Santa Barbara, Calif., 1981), packed with important information, its main lines of argument somewhat obscured by detail; J. B. Conacher, *Britain and the Crimea, 1855-56: Problems of War and Peace* (New York, 1987). Leo Tolstoy, *Tales of Sebastopol* (many editions) records the heroism of the Russian soldiers. Tolstoy himself was among the defenders of the city.

W. E. Mosse, *The Rise and Fall of the Crimean System* (London, 1963), makes the case that a peace treaty that cannot be defended will not survive; by the same author, a brief work on the successor of Nicholas I, *Alexander II and the Modernization of Russia* (New York, 1958). On the new state that emerged after the Crimean War, R. W. Seton-Watson, *A History of the Roumanians from Roman Times to the Completion of Unity* (Cambridge, 1934).

The Unification of Italy

Derek Beales, *The Risorgimento and the Unification of Italy* (New York, 1971), a judicious introduction; more detailed and eminently readable, George Martin, *The Red Shirt and the Cross of Savoy: The Story of Italy's Risorgimento, 1748-1871* (New York, 1969); see especially the works of D. Mack Smith, *Cavour and Garibaldi, 1860: A Study of Political Conflict* (Cambridge, 1954), critical of Cavour; *Garibaldi* (New York, 1956), a brief biography; *Cavour* (New York, 1985), a more substantial work; *Victor Emanuel, Cavour, and the Risorgimento* (London, 1971); and *Italy and Its Monarchy* (New Haven, 1989). C. Hibbert, *Garibaldi and His Enemies: The Clash of Arms and Personalities in the Making of Italy* (London, 1965), is very readable; Mack Walker, ed., *Plombières: Summit Diplomacy and Italian Nationalism* (New York, 1968), a collection of documents with excellent commentary; W. A. Jenks, *Francis Joseph and the Italians, 1849-1859* (Charlottesville, Va., 1978).

On the role of the Vatican: Ivan Scott, *The Roman Question* (The Hague, 1969); E. E. Y. Hales, *Pio Nono: A Study in European Politics and Religion in the Nineteenth Century* (New York, 1954); Lillian P. Wallace, *The Papacy and European Diplomacy, 1869-1878* (1948); R. A. Graham, *Vatican Diplomacy: A Study of Church and State on the International Plane* (Princeton, 1959); and J. B. Bury, *History of the Papacy in the Nineteenth Century* (London, 1930).

The American Civil War

D. P. Crook, *Diplomacy During the American Civil War* (New York, 1975), based on the same author's longer *The North, the South, and the Powers, 1861-1865* (New York, 1974), valuable works of synthesis with excellent bibliographies. On Southern diplomacy, the excellent older work of F. L. Owsley, *King Cotton Diplomacy: Foreign Relations of the Confederate States of America* (Chicago, 1931); and the biography of the Confederate secretary of state by Eli N. Evans, *Judah P. Benjamin, The Jewish Confederate* (New York, 1988); also R. I. Lester, *Confederate Finance and Purchasing in Great Britain* (Charlottesville, Va., 1975).

On relations with the European powers: D. Jordan and E. J. Pratt, *Europe and the American Civil War* (Boston, 1931); E. D. Adams, *Great Britain and the American Civil War*, 2 vols. (New York, 1925); L. M. Case and W. F. Spencer, *The United States and France: Civil War Diplomacy* (Philadelphia, 1970).

Adrian Cook, *The* Alabama *Claims: American Politics and Anglo-American Relations, 1865-1872* (Ithaca, N.Y., 1975) deals with one of the most troublesome postwar problems; and, on a more enduring problem, R. J. Jensen, *The Alaska Purchase and Russian-American Relations* (Seattle, 1975).

The Great Powers and Mexico: Napoleon III's Grand Design

Hubert Herring, *A History of Latin America* (New York, frequently reprinted) provides excellent background information. On Napoleon III and Eugénie, see the works cited under the Revolutions of 1848.

A. J. and K. A. Hanna, *Napoleon III and Mexico* (Chapel Hill, N.C., 1971), based on the archives of all the countries involved, marred by somewhat dull writing and insufficient grasp of European politics, includes an excellent critical bibliography; E. C. Corti, *Maximilian and Charlotte of Mexico* (New York, 1928), by a prolific but not uncritical writer on royalty who had remarkably wide access to royal archives; Nancy N. Barker, *The French Experience in Mexico, 1821–1861: A History of Constant Misunderstanding* (Chapel Hill, N.C., 1979), reliable and readable; A. Blumberg, *The Diplomacy of the Mexican Empire, 1863–1867* (Philadelphia, 1971), an exhaustive treatment; C. H. Bock, *Prelude to Tragedy: The Negotiation and Breakdown of the Tripartite Convention of London, October 31, 1861* (Philadelphia, 1966); and the valuable monograph of L. M. Case, *French Opinion on the United States and Mexico, 1860–1867* (New York, 1936).

The Unification of Germany

W. E. Mosse, *The European Powers and the German Question, 1848–1871, with special Reference to England and Russia* (Cambridge, 1958); H. Boehme, *The Foundations of the German Empire* (Oxford, 1973), emphasizes the socioeconomic background; W. O. Henderson, *The Zollverein* (Chicago, 1959) deals with a principal economic factor.

Otto Pflanze, *Bismarck and the Development of Germany*, 3 vols. (Princeton, 1990) is the best biography and in effect a history of Germany in the nineteenth century, but its overpowering detail may intimidate some readers. Also very detailed is the work of the German scholar Lothar Gall, *Bismarck: The White Revolutionary* (London, 1986). The brief biography of A. J. P. Taylor makes for lively reading, as does George Kent, *Bismarck and His Times* (Carbondale, Ill., 1978), which includes a valuable bibliographical analysis. Fritz Stern, *Gold and Iron: Bismarck, Bleichröder, and the Building of the German Empire* (New York, 1977) deals with the chancellor's relations with his banker and includes valuable social as well as political and economic insights.

Important stages in the unification process are covered in L. D. Steefel, *The Schleswig-Holstein Question* (Cambridge, Mass., 1932); E. Ann Pottinger, *Napoleon III and the German Crisis, 1865–1866* (Cambridge, Mass., 1966); Gordon Craig, *The Battle of Königgrätz: Prussia's Victory over Austria, 1866* (Philadelphia, 1964); L. D. Steefel, *Bismarck, the Hohenzollern Candidacy, and the Origins of the Franco-German War of 1870* (Cambridge, Mass., 1962), which fails to reach any clear-cut conclusions; Michael Howard, *The Franco-Prussian War: The German Invasion of France, 1870–1871* (New York, 1962), a model military history; R. Holmes, *The Road to Sedan: The French Army, 1866–1870* (London, 1984).

The Search for a New International Stability

W. L. Langer, *European Alliances and Alignments, 1871–1890* (New York, 1931, bibliography brought up to date in 1956) remains the best and most comprehensive survey.

Detailed analyses of international developments that culminated in World War I go back as far as 1871, for example, the classic work of S. B. Fay, *The Origins of the World War*, 2 vols. (many editions), and the even more detailed work of the Italian journalist Luigi Albertini, *The Origins of the War of 1914*, 3 vols. (Oxford, 1951–1957), which takes the story from 1878.

Klaus Hildebrand, *German Foreign Policy from Bismarck to Adenauer: The Limits of Statecraft* (London, 1989) provides an interesting contrast to the work of another German historian written soon after World War I, E. Brandenburg, *From Bismarck to the World War: A History of German Foreign Policy, 1870–1914* (London, 1927); A. Mitchell, *Bismarck and the French Nation* (New York, 1971) emphasizes the interrelation of foreign and domestic policy and includes a suggestive discussion of German imperialism during the 1880s.

New crises in the Near East are discussed with admirable clarity in Barbara Jelavich, *The Ottoman Empire, the Great Powers, and the Straits Question, 1870-1887* (Bloomington, Ind., 1973); and M. Stojanovic, *The Great Powers and the Balkans, 1875-1878* (Cambridge, 1939). Also of great value, B. H. Sumner, *Russia and the Balkans, 1870-1880* (Oxford, 1937); D. MacKenzie, *The Serbs and Russian Pan-Slavism* (Ithaca, N.Y., 1967); Charles Jelavich, *Tsarist Russia and Balkan Nationalism: Russian Influence in the Internal Affairs of Bulgaria and Serbia, 1879-1886* (Berkeley, 1958); R. T. Shannon, *Gladstone and the Bulgarian Agitation, 1876* (London, 1963); R. W. Seton-Watson, *Disraeli, Gladstone, and the Eastern Question* (London, 1935); W. N. Medlicott, *The Congress of Berlin and After: A Diplomatic History of the Near Eastern Settlement, 1878-1880* (London, 1938); by the same author, *Bismarck, Gladstone, and the Concert of Europe* (London, 1956); M. Swartz, *The Politics of British Foreign Policy in the Era of Disraeli and Gladstone* (New York, 1985); Bruce Waller, *Bismarck at the Crossroads: The Reorientation of German Foreign Policy After the Congress of Berlin* (London, 1974).

On the reemergence of the Egyptian question: K. M. Wilson, ed., *Imperialism and Nationalism in the Middle East: The Anglo-Egyptian Experience, 1882-1982* (London, 1983); and the fascinating work of D. S. Landes, *Bankers and Pashas: International Finance and Economic Imperialism in Egypt* (Cambridge, 1958). On the Suez Canal, the monumental work of D. A. Farnie, *East and West of Suez: The Suez Canal in History 1854-1956* (Oxford, 1969); and the works of Lord Kinross, C. W. Hallberg, J. A. Marlow, and H. J. Schonfield.

On the Berlin Africa Conference: Stig Förster, W. J. Mommsen, and Ronald Robinson, eds., *Bismarck, Europe, and Africa: The Berlin Africa Conference, 1884-1885 and the Onset of Partition* (Oxford, 1988) is a valuable collection of essays dealing with imperialism in general, the policies of the European powers, and the African reaction; R. Gavin, *The Scramble for Africa: Documents on the Berlin Africa Conference and Related Subjects, 1884-1885* (Ibadan, 1973); S. E. Crowe, *The Berlin West Africa Conference* (London, 1942).

The Breakdown of Bismarck's Alliance System

W. L. Langer, *The Franco-Russian Alliance, 1890-1894* (Cambridge, Mass., 1929); and the same author's *The Diplomacy of Imperialism* (New York, 1935), the most detailed and comprehensive treatment of international affairs in the period after 1890, with a superb bibliography brought up to date in 1956. George Kennan, *The Decline of Bismarck's European Order: Franco-Russian Relations, 1875-1890* (Princeton, 1979); and the same author's *The Fateful Alliance: France, Russia, and the Coming of the First World War* (New York, 1984) by the veteran diplomat and historian of Russian foreign policy.

J. A. Nichols, *Germany After Bismarck: The Caprivi Era* (Cambridge, Mass., 1958); J. C. G. Röhl, *Germany Without Bismarck: The Crisis of Government in the Second Reich, 1890-1900* (Berkeley, 1967); Michael Balfour, *The Kaiser and His Times* (London, 1964), a lively and readable biography, as are the more recent works of Alan Palmer and Lamar Cecil. J. C. G. Röhl and N. Sombart, eds., *Kaiser Wilhelm II: New Interpretations* (Cambridge, 1982) provides valuable insights. N. Rich, *Friedrich von Holstein, Politics and Diplomacy in the Era of Bismarck and Wilhelm II,* 2 vols. (Cambridge 1965) deals with a key figure in the German foreign office and provides a broad coverage of German diplomacy to 1909.

Imperialism

David Healy, *Modern Imperialism: Changing Styles in Historical Interpretation* (Washington, 1967), a brief bibliographical survey; W. J. Mommsen, *Theories of Imperialism* (London, 1980); G. N. Nadel and P. Curtis, eds., *Imperialism and Colonialism* (New York, 1964), a valuable collection of essays, especially the contribution by D. K. Fieldhouse, whose works *The Colonial Empires* (New York, 1966), *The Theory of Capitalist Imperialism* (London, 1967), and *Economics and Empire, 1830-1914* (New York, 1973) are judicious and suggestive studies on this controversial subject. E. M. Winslow, *The Pattern of Imperialism: A Study in the Theories of Power* (New York, 1948), a penetrating older critique; R. Koebner and H. D. Schmidt, *Imperialism: The Story and Significance of a Political Word, 1840-1960* (Cambridge, 1964) is a fascinating and original study, as is D. R. Headrick, *The Tools of Empire: Technology and European Imperialism in the Nineteenth Century* (Oxford, 1981).

On the imperialism of individual European powers: P. Porter, *The Lion's Share: A Short History of British Imperialism, 1850-1984* (London, 1975); W. Baumgart, *Imperialism: The Idea and Reality of British and French Colonial Expansion, 1880-1914* (Oxford, 1982); H. Brunschwig, *French Colonialism, 1871-1914: Myths and Realities* (New York, 1966); J. J. Cooke, *The New French Imperialism, 1880-1910: The Third Republic and Colonial Expansion* (Hamden, Conn., 1973); S. H. Roberts, *History of French Colonial Policy, 1870-1925*, 2 vols. (Edinburgh, 1963); T. F. Power, *Jules Ferry and the Renaissance of French Imperialism* (New York, 1944); and W. D. Smith, *The German Colonial Empire* (Chapel Hill, N.C., 1978).

On imperialism in Africa: J. D. Fage, *A History of Africa* (New York, 1979), brief coverage, good bibliography; D. L. Wiedner, *A History of Africa South of the Sahara* (London, 1964); Ronald Robinson, John Gallagher, and Alice Denny, *Africa and the Victorians: The Climax of Imperialism* (London, 1961), a challenging and original interpretation that the authors themselves later modified; L. H. Gann and P. Duignan, eds., *Colonialism in Africa 1870-1960*, 5 vols. (Cambridge, 1969-1975); H. S. Wilson, *The Imperial Experience in Sub-Saharan Africa Since 1870* (Minneapolis, 1977); P. Gifford and W. R. Louis, eds., *Britain and Germany in Africa: Imperial Rivalry and Colonial Rule* (New Haven, 1967); G. N. Sanderson, *England, Europe, and the Upper Nile, 1882-1889* (Edinburgh, 1965); E. Axelson, *Portugal and the Scramble for Africa, 1875-1891* (Johannesburg, 1967); R. O. Collins, *King Leopold, England, and the Upper Nile, 1899-1909* (New Haven, 1968).

The Struggle for Supremacy in South Africa

L. Thompson and M. Wilson, eds., *The Oxford History of South Africa*, 2 vols. (Oxford, 1969-1971); D. M. Schreuder, *The Scramble for Southern Africa, 1877-1895* (Cambridge, 1981); E. Pakenham, *Jameson's Raid* (London, 1960); B. Farwell, *The Great Anglo-Boer War* (New York, 1976); T. Pakenham, *The Boer War* (New York, 1979).

East Asia to the Russo-Japanese War

J. K. Fairbank, E. O. Reischauer, and A. M. Craig, *East Asia: The Modern Transformation* (Boston, periodically revised), superb introduction with good bibliography; P. Clyde and B. Beers, *The Far East: A History of Western Impacts and Eastern Responses, 1830-1975* (New York, 1975); Lea E. Williams, *Southeast Asia: A History* (New York, 1976); J. T. Pratt, *The Expansion of Europe into the Far East* (London, 1947); D. Gillard, *The Struggle for Asia, 1828-1914* (London, 1977); M. Edwardes, *The West in Asia, 1850-1914* (London, 1967); E. R. Hughes, *The Invasion of China by the Western World* (New York, 1968); J. K. Fairbank, *Trade and Diplomacy on the China Coast: The Opening of the Treaty Ports, 1842-1854* (Stanford, 1969).

On the policies of the individual powers: W. C. Costin, *Great Britain and China, 1833-1860* (Oxford, 1937); L. K. Young, *British Policy in China, 1895-1902* (Oxford, 1970); J. K. Fairbank, *The United States and China* (Cambridge, Mass., 1971); A. W. Griswold, *The Far*

Eastern Policy of the United States (New Haven, 1938); E. O. Reischauer, *The United States and Japan* (Cambridge, Mass., 1957); W. L. Neumann, *America Encounters Japan: From Perry to MacArthur* (Baltimore, 1963); C. E. Neu, *An Uncertain Friendship: Theodore Roosevelt and Japan, 1906-1909* (Cambridge, Mass., 1967); by the same author, *The Troubled Encounter: the United States and Japan* (New York, 1975); Akira Iriye, *Across the Pacific: An Inner History of American-East Asian Relations* (New York, 1967); and the same author's *Pacific Estrangement: Japanese and American Expansion, 1897-1911* (Cambridge, Mass., 1972); A. Lobanov-Rostovsky, *Russia and Asia* (New York, 1933); D. J. Dallin, *The Rise of Russia in Asia* (New Haven, 1949); R. A. Pierce, *Russia and Central Asia, 1867-1917* (Berkeley, 1960); G. A. Lensen, *The Russian Push Toward Japan: Russo-Japanese Relations, 1697-1875* (Princeton, 1959); B. H. Sumner, *Tsardom and Imperialism in the Far East and Middle East, 1880-1914* (New York, 1942); A. Malozemoff, *Russian Far Eastern Policy, 1881-1904* (Berkeley, 1958); S. G. Marks, *The Road to Power: The Trans-Siberian Railroad and the Colonization of Asian Russia, 1850-1917* (Ithaca, N.Y., 1991).

On the Russo-Japanese War: J. A. White, *The Diplomacy of the Russo-Japanese War* (Princeton, 1964); I. Nish, *The Origins of the Russo-Japanese War* (London, 1985); S. Okamoto, *The Japanese Oligarchy and the Russo-Japanese War* (New York, 1970); David Walker, *The Short Victorious War: The Russo-Japanese Conflict, 1904-1905* (New York, 1974); E. P. Trani, *The Treaty of Portsmouth* (Lexington, Ky., 1969).

The Reemergence of the Eastern Question

See the works on the Eastern Question cited earlier. Further, A. O. Sarkissian, "Concert Diplomacy and the Armenians, 1890-97," in A. O. Sarkissian, ed., *Studies in Diplomatic History and Historiography in Honour of G. P. Gooch* (London, 1962), pp. 48-75; M. K. Chapman, *Britain and the Bagdad Railway, 1888-1914* (Northampton, Mass., 1948); J. B. Wolf, *The Diplomatic History of the Bagdad Railway* (Columbia, Mo., 1936).

The United States Enters the Great Power Arena

E. R. May, *Imperial Democracy: The Emergence of America as a Great Power* (New York, 1961); by the same author, *American Imperialism: A Speculative Essay* (New York, 1968); A. Iriye, *From Nationalism to Internationalism: United States Foreign Policy to 1914* (Boston, 1977); C. S. Campbell, *The Transformation of American Foreign Relations, 1865-1900* (New York, 1976); R. L. Beisner, *From the Old Diplomacy to the New, 1865-1900* (Arlington Heights, Ill., 1986); J. W. Pratt, *Expansionists of 1898: The Acquisition of Hawaii and the Spanish Islands* (Baltimore, 1936); H. K. Beale, *Theodore Roosevelt and the Rise of America to World Power* (Baltimore, 1956); H. Sprout and M. Sprout, *The Rise of American Naval Power, 1776-1918* (Annapolis, 1990); R. D. Challener, *Admirals, Generals, and American Foreign Policy, 1898-1914* (Princeton, 1973); D. F. Trask, *The War with Spain in 1898* (New York, 1981); W. LaFeber, *The Panama Canal: The Crisis in Historical Perspective* (Oxford, 1978); David McCullough, *The Path Between the Seas: The Creation of the Panama Canal, 1870-1914* (New York, 1977), superbly written, especially good on medical and engineering problems.

The Collapse of the Sick Man of Europe; The Balkan Wars

E. C. Thaden, *Russia and the Balkan Alliance of 1912* (University Park, Penn., 1965); A. Rossos, *Russia and the Balkans: Inter-Balkan Rivalries and Russian Foreign Policy, 1908-*

1914 (Toronto, 1981); E. C. Helmreich, *The Diplomacy of the Balkan Wars* (Cambridge, Mass., 1938); J. Heller, *British Policy Towards the Ottoman Empire* (London, 1983); Marion Kent, ed., *The Great Powers and the End of the Ottoman Empire* (London, 1984).

The European Great Powers Before 1914

O. J. Hale, *The Great Illusion, 1900-1914* (New York, 1971), a good general coverage of the period, excellent bibliography.

On Britain: C. Howard, *Splendid Isolation: A Study of Ideas Concerning Britain's International Position and Foreign Policy During the Later Years of the Third Marquis of Salisbury* (London, 1967); J. A. S. Grenville, *Lord Salisbury and Foreign Policy: The Close of the Nineteenth Century* (London, 1964); G. Monger, *The End of Isolation, British Foreign Policy, 1900-1907* (Edinburgh, 1963); C. J. Lowe and M. L. Dockrill, *The Mirage of Power*, vol. 1, *British Foreign Policy, 1902-1914* (London, 1972); Z. S. Steiner, *Britain and the Origins of the First World War* (London, 1978); F. H. Hinsley, ed., *British Foreign Policy Under Sir Edward Grey* (Cambridge, 1977); H. C. Allen, *Great Britain and the United States: A History of Anglo-American Relations* (New York, 1955); A. E. Campbell, *Great Britain and the United States, 1895-1903* (London, 1960); Bradford Perkins, *The Great Rapprochement: England and the United States, 1895-1914* (New York, 1968); I. Nish, *The Anglo-Japanese Alliance: The Diplomacy of Two Island Empires, 1894-1907* (London, 1966); P. Lowe, *Great Britain and Japan, 1911-1915: A Study of British Far Eastern Policy* (New York, 1969); D. French, *British Economic and Strategic Planning, 1905-1915* (London, 1982); P. J. V. Rolo, *Entente Cordiale: The Origins and Negotiation of the Anglo-French Agreements of 8 April 1904* (London, 1969); F. R. Bridge, *Great Britain and Austria-Hungary, 1906-1914: A Diplomatic History* (London, 1972); J. Gooch, *The Plans of War: The General Staff and British Military Strategy, 1900-1916* (London, 1974); on British naval policy and fleet building, see the numerous excellent works of A. J. Marder. There are comparatively recent biographies of Balfour by S. H. Zebel and R. F. Mackay; of Grey by K. G. Robbins.

On Anglo-German relations: R. J. Sontag, *Germany and England: Background of Conflict, 1848-1914* (New York, 1938); Paul Kennedy, *The Rise of Anglo-German Antagonism, 1860-1914* (London, 1980); R. J. S. Hoffman, *Great Britain and the German Trade Rivalry* (New York, 1964); P. Padfield, *The Great Naval Race: The Anglo-German Naval Rivalry, 1900-1914* (London, 1974); E. L. Woodward, *Great Britain and the German Navy* (Oxford, 1935).

On Germany: V. R. Berghahn, *Germany and the Approach of War in 1914* (London, 1973); Fritz Fischer, *War of Illusions: German Policies from 1911 to 1914* (New York, 1975), a scathing indictment; K. Jarausch, *The Enigmatic Chancellor: Bethmann-Hollweg and the Hubris of Imperial Germany* (New Haven, 1973); E. Kehr, *Battleship Building and Party Politics in Germany, 1894-1901* (Chicago, 1975), an influential pioneering work on the influence of big business on politics; an excellent work by J. Steinberg, *Yesterday's Deterrent: Tirpitz and the Birth of the German Battle Fleet* (London, 1965); and I. N. Lambi, *The Navy and German Power Politics, 1862-1914* (London, 1984); O. J. Hale, *Germany and the Diplomatic Revolution: A Study in Diplomacy and the Press, 1904-1906* (Philadelphia, 1931).

On France: J. Keiger, *France and the Origins of the First World War* (London, 1983); C. Andrew, *Théophile Delcassé and the Making of the Entente Cordiale: A Reappraisal of French Foreign Policy* (New York, 1968); G. Krumeich, *Armaments and Politics in France on the Eve of the First World War* (Leamington Spa, 1984); E. Weber, *The Nationalist Revival in France 1905-1914* (Berkeley, 1959); D. R. Watson, *Georges Clemenceau: A Political Bi-*

ography (New York, 1976); G. Wright, *Raymond Poincaré and the French Presidency* (Stanford, 1942).

On Austria-Hungary, Russia, and Italy, see the works cited earlier; further, S. R. Williamson, Jr., *Austria-Hungary and the Origins of the First World War* (New York, 1991); D. Lieven, *Russia and the Origins of the First World War* (London, 1983); R. Bosworth, *Italy and the Approach of the First World War* (London, 1983).

On the major diplomatic crises, see the general works cited earlier; further, E. N. Anderson, *The First Morocco Crisis, 1904-1906* (Chicago, 1930); B. Schmitt, *The Annexation of Bosnia* (Cambridge, 1937); G. Barraclough, *From Agadir to Armageddon: Anatomy of a Crisis* (New York, 1984); J. Remak, *Sarajevo: The Story of a Political Murder* (New York, 1959) contends that the assassination was planned by the Serbian chief of military intelligence, Col. Dimitrievich, an interpretation contested by V. Dedijer, *The Road to Sarajevo* (New York, 1966).

The Coming of World War I

James Joll, *The Origins of the First World War* (London, 1984) includes coverage of the role of domestic politics and economic and imperial rivalries; I. Geiss, ed., *July 1914* (London, 1972), excellent collection of documents; see the works of S. B. Fay and L. Albertini, cited earlier; further, B. Schmitt, *The Coming of the War, 1914,* 2 vols. (New York, 1930); D. E. Lee, *Europe's Crucial Years: The Diplomatic Background of World War I, 1902-1914* (Hanover, N.H., 1974), with a good bibliographical essay; L. C. F. Turner, *Origins of the First World War* (New York, 1970), emphasis on military problems; L. Lafore, *The Long Fuse: An Interpretation of the Origins of World War I* (Philadelphia, 1965), emphasis on Balkan problems; H. W. Koch, ed., *The Origins of the First World War: Great Power Rivalry and German War Aims* (London, 1972), a valuable collection of essays. On German responsibility, see the work of F. Fischer, cited earlier, and for a recent survey of the seemingly endless debate on the subject, Gregor Schöllgen, *Escape into War? The Foreign Policy of Imperial Germany* (New York, 1990).

On military planning: S. Miller, ed., *Military Strategy and the Origins of the First World War* (Princeton, 1985); P. Kennedy, ed., *The War Plans of the Great Powers, 1880-1914* (London, 1979); S. R. Williamson, Jr., *The Politics of Grand Strategy: Britain and France Prepare for War, 1904-1914* (Cambridge, Mass., 1969); G. Ritter, *The Schlieffen Plan: Critique of a Myth* (New York, 1958), a devastating analysis.

Index